Triumphant Capitalism

Henry Clay Frick, circa 1915. *Photograph by Pach Bros., N.Y., N.Y. Courtesy of Frick Art and Historical Center, Frick Archives.*

Triumphant Capitalism

HENRY CLAY FRICK

and the

INDUSTRIAL TRANSFORMATION

of

AMERICA

Kenneth Warren

University of Pittsburgh Press

Published by the University of Pittsburgh Press, Pittsburgh, Pa. 15261
Copyright © 1996, University of Pittsburgh Press
All rights reserved
Manufactured in the United States of America
Printed on acid-free paper

10 9 8 7 6 5 4 3 2 1

Library of Congress Cataloging-in-Publication Data
Warren, Kenneth.
   Triumphant capitalism : Henry Clay Frick and the industrial
transformation of America / Kenneth Warren
        p.   cm.
   Includes bibliographical references and index.
   ISBN 0-8229-3889-8 (cl) — ISBN 0-8229-5744-2 (pbk)
   1. Frick, Henry Clay, 1849–1919.   2. Industrialists—United
States—Biography.   3. Steel industry and trade—Pennsylvania—
Pittsburgh—History.   I. Title.
HD9520.F75W37 1995
338.092—dc20
   [B]   95-14572

For Jean

Contents

Illustrations

Tables

Preface

━◦⟪⟪⟪⟫⟫⟫◦━

H enry Clay Frick was one of an outstanding group of American businessmen living and working in the United States as that country became the world's leading industrial economy. He was not so central as to
qualify as one of Jonathan Hughes's "vital few," but he stood not far behind
this select group. Indeed, the tremendous achievements of one of them—
Andrew Carnegie—would have been greatly reduced without him. Frick's
importance has long been recognized, but his work and his standing have
been difficult to assess in detail because of the partial nature of the record
that is accessible to researchers. He died in 1919, but for family reasons his
papers remained closed until after the mid 1980s. Given the circumstances
of his career and, particularly, his involvement in the Homestead strike (one
of the most dramatic and emotive episodes in American labor history and
the event that brought Frick to the attention of the whole nation), this was
unfortunate, for in the absence of knowledge, speculation and myth flourished. As a result, although working among a group of men who for long
were commonly regarded as folk heroes, Frick stood out as the villain, a
man lacking in human warmth, a character both harder and less colorful
than his peers.

The account that follows is not an attempt to rehabilitate him, still less
to promote him, but to provide the first full and critical account of his
career using mainly his own papers. Based largely on the abundant correspondence between the principals of Carnegie Steel or to and from the leaders of other major companies, this account may claim to be an inside view
of the making and the shaping of America's economic might. Through
everyday letters written in the heat of action, one may gain a subtle insight
into the workings of industrial capitalism in a most strident but also most
successful phase. Yet, although my aim has been in the first place to adopt
the actors' perspectives on the processes of industrialization, I have tried
throughout to set this view within the wider framework of the economic
environment of the times and, with the benefit of hindsight, to assess opinions, actions, and results with a critical eye.

xiii

As far as Frick is concerned, the records reveal a man with clearly envisaged business objectives and an inflexible will in steering toward the goals he set himself. He had a sense of what was and what was not justifiable behavior in getting to those goals, and these standards he applied also to his business associates and relations with labor. Above all he spurned dissimulation. Many of his contemporaries in the top ranks of business were happy to masquerade as public benefactors. Their occasional business peccadilloes were represented as inevitable concessions to the griminess of capitalist processes that nonetheless always seemed to issue in the greater well-being of society at large. In contrast, Frick never affected to regard business as anything other than a struggle for survival or, more usually, for supremacy. There were rules, but no recourse to cant about public benefit; except in that most general of senses so popular in that age (as in our own) that the welfare of humankind would increase as more goods become available at more reasonable prices. For him, labor was a factor of production to be sold or bought under much the same terms as other inputs. There is no record that Henry Clay Frick read Adam Smith, but his business philosophy was of the early classical mold, spiced (as commonly at this time) with social Darwinism.

Yet Frick was not a business tyrant. He played the game within the rules but was utterly without pretence in the face he turned (and even then reluctantly enough) to public scrutiny. He was charitable to individuals and to worthy institutions but—in contrast to other, better-known examples—was so averse to any public parade of his generosity that he insisted on anonymity. He had relatively few friends, but those few affirmed his loyalty. Outside business it has always seemed that he was a warmhearted family man, though more recently some have questioned this. Unlike many of his fellow tycoons, he was discriminating in the style of living he chose as great wealth came his way. Like them, he erected fine houses and enjoyed world travel. He became an art collector, but one who not merely amassed objects but also learned much about this new field of endeavor; from being a tyro, he became a discriminating buyer. Above all he genuinely enjoyed the beauty he had brought together, so that the accumulation of things became merely a step toward a genuine appreciation of their qualities. In short, not only was he a little-known and generally misunderstood business leader, but in many respects he was a deviation from the type. In some respects, he represented the transition to the next stage of business organization, the step from the captain of industry to the conditions of the managerial society: as Herbert N. Casson remarked almost ninety years ago, Carnegie stood for a patriarchal system of industry, Frick represented the corporate system.[1]

A brief explanation of the structure of what follows is in order. My object has not been to provide a full biography of Henry Clay Frick. There are two straightforward reasons for this. The archival material available above all concerns his business career, and my interests and abilities do not extend in equal degree into the other areas of his life. It would be wrong to pretend to competence as an analyst of "complexes" or to be able to delve deeply into the significance of childhood or family experiences—even were there evidence enough to undertake such a study. However, the whole man provides an essential context for the working part of life, and therefore this background must be briefly sketched in. Even in relation to Frick's fifty-year business career the record is uneven. There is relatively little on the first ten years. On the last twenty, there is a good deal more, but the bulk of the archive is concerned with the middle period from 1880 to 1900. These were the peak years of his impact on American economic growth, and they have left us the most systematic coverage of his activities in other papers besides his own. After this, he remained intimately involved with decision making within big business, and especially in the counsels of the U.S. Steel Corporation.

Frick was a key figure in two industries that were central in these unparalleled years of American economic growth, fuel and steel—the energy to move goods and people and to transform raw materials into finished goods, and the most important material used in building the national infrastructure. He was popularly referred to as "king of coke"; for thirty years he was one of the key decision makers in the iron and steel industry. The wider economic framework is the ever present backdrop to his life, and thus his career provides yet one more perspective on this great process, a further insight into the mechanisms of capitalist development.

What follows is a study of industrial dynamics, which were shaped by key businessmen, who were in turn molded by the manufacturing framework within which they operated. There is a two-way relationship here. The general processes of economic development may be of a scale and a power far beyond the influence either of one individual or even of a small group; but such individuals or groups particularize the process, giving it substance at particular times and places. A single-minded, sometimes ruthless individual like Frick could use the business circumstances of the time to advance his own interests, but in doing so, he helped change the industries concerned. What follows is not only an "industrial biography," but also a biographical perspective on whole industries in their most formative periods. Looking outward rather than inward, I hope this study may be a contribution to the understanding of the history of the basic industries, the shaping of society, locality, and region, and thereby of foundation-laying for the value systems and landscapes of present-day America.

I have tried to avoid grand paradigms—either of an inevitably beneficent process involving the broadening out of the benefits of economic growth or, on the other hand, of capitalists invariably exploiting workers and creating ever deeper class antagonisms. In this respect (though not it is hoped in others), this study may merit the description "uncritical." Its focus is not a system but a life, though one inextricably enmeshed in contemporary economic and social structures. The course of Frick's working life coincided with a series of vital stages in national economic development. It began around 1870 as post–Civil War reconstruction passed over into a surge of new development, a true drive to economic maturity. It matured in the years of ruthless competition and company conflict in the 1890s, which culminated in a great period of trust building. It ended in the early aftermath of World War I as America stood on the edge of the age of mass consumption, and, much more diffidently, set out as the world's economic superpower.

In the 1880s, Carnegie produced a thought-provoking book, *Triumphant Democracy*. The material progress he depicted in such vivid detail was undeniably "triumphant"; how fully it was "democratic" (in a sense the Founding Fathers would have been happy with) is more debatable. The industrialization examined in this book was undoubtedly a triumph of capitalist enterprise, but the achievement was ambivalent. Whatever the debate on such issues, however, there remains the fascination of Frick's career within the context of nationwide development. Some of the features of this life are features of a great tragedy. Well-placed to completely dominate one industry, coke, he sold his controlling share in order to gain entry and then increase his power in another, steel. Eventually, he was in a position to bid for overall control of the key company in this industry, only to be frustrated by the very man to whom he had sold his coke firm and to whose unrivaled successes in steel he had contributed so much. He lost his direction of the coke industry. Then by a sudden turn of fate he became the power behind the throne in the far greater concern that emerged as the steel industry was consolidated. He used his great wealth and reputation to extend and broaden the nation's capitalist structures. Then, in his last months of life, he lent both wealth and reputation to the struggle against the United States' membership of the League of Nations and thereby helped to defeat the attempt to match America's new role as world economic leader with a formal recognition that it faced similar responsibilities in the political realm.

Acknowledgments

M any have been generous in helping with my research. Support from the University of Oxford, from Jesus College (my academic home there), and from the Nuffield Foundation financed a number of research visits to the United States. Over the years I have received willing, friendly, and much-valued assistance in a number of American libraries and archival centers. Noteworthy among them were the library and record collections at the Pennsylvania State Capitol in Harrisburg, the Carnegie Library in Pittsburgh, and the Library of Congress. On a number of occasions I enjoyed working within the superb facilities and the beautiful setting of the Hagley Library near Wilmington, Delaware. The U.S. Steel Corporation generously opened their files for the period in which Frick was a director. Above all I wish to thank the Trustees of the Helen Clay Frick Foundation in Pittsburgh and especially the Foundation's executive director, Dick McIntosh, for giving me access to the papers of Henry Clay Frick and for their friendly interest in my work. Joanne Moore, at that time the keeper of that excellent collection, was invariably helpful and cheerful, qualities that made research at the Foundation pleasurable as well as fruitful. Fred Hetzel, until recently the director of the University of Pittsburgh Press, provided steady support and helped me directly in the shaping of the final chapter. His encouragement and hospitality have been much appreciated. The readers of my draft made valuable comments that I have tried to take into account. Finally I would like to record my thanks for the skill and care of my copy editor, Pippa Letsky. It goes without saying that none of those who helped me in these various ways are responsible for any mistakes of fact or interpretation that may remain.

Triumphant Capitalism

1

Prologue

Foundations for a Business Life

—◅◅◅﹖◌﹖▻▻▻—

The Industrial Setting

The life of Henry Clay Frick spanned an era of unprecedented national
economic growth. When he was born, the wealth of the United States
was much less than one-third that of the world's pioneer industrial nation,
the United Kingdom; when he died, it was more than three times as large.
During his lifetime the nation's wealth increased more than fortyfold, and
both the structure and the geographical form of the economy were transformed almost out of recognition. Ideas and expectations were dramatically
altered. Such changes were the result of great forces and movements both
within and from outside the United States, the product of the abilities and
ambitions of millions of people. Yet they were also greatly influenced by
outstanding individuals who helped determine which businesses—and
therefore which areas and places—were most affected. Henry Clay Frick was
to play a prominent part in these transformations of an era of unprecedented material progress.

During his seventy-year life the population of the United States grew
from 23 to 105 million. The spatial distribution of the people changed even
more dramatically. The 1850 census was taken just a few months after Frick's
birth, and at that time, only two million people—just over one in every
twelve Americans—lived west of the Mississippi. More than half of these
were in Louisiana or Missouri, and California then contained well under a
hundred thousand. There were only four states and seven territories
throughout the entire West. Long before the end of Frick's life, the frontier
had disappeared and the United States was declared fully settled. When the
1920 census was taken, a few months after his death, twenty-two states lay

1

west of the Mississippi, and they contained almost 32 million people, or 30 percent of the national population. California, with 3.4 million inhabitants, was already eighth in number of the forty-eight states.

During Frick's life, American society passed from an early stage of industrialization to the beginnings of an affluent consumerism—in W. W. Rostow's terminology, from a stage shortly after "take-off" through sustained growth and the "drive to maturity," to the start of an "age of mass consumption."[1] In the process, the industrial requirements of the nation changed. At first a basic economy had to be established—lines of communication, sources of energy, farms, mines, factories, homes, and public buildings. While this was happening (although wealth increased rapidly), investment was above all in capital equipment rather than in widely diffused high levels of private consumption. Apart from essential goods such as furniture, clothing, footwear, and food, the emphasis was on heavy industry and the provision of public infrastructure.

The opening of the West dramatically altered the distribution pattern for the products of the basic industries. In the year of Frick's birth, for example, the length of the nation's railroads reached 7,365 miles. When he entered the coal and coke business in 1870, this had increased to 52,922 miles, by 1900 to 193,346 miles, and at his death nineteen years later, there were 253,152 miles of railroad in the nation. For most of Frick's life, railroads dominated long-distance passenger and freight transport, but before he died, the automobile industry was already assembling almost two million passenger and commercial vehicles a year.

Changes in the basic industries were equally if not more dramatic than those in transport. In the roughly seventy years of Frick's life, the output of bituminous coal increased from under 4 million to 516 million tons. Between 1850 and 1920, pig iron production went from under 0.6 million to over 37 million tons. By value added in manufacturing, iron and steel as a combined industry was seventh in 1860 but ranked first by World War I. Never again would there be such rates of relative overall economic growth nor would these industries be so prominent. As the demand for coal and steel grew, so the patterns of their production shifted. Whereas in the early 1870s the output of anthracite and the output of bituminous coal were at comparable levels, by 1900 the tonnage of anthracite was only a little more than one-quarter that of bituminous coal; in 1918, anthracite production reached what was to prove its highest ever figure, only a little over one-sixth that of the bituminous coal mines.

Geology as well as the distribution of demand led to a concentration of the mining of bituminous coal and the associated manufacture of coke in the northern parts of the Appalachian plateau. In comparison, the manufacture of iron and steel was freer in terms of locational choice. The opening and large-scale development of the Lake Superior iron ranges and the use of furnace fuel from the Appalachians helped concentrate the centers of iron and steel manufacture in the broad swathe of territory between the lower end of the Great Lakes and the coal plateaus, but within this area the increasingly complex network of railroads left open a wide range of possibilities. Variations in plant efficiency decided which would be the successful operations and the greater growth points. Efficiency, in turn, was determined above all by the quality of management. Western Pennsylvania became the greatest single focus for the growth of these industries in the late nineteenth century, because of its natural advantages for coke manufacture and the acquired attractions for steelmaking, and it remained of outstanding significance in each industry far into the twentieth century.

Considerations involved in the growth of any industry are complex. Some factors are general to any activity, at any time and place; others are specific to particular trades, eras, and locations. The demand side of an industry is of primary significance. Entrepreneurial skills cannot normally create a demand, although they might foster its expansion. The market, its growth, and changes in its composition and distribution are the largely exogenous factors to which an industry must respond. National economic growth provides the overall context. Competition from other producers determines how much of the market a particular firm can control, although in order to simplify market access it may choose to collaborate with other firms, through understandings, pools, quotas, and so on. The supply side of an industry involves the availability and cost of raw materials, forms and cost of delivery, the quality and price of labor, and the availability of and charges for capital. Then there is the production process itself, its technology, its scale, the type and degree of integration with other processes. All of these aspects may be brought within the control of an individual company, but there may still be unexpected influences (notably technological change) from outside. Such changes may occur in other industries but may even so affect the pattern of demand for the activity under consideration; if technical change comes from within, it will alter inputs, scales of production, probably the association and integration of processes, and the nature of outputs.

Management has to take initiative in response to all these aspects of business. It must meet demand efficiently and keep pace with changes. It has to balance the mix of inputs so as to secure the most cost-effective combination—replacing one material with another, changing relative proportions, substituting capital for labor within the limited bounds that this is technically possible. In addition to the vital day-to-day decisions, there are also medium-term responses involving the taking up of opportunities and the minimizing of liabilities, as well as long-term perspectives on development. Management structures and conditions provide many variations, of individual relationships, delegation of powers, incentives, and so on. Inspiring top management may motivate a whole concern, a healthy emulation among the top servants of the firm maximizing its progress. For better or worse, the leadership of the firm is the central most important factor that determines the coordination and efficiency of production, the vigor of the response to rivals, the perception of possibilities, and attitudes to workers. An excellent location, efficient plant, able and willing workers, abundance both of capital and of markets—all such assets can be vitiated by uninspiring management. Conversely, a good managerial team operating within an indifferent situation with respect to all these important factors may yet be able to produce an operation that is distinguished by its excellence and success.

COKE AND STEEL DURING FRICK'S LIFE

Such generalities must now be set within a specific context. In the coke and steel industries during the working life of Henry Clay Frick there occurred large-scale growth and technical change. A cogent case could be made for the thesis that in both industries the changes of the 1870–1920 period were more fundamental than those of any other period either before or since. At the beginning of this period, coke manufacture was highly localized and was fragmented into a large number of individual operations. The processes were conducted separately from iron manufacture and were simple and wasteful. During the last twenty years of his life, production became more scattered throughout the industrial Northeast but was grouped into fewer, larger, more complex, and more efficient plants and became intimately integrated with iron and steel manufacture.

Until roughly 1900, expansion depended on the beehive coke oven; after that the by-product oven became increasingly important. The former process involved the burning of coal with the minumum access for air in a circular, dome-shaped oven. Excellent coke was produced but all the gaseous and liquid by-products were lost. The by-product oven was more elaborate but recovered these products.

In metallurgy too there was a large-scale shift. In the first half of the 1870–1920 period, bulk steel production became firmly established in the form of the Bessemer process, which in America was associated mainly with rail manufacture. In the second half of the period, there occurred the gradual replacement of this process by open-hearth furnace manufacture of bulk steels, which were by then being finished in a much wider variety of forms. Scale of plant grew as industrialists became aware of the economies to be derived from bigger operations with combined processes of by-product coke manufacture, iron making, steelmaking, and steel finishing.

Thus, fundamental changes took place in both the technological and the business environments. At the beginning, both in coke and in iron and steel, there were large numbers of mines, plants, and firms. Competition led to attempts to fix prices, to form pools, to allocate quotas. There followed a much more radical reorganization involving amalgamations and programs of rationalization of plant. Finally, in coke and still more in steel, came an era of concentration of economic power, but exercised in a paternalistic fashion. In both industries, this last phase was under the leadership and tutelage of the United States Steel Corporation. At this stage, outsiders might be excused for believing that change had come to a stop; but in fact, within this congenial operating environment new processes, locations, and firms were emerging and problems were being laid up for the future. Frick's working life spanned all these periods.

THE CHANGING ETHOS OF THE TIME

As well as technical and organizational changes, an important context for this case study is the business ethos of the time. For most of the period, there was optimism about the future state of the economy and a conviction (naive though it seems in retrospect) that progress could only be secured by a relentless and competitive struggle, that this would produce material well-being, which in turn would increase human happiness and indeed, if undisturbed, would lead on to the millennium. Such a belief that soon all would be well could ignore short-term struggle, hardships, and uncertainties. The age was well provided with persuasive apostles of this doctrine, and nowhere were they more confident or explicit than in America. The highly respected publicist Edwin Lawrence Godkin proclaimed that "the principle of competition . . . is the law by which Providence secures the progress of the human race." He drew logical conclusions from his statement, conclusions that were very comforting to the great captains of industry:

> The great law which nature seems to have prescribed for the government of the world, and the only law of human society which we are able to extract from history, is that the more intelligent and thoughtful of the race shall inherit the earth and have the best time, and that all others shall find life on the whole dull and unprofitable.

The pioneer Yale sociologist William Graham Sumner was even more unequivocal about the universal worth of the process, whatever the surface appearance of things:

What matters it . . . that some millionaires are idle or silly or vulgar? . . . The
millionaires are a product of natural selection, acting on the whole body of men
to pick out those who can meet the requirement of certain work to be done.
They get high wages and live in luxury, but the bargain is a good one for
society.[2]

Questions of private gain in relation to public good lead on naturally to a
fuller consideration of the role of the individual in the shaping of great
industries and national economies. The heroic perspective on economic history is out of favor. We may still speak or write of business leaders or captains of industry, but are we not dealing with forces beyond the control of
any individual? Developments in technology, forms of industrial organization, relations between capital and labor (in short, forms and systems of
production) are not these the real points of reference? Under these circumstances individual entrepreneurs, managers, or particular firms seem little
more than agents of historical necessity. True, some modern historians are
still willing to allow some role to special circumstances. Writing specifically
about changes in demand for steel, Peter Temin made allowance for disturbing effects:

It is apparent that most gradual trends are aided, obstructed, or at least altered
by the presence of temporary developments that produce their own highly specialized effects. The differences between times and places may be the result of
the extent to which these temporary influences correspond with the requirements of the general trends.[3]

This applies at least equally to individual economic actors. Their successes
may indeed do more, speeding change or (as with the individuals considered
here) holding back for decades the gradual drift of locational change in a
basic industry. Frick himself deprecated the role of an individual or small
group of businessmen: "The demands of modern life called for such works
as ours; if we had not met the demands others would have done so. Even
without us the steel industry of the country would have been just as great as
it is, though men would have used other names in speaking of its leaders."[4]
However, in that case the form of the industry would have been different,
and its size, efficiency, and role in national economic development probably
less. The fact remains that in such a large, complex, and vibrant organization
as Carnegie Steel, itself the front-runner in what was then the largest or
indeed the key manufacturing activity in the nation, there was ample scope
for the exercise of individual talent and initiative. All within the company's
top management were straining to make it still more successful, but they
contributed different qualities. Sixty years ago, Burton J. Hendrick summed
this up:

[T]he Carnegie Minutes, technical as the contents are, teem everywhere with personality. The characteristics of each partner stand out clearly as in a well-written play. Here is Henry Phipps, cautious, penetrating, conservative, especially alert in matters of finance; [Henry Clay] Frick, abrupt, down-right, grim, occasionally cynical; [George "Dod"] Lauder, quiet, thoughtful, deliberate, anxious always for the views of "absent partners"; [Charles M.] Schwab, dashing, self-confident, quick to decide, vain, sensitive to criticism; [Thomas] Morrison, brief-spoken, exact; and [Alexander] Peacock, animated and optimistic, as a good salesman should be.[5]

One may not agree with all of Hendrick's characterizations, but his evocation of the expression and interplay of individuality can scarcely be bettered.

In the operational conditions of mushrooming basic industries and of an expansive national economy operated according to a heady mixture of the thinking of laissez-faire economics and social Darwinist thought, the exceptional business skills of Henry Clay Frick flourished. The interplay between favorable external circumstances and personal talents of a high order shaped the course of his career and, in the process, played a significant part in the national processes and forms of growth at this most propitious of times. Yet, as will be seen, these concerns by no means wholly excluded other, wider, gentler interests. In short, the man was to prove worthy of his times.

Family Origins

During the decades before the War of Independence, one Abraham Oberholtzer from the Palatinate emigrated to the British colonies in North America. He settled near Point Pleasant on the Delaware River, in Bucks County, Pennsylvania. In 1800 the Overholts (having simplified their family name) moved across the Appalachians to Westmoreland County in southwestern Pennsylvania. There, another Abraham took up a large tract of land some fifteen miles south of the small settlement of Greensburg, a holding that came to be known as "the Overholt place." On it was established the settlement of West Overton. By 1810 Abraham Overholt had established a distillery, which by the standards of this region eventually became a major operation. He also raised livestock, put up large flour mills, and worked some local coal. Before he died in 1870 he was the wealthiest man in the area.

Abraham's daughter Elizabeth married a man, John Frick, whose Swiss ancestors had come to America over thirty years before the Overholts. John W. Frick is said to have had ambitions to be a painter; instead he was a not very successful farmer, showing little enterprise and receiving little reward. John and Elizabeth settled in West Overton. Their second son was born in the village on 19 December 1849 and was baptized in the names of the Great Compromiser, Henry Clay.

Some time after this, the family moved a mile or so away to a farm south of Mount Pleasant. Their son—commonly known, at this time and in his youth, by his second name—grew up as a farm boy. He was a sickly child, but already there showed through his physical weaknesses, as the biographer J. F. Wall put it, "a kind of inner strength and inflexibility of purpose." One of the joys of his childhood was to ride in his grandfather's fine carriage, an outward symbol contrasting with the impecunious lifestyle to which John Frick's indifferent achievements in farming committed his wife and children. It became Clay's boyhood dream to at least rival Abraham in wealth. Meanwhile, in the school holidays, Clay labored at chores around the farm, carrying wood and water, gathering sheaves, and so on. In this way he earned the money to buy his own clothes.[6]

He attended the district school, in which he was taught by a relative, Henry Overholt. Before he was sixteen, he had left home to live with his uncle Christian S. Overholt, one of the leading merchants in Mount Pleasant and president of the First National Bank. This move was designed to allow him to attend Westmoreland College. In 1866, he went much farther afield, for a short period attending a college organized by the United Brethren, Otterbein University in Westerville, twelve miles north of Columbus, Ohio. Here he showed evidence of some artistic and literary taste, but the only academic subject that interested him was mathematics.

After this brief period away from his home area, he returned to live in the Overholts' brick mansion in Mount Pleasant and to work as a clerk in his uncle's general store. In autumn 1868, he moved to Pittsburgh where he obtained a position in the important store of Macrum and Carlisle, in which his efficiency and courtesy made him a top salesman, especially popular with women customers. He lived on Anderson Street in Allegheny City, just across the Ninth Street Bridge from downtown Pittsburgh. But illness and the ambition to better himself together then brought him back to the country districts, to Broadford, where he was installed by his fond grandfather as chief bookkeeper, at a salary of a thousand dollars a year (which was high for a man not yet twenty). He was there when, in January 1870, Abraham Overholt died at the age of eighty-six.

Clay's business career then took a new direction. His grandfather had mined some coal; his father is alleged to have sometimes exposed its infertile outcrops with his plough; now Clay was to become involved in its more profitable utilization. Others had already realized the possibilities, but it was to be Clay's peculiar achievement to follow the logic of those possibilities

with unrivaled resolution and exceptional success. The natural resource en-
dowment of the area he had been familiar with from birth provided him
with the necessary opportunities to embark on an industrial career.

THE LAND OF HIS YOUTH

Two prominent, level, and continuous ridges run from northeast to southwest across Westmoreland County. They constitute a small part of the western limbs of the Appalachians, a mountain system that wonderfully displays
in its topography the fold structures of which it is built. The larger ridge is
Laurel Hill; parallel to its northern side is Chestnut Ridge, which forms an
attractive forested backdrop to the landscapes of the county. Here are scenes
that even now, almost a century and a half after Clay's birth, are pleasing in
their gentle swelling contours and occasional wooded valleys, the whole
forming a context of deeply rural, traditional America. Seeing it thus (either
today or reconstructed in the mind's eye in Clay's childhood), it is not easy
to imagine that for well over half a century this area was a seething cauldron
of development, intimately involved in the industrialization of the entire
country. In the processes involved in that phase, the young Clay Frick was
to find the business success that gave him wealth far beyond the dreams of
even his rich grandfather.

North of Chestnut Ridge stretch the lowlands through which the main
streams of the Youghiogheny and the Monongahela Rivers meander through
Fayette County toward Pittsburgh. This lower ground contains no strong
landscape features. It had been covered by forest, but by mid century much
of this had been cleared. Farmed, the land gave a reasonable living, though
it was by no means a rich agricultural area. In 1840 in Westmoreland County
there were 43 people per square mile; in Fayette County there were 41; at
the same time Lancaster County in southeastern Pennsylvania, much longer
settled and already a byword for good farming, had a density of 91 people
per square mile. In southwestern Pennsylvania, the potential wealth lay not
in the surface but below it, in its mineral resources. So effectively were these
developed over the next few decades that by 1910 Fayette County was equal
in population to Lancaster County, and Westmoreland County was 40 percent more populous.

The headwaters region of the Ohio River system was well located to serve
the needs of the huge pioneer country lying within or beyond its basin with
lumber, food, and other supplies. Soon after the Revolutionary Wars, ironworks were established here to smelt local ores with charcoal made from the
then abundant woodland. In November 1790, Philadelphia interests blew in
the first blast furnace west of the Alleghenies. It was in Fayette County, on

Jacobs Creek, a few miles above the junction with the Youghiogheny River. This Alliance works was also equipped with a forge. Within another four months, the Union furnace was in blast on Dunbar Creek, four miles south of Connellsville. Over the next twenty years, there was a great growth of furnaces, forges, and mills in the district, so that by 1810 Fayette County contained ten furnaces, eight forges, and three mills.[7] Within another thirty years, practically all this early iron industry had disappeared, mainly because of the reduced availability and rising cost of raw materials. Shortage of woodland that was well placed to provide charcoal seems to have been the major problem; the progress of agriculture (which involved clearing the forests) helped the industrial decline.

It had long been known that this area was richly endowed with coal. As early as autumn 1770, after visiting William Crawford's pioneer farm on the banks of the Youghiogheny, Washington recorded that local coal was burned there. Twenty years later, a new village was laid out nearby. It was named in honor of another pioneer of the area, Zachariah Connell. By the mid 1830s, Connellsville was still known above all as a center of furnaces, forges, and mills, but soon afterward the local coal was recognized not only to be easily accessible but to have physical qualities that made it a prime resource.

The finest coals lay in a shallow basin stretching along the northwestern edge of Chestnut Ridge, a strip of country only three miles wide but some fifty miles in length, extending from just south of Latrobe, southwestward through Mount Pleasant, Connellsville, and Uniontown, and on toward the Monongahela River and the West Virginia line. Within this area, the seams contained scarcely any faults and yielded from 8 to 10 feet of a coal that was of high grade, soft and easily worked. To the east, the coal beds thinned; to the west, the coal became harder. Above all, this "Connellsville" coal was remarkably free of ash and sulphur, and when coked it produced a fine, hard, dense fibrous fuel for the furnace man. Gradually, during the middle decades of the nineteenth century, it was realized that here, beneath cleared forests and farms of only middling grade, under the cold hearths of furnaces abandoned for want of charcoal, was a coal that was ideally suited to the manufacture of the finest metallurgical coke.

FUEL FOR THE IRON INDUSTRY

In Britain, coke iron manufacture had begun in the first decade of the eighteenth century and was overwhelmingly dominant by the end of the century. Under American conditions, coke made its way with much greater difficulty. It was used in the Fairchance furnace, Fayette County, in 1837, but after that this works reverted to using charcoal. By the year of Clay's birth, there was not one coke furnace in blast in Pennsylvania. At that time, following a boom from 1846 to 1848, pig iron production was at a low ebb. Activity revived after 1852 and, within four years, national production was back to the level of ten years before. In a survey, J. P. Lesley then recorded twenty-one iron furnaces in Pennsylvania and three in Maryland.[8]

Between 1850 and 1860 the number of coke-making establishments in the nation increased from four to twenty-one. At the end of the 1860s, national output of coke iron first exceeded that of charcoal iron; six years later coke iron pushed ahead of anthracite iron. This expansion boosted the economy of the prime coking coal district. In turn this area became closely linked to the fortunes of Pittsburgh.

One of the major events of the year in which Clay was five was the building, less than ten miles west of his home, of the track of the Pittsburgh and Connellsville branch of the Baltimore and Ohio Railroad, the pioneer bulk supply link between the new source of fuel and the thriving metallurgical center. At that time, however, there were no blast furnaces in Pittsburgh, so that its expanding requirements for pig iron had to be supplied from furnaces scattered throughout Western Pennsylvania and eastern Ohio. Four years after the opening of the Pittsburgh and Connellsville Railroad, Connellsville coke proved itself in the first successful ironworks built in Allegheny County. The Clinton furnace was erected by the long-established rolling mill firm of Graff, Bennett, and Company at their works in the Birmingham district, just opposite the Point. Succeeding with the new fuel, they then tried to substitute coal from nearer at hand, but the results were unsatisfactory and they went back to the use of Connellsville coke. Their example inspired others to build coke furnaces, and by 1870 there were already seven in Pittsburgh. This in turn spurred further expansion of coke-making capacity. In 1841 there were two ovens in the Connellsville district, in 1850 four, but ten years later there were seventy. By the mid 1870s the number was 550, which by 1879 had increased to 4,200. It was in this decade of feverish growth that Henry Clay Frick's working life and fortunes became inextricably linked with coke.

Beginnings in Coke

In 1859 Clay's cousin Abraham Tinstman, in partnership with Joseph Rist, bought six hundred acres of coal lands. Nine years later, along with Colonel A. S. Morgan, Tinstman began to manufacture coke at the Morgan mine. Morgan soon left the partnership. There is evidence (although it is slight) that, shortly after his grandfather's death, Clay worked for a time for Morgan and Company, coke dealers. It appears that, possibly in the first months of 1871, he may have acted as their agent in Poughkeepsie, New York, which then had iron furnaces.[9]

Facing difficulties in maintaining his footing in the business, Tinstman looked for new partners. Still only twenty years old, Clay came forward, borrowing money for the purpose from various members of his family, including his father who, despite his relative lack of wealth, proved willing to back the greater enterprise of his son. The reconstructed concern began trading on 10 March 1871. The first entry in its Day Book, made that day, is in Clay's hand. It reads:

> Jos. Rist, A. O. Tinstman, J. S. R. Overholt, and H. Clay Frick have this day commenced business as partners under name and style of Overholt, Frick, and Co., the gains and losses to be shared in the following proportions, viz—Jos. Rist the two fifths, A. O. Tinstman the one fifth, J. S. R. Overholt the one fifth, H. Clay Frick the one fifth.[10]

Frick soon proved to be the most go-ahead member of the partnership. They bought 123 acres of coal land near Broadford for over $50,000, and later that year he arranged for them to borrow $10,000 to finance a new plant. His loan came from the recently opened Pittsburgh banking house of T. Mellon and Sons.

It is interesting to speculate why a city banker, enjoying ample opportunities to make loans to local iron and special steel firms in a period of expansion, should have responded to a request from a very young man from the country districts who had little experience in the trade for which he wanted the money. Several reasons may be suggested. Mellon's father, Andrew, had come from Ireland in 1818 and had settled in Westmoreland County, where he became friendly with Abraham Overholt. Thomas had known Clay's mother, Elizabeth, when she was a girl. Family background may explain how Clay gained his appointment with Thomas Mellon, but his own qualities account for his success once there. It is not clear what he could offer as collateral, but the demand for coke was rising impressively, and the ex-judge was shrewd enough to realize that both the trade and the applicant were sound. A man who once remarked of his own courtship, "Had I been rejected, I would have felt neither sad nor depressed, nor greatly disappointed, only annoyed at the loss of time," must have warmed at once to the zeal, directness, and unremitting commitment to business that was shown by the young Clay Frick.[11]

Even before the fifty-oven plant named the Frick works was completed, Clay had applied to Mellon for a second loan of $10,000. This time a representative of the bank recommended that the request be refused. As a result Mellon had a report prepared by a mining partner, which provided a reassuring and perceptive assessment of the operation and its dedicated leading operator: "Lands good, ovens well built; manager on job all day, keeps books evenings, may be a little too enthusiastic about pictures but not enough to hurt; knows his business down to the ground; advise making the loan."[12] The endorsement "knows his business down to the ground" was high praise from an experienced engineer for a twenty-one-year-old who had been in mining and coking for little more than a year.

During 1872, trade continued to boom, fifty more ovens were completed, and a new hundred-oven plant was built and named Henry Clay. By 1873, the firm had been renamed Frick and Company. It now owned four hundred acres of coal lands and two hundred ovens. For a time the firm was able to sell all the coke it could make, being fortunate to be supplying the most rapidly expanding sector of the metallurgical industry, the sector supporting Bessemer steelmaking.

As late as 1867 (the year the Pennsylvania Steel Company made its first steel), there had only been three Bessemer works in the United States, compared with fifty-nine in Europe. Between 1871 and 1873, five more major steel mills came into production: the Cambria, Union, North Chicago, Bethlehem, and Joliet works. All of them concentrated on rails. Whereas in 1872 production of wrought iron rails reached a maximum of 808,000 tons, Bessemer rail output was rising rapidly. For peaking iron rail and expanding steel rail production alike, blast furnace capacity was being extended. In 1867 pig iron production was 1.3 million tons, but by 1873 it was 1.26 million tons more. Over the same period output of iron made using bituminous coal and coke went up by 588,000 tons (or 206 percent). Coal mine and oven capacity had to be extended to keep pace. Yet continued growth could not be relied upon.

In September 1873, the leading U.S. financial house of Jay Cooke collapsed, bringing on a period of retrenchment and depression throughout most of the nation's industries. The manufacturing trades producing capital goods were particularly hard hit. Between 1870 and 1873, the average annual increase in the mileage of U.S. railroads had been 6,243 miles; over the next two years it averaged less than one-third that level. Naturally the effects on the iron trade were severe. Hendrick has painted a dismal picture of Western Pennsylvania at this time.[13] A spectacular example occurred in the center of the coke region. The Connellsville Locomotive works failed and the sheriff had to sell the plant, its materials, and work on hand and on order. Good judges reckoned it was worth between $35,000 and $40,000, but E. K. Hyndman, superintendent of the Connellsville Railroad, was able to buy it for $2,500.[14]

In fact, Western Pennsylvania suffered less than the nation as a whole. Although demand for coke fell sharply, because coke iron was still making headway at the expense of charcoal and anthracite iron, the decrease was smaller. (National pig production fell from 2.6 million tons in 1873, to an average of only 2.1 million tons over the next four years. In 1873, iron made with coke and coal totalled 873,000 tons; over the next two years, it averaged 830,000 tons. By 1876, the level of 1873 production had been surpassed. Anthracite iron production was not back to the 1873 level until 1880; and charcoal iron not until 1881.) Even so, coke makers suffered severely, and the sellers' market now became an arena where buyers could pick and choose their suppliers. The price of coke per ton fell to as little as 90 cents. In these difficult circumstances, Frick had to add to his early managerial achievements the functions of an indefatigable salesman, determined not to lose heart. At the end of his life he still recalled this period as "an awful time."[15]

He retained an apparent unremitting commitment to expansion when opportunity offered, buying coal lands and increasing the number of ovens his company controlled. To this end, he carefully accumulated capital. In 1874 he borrowed more from the Mellons and returned to them again in 1876—in the two years securing, in loans and credits, over $100,000. One coup concerned the ten-mile-long community-built Broadford to Mount Pleasant Railway. He gathered together the options on this and then offered it at a competitive price and with eloquent promotion of its development possibilities to the Baltimore and Ohio Railroad. They bought it and paid him a commission of $50,000. Profits from company stores also provided funds for development.

During the summer of 1875, Franklin Platt examined the coke region on behalf of the Second Geological Survey of Pennsylvania. His report showed that Frick and Company controlled only 2 of the 45 coke works, and 201 of the 3,578 ovens. Frick's works were somewhat bigger than average (by 26 percent), but there were nine bigger ones. After this, the carefully garnered capital resources of Frick and Company were judiciously invested to extend its influence in the region whenever opportunity permitted.

In spring 1875, Frick and Tinstman had negotiated for the purchase of the properties of one of their chief rivals, Morgan and Company. The deal fell through when it was found how weak Morgan's financial situation really was. Shortly after this, Frick bought out his partners, who needed cash to pay debts of their own. In 1877, he loaned money to Daniel Davidson and Alfred Patterson, who were trying to reestablish Morgan and Company.

Over a year later, he refused to extend them any further credit and, having sold an interest in his business to Edmund Morewood Ferguson, used this increase in capital to complete the purchase of the Morgan interests. In 1877 he leased the 102 ovens of the Valley Coke works south of Scottdale. On 9 March 1878, his business was again reconstructed, this time as H. C. Frick and Company, and leased the idle Anchor works west of Dunbar and the Mullen works near Mount Pleasant. Over the next four years, the partnership extended its control of lands and works and, as a result, by 1882 H. C. Frick and Company owned 3,000 acres of coal and 1,026 coke ovens. Meanwhile, on his own account, Frick had organized the Morewood Coke Company and built the 470-oven Morewood works, then the largest in the coke region.[16] When the 1870s began there had been about 300 ovens in the Connellsville district; by 1876 there were 3,500; and in 1879 in excess of 4,000. In addition to making him a dominant force in coal and coke, Frick's experiences in the difficult and uncertain conditions of the 1870s helped shape his attitudes to raising capital, to business methods generally, and above all to labor.

He had proved a shrewd operator, but as demand for coking coal was likely to increase, he usually had to pay a high price for what he bought. In the early 1870s, Wilson, Ewing, Boyle of Uniontown had purchased a 440-acre coal tract, for most of which they paid $2.50 an acre. It was underlain to the extent of three-quarters of the whole area by the Connellsville seam. In 1882 Frick bought it from them for $180,000 (or $409.09 an acre).[17] At about the same time he was hoping to buy flat bottomland near the Valley works from the Sherrick interests. He gave Thomas Lynch, his manager, careful guidelines for the negotiations:

> [You are] to call upon Mr. Sherrick on Monday and get the option on that land near Valley on the best terms you can. He may want to include his entire farm and if he does and insists upon it, and you cannot get the option on the other without that, take the option on the whole thing. His price heretofore has been $300.00 per acre for the flat land. You can probably do better with him.[18]

He sold as well as bought. Occasionally this was for general development. Always he was businesslike. To Lynch he wrote, "I gave a letter of introduction to a gentleman from Cincinnati who will call on you on Monday, and who is desirous of locating a facing mill somewhere in the Connellsville region. I would like you to show him our land near Valley . . . and also our land near Summit. . . . Let me know what he thinks."[19] He also sold coal lands that, once bought, had proved unnecessary. In 1885 he wrote to John G. Leishman (with whom he was a little later to be closely connected in business), who at this time was acting on behalf of an undisclosed party for purchase of coal lands on the John K. Ewing farm. Frick wanted to appear reasonable:

> [T]o a party such as you represent we would be willing to sell an undivided one-half interest in that farm, together with an interest in as much coal adjoining it as they might want, upon as fair terms as they could purchase from anyone in that locality. . . . If your party means business, we would be very glad to meet them personally and show them over the ground. Think we could suggest an arrangement which would be mutually beneficial. In regard to the property near Mount Pleasant, we would sell it at a very much less price per acre than we would this property, for the reason that the latter is nearer a good supply of water and the vein is somewhat thicker.[20]

Early attempts were made to interest him in coal and coke possibilities in other districts. It is difficult to know how many of these inquiries he initiated, and how many other businessmen wrote to him unasked. He resisted attempts to involve him in western coals, but once he had to write replies to two men on the same day to convey his reactions to coal, limestone, and (in one case) iron ore specimens sent to him from Colorado, which suggests that in this instance at least he may have set the matter in train. To one Colorado correspondent he wrote, "I have made up my mind not to extend my interests further at the moment." The other one had also suggested that he take a financial share in a project, to which Frick replied, "I have so many interests that need my attention that I do not believe, even if I joined you in this, I could be of the service that you expect of me."[21]

However, by as early as 1881, he was showing much more interest in prospects for coke making from the coals of the Hawks Nest area of the Great Kanawha Valley in central West Virginia. He wanted to lease two oven plants there from W. N. Page, and he was keen enough to be willing to pay the price asked and to send his own men to see Page about the trial. He indicated that this serious approach was because he was thinking of investing there: "Before buying the Loupe Creek tract we should like to make some coke and ship it to some of our trade, in order to give it a thorough test."[22] It is unknown whether the tests ever took place and what the results were, but later that decade, he consistently declined to become involved in coking coal and coke developments in the various mineral districts of West Virginia and Virginia.

At this time, like other Pennsylvanians, he ventured outside his own trade to speculate in oil. On 3 October 1881, he reported that he had looked out at the club for C. C. Beggs in the hope of consulting him about the oil situation. Not finding him there, he sold twenty thousand barrels of oil, but (as he wrote to Beggs), "It looks to us a little as if oil was going to hang around at these figures for some time and we will keep the run of the market and get it back if possible before any material advance." Less than two years later, he sold five thousand barrels at 92 cents for W. J. Hitchorn of Mount Pleasant. It was not a profitable sale: "I regret that you have made a loss in this and hope that you may have better luck next time."[23]

He made investments in non-ferrous metal mining in the west but quickly drew in his horns. During 1881 he acquired a two-fifths stake in the Anna Bella Lode and a half-interest in the Baker Lode, both in Colorado. This was followed by correspondence concerning prospects in western mineral investment with George D. Nickel who, after living in Pennsylvania until the second half of the 1870s, was now based in Del Norte, Colorado. Shortly afterward, prices for lead, copper, and zinc fell sharply, and Frick became unwilling to risk further involvement. He thanked Nickel for materials sent but went on, "I do not desire to increase my interest in mining property; would much prefer to sell out."[24]

All these activities may perhaps have increased his accumulation of capital or they could have been a drain on his resources; in any case his main source of income remained coke. In the depression of the mid 1870s, the price had been as low as 90 cents a ton, at which level operations yielded no profit. At the end of the decade demand recovered. In 1875, the region shipped 666,000 tons of coke, representing utilization of about half the capacity of the ovens. For the following two years, output was 770,000 and 869,000 tons respectively, but in the first half of 1878, it was running at an annual rate of 1,076,000 tons. Prices advanced to $2 and then further until eventually they reached $5 a ton. At that price, sales yielded a profit of $3 a ton.[25] A few years before, Frick had been hawking his wares from one ironworks or foundry to another; now the ironmasters of Pittsburgh came to his office in the coke region to request that their orders for coke be supplied. Before the end of 1879, as he passed his thirtieth birthday, Clay Frick was a millionaire.

In the early 1880s, although coke prices were not so high, consumption was increasing rapidly, and the tonnage of iron made in 1882 was twice as great as in 1878. Levels of income remained high. Thus in the fourteen months to the end of February 1883, the H. C. Frick Coke Company mined eighty-two acres of coal, and from it made and sold 596,000 tons of coke. It also bought 350,000 tons of coke from other producers, which it sold with its own product. Sales of coke, made and bought, resulted in a profit of $378,000 (an average per ton amounting to 27.05 percent of the selling price).[26]

As a producer, Frick was always concerned to lower costs. To do so, he improved methods, pared away at freight rates, but above all (in what was still a labor intensive industry) struggled to maintain "competitive" wage rates. Much of the coke region workforce consisted of recent immigrants, men who were used to the deprivations of European rural areas. The district was relatively isolated from bigger centers of population, even Pittsburgh being more than forty miles away. Lack of financial means on the part of the men, and language difficulties for many of them, meant that in real terms they were even more isolated than such distances might suggest. Given these circumstances, not surprisingly, the coke operators provided their workers with low wages and minimal living conditions. Strikes were dealt with firmly. Because of the distance of some of the mines and oven plants from preexisting rural settlements, the firms opened company stores. The H. C. Frick Company even printed their own scrip to be used in stores, hotels, and saloons in place of U.S. currency.[27] Whether by intention or mere effect, this practice helped produce still more "surplus value" from the laboring population.

Evidence was given in 1878 and 1879 to the Pennsylvania Secretary of Internal Affairs concerning the Frick Company stores. Although Lynch was to take delight in instances when their produce was cheaper than in other groceries or general stores, at this time, Frick Company stores were said to be selling flour at $9.60 a barrel at a time when it was available elsewhere at $8. The company might legitimately have claimed that it had a narrower clientele over which to spread its overheads, or that it had to bear extra costs for delivery, but—the Secretary was also informed—the men were given to understand that if the scrip was not spent in the company stores, they might eventually lose their jobs. In the fourteen months in which coke made profits of $378,000, the Frick stores added another $33,000, a sum that (as Frick's own figures showed) was equal to 16.86 percent of the total sales income of those stores.[28]

During these hard formative years in the coke industry, Frick was developing a view of labor that all too often resulted in its being treated as merely another input, which the capitalist must strive to obtain at the lowest possible price. Commercially this view was a logical position to take, but it could scarcely commend the manager who practiced it to his men. Labor disputes were inevitable. Frick was to pay a price for his success in these struggles in terms of his own character. As time was to show, below the icily efficient business exterior there was passion as well as concentration and intensity. Together such qualities formed a dangerous combination.

A new, more diverse stage of Frick's life began in his early thirties. He had known Thomas Mellon's son Andrew since 1876. They became firm friends, a friendship that was to be lifelong, although Mellon never used a more intimate form of address than "Mr. Frick," and the latter always referred to Andrew, four years his junior, and his brother Richard Beatty as "the Mellon boys." In spring 1880 Clay suggested that Andrew go with him on a holiday visit to Europe. They were joined in this four-month trip by the journalist Frank Cowan and a coke maker, A. A. Hutchinson (some of whose coal lands Frick managed to buy during the course of their journeys). They traveled around the British Isles, to Paris, and on to Venice.

Some months after he returned, Frick moved his home from the coke region to Pittsburgh, renting rooms in March 1881 at the Monongahela House, then reckoned one of the city's best residential hotels. In the "season," Frick and Mellon—both normally taciturn men—became largely involved in the functions of Pittsburgh's social round, and in the late spring of 1881, Clay met Adelaide Howard, the daughter of Asa P. Childs, a man whose wealth had come from the import and the manufacture of footwear. The Childs home, at Halket and Forbes Streets was then regarded as one of the show pieces of the city. Clay fell in love with Adelaide, and three months later they announced their engagement. They were married on Thursday, 15 December 1881, in what was described by a local paper as "one of the most notable weddings of the season."[29] Frick was fortunate in the family life that he and Adelaide now embarked upon. Adelaide understood the demands of business, and he could now turn to his working routine with renewed vigor and a widening sense of purpose. In fact it was during their honeymoon visit to the East Coast that Frick first met Andrew Carnegie and their business association began.

INDUSTRIAL CONNECTIONS

A distinctive feature of the headlong American economic growth that characterized the later decades of the nineteenth century was the frequent extension of productive capacity well beyond the needs of all but exceptional years. This was undoubtedly the case in coke manufacture. Apart from restraint in expansion, which might end up giving the market to the other man, there were two important ways of tackling the problem. One was to fix prices and allocate shares of the expected demand so as to keep all producers reasonably happy. The other was to secure outlets for one's own ovens through arrangements with major consumers. From the other side, that of demand, although a free market might give them advantages of low prices in times of slack business, buyers might at times of boom be caught out by high prices or even physical shortages of fuel. In such circumstances the result could be disastrous: highly capitalized operations in iron smelting, steelmaking, and rolling mills being disrupted or even made idle by bottlenecks in fuel supply. In short, both large coke producers and major concerns in iron and steel could see advantages in associating with each other.

By the early 1880s, in a rising market, the Frick Coke Company was already the leading single firm in its trade. Both the firm and the district were carried along still more rapidly because the growth of the Pittsburgh iron trade was even more rapid than that of the nation generally (Allegheny County made 5.3 percent of America's pig iron in 1874 and almost 7 percent six years later.) Within Pittsburgh, the pacemaking concerns were owned by the Carnegie associates. Construction of their main steel plant—the Edgar Thomson works in Braddock—had begun only in 1873, and the works came into production two years later. This was a time of generally inauspicious market conditions, but steel rail production was still rising strongly. In 1875, national output of steel rails was over three times greater than in 1872; by 1879, output was 138 percent above the 1875 figure. Edgar Thomson increased its net profits from $18,642 in 1875, to $512,068 in 1879, to $1,557,771 the following year. From 1879, Edgar Thomson was equipped with blast furnaces. The Carnegies also operated the Lucy furnaces in Pittsburgh. A considerable proportion of the increasing Frick shipments of coke were delivered to these two furnace plants, and it soon became logical that there should be a coming together of the leading interests in their respective trades. Before they reached that stage, however, the Carnegie associates had spent a great deal of time, effort, and expense looking for other sources of furnace fuel. Their failure in this endeavor was to bring Henry Clay Frick and Andrew Carnegie into close association.

2

Complexities in Coke and Steel

―⸲⸲⸲∫∫⸲⸲⸲―

Iron and Coke Since the Civil War

After the disturbances of the Civil War years, U.S. iron and steel production advanced rapidly. The raw materials on which this increase depended became the iron ores of the upper Great Lakes and the coals of
the northern Appalachian plateau. The main outlets were in the expanding
infrastructure of a subcontinent now experiencing the full tide of economic
growth. In 1860 pig iron production had been a record 835,000 tons, but by
1869 output was already more than twice that. In the boom of the early
1870s, output rose to more than three times that on the eve of the war. After
the general depression of the mid 1870s output resumed its upward course,
so that in 1881, at 4.2 million tons, output was more than five times the 1860
figure.

Not only was the economy developing rapidly, but its westward movement was becoming more pronounced. A matching shift occurred in the
railroad system, whose track requirements constituted the largest single outlet for iron and later for steel. In 1860 New England and the Middle Atlantic
states contained almost 33 percent of the mileage of railroads; in 1880 their
share was 22.6 percent. Purchases for track renewal meant that the Northeast
remained more important than these changes suggest, but the geographical
shift in demand was undeniable.

THE ROLE OF PITTSBURGH

In terms of location, increasing use of Lake ore gave the iron and steel industries an impetus toward the Lakes in order to minimize further land
haulage on ores that were, year by year, being carried at lower costs in bigger

21

(and eventually specially designed) ore boats. Market changes added a strong westward component. Yet in spite of both these trends, another leading feature of the iron trade at this time was the persistence (indeed the increased significance) of the Pittsburgh district, whose share of the entire U.S. rolled iron production in 1874 was 24.73 percent; between 1896 and 1898 it averaged 30 percent of the national total of rolled iron and steel. Although Pittsburgh did not make steel rails before 1875, by 1878 it rolled 13.13 percent of the total, and in the late 1890s it rolled as much as 29 percent.

In pig iron, Pittsburgh registered an even more impressive advance (5.8 percent of the U.S. total in 1875, 14.5 percent in 1890, and 27.6 percent in 1897) at the very time that a relative decline might have been anticipated. Much of this large growth represented a movement to self-sufficiency, with accompanying reductions in purchases from other areas, notably from the Valleys district. Given the large growth in national output, these increased proportions represent a massive rise in Pittsburgh tonnages, from 132,000 to 2,663,000 tons over the twenty-two years from 1875 to 1897. Such a situation at variance with the trend of locational influences is puzzling at first sight, but the answer can be found partly in the fuel supply and partly in the way iron and steel production was managed so as to lower processing costs and make the area highly competitive. Frick played an important part in both these respects.

Successful pig iron production in the Pittsburgh district dated only from 1859. From that late start, the supremacy of Connellsville coke not only over other fuels but over other cokes became universally recognized. The city's proximity to the coke district was a major asset. Elsewhere, users of Connellsville coke faced not only higher freight charges but another (though relatively minor) disadvantage, the slight degeneration of the coke in long-distance carriage. Coke production in 1880 (at 1.85 million tons) was just short of three times the level of 1875. In 1876, the Connellsville district had 3,578 ovens, but by the end of May 1880 there were 6,237 ovens, with another 1,242 building.

In spite of this dramatic increase in coke, the advance in iron production, especially in Allegheny County, kept pace. Given the headlong growth of both, there was always a possibility that their prices would get out of step, thus increasing the swings in the prosperity of the iron and steel industry— its character as "prince" or "pauper," as Carnegie once put it. His own concern's involvement in pig iron was increasing. In spring 1871 (almost at the same time as Frick was first venturing into coke) Carnegie, Kloman, and Company began building a blast furnace at Fifty-first Street in Pittsburgh. This, the first of the Lucy furnaces, was completed in early summer 1872.

Concern for its operating conditions marked the beginning of Carnegie's interest in coke.

The Carnegies' Search for Improved Fuel

The Carnegies' cousin George Lauder ("Dod") was trained as a mechanical engineer at Glasgow University. On one occasion of unknown date he took William Coleman, one of the Carnegie partners, on a visit to the works of the Wigan Coal and Iron Company in Lancashire. The coal there was of inferior quality and consequently had to be washed before being charged into the coke ovens. Coleman realized that a similar process might make usable the small coal or slack then being thrown away at Pennsylvania mines. In December 1871, Andrew Carnegie agreed to advance money for a washery and ovens to be erected along the Pennsylvania Railroad at Larimer Station, just east of Turtle Creek; Lauder was to be manager. Six years later, Larimer was brought into the Carnegie association.

In addition to investing in this plant, the Carnegies considered other possible sources of fuel. For instance, in 1872 Carnegie corresponded with F. B. Hubbell about leasing three hundred acres of coal and building two hundred ovens. He stressed that they wanted an option to buy if the arrangement went well. Gradually and for various reasons the Larimer operations proved disappointing. Early in their development, Lauder had gently chided his cousin for, not untypically, expecting more from them than was reasonable: "I judge from your telegram that you must have got imbued with some strange notion of the magnitude of our works here. Have only 80 ovens and usual calculation is one ton of coke a day [per oven]. At present are getting 14 cars of slack a day and this supplies only 68 ovens."[1]

Difficulties with supplies of small coal continued, and as a result E. C. Biddle of the Westmoreland Coal Company and his brother became objects for Carnegie's anger. He accused them of utilizing the slack their ovens might have carbonized in constructing sidings and for ballasting a new track up Timber Run. He also objected to paying more than 10 cents a gross ton for the material and suggested that to ensure they got fair treatment, Biddle should send his superintendents a copy of their contract. He ended, "We are all weary of being apparently considered as only poor pensioners upon your bounty, dependent upon your own sweet will for any crumbs you may in your own good nature see fit to shower upon us." Their capital outlay, he revealed, had been three times and their profits only half as much as expected.[2]

Increasing requirements for coke were more important incentives to fur-

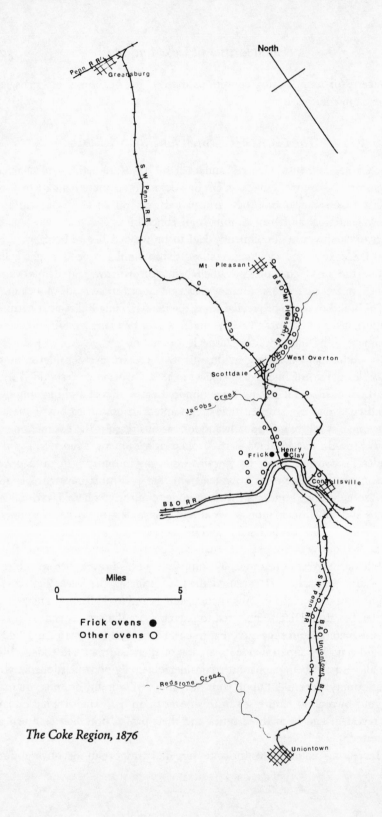

North

Penn RR /
Greensburg

S W Penn R R

Mt Pleasant

B & O Mt Pleasant Br

West Overton

Scottdale

Jacobs Creek

O Frick Henry O
         O Clay

Connellsville

B & O RR

Miles
0 — — — — — 5

Frick ovens ●
Other ovens ○

S W Penn RR

B & O Uniontown Br

Redstone Creek

The Coke Region, 1876

Uniontown

ther efforts than all these discontents. By early February 1872, their first car-loads of Connellsville coke arrived, ready for the lighting of the Lucy furnace.[3] A second stack was built there five years later. By the early 1880s, annual capacity at these furnaces was 95,000 tons iron. At current rates this would require almost 200,000 tons coke. In the late 1870s, they also put up two furnaces at Braddock to supply the Edgar Thomson converters. Relative to the needs of these four furnaces, their capacity to produce coal and coke was slight. By 1877 Larimer contained 140 ovens; in 1880 they built another 60 there. By the time of the consolidation of Edgar Thomson and the Lucy furnaces in spring 1881 to form Carnegie Brothers and Company, they also owned the Monastery works near Latrobe, with mines, 50 ovens dating from 1874, and another 60 that were installed in 1880. Together, the 310 ovens of the two works gave them an annual coke capacity of about 140,000 tons, no more than about two-thirds of the tonnage used by the Lucy furnaces alone. Consequently the Carnegies remained large purchasers of coke. Their de-pendence on the open market brought with it unacceptable levels of uncer-tainty, and they continued to search for either coking coal of their own or coke firms with which they could associate.

One of the most intriguing episodes of this search concerned the possible purchase of the Valley works near Everson. The puzzling thing is that Frick had leased this property three years before. A detailed memorandum on Valley was produced by Lauder in December 1879. In it he noted that the plant had 102 ovens and 379 acres of coal land—but behind the works were "at least 2,000 acres not yet touched." Frick had paid $200,000 for it. Lauder thought they could build another 150 ovens and provide the necessary 90 cars for an estimated $82,000. An installation of 250 ovens would provide 110,000 tons coke annually. With operating expenses of $0.84 and interest and depreciation at $0.42 a ton they should make coke for $1.26, whereas the current selling price was $1.75. He reckoned they might have net earnings of $54,000 or almost 20 percent on their outlay.[4] He was negotiating not with Frick but with the independent coke makers Wilson, Boyle, and Play-ford of Uniontown, who offered the property at $200,000. The correspon-dence did not result in the acquisition of Valley works.[5]

Early in 1880 Carnegie wrote to Samuel Felton—president both of the Pennsylvania Steel Company and of the collective organization of the indus-try, the Bessemer Steel Company—to sound him out on the possibility of joining with other steel companies in making coke. A few weeks later, the Edgar Thomson Steel Company authorized Tom Carnegie and John Scott to purchase the Morgan coke property. At this time David A. Stewart, one of the original partners in the Edgar Thomson plant, provided a clear ratio-

TABLE 1

The Connellsville Coke Industry, 1870–1871, 1876, 1901

Year	Companies	Coke Works	Ovens
1870–1871	na	7	550
1876	42	45	3,455[a]
1901	34	96	21,919

Sources: Platt 1876; Fulton 1884–1885, p. 334; Coal and Coke, 8 Feb. 1901; Eavenson 1942.

Note: [a] Some accounts indicate 3,578 ovens.

nale for backward integration, the avoiding of an underuse of their finishing capacity at a time when they were rolling about two thousand tons of rails a week: "I do not like to depend on the chances of getting coke from the manufacturers and we may have one of our furnaces out of blast or stop converting works. This would cost us more than a few dollars in coke property."[6]

On the other hand, Henry Phipps, always a key figure, wanted them to advance cautiously and above all to be sure that they should not make a link that involved the second best. He pointed out that extra costs would be involved in crushing and washing Latrobe coal as compared with that from the main Connellsville area "and unless that can be compensated for, Morgan's is not what we are hunting. . . . Before proceeding any further in the Morgan purchase, it is important that we should have an arrangement as to the rate of freight to Bessemer—also to Lucys." However, by early March Stewart reported they had the Morgan works in good shape and would soon get a good supply from there.[7] At this time they were also considering association with Mullen (who had interests in eight thousand acres of coal), a link with the Davidsons, or the purchase of a half-share in the Globe and Standard coke works of A. A. Hutchinson (for the former of which Frick had already offered $240,000, although $300,000 had been asked).[8]

Early in 1881 the search for coke-making associates brought Carnegie to William J. Rainey who had been a coke producer for only two years. Apparently they thought of a jointly managed concern, but Carnegie was keen to stress that for his company's part they wanted independence of action. Clearly he was most unwilling to risk being tied to an unreliable or inefficient producer: "We wish to burn our coke longer . . . in unusual ways, as we consume the product ourselves and our coke operations based upon market prices may not show much profit."[9] The implications for future coke-making associates were ominous.

A final line of possible investment was to open up new areas that were well placed to ship coke at low cost by water. To this end, Tom Carnegie and George Lauder inspected coking coals along the Cheat River inside West Virginia. Both were highly optimistic about the prospects. Lauder was clear and brief: "Tom and I are going up with Davidson to see his coal on Cheat river, if you want something for the future that is the place." For his part, Tom was attracted by the possible economies in carriage:

> The present rail rate Connellsville region is 86$^2/_3$ cents per ton to Bessemer. Shippers *load* and *unload*. From Cheat River to Bessr., Slackwater would not exceed 15 c for transportation, the expense of loading remaining the same as by rail, and unloading say 5 c per ton more. . . . The cost of coke in the Stockhouse at Bessr. for transportation and loading and unloading would be say 20 cts pr ton—when Connellsville costs 86$^2/_3$ c less 5c or 81$^2/_3$ c per ton. This for Bessr. if we figure for Lucys—the gain is very much greater and if we look to a market on the river below Pittsburgh, Wheeling, Cincinatti, St. Louis etc. it is not necessary to figure the advantage of mines on the Slackwater. So much for water—Rail Transportation will be within our reach as soon as we will say to the PRR that we will build 200 ovens.[10]

However, the finest coking coals were confined to the smaller area of Connellsville proper, and their quality more than cancelled out the undoubted benefits of all-water transport from possible Cheat River ovens to the furnaces. The attractions of the Connellsville area thus remained strong.

Lauder realized that building more of their own ovens would be a costly business, and they could not be sure of the price of coke: "I cannot see my way to go into another big debt in Coke. To build another 100 ovens would run the cost up to over $200,000 and they could not be started for six months by which time coke will be God knows where."[11] Certainly prices had been volatile, but expanding iron production seemed likely to bring future rises in coke prices. During the second half of the 1870s, the price for coke at Connellsville ovens had ranged between $0.9 and $1.15 a ton. In 1879 pig production was 19 percent greater than in the previous year; in Pittsburgh the increase was 23 percent. The price for coke for a time had advanced to $4, and then to $5.[12] In 1881 iron production in Allegheny County was 168,000 tons (77 percent up on the 1878 figure). During 1881 prices for iron and steel fell; the decline in coke prices was smaller (see table 2).

As this happened, the Carnegies faced the prospect of needing a considerable increase in their coke supplies. In March 1881, in petitioning Alexander Cassatt of the Pennsylvania Railroad for fair rates on coke, Carnegie had affected to be nonchalant about the situation: "Our great consumption of Connellsville coke does not come until new furnaces are finished which I

TABLE 2
Iron, Steel, and Coke Prices, 1880, 1881

	1880	1881	Percentage Decline 1880–1881
Pig iron, no. 1 Foundry	28.48	25.17	11.62
Steel rails	67.52	61.08	9.54
Coke (U.S. average) at ovens	1.99	1.88	5.53

Note: Dollar amounts are per gross ton for iron and steel, per net ton for coke.

promise you will not be this year."[13] Yet the blowing in of those two new stacks in the following January would dangerously increase their dependence on the open market for coke. For an expansion-minded and perennially cost-conscious ironmaster greater control over this raw material was undeniably desirable.

From another point of view, as Frick's capacity increased, it might be of benefit to him to secure at least some tied outlets within his rapidly extending open-market operations. Another incentive for association with an iron company was that he might thereby obtain additional capital to finance extensions in coal mining and coke making, although it is well to remember that he was already investing some (though probably not very much) of his capital outside the coal and coke industry, as in western non-ferrous metal mining. By spring 1879, his company was selling coke to some fifty-four iron furnace companies over an area that stretched from New Jersey to St. Louis and Milwaukee. Seven of the customers listed at that time were in Pittsburgh, including both the Lucy Furnace Company and the Edgar Thomson Steel Company. Over the next two years these Carnegie outlets became more important, although there were wide variations in the destination of dispatches from week to week and even from day to day (see table 3).

Association at Arm's Length

Hendrick reports (but indicates neither date nor source) that the idea of association with Frick was first mooted by Carnegie during a Sunday afternoon stroll over the hills near Cresson in the healthy hill country of Cambria County: "We must attach this young man Frick to our concern. He has great ability and great energy. Moreover, he has the coke—and we need it." But this has the tone and flavor of a remark imagined by a later commentator. Carnegie himself was no help in filling out the steps toward an association. In his *Autobiography* he recorded, in the only reference to Frick by

TABLE 3

H. C. Frick Coke Company, Major Coke Shipments, 31 March 1881

	Cars	Tons
Edgar Thomson Steel Co., Pittsburgh	810	11,032
Lucy Furnace Co., Pittsburgh	4	74
Joliet Steel Co., Illinois	129	1,677
Union Iron and Steel Co., Chicago	278	3,781[a]
Jones and Laughlin Ltd., Pittsburgh	12	212
Isabella Furnace Co., Pittsburgh	153	2,203
Wheeling Iron Nail Co., West Virginia	276	3,754[a]
A. A. Hutchinson and Co., coke region	502	6,827[a]

Source: H. C. Frick Coke Company Day Book, Frick Papers.

Note: [a] Indicates tonnage estimated by author at rate of 13.6 tons per car.

name in the whole of that fascinating (though not infrequently faulty) record of his own career, "a very thorough investigation of the question led us to the conclusion that the Frick Coke Company had not only the best coal and coke property, but that it had in Mr. Frick himself a man with a positive genius for its management. He had proved his ability by starting as a poor railway clerk [!] and succeeding."[14]

In fact, in mid January 1880, when the Carnegie interests were still looking in various directions for possible future coke supplies, it was Phipps who pointed them toward H. C. Frick and Company. He argued that investment there might not only solve their fuel supply problem but also prove remunerative. According to his reckoning, Frick's company was probably making a profit of $1.50 on each of the 720,000 tons of coke it produced: "take it say at half—and unless a great deal of boom has been added it might be a good thing."[15]

The coke capacity controlled by Frick early in October 1881 was considerably in excess of Phipps's estimate of the previous year, about 75,000 tons a month, or almost seven times the tonnage operated by the Carnegies. It was probably a few weeks after the reported Cresson walk that Tom Carnegie as chairman of Carnegie Brothers got in touch with Frick, apparently to ask advice about their own coke plants. The situation is by no means clear: it appears that costs at Monastery were high but that its prices for coke were also above average. (A year after these events, orders for Monastery coke were so large that it was priced at from $1.50 to $1.60 per ton; the 1882 average for the Connellsville region was $1.47 and in 1883 $1.14).[16] It was proposed that H. C. Frick Coke should acquire or control Monastery or at least buy and market its product. Frick replied on 30 November 1881, "I am called to the Coke Region this morning, consequently cannot see you as expected." Before he gave Tom an answer, he would go up to Latrobe to see their works: "I will go out there on Friday, unless something occurs that I do not know of now; and on Friday evening or Saturday morning will be able to let you know the best we will do."[17] Tom thought it best to sell Monastery coke (which they had been using to the extent of fifteen cars a day at the Lucy furnaces) and buy Connellsville coke: "I hope to arrange with Frick and Co. or Tinsman [sic] to take our Monastery coke at about $1.80 and give us Connellsville at present price for Lucy."[18]

A few days later Frick and Andrew Carnegie first met. In the course of their December honeymoon trip to the East Coast, Henry and Adelaide Frick visited New York. There they were entertained by Carnegie and his formidable mother, Margaret, to a formal midday dinner in the Windsor Hotel. Wall gives the impression that even Frick did not know what was coming; Harvey focuses on the contrast between Carnegie and Frick, "one voluble and hilarious, the other reticent and courteous." At the end of the meal Carnegie announced that he and Frick had become partners, and he toasted their future success. Further details are not available, but it seems Frick had accepted a proposal that Tom and Andrew Carnegie had worked out early in December. Margaret Carnegie reacted to her son's toast with the grating query, "Ah, Andra, that's a verra good thing for Mr Freek, but what do we get out of it?" The simple answer was security for long-term expansion in iron and steel.[19]

The first intimation of the agreement is in a cable, by no means clear, that Andrew sent his brother on 23 or 24 December: "Gentleman came to our original figure. January first one and a half instead of March first. Adds 25 if other be embraced at one ninety. Have written." Three days after Christmas, in a letter to Robert Garrett of the Baltimore and Ohio Railroad, who had been extremely tardy in quoting them freight charges on coke for the coming year, Carnegie triumphantly revealed their new situation. They were now to be a major factor in that trade as producers as well as consumers: "We have completed the purchase of one half of all Frick and Co. Coke Works. This with our own ovens makes us by far the largest manufacturers of the article."[20]

Over the next few years, the link was widened and deepened, and for a time things went smoothly. Within a few days of the New York agreement, Phipps was urging Carnegie to consult Frick at once about the desirability of buying half the A. A. Hutchinson coke interest. Already he had formed a high opinion of their new associate's business capacities: "If Mr. Frick de-

Andrew Carnegie in the late 1870s. *Photograph by W. Kurtz, N.Y., Courtesy of Old Westbury Gardens Archives.*

sires the transaction, his partners will of course be with him and this I presume would be recommendation sufficient to your brother." For Phipps, Frick stood far above his partners the Fergusons: "In our various negotiations I have found Mr. Frick clear-headed but can not say as much for his two associates. Mr. F. is the man to deal with."[21] However, Phipps's good business sense and caution was disturbed by any suggestion that, as Frick requested, they should contract exclusively with him for their future needs. He felt that Carnegie had taken a "broad and liberal view of this matter," and if their investment in his company was not sufficient earnest of their commitment, then Frick must be "the most lacking in faith of any man whom I have ever met."[22]

Meanwhile, Carnegie and Frick were in close contact. The first surviving direct communication between them is probably a cable sent by Carnegie on 6 January 1882 to Frick at the Continental Hotel in Philadelphia: "Will you be in Philadelphia tomorrow? If so will see you at Continental in morning. Answer to Windsor."[23] As usual, Carnegie was soon conceiving great schemes for development, which now included their interest in coke. This came out in a letter on 11 January 1882 to Alexander Cassatt, then vice-president of the Pennsylvania Railroad. At this time their fuel supplies had been secured, but the situation with respect to ore was uncertain, with various fields in possible contention (including Pilot Knob and Iron Mountain some eighty miles south of St. Louis). He informed Cassatt that they had bought half the Frick coke works, "extending in an unbroken line on both sides of the Valley three and a half miles from Broadford to Valley works with which your line is connected." His imagination then took wing, and he envisioned a shuttle-service exchange of coke and ore similar to the one that was later developed with the Lake Erie shore:

> We are the only party who could establish a trade from St. Louis to Steel Rail Works with ore and from Mines to St. Louis with coke. . . . I am satisfied we could use 500 cars in this East and West traffic to our mutual advantage. One thing you would be sure of in our case, viz, we have the coke and the ore to carry. It could be made a permanent growing trade if properly encouraged.[24]

In spite of Phipps's reservations, an agreement was concluded whereby all the coke required by the Lucy and Edgar Thomson furnaces was to be bought from the H. C. Frick Company. The financial terms were to be agreed by Tom Carnegie and Frick on 1 January each year. Andrew was now an enthusiastic advocate of their coke interests. By April he was commending it to Orrin W. Potter of the North Chicago Rolling Mill Company—even though Potter had said that he was not at present in the market for coke.[25] In May 1882, a new company—the H. C. Frick Coke Company—was formed with a capital of $2 million, of which (not withstanding Carnegie's claims to Garrett and to Cassatt) he, his brother, Phipps, and Carnegie Brothers and Company at first controlled only 11.25 percent, or little more than one-third of Frick's own interest. H. C. Frick Coke took a half interest in the Monastery works.

FRICK ADVOCATES EXPANSION

A year after their first meeting, Carnegie wrote to thank Frick for a report on their business: "I am much pleased with the statement sent me. I think

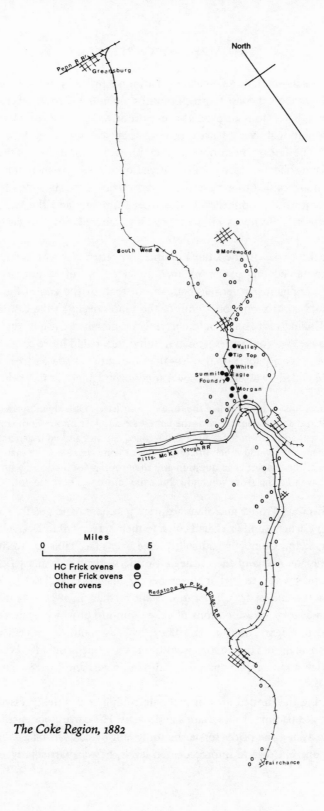

North

Penn R R'y
Greensburg

South West
Morewood

Valley
Tip Top
White
Summit Eagle
Foundry
Morgan

Pitts. McK & Yough RR

Miles

| 0 | 5 |

HC Frick ovens ●
Other Frick ovens ⊖
Other ovens ○

Redstone Br. P. Va & Ches. RR

The Coke Region, 1882

Fairchance

we can live in any kind of weather." Early in April 1883, Frick reported to Tom Carnegie on the last fourteen months' operations. In that period they had sold 946,000 tons of coke at a net profit of $377,909 (or 39.9 cents a ton—the national average price of coke that year was $1.77 a ton at the ovens).[26] The Edgar Thomson and Lucy furnaces had taken less than one-third of the coke, but even so, Frick urged on his new partners the need to allocate more capital to expand their oven capacity. He suggested that they should acquire the Connellsville Gas Coal Company and the Hutchinson coke properties. Tom was willing to give his approval, but Andrew had reservations.

Frick responded to the latter's doubts in a letter that was reasoned, but which contained one paragraph that indicated he might not necessarily prove a compliant partner. He pointed out that, by the end of the season, they would control only one-tenth of the 10,100 ovens in the Connellsville region. Coking coal lands could currently be obtained cheaply, and if they acquired the two companies he had in mind they could more or less double their oven capacity for $850,000 less than the outlay made on their existing plant. He ended by asserting his own superior judgment in this field:

> I am free to say, I do not like the tone of your letter. Outside of my desire to follow and accept your views as the largest stockholder in our Company—I have great admiration for your acknowledged abilities and your general good judgment, and would much prefer to defer to your views—in the matter of the values of the properties in question and the propriety of increasing our stock I shall have to differ from you and I think the future will bear me out.[27]

He got his way. Trotter and Standard were purchased and greatly extended.

When Carnegie and Frick had come to their agreement in December 1881, H. C. Frick and Company controlled 1,026 ovens (see table 4). To this were added the 208 ovens of the Carnegie Brothers' plant at Monastery, 400 at Trotter and 573 at Standard in November 1883, giving H. C. Frick Coke 2,207 ovens by the end of 1883. Expansion went further. In 1882–1883 they produced an average of 45,000 tons of coke a month, of which 25 percent was delivered to Edgar Thomson and Lucy. By 1885 about 40 percent of their monthly average of 130,000 tons went to the Carnegie works. Two years later H. C. Frick and Company had five thousand ovens and by 1889 almost ten thousand.[28]

Realizing the limited area of first-rate coking coal, Frick pressed ahead with the acquisition of more lands and ovens. His correspondence was full of letters asking the prices for farms underlain by coal. In 1882 as national iron production rose to unprecedented levels, he was particularly active in

TABLE 4

H. C. Frick Coke Company,
Location of Ovens, Early 1882

Henry Clay	100
Frick	106
Morgan	168
Foundry	74
White	148
Eagle	80
Summit	142
Tip Top	56
Valley	152
Total	1,026

Source: USX records, Annandale.

his search. On two occasions he negotiated with relatives, apparently in a very businesslike fashion. In June he returned a plan of his works to Tinstman: "At the price you name our party thinks it would not justify us to purchase at present." In November he was in touch with J. Overholt about the purchase of twenty-five acres on the north side of the Schoonmaker Railroad and west of the Morewood Railroad in the northernmost section of the main coking district. He wanted a small plot: "Will you sell us the additional five acres and at what price?" He treated with Dillinger, Tarr, and Company for their properties in this same northern part of the field: "I have not mentioned the matter to anybody, and on my return [from a trip to the West], if you are still in the notion of selling, it may be that we can come to terms."[29] Sometime later he acquired their two coke plants.

Not all went as smoothly as his negotiations with relatives or with Dillinger and Tarr, however. In April 1882, he agreed with the Chicago and Connellsville Coke Company to mine and work their properties. Apparently some remark or report was made suggesting that, as a leaseholder, he had not been a good steward. He protested he had not so "managed your mines as to render them dangerous or unsafe . . . on the contrary I have complied in all respects as to the employment of agents and the conduct of mining." He threatened that if they attempted to interfere, "I shall resist the same and hold you for damages." That fall, expanding in another direction, he pressed his manager Thomas Lynch to see the Sherrick interests in order to get land near their Valley works on the best terms he could manage.[30] In 1885 the H. C. Frick Coke Company paid $762,000 for the large Dawson Station works of James Cochran and Sons.

THE CARNEGIES' HOLDINGS IN H. C. FRICK COKE

In autumn 1883 Frick pressed Carnegie to buy Morewood and other ovens for $600,000 and also to take from him $500,000 of Frick Coke Company stock: "You will then be the owner of half of Frick Coke Co." He presented his case in an attractive light, although the calculations that lay behind his statements are not known. "I have a plan in mind how Morewood, South West, and Hutchinsons—making a total of about 3,700 acres of coal and 1,200 ovens—could be consolidated—made auxiliary to H. C. Frick Coke Company without them investing any money. . . . When you come out I would like to present it to you." As so often, Lauder advised his cousin to move with care. Although the coal lay "quite normal" and the improvements made were "all of the best class of the district," he reported almost all the coal was under water level and this represented an extra cost of 10 cents per ton of coke. As compared with coking coals around Broadford, the heart of the early Frick works, it had disadvantages: "I do not see *why we* should wish to take these properties into the Frick Co. They are well enough as they are. Coke would require to be $1.25 to make Morewood return interest and depreciation. The South West would be a dead load till more ovens are built. Let Frick worry with them is my verdict."[31] South West, Morewood, and the Dillinger works were to become the nucleus of the South West Coal and Coke Company, through which Frick established a link with Chicago steelmakers somewhat similar to his connection with the Carnegies.

In spite of refusing to follow Frick's advice about these particular coke properties, by autumn 1883 the Carnegies had increased their holding in the H. C. Frick Coke Company to over half the total by investment in the expansion of coke capacity and the purchase of some of the stock held by the Fergusons. Later that decade, the Fergusons withdrew and the Carnegie associates' share increased still further (see table 5).

Frick was left to operate and expand the company with the increased capital resources that had become available, but he now had a minority interest in the growing concern that continued to bear his name. The linking of coke and steel was superficially a satisfactory arrangement, giving each party what it desired. It was potentially extremely dangerous, however, with expertise and management in coke on one side, and on the other side a majority owner whose main interests were in another industry. The gains to the Carnegie associates were substantial. In the year to March 1885, all the coke handled by H. C. Frick Coke netted that company 17.41 cents per ton more than the coke it supplied to the Edgar Thomson and Lucy furnaces.

TABLE 5

H. C. Frick Coke Company, Capital and Shares, 1882, 1885, 1888

	May 1882	August 1885	July 1888
Total capital (*in thousand dollars*)	2,000	2,600	2,750
Percentage shares			
H. C. Frick	29.60	16.67	21.01
Ferguson brothers	59.15	33.33	withdrawn
Carnegie associates	11.25	c.50.00	73.53
Other minor interests within H. C. Frick Coke	—	—	5.45

Source: Frick Papers

That year the Carnegies took 303,138 tons of Frick coke. They thereby saved $52,776 (equal to 4 percent of their net profits that year).[32] As Phipps had anticipated, the leading Carnegie associates made substantial profits from their investments in coke. In 1888 the dividends on H. C. Frick Coke amounted to $2 million, on a capital of $3 million. (They were thus slightly higher than the net earnings of the Carnegie works.) Of this total, some three-quarters were taken by individuals who were from the iron and steel side of the association (see table 6).

Already there were occasional disputes between the principals in coke and steel. Given a touchiness on Frick's part whenever he felt the interests of "his" company were being sacrificed or put at risk, these were sometimes lively episodes. His August 1883 assertion of his superior knowledge of priorities in the coke business was an early example. One disagreement in 1884 was a dramatic illustration of the tensions below the surface, although it is unfortunately not fully documented. Over the previous few years Connellsville coke capacity had increased rapidly; there were 4,200 ovens in the district in 1879, and 10,364 ovens five years later. Demand had not kept pace, and ironmasters pressed the coke makers for lower and lower prices. The year 1883 was one of exceptional depression, and by December coke prices were said to be at a "bed-rock" of from 95 cents to a dollar a ton. By August 1884 nearly half the ovens in the area were idle, and others were out of production one day each week. Even now the Carnegie interests, through their interest in H. C. Frick Coke, obtained their fuel at much lower prices than most other iron makers. As Frick informed Carnegie, during the year to March 1885 all the coke handled by the coke company netted them 17.41

TABLE 6

H. C. Frick Coke Company,
Dividends Declared 8 April 1889

A. Carnegie	498,333
H. C. Frick	420,367
Carnegie Bros and Co.	531,833
H. Phipps	143,833
T. M. Carnegie estate	137,500
J. Walker	37,100
C. A. Spencer	54,533
T. Lynch	18,167
D. A. Stewart estate	31,000
All others	127,334

Source: USX records, Annandale.
Note: Figures are in dollars.

cents more per ton than the 303,138 tons they delivered that year to the Edgar Thomson and Lucy furnaces.

Given both the difficult general circumstances of trade and their highly beneficial terms for it, Frick resented further intervention by the Carnegies, especially when it was seen to undermine his standing with others in the coke trade. Under his chairmanship, a meeting of the Coke Syndicate fixed the price of coke at $1.50 a ton. At that point John Walker arrived and asked the price on behalf of the Carnegie interests. When told, he made it clear that the party he represented would pay only $1.15. Frick at once resigned his position in the Syndicate, saying to his colleagues: "Gentlemen, I have nothing else to say. You have just heard what the worthy representative of the majority stockholders in the H. C. Frick Coke Company said." He left the room. Shortly afterward he sailed for Europe and returned only when Carnegie, through a friend, apologized for the episode.[33] Eventually his new colleagues became more aware of the likely strength of his reactions to what he regarded as infringements on his sphere of decision making in coke. Phipps once put it to Carnegie: "Frick and Company [sic] is almost his all, his ewe lamb, put yourself in his place."[34]

ANDREW CARNEGIE AND THE MAN

There was a counterbalance to the interest and occasional interference of the Carnegie associates in coke. Gradually Frick became more involved in steel. His progress in doing so was linked with one of Carnegie's particular characteristics. No one who knew him could doubt his extraordinary abilities. He often showed an unexpected grasp of technical details, was extremely acute in all his observations, and had a never relaxing acuity in overseeing the performance of the various departments of his growing industrial concerns. However, he liked to find a man in whom he could place absolute confidence to run the business in a closer, day-to-day contact with operations. With such a man he would show friendliness and often an annoying condescension. In almost thirty years in steel, he put this sort of trust in four individuals: William P. Shinn, William A. Abbott, Henry Clay Frick, and Charles M. Schwab. With each of the first three he was eventually disappointed; with Schwab he remained satisfied, but Schwab continued after Carnegie left the industry and in that period Carnegie was disillusioned with at least some aspects of Schwab's behavior. With Abbott and especially with Schwab, personal friendship survived business divorce or disagreement; in the cases of both Shinn and Frick, dependency and trust were to end in acrimonious partings. Insofar as it has many parallels with what was to happen again later, the experience with Shinn is worth summarizing.

When Edgar Thomson works came into production in late summer 1875, it was under the excellent superintendence of William R. Jones. Carnegie thought he had also secured an ideal general manager in the vice-president of the Allegheny Valley Railroad, W. P. Shinn, and pressed him to become more involved in their business. In spring 1876 he wrote, "My Dear Friend, I like the tone of your personal letter—much. Have always known you would find it necessary if ET proved what we expected to give it all your time and thought. . . . With you at the helm, and my pulling an oar outside, we are bound to put it at the head of rail-making concerns." Four months later, he again stressed his conviction that Shinn should be wholly devoted to the concern and his own complete confidence in him: "My Dear Friend, I have your letter. I am naturally anxious to get *all* of you for ET. I do not know your equal as an Ex. officer and I always feel with you at the helm ET is safe, but it makes all the difference whether your entire mind is bent on the concern." In October 1878, leaving for an extended trip overseas, he scribbled a penciled note to Shinn: "Goodbye my friend. I feel so perfectly satisfied to leave ET in your hands. This absolute confidence is worth everything and I daily congratulate myself that I have met you and got such a man bound in the closest possible manner to our party."[35]

Soon afterward, however, this confidence was shown to have been misplaced. The Edgar Thomson chairman died while Carnegie was away, and Shinn asked if he could take his place, to which Carnegie responded with a request that they should proceed more slowly. On his return home, he found that Shinn had acquired limestone properties in Western Pennsylva-

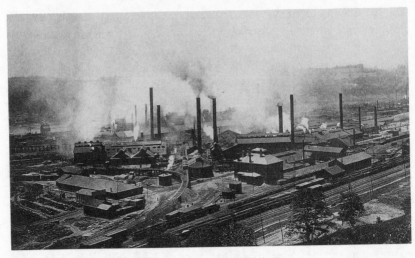

Edgar Thomson Steel Works and Furnaces, 1897. *Courtesy of USX.*

nia and, instead of selling them to the Carnegie concern, was supplying lime to Edgar Thomson works to his own profit. It also became known that he was negotiating to become the general manager for the Vulcan Iron Company in St. Louis. Shinn left Edgar Thomson with blunt words from Carnegie and eventually took his old employer to court to secure his rights. Some of these same themes were to recur more than a decade after Henry Clay Frick obtained his wished-for closer association with the operations of the Carnegie businesses.

From an undetermined but fairly early date in their association, Frick had been involved in fields beyond coke on behalf of the Carnegies. In autumn 1884, for instance, he negotiated for them about natural gas prices, drawing upon other personal connections. If he could not come to an agreement with the Philadelphia Company about gas, he wanted the price to be fixed by the arbitration of Andrew Mellon, "a gentleman on whom I can rely." He corresponded in spring 1886 with the Pennsylvania Railroad's general freight traffic agent, John S. Wilson, concerning new freight rates for the shipment of raw materials to and products from all the Carnegie works.[36] In addition to his expertise and power in coke, and the evidence he provided of abilities in these widening fields of activity, Frick at this time came across as a generally congenial business companion. James H. Bridge—the young Englishman who had been Herbert Spencer's secretary before becoming Carnegie's literary assistant—first met him in Carnegie's rooms in the Windsor Hotel early in 1885. Many years later he recalled the striking impression this young capitalist made:

[He was] a well-groomed man, not noticeably taller than Carnegie, who was puny-built. He wore a full brown beard. . . . His friendly smile was the most noticeable thing about him—that and his extremely courteous, almost deferential manner. . . . He seemed more polished, more refined than the Carnegie partners, who often came to the Windsor for dinner, and had the rough friendliness of Western men who do big things. He spoke little, his smile serving as an answer to, or acknowledgment of, Carnegie's jests and habitual enthusiasms.[37]

FRICK'S INTEREST IN STEEL: A WARNING

Distinguished by both his business and personal qualities, as well as by his inflexible sense of purpose, Frick set out to make his way into the Carnegie businesses. He got on well with Tom Carnegie, a man nearer his own age than Andrew and (unlike Andrew) accessible on the spot. (It is however well to remember that in some respects the record of relationships was retrospectively adjusted by partisan interests—so that, for example, Bridge's fulsome tributes to Tom may in part be designed to reflect badly on his brother.)

Four years after his association with them began, Frick approached both men about taking an interest in steel. He planned to do so by the same device used in the purchase of more coke capacity, acquiring the new stock by reducing still further his interest in H. C. Frick Coke, apparently to the very small share of 4 percent of the total stock. Henry Phipps supported him in this, but from the Carnegies his overtures brought two different but unfavorable responses. Tom replied in a penciled note—slightly obscure and unfortunately undated—that was probably written in the early weeks of 1886. It indicates that Frick had been pressing his case.

I am somewhat tenacious of my opinions—no doubt they are often wrong. I do confess so much. In the matter of your prospective interest with CB and Co. I cannot help but think that you should become a *manager*—I know that you have weighty arguments against it and HP Jnr. and the general judgment outweighs mine, but because of the infirmity which I have alluded to (my tenacity) I wish you to reconsider and submit the matter to AC—good bye—I'm off for Florida—nothing can trouble me further for months, Yours TMC.[38]

From Andrew he received a longer, more considered, and very perceptive letter, written from his New York office on 25 February 1886, in which, although allowing fully for Frick's ambitions and potential, he also pointed unerringly to a weakness in the situation Frick desired. At one point the letter indicated that Carnegie had changed his mind, so that he was less willing to consider the matter than formerly:

Excuse me for saying that in my opinion you propose what would be the mistake of your life. Your career must be identified with the Frick Coke Co. You never could become the *Creator* of CB and Co. Twenty years from now you might be a large owner in it, perhaps the principal, still the concern would not be *your work and you could not be proud of it.* Now money is very good, but I say that H. C. Frick, Principal in Frick Coke Co. would occupy a position, both as to power and influence—and as regards himself in his own judgment— infinitely more satisfactory than he ever could do in CB and Co.—even if his private ledger showed a million more money if he bartered away the headship of his own Company to be one of the tails of CB and Co. I cannot imagine how your pride permitted you to think for one moment of sinking to an insignificant holder of 4 percent in your own Creation. To think that you could ever be influential in its councils with such a petty interest is absurd. You would merely be the agent of the real men in the concern— . . . officials and the business community generally would look upon you with suppressed contempt. *The idea is suicidal.* Now listen to me. Were I you, not one dollar would I hold in anything, not even CB and Co., nor Banks, nor anything. Every dollar I had, all I could get credit for, I should put in *My Company,* and be the Frick of the Frick Coke Co. Buy the dead wood out, all you can't stagger under, or that my partners or your friends don't want. If you want me with you, I'll take and support you in progressive development. I see the *possibilities* very big—the probabilities—if you became the head. If you don't increase your interest to the full extent of every dollar you can command I don't want to increase mine. I can't consider the idea of loading CB and Co. with the control of Frick Coke Co. Think over this. I know I counsel wisely if you aim to become a power, and even if dollars merely be your idea of power (which is a mistake), I believe you will make more millions by *Concentrating* than by scattering. Remember when I thought you would do well in CB and Co. control of your own concern was not within your grasp. I never could advise you to divide your thoughts and time between concerns when your own field was fully open before you. *Go in and possess it or sink into merited insignificance.* Your friend, Andrew Carnegie. [And he added as an afterthought] File this for future reference. AC.[39]

Many years later, Carnegie recorded that after he had resigned from the Pennsylvania Railroad in spring 1865, he had never again worked for a salary. He must have thought of Frick when he added, "A man must necessarily occupy a narrow field who is at the beck and call of others. Even if he becomes president of a great corporation, he is hardly his own master unless he owns control of the stock."[40]

The situation—and with it Carnegie's attitude to Frick's closer involvement—was dramatically changed by events in early autumn 1886. At that time Andrew was ill with typhoid fever at Cresson. As late as Thursday, 14 October, Tom was at his chairman's desk in the Pittsburgh offices of Carnegie Brothers. He too then fell ill with pneumonia. Although he was only forty-three his constitution had been weakened by hard drinking, and he rapidly worsened. At noon on the following Tuesday, 19 October, he died at his home in the Homewood district of Pittsburgh.[41] Carnegie Brothers was left without an everyday leader.

Henry Phipps was appointed chairman, but it was clear that this was only a caretaker appointment. Phipps had some very positive business qualities, which historians have sometimes overlooked, but he lacked the stature of command that such a concern required. Frick was soon being brought in to other important decisions in the steel company. Within less than three weeks of Tom's death, one of the managers, Henry Curry, was corresponding with him about shipments of ore from Lake Champlain, and soon afterward concerning the considerable tonnages of foreign ore to be railed to them from Baltimore in 1887.[42] On 1 November 1886, Frick gained his wished-for first entry to stockholding in Carnegie steel, when Carnegie agreed to sell him $100,000 stock for $184,000, payment to be made from future dividends. The way to still fuller involvement was complicated and delayed by serious problems in the middle months of 1887, when events in the coke region exposed those very weaknesses that Carnegie had warned Frick about in the letter he had urged him to keep for future reference. The result was Frick's angry, short-term withdrawal from business.

Problems in Coke: The Strike of 1887

In the 1880s, the output of charcoal and anthracite furnaces had reached unprecedented levels. However, fuel shortages were forcing the former into remote areas, and anthracite works were now finding it advantageous to mix coke with their traditional fuel. In 1883 the tonnage of iron made from anthracite alone was greater than that using an anthracite and coke mixture; by the last two years of the 1880s, it was less than one-fifth as much. Neither charcoal nor anthracite furnaces could meet the spiraling demand for iron. As a result, the share of total iron output represented by bituminous coal and coke iron (overwhelmingly the latter) increased rapidly. In 1871 their proportion of the total had been 30.6 percent, by 1880 45.4 percent, and in 1890 69.4 percent. The increased significance of coke, and the dominance of Connellsville in production, meant that in the keen competition for business, big iron and steel firms were (like the Carnegies) concerned to ensure supplies and to keep the price low.

In what was then a labor-intensive industry, wage rates were a prime consideration and industrial conflict an ever present threat to the steady course of the coke trade. On the other hand, the need for a reliable flow of fuel for their ironworks meant that steel firms were not always willing to struggle for cuts in coke wages, or even to resist wage increases, if this resulted in idleness in their costly iron, steel, and rolling mill operations. In short, coke operations were of great significance to the success of the steel companies, but their interests were by no means always identical.

In the early 1880s, immigrant labor from Eastern Europe began to be important in the coke region. For a time this group of workers, undiscriminatingly called Hungarians (and more commonly "Huns"), was regarded as a conservative element; within a few years they were active in labor disputes and were important contributors to the often violent nature these disputes could take. By the mid 1880s, although he was the most successful of all the coke operators, Frick was being pressed between the aspirations of his workers and the priorities of major associates from beyond the industry.

The 1886 strike was a foretaste of what was to come. Carnegie wanted to ensure that coke got through to their furnaces. Making his point, he wrote one of his annoying letters to "My Dear Pard" in which he said, "Of course you won't let us stop again at Bessemer *if possible to prevent it.* We do want to go along there regularly now."[43] He had every reason to be concerned, for 1886 was to turn out to be a record year for rails, with the national output 21 percent higher than in the previous best year. On the workers' side, action at the start was confined to a few "Huns," but their combination of earnestness and violence caused others to join, and by the latter part of February 1886, about 75 percent of the ovens were idle.

The men's grievances were varied. As always, wages were an important matter, but the men also alleged that false weights were being used, causing them to be paid for less than they had produced. There was agitation against company stores, some of it from those who had to use them, but fostered partly by other storekeepers who suffered from the competition. Within a month, most men had returned to work, to be paid at 1884 rates—before wages had been cut by one-third—and with the understanding that complaints about stores and weights would be looked into later. Quite unjustifiably, one trade paper believed that another outcome might be to rid the coke region of the "Hungarians."[44]

The next year's strike was of far more moment, and for Frick it highlighted the problems of the business associations he had chosen. A new labor dispute was already looming by the end of 1886. There followed an advance in coke prices. In February 1887, Father M. A. Lambing—a priest who had worked in the coke region since 1879 and who was already becoming a friend—sent Frick an assessment of the situation, an opinion the latter had requested. Lambing feared a strike and was independent enough to indicate that he hoped for an amicable settlement rather than domination of the region by the coke operators. Some men had demanded a 20 percent in-

Miner at work in Connellsville coke region, circa 1893. *Courtesy of Frick Art and Historical Center, Frick Archives.*

crease in wages, but he thought that because of the "conservatism" of the Knights of Labor a 10 percent increase might be sufficient to avert a strike. As for the other union, the Amalgamated Association of Miners and Mine Laborers, he reckoned it was unlikely, as some owners hoped, that there might be defection by the Slavs if a strike caused them protracted idleness.[45]

The leading operators were at this time still working together in the Coke Syndicate. After their proposed new wage scale was rejected by the men, the matter was referred to arbitration. National union officials accepted the arbitrator's decision, but the local lodges determined to hold out for a higher scale. A strike began on 7 May 1887. It struggled on into late summer, its course being marked by the usual features—negotiations, rallies, the im-

portation of scab labor, the use of Pinkerton detectives and the Coal and
Iron Police, "drilling" by the more militant strikers, periodic outbreaks of
violence from both sides, and in some instances the eviction of strikers'
families. The center of greatest disturbance was Leisenring. By late June,
before the conflict was at mid point, it was calculated that the operators had
lost $42,000 in potential profits and the men $689,000 in wages, with still
wider losses to other businesses and employees in reduced iron and steel
production, lower retail and railroad receipts, and so on.[46] Most important
of all, the strike showed the weakness of a primary producer industry when
controlled by a finishing operation. In this way, it gave substance to the
warnings Frick had received from both Andrew and Tom Carnegie a year
before. It also indicated how much he had already compromised his freedom of action, not only in relation to Pittsburgh steelmaking but also (although to a lesser extent) with that of Chicago.

The 11 June 1887 issue of the *Pennsylvania Press* carried a dramatic headline: "Coke Men Crushed. Carnegie Thunders from His Castle in the Scottish Highlands. His Bolt Wrecks the Syndicate. Millionaire Operators
Mourn and Hungry Hungarians Dance with Glee. President Frick, Overpowered, Resigns." Despite its crudity, the message was essentially correct.
The strikers had begun by regarding the demands from furnace men for
cheaper coke as a bluff, but by the end of May they had realized that the
demands were genuine, which would entail a long dispute. Yet for integrated
iron and steel concerns, the need to keep the Carnegie Brothers' Bessemer
shops supplied with iron outweighed the gain of a few cents on the cost of
one of the materials used in their associated blast furnaces. It was reported
that, as his firm had commitments for delivery of rails over the summer
months, Carnegie had given orders to concede to the coke men, and that
when Frick protested that his honor was at stake, Carnegie had expressed a
willingness to accept Frick's resignation from the coke company in which
(although it bore his name) his share of the stock was now less than one-
third that of the Carnegie interests.[47]

When the strike started, Frick had been one of the most resolute of the
employers. Yet his coke industry colleagues had realized that he might be
put under pressure to desert them. On 4 May 1887, Colonel Schoonmaker
(with whom his relationship had by no means always been happy) wrote a
very purposeful if rather coded letter to "My Dear Frick." With less disinter-
est than Andrew and Tom Carnegie, he made more or less the same points
as they had a year before. He asked that Frick

   accept a suggestion at my hands in the same kind spirit in which it is offered.
   ... There never was and probably never will be a better opportunity than now

Leisenring No. 3 Works, circa 1893. *Courtesy of Frick Art and Historical Center, Frick Archives.*

for you either to be the President of the H. C. Frick Coke Co. for all time in the future or merely a representative of other interests at the sacrifice of your own. The present issue is simply one of self-interest. You are bound by all the ties of honor to stand by those whose interests are identical with yours and who in the past have seen yours and their interests suffer rather than force you into an issue with others we have no common interest with. My sincere wish is that this issue will not arise in the present Crisis but if it does that you may see your way clear to stand square and firm with those who have and will stand with you as being the *right* course under all the circumstances, the only one you can in justice to everybody assume, and what is better the correct one for the pecuniary welfare of every stockholder in your Company and all who have a dollar in the Connellsville region. We are bound to come out all right if you stay with us and I never have doubted your nerve or manhood in any issue past or present.[48]

The fears that motivated this supportive message were soon shown to be well justified.

The shutting down of coke ovens soon began to affect Carnegie steel. Henry Phipps as chairman of Carnegie Brothers and John Walker who now headed Carnegie, Phipps, and Company, whose Homestead beam mill had only recently begun work, were reluctant to suffer an interruption of production. They had contacted Carnegie in Britain, and he had sent his "thunderbolt" response. On 13 May 1887, Frick tendered his resignation from "his" coke company. In identical letters to Henry Phipps and to John Walker, he expressed his anger concerning the way they had "temporized with our employees and made concession after concession to satisfy them and against the interest and judgment of all the other coke producers." He believed that "cost what it may," they should not restart their coke works until their employees resumed at the old wages. At the same time he revealed that—despite Carnegie's clear statement only a little over a year earlier— Frick had not fully recognized the power that financial control gave (or that its absence removed). In a second angry letter to the two chairmen he wrote, "The loss to the coke company . . . may be far more than made up in your steel interests, but I object to so manifest a prostitution of the Coke Company's interests in order to promote your steel interests. Whilst a majority of the stock entitles you to control, I deny that it confers the right to manage." He predicted that their action would lead to even more unreasonable demands from the men in the future.[49]

After he had given notice of his intended resignation, there was a waiting period of over three weeks. By the beginning of June most of the furnace capacity at Edgar Thomson had been banked, and the last two furnaces were ready to follow. The rail mill was to close a few days later.[50] On 1 June, Carnegie sent a cable that, although by no means lucidly phrased, was unambiguously an ultimatum to Frick: "Please don't mislead me second time remember suffered enough last time make no mistake now no stoppage tolerated reply." Six days later, Frick confirmed his resignation. In doing so, he made a vigorous defense of his own position.

Others in the coke and iron industries saw and deplored the necessities under which he had to operate. On 4 June 1887, the Cambria Iron Company was standing with him, believing him to be a leader in the dispute, but their letter of that date indicates their lurking uncertainty that he might give way, and that they could trace weaknesses in his policy:

> Our disposition is and has been from first, to stand firm with you in this fight, believing the men were in the wrong, but I have always felt that it was an unwise act on your part to advance the price of coke to $2.00 and think it should be reduced. I earnestly hope your predictions may prove correct as to men going back to work at old rates on Tuesday next.

Ten days later, J. H. Bailey of the Sligo rolling mills of Phillips, Nimick, and Company in Pittsburgh wrote to sympathize:

> I see by the papers that you have carried out your intention in the coal strike. It is I fear a very grave mistake on the part of Carnegies and really do not see what else you could do under the circumstances. I hope something may occur to place you back again at the head of the concern you built up, before a great while.[51]

On 7 June, Frick had resigned as president of the H. C. Coke Company and was succeeded by Henry Phipps. John Walker was elected a director.

Frick's disagreement with the principals in steel, although sharp, was not protracted. He left New York on 20 July 1887 for Bremen and from there traveled through Germany and Switzerland to Venice, returning through France to England. It is significant that in Britain he went on to visit Andrew and Louise Carnegie, who were spending the first summer since their marriage in Scotland. At the H. C. Frick Coke Company meeting on 5 November 1887, Phipps resigned as president and Frick was reelected to the post. Two days later, Thomas Lynch wrote, "I am very glad to know that you have returned to your old place at the head of this Company. I think it is in the interest of all the stockholders to have you do so."[52] Frick also resumed his progress toward a more active role in steel. He already had links as a coke supplier with steel firms in another major center of production.

THE CHICAGO STEELMEN

Although this crisis had temporarily broken his command over the H. C. Frick Coke Company, Frick retained control of another major coke concern, the South West Coal and Coke Company, which was linked to Chicago steel interests. In spring 1882, he had mentioned to Carnegie that his contract to supply coke to the Union Steel Company in Chicago expired in the middle of the year and that he was going over to Chicago within the next few days. He particularly wanted to see Orrin W. Potter of the North Chicago Rolling Mill Company, which was then completing construction of its second Chicago plant, the South works, and whose order for coke they would much prefer to that from the smaller Union Steel Company. Very soon after his link with Frick had been made, Carnegie had written to Potter championing "their" coke. Potter had said that he was not in the market for coke, but this was not the sort of thing to dampen Carnegie when he was in an expansive mood. He threatened (gently) that supplies might not be so favorable in the future:

> I suppose before very long you will want a largely increased supply for your
> new works. I know so well that our coke is superior, and that in some seasons
> of scarcity of coke we have means of getting a large share; that I hope you will
> give us a trial for a portion of your trade. Any time you would like to see our
> people about coke, one of them will go and confer with you, or if you are to be
> here to see Miss Potter sail, I will have Mr. Frick meet you.

At the end of the following year, Frick told Carnegie that Potter had entered into a coke supply agreement for a term of years with another major Connellsville company, McClure Coke Company, the price for coke to be on a sliding scale related to the price of rails.[53]

However, soon after this the H. C. Frick Coke Company replaced Mc-

Clure. It was said that this avoided the need for the steel company to build its own ovens. Yet some of Potter's reservations persisted, so that more than eighteen months later Frick was again explaining to one of Potter's associates that Potter "does not like the idea of taking the risk of having Mr. Carnegie say to his friends in the east that he is getting a dividend out of the Chicago Rolling Mill Co. by supplying him with coke," which was just the sort of thing that Carnegie would have delighted to do.[54] The necessity to secure the best coke eventually made Chicago iron makers take a direct interest in Connellsville. Although already associated with Carnegie, Frick was ready to cooperate.

Having failed to get the Carnegies to buy Morewood, Frick next tried to interest the Cambria Iron Company. He expected in exchange a share in the Cambria coke works. Disappointed again, he formed the South West Coal and Coke Company. In autumn 1885, he came to an understanding with two of the three leading Chicago steelmakers, Union Steel and Joliet Steel, whereby they agreed to joint ownership—with H. C. Frick Coke—of this new company and of the properties of the Chicago and Connellsville Coke Company, which Joliet Steel already controlled. A few weeks later, this was followed by an agreement to supply the other major firm, North Chicago Rolling Mill Company. As with the Carnegie link, Joliet, Union, and North Chicago were to obtain supplies at a concession rate—for $1.10 a ton, at the beginning, when the Syndicate price was $1.20.[55]

His new Chicago colleagues took a great deal of interest, through correspondence, in what was happening in Pittsburgh steel and in the affairs of the H. C. Frick Coke Company. They asked for general information, as well as for specific information concerning coal and coke. On one occasion Jay Morse, president of Union Steel, even asked Frick to make out a comparative balance sheet of their own coke firm and of H. C. Frick Coke, with figures of output and cost. Another time, when men at Edgar Thomson works had already been on strike for over three months, W. R. Stirling of Joliet noted in a memorandum that he had seen from the papers that Carnegie's offer to his men had been rejected. He wanted to know, "Has this brought about any lock-out or any further suspension of work than that already in existence? . . . Your reply will oblige."[56]

When there were labor difficulties in the Connellsville field, the Chicago steelmen, like Carnegie, became alarmed. Although late in 1886 Morse acknowledged that the men's demands were "simply outrageous," he saw that the situation of an approaching strike had unfavorable implications for the Chicago companies: "you certainly are in mighty bad shape and it is liable to place us in one equally as bad." Morse was seeking reassurance that their interests as steelmakers would be taken fully into account: "Do not let a strike occur—If it has got to come let the steelmen get together and decide when they will have it." If they were given two or three months to prepare, they would try to be ready. They were given even longer, but by early May 1887, they were still disturbed. Morse then wrote:

> [N]ote what you say about the strike. I trust some settlement can be made satisfactory to yourself within a reasonable time. We can keep alive, here, about 8 days, I think—possibly 10. The Joliet Steel Co. say they are good for 30 days. I don't know what shape the North Chicago people are in. How is the Edgar Thompson [*sic*]. I suppose they are good for 40 or 50, are they not?

A week later he was asking that if, as they hoped, their men returned to work the following week, perhaps Frick "would have some coke rushed through as rapidly as possible—it may save us banking our furnaces."[57]

The capitulation that Carnegie forced on H. C. Frick Coke in 1887 left the Chicago firms in a difficult situation. Their workers remained on strike and their mines and ovens were still idle. Morris Ramsay—brother of Robert Ramsay, one of the H. C. Frick officials—was superintendent of the Morewood mines of South West Coal and Coke. On Saturday, 11 June 1887, he informed Frick of the confusion that had resulted from the concession to the strikers, at a time when in his judgment their resolution had been waning and they were ready to concede defeat: "I was much surprised to hear that the H. C. Frick Coke Co. had paid the advance this morning, and not any more than the men themselves were. When the report reached here they did not believe it. It was generally thought by the leaders here that they would all be at work by Monday at the old wages." The fact that the biggest coke company had given way naturally put new heart into the men. A week after Frick resigned, the general agent of Union Steel, Robert Spencer, was already pressing him (though with a gentleness that the recipient must have contrasted very favorably with Carnegie's approach): "Mr. Porter desires me to say, without urging you to any undue haste, that he would like you to appreciate the fact that it is very important for us to get started now as early as any one else and requests that you give us our full share of first shipments as soon as the coke is suitable for our use." Later that month, Stirling was contemplating the possibility that they too would have to give way:

> The chances of victory are now greatly reduced by Carnegie's action, and I think we should face the situation and determine upon an *absolute date* by which, if the strike is not over, we should compromise with the men, either on the same terms as Carnegie or whatever better terms we could make, but by said date we should cease to fight for the original position.

A week later he considered the implications of holding out: "To win will I think require more men willing to work; more men to protect them; more evictions and consequent legal work and more time than I believe most of you are calculating upon." For his part, Spencer now recognized that even if they got the men back to work on the old terms, the fact that Carnegies were paying higher rates would mean that the settlement would not last, so that "we would be kept in hot water for some time to come."[58]

The uncertainties of the period were reflected in the shifts made in the positions adopted by some of the Chicago people. This is well seen in the letters from H. A. Gray, the secretary and treasurer for Union Steel. While stressing their wish not to do anything to weaken Frick's position, he argued for conceding at once—it would be a "great relief" to them if Frick would start up the ovens at the South West and Leith works "giving the men what they ask now, trusting to the future for an opportunity to recover the lost prestige and control of the works." Yet within only a few days he had shifted his ground. He now advocated sticking to an aggressive policy, conducting it "as Grant conducted his campaigns, i.e., keep it up along the whole line and pound them hard." Next day he went back on this, acknowledging that they had not made much progress and, taking much the same position that Carnegie had adopted, stressing that "we have made up our minds that we must have coke or we must disappoint all the railroads that we are under contract with for our rails."[59]

Gradually this attitude prevailed, and resumption of supplies was seen as more important than victory. On 26 August 1887, Gray and Stirling side-stepped Frick by writing a joint letter to E. M. Ferguson. They pointed out that they had lost more than they had gained by being associated with the Syndicate and were now "decidedly of the opinion that no time should be lost in coming to an accommodation with our men." Driving home the message, they went on, "we desire to receive your very full and prompt reply, would like to hear from you by return of mail and wish you to under-stand that this is an explicit statement of our views as partners with you and others in the South West Coal and Coke company and in the Chicago and Connellsville Coke Company."[60]

The Chicago associates took advantage of the circumstances to preach to Frick in ways he must have found galling. As compared with Carnegie, they had been mindful of his interests and feelings, but gradually the tone of their letters stiffened. This led them on to expressions of greater concern for social justice in the coke region. Morse suggested that they should weigh the tonnages produced both accurately and openly to ensure that men were paid fully for their work. He doubted the wisdom of having company stores.

Then he went on to a very provocative generalization: "I think that the trouble you are having is largely due to the fact that the men have not been used honestly in times past—and the sooner you get on an honest basis the better." Stirling and Gray made much the same points to Ferguson and also recommended that he take a couple of days to go to the coke region to find out whether the men's grievances were

> real or imaginary, outside the question of wages, and arrange to have all reasonable remedies applied, and when the grievances are only imaginary and demands are unreasonable, endeavor to make it apparent to the men and, at all events, create the impression among them that the company wants to do what is fair and liberal with them in the future. . . . It is not a matter of sentiment, however, but of good business policy, and, if carried out wisely, will put money in all our pockets.

Stirling was said to concur in Gray's view that "it is better to be liberal with the men, and while it may curtail our present profits, we are likely to make more money in the long run." A few weeks later, when a new wage scale was coming in, it was Gray who pointed out that the men would now be getting the same payment for making coke selling for $2.00 a ton as they had earned in the previous January for $1.50 coke.[61]

At the end of the summer an estimate was made of the cost of the strike to Union Steel. They had, Gray wrote,

> tried to look at this matter as coke operators without being prejudiced by our interests as steel makers, [but] . . . Looking at this matter from our standpoint as steel-makers, we have lost $150 to $200,000 this summer, which we would not have lost if we had been able to control our own coke works. As it is, our principle competitors have not only been able to obtain a supply of coke while our furnaces were idle, but they have also obtained it at lower prices than we have had to pay.

Some weeks later Morse was even more direct than Gray had been and drew some harsh conclusions:

> Isn't Schoonmaker about right when he says that the Frick Coke Company did not keep good faith with the Syndicate in advancing wages? Didn't the Frick Coke Company agree to stand with the other coke makers of the Syndicate in declining to make an advance, and then, afterwards, allowed the 12 percent? Of course I am not clear on this point, but I had supposed that was the reason you resigned the Presidency.

He went on to spell out a further consequence of their recent experiences. To protect themselves against high freight rates (and presumably also against the collective ownership pressures) of the Connellsville district, they felt they must acquire coal lands in Virginia.[62]

With such a move Frick's overwhelming power in the coke industry would be reduced. In the short term, things seemed to drift back to normal and Frick was eventually reelected president of the H. C. Frick Coke Company. In the longer term, however, scars from the 1887 strike remained. They were later to be traced in new conflicts both with the coke workers and with the owners of the steel plants, notably with Carnegie.

FRICK AT THE HEAD OF CARNEGIE'S, 1889

During 1888, Frick was further involved in aspects of the management of Carnegie Brothers, although he was still without a formal position. He negotiated with the Pennsylvania Railroad about tonnages and rates for the coming season's ore movements from Lake Erie to Pittsburgh and pressed for freight charges on blooms and billets from Homestead to Cleveland to be reduced to $1.25, the same rate as for shipments in the reverse direction.[63] By the end of that year, two senior men were removed from his path to advancement. In October Phipps wrote to the board of managers of Carnegie Brothers and Company. He pointed out that by the following month he would have been in the iron and steel business for twenty-eight years. This, "and the fact that I have reached the age [forty-nine] and estate that may perhaps entitle me to withdraw from active business," had persuaded him to give up the chairmanship, though he would remain a partner and Carnegie's close friend.[64] He was succeeded by David Stewart. But almost immediately after this, Stewart died. On 14 January 1889 Frick was appointed head of Carnegie Brothers. From this time onward, he further proved his worth and became a major power in steel as well as in coke.

Initially he was eager to learn and seemed cooperative. Three weeks after his appointment, he ended a letter to Carnegie, "Please advise me a day or two before you arrive in Pittsburgh. Don't want to be away on your arrival, as I have many things to ask you about." Gradually he became more confident of his abilities in managing the concern and was then ready to assert his right to do so. By midsummer he had forced their accountant to resign on grounds of neglecting his duties. He replaced him with Francis Lovejoy.[65] Soon after that he was warning Carnegie not to hedge him round too closely:

I could not and would not remain the official head of any concern that was not well managed. . . . I cannot stand fault-finding and I must feel that I have the entire confidence of the power that put me where I am, in a place I did not seek. With all that, I know that I can manage both Carnegie Brothers and Co. and Frick Coke Co. successfully.

TABLE 7

Frick's Financial Involvement in Carnegie Associations, 1886–1892

Date	Investment Involved	Dollars
Nov. 1, 1886	$100,000 at $1.84	184,000
Dec. 31, 1888	Transfer from H. Phipps	190,511
Oct. 31, 1890	1% of total capital—$50,000 at $2.46	123,336
Dec. 31, 1891	From funds held for him	220,000
Jun. 30, 1892	Increase to 11% of C. Steel capital	2,200,000

Source: USX records, Annandale.

Early in September Carnegie, acknowledging his worth, tacitly committed himself to non-interference: "Let me express the relief I feel in knowing that the important departments of our extended business are in the hands of a competent manager. Phipps and I exchanged congratulations upon this point. Now I only want to know how your hands can be strengthened." Two months later, writing to Carnegie from Dresden, Phipps gave his own endorsement: "With Mr. Frick at the head, I have no fear as to receiving a good return upon our capital."[66]

Frick now applied all his formidable energies to both coke and steel. He worked long days, took no holidays, and kept himself informed of all that was happening in all departments of the business. As his biographer naively put it, "He revelled in doing and gloried in achieving big things"; and he received satisfaction from his efforts.[67] Bit by bit he increased his financial stake in the Carnegie enterprises until he was equal in standing to Phipps (see table 7). By summer 1892, his achievements at Carnegie Brothers had persuaded Carnegie to withdraw his original opposition to its merging with Carnegie Phipps. The resulting single concern was named the Carnegie Steel Company. Frick became chairman and chief executive, committed to devoting his talents to the pursuit of excellence in this wider sphere. By now his reputation was firmly established as a manager of exceptional quality. It was a high point, possibly the peak, of his working life, but at this very moment, with all the drama of a great tragedy, he was plunged into its deepest crisis.

3

Carnegie Company Growth
and the Homestead Crisis

⟨ornament⟩

The opposition of capital and organized labor, which reached a violent culmination in the strike and lockout at the Homestead works in the summer and autumn of 1892, has been widely written about and much studied—as it was happening, in its early aftermath, and since. Recent interest and research activity reached a new peak at the time of the centenary. Much of this considerable body of work is excellent, and no claim is made that the following account represents or requires a major reinterpretation of the events of those painful months. This analysis aims to do three things, which have not always been adequately represented elsewhere. First, it sets Homestead in the wider context of labor relations at Carnegie Steel. Second, it gives far more attention than is usual to the period following the strike, the hard years in which Homestead was stamped and shaped into the very epitome of an efficient, hard-driven steelmaking operation by a careful admixture of inducements, persuasion, compulsion, and surveillance. Third, it studies both antecedents and aftermath above all through the contemporary viewpoints of the principal actors on the side of management as recorded in their day-to-day correspondence. History is rewritten and myths are created during leisured retrospection; it is less easy to dissimulate in a letter written during the very heat of battle.

The way in which the Carnegie Steel Company conducted the Homestead strike helped shape Frick's reputation more than any other event in his life. In the public perception it separated him from his senior partner. The popular view was that Carnegie was liberal in his attitudes to labor. In 1886, in two articles in *Forum* he had presented an idealized conception of relationships between capital and labor. Although his actions by no means always tallied with his alleged convictions, the general public were less aware of the details of disputes than they were of his widely disseminated statements, and consequently he was for long taken at his own valuation. A newspaper review of the *Forum* articles concluded: "No manufacturer has done more for his employees, or thought more earnestly on all the practicable methods for improving the conditions and rewards of labor, than Andrew Carnegie." A contemporary recorder of the strike at Homestead remarked that Carnegie had a "high reputation for liberality and sympathetic regard for the well-being of his employees." Looking back on the most violent incident, a House of Representatives report even went so far as to record that Carnegie Steel's labor attitudes had previously been "kind and considerate in many respects." By contrast, conflicts in the coke region had proved that, in labor matters, Frick was a hard man. He had no "dilettanteism or liberally-advertised philanthropy of the Carnegie stripe. . . . He was a man of blood and iron like Bismark . . . [who] cared not a penny whether his underlings loved him or hated him."[1]

For Frick such a harsh characterization was not wholly unfair; in the case of Carnegie the favorable image flattered. Carnegie was to receive a good deal of opprobrium as the strike progressed, but eventually his image was largely refurbished; Frick's reputation was irreversibly blackened in the general consciousness by his association with the dispute. The Homestead strike can be understood only in the context of the broader framework of labor conditions in nineteenth-century America and in that of the growth of the Carnegie operations and the company's stance in previous disputes.

Plants and Personalities

Things went well for many months after Frick replaced Henry Phipps as chairman of Carnegie Brothers and Company in January 1889. Market conditions were favorable for a man striving to make his mark. National output of rolled steel in 1889 was at record levels, almost 19 percent higher than in the previous year. Carnegie's share of this output and their net profits both went up sharply. In spring 1890 Phipps, holidaying in the Levant, wrote a generous appreciation of the first period of his successor's performance. It was obviously a response to news he had received from Frick:

I enjoy the satisfaction you must naturally feel in the success of the business you so lately assumed, not only in the profits, which may be largely controlled by the market, but by the good practice which has prevailed and been inspired and watched by you. The smoothness you mention, with which things are running is also very gratifying.

Less than a year after Frick's chairmanship began, however, they had to weather a serious crisis in management, one that, exceptionally, was not due to human failing or dispute.[2]

Until the early 1880s, the Carnegie interest in steel was confined to the Edgar Thomson works. Designed by Alexander Holley, the Bessemer plant and rail mill there were erected under the supervision of William R. Jones, aged thirty-four, who had been assistant to George Fritz, general superintendent at Cambria Iron. Jones, generally known as "Captain," established a nationwide reputation for excellent results at the new works. He was a ruthless competitor, driving both himself and his men, developing and exploiting their feelings for rivalry yet concerned not to push them beyond breaking point. Occasionally he could be brutal to those he felt might hinder the work's progress. Altogether he was an excellent steelmaker and an outstanding leader of men, a very human figure of mixed talents, qualities, and defects, all on a heroic scale and suffused by a colorful personality. One who knew him well summed him up as "big-hearted, open-handed, good-natured, genial, level-headed, hard-working."[3]

In the course of 1889 Jones, renowned throughout the metallurgical world and revered by the men he both led and drove, had to deal with a new company chairman, a man ten years his junior, and a relative newcomer to the industry. Frick was a resolute learner, and he soon showed that he had very definite ideas about the way the business should be conducted. It has been suggested that the new chairman and his superintendent did not get on well. The evidence is slight, but as they differed so much in character and personality, it would not be surprising. Jones wanted to be left to run "his" works his own way; in March 1889, for instance, he wrote to protest against plans for the Pennsylvania Railroad to lay another track through the works, stressing that they were already very cramped. Each day they brought in or dispatched a total of 6,500 tons of material; a further 2,500 tons were moved within the works.[4] During the summer he wrote optimistically to Frick about the level of rail production he anticipated for that season's campaign.

On Thursday, 26 September 1889, Jones was fatally injured in a tragic accident, an event that completed his establishment as an industrial folk hero. That evening a group of men under his supervision were struggling to improve the working of blast furnace C at Edgar Thomson by releasing the cinder that had blocked it. The furnace wall burst. Flames and gas flashed down on the men standing below, and then hot ore, coke, and limestone fell on them from the ruptured stack. Twenty men were burned, to varying degrees. Jones was hit by falling materials and was swept into the casting pit, where he narrowly escaping instant death. He was lifted out and taken to the

Pittsburgh Homeopathic Hospital. Colleagues and competitors alike were shocked and expressed deep concern. Orrin W. Potter of Illinois Steel cabled Frick and received the reply, "Very sorry to say it is too true. Captain Jones was dangerously burned yesterday evening but not fatally. He is resting easily and we think he will pull through all right." Frick sent a similar message to Jay Morse. By Saturday afternoon, two of the men who had been burned were already dead, and without once regaining consciousness Jones died that evening. His funeral the following Wednesday brought forth a great public demonstration of affection and grief. The works were closed, the town of Braddock was draped in black, and thousands of workmen followed the procession from his home.[5]

The expressions of condolence and sadness by the company's principals were doubtless sincere, but such men speedily returned to the values of the marketplace. Within two days of the funeral, George Lauder had visited Jones's home and secured from his invalid widow the exclusive rights to his patented improvements to steel practice and equipment. The price paid was $35,000; the savings to Carnegie Steel over the next few years were certainly vastly greater. Frick's own detachment from the tragedy (or, perhaps more accurately, his awkwardness in such situations) was brought out by the strange manner in which he signed the memorial of condolence to the family, "With kind regards—H. C. Frick."[6]

The death of Jones brought sudden greater prominence to his protégé Charles Michael Schwab, a man whose reputation was eventually to rival, and to some extent overshadow, that of Frick. In 1886, on Jones's recommendation, Carnegie had appointed Schwab (still only twenty-four) as general superintendent of their Homestead works. Moving now from Carnegie Phipps to Carnegie Brothers, he was brought into closer contact with the latter's still relatively new chairman. The next three years highlighted the contrasts between the policies and attitudes of these two men and showed how Frick related to a business genius as great as his own.

On 10 October 1889, Frick introduced Schwab as the new general superintendent at Edgar Thomson. He reported that he was very favorably received and quickly demonstrated his commitment, drive, and imagination. Less than three weeks after Jones's death, Schwab had already written to Frick to suggest that a fourth converter be installed. By mid autumn he was proposing other considerable changes there, and Frick supported him: "As you have gone over the ground carefully and given excellent reasons for the new straightening presses, we hereby authorize you to proceed at once and make the improvement as stated in your letter."[7]

The new plant and Schwab's unremitting attention to business yielded good results. As Frick reported to Phipps early in 1890, a new rolling mill was at work, the fourth converter was a great success, and the Bessemer shop generally was in splendid form. "The men are extremely pleased with the new order of things and it is considered by everyone that the Works certainly are in better shape than ever."[8] Through much of 1890, the flow of suggestions from its general superintendent for improvements to Edgar Thomson works and a return flow of approvals from the chairman continued. Some were for mundane items, others for more costly or radical projects. All bore witness to their good fortune in having a man of Schwab's quality to step into the place of Jones.

Elsewhere the consequences of their reactions to Jones's death were not so unambiguously successful. Schwab's place at Homestead was taken by John A. Potter. At that time, Homestead was a smaller works than Edgar Thomson, although it was expanding, widening its product range, and becoming more important within Carnegie Phipps and Company.

In 1890 another independent venture was absorbed and became the group's third major works. As Homestead was being revamped, trade and steel consumption—having fallen away slightly in 1883, 1884, and 1885—revived and then went on to new highs. By mid 1886, a group broadly similar to that of the promoters of Homestead was ready to try again to compete with Carnegie in the more rapidly expanding bulk steel trades. This time the Carnegie associates took a rather more active part in routing the opposition. The Duquesne Steel Company was organized in June 1886, and construction began on a site on the west bank of the Monongahela River, well above existing steel mills. Although national output of crude steel in 1887 was almost twice that of any year before 1886, the Duquesne project ran into difficulties. There was dispute among its promoters and a need for more capital. Work stopped and was not resumed until the concern was relaunched in March 1888 as the Allegheny Bessemer Steel Company, which had double the capital of the previous project and then had to raise yet another $300,000.

Duquesne blew in its first converter early in February 1889; rail production began next month. The plant was well built. Its practice, too, broke new ground, ingots being rolled down into finished rails with no reheating. The new chairman of Carnegie Brothers and his senior colleagues recognized that they now had a serious local rival in their largest single line of business. However, although Duquesne stayed outside the Steel Rail Association and became a troublesome competitor in western markets, it was not successful commercially. The Carnegie management kept a close eye on what went on and did what they could to frustrate their near neighbor's chances of success. Within three months of their starting, Frick reported, "Allegheny Bessemer not doing very well. Have not completed their New York order yet, but the condition of the rail market is such that I fear with all our efforts they will be able to secure plenty of orders to keep them running."[9]

One method resorted to in the attempt to impede them was to persuade the railroad companies that direct rolling without reheating was injurious to the quality of the rail. To emphasize this message, through into autumn 1890, the stationery of Carnegie Brothers carried a "Special Note" at its left head: "To guard against danger of flaws and ensure uniform quality, all rails are reheated and re-rolled from the bloom." Naturally Allegheny Bessemer's management endeavored to fend off the various attacks made on them. By July 1889, although still not as successful as the quality of their plant might have warranted, they had tried to get information through to the Carnegies that they were not selling at the low prices being reported. Two weeks later, George Lauder suggested finding out what prices they really were offering. It was scarcely a sophisticated approach: "Wouldn't it be worthwhile to have an inquiry made by some party for rails from Allegheny Bessemer—and so ascertain the price at which they think they can deliver?" Throughout that year and the next, Duquesne was a source of concern.[10]

In summer 1889, Jay Morse contacted Frick about the prices both their companies should quote for a 5,000 to 7,000 ton rail order from an old Union Steel customer, the Cleveland, Cincinnati, Chicago, and St. Louis Railroad. He asked for Frick's considered views as soon as possible, "bearing in mind the position at the Allegheny Bessemer and the necessity of considering them a possible if not a probable competitor." At the beginning of 1890, reporting that Edgar Thomson was in "splendid trim," Frick also recognized that Duquesne was still "a great nuisance." A few months after this, Morse again pressed him for news: "now that Mr. Stegle has been made President of the Allegheny Bessemer Steel Company, will it make any difference in their position in trade? Will they continue to make rails and billets as heretofore? Is there any idea of enlarging their works?"[11]

The new plant, despite its nuisance value, did not stop the Carnegies' successes. Early in April 1890, although the president of Allegheny Bessemer was "on hand," the Carnegie agent John Fleming won an order for 17,100 tons rails. However, as Frick revealed to Morse, they had to cut prices to meet the competition: "This Allegheny Bessemer business has been costing us a great deal of money, but I think we are pursuing the right course." Looking ahead to the August meeting of the Railmakers Association, Frick stressed to Carnegie the continuing importance of their understanding with Illinois Steel, which "will to some extent non-plus the Allegheny Bessemer [*sic*]."[12]

The rail pool tried to block the new firm from getting business; and in response it had to accept lower prices. In spite of these pressures, in August 1890 Duquesne made 20,000 tons of steel and 17,000 tons of rails. At an annual rate this would have amounted to almost 11 percent of that year's national production and almost three-quarters as much rail tonnage as was made at Edgar Thomson. At the start of 1890, Carnegie had obtained rail orders from the Texas Pacific Railroad for $35 at works; by midsummer they were taking small orders for autumn delivery at $31 at works.[13]

Although it was an annoyance to others, all was not well at Duquesne. There were disputes between owners and managers as well as between the company and its employees. Occasional stoppages caused by labor disputes increased costs at the same time as the difficult competitive situation squeezed prices. These conditions gave Frick an opportunity, and as early as fall 1889, he made an offer to buy the works on behalf of the Carnegie interests. His bid of $600,000 was little more than half the cost of building, and the offer was declined. A year later falling prices provided him with a second chance. Protracted negotiations in New York were broken off, then resumed, and eventually the Allegheny Bessemer partners agreed to sell their works for $1 million, to be paid in bonds. On 14 November 1890, the triumphant Frick cabled Carnegie: "Papers signed. They stop in morning. We assume control 21st." The timing turned out slightly different. On the evening of Friday, 15 November, superintendents of the various departments at Duquesne posted notices informing their men they need not report to work the following day and that, if they reported to the general office, they would receive the wages due them.[14]

When Carnegie took over, Thomas Morrison was appointed general superintendent at Duquesne. Although its labor troubles recurred in midsummer 1891, the plant showed up well under his direction. Within the group, it constituted a new competitor to force up the pace of work; as Frick put it when sending figures to Carnegie, the efficiency of Duquesne meant that at Edgar Thomson, "Schwab will have to hump himself." By the August following the acquisition, they had analyzed the direct rolling process, which previously they had been at pains to denigrate. There was agreement that the process represented a cost saving, but there was dispute as to its extent. Schwab reckoned that direct rolling would not save them more than 45 cents per ton of rails and that it would increase the number of seconds. Leishman put the figure at 75 cents per ton and quoted the mill superintendent's belief that the quality of the rail might in fact be improved.[15] On the Carnegie 1890 rail output, even the smaller of these savings would have increased their income by $135,000, an amount equal to 2.5 percent of their profits. Both Edgar Thomson and Homestead were quietly converted to direct rolling and no more was heard of the alleged threat to quality.

Morrison further improved an already good plant. In December 1893 an independent Pittsburgh engineer, D. Ashworth, gave Duquesne a general audit and was impressed by what he found: "I find everything working in an admirable manner and a general neatness and evidence upon every hand of close attention which certainly reflects credit upon those in immediate charge."[16] Yet, despite its modern construction and efficient operation, Duquesne was soon taken out of the rail trade. The rumor was that it might be turned over to bridge and angle steels, in order to complement the production range of Homestead, but instead it was concentrated on billets, to be sold for further rolling. As well as these benefits from large-scale specialization, the Carnegies soon determined to provide the cost savings associated with backward integration. Early in 1892, Morrison was instructed to draw up plans for two blast furnaces, but work on putting these plans into practice was delayed by adverse circumstances: first by labor troubles at Homestead and then by trade depression, which in 1893 cut Carnegie profits by 25 percent. Construction of the first Duquesne furnace was begun in autumn 1894, but it was not blown in until June 1896.

Before the five-year bonds with which it had been purchased had matured, Duquesne's earnings had already paid for itself six times over. Carnegie was thrilled by this coup but was not willing to follow the chairman who had engineered it in his other (more vague) ideas of plant acquisition or construction. Within eleven months of the purchase of Allegheny Bessemer, Frick had written to him, "If we could purchase Sparrows Point works on about the same basis of Duquesne, and pay in 20 year bonds, would it not be a good thing to have?"[17] Some time later, he was contemplating ventures in the Chicago area, this time in the form of new building. In each instance Carnegie proved both skeptical and unmovable. Meanwhile, having built up and consolidated their steel interests in Pittsburgh, the Carnegie associates were now facing labor troubles of increasing severity. In the course of these, Frick came to the greatest crisis of his life.

Early Labor Disputes

Long-term trends or general situations are often summed up in isolated symbolic events. In labor relations, the Homestead strike of the summer and autumn of 1892 was an outstanding representation of a major shift in busi-ness thinking about the role of the workforce. Essentially, the strike indi-cated how changes in the structure and nature of manufacturing processes, already underway for many years, meant that labor was now to be treated as just another factor of production, wages being regarded as a cost consid-eration on a par with charges for raw materials, energy, or transportation. To reduce the price paid for inputs used was obviously good business prac-tice. As a general principle (that of securing efficient use of scarce resources), there is nothing exceptionable about this; but in dealing with men, rather than things—with communities, families, and individuals, not physical plant, mines, or utilities—this principle led to ruthlessness on the part of management and to dogged resistance on the part of the men.

It was Henry Clay Frick's misfortune to become the management exem-plar of this already fully developed capitalist attitude to labor. He was, in fact, only a prominent representative of a large class of businessmen who were all moving in this direction. On the other hand, it must be recognized that he was happy to carry the search for efficiency to its logical conclusion and, in so doing, acted as the figurehead for a company that was already generally committed to this policy.

For long it had seemed to idealists and realists alike that, in a nation as richly endowed as the United States, conditions for workers—and perhaps relations between capital and labor—could be different from those of the old antagonistic patterns in Europe. The idea that this new nation might still be shaped into an earthly Eden survived the Civil War. At that time, the flood of immigration resumed, and newcomers from Europe usually achieved a standard of living and of self-respect far higher than they had left behind. At the beginning of this post-bellum period, the major British rail-road contractor Sir Morton Peto, when asked what had struck him most favorably during his American travels, replied that it was the lack of pauper-ism: "Nothing is more striking to a European than the universal appearance of respectability of all classes in America. You see no rags, you meet no beggars." Ten years later while traveling in the United States as a special correspondent, the young Polish novelist Henryk Sienkiewicz remarked on the open-handed manner in which foreigners were received: "Other lands grant only asylum, this land recognizes the immigrant as a son and grants him rights." Unfortunately it was soon to become clear that in the field of labor relations, these rights were by no means unalienable and that not all immigrants were to be treated equally. In the course of a letter concerning a strike in the coke region, only a decade after Sienkiewicz's praises, Carne-gie wrote to Frick, "I agree these foreigners must learn they can't quit work and riot in this free country." It was an interesting comment from a man who was working on (or had just completed) *Triumphant Democracy*.[18]

In the mid nineteenth century, the supply of labor in America was often tight, and it has been commonly suggested that, in response, capital was substituted for workers.[19] There is some evidence for this, though the situation was more complex than is sometimes depicted. Capital was also short, and Europeans often commented on the flimsy nature of the machinery American concerns could then afford. In the metal industries, labor-intensive processes survived, and American works still lagged behind their leading European rivals.[20]

In 1867 the East Coast ironmaster Abram Hewitt attended the Paris International Exposition as one of the American commissioners. While in Europe, he visited steelworks in Britain, including mills in Sheffield and South Wales. He reported back that the crane power and other mechanical equipment available in these works beat operations in his own country "to death."[21] Yet, after that, it was not long before the balance of advantage began to swing the way of the Americans. One factor in helping it was to keep down wages as much as possible.

The home economy grew with unprecedented rapidity following the reconstruction from the Civil War. (At constant prices, in the 1850s the increase in GNP was 37.5 percent; in the 1860s it was 35.7 percent; in the 1870s it reached a remarkable 86.3 percent.) Emphasis on high productivity to meet burgeoning demand led to more capital being invested in plant and equipment. The whole distinctive phenomenon later to be described as the American system of manufacturing was coming into being. This had direct implications for labor, and some of these were clearly anticipated by a speaker at an early meeting of the American Institute of Mining Engineers, who advocated yet more capital outlay:

> [M]oney must flow like water, there can be no such thing as economy in the construction of a blast furnace. Whatever is proved to be the best adapted for the particular purpose to which it is to be applied, must be adopted, regardless of cost. . . . Whatever can be done by machinery, let machinery do, for it at least is insensible to Fourth of July, Washington's birthday, political meetings, pay-days and whiskey.[22]

This was to lead on to a preoccupation with output at all costs. Nominal wages might be good, but unit labor costs would fall, and workers would become enslaved to the machine.

Sometimes the results of this urge to mechanize and to speed processes could be an innocent enough search to minimize operational inefficiencies.

In other instances, stories carried a fuller flavor of the driving of plant and of labor. In 1890, for example, the members of the Iron and Steel Institute from Britain visited the United States. The doyen of British producers, Sir Lowthian Bell, expressed surprise about the hard driving of American blast furnaces, which, though resulting in high yields, required frequent relinings. The superintendent of the Cambria works responded, "What do we care about the lining? We think that a lining is good for so much iron and the sooner it makes it the better."[23]

The danger was that the same argument could be applied to the men who operated furnace, converter, or mill. It was reported once that the manager of a works had chalked up the output of the departing shift on a board. The next shift arrived, took up this target, and bettered it, and the process of rivalry between teams soon vastly improved this mill's performance. In an address to the Iron and Steel Institute in Britain in 1881, "Captain" Jones of Edgar Thomson explained that interplant rivalry was a means whereby productivity could be steadily increased. In the discussion that followed, the manager of the Eston works on Teesside—a plant even more recently built—revealed that it could produce only half what Jones and his men could turn out.[24]

It was "common" labor that paid the highest price in this struggle for tonnage. There continued to be satisfying jobs for engineers and managers, but the bulk of the workforce was gradually reduced to obedience to the rhythms and pace of the machine. To the employer, the workingman could become just an awkward and intractable factor of production, although he could be driven, laid off, or dispensed with in some other fashion. The quintessence of the system, "hard driving," ruined men as well as machines. Although, like physical plant, they could be replaced, a consequence of this practice was that in some trades a man was worn out by the time he was forty.[25]

Investments made in expensive plants made it possible either to do without many of the men formerly employed or to get more output from the same workforce. Sometimes the change to more modern machinery could be cataclysmic in its effect on employment—in 1885, for example, improvements in two departments of Edgar Thomson laid off 108 men out of 132.[26] It also became necessary to reduce tonnage rates, for otherwise the men might get what could be regarded as a disproportionate share of any gains from the newly installed plant. To achieve these reductions, the collective power of the workingmen had to be contained; and unionization, at least of a kind that extended widely throughout the industry, was anathema to cost-reducing managements. In steel, this meant that the powers of the Amalgamated Association of Iron and Steel Workers especially would have to be broken. The Carnegie associates were to play a major role in breaking this union, and in the most critical stage of the conflict their power was deployed under the leadership of Henry Clay Frick on the battleground of Homestead. However, the early engagements were fought elsewhere and under less competent or less unswervingly resolute commanders.

"Captain" W. R. Jones was insistent in his pursuit of output, for which he would drive both himself and his men. He took care to secure a loyal workforce whose members would not resort to strikes at the slightest provocation (as he believed Englishmen in particular would). Yet he managed to avoid dealing with his men as mere cogs in the production machine. On one occasion, he summed up his labor philosophy: "I have always found it best to treat men well. They should be made to feel that the Company is interested in their welfare. Make the works a pleasant place for them. All haughty and disdainful treatment of men has a decidedly bad effect on them."[27] Not all of his seniors or successors shared these convictions, and in the end even Jones was forced to compromise his beliefs.

In the late 1870s the Carnegies had adopted the eight-hour three-shift day at Edgar Thomson works. Almost a decade later, the other Carnegie works were still operating two twelve-hour shifts. At this time, Carnegie decided they could no longer afford the Edgar Thomson regimen, which was easier on the men. As a result Jones was instructed to adopt the standard twelve-hour-shift system from the beginning of 1888. The men struck, and three thousand of them remained out for over four months. Eventually, and notwithstanding the liberal sentiments he had expressed *Forum* only two years before, Carnegie decided that the strike must be broken. Jones was called to New York for consultations and from there sent on to Philadelphia to engage Pinkerton detectives for service at Braddock. With their protection (whose hiring Carnegie long afterward conveniently forgot) the works were put back in action with nonunion men. Bridge remarked laconically, "The usual disorders took place, resulting in a slight loss of life; but eventually the contest was won by the Company. . . . Thus ended the eight hour day in a night of sorrow and suffering." In this dispute, the men lost wages amounting to an estimated $560,000, and the 1888 earnings of the Carnegie associates were $1.5 million down on the previous year.[28]

After Jones's death, Schwab became responsible for labor conditions and relations at Edgar Thomson. He got off to a good start on this front. In February 1890, he met with a committee representing the Edgar Thomson locomotive engineers. Frick wrote, "From the notice furnished, I am much pleased with the way you handled this matter, and am glad to see from the

tone of your letter that you think the matter is settled." However, later that
year harmony between chairman and superintendent was decreasing. On 1
October, Frick asked for an assessment of the Edgar Thomson labor situation. Remarkably, Schwab delivered a sixteen-page typed report the following day (he admitted he had started to put it together before he got Frick's
letter). He gave a résumé of the plant's labor situation, because (as he put
it) Frick's information had been "so broken up and detached."[29]

All had been quiet until six weeks before this report. Several lodges of the
Amalgamated Association had arranged a meeting for the evening of Saturday, 13 September, at which their national president, William Weihe, was
present. Schwab had "placed [him]self in position to get all the information
possible from this meeting," presumably by arranging that his own infor-
mants should be there. Almost all the men present joined the union, signed
a paper, and paid their "initiation" fee. A committee was appointed to negotiate the restoration of the eight-hour day. At this point in his report he gave
his opinion that, as shown by a table of earnings he had already sent to
Frick, the wages of the rail mill men were unjust "and there was good
ground for dissatisfaction." On 28 September, the blowing engineers in the
converter shop wrote a well-reasoned letter to Schwab, pointing out that,
although so vital to the operations, they received well below half the pay of
the converting mill men. They gave notice of a request for an increase in the
sliding scale then in force but ended with a paragraph that indicated how
far they were from the popular image of the militant proletariat: "We re-
frained from bothering you in regard to wages, as others have done, until
now, the time named in the agreement, and we hope that our request will
be received in the same spirit in which it is made, and that our case will
receive just consideration and hoping that your answer will be favorable to
us, we remain, Yours respectfully. . . ." There followed eight signatures.

In the next few days, Schwab was contacted by various departments in
the steelworks, all requesting the eight-hour day. In each case he caused the
men to withdraw their request by pointing out that it was tantamount to a
notice to end their contract and negotiate a completely new one. To Frick
he again pointed out that there were inequalities and injustices in the present scales. The blast furnace men wanted to renegotiate both hours and
rates, doing away with a sliding scale tied to the price of rails. Schwab con-
fessed he had not been able to make the delegation that visited him (two
Hungarians and an Irishman) comprehend the situation. But, he acknowledged, the output of the furnaces had increased from 25 to 30 percent in a
period when the wages per day had remained the same. He ended by posing
some questions: Should all departmental scales be renegotiated together?

Should they have a new scale every three years, a time over which "all the conditions about a large works like Edgar Thomson are likely to change?"[30]

Later in October, Schwab began to press for wage increases to correct some of the injustices he had identified. In the last clear month before his fatal accident, Jones had hoped to make 25,000 tons of rails. In the eight months to the end of August 1890, monthly output averaged 27,500 tons. Yet, despite these increases, Frick remained parsimonious about labor. Within less than five weeks of Schwab's taking control of the works, he had been asked to notify James Gayley that the number of men at the furnaces was increasing. He pointed out that the furnace department was doing some 27 percent more work than in the previous year without any material increase in the workforce. He suggested, "it seems only just that these men should have some advance," and reckoned that the increases would have little adverse effect on costs (see table 8).[31]

The profits made by the Carnegie companies in 1890 topped $4.8 million. Two days after these splendid results were to hand, Frick explained to Carnegie that in several recent talks with Schwab he had "told him that it was out of the question to think of advancing the wages of any of the men." Within a few weeks they were faced with a strike at Edgar Thomson. The blast furnace men informed their chief superintendent that, unless hours of work were cut to eight, they would stop work on the morning of 1 January 1891. As Frick put it to Carnegie, "it is a question of hours he says more than wages but of course [it] means the same thing in the end." Because of current depressed conditions and outlook, he felt no concession was possible and suggested that Schwab should call the men together and send some of them to the furnace plants of other steel companies and thereby come to realize that the idea was unrealistic.[32]

At this point, they were on the edge of a crisis in labor relations. It was a brief episode, but one whose color and heat come across vividly in the accounts of its course written hour by hour. Schwab, author of the following reports, asserted a measure of independence in adopting a stance somewhat distanced from that of his chairman. On 1 January 1891, Frick sent Carnegie some correspondence between himself and Schwab concerning what he described as "not anything more than a drunken Hungarian spree. . . . A little nerve and patience will certainly bring this matter through all right." Next day he sent on a reassuring message: "All quiet last night and this morning. Think it is working itself out all right. Newspaper reports greatly exaggerated." He followed this with a private wire: "Everything quiet at Bessemer. No new developments. Schwab was just in and says they expect to make a start Monday or Tuesday. Nothing else of special interest here today."[33]

TABLE 8

Edgar Thomson, Wage Increases Suggested October 1890

Department	Number of Men Involved	Total Extra Monthly Cost	Cost per Ton of Product
Furnaces	442	1,095[a]	2.0[b]
Converters	na	567	1.6
Blooming mill	na	60	na
Rail mill	32	640	2.1

Source: CMS to HCF, 20 Oct. 1890, Frick Papers.
Notes: [a] Figures this column are in dollars.
[b] Figures this column are in cents.

Very early on the morning of 1 January 1891, Schwab reported that the main body of stockyard men had left the works the previous evening, six hours before their contract expired. Fifty men from "Cosgrove's gang" had remained filling coke. His account is vivid with the harshness of the current labor relations; it also indicates both his own decisiveness and his distinctive methods:

> About 12 o'clock . . . I received a message from the works stating that the Hungarian element were organizing at the corner of 13th street, near Wolfe's saloon, and were going to the works to clean out the men who were at work, and I then at once started for the works and arrived there about the same time the mob did, there being about 60 in the crowd. They immediately went down to the Stock House and of course after considerable skirmishing managed to chase all the men away from there. They then turned their attention to the men unloading material on trestles and succeeded in cleaning these men out. The crowd was made up largely of drunken fellows with whom you could neither reason, nor induce to leave by any argument and inasmuch as our force at the works was comprised of but few foremen it was impossible to do anything with them. After they cleaned out the trestle, however, they went down into the Stock Yard and commenced doing injury to our property by upsetting barrows, etc., when our loyal men from the trestle made an attack upon them and succeeded in beating them off from the stock house. I do not know that we have gained anything by this, but at this writing, 3 A.M, stock yard is entirely clear.

He intended to file information the following morning against those who had trespassed and caused disturbance and to have them jailed. He had sent Cosgrove, his assistant, to the city to get the sheriff to come out in order to swear in twenty or thirty police and to deputize their foremen:

> We are going to make a vigorous fight, and we are going to try and carry it through with a rush if at all possible. Have better hopes at this writing than have had at any time. . . . Am quite tired and worn out and go to rest for a few

hours. . . . It was a great mistake that we did not arrange with Mr. Wolfe to close his saloon tonight. He has promised to do so tomorrow. . . . . Our front men at the furnaces have remained firm. They have themselves pretty well armed with clubs etc. and state will resist any attempt to make attacks upon them by the Hungarian element.

Schwab's "better hopes" were disappointed. Later that day he reported that a "posse" of about 250 drunken Hungarians had organized between noon and 2 P.M. and had moved on the furnace department causing all the men there to quit. At this point, he outlined two policy options open to them, one that Frick was later to favor and the other that was to be championed both by Carnegie and Schwab. If it was a priority to get their furnaces working as soon as possible, he suggested to Frick that they should bring in Pinkerton men:

> [I]t seems to me that this method would ensure a quicker breaking of the strike than the second method which I am about to propose, and that is that we send everybody away from the works, having nobody there but a few foremen and Superintendents who can watch the furnaces, and do other work which may be necessary from time to time. I think if this was done and the furnaces and works generally were allowed to stand idle for a considerable length of time, say two to three weeks, that these people may have regained their senses and will not be inclined to adopt the methods which they are now pursuing. This, coupled with the fact that I intend having arrested and put in jail all of these men that I can get a hold of, should have the desired effect. Your early advice is desirable.

Frick replied from their head office on the same day:

> Am opposed to bringing Pinkerton men to protect our property. Mr. Knox has gone to see the Sheriff and to find whether the Sheriff will agree to protect our property. . . . In case the Sheriff will not consent to protect our property and the men who are willing to work, we will have to adopt the second method which you propose. This I hope will not be necessary.

A little later, sending that day's correspondence on to Carnegie, Frick reported that the sheriff had agreed to give them protection and had gone to Bessemer on the afternoon train to examine the situation. He did not think the episode would lead to anything. They were, he believed, being very reasonable with the men: "We are asking for no reduction even in these depressed times, when furnaces all over the country are either banking up or their employees accepting a reduction in wages. A little nerve and patience will certainly bring this matter through all right."[34]

In his final letter on what must have seemed a very long day, Schwab reported that he had arrived at Edgar Thomson about fifteen minutes after the sheriff:

> Since my arrival at the works I have called together all the workmen who were then at the works; brought them into the office; addressed them, saying it was simply ridiculous for three thousand honest workmen to allow four or five hundred Hungarians to deprive them of work which they so much desired doing. I told them that the Sheriff was here and would swear them in as Deputy Sheriffs. . . . The result is, that I expect to have a force of at least 100 men at Furnace Department tonight, well armed. Have twelve Winchester Rifles (repeating) which I have placed in the hands of Kileen with instructions to put them in the hands of the best men, with permission of the Sheriff. Besides this, I have a large number of other men who are armed with small arms and clubs. I understand the "Huns" intend making another attack tonight, and I can assure you that if they do, they will meet with a pretty lively reception as I am determined to drive them out, no matter at what cost or sacrifices. [The Sheriff said] it was the best thing in the world that we did not force an attack today. My plan now is, to appeal to the sympathy of the other men, get them to come to work, be sworn in as Deputies, and will then try and start some of the furnaces as soon as we possibly can, protecting ourselves all the while. All I ask of you Mr. Frick, is to have a little more confidence in me in this respect. Have felt right along that you do not have the confidence in this matter that you have had in the others, but I can assure you that should the opportunity come tonight we will make it mighty hot for these people, unless I am much disappointed in the men I have back of me. If, in this manner, I can get our men to stand right by us, I would much prefer this to getting Pinkerton detectives. Am going to adopt the policy laid out and fight it through as hard as I can.

By this time, Gayley was "played out" and was to go home to rest. Next day he would come in to relieve Schwab of the leadership of their forces. Schwab ended, "As I before stated, have a little more confidence, and I assure you I will pull it through, and quickly at that. If you have any instructions to give me tonight Mr. Reinhardt will be glad to return to the works with them."[35]

Two letters from Frick on 2 January show how potentially explosive the situation was. To Gayley at the Edgar Thomson furnaces, he wrote that they had probably twice as many revolvers as he had asked for, and that they would be taken out on the 12.30 train by Utley: "I wired you that, as this train did not go any further than Braddock, that you should meet him there with a team. Of course you must exercise care as to who you give these revolvers to; they must not be given . . . to any except Deputy Sheriffs. I have no doubt, though, but that you will use great caution in this matter." His other letter concerned a threat of a widening of the labor dispute:

> Mr. Potter of Homestead telegraphs Mr. Curry as follows:—"There is a rumor that the Huns are arranging in Homestead to go to Braddock tonight in full

force. I think it is all idle talk but thought it best to give it to you to be used for what it is worth." I agree with Potter, I do not think there is anything in it, but thought I had better repeat it to you. At the same time I told Mr. Curry to tell Potter to have a man on the lookout and advise you from Homestead direct of anything that might take place in that direction.[36]

Concern of this sort, surveillance of the mood and of moves at other works, and preparations for possible violent action in defense of property were to be recurrent themes at this period of the company's history.

These Edgar Thomson troubles are significant in a number of respects. There was violence, but it was contained and (especially valuable from the company point of view) was not widely reported. Frick was not unsympathetic to calls for help for innocent victims of their labor troubles, although (perhaps because of his position at the head of the firm) his response seems to have been efficient rather than caring. In mid January he sent a brief note to Schwab:

> I understood you to say today that Michael Quinn, who died recently from injuries received at the hands of some Hungarians, while he was on duty at our works, was a widower, and left three children, a boy 12 years old and two girls younger. Such being the case we feel that we should make some provision for the children, and you are hereby authorized, when there is a satisfactory guardian appointed for them, to say that we will pay him, for their use, $3,000.[37]

Although he had agreed with Schwab that they should not bring in the Pinkertons, subsequent events show that this was on the basis of expediency rather than principle. If they had done so it could easily have united the rest of their workers against them, and if anything had gone wrong it might have alienated the public as well. During the dispute, Schwab had made it clear that he felt he lacked the complete confidence of his chairman. He had asserted himself in pursuing an independent line. It was by no means a weak one, for he was able to secure the support of the majority of the workforce. Inevitably the circumstances of every dispute were different, and when Frick's attitudes came to the test the case was to prove a harder one, but the younger man had shown a flexibility that was foreign to his superior. This brief flare-up at Edgar Thomson also introduced a sour note to their relationship, although it was not to be permanent.

Two weeks after this violent episode, Frick was reproving Schwab for not building up their coke stockpile. That month they had added less than eight cars a day. His letter had a peremptory tone: "This will not do. I am disappointed that you have not given this more attention, and from this on, and until further advised, I want you to arrange to unload at least 50 cars daily into that stockpile." The urgency was in order to meet the threat of a strike in the coke region that was expected to start about 10 February 1891. In April, he criticized Schwab for allowing information as to which rail orders they were working on to leak out of the mill. He wanted him to inquire into the matter "quietly and intelligently," although it might involve the discharge of some of their "pretty prominent" men.[38] By early autumn he had become less willing to endorse continuing requests for spending on plant improvements, which included changes in the converting department; "something of a new departure" Frick called them, and he asked Schwab to be quite clear that they would yield the benefits claimed and that their cost would not be more than $25,000:

> The next time you are in I should like you to call on Mr. Lovejoy and let him show you the amount of money you have already spent at Edgar Thomson this year for improvements. I think it will make you open your eyes. However, I will talk this matter over with you the next time you are in, or I am out, and if, on further investigation, you still think that you are correct, it is likely I can prevail on the Board to agree to the expenditure.

In late October, Schwab wrote in a not untypical tone of almost boyish enthusiasm to report that he had been able to secure a new labor settlement in all departments for the three years from 1 January 1892, involving major reductions of scales, reflecting higher outputs secured by installation of more or higher capacity equipment—reductions greater than Frick had suggested were acceptable and more than he himself had expected to win: "I take this occasion of saying that the reductions secured this time are by long odds the heaviest reductions we have ever secured at Edgar Thomson." In 1888 the company had negotiated scale reductions there averaging 21 percent; this time the figure was 32 percent. Altogether he expected that they would be able to save $8,771 a month, and that a further monthly cost reduction of $5,358 could result from new equipment and the consequent laying-off of thirty-eight men (see table 9).[39]

A week after this news of a successful wage settlement, and again a little later, Frick expressed reluctance to increase the salaries of Schwab's assistants in the works—Kerr, Kileen, Benn, and Reinhardt—as Schwab had requested. A clear indication that Frick felt he was being hustled by his general superintendent comes in a letter he wrote when Schwab's review of scales was underway:

> Mr. Lovejoy has shown me your message wherein you want the comparative wages and comparative earnings of Homestead, Braddock and Duquesne. I told you very plainly, the other evening, that I did not wish you to bring in the

TABLE 9
Edgar Thomson, Savings in Labor Costs from New Scales, from 1 January 1892

Department	Number of Men Involved	Monthly Saving	Average Reduction
Converting works	114	5,824[a]	32[b]
Blooming mill	39	1,656	25
Rail mill	91	1,291	14

Source: CMS to HCF, 22 Oct. 1891, Frick Papers.
Notes: [a] Figures this column are in dollars.
[b] Figures this column are percentages.

question of what wages were paid at Duquesne and Homestead, and I do not think you would gain anything by it if you did. Make no mistake about this.[40]

Homestead was soon to be the setting for a far more serious dispute.

The Homestead Plant

Prospects for the iron and steel trades looked bright as 1891 ended. Whereas the year's production of crude steel in the rest of the nation was 14.1 percent less than in 1890, the Carnegie plants had made 20.7 percent more. The net profits of Carnegie, Phipps, and Company and of Carnegie Brothers were only 80 percent those of the previous year, but their increased share of U.S. production (up from 15.43 to 20.42 percent) was a striking indication of their exceptional efficiency and of their ability to do well when the trade generally was in the doldrums. Now rail prices were rising rapidly. All in all there was every justification for the telegram of happy, if not particularly well-expressed, Christmas sentiments that the associates sent to their head: "Your partners gladly, and probably at no previous time, have had greater reasons to extend congratulations, or with more cordiality than at present." A few weeks later, Carnegie was encouraging Frick, who had worked so unremittingly for so long, to take a European holiday: "There never is a time when it seems wise to leave, and there scarcely ever comes a time when it is not wise to do so. In your own case it is the highest wisdom, indeed I consider it a duty to yourself and others." He ended, "Truly I never knew a time when you could leave so well as just now; plenty of work, plenty of money."[41] Within a few months there occurred what was in many ways the greatest trial of Frick's working life, the event that without doubt stamped the nature of his work and attitudes most firmly in the popular imagination—the Homestead strike.

Homestead had been farmland until the 1870s. In 1879 its first industrial plant (a glassworks) was built, and work also began on construction of the plant of the Pittsburgh Bessemer Steel Company. Its two small converters made their first steel in March 1881, when it embarked on what seemed likely to be a successful career in rail making. Overall, 1882 and 1883 were good years for national steel production, but there were serious labor difficulties at Homestead. In October 1883, still troubled with disputes in a year during which rail production fell and prices tumbled, the mill was sold to the Carnegies. Three years later, the decision was taken to install open-hearth furnaces. These additions were made with the frenetic speed that became a hallmark of the way Homestead conducted business. Work on four thirty-ton furnaces with a combined weekly capacity of 900 tons started on 26 April; less than six months later the first furnace was making steel. The rolling of rails was replaced by the rolling of plates and structurals. Capacity steadily increased, and by the end of the 1880s, as the core enterprise of Carnegie, Phipps, and Company, Homestead was already the nation's biggest unit in its new rolled products—although among the Carnegie plants it was still a smaller operation than Edgar Thomson. With the growth of the works went that of the community, which in less than a decade grew from a village into a mill town (at the 1880 census, Homestead borough contained 596 inhabitants; a decade later there were 7,911). The works also drew labor from other nearby mill towns.

Homestead had passed to the Carnegies in a context of labor disputes, and labor relations there continued to cause periodic trouble. The Amalgamated Association of Iron and Steel Workers had been formed in 1875–1876. It was not a radical union. As the editor of its paper, the *National Labor Tribune,* put it in the mid 1880s, it had not "been a strike machine; on the other hand its history proves it to have been conducted on the theory that the labor organization which secures to its members their rights with the least friction is the one that recommends itself most highly to workmen, to employers and to the public."[42] These qualities did not prevent the union from being a target for company attack.

Although it was Frick who, in the popular imagination, was to become inseparably linked with the name and reputation of Homestead, it is important to record something of its earlier labor history, for Carnegie and other partners were also deeply involved. In 1886 a thirty-four-year-old engineer, William Abbott, was elected vice-chairman of Carnegie, Phipps, and Company and thereby assumed overall responsibility for Homestead. In 1889 he became president. Abbott was not so "hard" as a number of his peers, but his relatively humane qualities proved a mixed blessing in his management

Homestead Steel Works, 1897. *Courtesy of USX.*

career. As with other partners, his relationship with Carnegie followed an uneven course, for which personnel management was only partly responsible. During the summer of 1888, for example, Carnegie had alternatively praised and criticized his handling of negotiations for armor plate contracts, including those for the battleship *Maine*.[43] At the end of 1888, Carnegie drew Abbott's attention to the Homestead labor situation. They had "an enormous number" of machinists, watchmen, and general employees—men whose occupations the Homestead superintendent, Schwab, had listed in his payrolls as "various." As ever, Carnegie wanted to chisel away at costs, even if this meant reduced standards of living for those whose rights he was so warmly endorsing in his writings: "I do think that if you and he went over it carefully, the force could be considerably reduced from January 1st. I notice we are paying 14 cents an hour for labor, which is above Edgar Thomson price. The force might perhaps be reduced in number 10 percent so that each man getting more wages would be required to do more work."[44]

Labor problems at Homestead came to a head in 1889. On 29 March, three months before the current wage contract expired, Carnegie and Abbott met in Pittsburgh to look into the situation. In mid May, it was announced that the renewal of contracts would be made conditional on the men's acceptance of a sliding scale; they would be required to sign individually to indicate a willingness to work under this arrangement. For a time it seemed that the company would get its way, and in mid June Frick reported, "Mr. Abbott is managing Homestead matters well. It looks very favorable, and, to me, as if he would be able [to win] the Amalgamated to his terms."[45] In the end, however, sticking to their opposition to individual contracts, the local lodges of the union determined to fight, the majority of the men refused to sign the undertaking, and the mill closed on 1 July 1889.

Carnegie's advice to Abbott was that he should wait for the workers to return on company terms; but instead Abbott tried to break the strike by bringing in black and immigrant workers. Their arrival was opposed by a mass of angry strikers. Wishing to avoid violence and the possibility of sympathy walkouts at their other plants, Abbott gave way and conferred with the men. In exchange for recognizing the Amalgamated as the sole negotiating agent for Homestead, he won acceptance of the proposed wage rates and the sliding scale for the next three years. Under the terms of the sliding scale, wages were linked with the price of billets, although there was a "minimum base" fixed at $25 a ton below which wages would not be allowed to fall (at that time billets were $26.50). Except as a financially interested partner and a powerful and respected commentator, Frick was not involved, and although Schwab was in everyday command of production at Homestead, he too seems to have played an unimportant part in this dispute.

During the 1889 strike at Homestead, Abbott as president of Carnegie, Phipps, and Company had conducted negotiations with the men, but after the dispute was settled, Schwab further proved his worth in rapidly restoring normal operations. His success caught the eye of Carnegie, who (perhaps with a touch of sarcasm) wrote to Abbott, "So glad Schwab proved so able. If we have a real manager of men there Homestead will come out right now. Everything is in the man." Less than eight weeks after his letter, Jones was killed, and at his own request Schwab was moved to Edgar Thomson to replace him. The superintendency of Homestead was taken by John A. Potter. Frick thought highly of him: "I would like to say that I do not think there is in the service of either Association [a man] who will make a better record than Mr. Potter. He is truthful, direct, and has good judgment, plenty of energy, and will be the idol of his men." It proved too optimistic an assessment.[46]

After the return to work in summer 1889, investment continued in expansion and cost reduction at Homestead. Carnegie pressed for what he always regarded as the keys to commercial success, "product" and reduced factor costs, including labor: "I am glad to see that Homestead is receiving attention. I judge from the newspaper items somebody is getting things down to bearings there. We can afford to insist on a very fair scale in the new open-hearth plant." In fact, wages based on tonnage had gone up as a result of the plant improvements they had made.[47] As these developments occurred, the general trend of prices was downward (the average for billets fell by $5.82 or almost 19.8 percent between 1889 and 1892). Taking into account capital outlay, the consequent increase in labor productivity, and the effects of price reductions, management let it be known early in 1892 that it would be looking for reduction of the minimum base to $22 in the new contracts, which had to be agreed by midsummer.

In the local community, if not in the higher echelons of the firm, there was already a sense of looming conflict. In January 1892 a representative of Cramp (the Philadelphia shipbuilders) while in Pittsburgh met J. W. Allen, a member of the Amalgamated Association, who told him that, because the tempo of work was being geared to that of the new machinery, real wage levels were already being lowered: "you will see seven men doing the work that formerly required 24 men in a crew, and yet they say that the seven ought to be content with a lower scale than used to be paid to the 24."[48]

During January 1892 the formal processes of negotiation began. Potter sent for the joint committee of Amalgamated's local lodges and asked them to propose a scale of wages. When this was submitted a month later, he handed the men counterproposals prepared by Frick. Discussions proved fruitless, and both sides pushed ahead with preparations for battle. The Amalgamated Association conducted a recruitment drive at Homestead and its membership almost doubled from the four hundred with which it had begun the year; even so by midsummer only about one-fifth of the workers were in the union.

The company was also squaring for a fight. On 4 April 1892, Carnegie sent a draft notice for their Homestead employees, which announced that, in the light of the planned 1 July amalgamation with Edgar Thomson and Duquesne to form the Carnegie Steel Company, Homestead must become non-union. The labor force would be reduced, although hope was expressed that extensions at all the mills might soon make it possible to reemploy those who lost their jobs. At the same time, he recommended that Potter should roll a large tonnage of plates ahead of demand to cover their needs if a strike resulted.[49] Frick disapproved of the Carnegie notice and did not issue it, but he made sure that plates—including armor plate—were produced in excess of immediate demand, to be stockpiled awaiting their final treatments. Meanwhile he kept negotiations open, even going so far as to suggest that the company was not concerned to break the union.

In the early part of April 1892, Carnegie left for Europe. Just before he sailed, he met with Frick in his library in New York and handed him a memorandum recording his view of the Homestead situation. This involved closing the works and waiting for the men to give way, the approach he had commended to Abbott three years before. By 21 April, when Frick wrote to Carnegie at Coworth Park, Sunningdale, Berkshire, in southern England, he tried to prepare his senior partner for what might be involved. He made his own approach clear:

> The wages question at Homestead is a most serious one and it may become necessary to fight it out this summer. No better time can be selected or expected. We will get ready for a fight immediately. If it be unnecessary, all the better. It may be a stubborn one, but if once gone into, without regard to cost or time, it will be fought to a finish.[50]

Six weeks later, he sent Potter (and on the following day, Carnegie) a list of the scales to be presented to the men. According to his reckoning, they required reductions of nearly 15 percent, with a further 4 percent decrease for each dollar the price of billets fell below $26.50 (see table 10). Frick added that he hoped to use the dispute as an opportunity to improve the standing of their superintendent in the eyes of his men: "Want to put Potter in the position of having used his influence with us to make a deal with the Association if possible and to have used his influence toward securing for the men as high a rate of wages as possible. In other words to strengthen him with his men." He had asked Potter to present the proposed scales to the men's joint committee as soon as possible. Even at this stage, he implied that he was still open-minded about union membership:

> These scales have had most careful consideration, with a desire to act toward our employees in the most liberal manner. . . . We do not care whether a man belongs to a union or not, nor do we wish to interfere. He may belong to as many unions or organizations as he chooses, but we think our employees at Homestead Steel Works would fare much better working under the system in vogue at Edgar Thomson and Duquesne.

Union response was requested not later than 24 June.[51]

In view of comparisons later drawn between Frick's approach to the dispute and that of Carnegie, it is important to stress that the latter was also insistent on the need for new wage rates. Early in June, Carnegie remarked that plate makers in the East could compete with them because fewer men worked in the mills there and they were paid less: "I hope you will put labor at Homestead once for all upon its proper basis." To this end he was willing to close the works, believing that dispute over new scales would provide a pretext for breaking the Amalgamated Association: "Perhaps if Homestead men understand that *non-acceptance means non-union for ever* they will accept." He had forgotten that, six years before, he had written in *Forum,* "I would lay it down as a maxim that there is no excuse for a strike or a lock out until arbitration of differences has been offered by one party and refused by the other."[52]

TABLE 10

Daily Wage Rates at Homestead, Actual and Proposed

| | On $26.50 Basis | | On $23 Basis |
	1889–1892 Scale	Proposed 1892–1893 Scale	Proposed 1892–1893 Scale
32″ Slabbing Mill			
Heater	6.37	7.68	6.67
Heater, 1st helper	4.53	5.47	4.75
Heater, 2nd helper	2.56	2.62	2.27
Craneman	3.29	2.37	2.06
Shear tongsman	2.27	2.23	1.94
Open-Hearth Furnaces			
Melter's helpers 1	3.60	3.76	3.26
Charging machine	3.00	3.29	2.86
Ladleman 1	3.40	3.76	3.26
Pitman 3	2.70	2.83	2.45

Source: Pennsylvania Department of Internal Affairs 1893, p. D-5.
Note: Figures are in dollars. The $23 basis was a company concession offered during negotiations.

At this critical time, Abbott retired from active involvement in the company, and Frick became chairman of the new Carnegie Steel Company, which incorporated both Carnegie Brothers and Carnegie, Phipps, and Company and therefore encompassed the whole of their steel operations. Personally he had no doubt that he could do better than his predecessor had done three years before. He even seems to have expected a speedy victory. On 2 June 1892, writing to Carnegie care of the London office of the financier J. S. Morgan, he was scathing about his predecessor's policies and sufficiently sanguine about his own that, taking up his senior partner's advice of a few months before, he referred to the possibility of a late summer vacation: "Dear Abbott (and he was *very* dear) is wrong as usual. . . . I note that you have taken a place in Scotland. Have no doubt it is a very fine one and I might take a notion to run over for a short time in the latter part of August, say 30 day trip if everything should be going all right."[53]

Meanwhile, he had not allowed such happy expectations to distract him from preparations for confrontation with the Amalgamated. In May 1892, he set in train work on a solid board fence, three miles in length, around the Homestead works. It was topped with strands of barbed wire. This was

Henry Clay Frick, circa 1890–94. *Photograph by B.L.H. Dabbs, Pittsburgh.*
Courtesy of Frick Art and Historical Center, Frick Archives.

completed in June. Platforms, twelve feet in height and equipped with elec-
trically powered searchlights, were built at the ends of the mill buildings.
Not surprisingly the men nicknamed the works "Fort Frick."

Warnings were given to customers of difficulties that might lie ahead. On
9 June 1892, Frick wrote to William C. Whitney, an important purchaser,
formerly as Secretary of the Navy but now as joint owner of the Metropoli-
tan Traction Company of New York. He attributed slow deliveries of beams
to the disappointing performance of their new mill but had to admit that
there might be more delays. The words he used about the first problem
provide an interesting insight into his attitudes to labor: "The mill is going
to be all right, but it takes time to break in the men and get things to work
smoothly." Two days later, to their New York agent, Sylvanus L. Schoon-

maker, he again referred to beam deliveries, but this time specifically identi-fied the new disturbing factor: "Another trouble has been that in view of the expiration of the scale, July 1st, and the preparation being made by us to enforce a new scale if necessary, has made the men somewhat careless. So that the product of the mill is not what it should be. We will overcome all this, however, in a short time." In any lengthy strike they would unavoidably lose some business they had hoped to win. In this particular instance, they had to forgo the contract to supply steel for the Monadnock Building, one of the new Chicago skyscraper office blocks.[54]

As he went about his business of warning the trade, Frick was also taking further steps to protect the property whose defensive works were already taking shape. On 9 June, he contacted J. Ogden Hoffman in Philadelphia, informing him that they would probably need some guards. He wanted the matter to be all lined up "in case I wire you. . . . All this must of course be considered strictly confidential." Hoffman replied promptly and was in-structed not to send his representative to the Carnegie Steel offices, but to those of the Frick Coke Company, where he would be less likely to be no-ticed. Between 20 and 25 June 1892, arrangements were made with R. A. Pinkerton for the employment of three hundred of his men as guards or watchmen.[55]

Having made their dispositions, the management of Carnegie Steel con-tinued their negotiations with the men. As these went on, the differences of approach among the principals became more obvious. The outside world might conclude that the dispute was a straightforward struggle between cap-ital and labor, but in fact the former party at least was divided. In mid June, Carnegie advised Frick to hold no more meetings with the union representa-tives but to make a stand. However, Frick kept up contacts with the Amalga-mated until late that month.

The company had set itself three negotiating aims: a change in the date for fixing new scales from 30 June to 31 December; reduction in tonnage rates to take account of the benefits from new machinery; and a cut in the minimum base from $25 to $22 a ton to reflect the fall in steel prices. The first of these aims reflected different perspectives on the part of the firm and of the men. The company claimed that a year-end date would better fit in with times of contracts with customers, and that with business then less active than in midsummer it would be easier to accommodate new arrange-ments for employment. The men believed that midwinter was chosen be-cause they would then be unable to put up a long-term resistance to wage cuts.

On the evening of 21 June, three days before the deadline set for their response, the Amalgamated Association requested a meeting on Thursday, 23 June, and Frick, punctilious in following the due procedures, agreed. For the men the conference was attended by William Weihe, the Amalgamated's national president, and by twenty-five local representatives. In the course of the discussions, Frick expressed his willingness to raise the proposed minimum base to $23; the men stuck out for $24. On this difference of $1 per ton the possibility of resolving the dispute foundered. Next day Frick reported on the meeting to Carnegie, who was now at Rannoch Lodge in the Scottish Highlands: "While harmonious it did not result in anything. . . . We are now preparing for a struggle. . . . It may be, of course, that they will yet propose to accept our ultimatum, but we will have no more conferences with them."[56] Closure of the various departments at Homestead began at the end of the month. As this happened, effigies of Potter and Frick were hung from the town's telegraph posts. By 1 July 1892, all work had ceased.

Frick was now paying attention to the desirability of presenting their case in the best light to the wider American public. He sent copies of an *American Manufacturer* article on Homestead to Hoffman, asking, "if you think it would serve our interests" to arrange that it should be included in two or three Philadelphia papers.[57] He sent a similar message to Schoonmaker. The events of the weeks that followed have been extensively related and debated on innumerable occasions, not least at the time of their centenary.[58] Here it is necessary only to consider the highlights and Frick's reactions to them.

The Strike

In the first days of the strike, the sheriff of Allegheny County failed to gain control of the situation. By Independence Day, Frick was looking ahead to the arrival of the Pinkertons, planned for early on 6 July, and was seeking to assure Carnegie that all was in order: "We expect to land our guards or watchmen in our property at Homestead without much trouble, and this once accomplished we are, we think, in good position." They would be able to land these men by boat and all was ready to "receive" and "care for" them there:

> Homestead seems to be the center of attraction, and I do not think anything has been left undone toward securing for us a complete victory at that place. Doubtless by the time this reaches you it will be uninteresting, at least I trust so. . . . We shall, of course, keep within the law, and do nothing that is not entirely legal.

During the first week of the strike they advertised for workers in newspapers in Boston, St. Louis, and Philadelphia. They also received numerous applications for jobs from nonstrikers. Helped by these new workers, Frick planned to restart operations as soon as possible under Pinkerton protection.[59]

The Pinkerton men arrived as expected; but they were spotted by a look-out as their tugboat and two barges laden with men moved up the Monongahela River under cover of darkness. They were followed, and a warning was sounded in Homestead. For the last mile of the journey upriver, they were subjected to rifle fire from the banks. When they tried to land at the works, there was more firing, and they in turn began shooting. The tugboat left the barges and their occupants helplessly exposed to the violence of those on shore, who now attempted to set the boats on fire. Eventually, the Pinkertons surrendered, having been assured that they would not be harmed. After landing they had to make their way for almost a mile through a crowd of strikers and their families and supporters. As they ran this gauntlet, they were submitted to the most vicious assaults. Varying statements of the number of people injured and killed as a result of the events of the day range from ten killed (three Pinkertons and seven workers) and over sixty wounded, to sixteen killed.[60] The violence, loss of life, and material destruction left the works still under siege.

In spite of these terrible incidents, Frick remained convinced of the soundness of their position; he was not so concerned about the suffering as might have been expected. Next day, when interviewed by the *Philadelphia Press*, he was as inflexible as ever: "While nobody could regret the occurrences of the last few days more than myself, yet it is my duty, as the executive head of the Carnegie Company, to protect the interests of the association. We desire to and will protect our property at all hazards."[61] This was a very different reaction from the one Carnegie expressed to Gladstone later that summer: "The Works are not worth one drop of human blood. I wish they had sunk." On the other hand, whereas Carnegie was concerned for the preservation of his public image, he had left others to bring Homestead into shape. A few days after the battle, Frick reported: "There is no question but what the firing was begun by the strikers. All that I have to regret is that our guards did not land, and, between ourselves, think that Potter was to blame. He did not show the nerve I expected he would. He was most anxious to accompany the guards to Homestead, but failed at the critical time." Frick wanted to vindicate himself, and to emphasize the brutality of the men with whom they were dealing. In a second letter on the same day, he remarked:

> Feel sure that when you become thoroughly acquainted with all the details you will be satisfied with every action taken in this lamentable matter. The best

The Tennessee River Navigation Company barge, which transported the Pinkerton agents, several minutes after being set ablaze by strikers at Homestead Steel Works, 1892. *Photograph by B.L.H. Dabbs, Pittsburgh. Courtesy of Frick Art and Historical Center, Frick Archives.*

evidence of the character of the men employed at Homestead is shown by the manner in which they treated the watchmen after they had surrendered, and also, it would not have mattered who the men were that were in those boats, their treatment would have been just the same. They did not know they were obtained through Pinkerton at the time they fired on them.[62]

On Monday, 11 July, the day Frick wrote those two letters, a special committee appointed by the House of Representatives arrived in Pittsburgh to gather evidence about the "battle" and its background. Frick was their first witness on the evening they arrived. He was called to testify again before the inquiry closed three days later. That morning he received a cable from Rannoch, in which Carnegie claimed the press had published a bogus telegram allegedly from him. He gave his unqualified support: "have not spoken, written or cabled one word to anybody. Shall continue silent. Am with you to end whether works run this year, next or never. No longer question of wages or dollars." After the House committee left for Washington, Frick sent off a reply: "Much pleased with your cable. Did not doubt your position. Congressional inquiry ended. Business men and the impartial public without exception concede that we substantiated by good reason our position." He followed this up with a letter:

This Congressional investigation has kept me rather busy. . . . Your cable of this morning was received, and I cabled a reply. Never had a doubt but that you would thoroughly approve of every action taken in this matter when you would once be made acquainted with all the facts of the case and have felt that you had sufficient confidence in the management here not to form an opinion unfavorable to it, even with the meager information that you would receive or gather from newspaper dispatches. In my testimony was as frank as I could well be.[63]

His letter was positive and optimistic, but even so, it seemed to hint at a suspicion that Carnegie might not agree with all he had done.

On the morning of 12 July 1892, some eight thousand troops of the National Guard of Pennsylvania entered Homestead, and the company again took over the mill and made preparations to resume work with non-union men. Frick had testified to the congressional committee: "I can say with the greatest emphasis that under no circumstances will we have any further dealings with the Amalgamated Association as an organization. That is final." He now went on to the next stage of the struggle. On 15 July, he contacted his brother-in-law, Otis H. Childs, concerning accommodation for strikebreakers: "It seems to me we should proceed at once to arrange with good contractors for the erection of 50 or 100 good houses at Homestead and probably one or two large boarding houses."[64] While making preparations for resumption of work at Homestead, he had to cope with threats of sympathy action at their other works.

On 11 July, Patrick R. Dillon had warned him of an impending visit from a committee representing men at Beaver Falls. They came, and Frick replied to Dillon, all on the same day. He made clear that the company would not be deflected from its refusal to deal with the union even if other mills gave their support: "They plead very hard, but I was just as firm at the end as I was at the beginning. . . . Of course I hope that we will have no trouble at the mills under your control, but if we do have it only means that we will have a little harder fight and probably a little longer, and a few more men to bring into line." A week later, he agreed it was advisable to get some police into Beaver Falls. Arthur Thornton, chairman of the committee of the Amalgamated Association there, sent a telegram informing him they would not return to work until he was willing to confer with the union at Homestead. Frick responded promptly and implacably, through the superintendent:

You will please say to Mr. Thornton . . . and ask him to so notify the men, that if they, composing the Amalgamated Association at Beaver Falls Mills and who signed an agreement with us for one year, do not go to work on Monday next, or when you are ready to start, we will consider their failure to do so as a cancellation of the agreement existing between us, and, when those works do resume, it will be as non-union, and former employees satisfactory to us, who desire to work there, will have to apply as individuals. You can say that under no circumstances will we confer with the men at Homestead as members of the Amalgamated Association.

Although their men were unsettled, trouble at the other mills was in fact slight. On 14 and 15 July, the men at Beaver Falls and those at Union Iron Mills struck in sympathy with Homestead; Duquesne was out for a week; Edgar Thomson was unaffected. Frick wrote twice in one day to Morrison at Duquesne, asking him to "look after" four named individuals there, who had presumably involved themselves in the disturbances at Homestead.[65]

Frick's generalship not only encompassed the problems at Homestead and the other works but extended further abroad. He even found time to write to the U.S. Postmaster General, requesting an investigation into the character of the postmaster at Munhall, Thomas B. Dodds, who a few days earlier had publicly boasted, "We cleared the Pinkertons out." To Major Bent at Pennsylvania Steel, Frick reported, "We are having a pretty lively time here but we will come out all right eventually." Another interim assessment of the situation was made for Carnegie, in which he once again vindicated himself: "Looking back over the transactions of this month so far, or previous to that, I cannot see where we have made any serious blunders, or done anything that was not proper and right." Gaps in their defenses were being plugged. For instance, on 21 July, he pointed out to the vice-president of the Pittsburgh and Lake Erie Railroad, "Your track through our works is used by reporters. Is there no way that you could stop this?" Next day, he urged the sheriff to help end attempts to incite their other workers:

> We are just in receipt of information that a crowd, aggregating probably 150, are congregated about the entrance of our works at Duquesne, intercepting workmen and preventing them from going to work. We respectfully request that you send a sufficient force of deputies at once to Duquesne to prevent this unlawful interference with the operation of our plant and the prevention of our employees from pursuing their usual avocations.[66]

After the terrible conflict of Wednesday, 6 July, events seemed to be following an unhappy but less violent and more predictable course. On Saturday, 23 July, they took a completely unexpected and grimly dramatic turn. In the early afternoon a twenty-five-year-old anarchist, Alexander Berkman, contrived an appointment to see Frick in his office on the second floor of the Chronicle-Telegraph building on Fifth Avenue. Pushing his way into the room ahead of a formal introduction, he found the chairman talking to

John Leishman and shot and stabbed him. Berkman was overpowered and Frick was taken home, although not before he had shown remarkable coolness and courage in guiding the physician in probings for the bullets and in settling urgent business. This included sending a brief but pointed cable to Carnegie: "Was shot twice, but not dangerously. There is no necessity for you to come home. I am still in shape to fight the battle out." When he received news of the attack, Carnegie was deeply concerned. A penciled jotting of his cabled response to Leishman survives. It points to his own disturbed state: "Early anxiety his recovery. . . . Close all works until recovery complete. We regard it is necessary something must be done to save Frick anxiety—his recovery before all—if others are willing we can close. Can you see daylight?"[67]

Frick recovered, and his bedroom on the first floor at Clayton, his impressive mansion in the Homewood district of Pittsburgh, became for almost two weeks the headquarters from which he continued to mastermind the struggle. His injuries—and the fact that his baby son, Henry Clay, born on the day of the Homestead battle, lay dying in the same house—give his normal cool resolution something of a fanatical quality. A week after the attack, he was visited by John Elmer Milholland on behalf of Whitelaw Reid, Republican nominee for vice-president in the forthcoming election. Milholland found him in bed, his face and head still swathed in bandages, but in "fairly vigorous condition." He showed "considerable excitement" as they talked. The visitor explained that Hugh O'Donnell, one of the more conservative strikers, had asked Reid to contact Carnegie in hope of bringing about a reconciliation. Frick's response startled him: "in the heat of passion," he denounced O'Donnell as "a blood-thirsty villain" and as "the red-handed murderer." Although a Republican and an admirer of Harrison, Frick declared that he would not settle except on his own terms, even if the president and the cabinet asked him, or if Carnegie was to "order me peremptorily to do so. . . . Somebody has got to be a boss, and I propose to be that individual so long as I am in charge." By now considerably "wrought up," he added with much emphasis, "I will fight this thing to the bitter end. I will never recognize the Union, never, never!"[68]

He made a remarkable recovery. During Wednesday, 3 August, his four-week-old son, Henry Clay junior, died. Frick attended the funeral service next day. On Friday morning, thirteen days after Berkman's attack, he traveled by streetcar into Pittsburgh and returned to his office to resume his duties. Outrage for Berkman's crime and sympathy and admiration for Frick's courage, from all sections of society, now cancelled out much of the anger aroused by his conduct of the strike. The attempted assassination was in no way supported by the Amalgamated Association, some of whose members saw clearly that it had undermined their public support. Already, a drift back to work had begun. There were only about 150 men in the mill on 21 July, but within ten days there were almost a thousand. For his part, although still resolute, Frick was already wearying of the conflict: "I shall be most happy when it is all over, as the magnitude of our business is such that there are plenty of important matters to take up at this time without being troubled with strikes." By late August, as fears mounted of a possible cholera outbreak in Homestead, he wrote to Jay Morse in Chicago, "We are making slow but satisfactory progress at all our works: as you know, however, these matters are usually long drawn out."[69] On 31 August, accompanied by a detective, he visited Homestead for the first time since the dispute began: in spite of all they had gone through the men there showed no anger. He made a thorough inspection, concluded that all departments were in excellent order, and remarked to reporters that the strike was a thing of the past. Its formal end was to be delayed for almost three months.

September shipments from Homestead were just under 44 percent of the average for that month over the previous two years, but as tension eased, Frick was now able to travel east to a meeting of the Railmakers Association. By this time Carnegie Steel was pressing other companies for supplies of steel—from the Dewes Wood works in McKeesport, from Hainsworth and from Pennsylvania Steel at Harrisburg. Such arrangements were by no means straightforward. Frick had to ask Henry Oliver for help in sorting out their arrangements for 200 tons of steel from "the Hainsworth people." Although it had been purchased, shipment was delayed because of that company's fear of trouble with its own men. Meanwhile, he continued to refuse meetings with union representatives.[70]

Carnegie appears to have given Frick the impression that he was becoming impatient. Frick meanwhile periodically permitted himself to look ahead to a rosier future in labor relations, a future in which the men's wages and welfare would be in their hands, a paternalistic arrangement. Such a situation—in which the company would be in control—was the essential foundation for remarks that, if taken at face value, give an impression of a utopian vision quite out of character with their author. As early as mid August, Frick wrote: "I feel we will be amply repaid for all our trouble. . . . . We shall be able to get closer to our men and when they become acquainted with us they will find that we are probably the best friends they have." On 12 September, he again speculated about the future in an optimistic (but decidedly strange) manner. Reaffirming his resolution, he yet looked ahead to after the strike was settled, when they would enter a new era, happier for all:

> I, with you, most heartily wish the break would come, but we will have to exercise a little more patience, and it will come eventually, and when once we demonstrate to our workmen that they can only have one master, and that it is better for them that it should be so, we will be able to accomplish wonderful results at all of the works. We cannot expect that the public should understand just how kindly we do feel toward those who are in our service; that we are just as anxious for their welfare as we are for our own. We must expect to be misrepresented, but time will cure this all, if we are right, and there is no question but what we are right in this matter.

A few weeks later he returned yet again to this theme: "we have been right, and have not tried to oppress any one, and have put ourselves in position so that we can treat our men most generously, as has always been the case."[71] It is impossible to read these statements of hope without concluding that Frick was either naive (which clearly he was not), concerned to dupe the public (which was quite uncharacteristic of him), or that, finally, he had a conception of the welfare of the men radically different from their own. Perhaps he was in desperate need of optimism (even unrealistic optimism), to balance the fear caused by the assassination attempt and the pain of losing his son.

On 28 September, writing from Sunningdale, Berkshire, Carnegie appeared to take up Frick's criticism of Potter's role in the strike: "I am expecting daily to hear that a break has occurred. Believe me, he is a poor manager who has not sufficient influence over part of his men to draw them to him." At the end of that month, Frick again refused a suggestion that he should meet the Amalgamated Association. When the last troops were withdrawn on 13 October, Homestead was said to be in full operation with non-union men, but some of these men still slept at the mill for fear of those who remained on strike. Even at the end of October, when old employees were coming back daily, Frick was forced to admit that, "the firmness with which these strikers hold on is surprising to every one."[72] The dispute dragged on for another three weeks. On 17 November, the mechanics and laborers declared their strike over, and next day there was a rush of men back to work. On Sunday, 20 November, the lodges of the Amalgamated met in Homestead. In spite of opposition from some delegates, union officials advised them that the strike was lost. On a vote, 101 delegates favored a return to work; as many as 91 wished to struggle on. Next day, the local lodge called the strike off. The *Pittsburgh Post* ran a bluntly worded headline: "They

Surrender." That was far too simple a conclusion, for indeed the effects were to rumble on through the years. Even a more immediate costing of the strike was almost impossibly complex.

In violence alone, Homestead was a dispute of the first rank. One estimate (made by the employers' "side" of American industry) was that—taking into account both the "battle" of 6 July and subsequent losses due to violence, accident, disease, and suicide—thirty-five people died as a result of the strike. Production at Homestead fell sharply. In monetary terms, the cost was considerable (see table 11). Although the financial implications were to some extent offset by reduced bills for materials and labor, Carnegie Steel profits fell by $300,000 (7 percent). The direct cost to the men in wages lost was estimated at about $1.25 million. The action by the National Guard cost almost half a million dollars. Wear and tear on Carnegie Steel's principal officers could not be measured but was certainly great. This applied particularly to Frick. On the day the strike ended he was naturally in a happy mood. He expressed his relief and satisfaction to Carnegie:

> Our victory is now complete and most gratifying. Do not think we will ever have any serious labor trouble again and should soon have Homestead and all the works formerly managed by Carnegie, Phipps and Company in as good shape as Edgar Thomson and Duquesne. Let the Amalgamated still exist and hold full sway at other people's mills. That is no concern of ours.

But a week later he admitted, "The cost of the strike was, as you say, simply awful," though "we had to teach our employees a lesson and we have taught them one they never will forget."[73]

The House of Representatives report was critical of the way the dispute had been handled: "[W]e do not think that the officers of the Company exercised that degree of patience, indulgence and solicitude which they should have done." While they praised some of his qualities, there were hard words for the chairman: "Mr. Frick, who is a businessman of great energy and intelligence, seems to have been too stern, brusque and somewhat autocratic."[74] Although others admired his physical and moral courage during and after the attempt on his life, his methods were widely condemned.

The strike had exposed a lack of unanimity among the principals of Carnegie Steel. Carnegie was unquestionably relieved that the union had been broken and was outwardly loyal to Frick, but in his correspondence, he criticized his methods. Writing Lauder in mid July, Carnegie deplored the execution rather than the principle or morality of their chairman's actions: "Matters at home *bad*—such a fiasco trying to send guards by boat and then

TABLE 11
Production at Homestead, Early 1890s

Department	1890	1891	1892
Bessemer plant	140,939	145,691	97,134
Open-hearth plant 1, Basic	66,406	43,390	23,404
Open-hearth plant 2, Acid	14,010	7,334	1,868
Open-hearth plant 2, Basic	11,373	56,725	68,354
Crude Steel Total	232,728	253,140	190,760
Plates	40,430	44,498	33,899
Beams	33,150	33,718	22,220

Source: Carnegie Steel Company papers (USX).
Note: Figures are in tons.

leaving space between river and fences for the men to get opposite landing and fire—still we must keep quiet and so do all we can to support Frick and those at seat of war. . . . We shall win of course, but may have to shut down for months." A few weeks later, after his recovery, Frick was still convinced he was right, and he expressed his regrets about Carnegie's public timidity and failure to make clear to Whitelaw Reid that "you [Carnegie] did not propose then or at any time in the future to urge your partners to treat with law-breakers and assassins," but "It is too late now, however, for you to say or do anything in the matter." A few days later, he again made reference to Reid's attempted intervention: "Frankly, I do not think that you sent the proper message to Reid. You should have said emphatically, in my opinion, that we did not propose hereafter, under any circumstances, to deal with the Amalgamated Association."[75]

To friends outside the business world, Carnegie made plain he disapproved of the tactics used in the strike and the violence that had resulted. In turn, his friends generally exonerated him from blame for what had happened. This was certainly the case with his British friends, who were far enough away from the events to be ignorant of their context, true character, and significance. Carnegie told Gladstone that "the pain I suffer increases daily," and he reiterated that his own experience would have caused him to close the mill and wait for the men to return: "This our partners should have done, and I had written sketching the plan, alas! too late. My letter did not reach." A naively trusting Lord Rosebery assured Carnegie that he regarded him as innocent: "I know nothing of the rights and wrongs of the Homestead case, but I cannot believe that you would ever be illiberal or unjust." A little more than a year later, after Carnegie had taken the first small steps to heal the wounds in Homestead, John Morley praised him: "I note what you say about Homestead with much pleasure and much admiration. Such handsome and humane conduct ought to wipe out every trace of the mischief of last year—mischief for which you, I verily believe, were no more responsible than I was."[76] It was all very touching, but far too kind. On the other hand, it was undoubtedly true that it had been Frick's wish to keep Carnegie away during the strike, leaving him free to conduct the dispute as he wished. He was treated unkindly by the critics.

More than forty years later, Schwab gave his assessment of the people and the policies adopted. In this he was both recollecting events long past and rationalizing his own attitudes. (Evidence shows that even over much shorter periods his memory was fallible.) Some at least of his opinions he could not have held at the time; but on the other hand, they do represent a mature evaluation of the problem:

> At Homestead, had I been running affairs, I would have called the men in and told them it was impossible to meet their terms. I would have told them we would simply close down until the justice of our position had been demonstrated—even if we had to close down for ever. But I would have told them that nobody else would be given their jobs. . . . There is nothing a worker resents more than to see some man taking his job. A factory can be closed down, its chimneys smokeless, waiting for the worker to come back to his job, and all will be peaceful. But the moment workers are imported, and the striker sees his own place usurped, there is bound to be trouble. . . . Johnny Potter was not the proper man to have been in charge at Homestead. He was a handshaker, but there was no sincerity back of his interest in the working man. You can tell a working man you like him, but he *knows* whether you are sincere or not. You can't make him believe you are interested in his welfare unless you are. . . . Frick had a fight on his hands before he started, because he didn't understand men. . . . Frick was by nature a fighter, and when he saw it was to be war, he imported 300 men from New York "to make war." If Carnegie had been here that wouldn't have happened. Carnegie and I would have agreed on the same policy—that of closing the mills until an adjustment could have been made.

The last was a logical and persuasive policy, but there were things to be said for the other side. Frick had given his reaction to the idea of closing the mill and waiting for the men to return, in a letter written to Carnegie on 12 October, as the strike began to crumble:

> If we had adopted the policy of sitting down and waiting, we would have still been sitting, waiting, and the fight would yet have to be made, and then we would have been accused of trying to starve our men into submission. This is the way I think. Of course, I may be wrong, and if we had eventually been compelled to make a deal with the Amalgamated Association just think what effect that would have had on Edgar Thomson and Duquesne, and when this

victory is won it will not take very long to show our men at Homestead how much better it is to deal with us direct, and anything we do for them will not be credited to the Amalgamated Association, or any other Ass'n, but the one that we are most deeply interested in.

As he had argued on 8 September, even in the midst of it, the struggle would prove to have been worthwhile in the end: "I do not agree with you as stated in your cable, that we are going to suffer for years at Homestead. We are not going to suffer for years as we have in the past, and would have continued to have done, unless the struggle had taken place."[77] Events were to show that his firmness had indeed set in train a wholesale and irreversible decline in the union, but hopes of happier relations with the men were totally unrealistic and were quickly to be disappointed.

Among the less obvious costs of the Homestead strike was the effect on Frick himself. Some of this was physical. As Bridge long after recalled, it was the tension and tragedy of Homestead that whitened what had till then been a full brown beard. Above all, however, it brought about an undermining of his relationship with Carnegie, who had given him public support throughout but who had lost faith in his methods. In mid October, Carnegie wrote a perceptive letter, identifying what was to be one of the long-term effects of the strike:

This fight is too much against our Chairman; partakes of personal issue. It is very bad indeed for you—very, and also bad for the interests of the firm. . . . There is another point which troubles me on your account, the danger that the public, and hence all our men, get the impression that it is all Frick. Your influence for good would be permanently impaired. You don't deserve a bad name, but then one is sometimes wrongly got. Your partners should be as much identified with this struggle as you. Think over this counsel. It is from a very wise man, as you know, and a true friend.

Frick replied in a restrained, clear manner, but one that completely missed the full import of Carnegie's remarks:

I am at a loss to know just why you should express yourself so. I know it is not from any other than a friendly interest, but, as you should know, it seems to me that I am particularly anxious that no action of mine should under any circumstances cause loss of any kind to the firm, and that I am not naturally inclined to push myself into prominence under any circumstances. It seems to me wherever it was possible to put any of our people forward I have not let the opportunity go by. That is to say, when they have been asked by any one whether some arrangement could not be made by which this thing could be fixed up they have had instructions to reply, on their own responsibility . . . and I think that when any of our people have had such an opportunity presented to them they have most promptly acted, and thus identified themselves with the struggle. I note the counsel you give, but I cannot see wherein I can profit by it, or what action could be taken by me that would change matters in respect to that which you mention.[78]

Although Carnegie continued to present himself to the world as a friend of labor, privately he was well satisfied that the men had been put in their place. In mid November, he mentioned to Frick that he had received a letter "extolling the public service our great firm has done—etc., etc.—All right—No doubt—right thing done by the wrong firm. I hope next 'great duty' will devolve on one of our dear, kind eulogistic competitors that's all." Even so, a few months later, he was yet again presenting a different perspective on things to Whitelaw Reid: "I have been in misery since July, but I am reconciled somewhat since I have visited Homestead and gone through all the Works and shaken hands with the chief men." He warmed to his theme, "No one knows the virtues, the noble traits of the working-man who has not lived with them, as I have, and there's one consolation in all my sorrow; not one of them but said, 'Ah, Mr. Carnegie, if you had only been here it never would have happened.' "[79] Despite this sort of humbug, Carnegie did show initiative and courage in trying to build new bridges outward toward their men.

On the evening of Thursday, 26 January 1893, just over nine weeks after the end of the strike, Carnegie arrived in Pittsburgh after an absence of about a year. He looked much older. The *Commercial Gazette* reported that Frick met him at the Baltimore and Ohio Smithfield depot and took him to stay at Clayton. That weekend Carnegie went out to Homestead. Bridge in reporting this visit allowed a malicious streak to creep into his account: "In January 1893, all being quiet on the Monongahela, Andrew Carnegie returned from Europe." When he arrived in Homestead, he stated he was concerned to "bury the past . . . of which I knew nothing." Yet even in this setting he was brave enough to speak favorably about Frick:

> And now one word about Mr. Frick, whom I recommended to the Carnegie Steel Company Limited as its Chairman and my successor four years ago. I am not mistaken in the man, as the future will show. Of his ability, fairness and pluck, no one has now the slightest question. His four years management stamp him as one of the ablest managers in the world. I would not exchange him for any manager I know. People generally are still to learn of his virtues, which his partners and friends well know. His are the qualities that wear. He never disappoints. What he promises he more than fulfills.

His remarks were reported in the Pittsburgh papers on 30 January 1893. They were read that morning by the eighty-year-old Thomas Mellon, who wrote to Carnegie at once to congratulate him on his "noble utterances," public statements that were "worthy of yourself and deserved by the Board of Directors." The old banker went on to take up the praise of the man he had helped start in business twenty-one years before: "The recognition of Mr. Frick's good qualities shows remarkable discrimination on your part. He is by no means the hard and arbitrary man depicted by labor parasites. I have never known one in like position who would lend more willing ear to just complaints of working men."[80] Notwithstanding these ringing endorsements and the undoubted services that Frick had provided to Carnegie Steel's drive for cost reductions, the Homestead strike marked a divide in the history of the relations between Carnegie and Frick. Carnegie could still occasionally slip into his annoying habit of addressing Frick as "My Dear Pard," but he was now no longer so convinced he had found "The Man."

The Aftermath

The effects of the strike on Carnegie Steel overall seemed relatively small in material terms. Their total output of crude steel in 1892 was 80,000 tons more than in 1891, an increase of 10 percent. True, profits fell, but some of this was due to a general fall in prices for finished products. In many ways the impact could not be quantified, but the hurt went deep and the effects were long-lasting. For many years visitors to Homestead found the evidence for this almost tangible.

Less than eighteen months after the capitulation of the Amalgamated Association, the young social realist writer Hamlin Garland came to Homestead. He wrote a depressing account of it for the June 1894 issue of *McClure's Magazine*. Every sentence in his article is a dismal evocation of the spiritual as well as the physical degradation of the area. Such places were common in the hills of Pennsylvania, but "They are American only in the sense in which they represent the American idea of business." Over the next few years, others commented on the cheerless, sullen, almost soulless atmosphere of Homestead, but Garland's "they represent the American idea of business" was most thought-provoking, for the Carnegie Steel Company under Frick's direction—yet with the approval of Carnegie himself—had fought the union to that very end.[81] The company was now more determined than ever to be master in its own house, free to pursue technical excellence and economic efficiency, untrammeled by any restrictions organized labor might seek to impose. After the struggle had been won, the company was in a position to push through a wholesale reconstruction of the operations.

At the end of October 1892, as the dispute neared its end, Frick had reck-

oned that Homestead had not been well managed and consequently a large
potential profit had been lost. Although the strike had cost a great deal, "we
will get it all back in the next two or three years." Their troubles had been
due not only to the obduracy of the Amalgamated but to the inadequacies of
their previous chairman's stewardship. About these, Frick continued caustic:

> You have no idea in what a mix most matters were that Abbott had to decide
> on and manage, and it is hard to estimate just what he cost the concern in his
> management of its interests in the Beam Pool. But outside of that, thousands
> of dollars have been wasted by his incompetency. He is a very dear, nice fellow,
> but should have been in charge of a peanut stand.[82]

The first step toward a new order was to change the Homestead superintendent. As early as mid July, Carnegie wrote to Lauder suggesting that Potter
should be replaced ("sent abroad" was the euphemism). Schwab should take
over for "He manages men well and would soon draw around him good
men from E.T. and other works." Frick did not wish to act on this early in
the strike, for to do so would have been to undermine the present authority
of the post; by early autumn, as the men drifted back to work, however, he
judged the time was right. He revealed these thoughts to Schwab. On Sunday, 16 October, Schwab was unwell and confined to his home, but he wrote
to say that he hoped to be fit enough next day to meet Frick at City Farm
Station and to go on from there to Homestead. He expressed reservations
about displacing Potter, though his words showed that his concern was not
wholly disinterested:

> In talking to John try to impress him with the fact that my greatest regret was
> supplanting him and that I was most anxious to see him well provided for,
> which as you know is quite true. In this way I can get better service from him
> in the future. If he gets an idea that I rejoice in his failure he might not be of
> much use to me afterwards.

He planned to spend the rest of Monday with James Gayley, his own successor at Edgar Thomson, for when he went to Homestead he wanted to be
able "to stay right there. For the first few weeks I will be obliged to be there
almost night and day so I can learn and become acquainted with both turns
fully and quickly." He disliked leaving his present post: "But one thing sure.
I am determined to make this the greatest work of my life—and am eager
to get at it. Only have patience with me and don't expect too much until the
strike is broken. Give me the same support you have always given me and I
will take care of the rest."[83] This proved to have been a proclamation for a
thoroughgoing overhaul of the whole of the Homestead works.

On 18 October, a notice was issued announcing that a special post had been created for Potter, as superintendent of general engineering for the whole Carnegie group. It was said that it was something he had wanted since before the strike. A few weeks later, Schwab suggested that his predecessor might become superintendent of their armor plate department, "for which he would be well suited." However, this would have involved a demotion and was therefore unacceptable. A year later, Potter resigned and left Carnegie Steel to take over the management of a plant in Cleveland.[84]

When Schwab took charge at Homestead, he was thirty years old, a man of unbounded ambition and talents, backed by drive and the attractive qualities associated with an easy congeniality. A few days after his appointment, Frick wrote to add a material incentive, if one was needed. It was a share in the partnership of two-thirds of 1 percent, backdated to 1 July, the day on which both the new company and the strike had begun. At the level their profits had reached, even this very modest interest was of great value. Notification of this share in their stock was accompanied by Frick's congratulations—and a challenge: "I hope it will prove as profitable to you in the future as such interests have been to others in the past. It largely rests with you, however, and I have no doubt that it will not be your fault if it does not prove profitable."[85] In short, Schwab was being transferred to Homestead to sort out the mess there and was to be rewarded handsomely for the unstinted exercise of his singular talents.

He fully lived up to his own promises and the hopes of senior partners, although it must be recorded that Bridge at least attributes much of the cost saving by plant improvement and pruning of the labor force to Patrick R. Dillon, formerly of Beaver Falls, but for whom Frick now created an advisory post covering all of their works. On the day Schwab took over, Frick issued instructions for a telephone connection to be made between Homestead and the new superintendent's Braddock home. However, as Schwab had anticipated, for a time Homestead became home as well as workplace. For the first four months, he lived in one of the five executive houses that had been erected inside the works; he claimed (though apparently with some exaggeration) that he did not set foot outside the perimeter.[86]

During the early days, at least, Schwab was heavily dependent on encouragement and advice from Frick. Apparently, on 18 October, he asked him to visit him. With his greater experience, Frick realized that it would not necessarily be helpful to comply at once, but he wrote a supportive letter next day:

> As you know, would take great pleasure in going out to Homestead frequently to see you. In thinking the matter over, since yesterday, have decided that it is

far better for you that I should not visit the works for the next week or ten days. Want to make you as strong there as possible, and show all parties that I have the greatest confidence in your management by staying away for a while. If, however, there are any matters which you would like to consult me about, of course will go out any time.

Frick had planned a visit east in the week following this letter, but on that same evening, Schwab's secretary, Reinhardt, came with a letter to Clayton. It contained evidence of Schwab's enthusiasm and impatience to get things under way, but also a further cry for help, and especially for moral support:

Have met many discouraging things indeed, since starting at this place that it would be impossible for me to tell you by letter. The converting mill is in terrible condition and with their present machinery it is going to be a very difficult matter to increase product materially. Coupled with this fact, it seems impossible to urge the men. Started in the converting mill this morning with the Foremen, to shove things along a little and endeavor to make 25 to 30 heats. Things went along pretty well until about ten o'clock when every man employed in this department, with the exception of two old men who returned, quit, leaving us in a very bad condition I can assure you.

They had also had a big break in the slabbing mill and had no spares to enable them to put things right. However the main problem was demoralization of the workers: "All our Foremen and Superintendents here lack energy, vitality, and it seems impossible to get them started up, in fact, the men seem completely worked out, and they will have to be very gently nursed, as their positions are not the most desirable under the circumstances and might leave us in a still worse condition." He wanted advice: "I wish I had an opportunity of talking to you about this matter and I hope I will get to see you before you go East. Could you not arrange to come out some time tomorrow?" Frick immediately dictated a reply to Reinhardt. He has often been represented as a hard, inflexible business machine (among others, by Schwab himself in later years), but few beleaguered executives can have received a more helpful letter than the one he sent that evening. Its essence was that everything would come out all right eventually. He added that he had been intending to write even before Reinhardt called:

You must not allow anything to discourage you in the least, even if things do not go well for some time to come, or even if they should get much worse than they have for some time past. Do not be in the least bit discouraged. We all expect that it is going to take some time yet to settle this matter properly. I am perfectly aware that you will put into it all the energy and good judgment that any one can, but with that I know it is going to be hard work to make things run smoothly, or show any decided improvement. I am perfectly aware of the fact that things generally are in bad order and of course that will operate against you for a while, but let me repeat, do not allow anything of that kind to worry you; just keep at it, doing the best you can, and, as I said to you before, do not allow the fact that you are not getting along as well as you would like, to lead you to put yourself in a compromising position with any of the old employees who are still on strike. I decided not to go East this week, but intend to go to the coke region Friday morning, to be gone that day. If, after you get this letter, you would like me to come out tomorrow, please wire me and I will go out on the one o'clock train tomorrow afternoon.[87]

Schwab recognized immediately that one of his priorities had to be attention to physical plant. Homestead was a heavily capitalized operation. Large outputs were needed to cover the high standing charges, for in terms of day labor the works cost almost as much to run with a daily output of 100 tons as with 400 tons. Schwab responded to this situation with startling speed. Within as little as three days following his appointment, he wrote to Frick more fully about the deficiencies he had found in one of the Homestead mills: "It is the most surprising thing I ever encountered, the utter disregard of details in constructing this mill. Please understand that I am giving this matter every possible effort and it is up-hill work, but I think that you will find each day and week will add to our efficiency." Less than a week later, he had "figured" that next month they could produce two-thirds of their usual output there. The four months he spent working and living within the works were, he later recalled, "devoted wholly to reorganization." After this, he took a "holiday" to visit Carnegie in Scotland, in the course of which he secured approval for further large new expenditures on plant and equipment.[88]

Extension and modernization were to go on almost without stopping throughout the 1890s. Within five years, steel production there was already 128 percent greater than in the last operating year before the strike. After that, expansion was even more rapid; by 1901, Homestead was almost certainly the biggest steel plant in the world. It was also one of the most efficient. Unfortunately the evidence is that it was not equally distinguished for good working conditions or for harmony.

Action on labor policy was clearly vital after five months of bitter conflict. Even before the formal end of the strike, Frick had spelled out his general approach to Schwab. It was clear, hard, and inflexible. The cornerstone was that he would have nothing to do with the union:

> I would not meet the Committee [the Advisory Committee of the Amalgamated] either as a committee, as individuals, or in any way. . . . The only way our former employees could get back to work would be as individuals, and by applying to the General Superintendent of the works in question. . . . Work

would be given them, in case they were needed, and had done nothing we considered objectionable.

As the strike collapsed, the first steps were taken to get the labor situation into the shape the company wanted. This involved choosing who should and who should not be taken back. On Thursday, 17 November 1892, Frick noted that so far that day sixty-five men had requested employment from Schwab, and fifty more were standing around the office waiting to get in their applications. On Friday, 18 November, things went even better: "Just come from Homestead. Over 500 men applied individually for their positions while I was there, many of them valuable men in all departments. Not being able to get their positions, all were willing to take anything they could get." By Saturday, 19 November, Frick estimated that more than twelve hundred old employees had applied, but the presence of the newcomers brought in during the strike enabled the management to be selective: "There are no new men put off that are efficient. This rule is adhered to strictly. If any man who took work at Homestead during the strike is retired from duty, it is only because of his inefficiency."[89]

Schwab was provided not only with general principles but fuller guidelines on employment policy. These showed how Frick was determined to exploit the dominating position the company now occupied:

We have now put the labor matter in a most satisfactory shape at Homestead, and it rests entirely with you as to how long it will be kept that way. It is not who you can get to work for you, but who will you have? It is not, "How much will you take and come and work for me?" but it is, "What will you give me if I take this position, or that?" I like the way you are going about this matter, treating the men kindly, and considerately, but at the same time keeping in view that, as the Democrats have been overwhelmingly successful on a platform plainly against a tariff for protection, we must expect a great reduction in the tariff on the articles we make, and of course in order to live, we must manufacture at very much less cost than heretofore, and to do that you must have men that you can depend upon under all circumstances. . . . Let us settle with all . . . inefficient men as soon as possible or rather as soon as we can secure efficient and reliable men to take their places, but let us pay the bill and be done with it. No man had a better opportunity than you now have to make a perfect organization, and I am glad to be able to say I believe no works had at their head, as General Superintendent, a better man to make a complete and efficient organization. The stock-holders of this Association will, and do, expect great things from you at Homestead, and I do not think you will disappoint them, and so far as my counsel and support goes, you shall have it at all times.[90]

This letter provides a valuable insight into Frick's mind and value system. Like his other letters to Schwab at this time, it is an admirable example of a senior colleague's endorsement, encouragement, and support. It is logical. There is a dispassionate assessment of the qualities of the younger man (of whose popularity he might well have been expected to feel envious) and a generous offer of advice and help in times of trouble ahead. But there is no suggestion that Schwab might act as a conciliator, a healer of the grave wounds inflicted on the relationships between capital and labor over recent months. Here is no conception of a new, happier order of relations with their men such as he had appeared to entertain only a short time before. Labor is to be treated only as a commodity offered by men who have to seek sustenance and shelter for their families; management is expected to exploit its favorable position in this marketplace to the full. Men are not looked upon as individuals whose needs call for solicitude on the part of an employer, but as labor units, and apparently nothing more.

In this field as in others, Schwab did not disappoint the trust placed in him. It is said that at times he stood with a checklist of the men and their performances and reliability as they lined up to be vetted for employment. Soon after the strike, a system for surveillance was introduced that required all employees entering or leaving the mill yard to pass over the bridge at the main entrance. This proved inconvenient to many men who were thus forced to walk an extra quarter- or half-mile to get to their place of work.[91] On the other hand, Schwab also adopted a few features of a more progressive labor policy, one that in some ways anticipated twentieth-century practice. Under his direction, labor relations became a matter of both stick and carrot.

Frick initiated and—together with Schwab—carried through a campaign against those whose loyalty was suspect or those who had some other defect. They were to be weeded out. On 26 October 1892, Schwab was away from the works, spending the night at home. While there, he was visited by three men—Crawford, Roberts, and Vogel—who had been sent to see if there was any way of arranging talks to settle the strike. Schwab replied "plainly and very bluntly" that company policy had been outlined, and "it would not be deviated from, one iota." Three weeks before the end of the strike, Frick was in contact with Carnegie Steel's counsel, Philander C. Knox. He asked him for a list of parties owning their own properties in Homestead, but who were "bad" characters: "It seems to me that any very objectionable party whose property could be bought right quick should be bought out so that they could get out of town as soon as possible." In the works, they carried through a drive against the inefficient—in itself a natural enough, unobjectionable aim of good management, but now combined with a resolve to eject those with union affiliations or sympathies. An early instance was that of John Elias Jones, a roller on the beam mill. Jones had been a leader of the first lodge of the Amalgamated Association of Iron and Steel Workers, which opened in Homestead in 1881. He was involved in labor disputes there in 1882 and 1889. Two days after Frick had mentioned his name to Schwab, the latter wrote back: "Have notified John Elias Jones that he will not be employed again at these works."[92]

Other approaches to man management were not quite so straightforward, involving the collection of "information" and the employment in the mills of what were, effectively, secret agents. A few weeks after Schwab took up the superintendency, he received a letter from Frick about methods of gathering data on labor attitudes. A generally cautious approach was recommended:

> It is all right for our people to secure information but the matter must not be pressed so that the men who have gone back to work will feel that they are persecuted, or it might place us in an awkward position. The obtaining of information should be skillfully and quietly handled so as not to attract too much attention or look too much as if we were making a regular business out of it.

He carried this further a few weeks later:

> I would nip in the bud the formation of any labor organization at Homestead. I would act with judgment and discretion, but without any fear whatever and give any man (no matter what his position may be at the works) to understand that you do not propose to have any organization of any kind there. The prompt discharge of men whom you know to be leaders will have a good effect. You should at once take such means as will keep you fully informed of all that goes on.

Schwab sometimes seems to have been as aggressive as his chairman. Early in 1894 he reported "considerable rumor and uneasiness" about the possibility of Homestead men either joining the Amalgamated Association or forming a new union of their own. Despite his easy manner and approachability, he was decisive enough on this occasion: "My own idea is that if the men hold any meetings or attempt to form any organization, we should be prepared to be fully informed of all that goes on and unhesitatingly discharge any man connected with this movement." Some of their inquiries were about general conduct, others directly concerned their fears of renewed labor agitation. An example of the former came in a letter sent on by Frick in May 1894. It came from Charlie Tientarski. Frick wrote a covering note:

> If Mr. Adam Burger is the kind of man he is described to be in the enclosed letter, the sooner he is discharged the better. It does seem from information which reaches me from time to time that there are a good many men employed

at the works who are addicted to drinking while on duty. I have no doubt that some misstatements are made to me, but it will do no harm for you to investigate some of these reports.

Two letters Frick wrote on the same day two years after the strike show how information gathering still centered around the events and personalities of that time. One was to Joseph R. Skewis in Fayette County, who had apparently asked for a reference:

> As you know, Mr. Curry [presumably Henry Curry, the Carnegie treasurer] gave a good deal of attention to Homestead during the strike, and he tells me that you were quite luke-warm, hobnobbing with the opposition, he was told, and, while I hold no resentment whatsoever toward you, yet I do not see that we should, or could[,] give you a letter of recommendation.

The other referred to a man who, during the strike, had been suspected of being an informer against its leader, O'Donnell, but who, in the following February, was tried and acquitted for the murder of a detective during the same period. Frick now wrote to Schwab: "The famous Jack Clifford called this morning to secure a pass to go into the works to solicit aid for some men who used to work there. Of course, I told him that he could not get into the works. I merely write you so that you will be on the lookout that he does not get in."[93]

The key figure in their oversight of labor and the attempt to pry into its thoughts was Homer J. Lindsay. On 6 January 1893, less than seven weeks after the strike was called off, he reported new moves among the workers. A letter had come to him from a Dr. Chandler of Rochester, Pennsylvania, two of whose sons worked in the armor plate machine shop. One of them had been approached by former strikers who said that their association was being reformed. They wanted as many non-union men as possible to join them so that they could do something definite by March. Frick instructed Lindsay to "quietly" get the names of the men concerned and to pass them on to Schwab. Within three days, Lindsay had obtained a statement from Benjamin Chandler. This revealed that, as he and another man walked through the mill a week before, they had been approached by a locomotive engineer, who spoke about the strike and then said, "we will have another smack at them before Spring; we have 500 of the best make of Winchester rifles in the market; we will show Frick and those others that they won't have everything their own way this time." He added that, if they wanted to hold their jobs, they had better join this group, for "any man that goes back on us this time we will kill him." Lindsay added to his report, "I don't know the man's name, but will get it for you just as soon as possible."[94]

Frick was away from Pittsburgh for three months during spring 1893. When he returned, in May 1893, Schwab sent a long report to bring him up-to-date on labor matters. It proved that, for all his charisma and bonhomie, he too could be ruthless, and that the company's writ extended well beyond the confines of their works. He reported that since Frick left they had carried out the agreed labor policy "to the very letter":

> I have kept an exceedingly close watch on everything pertaining to this point and feel that nothing important has escaped me. All through March and April matters were very much as they were in January and February, occasional rumors of trouble, street fights, annoyances to non-union employees etc., but nothing of any consequence. Commencing in April, I decided to take a very strong hand in such proceedings and thought it time they should end. So I undertook to investigate every squabble whether it occurred in the town, or works, and deal with the guilty parties severely. As an instance of how this was conducted. One day I heard that an employee of the Plate Mill, a head shearer, and an old hand, had called another man a scab. I immediately went down into the mill, brought the parties together, found that the charge was true and instantly discharged the offender, at the same time taking occasion to state that any employee, no matter how important, would be dealt with in the same manner. I had probably six or eight of such cases all told, within the two months of March and April. I also watched the town closely. As an example, an old German employee who resided in Homestead, and one of our new men was being constantly annoyed by people yelling in his yard and about his house. I had a policeman secreted in his yard, and when two young men came into his back yard and started to annoy him they were then promptly arrested and fined by the magistrate of the town and discharged from our employ.

The result of such policies was that they had not had any complaints for four or five weeks, "and the works now seem to be in more harmonious condition than any time since our trouble. Our men are working together nicely and are commencing to settle down to peaceful work, and gradually forgetting the past." As usual, Schwab was optimistic about the outlook, perhaps in excess of what could be justified by the evidence. Their policies were proving successful:

> [T]he labor situation could not be in better shape . . . and men are working in greater harmony than ever before. As an instance of this better feeling. On May 1st, I had a party at my house (tenth wedding anniversary) and was agreeably surprised by being greeted by a body of Homestead and Braddock workmen, headed by the bands from both works, playing as one body and acting very nicely indeed. This is only a little incident, but they sometimes have an important bearing on greater matters.[95]

For his part, Frick was less easily persuaded by "nice" actions on the part of their workers. A note in his hand indicates that he had shown this letter to

Knox: whether or not this was in order to obtain his opinion about the legality of Schwab's intervention in Homestead borough is not known. Some interesting statistics were attached to the report. They showed that on 15 May 1893, of their skilled men (that is, excluding mechanics and day laborers) 46 percent were "new" men and the other 54 percent were "old" men, (that is, had worked there before the strike). However only 18 percent of the workers occupied the same position as a year before. Such figures scarcely seem to point to unprecedented harmony in the works.

An essential complement to the attempt to weed out the inefficient and the malcontents was to try to prevent, as far as possible, unfavorable public impressions of company action. Although Carnegies had already had a bad press throughout the nation and beyond, Frick did his best to stem the tide. Less than a month after the end of the strike, he corresponded with Jacob Barton, of the tiny Illinois village of Sublette, who had written an account of the strike. He disclaimed interest in media coverage on the grounds that it was hopelessly biased against them but, at the same time, attempted to undermine the credibility of a local clergyman who had spoken out during the strike. The Reverend J. J. McIlyar had conducted the funeral service at the Fourth Avenue Methodist Episcopal Church for one of the workers who had been a victim of the violence of 6 July 1892. In his address he inferred that arbitration might have resolved the dispute and deplored the bloodshed that had resulted instead. All this was, as he put it, "brought about by one man, who is less respected by the laboring people than any other employer in the country." For good measure, he added, "There is no more sensibility in that man than in a toad." In his letter to Barton, Frick wrote, "The public press have been so unfair and vicious in treating of our Homestead trouble that I have never thought it worthwhile to attempt to have them correct many of their misstatements, in this city particularly where they cater to the worst element in order to increase their circulation." In a postscript he wrote: "McIlyar is generally considered a crank in this part of the country and certainly is no credit to the church."[96]

Frick's sensitivity to press coverage persisted. There was concern as the first anniversary of the "battle" of Homestead arrived. Schwab received and sent on to him a report from T. S. Newton concerning what "Special Service Men" had found in four of the Homestead mills and in the converting department. Reviewing the proposed workers' celebration, Newton wrote, "Some few Bums and Sore-heads will, no doubt, have a blow-out on the 6th, but it will have no effect upon the employees of this plant." One former employee, Ackers, who had been discharged for drunkenness before the strike, was trying to get up an anniversary "Pic-Nic," but he was already under indictment for riot, and Newton had "arranged it so that the local papers will take the matter up." He ended, "The outlook for peace and quietness at this plant were never better than at present. I hear on all sides expressions favorable toward the Company. . . . Everything is certainly very satisfactory from a Police Standpoint." In sending on Newton's report, Schwab wrote on it, "Please note I believe above to be a correct report." A year later, Frick was so disturbed by the Hamlin Garland article that he wrote to ask Schwab how Garland and his illustrator, Orson Lowell, could have got into the mill.[97]

The struggle to improve Homestead's efficiency with both better plant and more tractable men was kept up year after year. Judged by the criterion of the balance sheet, the result was success. Frick was delighted and warm in his praise of Schwab. As he reported to Carnegie in September 1895: "Homestead is in remarkably fine condition. Schwab tells me and shows me costs for last month are lower than ever before, notwithstanding the bonus. If that works could be run smoothly, the output would be enormous and cost exceedingly low." Success there threw into relief their lesser achievements elsewhere in the organization and consequently made Frick contemplate an extension of Schwab's powers: "Duquesne it seems to me lacks the presence of a good engineer; do not think Mr. Miller has the qualities necessary to get furnaces down to a good working basis, even with the help of Mr. Gayley who, of course, does understand metallurgical part of the business, but has demonstrated in the past that he was not a good manager of men." He suggested that Schwab's jurisdiction might be extended to Duquesne.[98]

Although Homestead capacity, output, and productivity had all been increased, working hours had also been adjusted in order to maximize production and cut unit costs. Effectively men were being reprogrammed to become adjuncts of the machine. Naturally such a situation had to be rationalized. Already, before the Homestead crisis, the metallurgist Henry Marion Howe had considered harmful overwork from the perspective of an academic and research scientist. As a humanitarian, he remarked, one might perhaps regret it, but "as managers . . . we would not be justified in diminishing our employer's profits." Twenty years later, Percival Roberts, a director of U.S. Steel (itself a beneficiary of the tractable labor the Homestead struggle had secured), referred to the question of excessive hours. He was even more explicit than Howe: "Who shall say [what] is the proper limit? There is no doubt that the minimum number . . . is the pleasantest; but in the economies of this world, how shall we determine what the limit may be?" Like some others, he saw the answer in "the laws of nature."[99]

At Homestead the laws of nature worked well enough—for the company. Between 1892 and 1897, as output went up sharply, the workforce was cut by about one-quarter. It was a continuing process of paring away at costs. In December 1894, Schwab committed himself to reduce 1895 costs at Homestead to $500,000 below the 1894 level, though he admitted to Frick that this would "take the best possible practice and close shaving in every department." He continued to pursue such improvements imaginatively. In January 1896, a visiting party from Bethlehem was impressed to find that every Monday at the time of the noon meal a meeting of the thirteen superintendents of departments was held in Schwab's private dining room at the works. The meeting acted as a "school" to consider any question that had arisen in the previous week. However, Carnegie was pressing for more. In August 1896, from Cluny, Scotland, he wrote to Leishman with his "Thoughts on Minutes." In the course of these he came to the item of bonuses: "There is a very easy way to stop bonus. When mills stop for a time, as they must, before starting them, let the men be told quietly that the firm regrets it cannot go on paying bonus under present conditions. The men will agree to start without the bonus; if not you can wait. No public notice need be given."[100]

Carnegie Steel made 1.37 million tons of crude steel in 1896, its best tonnage to date; net profits were $6 million. Next year the total product of the Homestead plant increased by 28.3 percent, but labor costs were cut by $467,772 (see table 12). Schwab wanted to bring wages into line with the increased mechanization of the plant. In December 1897, he pointed out to Frick that some of their tonnage men were being paid at rates that were "beyond all reason." Plate rollers at the Union Mills were earning $15 a day and men on the Homestead beam mill $12. He wished to reduce wages to an average of $6 and reckoned he could save from $20,000 to $25,000 a month at the two works. Meanwhile, Homestead was expanding to become the largest of the Carnegie works. In 1890, its annual capacity was 295,000 tons; by 1900, it was 2,260,000 tons.[101]

Further attempts were occasionally made to reestablish a favorable public image. In late summer 1893, for example, Schwab urged Frick to allow payments of rent on houses owned by the company in Homestead to "stand over" in cases where men were not earning enough to pay. When a senior representative of the Austro-Hungarian government came to Pittsburgh in autumn 1895 and went on to see the Hungarians in the mill towns, Frick stressed the importance of his visit:

I have put this gentleman in charge of our Mr. Bosworth who will leave for Homestead in the morning about 10.40. The Baron will have his wife with him.

TABLE 12

Output and Labor Costs at Homestead, 1896, 1897

Production	Tons		Percentage Increase
	1896	1897	
Bessemer	211,724	247,711	17.0
Open-hearth 1	137,032	191,954	40.1
Open-hearth 2	227,697	309,573	35.9
28″ mill	159,412	183,930	15.4
33″ cogging mill	90,017	125,510	39.4

Average Labor Costs	Dollars per Ton		Percentage Decrease
	1896	1897	
Bessemer	0.8076	0.6456	20.1
Open-hearth 1	1.6656	1.0931	34.4
Open-hearth 2	1.3776	0.9373	32.0
28″ mill	0.7110	0.6353	10.7
33″ cogging mill	0.6653	0.6279	5.6

Source: W. E. Corey to CMS, 27 Jan. 1898 (ACLC).

After he gathers all the information wanted at Homestead, would like you to have a nice lunch for them and then Mr. Bosworth will take them across to Edgar Thomson where of course he will find more Hungarians than at Homestead, especially at the blast furnaces. We are anxious that he shall receive a favorable impression in regard to the way we care for such labor.

But though Carnegie might still write with pride of the thundering progress of the great democracy compared with the crawling pace of the Old World, it was now widely recognized that, at Homestead and elsewhere, the price being paid was a high one. After their victory over the Amalgamated Association, Carnegie had sent his partners a congratulatory telegram that began, "Life worth living again."[102] Clearly the validity of that assessment depended on one's position in the company's hierarchy.

Schwab was also prepared to devote attention to more positive aspects of labor relations, not necessarily from disinterested goodwill but hoping thereby to gain the allegiance of the men. He explained these aims and policies in a letter to Carnegie in May 1896:

Ever since I assumed charge of the Homestead Steel Works, I have endeavored in every possible manner to eradicate the bitter feeling that once existed between the citizens and workmen of Homestead and the Company. . . . I have always felt that the best results at the works and the best workmen were obtained when everybody had our interests at heart and felt that we were in sympathy with them, as we expect them to be with us.

He believed he had changed things almost entirely since moving to the works, pointing out that, but for a similar situation they had created at Braddock, the Edgar Thomson men might have joined the 1892 strike. He had organized a musical contest for their Welsh workers. As he frankly admitted, he thought this would win them over: "They as a race are hard to control, but I think you will always find them on my side." He hoped to set up an industrial training school. He ended, "Homestead shall never again have strikes, if I can avoid it, and I think I can." Carnegie wrote in pencil on the front of this letter: "splendid, go ahead. No strikes in future. There would not have been any had you been in charge." By the end of the 1890s, Carnegie Steel was the largest employer of labor in Pennsylvania, with the single exception of the Pennsylvania Railroad. Early in 1899, it advanced the daily wage rate for common labor to $1.40 at a time when the average for the district was $1.35. In the previous year, payments in wages to all employees had been $13.5 million; profits were only $2 million less.[103]

In spite of Frick's reference to "kindness" in treating their men and the practical steps taken by Schwab to give expression to at least some aspects of that sentiment, more than a decade after the union was crushed Homestead was still a byword for the desolation—both physical and spiritual—that modern industrial organization was capable of bringing about. The town grew by four and a half thousand during the 1890s, and at the 1900 census, its foreign-born element was 28.7 percent, although this was smaller than at either Duquesne or Braddock. In the mid 1890s, the visiting Fabian socialist Beatrice Webb summed up the impression Homestead made on her: it was "a veritable Hell of a place." It may be best to end with the conclusions of another foreign observer, one familiar with conditions in heavy industrial areas of the Old World. The Englishman Arthur Shadwell visited the Pittsburgh area in 1903 or 1904. Having considered the situation of the city, he made his way out to the mill towns along the Monongahela. They made a strong impression:

> If Pittsburgh is hell with the lid off Homestead is hell with the hatches on. Never was [a] place more egregiously misnamed. Here is nothing but unrelieved gloom and grind; on one side the fuming, groaning works where men sweat at the furnaces and rolling mills twelve hours a day for seven days a week; on the other, rows of wretched hovels where they eat and sleep, having neither time nor energy left for anything else. Nor is there anything else for them to do if they wished. I was not surprised at the English workman who told me that if anyone would give him five dollars a week he would go home and live like a

gentleman in—the Black Country. Five dollars a day are no uncommon earnings at Homestead, but they are dear at the price. The output is enormous and there is an appearance of great efficiency, but such industrial conditions as these are not stable. The human element demands recognition and will obtain it. Trade unionism has been put down with an iron hand dipped in blood, and it is kept down. It has not been recognized since 1892, but it is a plant which does not die when it has anything to feed on, and here it has much. To watch and keep it under is anxious work, and eventually futile. The management shows obvious signs of nervousness on the subject, and nervousness is weakness.

To Carnegie, Schwab, and Frick, the outcome of the Homestead strike had been ostensible success, but they—and still more, society at large—paid dearly for that outcome. Krause recently wrote, "Homestead posed the urgent question that remains with us still: can—or how can—the new land of industry and technological innovation continue to be 'the land of the free'?"[104] As far as steel was concerned, for well over forty years Homestead showed that in some respects at least it could not.

4

Aspects of Management

Production and Supply

In many ways, Carnegie Steel was an exceptional business organization. Whereas ordinary public companies had to provide dividends to keep their stockholders happy, this was a close-knit private partnership dominated by the one man who held a predominating share of its grossly undervalued stock. As a result, for many years the company was able to pursue investment to secure maximum efficiency with scant regard to distribution of profits. Operating revenue was poured back into extensions of capacity, the securing of raw material supplies, and most impressive of all, the neverending pursuit of the highest productivity and lowest operating costs. Although it had always been a distinctive feature, this quest for efficiency peaked in the years after the Homestead strike. It enabled the Carnegie enterprise to prosper when others were floundering and to more than survive as failure spread elsewhere.

Carnegie Steel's high and increasing efficiency and the company's willingness to use pooling arrangements (despite its essential contempt for them), which for less well-endowed concerns might be a precondition for survival, are well illustrated by its part in the highly competitive rail trade, then the largest single sector of the steel business. By contrast, when a broad field of competing companies was replaced by a duopoly and when national government became involved, as in the special case of armor plate, scope for the exercise of Carnegies' unique characteristics was considerably reduced and their success was noticeably less. Pursuit of ever higher levels of efficiency caused them to play a key role in the almost revolutionary new organization of mineral supply during the 1890s, and to strive unceasingly for the modernization and further integration of their plants. Logically enough, keener conditions of trade, reduced costs of mineral delivery by water and railroad, as well as their own momentum, encouraged them to give serious consideration to the ideal location for lowest cost manufacture. Unending material reconstruction was accompanied by keen internal debate and dispute, and this led on to reconstruction in internal organization and a new hierarchy of power. At the end of the decade, this caused a crisis in which Frick was to be irreconcilably opposed to the large majority of his partners.

Competition and Collusion in Rails

In the late nineteenth century, demand for steel in America grew with a rapidity unrivaled elsewhere in the world (in 1880 consumption was 1.25 million gross tons, in 1890 it was 4.28 million, and by 1899 it was 10.64 million or equal to almost 40 percent of the world's output that year). However, there were major variations in consumption and production from year to year, and a striking feature was the large gap between installed capacity and production, even in good years. For instance, at 3.39 million tons in 1889, output was 440,000 tons below the 1888 level, and an estimated 3.04 million tons of installed capacity was not utilized. By 1898, national capacity for steel had more than doubled, to 14 million tons, but 5.1 million tons of that capacity was not used. Under these conditions, and taking into account also the high capital cost of the plant installed in this industry, there was an incentive to contain variations and to spread work around. This arrangement, desirable to most, was opposed by the urge on the part of some of the more successful companies to maximize their output at the expense of others. Given the efficiency of Carnegie Steel and the vigor with which its business was pushed, the company found itself frequently in the latter position, but it was also often willing to use pools or agreements as a convenience.[1]

POOL ARRANGEMENTS IN THE RAIL TRADE

The state of the market for rails was of major interest to Frick from the beginning of his involvement in coke manufacture to the end of the century. Liveliness or depression in railroad building—and to a lesser but not inconsiderable extent in the replacement of track—affected the demand for rails and thereby, through the chain of production, influenced iron making and the levels of activity in ore mines, limestone quarries, coal mines, and coke ovens. When Frick moved into steel, he became associated with one of the two leading rail-making concerns. Throughout his ten years as chairman first of Carnegie Brothers and then of Carnegie Steel, the rail business was the largest single part of the trade and therefore its well-being occupied a large part of his working life as central decision maker for the group and as negotiator with other leading steel firms. Although rails were already declining in relative importance as the leading sector of the industry (the ratio of rail tonnage to that of crude steel was 76.2 percent in 1881, 44.7 percent in 1889, and only 21.3 percent in 1899), few other products can illustrate better the complications of industrial capitalism in its unregulated heyday.

In the 1860s, and to a lesser extent through the 1870s, the increasing requirement for steel rails was supplied from European mills. Gradually, capital was invested to make rails at home. Protection was a precondition for this outlay. Although the duty fell over the years, the reduction lagged behind the fall in rail prices so that, effectively, tariff protection increased rather than fell, relative to home prices. This gave a great fillip to the establishment of a major industry. Even so, production increased less than rail-making capacity so that there was gross underutilization of plant both in the rail mills and in the associated iron making and steelmaking. The need for adjustment of the industry to lower and uncertain levels of trade encouraged the formation of pools in the rail business. Another factor was the economics of the production process.

Rail mills were big, complex, and costly. Their product was standardized and was consumed in bulk by one major market—though by many different railroad companies within that market. Demand not only varied widely over time but was also changing in its spatial distribution. Some of these aspects of the trade were vividly summarized in 1898 by one of Carnegie's leading rivals, E. C. Potter of Illinois Steel: "the rail is today the cheapest finished product in the whole domain of iron and steel manufacture, and is at the same time the most difficult to make. It requires an expenditure of at least $3 million before a single rail can be economically turned out."[2] Because overheads were so high, it was essential to keep the works in as near full production as possible, but this was difficult, as demand changed so much from year to year.

There were a number of possible ways for a company to increase its share of the available business. One way was to establish a consumer preference for your product. Carnegies tried this on at least two occasions. The first was as early as 1877, when they circulated to the other railroads copies of an endorsement of Edgar Thomson rails from the Vandalia Railroad.[3] Another attempt was made in 1890, this time to denigrate the product of their new local rival, the Allegheny Bessemer Steel Company. However rail specifications were fairly standard and straightforward, so it was difficult to establish a market niche of this nature. A second approach was to cut costs, so that the mill could survive and make money even when prices were low. Search for good ore supplies, the advantages of the connection with H. C. Frick

Coke, and constant attention to the costs of transport of materials and of freight charges to customers were major factors in an unrelenting Carnegie campaign along this front. The final possibility was to cut process costs. This could lessen or perhaps cancel out the increasing difficulty of reaching main markets.

For a number of years, it had been recognized that the natural drift of locational advantage had been toward the West. This applied especially to the rail trade, which served the needs of extensions now concentrated above all in that region (see table 13). By 1888, the trade journal *Iron Age* was reporting that it was rumored in Pittsburgh "that the great developments of the future in the manufacture of steel are to be made in Chicago, and that Pittsburgh manufacturers will be compelled to look more and more to the eastern market." In the following spring, speaking at the opening of the Carnegie Free Library in Braddock, Carnegie commented on the competitive environment in which local mills would now have to operate. He identified their main enemy: "The South will not trouble Pittsburgh. Our competition is not in the South—it is in Chicago." In 1887, in agreement with Frick, he had written to the general freight agent of the Pennsylvania Railroad, to question the rates charged for coke and the way (Carnegie felt) they had been penalized as compared with their rivals in Johnstown, at Steelton, and in Chicago. His worries were above all concentrated in Chicago:

> Even since I last saw you I am sorry to say that events have given to steel rail manufacturers of Chicago an advantage of three dollars per ton in cost, after allowing for the advantage which natural gas has given to us. Your rates upon coke to them have been reduced one dollar per ton; and by improved blast furnace practice pig iron is now made with one ton of coke per ton of iron, while a short time since one ton and a half would have been a fair average. These two causes have reduced the cost of making a ton of rails in the Chicago district no less than three and a half dollars, and you will see that unless something occurs to redress this change, the increased product of steel rails hereafter is to be in the Chicago district. Today there are four works there making rails against two in western Pennsylvania. I have made figures which show that the PRR receive upon rails made at Johnstown or Pittsburgh at least three times the revenue derived from rails made in the Chicago district; and upon my return from Europe I shall take the occasion to lay the details before you and also before Messrs. Roberts and Thomson. This is not a serious matter now when there are enough of rails to be made in the market for all existing works; but bearing upon the future, I know of no subject of deeper importance to the PRR than this. I am no alarmist, and I believe you will feel that I would not lightly make this statement. The circumstances have given me deep cause for consideration. I ask you to advance or reduce our rates upon coke as you ad-

TABLE 13
Railroad Mileage, 1870–1896

Area of USA	1870	1880	1890	1896
New England	4,490	5,980	6,730	7,130
Middle	10,580	15,180	19,740	21,500
South	12,560	19,570	39,240	45,650
Prairie and West	25,290	52,570	95,540	104,270
Total	52,920	93,300	161,250	178,550

Source: Poors *Manual,* quoted Mulhall 1899, pp. 507, 797.

vance or reduce the rates of our competitors, and as parties who made last month 46,000 tons of finished iron and steel, which required transportation of not less than five tons of material for every ton made, being equal to 10,000 tons of freight per working day, of which your lines received not less than three-quarters of the whole, I humbly submit that we have a right to ask you to oblige us upon the point in question. I am personally glad that the relations between the Pennsylvania Railroad and ourselves, through you and Mr. Frick, have been and are of such a friendly character; and I assure you that nothing shall be wanting upon our part not only to maintain but to strengthen these friendly relations.

This was all couched in his most persuasive style, but sweet reason could not completely cloak the harsher undertone. Two major factors could cancel out the advantages Carnegie and other less directly involved commentators saw moving in Chicago's favor—a failure to fully capitalize on those assets and, conversely, a strong response to the challenge elsewhere. Both were important.[4]

In the Chicago area there were four important, fully integrated plants—the North and South works of the North Chicago Rolling Mill Company, the Joliet works, and the Union works. In the good year 1887, they shared the 439,345 tons of steel rails made in Cook County. By contrast, Edgar Thomson was effectively the only producer of the 287,363 tons rails made that year in Allegheny County. Two years later, the four Chicago mills were consolidated into the Illinois Steel Company. Rail production was ended at North Chicago. Although their chief rail mill was idle for one-third of the year to June 1890, Illinois Steel still managed to roll 539,000 tons rails. With extensions then in progress, it would have an annual rail capacity of 850,000 tons.[5] It was never able to operate at anything near capacity, so that over the next six years, Bessemer rail production in Illinois averaged only 319,000 gross tons. Such large-scale underuse of plant pushed up unit costs of production. Meanwhile, the Carnegie associations were assiduously cutting their costs and by this means were able to cancel out much or all of the disadvantages due to location away from the Lake shores and well to the east of the main rail markets. As a result, they pushed back the boundaries between their "natural" market territory and the areas in which their rivals had apparent locational advantage. In doing so, they worked from behind the facade of pooling agreements.

Pools were designed to keep up prices and to contain their variations by controlling either or both output and price. The firms joining a pool were allocated shares of the market, might have a fine imposed if they exceeded their quota, or might receive a subsidy if they underfilled it. Money deposited by members provided something of a surety for good behavior. However, there were always weaknesses in such arrangements, conditions that threatened their gradual erosion or their dramatic collapse, which was often followed by cutthroat competition between the former associates. If pool prices were set too high, this might result in new entrants to the trade, although this could not occur too readily in a highly capitalized industry. A producer with low costs might, in times of generally depressed demand and falling prices, be tempted to withdraw from agreements in order to gain a higher utilization of his capacity. Carnegies, though benefiting from pooling arrangements, were always well placed to look after themselves if they broke down.

Another leading feature of the rail associations in the 1890s was a "pool within a pool," the close working understanding between the Illinois Steel Company and Carnegie Steel. In the negotiations to which rail pooling arrangements then gave rise, Henry Clay Frick was prominently involved either as a negotiator, or as being in close contact with those who were negotiating.

The westward shift of demand was to some extent mirrored in the allotments made by the rail pool year by year, but production did not always closely follow the tonnages allotted (see table 14). Some eastern works were almost prostrated before the decade ended; others managed to survive and sometimes performed strongly. From the mid 1890s, state law prevented Illinois Steel from participating formally in pooling arrangements. As a result, the large allowances to Carnegie at that time included tonnage to be passed on to the Chicago mills. Even so, Illinois Steel was often in distress, turning out less steel than at the start of the decade and sometimes registering heavy losses. Whatever the formal tonnages allowed by the pool, and in spite of the geographical shift in demand, mills in the East and West alike had great difficulty in holding their trade. A major reason for distress in both regions was the competitiveness of Carnegie Steel, which was main-

TABLE 14
Rail Allotments, 1880s, 1890s

	1887	*1888*	*1890*	*1895*	*1897*
Eastern works	43.04	40.7	33	39.35	38.25
Western Pennsylvania and Ohio, except CSC	12.99	12.8	8	7.87	8.25
Carnegie Steel	12.70	13.5	57	52.78	53.50
Illinois Steel	27.19[a]	28.5[a]			

Sources: Iron Age 16 Nov. 1893, 11 Feb. 1897; Berglund 1907, pp. 34, 35; U.S. Commissioner of Corporations 1911.

Notes: Figures are percentages of the total pool.

[a] In addition, "Western Works," which afterward disappeared from the pool, had a 4.10 percent allocation in 1887 and 4.5 percent allocation in 1888.

tained in a condition in which it made profits at prices ruinous to its rivals. Under such circumstances Carnegie Steel used formal pooling arrangements as an umbrella for operations that would have succeeded well enough without.

The first of a new series of rail pools was formed at a meeting held on 2 August 1887. There were fifteen members. The two Carnegie companies were represented and signed the agreement separately, John Walker as chairman for Carnegie, Phipps, and Company and David Stewart as vice-chairman of Carnegie Brothers. After record levels that year, the rail market fell away in 1888; it revived quite strongly over the next two years, but both the nominal pool price and "real" prices declined sharply.[6] It was at this time that Frick succeeded Henry Phipps as chairman of Carnegie Brothers. During summer 1890, he went on a trip to the Lake Superior ore fields and spent some time with Jay C. Morse, now president of Illinois Steel Company, with whom he already had a close working relationship through the South West Coal and Coke Company.

On Frick's return, he reported what he had learned to Carnegie, in a letter that revealed the uncertainties underlying pooling arrangements. Morse had agreed that his firm and the Carnegie companies should "work together in harmony" in rails. Writing to Carnegie soon after he increased his own involvement in the concern, Frick had put a rather different complexion on the matter: "I have written to Mr. Morse on the rail question and feel sure that we can keep the Chicago people in line and that they will be only too glad to continue to work in harmony with us." He had suggested to Morse their aim should be to operate the full capacity of the Edgar Thomson and South Chicago works, their respective key plants. The South Chicago works was big, ideally located, and well equipped. The Carnegie Company could scarcely fail to recognize the strength of its opposition. In late summer 1890, Schwab visited this works and was duly impressed. He reckoned the new blooming mill there could turn out 30 percent more steel than any other mill in the United States, rolling down a six-rail ingot in about one minute, whereas their own maximum capability was a four-rail ingot in the same time. On his return, his "only thought has been to re-model our mill to make it as nearly like Chicago's mill as possible without a large outlay of money."[7]

Sometimes the sharp conflicts were between others, and the Carnegie associates could look on as spectators. On one occasion, the Scranton Steel Company secured a low rail freight rate (from $1.25 to $1.35 a ton) on their rails to Buffalo and a very low Lake rate from there to Duluth and so into the natural market area of Chicago mills. Illinois Steel planned to retaliate by building boats to deliver their own rails to Buffalo and from there to invade Scranton home territory. That December (1889), Morse was fearful of the general trade outlook: "I hope that I am all wrong in my opinion as to the amount of rails required for 1890. I cannot, however, but be afraid that we will have hard sledding to fill all our mills."[8] In fact, 1890 was a good year (358,000 tons or 23.7 percent up on 1889); the average price was $31.78 a ton, the highest since 1887. But after that, output was lower for eight years, and prices were lower for ten.

Agreements could always be upset by new circumstances, which some-times came from outside, as for instance changes in the general economic situation and therefore in the rate of extension of railroad systems or expen-diture for renewals. There were increases in mill capacities, mergers, and a few new entrants. Amid such uncertainties, all producers had to do their best to preserve their positions. It was essential to remember that within the pool everyone was working for their own interest and cooperated only when that seemed on balance the most advantageous thing to do. Schwab summed up the situation vividly when he remarked later that some of the agreements, reached after long discussion, lasted only until the participants could get to the telephone and contact head office. John W. Gates, who became involved after he became president of Illinois Steel, later looked back and identified the chief disturbing element as a person rather than a situation:

> Well, in those days we used to have a few agreements. The boys would make them and Andy would kick them over. . . . I know that if Frick and I would agree to anything in the forenoon, as between our two companies, he might tell me in the afternoon that Carnegie would not stand for it. In other words, no one in the Carnegie organization controlled Mr. Carnegie, but he controlled every other man.

This was intriguing. In labor relations Frick had proved to be the hard man; Carnegie was generally more conciliatory and certainly more congenial in his contacts with their workers. By contrast, in the delicate relations with the leading representatives of their rivals, it was Frick who seemed cooperative and Carnegie who wished to capitalize on their advantages by crushing rather than accommodating them.[9]

Frick and Morse generally managed to act in concert, although there were occasional disagreements, some of which showed the pressures on their sales departments. Frick wrote to Carnegie that Morse "talked at one time as if it might be necessary for them to ask Pittsburgh prices at Chicago. This I do not think they will do, as he plainly understands it would mean a fight with us, and this I know he wants to avoid." A few months later, Frick was complaining about the obverse situation, Illinois Steel pricing that would enable them to invade Pittsburgh territory:

> We have pretty positive information that somebody in your interest is and has been quoting rails in our territory and also in territory which might be considered neutral at $27.00 Pittsburgh, that is to say, making prices that would equal $27.00 Pittsburgh. It seems to me that this is hardly in accordance with our understanding and that the price is much lower than we think it should be.

Prices generally were then between $28 and $29 a ton. Early in 1891, there was a particularly difficult period in their relations. On 10 January, Frick wrote to Morse:

> I do not think that it is either reasonable or right that you should ask us to protect you on the Michigan Central order, it is clearly in our territory, and, from the best information we can get, and I think that we can demonstrate to you that it is reliable, your people went to Mr. [Lewis C.] Ledyard and solicited his order before he asked for price. . . . Referring again to the order we took in July from the Big Four and the Chesapeake and Ohio people, when your Mr. Yale thought we should divide with you, and which I agreed to do just because you asked it, not because I thought it was right. These were orders all in our territory, and I do not think that you can point to a single order that we have taken in your territory, or to one instance where we have gone in and quoted in your territory except at a price that would amply protect you. We have an agreement based on a division of territory, and it seems to me that it should be strictly lived up to. I can well understand that you are pressed by your people frequently to ask of us things that are not altogether reasonable. On the other hand you must understand that our people naturally find fault when I concede anything in our territory to you. They feel particularly sore about this Michigan Central order. We, however, will protect you in this, not because it is right, but because you ask it, and because you say that you will give us other orders in place of it that we would not be strictly entitled to.

Within a week, on 16 January, he was pointing out that Morse's informant as to prices quoted by the Carnegie group "is entirely wrong. . . . We have not made any such absurd quotations. We have only made two small sales at less than $29 works."[10]

In general, the collaboration with Illinois Steel continued. A few weeks after they had taken over Allegheny Bessemer Steel and while they were still in dispute over markets, Frick agreed to let Morse know the tonnage rates of pay at Duquesne. In April 1891, sending other information, he pointed out, "You are about the only man that we would give, even confidentially, such information as you ask." Next year, the two companies cooperated further in passing on plant data or in opening their works to inspection by each other's officers, but (as was shown on such occasions) there was by no means complete frankness. In April 1892, Frick asked Morse for details of the Joliet works—the number and size of its converters, whether the direct method was used, and what their best month's work was when producing billets. In May he wrote, "I hope you will reconsider your determination to erect another mill at Joliet. Give us a show here in the east." That summer, Illinois Steel's assistant secretary, Green, visited Pittsburgh. Frick assured Jay Morse, "We shall endeavor to give him all the information he seeks." But when Green came back a little later with W. R. Stirling, asking for a tour of Edgar Thomson works, the letter Frick wrote to Schwab indicated the limitations of the understanding between the companies:

> Would like you to be on hand to show him around. You need not go to any extraordinary pains to enlighten them as to our various methods at Braddock yet give them sufficient information to satisfy them; that is to say, do not let them think that we are trying to keep anything from them. Green, I think, is the same man that was out to see you some time ago and I presume at that time you told him about all that was necessary.[11]

In November 1891, Frick was still complaining that Illinois Steel was not acting fairly by them:

> [D]id you know that your people have just taken an order right in our territory by selling your second quality rails, namely the Memphis and Raleigh Springs order. This is manifestly unfair. . . . If you could see the kind of rails that we scrap in order that we may not have the second quality go on the market, I am sure that you would at once adopt the same policy with yours.

Next month, Frick thanked Morse for his statement of rails sold for 1892 delivery and sent in return an account of the Carnegie orders. He went on to mention that the Western New York and Pennsylvania Railroad are in the market for 5,000 tons which we have about concluded to let Cambria Iron Company have. . . . We feel quite confident we could secure the order, yet in order to keep complete harmony all around we have decided to tell the Cambria people that we will not interfere with them in securing this order. They must have a certain amount of orders, and just at this time we had better let them secure a little more business.

In fact, Cambria supplied only 6.9 percent of 1892 association deliveries, an identical proportion to that of 1888; over those four years the Carnegie share increased from 11.6 to 25.8 percent.[12]

Another theme in the trade conditions of the time was the containment of new entrants. This involved two main approaches: one was to forge agreements with these companies, and the other was to secure favorable freight rates so that existing producers could meet the competition. In addition to Allegheny Bessemer Steel, there were three important examples of such arrangements with rail makers, one in Carnegies' home territory, a second in the East, and another in western markets. The Cleveland Rolling Mill Company had been a signatory to the 1887 combination, which allocated to it 96,549 tons or 4.8 percent of the total. In 1888, its share of actual shipments fell to 2.5 percent, and in 1889, to under 1.2 percent. The company then made moves to remodel its rail mill but was given inducements to leave the trade. At a pool meeting in New York, Frick—who had already been in contact with S. H. Chisholm of the Cleveland company—secured a resolution that Morse should see him on behalf of the members and offer $2.50 a ton on his potential output, now reckoned at 50,000 tons, to stay out of the trade throughout the rest of 1892 and the following year. Frick wrote to Leishman, who had already more than tested the waters: "This, you see, put the thing in good shape because it was having the Association agree to what you had practically arranged with Mr. Chisholm." After the New York meeting, Frick arranged for Morse to sign his acceptance of a Carnegie Steel proposal that, if the association should for any reason refuse to pay Chisholm the monthly amounts, Illinois Steel would pay thirty fifty-sevenths of the total—a proportion reflecting that company's share of the combined Carnegie-Illinois tonnage of association orders. After this, he telegraphed Chisholm at the watering place of Fortress Monroe, asking where they could meet to arrange details of the proposition that Chisholm had originally made to Leishman. Chisholm's return wire confirmed the arrangement. Frick told Leishman, "they will discontinue quoting on rails and turn the orders over to us." Toward the end of 1893, as Frick mentioned to H. A. Gray, Carnegie Steel was still paying Cleveland Rolling Mill a monthly "assessment."[13] In this way, to accommodate the resolutions of a trade association, jobs were lost in Cleveland and transferred to Pittsburgh. Later, Chisholm was to prove restless under this restraint, and his company had to receive more attention.

The eastern situation was simplified early in 1891 by the merger of the two operations in Scranton, when Lackawanna Iron and Coal acquired the Scranton Steel Company and was reconstructed as the Lackawanna Iron and Steel Company. Carnegie warned Frick of the powers of the new concern: "you have a clever man to fight in President Scranton." By this time, Bethlehem Steel was becoming more preoccupied with ordnance and armor and to some extent found compensation in this for its shrinking position in rails. In the hard conditions of the first half of 1893, Bethlehem's share of combination deliveries fell from 9.2 percent to only 6.15 percent. The other important eastern operation was Pennsylvania Steel at Steelton and its associated concern Maryland Steel of Sparrows Point, where steel was first made in 1891. In 1892, Sparrows Point took 7 percent of association deliveries and, as national production slumped in the first half of 1893, increased its proportion to 11.9 percent. Frick was suspicious of this group. In spring 1892, he complained to Lauder about Pennsylvania taking an 11,000 ton order for the Shawnee and Columbus Railroad delivered at Sandusky, "coming right into our territory," but he had to concede that "if the Major [Bent] is telling the truth and did get $30.00 at his works we can raise no objection."[14] Maryland Steel seemed likely to become a major long-term problem, although for a time in 1893 both it and its parent company were in receivership.

Sparrows Point was potentially a serious competitor because it could ship rails to Gulf Coast and West Coast points by water. An even more direct threat to expanding western business was the Pueblo works of the Colorado Fuel and Iron Company, which by 1885 was equipped to make Bessemer rails in a fully integrated plant, the only operation of this kind west of the Mississippi. It was strategically placed for many western areas of track construction and was over 900 miles from the nearest competing mills in Chicago. After early uncertainties, its career in rails promised success. In 1890, Colorado Fuel and Iron had a nominal annual capacity of 54,000 tons of rails, but next year, when national production was at its lowest since 1885, it turned out only 34,000 tons. At that time Frick wrote to Morse, "Am sorry that the Colorado Fuel and Iron company cannot be kept out of the rail business and think if we were situated as you are in Chicago we would make it to their interest to not make rails."[15] In 1893, with output and prices generally tumbling, Pueblo rolled almost 49,000 tons. It was clearly a potentially serious thorn in the flesh for eastern rail makers.

Given new producers, general overcapacity in rails, and a falling away of demand, production, and prices from the high levels of 1887 or 1890, Carnegie Steel was keen to obtain good quotations for delivery to distant outlets. This was brought out well in both 1891 and 1893, each a year of sharp recession from the preceding year. In February 1891, Frick contacted George Roberts, president of the Pennsylvania Railroad. He told him Carnegies were to make their rails the same price as those of the Pennsylvania Steel and Cambria Iron companies, and he went on, "In view of our large productive capacity compared with that of other steel rail mills on your lines, I think you should give us a larger share of your order, and have a suggestion to make which I think will meet with your approval." He wanted to see him for fifteen or twenty minutes some day during that week." During fall 1893, as rail prices tumbled, Frick wrote to the president of the Lake Shore and Michigan Southern Railroad Company, a system that was to provide an alternative route westward. He pointed out that outlets for Carnegie rails had been practically confined to nearby points or to southern and southwestern outlets:

> For nearby points we pay higher rates proportionally than any other Rail Mill in the country for same distances. For Southern business we compete with Eastern mills which have the advantage of still lower all Rail rates and privilege of shipping by ocean too. For South Western business our rates are much higher than those charged from Chicago, for while the Tariff is adhered to from here, it is practically not taken into account by the lines leading West and South from Chicago.

In these conditions, Frick had identified the locational disadvantages that were ultimately to erode the position of Pittsburgh in the steel industry, but before that happened, extremely high levels of processing efficiency in the plants of that district were to push its share of national output even higher.[16]

The 1893 depression was severe. Rail output was only 73.3 percent the 1892 figure, and prices were at a record low of $28.12 a ton. Illinois Steel was badly affected. The Joliet works operated for only about six weeks; then it closed in May, with twenty-five hundred men losing employment, and was to be idle for years. Apart from a short run on pig iron, Union works was idle all year. The North works was out of operation for the last half of the year, and even South works produced for no more than eight months.[17] The Pennsylvania and Maryland companies went into receivership and had to be reconstructed. In spite of Frick's complaints about their situation in marketing, Carnegie Steel—whose output in 1892 had been depressed by the long Homestead strike—suffered a much smaller decrease of business. They recorded their highest share of national steel production to that time, 21.47 percent. Under the strains of depression, late in 1893, the rail pool broke.

There followed a short period of harsher competition between its former associates. Within a few days, Maryland Steel had accepted an order for 15,000 tons of rails to be delivered on the Boston and Albany Railroad for $22, and Carnegies had sold rails for $21.90 at the mill. To outsiders it was clear that the pool had gone "all to pieces," but it was not easy to make out what would follow. The Pittsburgh newspapers wrote of the matter in heroic terms, reporting the dispositions of the local champion with great gusto: "the Carnegie has cut the price for steel rails about $5 a ton and proposes to knock out competition and make Pittsburgh the steel rail center of the world." Such sensational statements ignored the complexities of the trade, but already Frick was asserting their ability to do well under the new conditions. Contacting their senior representative, S. L. Schoonmaker, he exposed their aggressive intentions toward eastern producers, specifically Lackawanna and the Pennsylvania and Maryland plants, and the psychological weapons employed by a dominant concern:

> I have been thinking it would be a good idea for you to call on Mr. Scranton some afternoon—make it afternoon, because he will probably be feeling better after a good luncheon—and say that now that he has the Boston and Albany order for rails he would probably be willing to sell us his contract; that we would be willing to pay him what would be considered these times a handsome profit. If he asks how much, say fifty cents a ton. Would like you to do this, for the reason that I am satisfied if he fills the contract he cannot but lose largely on it, and he may feel obliged to bring the matter before his Board, and say that, while he was forced to take the contract at a loss, he can now dispose of it at a profit. And, for another reason, it will give you an opportunity to draw Scranton out, and learn just how he does feel since being compelled to go so low to secure this order, and he may be surprised to think we can still see a profit in it. You might incidentally remark that we are not making a fight against the steel rail manufacturers, but simply acting to protect ourselves against Major Bent, whom we think in the past has not acted fairly by the Rail Makers; and after reorganization was once secured might be still more arbitrary; that I told you the Major had said to me, in the latter part of May in Philadelphia, they were in position to make rails so very cheaply at Sparrows Point it was a serious question with him whether they should remain in the combination, when, in view of low costs, by running full, they could make much more money. You will understand how to handle Mr. Scranton, and draw from him anything you may think of interest to us.

Meanwhile an agreement signed by Frick and Morse on 18 October 1893 provided that, in 1894, tonnages and proceeds for rails obtained by either company at over $22 a ton should be divided equally between them. In order that they should work "in the most complete harmony," their representatives would have daily conferences, at which "there shall be an interchange of information as to inquiries, freight rates, credits and sales."[18]

The rail association was reestablished early in December 1893 and, this time, fixed prices at the mills. These prices emphasized Carnegie Steel's low costs and thereby helped the company penetrate the market areas of other, nearer producers. The price at Pittsburgh was set at $24 a ton, at Chicago at $25, and at tidewater at $24.80. The last would, it was believed, keep foreign rails out of the country, except on the Pacific Coast and the Gulf Coast, to the latter of which cotton steamers returned from Europe carrying steel at merely nominal freight charges.[19]

Even after the pooling arrangements were revived, hopes of a return to more profitable times were disappointed. Rail production in 1893 was 26.7 percent below the 1892 figure, and only 53.3 percent the output of 1887, the year the pool was formed. Rail tonnage was reduced by a further 10 percent in 1894. That year, the association cut prices and tried to buy off some of the newcomers to the trade, paying Maryland Steel for instance almost half a million dollars for its pool allotment. Under these difficult conditions, Carnegie Steel held up better than its rivals. In October 1894, Edgar Thomson alone rolled just twice the rail tonnage of Illinois Steel. Overall, Carnegie Steel made net profits of $4 million that year; Illinois Steel lost $1 million. When the rail makers met in Chicago in November 1894 to decide on arrangements for 1895, time and again they broke off in disagreement before coming to a decision. The penalty for overproduction was raised from $2 to $2.50 a ton. Carnegie and Illinois received 52.78 percent of the total tonnage allotted, a proportion ten points in excess of their share seven years earlier.[20]

In April 1895, the rail association arranged with a new producer, the Johnson Company, that in exchange for half the orders for track for electric railroads, Johnson would not make mainline material that year. This was a year in which demand recovered, though to no more than modest levels. Illinois Steel returned to profitability, but only to the extent of $360,000; profits at Carnegie Steel were $5 million. Negotiations about production shares for 1896 began in late summer 1895 and went on for at least two months. The limitations of pooling arrangements now became glaringly obvious, for there was a gross miscalculation of demand for 1896; the figure forecast was 2.2 million tons but production from all sources was only just over half that, 1.17 million tons, the lowest figures for eleven years excepting 1894. Such circumstances gave every incentive for producers to cut prices in order to keep their mills at work. Yet payments to firms to keep them from producing cost $1 million, and other firms producing little expected bonuses but found themselves paying penalties. Some time during 1896, Illinois Steel

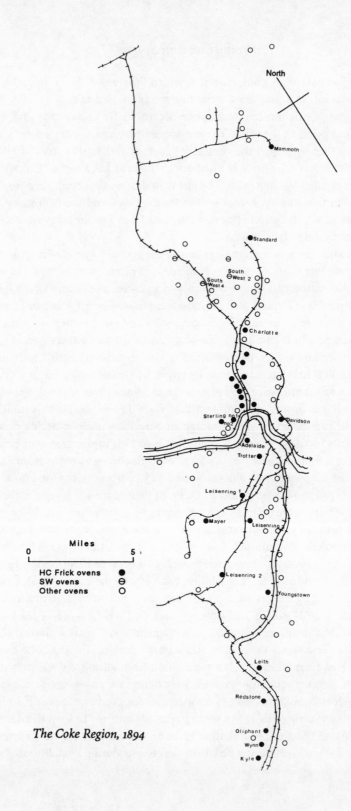

North

Mammoth

Standard

South
West 2

South
West 4

Charlotte

Sterling no.1
no.2

Davidson

Adelaide

Trotter

Leisenring 1

Mayer

Leisenring 3

Leisenring 2

Youngstown

Leith

Redstone

Oliphant

Wynn

Kyle

Miles

0   5

HC Frick ovens   ●
SW ovens   ⊖
Other ovens   ○

The Coke Region, 1894

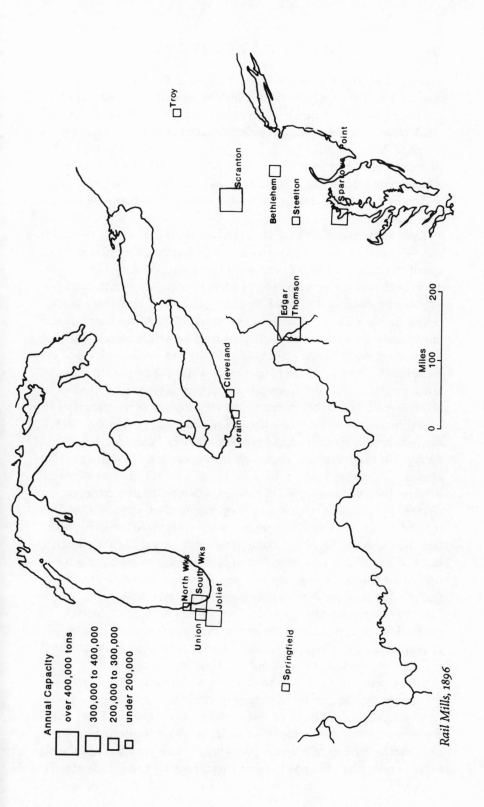

Annual Capacity

☐ over 400,000 tons

☐ 300,000 to 400,000

☐ 200,000 to 300,000

☐ under 200,000

Troy

Scranton

Bethlehem ☐

Steelton ☐

Sparrows Point

Edgar
Thomson

Cleveland

Lorain

North Wks

South Wks

Union

Joliet

Springfield

0   100   200

Miles

Rail Mills, 1896

is said to have come so close to receivership that the papers were already drawn. These were not conditions conducive to calm consideration of arrangements for 1897. A number of meetings were held in Philadelphia during December 1896, as *Iron Age* euphemistically put it, to "arrange matters for 1897." Some of the sessions were stormy, increased allocations being claimed by one or other of the producers. There were new "outsiders" to contend with—firms that, despite recession, had been attracted by prices held up by the pooling arrangements—but eventually matters were successfully "adjusted."[21]

Then, at the end of January 1897, the Lackawanna Iron and Steel Company—believing that not all its associates were honoring the prices they had agreed and that as a result it was losing business—gave notice of its withdrawal. On Friday, 5 February 1897, Lackawanna cut its price to $20 a ton and thereby threatened to break up the agreement. A conference was arranged for the following Monday in Pittsburgh. Heated arguments at this meeting brought to the surface disagreements between Carnegie Steel and Illinois Steel, which wanted concessions for staying in the pool. When the meeting adjourned, it seemed temporarily that the rail association had been saved; but Illinois failed to respond as promptly as expected, and when its management asked for deferment of their confirmation of the arrangements until their board met on Wednesday, 10 February, the pool broke. On Friday, 5 February, the price had been $28 a ton in Pittsburgh and $29 in Chicago. By early Tuesday, 9 February 1897, it was $20 in Pittsburgh. That afternoon, Carnegie Steel cut its price to $17 for both local and Chicago delivery. The result was a flood of business, which on the next day alone was reported to amount to 100,000 tons. As prices tumbled, wages were at once reduced. It seemed a calamity. That fervent advocate of the virtues of protection, James Swank, secretary of the American Iron and Steel Association, had to admit, "This is not the sort of 'prosperity' that we all hoped and worked for only a few months ago. The railroads get their rails almost as a free gift, the manufacturers lose money, and the men who make the rails have their wages cut down. But the Free Traders are happy." In 1897, rail production was 47 percent greater than in 1896, but average prices were only 67 percent as high. Illinois Steel returned to the black, recording a surplus of $21,000 on the year; Carnegie Steel earnings were $7 million.[22]

This general setting for the trade in the middle years of the 1890s was the context for the exercise of leadership at Carnegie Steel and for Frick's continuing chairmanship. Under his headship, his company still cooperated in actions that involved restraint of trade. This may be illustrated by two firms that had already affected the pool's negotiations, the Cleveland Rolling Mill Company and Colorado Fuel and Iron. There was a new flurry of activity about Cleveland in spring 1894. In response to an initiative from Morse, Frick wrote, "I note carefully what you say in regard to Cleveland Rolling Mill. I sometimes feel that I would like to take the risk of them making any rails. On the other hand it might cost us a great deal of money and much demoralization if we did not fix up with Chisholm." Next day, Frick and Morse talked the matter over on the telephone and arranged that Leishman, should go immediately to "make the best deal he can with Chisholm." Leishman returned with an agreement that the Cleveland concern, in return for an appropriate compensation, would not make any rails of fifty pounds or upward that year. As before, the costs of this arrangement were to be shared between Carnegie Steel and Illinois Steel, although "It is however hoped that we may be able to get the others to bear part of the cost." Apparently Chisholm followed up his agreement with a belated attempt to squeeze out more concessions, for Frick had to write him in a rather headmasterly tone: "Would say that you have from us all that we propose to say. Will not sign the agreement. Have told you that frequently, and it should be unnecessary for me to repeat it."[23]

In the fall of 1893, the Carnegie representative in Denver, Thomas C. Carson, reported that, excluding selling expenses, rail costs at Colorado Fuel and Iron (CFI) were $28 a ton. Next summer, Frick made a note of Carson's report that CFI had taken the order for rails for Indian Territory, and he added, "I would be glad if some arrangement could be made controlling their product." At the end of 1894, Carnegies' senior man in Chicago, John C. Fleming, reported that the CFI rails were of good quality. He had spoken to Paul Morton, the CFI vice-president, who was thinking of $25 as a minimum payment per ton for withdrawing from production on a guaranteed 60,000 tons. Fleming's opinion was that CFI would do well out of this, for although they could sell that tonnage at $26 or even $28 a ton, "if they had us to fight, backed up by the other Eastern mills to stand their share of cut prices, Pueblo would not be sure of even $22 or $23, which must be painfully near their cost."[24]

Through all these trade uncertainties, Carnegie Steel continued to be successful, but there were further signs of uneasiness in their relations with Illinois Steel. John Warne Gates was elected the Illinois president in 1894. He afterward conducted a correspondence with Frick that alternated between conciliatory and complaining. At the beginning of 1896, he affected to be the offended party but one who, though hurt, would carry out his part of a bargain:

> Your telegram at hand. I never for a moment thought of taking offense at your telegram, but I confess that I was surprised at your having any doubt that I

would forward the Penna RR order to you. I have been telling your Mr. Fleming right along that just as soon as we got any tonnage east of Chicago we would turn it over, so as to save both of us all the profit we could in the transaction. . . . Please bear in mind that several thousand tons of the Lake Shore rails which were transferred to you were not rolled by your company in December. If they had been we would have had less money to pay out. I did not think this was quite fair, but presume Mr. Leishman will have a satisfactory explanation. . . . I wish to assure you that I want nothing but what I think is fair and right. I may possibly allow my feeling for the Illinois Steel Company to warp my judgment, but I will try to avoid its doing so.

In April, Gates wrote personally to Frick about rail allocations asking him not to discuss the matter with Leishman, "but write me by return mail stating where you think I am wrong and where you think I am right and under no circumstances do I want you to agree with me simply because I make the suggestions." By September, he was in a more aggressive mood about three matters: "details of unpleasantness existing between our two companies." Only one of these concerned rails, the others being about billets and shipbuilding steels. On rail matters he adopted a fighting stance. He complained that Carnegies had "stepped in," unauthorized, and taken a small order for rails for the Chicago Great Western Railroad:

> [Y]ou took the order and did not report it to us. . . . Now, Mr. Frick, these are facts that cannot be controverted. I think, under the circumstances, that as your company does not hesitate to cut the soft steel pool price $4.50 per ton, and the rail pool price anywhere from $1 to $5 per ton, without asking our consent, and to put in bids for foreign rails at from 80c to 90c per ton less than the agreement, that there is only one thing to be done, and that is, to fight fair. Let us tear up all agreements existing between the two companies and let each one stand on their own bottom. . . . As for attempting to work with your sales department I will say frankly that we cannot do so, and I have today instructed Mr. Palmer and Mr. Yale not to have any future business with your Mr. Peacock, as I feel that it was his fault in deceiving us three times before we ascertained the facts, and now it will be our fault if he deceives us again. . . . I cannot consent to have this company hoodwinked any longer.

However, just before Christmas, he passed on to Carnegie Steel an order from the Missouri Pacific for 50,000 or possibly 100,000 tons: "I feel that this is your trade and I therefore quoted these people $20 per ton f.o.b. [free on board] trucks our works, and have since refused to reduce our price in any particular."[25]

A few months afterward, the pool fell apart. Even before the dramatic events of early February 1897, it was becoming clear to those at the head of Carnegie Steel that now was the time to go all out to command the market for rails. In the first half of January 1897, Pennsylvania Steel had cut wages by 10 percent. Carnegie concluded, "I think this forces us to take off the bonus to teach our competitors that they cannot take any advantage over us. . . . We are in for a year's business on rails at very low prices." Three weeks later, on the eve of the critical pool meeting in Pittsburgh, he wrote to Frick. After discussing the presidency of the company (Leishman was about to leave them), he turned to the rail situation. He made his own characteristically bullish assessment of their position and that of their competitors:

> Scranton seems to have acted recklessly—I fear his action renders maintenance agreement impracticable. Well it had to come sometime and we are prepared for low prices. It will break Pennsylvania Steel Co. again—and probably shut them up permanently, or at least for some years. Illinois Steel Co. also will have rough sledding and so will Scranton; they don't make cheap rails. Bethlehem will not be much affected.

His forecasts were only partially realized. Following the breakup, Carnegie and Illinois picked up a disproportionate share of the rail orders, but Lackawanna, Pennsylvania, Cambria, and Bethlehem all obtained business, survived, and in some instances even improved their financial standing.[26]

By the end of summer 1897, attempts were being made to revive the pool. Again, Lackawanna took the initiative. On Friday, 10 September, having already talked with Gates, Scranton met Frick and explained his wish for an agreement for 1898. Frick wrote Schwab:

> Scranton looks for large business and is pressed on all sides to name prices for next year [in which he had been led to believe that there would be greater business than ever before—which, except for 1887, was to prove the case]. Says Gates is sold up to the handle for this year and is anxious for him to make some rails for him. . . . He thinks that Penn. Steel Co. will have to be reorganized and says that he knows they are very hard pressed for money.

Frick's opinion reflected his realization of their superior position: "There can be no objection to an understanding with our competitors that does not lessen product and increases our price." A week later, Schwab met Gates and Scranton at Holland House, New York, and reported to Frick:

> Things looked bad for a while. After several hours' talk without accomplishing anything, I took Gates into the back room and had an hour's earnest talk with this result. He agrees to even percentage with us, both as to pool payment and tonnage. The scale as finally agreed upon between Scranton, Gates and I was— Carnegie 36 percent, Illinois 36 percent, Scranton 19¾ percent (same as he had in former pool), Cambria 8¼ percent (same as former pool). Orders now on books to be kept out of pool. Basis—$13 East, $14 West, mill price to be quoted everywhere and to be decided later. . . . With reference to Bethlehem and Penna

Steel, the idea was to tell them plainly what had been done. That we had agreed to take the business of the country. They cannot run on rails $18.00 or less. That if they keep out we will allow them their pool tonnage (old pool) as a basis to pay them $1.00 per ton on all the rails they might be entitled to if the proceeds were $19.00 per ton. If $20.00 they to get $1.50 per ton. If $21.00 they to get $2.00 per ton, etc. It is believed by Gates and Scranton that they will accept this proposition. If not, go ahead without them keeping price down where necessary in their district to take the business.

Schwab believed that if they added perhaps 360,000 tons of new business, secured under this pooling arrangement, to the 250,000 tons or so they would have on hand from orders already received, they would be well placed for 1898 business. The three participants in the discussion favored a three-year agreement.[27]

Schwab's optimism was soon tempered by events. Before the end of September, Powell Stackhouse had made clear that Cambria wanted 12 percent not 8¼ percent of the orders. This caused Gates to break ranks, refusing to cooperate with Carnegie and Lackawanna in adjusting to the Cambria demands. In turn, Scranton and Schwab refused to go over to Chicago to negotiate with him. "Scranton is awfully broken over the affair," and in spite of some talk "of a very friendly character" that Schwab had with Gates after the meeting adjourned, "matters now stand just as they did before negotiations were started. Each one to quote as he sees fit."[28]

That autumn, it became clear that not only was there deep division between the firms, but not all the Carnegie principals were of like mind either. Frick, as his early discussions with Scranton showed, was generally in favor of an agreement; Carnegie wanted to fight untrammeled by the pool. In November 1897, a committee of four representing Illinois, Carnegie, Lackawanna, and Cambria was set up to suggest a practical plan whereby the rail business could be "bettered"; or, as A. M. Moreland (representing Carnegie Steel) put it to Schwab, "Briefly to propose some method to stop the present industrial warfare amongst Rail Manufacturers." The committee was charged to agree tonnages or percentages and minimum prices for the four companies over a three-year period and to see what options on their business could be obtained from outside mills such as Pennsylvania, Maryland, Bethlehem, Johnson at Lorain, CFI, and the new mill at Ohio Steel. Moreland reported to Schwab that he did not think any rail producers would go out of business. The "pressure of their investment" was one factor keeping them in existence; another was their reciprocal relations with their customers, for "the railroads contiguous to their works are anxious that they do business and will assist them to get it so far as it is in their power to do so."

Yet the direct and keen competition of 1897 had shown up the weaknesses of some and the greater strength of others. Carnegie Steel had approximately one-quarter of the rail-making capacity of the eight main producers; in 1897 it made about one-third of their output (see table 15). Moreland adopted an aggressive stance toward the other members of the committee as well as toward the trade generally. Some years before (he pointed out) Lackawanna, Cambria, and even Illinois Steel had made more rails than in recent years, and in view of the decline in their competitive power, Carnegie Steel could not give them the percentages they were asking for: "We are not their rivals, rather their leader." He argued that the other concerns should not include the capacities of their second-grade mills in any calculations, for "They have been shut down for a long time. If I owned them, would sell them for scrap. . . . Capacity has nothing to do with the present issue. Ability to do business is preeminent." He pointed out that Cambria had only a small natural market area and that Lackawanna could not deliver cheaply except in New England and in areas east of Buffalo. Consequently, he was inclined to treat them both as second-rank producers. Moreland suggested that Lackawanna should not make over 200,000 tons of rails a year, and Cambria no more than 70,000 tons, and that they should be compensated for their restraint by Carnegie and Illinois, dividing the payments equally between them. Lackawanna would receive $3 a ton on 4 percent of total shipments made by the four pool members, and Cambria would receive $3 a ton on 3.5 percent of this total, which, on 1 million tons, would mean payment of $120,000 to the former and $105,000 to the latter. Moreland explained to the committee that he believed the average demand for rails, for home and export outlets together, would be less than 1,250,000 tons a year (see table 16). The others (he thought not very convincingly) reckoned it might be 500,000 or 600,000 tons higher. (In fact, even their projection was to prove too low; the average production of rails from 1898 to 1900 was 2,210,000 gross tons.) If the proposed Lackawanna and Cambria compensation schemes had been in operation, Carnegie and Illinois would have faced heavy calls.[29]

In December, Frick stressed to Scranton that they were serious about the pool: "Let me assure you that Mr. Schwab has been acting in the best of faith with you, and we are as anxious for a rail combination as you are." On the other hand, Carnegie was again in the mood for war. In September, he had advised a cautious approach in their negotiations:

> I would not have anything to do with the Illinois Steel Company under present management. . . . Our policy, in my opinion, is to stand by ourselves alone, just as we did last year, and take orders East and West. The Illinois Steel Co. in the West cannot get anything like the quantity of rails that we can get, reaching

TABLE 15
Rail Capacity and Shipments, 1897, 1892–1893

	1897		1892–1893 (18 months)
	Capacity	Shipments	Shipments
Carnegie	500	500	447
Illinois	500	430	567
Lackawanna	300	185	300
Cambria	250	140	131
"Low basis" estimates for other mills			
Pennsylvania, Maryland, Bethlehem, Colorado	each 100 +	each c. 60	av. 129 [a]
(Carnegie Steel share)	(25.6%)	(33.4%)	(22.8%)

Source: A. M. Moreland to CMS, 15 Nov. 1897 (ACLC); Iron Age, 16 Nov. 1893.
Note: Figures are in thousand tons.
[a] Pennsylvania, Maryland, and Bethlehem only.

both East and West, and any arrangement made with it should certainly be confined to competitive trade, that is, to the west of Chicago. . . . I say frankly that if I were running the business, I would have nothing to do with the Illinois Steel Company; should respectfully but firmly decline to have any communication with it. If you do arrange with them, you are simply bolstering a concern and enabling it to strike you in the near future. You began a great struggle wisely; it has been fought vigorously and we have triumphed. Now you are a good fighter, but there is something that comes after the fight is over, namely reaping the rewards of victory. Very few commanders have been able to do this. They fight well but are poor reapers. Now let us see that you can not only win victory, but also know how to gather in the fruits. [He added as a footnote] Please read to managers.

A little later, in October, taking up a theme similar to Moreland's "pressure of investment," he put an interesting new gloss on their own situation. Carnegie Steel's mineral holdings and the capital they had committed for the extension and modernization of the Pittsburgh, Bessemer, and Lake Erie Railroad, although major contributors to their low costs of operation, also meant that they had to make every effort to ensure high plant utilization rates in order to cover the extra overheads:

I suppose Illinois Steel will badger you about arranging a price for Rails. If you agree to equal division with them you are throwing away a great deal. . . . Since we have the ore mines on our shoulders and coke and the railroad, we cannot afford to do anything that will restrict us from taking the business of the coun-

TABLE 16
Estimated Annual Demand for Rails, 1898–1900

For USA (new track and renewals)	1,002,745
For export to:	
Canada	75,000
Mexico	20,000
All other countries	100,000
Total	1,197,745

Source: A. M. Moreland to CMS, 15 Nov. 1897 (ACLC).
Note: Figures are in tons.

try and running full; truly, my Pard, you can reap no advantage by arrangement with competitors that will in the end be so profitable to all our interests as go alone running 160,000 tons of steel per month. Do not be captivated by any temporary advantage. It is my advice.

By December, he was advocating an invasion of the Illinois Steel territory. He pointed out they could ship finished steel in ore wagons that would otherwise return empty to Conneaut, and from there "do a lively business during the navigation period, by taking Pittsburgh products to Chicago and bringing Chicago products, including scrap, to Pittsburgh manufacturers." By this combined rail and water route, they would be able to put steel into Chicago for not over $1 a ton. On the assembly and process cost account, he admitted there was now little to choose between them and Illinois Steel: "I cannot figure a dollar and a half per ton difference between the raw materials for steel assembled at Chicago and at Pittsburgh, but our immense product enables us, no doubt, to manufacture the materials at somewhat less cost, although I hear that our Chicago competitor has made wonderful strides, and is coming near our costs."[30]

Carnegie was justified in his surmise about Illinois's overall higher costs. Gates was feeling very vulnerable. A few days after Christmas, he wrote to Frick pointing out that Carnegies had quoted the Pennsylvania Railroad $18 fob at works for rails, "without saying anything to us. . . . We quoted $20 and telegraphed you we had done so. . . . It seems to me that your sales people ought to be a little more prompt in notifying us. If we had known you had quoted $18 we would have quoted $19." Gates followed this immediately with a commitment to cooperation that showed how weak his company's position really was: "I will state now that I will cheerfully tell you at any time just what quotation we make to any customer, and hope you will see your way clear to have the same done by your company." (Although

Illinois Steel just remained in profit, its difficulties under the cutthroat conditions of 1897 are vividly shown when comparison is made with the preceding year's output. Illinois state turned out 311,000 tons of rails in 1896,
compared with 305,000 tons from Allegheny County, Pennsylvania; in 1897
their respective outputs were 437,000 and 539,000 tons.)[31]

In addition to differences of policy between Frick and Carnegie, the rail
trade also brought out the changing positions of Frick and Schwab, who had
been president of Carnegie Steel since mid April 1897. It was now widely
recognized that Schwab combined ability, imagination, and vigor in a manner that amounted to industrial genius. When to that were added the qualities of youth and geniality, there was produced a mixture that it would
have been difficult for a man of Frick's qualities to accept with invariable
equanimity. Schwab conducted the difficult negotiations in autumn 1897, in
which Gates was accused of misleading the other parties to the discussions.
Frick had written to assure Scranton that, after the first interview he attended, Schwab had been given absolute authority to act on their behalf,
and that any agreement made by him would be approved by the partners:
"I have taken no active interest since that, for the reason that Mr. Schwab
had full power, and it only complicates matters to have two working on the
same thing." This gave Schwab an independence he had not had before, and
Frick felt its impact. In spite of the strong support he had given, there was
more than a hint of reproof in a letter he wrote to Schwab during the protracted rail negotiations: "I did not know until I saw in yesterday morning's
paper you were going to New York night before last. Presume you did not
know it when we went home together in the evening." Whether intention-
ally or not, a few days later Carnegie added to the potential tension when he
wrote from Cannes about financial interests in Carnegie Steel: "I think
Schwab should have half more than the Vice-Presidents, say 3 percent to
their 2. He's worth it and more, a genius. Lauder writes our business never
in such fine form and all pulling together. Let us get cheap freight rates and
defy the world." Early next year (and again probably quite innocently), he
added fuel to Frick's fire when, praising Schwab who had been to see him,
he employed about Schwab the very words he had used of Frick a few years
before: "Schwab's visit has made a great impression upon me, and you are
no doubt feeling as I do that a great load is off our shoulders. We have got
the man, and having him, there is no reason why we should hesitate about
going forward and keeping the lead."[32]

Meanwhile, the rail business remained a center of attention. At the beginning of 1898, Schwab came to an understanding with Gates, Scranton, and
Stackhouse for division of an order from the Gould railroads expected to

amount to 90,000 tons. The price was to be $18 at mills. For smaller orders, under 3,000 tons, they agreed to quote $18 at all Pennsylvania mills, $20 fob cars in Chicago, and $20 fob New York on all Pacific Coast business.[33] These levels were $5 or $6 below those of four years before. Shortly afterward, Carnegie came up with the idea of an alliance with Cambria (very much the junior partner) and the establishment of uniform prices for rails at Pittsburgh, at Tidewater, and in Chicago. In the East, he felt they would have a clear field with no effective rivalry from any of the concerns there: "Sparrows Point, Harrisburg, Bethlehem, it is all the same." He disagreed with Frick's high opinion of Lackawanna's ability to compete, pointing out that their last report showed they could not do so. Frick clarified his views to Carnegie: "if Lackawanna was well managed, with their cheap ore at Lebanon they would be quite a factor in the steel market in the East, and while I think Walter Scranton is a good salesman, do not think he is a manufacturer, and so long as he is at the head, we have nothing to fear." A day later Frick was generous enough to remark to the meeting of managers, "If they had a man like Mr. Schwab, they would make things lively for us."[34] Attempts to come to a new agreement over percentages with the main firms had been frustrated when the sum total of the percentages they asked for amounted to 124 percent.

Throughout the decade, Carnegie Steel remained uncertain about Illinois Steel. When Morse was president, Illinois had honored its agreements, but under Gates it sometimes did not.[35] And in the final years of the 1890s conditions changed yet again. Illinois Steel, as the key unit, was merged into a new amalgamation, the Federal Steel Company, headed by Elbert H. Gary; Gates was displaced. Into this new concern were brought additional Upper Lake ore properties controlled by the Minnesota Iron Company, as well as the Lorain plant on Lake Erie. Carnegie Steel now contemplated a bargain with Federal Steel, which they recognized as a more formidable competitor.[36] Before the end of 1898 Federal Steel was booking orders of a size comparable with Carnegie's. The company's South Chicago works had been remodeled to give it an annual capacity of up to 840,000 tons, and as Schwab reported to the board of managers, had "never showed such activity as now."[37] There was disagreement on the Carnegie board about the desirability of a new arrangement. On one occasion, when the matter was discussed in March 1898, the majority of members (including Frick and Schwab) were in favor; a minority (among them Carnegie and Phipps) opposed. At the end of discussion, Carnegie moved that because the senior partners—holding two-thirds of the stock—were against the association, it should not go through. This was then accepted unanimously, a striking example of the willingness of junior partners—and of some who were not so junior—to abandon their own convictions and fall in with Carnegie.[38]

In 1897 and 1898, Carnegie Steel's dominant position in the industry had been powerfully demonstrated. For some of the orders won, they had driven prices down to as little as $14 a ton. Even so, the results were not the elimination of competitors (as Carnegie had hoped), but their adjustment. South works was being modernized, and Lackawanna had decided to abandon Scranton and to build a bigger plant at Buffalo, which had some assembly cost advantages over Pittsburgh. In 1899 and 1900, prices rose dramatically, and works that had teetered on the edge of extinction were saved from disaster and able to make money again. During 1899, Lackawanna sold 325,000 tons of rails and Pennsylvania and Maryland 290,000 tons. In September, Schwab met representatives of the other companies in New York to try for an agreement for the next year. The price was fixed at $33 a ton, but under the new arrangement both the Pennsylvania and Maryland companies, which had received a bonus of $100,000 under the old scheme, had to recognize that they could not expect anything of that order. The $1 a ton differential between Pittsburgh and Chicago was eliminated. In the new allocations Carnegie and Federal were still dominant; Lackawanna was given a sharply reduced share.

However, things did not work out quite as planned partly because a new competitor, National Steel, came into production in 1899. In orders actually taken, most association members—including Carnegies—showed slight reductions from their allocations; only Lackawanna exceeded its share, though by a small percentage (see table 17). Clearly, despite its superb efficiency, Carnegie Steel could nowhere nearly command the rail trade of the nation. Within a further year, it was being considered as the key unit in a wider grouping. This involved not a loose and uncertain association, but amalgamation. Some of those who came in had been its rail-making competitors.

At the end of the 1890s, the rail trade was still of vital importance to Carnegie Steel, amounting to about 20 percent of their total output of finished steel, but it was a declining proportion. As recently as 1892 rails had been one-third of their tonnage; growth in recent years had been concentrated in other lines. It was symptomatic of the change that, whereas early in the 1890s Edgar Thomson was still their biggest plant, by the end of the decade Homestead was without doubt the major works.

Armor Plate

Late in 1887, the trade journal *American Manufacturer* carried an article on the new cogging mill and the large-scale manufacture of structural shapes

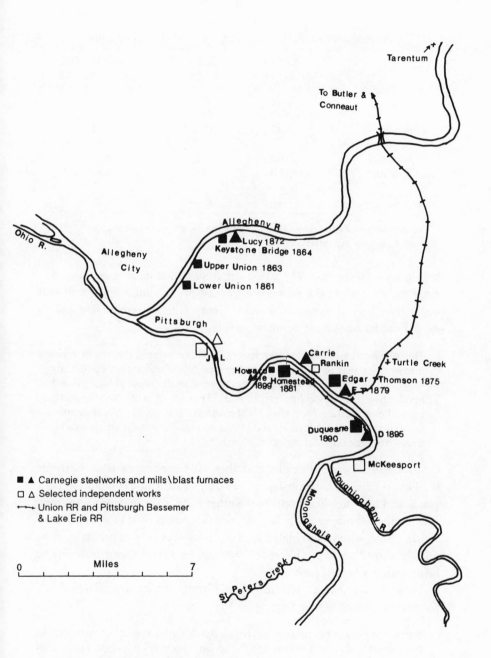

Ohio R.

Allegheny City

Allegheny R

■ Lucy 1872
▲ Keystone Bridge 1864

■ Upper Union 1863

■ Lower Union 1861

Pittsburgh

Tarentum

To Butler &
Conneaut

□ △
J L

Howard
▲ ■ Carrie
Rankin □

Mifle ■ ■
1899 Homestead
1881

■ Edgar ▼Thomson 1875
▲ E T 1879

+ Turtle Creek

Duquesne
1890

■
▲ D 1895

□ McKeesport

Youghiogheny R

Monongahela R

St Peters Creek

■ ▲ Carnegie steelworks and mills\blast furnaces
□ △ Selected independent works
←→ Union RR and Pittsburgh Bessemer
    & Lake Erie RR

0   Miles   7

Carnegie Steel Company Works, 1899

TABLE 17

Railmakers Association Allotments and Orders, 1899, 1900

	Allocation "old agreement"	Allocation for 1900	Share of Orders Taken Oct. 1899–Oct. 1900
Carnegie	26.75	30.01	29.64
Federal	26.75	30.01	29.55
Cambria	8.25	10.20	9.13
Pennsylvania and Maryland	11.0	11.0	10.82
Lackawanna	19.0	13.5	13.64
CFI	—	5.3	4.98
National	—	—	2.25

Source: Minutes of Carnegie Steel Company, 19 Sept. 1899, 6 Oct. 1900 (ACLC).
Note: Figures are percentages of total.

beginning at Homestead. The article emphasized that these operations indicated the strength of the movement to mass production, using words that might have been designed to describe Henry Ford's assembly line and its supporting facilities thirty or more years later:

> This step emphasizes another tendency of the day, namely, that the manufacture of any article of general use must necessarily be undertaken upon a large scale, and the returns be looked for not upon a small output at high prices but upon a large output yielding a small margin per ton of profit, and the margin secured only by the large divisor for the numerous items of expense common to large and small production, and by the manufacture of the article in all its stages from the ores and fuel to the finish.[39]

Generally these were principles that then, and even more later, Carnegie Steel exemplified in extreme degree, not only in structurals but also in rails, plates, and semi-finished steel. On the other hand, the company was already considering a departure in a very different direction, that of producing an article whose price was so high it held out prospects of large profits even on relatively small tonnages. However, the manufacture of armor plate was to bring with it a host of problems.

In November 1885, an account was published of some remarks made by Carnegie on Thanksgiving Day:

> Because in two continents man has begun the sickening murder of man [Britain was then at war in both Burma and the Sudan], while our Republic stands forth preaching by her example—the most eloquent of all preaching—the gospel of "Peace on earth, among men goodwill"; because we have neither army nor navy—chief tools of the devil—worthy of the name, but are blessed with an

educated people who value the victories of peace, who stand pledged to offer amicable arbitration to their adversaries; because of all this, and more, I am moved to join with full and grateful heart in the National Thanksgiving.

Next year Carnegie published *Triumphant Democracy,* a eulogy of American achievement. In the course of the book he spelled out his pacifist principles once again, making a favorable comparison of the policies of the United States with those of the quarrelsome and often imperialist nation states of Europe: "It is one of the chief glories of the Republic that she spends her money for better ends and has nothing worthy to rank as a ship of war."[40] Within a few months of this commendation of a non-military state, Carnegie had given his approval for the building of an armor plate mill at Homestead. However, he did refuse to countenance the manufacture of ordnance, it was said because this would contribute to offensive action rather than, as with armor, merely defending against destruction. Explanation for even his partial denial of his cherished, apparently genuine, and certainly loudly proclaimed principles lay in two rather different circumstances. One was his undoubted deep loyalty and sense of obligation to the Republic. The other was his insatiable desire for financial gain. Wall sums it up neatly, though at the same time putting a generous gloss on the whole episode:

> Quite clearly, Carnegie had given in to the pressure of his partners and his own desire for the profits and prestige involved in these contracts. He regarded it not as a surrender, but only a minor compromise of his pacifist principles. He would only make armor plate—a defensive item of armaments, not guns. On this point he was, at first, very insistent.

The correspondence indicates that it was he, rather than his partners, who strongly favored going ahead. In time, Carnegie warmed to his commitment—although as late as 1911, speaking to the Republican Club in New York, he explained that he had undertaken armor plate manufacture reluctantly and only because President Harrison had asked him to do so as a duty to his country.[41] (His reservations about making guns eventually also evaporated.)

Some years before Carnegie's 1886 uncertainties, President Arthur's Secretary of the Navy, William E. Chandler, had urged American steel firms to build plant to produce armor and gun forgings. But he made no specific promises of orders, and consequently his invitation brought forth no positive response. William C. Whitney, Chandler's successor, adopted a different approach, obtaining congressional authority for naval construction and offering several years of warship orders for tender, in the hope that companies would find the prospect attractive enough for them to install the necessary and expensive plant. In February 1886, Carnegie rejected Whitney's request, however, sending him two pages from *Triumphant Democracy* with the sentence quoted above underlined. Yet preparations for a change of direction were soon underway. In the course of that year, Schwab, then the twenty-four-year-old superintendent-designate of Homestead works, was sent to look at European works, including the Krupp and Schneider armor plate mills. His experiences there helped him realize how different this business might turn out to be, in comparison with the business of rails, billets, and beams. However, decision was taken to go ahead, and under the general superintendence of Julian Kennedy and his assistant Henry Aiken, outline plans were drawn up for an armor mill at Homestead. In December, Whitney invited bids for 5,000 tons of armor plate.[42]

The trade on which both Carnegie and Bethlehem Iron now embarked was full of both technical and commercial uncertainties. In contrast to regular (though varying) levels of demand from a large number of customers for commercial grades of steel, there was the prospect in this instance of only fitful consumption by a monopsonist, one who would even want to specify the processes to be used. Considering some of these difficulties, Carnegie had second thoughts and decided not to go ahead. However, Bethlehem Steel then failed to deliver the armor for which it had contracted, and this caused Carnegie to overcome his doubts and complete the Homestead mill. In summer 1890 he obtained specifications of proposed U.S. warships—from the U.S. naval attaché in London—and during that autumn Carnegie, Phipps, and Company put in its first bid for armor. By mid 1892, more than five years after he had first endorsed their entry to a trade he had previously deplored, their armor mill was completed. Carnegie was anticipating great results, but problems were quick to emerge.

In summer 1889, Carnegie had written to William Abbott at Carnegie, Phipps, and Company in a manner that might have surprised those who took his written pacifist statements at face value: "There may be millions for us in armor." Next year he was even more optimistic: "Sure we never had such a chance for returns." There is indeed some evidence that, later in the decade, they may have been making profits of 200 percent over their costs of production.[43] If so, it would have made the returns on the rail business look minuscule but for the fact that armor tonnages were, relatively speaking, so small. In addition, even before their new department was in regular production, it had become obvious that production schedules would be uncertain. In addition to the difficulties of getting in the right equipment and of training managers and men and the constant threat that plates—which cost so much to make, and which might yield so much profit—would at the last be rejected by Navy inspectors, there were wearying days of negotiations with national government. Carnegie, Phipps, and Company did not start out well in the last of these fields.

In summer 1888, Abbott earned Carnegie's strongly expressed disapproval for a bid he had made for plates for cruiser construction. The Carnegie price was $89,000; they soon learned that the lowest competing price had been $120,000: "seems the wildest bidding I ever heard of. . . . one cent per pound absolutely thrown away. . . . If we can't gauge competitors better than that we are not likely to make much of a success." Not receiving adequate answer to his complaint, he pursued Abbott further: "Am anxious to hear why we misjudged competition so seriously about government plates that $30,000 thrown away. *Gravels* me—too bad—too bad. Besides it exposed our hand for all future." Abbott now responded with an eloquent defense of his position, and Carnegie had the grace to admit he had been wrong. He did so in a manner that showed both his affection for Abbott and the ease with which he could descend to patronizing: "My Dear Boy, On the Maine *I cave*. You did well and let me say that your letter is creditable as a literary production—not one superfluous word and all excellent English."[44] In spite of this, memory of Abbott's deficiencies as a negotiator remained, and was to resurface.

The beginning of 1890 was a time of cheerfulness about armor prospects. As Carnegie put it in a letter to Frick, which also conveyed the not necessarily welcome news that he was to spend the week beginning 3 February 1890 with the managers in Pittsburgh: "There is a *possible* fortune in Navy Department's attitude toward us and I am to confer with Secretary Tracy next week. So glad we can oblige him by rolling a trial plate with 1 percent nickel. He will pay us same as he did for one abroad, $4,500, which will let us out." Sometime later (the letter unfortunately is undated but may well be the "very comprehensive" one acknowledged on 3 July), Carnegie wrote to Frick in a less satisfied tone and exposed some of the problems of top management in Carnegie, Phipps. Armor plate, he now recognized, could be so managed "as to make us much, or to land us in complications with the Government." Abbott had again proved inadequate in negotiations at the highest level, and Carnegie wanted a better representative for their interests. As so often, both before and later, he was—rather touchingly—looking for someone on whom they could wholly depend. It was a typical Carnegie letter, a veritable torrent of ideas, asides, self-confidence. He wondered if Leishman could be spared for the job, for apart from anything else, Abbott had many other calls on his time:

> The Chairman of Carnegie Phipps and Co. cannot be at the beck and call of anybody, even Washington officials—has higher duties—therefore Leishman

Frick with Andrew Carnegie (seated) at Cluny, circa 1893. *Courtesy of Frick Art and Historical Center, Frick Archives.*

who can be spared and *has not much to do,* better be made useful. . . . *Next to yourself,* I bet on Leishman getting deep into all these officials and running out ahead. He has done brilliant things—I think I told you Ingalls [M. E. Ingalls, president of the Chesapeake and Ohio Railroad] said he was the nicest man he ever had to do business with—(except one he said of course, but didn't quite mean). With Leishman in charge of Government things, I for one should be able to rest entirely confident. It's too harassing to be always dreading one false step which may lead to so great a loss—For instance, Abbott really said to me, "I propose to just say to Commodore Folger [the government officer in charge of the nickel plate trials] '*We are in your hands*' "—Just think of it!—Now if we are so in this one instance, it would be a precedent and ever after we should be in for *nickel* results. What can you do with a man so lost to the key of a position? However no partner is good for all kinds of work and I do not at all disparage Abbott's value to his partners, nor his zeal nor his splendid record.

He thought that if his suggestion of Leishman proved impracticable, then perhaps W. P. Palmer, the Carnegie Phipps secretary, could do the job, "but my feeling is that we could only be dead sure with Leishman." This was the only matter, in all their affairs, concerning which he had not been able to dismiss fears by the thought "all is in able hands." Finally he came back to Abbott, again revealing his affection for the man notwithstanding his failings as a negotiator. At the moment, "In Washington we have the wrong dog in the field for the game we are after—a good, true, fine dog, but not *the* one for this special hunt and he will spoil the affair."[45]

At this time, there was a good deal of uncertainty and indecision— accompanied alternately by euphoria and by depression—about armor. Carnegie first refused a request that they should complete the Homestead armor mill but then, when asked directly by President Harrison, agreed to do so. They then had to secure the necessary expertise, equipment, and site. For the first two of these, they had to look to Europe. Carnegie reported to Benjamin Tracy, Secretary of the Navy from 1889 to 1893, that Lauder had seen and been much impressed by nickel plate at Schneider's. Now Carnegie Steel had obtained a license to manufacture from Charles Cammell, which firm would furnish all the information and help needed, and they reckoned they could also get a license from the other long-established Sheffield armor firm, John Brown. The extensions needed at Homestead would require the land of the City Poor Farm. Carnegie suggested they offer $25,000 rent for it. Within a few days he was drawing back yet again. He contacted Secretary Tracy: "There is but one basis. We can accept perfect equality with our competitor. Ask no more, will accept no less. Offer therefore declined." Frick as always was less subject to mercurial changes of mood. He had remained cautious: "we certainly should go very slow."[46] Returning home that autumn, Carnegie thought they might negotiate with Tracy in the hope of providing the entire requirements for U.S. yards—presumably cutting out Bethlehem, which was now having difficulties meeting its contracts.

Having at last made the decision to go into armor, Carnegie was once again optimistic, affecting to believe that either there were few obstacles or that any that emerged could easily be overcome. On 3 August, he wrote to Frick from the Royal Hotel, Thurso, Scotland (a strange place from which to pen a message about the industrial maelstrom of Pittsburgh or about steps in the preparations for future naval wars):

> No specialty can be had equal to this. Further study of the situation convinces me that we can easily succeed. Lauder shows me that we require little ground for new machine shop. . . . Lauder says it's not half the task I thought. . . . I propose having Lauder visit Sheffield next week. . . . I think we can average a million per year out of this department with ease.

He was sanguine both about competition at home and about prospects for foreign orders: "Russia will not buy an English plate if she can buy in

America and she is constantly buying . . . nobody will follow us and we can agree with Bethlehem. . . . They can't make over a plate per day and won't do that for years—we can do it within a few months."[47]

A few days later Lauder reported back to Pittsburgh from Helmsdale, also in the far north of Scotland, where he was completing a coaching trip. Next week he was to go to Sheffield "to get up particulars of all that is necessary for armor plate." He was less convinced of how easy the business would be than Carnegie had indicated. He quoted Frick's own remark "it takes money to go into armor" but promised he would try to ensure that nothing turned up afterward to double estimates and time. Meanwhile, at the end of the month, Carnegie gave two conflicting signals of his own feelings. To Abbott he sent one of his warm messages: "Good boy. Shall have Lauder get offers tools. Best specialty going sure—millions in it." But next day, cabling Frick, he gave a rather different assessment. He recognized that, although Abbott was still chairman of the company that would be making the armor, central power now lay in other hands: "Fear Abbott has agreed to penalty time of delivery . . . reckless folly. No man can fix deliveries within 6 months. Certainly hope you will instruct him to sign no contract with penalty." Carnegie became more convinced about this. A year later when again discussing armor plate with Frick, he wrote, "we cannot entrust important matters to Mr. Abbott."[48]

Major problems dogged their early attempts to make armor—technical problems, negotiations with the government, and the need to cooperate, in technology, in submissions, and in bids, with Bethlehem Iron Company. Schwab explained to Leishman how difficult it was to cost the armor plate they made. Production was irregular and the making of a single plate might extend over six or seven months. The call on other facilities was heavy. By 1896, when their annual armor capacity was 3,000 tons, Schwab reckoned that possibly one-tenth of the general charges of the Homestead works should be allocated to that department, but he wondered if he should have allowed even more, perhaps even up to one-quarter of the whole. Frick periodically met or corresponded with Bethlehem's president, Robert P. Linderman. Within Carnegie Steel the armor business was instrumental in causing important changes of personnel and rank. As for relations with government, Carnegie sent Frick a statement made by the Secretary of the Navy that proved "what dangers we run in dealing with politicians."[49] That was to prove a very moderate assessment.

The necessary technical collaboration involved exchanges not only with Bethlehem but also with European companies. There were visits to the works of such continental concerns as Schneider, Krupp, and Hoerde. Information was obtained from—and a certain amount of data given in return to—the Admiralty in London, through William H. White, the director of Naval Construction for the Royal Navy. Agreements were made for the transfer of expertise from Sheffield. Plant—especially a heavy forging press with accompanying "tools"—was purchased from the Manchester engineering firm of Whitworth and Company. Contract for the press—needed for the heavier plates, which could not be rolled throughout—was signed in December 1892, after one of Whitworth's managing directors had visited Pittsburgh. The pace of change in the processes of armor manufacture was at this time extremely rapid. In the light of this, the U.S. government forced continuing adaptation on its suppliers. For instance, in mid December 1892 (Millard Hunsiker reported to Frick), the Secretary of the Navy informed them he wanted quotations for the new "Harveyized" plates. This alone would require new heating furnaces and cranes.[50]

Constant attention to the pressure of business, the necessity to respond to rapid technical change, negotiations for orders with customers operating in very different spheres, and the uncertainty of meeting the specifications they provided—all these severely taxed those in charge of this part of the company's business. In December 1891, Carnegie reported to Frick that he had told Commodore William M. Folger, chief of the Bureau of Ordnance something of the toll: "Mr. Abbott was indisposed. Like all our men he had been too anxious about this armor business and had worked too hard to please him and the Secretary. He expressed great regret, adding that Potter was a bright fellow—to which I said, 'Yes, he will probably be down too, if he has much more trouble.'" This prediction was not ill-founded. Three months later, Frick reported that, having concentrated for several months on armor plate, Potter was now away on a short vacation: "To use his own words, he is '. . . a physical wreck,' so it was thought advisable by Messrs. Abbott and Childs that he take a rest of a week or ten days."[51]

As indicated above, for a number of years, the Carnegie and Bethlehem companies were net importers of Old World technology. Even so, Andrew Carnegie, having but a smattering of technical knowledge and no experience at all in this line, yet had the audacity to denigrate the long-established producers on whose expertise his company was drawing. As early as summer 1890, from Cluny Castle in Scotland, he wrote to Benjamin Tracy: "After seeing the inferior facilities for armor plate making here, and the small amount of work which is given the steel, compared with what we should give, I am not so sure that solid steel plates can be excelled by compound plates of iron and steel." His company would be able to supply solid steel plates for the Navy to test within less than six months, and "I think it will repay you to await the result of such tests." If they were given orders for 12,000 tons of plate, say, they would put into them more than double the work done on such plates in Britain. Next summer Folger came to Homestead, and in June Frick reported on his visit: "[he] was evidently much impressed with our facilities for manufacturing and progress being made toward getting ready to manufacture armor." A few months later, Frick wrote that he hoped the Secretary of the Navy would also pay them a visit. Just before Christmas, Carnegie saw Tracy, and on 26 December 1891, Frick expressed the wish that all questions with him had been settled. Two weeks later, sending Philander C. Knox's opinion of a government contract for armor, Frick added: "I understand that someone has been saying to the Secretary that our plant was not as complete as represented; . . . A visit by the Secretary to Homestead would open his eyes and satisfy him on all points."[52]

The contract for armor for the monitor *Monterey* showed how complex their new business was. During the last days of 1891, Tracy was pressing them for the earliest possible delivery date. Even this pressure was seen to have its advantages, Frick wrote to Carnegie: "The Inspector at Homestead has received instructions to have us work night and day on the *Monterey* armor, shipping it as rapidly as possible, so tests of all kinds will be practically lost sight of, and we should be able to make a good showing on this lot of armor." Next summer, Frick was in touch with Irving M. Scott, the vice-president and general manager of the Union Iron works in San Francisco, reporting that all of the parts of the conning tower were now at the Mackintosh, Hemphill, and Company works in Pittsburgh where that firm's workforce was working day and night boring and turning them. Meanwhile, Homestead was finishing the thirteen-inch plate. It would take about ten days to get it out after they started. Frick apologized for the delay: "we have been however, more or less interfered with at the Homestead Works for a long time by the arbitrary actions of the Amalgamated Association." At the end of that summer, Carnegie was complaining that they had been misled by the government, which had given more of the work to Bethlehem. He was again at a low point in his appreciation of the trade: "The armor business has been a disappointment all through."[53]

It is clear that the company did not want too many of its processes to be understood by the Navy, in spite of their wish to have Tracy visit and be impressed by Homestead's facilities. This came out well in a letter from Frick to Schwab shortly after the latter took over at Homestead:

Please have it understood that any employee that is found answering questions as to the manufacture of armor, or its treatment in any way, will be summarily dismissed. . . . I am told by some of the Government men that they asked Mr. [W. A.] Cline, in charge of the press shop, yesterday, in regard to bending armor, who told them that it was much easier to bend nickel-steel than all-steel. This makes it rather awkward for us, in view of the fact that we are endeavoring to secure more for working nickel-steel than all-steel, and you can readily understand the situation that it puts us in.

In cables to Carnegie, Frick resorted in part to cryptical forms concerning this high-security section of their business. In the course of a week in February 1891, he sent two of these "cryptograms" to Carnegie en route to England. The first was to meet the liner *Teutonic* in Liverpool: "All well, Business quiet, Navy contract executed, Piety matter getting into good shape." The second, sent care of the Morgan Company's London office, was even more intriguing: "January net piano command, copy condition look piety copy. Repairs progressing well. Piety matter working into good shape. Picture orders good. Piano fair. Pig dollar better. Money plenty, five per cent. New Amity well seven hundred pounds. Slumber."[54]

During the early 1890s, Carnegies gradually made their way into ordnance manufacture as well as into armor. By this time, Carnegie seemed no longer reluctant about offensive armaments. In August 1891, he reacted to news of a rival's success in this field: "Bethlehem's 3 million contract for guns is a 'stunner.' With one more tool—a boring mill—we should be ready to compete for the next lot." By the end of the following year, they were planning production of gun forgings. Early in autumn 1894, the press carried reports of bids from Bethlehem and from Midvale for gun forgings. Carnegie sent some of these news clippings on to Frick with a note: "Surprised apparently no bid from us. We can make gun forgings as well as anybody by getting two small tools." Schwab was opposed to entry to this trade on the grounds that the investment in plant required would be considerably more than Carnegie anticipated. He estimated it might need $200,000 at least: a few months later, Lauder reckoned it could be as high as from $600,000 to $650,000.[55]

Gradually Carnegie Steel built up its system of liaison with the Navy and Ordnance Departments in Washington. They also followed the practice of their European rivals, securing expertise from these departments. Millard Hunsiker, who had been Frick's personal assistant, was put in charge of armor matters and conducted at least some of the negotiations with the Secretary of the Navy. In 1893, William M. Folger left the Ordnance Bureau. For a time, he contemplated becoming associated with Carnegie Steel, but then he withdrew with good grace. Lieutenant C. A. Stone, who had been in the Bureau of Ordnance, was appointed the company's representative in

Washington. In November 1892, after negotiations there, Frick commented on various aspects of their relations with the departments of government. The implications in terms of the installation of further costly plant soon became obvious:

> Had a very satisfactory interview with the Secretary of the Navy yesterday. Present; His Assistant (Sole), Com. Folger, Stone and Hunsiker. He started in rather severely, but at the close promised to adjust all unsettled matters between now and Jan. 1st, the principal of which are an extension of time on our contract and proper price for the sponsons we have made, and will have to make additional compensation for nickel over all-steel. He expects to advertise for the additional armor very soon. Wanted us to agree to a transfer of heavy armor to Bethlehem, for the "Oregon," which is the last on our schedule. We declined to agree on this, for the reason that it might operate against us in securing our share of the heavy armor to be assigned shortly. . . . I was much pleased to see the esteem in which Stone and Hunsiker are held by the Secretary, Folger and all other officials in Washington. Am satisfied that if Hunsiker had been the man—in place of Abbott—to have visited Washington from time to time, our armor matters would have been in much better shape. Since Hunsiker has had charge, we have entered no orders on the books but what we could make. Previous to that, Abbott agreed to make anything they asked him to make.

He ended his report on an optimistic note: "All that is necessary is to show those people the impossibility of doing certain things, and they will not insist, but will change to suit our facilities."[56]

Events were to prove that this was far too sanguine an assessment. Before long their decision to enter the armor business was to make Carnegie one of the world's great armament suppliers. But although the company's relations with the U.S. government had started out happily enough, the two parties were soon to be in confrontation. In autumn 1892, Carnegie and Frick both subscribed to the presidential campaign funds of Benjamin Harrison. He was unsuccessful, an outcome to which the horrors of the Homestead strike are said to have made some contribution. On 9 November, Carnegie added a postscript to a letter from Milan. He anticipated some trouble with the incoming administration of Grover Cleveland:

> Will be important to get some matters fixed with Dept., Washington—New contracts Armor, etc., etc., prices, extras, etc. May be in very bad odor with new people—Think hereafter better decide C.S. Co. give nothing—remain neutral—Bethm. will have inside track I fear, altho my personal relations excellent Whitney and New Prest.—Whitney fair and big broad man—not much fear of him. Altho' he hurt Roach (unknowingly I think). Will be home January some time—May be about middle or may be 1st week—so can help get Armor matters Washington in best possible shape—Think we ought to do so—any loose ends left over might be troublesome.

Although he had helped in Cleveland's campaign, W. C. Whitney did not return as Secretary of the Navy. Instead, the southern lawyer Hilary Abner Herbert was appointed, and he retained the post throughout Cleveland's second term. It was during this administration that a scandal over Carnegie armor plate became a national issue. The episode has often been referred to in a superficial manner, one almost always detrimental to the reputation of Carnegie Steel and of its principals, but in more recent years a full and well-reasoned account has been published by Robert Hessen.[57] A neglected aspect of the affair has been its impact on relationships between individuals within the company, and this will be the focus in what follows.

There was always ample scope for dispute between manufacturers and the government over armor orders. Rumor was rife. In summer 1892, Folger had to deny reports that some Carnegie plates had been returned to Homestead because they contained inferior metal.[58] Afterward, conditions were made yet more uncertain by the discontent that seethed below the surface in the aftermath of the Homestead strike. It was an explosive situation. Then in late summer 1893, Frick received a message from an attorney acting on behalf of four men from their armor department, offering to sell him evidence of fraud in the execution of government contracts to prevent his going directly to the Navy Department. Frick refused to treat with such blackmailers, and the attorney then approached Herbert. After haggling, it was agreed that the men should share 25 percent of any penalties charged against Carnegie Steel as a consequence of their evidence. The matter was investigated by a board under the chief of the Bureau of Naval Ordnance, William T. Sampson. The company was found guilty of the alleged offenses and Frick was informed that the board intended to levy a fine equal to 15 percent of the value of all plate delivered to date.

Carnegie wrote personally to Cleveland to request a new inquiry, criticizing the way Sampson's board had operated, and pleading that the company had "spent millions, subordinated every other branch of our business to the Government's needs, succeeded" (claims that could not legitimately be made without reservation). He stressed that Schwab and others were "quite as incapable of attempting to defraud the Govt. as the Hon. Sec'y himself."[59] At one point, he even offered to have all the armor removed from the ships for which it had been made in order to have its resistance tried on the ranges, all at the expense of Carnegie Steel—which provoked a newspaper cartoon showing Carnegie cowering behind a trial plate on the test range, shouting: "Don't shoot, I made this plate."

Cleveland confirmed the Sampson decision but reduced the fine to 10 percent. Both critics and friends of the company complained, and the result was an investigation by the House Committee on Naval Affairs. The most popularly emotive charge—the infilling of blowholes in the surface of the plates—was shown to be no more than cosmetic; all armor plates were said to have blowholes. A second charge, failure to follow set manufacturing procedures, was a breach of contract, but it could be argued that it illustrated the steelmakers' frustration with imposed means of attaining the results which they thought should alone be specified. The steelmakers undoubtedly had contempt for the lack of technical knowledge on the part of the government inspectors. The attempt to explain away the third charge. that test results had been falsified, was less successful. To argue that the tests were inexact, or not appropriate to the role the plate was required to fulfil (although true), could not disguise that deceit had been practiced. Finally, it was shown that retreatments had been applied to six plates selected for test, and the inspectors had not been informed. This, the company claimed, had been in order to explore various ideas for the strengthening of armor. Such a plea was again only superficially persuasive: retreatment in any form was deception.[60] The Committee on Naval Affairs unanimously endorsed Herbert's original decision, although the fine imposed was to be at the reduced rate approved by the president.

Within Carnegie Steel, as chairman and chief executive, Frick played a central part in this crisis. As early as Friday, 15 September 1893, Lovejoy had warned him of "possible irregularities" in one department of the Homestead armor plant. The information at this stage had been unspecific. That day, after discussing the matter with Curry and Schwab, Frick sent a telegram to Herbert, in which, without specifying the business, he asked for an interview on the following Tuesday. On the Saturday, he wrote to Schwab:

> Would say that I cannot too forcibly impress on you the importance of not permitting the heads of your departments there, or any employee under them, to do anything that would even look like slighting work that we turn out for the Government, and I trust you will give this matter your close personal attention and see that all matters and things in connection with armor are done strictly in accordance with specifications in our contracts with the Government.

He suggested Schwab should ask the government inspectors to be on the alert for reported carelessness in manufacture—which was indeed their normal responsibility. After this, bearing in mind the frequent "plots" against both himself and the company since the Homestead strike, he decided to lie low and "see how the matter would work out." Thinking he had now done all that he could, he wrote to Herbert again, this time withdrawing his request for an appointment but renewing the invitation for him to visit their works.[61]

The company learned more, which confirmed that an attempt at black-mail was underway, but when called to appear before Herbert in early December Frick was "surprised" to learn that "we had been tried, found guilty and sentenced on specific charges of deviation from the contract." He rebut-ted the accusations concerning blowholes, the retreatment of pieces selected for physical test, and the treatment of plates chosen for ballistic tests after their selection, in much the way that Schwab was to have the opportunity to do more fully before the Naval Affairs Committee. Frick invited examina-tion of their plant, their methods and product, and comparison with any armor plant in the world. At the same time he explained to Herbert the likelihood of divergence between theory and practice, in a large and new undertaking, and placed the responsibility firmly with individuals within the company—an interesting, if dangerous, doctrine of corporate innocence:

> It must be obvious to any mind sufficiently broad to comprehend the nature and scope of our business that when the responsible and controlling officers of a Company employing as many thousand men as we do, have conscientiously acquitted themselves of their personal and official obligations to their custom-ers by the most careful selection of the best materials, the purchase and erection of the most improved and expensive machinery and plant, the promulgation of the most rigid rules looking to uniform practice and results, that we are to a large extent, if not wholly, dependent on the good faith and honor of our employees to see that the ends are accomplished for which the means have been thus carefully and liberally provided.

Four months later, as invited, Herbert paid a visit to Homestead. Before he did so, Frick sent him further evidence of the link between the suspicion and bitterness left by the strike and the present scandal. He included a copy of a confidential letter from John A. Wiley who had commanded the Third Brigade during their occupation of the Homestead area. It concerned Cap-tain O. C. Coon, a man Herbert was reported to be planning to see. Coon had spoken up on behalf of the Amalgamated Association and given evi-dence at the trials of the strikers. He was someone, Frick wrote, "whose reputation, I assure you, is not of the best, and who would go very far out of his way to do us an injury. . . . It is important that you should know the character of the men who make statements to you regarding matters at Homestead."[62]

Well before this, Frick had begun to seek out the truth from the personnel in the works. He sent Schwab the memorandum of charges he had received from the Secretary of the Navy. In turn, Schwab explained that the men who had made the accusations had come in to their employment during the Homestead strike but had been disappointed in their hopes of securing positions "that would pay enormous wages." There was another reason for their discontent. They had been under the supervision of William Ellis Corey's chief assistant, W. A. Cline, who, as Schwab put it, "is very strict and hard on men and very unpopular on that account." Three months later, it was reported in the *Pittsburgh Dispatch* that Schwab had offered his resignation over the armor issue. A little later, Schwab referred to the possibility of retiring from Homestead and asked in the meantime for two months to "run these works in my own way."[63] He stayed on, but others were not so fortunate.

It seems incontrovertible that, in the weeding out of their workforce during this crisis in their affairs, Schwab was cautious, seeking to defend his men against precipitate dismissal; Frick, on the other hand, was inflexible. Late in March 1894, Millard Hunsiker ordered the discharge of a man named Buck from the plate mill testing laboratory. Buck had approached an attorney with evidence that he had received orders from Leo Bullion (in charge of the 119-inch plate mill) and from Packer (a clerk in that mill) that certain plates for commercial buyers "must pass." Schwab delayed Buck's dismissal and reported that Buck also had "records of private tests on Government ship plate, and final test on Government ship plate, which show marked differences." Schwab thought Buck was unaware that he was to be discharged and had not given the details of the tests on government material to the attorney. He asked for Frick's instructions. His letter was delivered by his personal assistant, Reinhardt. Frick wrote a note on it: "Told Schwab to carry out Hunsiker's instructions."[64]

The next step was to deal with Bullion. On 30 March 1894, Schwab wrote him to ask for his immediate resignation from the plate mill. Having worked in various departments of the Carnegie enterprises for twenty or twenty-one years, Bullion was surprised by the abruptness of this request. On the following Tuesday, he was informed by Schwab of the reasons. The main charge was irregularity in the preparation of test plates—other than armor plates, which, as Bullion explained to Frick, had always been in the hands of Corey, superintendent of the armor mill. Two other grounds given for his dismissal were that he had not served a regular mechanical course and that he lacked executive ability, which in turn led to claims from Lauder and Frick that he had failed wherever he had been employed.[65] That he had been appointed to superintend the plate mill would indicate that, although they must have been known, these further grounds for dismissal had not previously been thought important, and that he had proved his ability and his suitability for his post. He admitted there had been irregularities since the 119-inch mill began operations in 1887, but he accused his previous assistant of getting even with him by fabricating charges against him. He also demonstrated how easily the test machine could be given an extra slight pressure to ensure that a piece was accepted. Tests of government plates had sometimes been rigged. He asked to be transferred to another department. Schwab, in a covering note, remarked to Frick that Bullion had an exceedingly good record during all their difficulties, notably in restarting after the Homestead strike. He recommended him "to your kindest consideration."[66]

Frick was unbending. Two days later he wrote angrily to Schwab:

> It seems to be very difficult to get anything into your head, or to have you follow out instructions as given you. I told you that I wanted Mr. Bullion's services dispensed with. You assured me last Saturday that he would go at once. . . . I find that Mr. Bullion is still in charge of the 119″ mill. I shall expect prompt action on your part in this matter, on receipt of this.

Schwab had the courage to make an immediate response to what he recognized as severe criticism of his own conduct. He pointed out that he had replaced Bullion but had asked him to remain during that week so as to give his successor all necessary information about the department. He stood firm: "Inasmuch as you expressed no special desire that very great haste be made, I think the matter received the most prompt attention possible, and I fail to recall any instances in which instructions given me were not promptly carried out."[67]

The effects of the armor scandal lingered. Even Andrew Carnegie was deflated. By September that year, he was "sanguine that we are now entering upon smooth waters and will make a splendid record for years ahead. The only weak department is the armor department, which may have to close." A few days later, Frick reported, "this armor mess handicaps us in many ways, as the Navy Dept. are anything but friendly to Schwab and have no confidence in him." At the year's end, Frick again displayed prejudice against Schwab, quoting remarks made in a letter from Hunsiker, with sarcasm that provides eloquent testimony of the tensions then lying below the surface of their organization:

> Please say to Mr. Schwab, if the trial shield plates have not been shipped to Indian Head yet, to send down to my room and get my Austrian rifle, with some of the ammunition and shoot at the plates himself or have Curtis [the Navy Department's inspector at Homestead] do it. He can tell then about what they will do. Perhaps he might want to machine them over.[68]

After this, Frick now and then still remarked about the excellence of Schwab's conduct of their affairs and Schwab expressed admiration of Frick's qualities, but the sharp divide between the two men in temperament and business methods had been clearly demonstrated. Within little more than two years, Schwab had achieved a power and influence within Carnegie Steel at least equal to Frick's.

Organizing Mineral Supply

In the course of the 1890s, the Carnegie Steel Company became the world's largest iron- and steelmaking concern. It was also probably the most efficient. The remarkable success obtained in both expansion and in cost saving required unremitting attention to market opportunities, readiness to install the newest, most productive plant, and care to reap the economies of integration. The latter required investment in blast furnace capacity to match the extension in mills, converter plant, and melting shops and (moving still further upstream) the development of matching capacity to produce and to deliver necessary minerals to the furnace stockyards. In the ten years that Frick was chairman of Carnegie, Phipps, and Company and then of Carnegie Steel, the steel production of the Carnegie plants increased by almost 400 percent. In April 1892 Edgar Thomson, Homestead, and Duquesne produced at an annual rate of 971,000 tons; their March 1898 production represented an annual output of 2,892,000 tons. Over the same period, the output of the blast furnaces of Edgar Thomson and Lucy increased from only 743,000 to 1,159,000 tons, but the company also built furnaces at Duquesne and bought the Carrie furnaces. Together these added another 1,070,000 tons of iron production.[69]

Large additional supplies of minerals had to be made available—for every ton of iron about 2 tons of ore and 0.8 tons of coke were now required in Carnegie Steel practice. For fuel, their controlling interest in the H. C. Frick Coke Company and its large-scale extension of existing plants or acquisition of new ones ensured that there would be no problem in supplying the tonnages required. The difficulties there would be confined to prices and conditions of production. Limestone could easily be obtained not far from Pittsburgh; the tonnages involved made limestone a secondary consideration that, however, was not too small to escape Frick's attention. When he met with Jay Morse in 1890, he learned that Illinois Steel's supplies of limestone were delivered to their stock houses, already crushed, for only 90 cents a ton. In July 1890 he wrote to Carnegie, "We must look into the matter, and see whether we cannot make a permanent arrangement with the owners of limestone quarries on the Juniata for crushed limestone and also 5 or 10 year arrangement with the Pennsylvania Railroad on freight on limestone."[70]

IRON ORE

Iron ore presented more serious problems. The tonnages involved were large, and the sources of high-grade Bessemer ore limited in area. The iron ranges of Lake Superior were up to a thousand miles distant by a route involving two rail journeys and a long lake haul, yet it was this source that had to be organized as the main supply for their furnaces. In this decade, although a slow starter, Carnegie Steel came to occupy a dominating position in Upper Lakes ore. The role of Frick in this achievement has been disputed. Some (Bridge, for instance) have suggested that Carnegie had to be cajoled into taking large interests and that Frick was the active agent in their progress on this front; others, though not making Carnegie a pioneer, have found Frick also often ambivalent about the ore trade (Wall illustrates this from the early 1890s).

The Marquette range in Michigan had been opened as early as the mid 1850s. By 1880 almost one-quarter of U.S. ore production came from the Upper Lakes states, but 52.7 percent was still supplied from mines in New York, New Jersey, and Pennsylvania. Over the next ten years there was a dramatic change. The mines of Menominee (south of Marquette) and of Gogebic (straddling the Michigan-Wisconsin border) were brought into production. Minnesota production began with operations on the Vermilion range. By 1890 the relative positions of the Upper and Lower Lakes districts had already been roughly reversed: New York, New Jersey, and Pennsylvania produced 19.4 percent of a much increased national total, whereas Michigan, Wisconsin, and Minnesota now supplied 56.1 percent. Within another decade, the share of the three eastern states was more than halved (to 9.3 percent), whereas the Upper Lakes now mined 64.7 percent of the national total. Most of this growth had been in Minnesota and above all in the newly opened Mesabi range.

The iron firms of the Great Lakes–Ohio River belt had for a long time bought their Lake ore through merchants, but in the 1890s, as scales of production in pig iron increased and competition became keener, they began to acquire mines and in some instances to organize ore delivery through their own railroads and lake carriers. There was a strong drive to improve the efficiency of the ore trade. As a result, by the second half of the 1890s, the largest ore carriers on the Great Lakes were already five times the level of twenty-five years earlier; loading times were three hours whereas they had been two days; and rail and lake freights were about one-quarter and one-eighth respectively of the levels that had then obtained. Ore was now sold at Lake Erie ports for $1 a ton less than it had then cost to mine it on the range itself; the price of steel rails was now no higher than had then been charged for one ton of ore delivered in Pittsburgh. The ore trade expert John Birkibine graphically summed up one major aspect of the changes that had occurred over a longer period: "At the present time the ore supply is a local consideration for but a small proportion of American blast furnaces, and 700 miles or more separate a greater number from the mines producing the ore in 1897 than was supplied in 1857 with ore carried 50 miles."[71] The costs of mining and delivery to the Lower Lakes were now being cut even below the most sanguine expectations of only a few years before (see table 18). As the largest and most cost-conscious firm, Carnegie Steel was closely involved in this process.

Carnegie had an early, unhappy involvement in Lake ore, with the mine that his partner Andrew Kloman had owned on the Marquette range in the 1870s. Kloman's unwise investments there brought him to bankruptcy, and Carnegie had to help rescue him. In 1880, after eight years, Carnegie at last freed himself from these entanglements. This experience must in part explain his subsequent caution about ore investments in that region. Frick had no similar memories to condition his responses. On 2 July 1890, he left Pittsburgh to join up with Jay Morse for a journey to the Upper Lakes mines. His most vivid impression from that tour was of their disorganized state rather than of their natural riches. He wrote to Carnegie in July: "I arrived back from the North West Monday morning. Had a very enjoyable and interesting trip. Visited the Menominee range; examined the Chapin, Ludington, Hamilton and other mines there including Pewabic. Was not favorably impressed by the management of any of them." Men were not plentiful and were "very independent." In both respects the labor situation must have seemed to him very different from and less satisfactory than that in the coke region. In April 1891, he reported to Morse on negotiations with ore companies. Mark Hanna had been in Pittsburgh, offering Chapin ore from the Vermilion range for $4.50. Frick reported he had told Hanna he thought they would be able to get it for $3.55, although "of course, we would not expect it quite so low, and intimated that we might pay $3.75." They would not, he assured Morse two days later, make any arrangements with the people from Norrie mine before first advising him.[72]

Next year, 1892, brought the most important development of all, the opening of Mesabi. In a number of important respects, Mesabi differed from the other ranges. Their production was derived from mines containing hard ore; the Mesabi range contained a large number of various-sized surface pockets of ore that was in a loose, often powdery, condition. This meant that although the ore was more easily worked in open pit operations, when

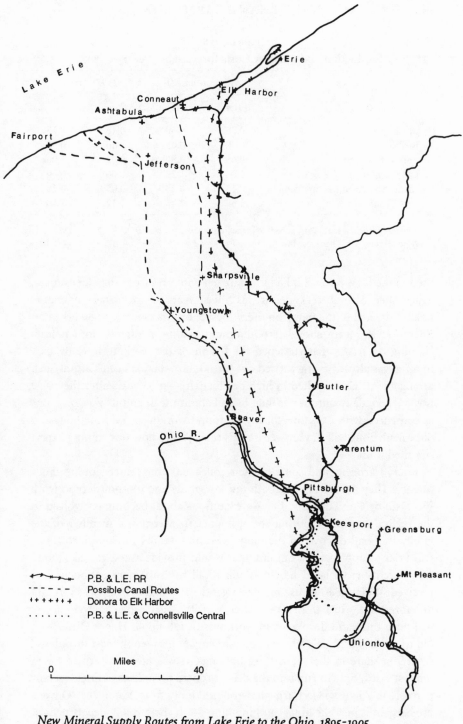

Lake Erie

Erie

Elk Harbor

Conneaut

Ashtabula

Fairport

L

Jefferson

Sharpsville

Youngstown

Butler

Beaver

Ohio R.

Tarentum

Pittsburgh

Keesport

Greensburg

Mt Pleasant

+—+—+—+—+ P.B. & L.E. RR
– – – – – Possible Canal Routes
+ + + + + + Donora to Elk Harbor
. . . . . . P.B. & L.E. & Connellsville Central

Miles

0   40

Uniontown

New Mineral Supply Routes from Lake Erie to the Ohio, 1895-1905

TABLE 18

Production and Delivery Costs for Mesabi Ore, 1892, 1897

	1892 (Estimated)		1897 (Actual)	
	From	To	From	To
Mining costs	0.25	0.50	0.15	0.75
Royalty	0.50	0.65	nil	0.35
Rail to lakehead	0.65	0.80	0.32	1.00
Lake freight to Lake Erie	1.00	1.25	0.60	0.80
Insurance, commission, loss	0.15	0.25	0.05	0.20
Total	2.55	3.45	1.12	3.10

Sources: Winchell 1892–1893, p. 686; Winchell 1896–1897, p. 545.
Note: Figures are dollars per ton.

used in the blast furnace it had to be mixed with ores from the older ranges. Much later, Schwab reckoned it was fifteen years before furnace operators finally adjusted to the new iron ore.[73] Mesabi ore was soon being worked on a large scale, steam shovels scooping and loading it directly into railcars running on tracks that stretched the length of the working face. By 1896 mining was already being carried out for no more than 20 cents a ton. Such arrangements also resulted in high productivity—nine years after the range was opened, daily output per man in and about the open pits was 21.53 tons as compared with 4.69 tons for underground workings. "Old methods and old calculations will not answer on this range," was how one mining expert summed it up.[74]

Frick, Carnegie, and some of their colleagues entertained doubts about Mesabi. They thought its ore both too low-grade and too powdery to work successfully. Consequently they were cautious about becoming involved in the region. Sometime during spring 1891, Lon Merritt—a member of the family that had discovered the range's wealth—visited Pittsburgh to try to win Frick's support for a rail link that would provide access to Lake Superior. Twenty years later, he could still recall the sort of reception he had received: "Frick did not use me like a gentleman, and cut me off short and bulldozed me." Just over a year after Merritt's visit, when railroad access had been built and development work was in full flood, Henry Oliver—an old friend of Carnegie's who had investments of his own in blast furnaces—secured a share in the Merritt ore holdings. It was now his turn to try to interest Frick, only to run into the deeper rooted prejudices of Frick's senior partner. In August 1892 Carnegie wrote unkindly from Rannoch: "Oliver's ore bargain is just like him—nothing in it. . . . If there is any department of

business that offers no inducement it is ore. It never has been very profitable, and the Mesabi is not the last great deposit that Lake Superior is to
reveal."[75]

In the last point he was wrong; his more general conviction that ore was
not a profitable investment ignored the wider contribution that its assured
supply could make to the efficiency and long-term security of operations on
the major scale now reached by Carnegie Steel. By now Frick thought differently. In spring 1894, in return for a loan of half a million dollars to help
him surmount the aftereffects of trade depression, Oliver made over to the
Carnegie Steel Company a half-interest in his mining company. This proved
an excellent bargain for the steel firm, and the Oliver Mining Company
remained one of the firmest foundations for the ensuing success of Carnegie
Steel and of its successor company. Yet for another two years, Carnegie retained his skepticism about further Lake ore investments. In September
1894, writing to Frick, he indicated both a general and a particular prejudice
against involvement:

> If Massawba [*sic*] ore requires special form of furnaces, it will add force to my
> instinctive aversion to making investments hundreds of miles away. These, in
> my opinion, are all wrong. The ore mining business is a business by itself, and
> ten dollars can be made at home to any one that you can make in these outside
> ventures. Two furnaces at Duquesne will beat all the money you will ever make
> elsewhere.

Given Carnegie's usual astuteness, it is strange he did not recognize that the
very extension in their iron capacity represented by the Duquesne furnaces
made it even more desirable to control a larger part of their own mineral
supply. Yet, although Frick had been more open to Oliver's persuasion than
Carnegie, he too was still cautious (and not as constantly concerned to extend their ore holdings as Harvey, for instance, makes out). Thus, when in
January 1893 C. A. Turner of St. Paul, Minnesota, wrote him about ore mining projects, Frick at once poured cold water on the idea: "Would say that
we have had the new Mesabi Iron Range very thoroughly examined and it
is certainly a wonderful deposit of ore. We, however, are not in the market
for any ore mines in any district whatever." He found it difficult to keep up
with what was happening in the ore districts. In summer 1895, he again
traveled in the Lake region and informed Carnegie: "Had no idea there was
so much ore mined and in stockpiles as we found."[76]

Meanwhile Carnegie's hopes for their future supply had turned for a
short period in another direction. In 1895 he set in train an examination of
what he was led to believe were "unlimited" supplies of ore in the Appala-

chians in northwestern Virginia. They were said to be suitable for concentration to a burden containing 55 percent iron and were located near White
Sulphur Springs, just across the West Virginia state line, west of Covington.
From there they could be delivered to Pittsburgh for less than the company
was then paying for haulage from Lake Erie. This rosy prospect proved a
chimera, and although he took an interest in prospects for Cuban ore purchases, Carnegie was finally compelled to acknowledge they must look to
Lake ore: "I am disappointed at the result in Virginia so far, but it was well
worth knowing just what was there. Lake Superior, after all, is to be our
source of supply."[77] There they were brought into potential conflict and
eventually to cooperation with another great business group.

In 1894 J. D. Rockefeller bought a major share in the Merritts' ore mines,
railroad, and docks under the title of the Lake Superior Consolidated Iron
Mines Company. During the first ten months of 1896, he had twelve large
ore carriers built on the Great Lakes and purchased another four to create
the Bessemer Steamship Company. The two moves gave him, at a cost of
$3.4 million, the capacity to carry two million tons of ore down the lakes in
each navigation season. Before this new ore fleet had been completed, Oliver
sensed the possibilities presented to Carnegie Steel if it could lease the
Rockefeller mines, railroads, and boats, and he began negotiations to that
end. This time Carnegie gave his support, even to the extent of proposing
to Rockefeller that they meet to sort out any difficulties: "I believe you and
I could fix it in a few minutes." By the beginning of December, an agreement was ready for completion. It provided for a fifty-year arrangement,
under which Carnegie Steel was to lease all the Consolidated ore, paying 25
cents royalty on each ton extracted. The steel company was to guarantee to
take 600,000 tons each year, and to ensure that an equal tonnage from Oliver mines was shipped over Rockefeller's railroads and in his steamships to
the Lower Lakes. Frick was cautious about the arrangement, at the board
meeting of 3 November going so far as to say: "I would not favor the proposition as made." On 4 and 5 December, Carnegie wrote him about the
scheme, with which he was generally happy, although he had reservations
about a so-called gold clause, a requirement that they pay in gold, something
Rockefeller insisted on as there was a threat at this time of introduction of a
silver standard as advocated in William Jennings Bryan's presidential campaign. (Hendrick wrongly implies that the reservations on the gold clause
were Frick's rather than Carnegie's.) On 12 December, Frick reported:
"Board approved Rockefeller lease today, subject to your approval of payment of royalty in gold."[78]

The result of the arrangement with Rockefeller was to confirm Carnegie

Steel's unrivaled leadership in the industry. A month after the deal, the *Engineering and Mining Journal* recognized how momentous the consequences were: "This company is not only in a position to make steel cheaper than any other producer; it is so situated as to be absolutely in control of the market, and make the price of steel what it will. . . . The situation is not altogether a comfortable one, and many are looking anxiously for the result." *Iron Age* was more circumspect, recognizing that years of further work and large investments would be required before such an outcome could be achieved. A more immediate result was that Carnegie Steel decided to go still further in controlling Lake ore. Even before the Rockefeller bargain was finalized, Frick had sent Carnegie costings in connection with a possible lease of the Norrie mine on the Gogebic range. Including royalty, the cost of mining there was about $1.25 per ton or probably less. Charges for delivery to Lower Lake ports would be $1.23 and carriage from Lake Erie to Pittsburgh another 70 cents. With 25 cents to the Norrie people this would give them a ton of 57 percent iron ore for $3.43, or 6 cents per iron unit: "Cost of Mesabi on Rockefeller lease, 5 cents per unit—using half each, we have a unit cost of 5½ cents. The Norrie Mine is capable of producing 1 million tons per annum."[79]

The prospects of other producers were obviously worsened by the Carnegie-Rockefeller agreement, and depression in iron and a wider shrinkage in the ore trade soon gave Oliver the opportunity to take the initiative yet again. In July 1897 he wrote to Frick, "We simply knocked the price of ore from $4.00 down to say $2.50 per ton. Now let us take advantage of our action before a season of good times gives the ore producers strength and opportunity to get together by combination." Oliver suggested they should obtain control of the Norrie and Tilden mines in the Gogebic range and Pioneer mine on Vermilion, with a combined annual production capacity of 1.6 million tons. Only Norrie would involve purchase. On this last point Carnegie demurred, repeating once more his old conviction that they could make greater savings by spending an equivalent amount on improving their manufacturing plant. Although he too thought Oliver had been unwise to threaten their credit in this way, Frick eventually came up with the idea of offering Norrie stock to Rockefeller and then leasing it back, as with the Lake Superior Consolidated Iron Mines, but this time Rockefeller refused to cooperate. The danger that they would lose their bargain was averted at the last minute when Carnegie, Frick, and with them the whole Carnegie board, approved purchase of the Norrie mines. Now, at last, Carnegie was willing to revise his cautious approach to the extension of their ore resources. Less than two weeks after they had acquired Norrie, he admitted to Frick, "I am happy that we are now secure in our ore supply; it was the only element needed to give us an impregnable position." Within another year, Oliver had purchased the Pioneer mine. In 1899 he added still more ore properties. As a result of these developments, Carnegie Steel was now wholly independent of the open market for Bessemer grade iron ore. In 1899 it shipped 3.5 million tons of ore down the lakes.[80]

The evidence suggests that neither Carnegie nor Frick was consistently positive in his efforts to secure ore supplies. Carnegie later wrote a memorandum stating that it was when he and others went with Oliver to the Upper Lakes mines that they were convinced about the wisdom of ore purchases there. There seems to be no evidence of such a sudden conversion. On the other hand, Harvey wrote of Oliver and Frick as "still persisting in the face of constant discouragement," and of "the far-seeing Frick and the indomitable Oliver." This too simplistically links Frick to a man who was indeed more consistently hawkish. When the ore supply situation was at last satisfactorily arranged, it was necessary to build up the system for the effective delivery of the ore to Pittsburgh. There it connected with their established coke supply.[81]

CHANGES IN THE COKE REGION

In 1890, the United States had first produced more iron than the United Kingdom. Over the next ten years, American output went up by a further 50 percent. The 1900 iron output, at 14 million tons, was almost three and a half times the tonnage of the year Frick and Carnegie first met. In the 1890s, production of pig iron using charcoal, anthracite, or mixed charges of anthracite and coke fell by nearly 27 percent, and production of coke iron (including very small tonnages made using raw coal) went up by 83.6 percent. Although there was a significant reduction in the coke rate (the amount of coke used per ton of iron made), a great increase occurred in the tonnages of coke used. Connellsville still supplied most of the demand, and within that coke district, the H. C. Frick Coke Company became ever more dominant. Even so, there were signs of changes to come.

By-product coke ovens, for many years prominent in continental Europe, in the early 1890s were first used in the United States. The first came into production at Syracuse in the early part of the decade and was built not to feed the ironworks but to supply the needs of the new American soda ash industry. The first steel company to install this type of oven was Cambria in 1895. For long the impact of the new technology was small—by 1900, only 12.2 percent of the increase of 8.2 million tons over the level of 1890 had come from by-product ovens. There was expanding production of beehive coke in West Virginia and Alabama and to a lesser extent other states of the Appalachian plateau, but Pennsylvania remained far ahead, its southwest corner now the world's leading coke district. In this region, production was extending into sections neighboring the old Connellsville core area, to Upper Connellsville (to the north around Latrobe) and to the Lower Connellsville area (further to the southwest). Together, Lower Connellsville and Connellsville "proper" more than doubled their already huge output of coke between 1894 and 1899. In the former year, this small tract of mineral land shipped 54.2 percent of all the coke made in the United States; in the latter year, 51.5 percent. The increase of over five million tons came from new coke works and from large extensions made to existing plants. H. C. Frick Coke was deeply involved in the expansion of capacity but stubbornly refused to countenance installation of the new-style ovens (see table 19).

H. C. Frick Coke continued to purchase other coke companies, although the rate varied with the state of trade; there was a falling away of acquisitions in 1893 and 1894 and a strong revival in 1895. During the great iron expansion of the remainder of the decade, interest in coke extensions again increased. In 1890 H. C. Frick Coke bought the coal lands of the J. A. Strickler Coke Company and half the stock of the much bigger properties of the Hostetter-Connellsville Coke Company. There was a flurry of activity in 1895, when they purchased the Youngstown Coke Company and then spent $3 million to acquire McClure Coke. In 1899 they obtained the remaining half of the capital of the Calumet Coke Company. A few days before these last properties were bought for $185,000, Lynch estimated the value of the H. C. Frick Coke Company at over $45 million; Frick's own figure at the same time was $40 million. That year, the estimated net earnings of the company and of its associated concerns were $4.6 millions. H. C. Frick Coke Company paid $2.4 million in dividends; a further $225,000 was paid by Union Supply Company, the rates of dividend on capital for the two companies being 24 percent and 300 percent respectively. Although Carnegie Steel controlled most of the coke company's capital and Thomas Lynch was now its chief executive officer, H. C. Frick Coke still remained the apple of Frick's business eye, and he could not bear to have it criticized. Schwab, for instance, recalled an occasion when James Gayley complained that the coke had so shaken down in the gondola cars that he was not getting full measure at the blast furnaces. "Frick flew up in a tantrum and almost frothed at the mouth he was so enraged to think anyone would say a word about his Coke Company."[82]

Labor relations in the coalfield remained a source of difficulty, although from the mid 1890s rates of pay were increased. Two disputes of the earlier

TABLE 19
The Coke Industry, 1890, 1895, 1900

	1890	1895	1900
Production of Coke			
Beehive	11,508	13,315	19,458
By-product	nil	18	1,076
Tonnage of Coal Used in Beehive Ovens by District			
Connellsville	9,748	12,174	14,947
Lower Connellsville	neg.[a]	neg.	580
Upper Connellsville	889	319	1,042
Other Western Pennsylvania	1,353	970	2,329
West Virginia "Mon" Valley	276	392	584
Other Districts	6,628	7,312	13,673

Sources: Eavenson 1939; Bureau of Mines, *Mineral Resources of the United States.*
Note: Figures are in thousand net tons.
[a] "negligible"

part of the decade are worth brief attention, for they show how slowly things improved. The first, as Homestead did, highlighted the different approach to labor relations on the part of Carnegie and Frick. The second showed how Frick's immovability in labor disputes was matched by his deep loyalty to those who had served him well.

COKE STRIKES IN 1891 AND 1894

The strike of 1891 lasted from February to May and cost over one million tons of coke production. Carnegie advocated his own approach to the problem. In this he showed greater psychological insight than Frick, though not necessarily more real sympathy with their men. As always, he suggested a wait-and-see approach, and a willingness to make workers think that their ideas were being adopted. The methods of taking time, allowing desperation to build on the part of the employees and their families, and an apparent willingness for conciliation on the part of management seemed to him, then as in other disputes, better than blank confrontation. Rather than present an ultimatum, he would wait, realizing that this would put more pressure on the striker. As he wrote in March:

> To announce terms and try to start ovens is a very serious step to take. It should be postponed until the last day possible, as every day's idleness will render starting easier. I should not think of making a move this month. Cannot Lynch get some of the men to *suggest a sliding scale* and *you offer in compliance with*

the request? This is the shape to get it in, and I think that Lynch could lead up to that subject and get enough from the men to base your action upon. I do not like the idea of you thrusting it upon them. It would show too clearly your desire to start.

Less than two weeks after this (as at Homestead the following year), events on the spot changed industrial disagreement about labor policy from private correspondence to the stark realities of violence, damage to property, bloodshed, and notorious publicity. On 2 April 1891, a report on the dispute was sent to H. B. Tate, the Private Secretary in the Executive Chamber in Harrisburg. Even though a state government report, it conveys a vivid sense of the anarchy prevailing:

> The rioters marched on Morewood last night and Clawson's deputies met them, result seven strikers dead and several wounded; one of the clerks in the office at Morewood reports they got information that they were to be attacked from three points and the deputies were divided into three squads; one stationed at the barn under Loar; the crowd passed the store and threw stones into the windows but they were allowed to pass on unmolested; they then went to gate leading into the barn and were breaking it down. Loar commanded them to halt, their response to his command was to fire on them. He then ordered his men to fire with the result above stated; it is said, however they fired twice before the rioters dispersed. The crowd numbered about 450 and left Standard at 2.50 AM and before leaving broke down the telephone so that Morewood could not be communicated with, but the Standard men fixed up the line and notified Morewood of the movements of the mob.

Frick learned of the tragic turn of events at Morewood from a telegram delivered to his home at about 7 A.M. that morning. One and a half hours later, he sent a copy of it to Jay Morse as head of one of the joint owners of South West Coal and Coke. He added a brief but remarkable note: "I have no further particulars. This will likely have a good effect on the riotous element up there." Carnegie too recognized that these events had changed the situation in the coke region, but he still would not concede that his approach could be bettered:

> It is probable the Fabian policy would have been better had Lynch not acted in pushing scale but now we have to go ahead to the end. My idea of treating in a dispute with men is always to shut down and suffer, let them decide by vote when they desire to go to work—say kindly, "All right gentlemen, let's hear from you, no quarrel, not the least in the world. Until a majority vote (secret ballot) to go to work have a good time—when a majority vote to start, start it is." Such an approach will mean no long stoppages and not much ill feeling. We did it at Edgar Thomson *but* Abbott failed at Homestead and *we* have lost ground to recover.

Mention of Abbott's "failure" proved to have been sadly prophetic of the next major occasion and place of the difference of Carnegie's and Frick's approaches to labor disputes.[83]

Three years after the Morewood incident, another coke strike brought with it what the *Connellsville Courier* called a "reign of terror." Striking coke workers were "marching" to and fro in mobs of between five hundred and a thousand. On Tuesday morning, 3 April 1894, the works at Trotter, Leith, Youngstown, Kyle, Elm Grove, Juniata, Paul, Fort Hill, and Rainey were all visited by groups of between two hundred and six hundred strikers. By Thursday, 5 April, the men who had remained at work had been so intimidated by these roving bands that, in the center of the coke field from Scottdale to Fairchance, only three plants were still in operation. On the previous day, the men had walked from Adelaide, crossed the river at Broad Ford, driven the men from their jobs at Henry Clay, and then set out southeastward toward Davidson. There, a shot or a stone brought down the chief engineer of the H. C. Frick Coke Company, Joseph H. Paddock, who was then beaten by clubs and stones until he was dead. More than twenty years later, Frick was to remember the costly loyalty of his chief engineer and act to help his son. In the meantime, only weeks after Paddock's death, Frick showed how much he appreciated another of his leading officials, the general superintendent. He wrote to William Ramsay at Mount Pleasant:

> It would seem that by the judicious expenditure of even a considerable amount of money you ought to be able to reach out to some of the leading Hungarians, or others, and get them to make a break looking toward the resumption of work. Do not hesitate to spend some money if that will accomplish a decided break. Of course the money would better be not expended, or payable rather, until the goods are delivered. There is not anything in running coke works at present, yet it is annoying to see our trade going to some of our competitors, and to other coke districts. I congratulate you, however, on doing remarkably well so far.[84]

CHANGES IN COKE TECHNOLOGY

As indicated above, the question of technological change in coke making became a lively issue in the 1890s. Slot ovens had replaced the old beehives in continental Europe because their narrow dimensions made it possible to coke the inferior coking coals that predominated there. A major additional benefit was gained in the form of chemicals extracted in recovery plants that were increasingly and soon invariably attached to the new batteries of slot-type oven—hence the common name, by-product oven. An abundance of excellent coking coals and a lesser need to use coal derivatives for fertilizers, dyes, or tar, or to burn oven gas in industrial regions that could easily pipe in natural gas were the considerations that largely explained the much delayed switch to the new technology in the United States. However, by the 1890s, by-product coking was becoming increasingly attractive. The weight and prestige of the H. C. Frick Coke Company was thrown into the balance against the new technology.

In his chairmanship of Carnegie Steel, Frick usually proved ready to support innovation. His frequent approvals of Schwab's proposals for spending at Homestead from autumn 1892 onward are indicative of this. He also proved to be more open-minded than most of his colleagues about locational change in steel. But by contrast, in relation to by-product ovens, he was decidedly conservative. Time and again he gave short shrift to proposals for trying them. His refusal to entertain such suggestions indicated a lack of appreciation of their technical superiority; much more likely it reflected his recognition that advance of the new process would lead to the wholesale depreciation of the exceptional asset of Connellsville coking coal. Such ovens could operate with inferior coals; the opening of poorer coking coals would in turn encourage the establishment of more of the new-style ovens in areas far from the coke region. The common result would be a devaluation of both coal lands and the many thousands of beehive ovens that depended on them in the Connellsville district.

The special qualities of Connellsville coal were universally recognized and praised. Lynch summarized them well in a memorandum of summer 1899. He pointed out, apparently for their steel associates, that the coal was remarkably soft and free from faults. No machinery or powder was needed in its extraction. As a result, though H. C. Frick Coke was then paying the highest wages ever paid in the region, mining costs were as low as 25 cents per net ton, below the cost anywhere else. The coal was still charged directly into the ovens with no screening, crushing, or washing; the coke they drew from the ovens was unequaled in chemical composition, hardness, and cell structure. Apart from the purity of the coal and the quality of the coke, the other factor contributing to the high value of Connellsville coal lands was their limited extent. At the current rate of coke consumption, the 55,000 acres of coal (of which H. C. Frick Coke owned about 73 percent) would be used up in fifty years. If, as in the past, rates of consumption increased, the life expectancy of the field would be shortened but its value would increase still further. Lynch was convinced that, either way, the result would be favorable: "Therefore I conclude, from the foregoing facts, that the value of Connellsville coal will continue to increase as surely as effect follows cause." At the present price fob at the ovens ($1.50 per ton), he reckoned that each acre yielded a profit—over and above interest, taxes, and so on—of $3,500. If only that price was maintained, the coal lands they owned represented a prospective income of $140 million.[85] In making these calculations, however, Lynch did not allow for the advance of the by-product oven, a development that came between the cause and effect of which he wrote. Frick's sustained hostility to the new process may have owed something to his realization that it would undermine Connellsville's position, as well as his doubts about its economic viability.

By-product coking required a larger capital outlay than beehive coking; on the other hand, it not only made possible the use of coals of inferior quality but increased the ratio of the tonnage of coke turned out to that of coal charged and also yielded revenue from the sale of by-products. (Apart from the private saving this represented, there was an immediate social benefit in the form of a cleaner environment as well as a wider gain to future generations in the reduced rate of resource depletion. However, this does not appear to have been a consideration of any moment at that time.) In spite of these well-known and frequently costed savings, time and again from the 1880s until the end of his direct association with Connellsville coke in 1900, Frick refused to countenance not only their introduction but even any experimentation with the new ovens. He was willing to sanction capital spending to improve beehive operations for this would reduce operating costs, but his face was set against a process that would lead to the writing off of the huge capital assets tied up in the old technology. Various suggestions were made to him that pilot plants should be built to demonstrate the pros and cons of the by-product oven, and he even had reports from senior staff on installations made by others, both in Europe and in the United States. He would go no further. However, after the turn of the century, he witnessed the uneven but inexorable advance of this new technology, and in the last years of his life, he had to recognize that it could no longer be rationally fought.

Through the 1890s, H. C. Frick Coke remained preeminent among coke firms, although the company's expansion was less spectacular than in the 1880s. In January 1900, the coke works of the Connellsville district contained 18,992 ovens, of which H. C. Frick Coke owned 10,166 as well as handling sale of the product for a number of other, smaller concerns. Altogether well over three-quarters of the region's coke trade was under the company's direction. Less than seventeen years before, Frick had reported to Carnegie that his company controlled "but one-tenth of the 10,100 ovens" in the district. The situation had been transformed by the vigor with which he had followed out his own commission from that time: "we must do something toward securing new properties."[86]

In coke as in iron ore, the prime motive for the acquisition of raw materials was to gain ample assured supplies at competitive prices amid all the uncertainties of the markets. The connection with H. C. Frick Coke undoubtedly helped Carnegie Steel in all these respects, and (as in steel so in coke) the associated properties were examples of the best practice of their kind. In summer 1898, Schwab led a visit of inspection to the coke region. His report to the board of managers was highly appreciative. It spoke of "the cleanliness and excellent condition of the mines" and concluded that, "The operations of coke making, while comparatively simple as compared with steel, were carried on in an excellent manner, and that above all, the condition and equipment of all the works we visited were model in every respect." Frick was delighted: "I am very much pleased to hear so favorable a report"; he asked that a copy be sent to Lynch "for his information and encouragement."[87]

THE PRICING OF COKE

Carnegie Steel gained from its association with H. C. Frick Coke in the reduced price it paid for coke, although over the 1890s this benefit lessened. When the large capital tied up in coke was taken into account, the advantage was still more reduced. Over the five years from January 1894, the coke company sold Carnegie Steel 7.26 million tons of coke at an average price of $1.42 a ton. Over the same five years, the ordinary market price for Connellsville coke averaged $1.49. Frick had his own men—Bosworth and Keller—go carefully over the H. C. Frick Coke books for a longer period, the ten years from 1 January 1889. Lynch reported they found that the average price realized on all coke sold in that period was $1.66 per ton; the average on all they had shipped to the Carnegie interests was $1.54 (see table 20).[88]

Not only did their investment give Carnegie Steel at least some cost advantages over coke purchasers in general, but in particular against their main western rival, Illinois Steel. Yet, here too, there occurred an erosion of that advantage in the second half of the 1890s. In January 1892, H. C. Frick Coke charged Illinois 9.4 percent more per ton than Carnegie; in July 1894, 35 percent more. Early in 1896, Frick suggested at a Carnegie Steel board meeting that the price at which coke was offered to Illinois Steel should be cut in order to stop them developing the large coal properties they now owned in the coke region. Schwab argued that Carnegie should be supplied at prices at least as low as those quoted to Illinois Steel. At the beginning of

TABLE 20
Price Trends, 1890–1898

| Date | Steel | | Connellsville Coke | H. C. Frick Coke Prices to Carnegie | |
	Rails	Billets			
1890	31.75[a]	30.32[a]	1.94[b]	Jan.–Feb.	1.32[c]
				Mar.–Dec.	1.41
				Jan.–Apr.	1.44
1891	29.92	25.32	1.87	May–Dec.	1.70
				Jan.–Nov.	1.60
1892	30.00	23.63	1.83	Dec.	1.45
				Jan.–Jun.	1.45
				Jul.	1.50
1893	28.12	20.44	1.49	Aug.–Dec.	1.35
				Jan.–Feb.	1.00
				Mar.	1.85
				Apr.–May	1.00
				Jun.–Jul.	1.50
1894	24.00	16.58	1.00	Aug.–Dec.	1.00
				Jan.–Mar.	1.00
				Apr.–Jun.	1.15
				Jul.–Sep.	1.25
1895	24.33	18.48	1.23	Oct.–Dec.	1.30
1896	28.00	18.83	1.90	Jan.–Dec.	1.75
				Jan.–Jul.	1.50
				Aug.–Nov.	1.35
1897	18.75	15.08	1.65	Dec.	1.50
				Jan.–Jun.	1.50
1898	17.62	15.31	1.55	Jul.–Aug.	1.45

Sources: For Rails and billets, Temin 1964, p. 284; for coke prices, Connellsville Courier, quoted in AISA Annual Statistics; for Carnegie prices, Lovejoy to AC, 19 Sept. 1898 (ACLC).
Notes: [a] Figures this column are dollars per gross ton.
[b] Figures this column are average dollar price per net ton.
[c] Figures this column are dollars per net ton.

1897, Frick explained the difficult situation that had resulted in the prices charged to both of them now being identical at $1.50 when most other companies were being charged $1.75: "The Illinois Steel Company worked Virginia coke against us and we had to make the price low." In midsummer, the price for both companies was further reduced to $1.35.[89]

Sometime during the summer of 1897, Carnegie met his most senior colleagues for general discussions of issues connected with the business. Later, he was to claim that they had come to an understanding that coke prices should be fixed at the then current but fairly low level. In August 1898, he wrote about this to Lovejoy, who replied:

> Mr. Frick directs me to say that he does not recall any conversation on the subject of Coke prices, but he has no doubt whatever that he named you $1.35 as the then price. He is confident, however, there was no discussion of the price, and no promise, express or implied, that coke would remain at that figure. On and about August 1897 you, Mr. Phipps, Mr. Lauder and Mr. Frick had several consultations on the subjects of Bonus, Norrie mines, Rockefeller negotiations, improvements at Homestead etc. and it is probable it was during that visit that the question was asked and answered.

Carnegie penciled a note on Lovejoy's reply: "Those of rates all wrong from $1.35 to $1.50." A few days later, in September 1898, he expressed his frustration to Lauder, obviously attributing problems he thought they had over prices to their own president rather than to Frick:

> I cannot understand how Mr. Schwab promised to change the rate of coke from $1.35 to $1.50 without submitting it to the Board. It means $300,000 a year, and if he thinks he is authorized to do such things without discussion in the Board, he takes a different view of his authority from mine. There has been no advance in coke. 4,000 ovens are still idle. We could have bought coke at $1.25. If we had not concurred in the combination we could buy it at 90 cents. It was very liberal in the Steel Co. to give the Coke Co. $1.35. . . . You need not raise the question, however until we meet in Pittsburgh.

He reckoned that Illinois Steel could get coke at $1 from its own ovens: "if we pay $1.50 we are at just 50 cents disadvantage." Soon this resentment was to induce them to try once again for a fixed price, as Carnegie fancied they already had done during the previous summer.[90]

There were also problems over the shipping of coke, and another divisive issue concerned rebates from the major railroads. On 11 May 1896, Carnegie and Frick met officials of the Pennsylvania Railroad in Philadelphia. They reported to their colleagues that, helped along by plans for their own rail link from Butler to Pittsburgh, they had been able to secure advantageous freight arrangements on ore, limestone, and coke. These new rates took effect on 8 June 1896. They included rebates from the normal charges, which reflected the fact that some of the haulage was undertaken by Carnegie Steel's railroad subsidiaries. Carnegie thought that these rebates were not equitably redistributed. In 1898, Lovejoy tried to explain to him why a 10 cent per ton rebate had been passed on to the coke company. Coke was being billed by the railroad companies at 40 cents, but from this they paid 5 cents to the Union Railroad and 10 cents to the coke company, leaving a net freight rate of only 25 cents. H. C. Frick Coke had been collecting this 10 cents from as long ago as 1892, and since 1894 both the steel and the coke companies had been taking this rebate into account when fixing the price for coke. Again, Carnegie was not satisfied and scribbled a note on Lovejoy's letter: "This is all wrong. No ten cents are due the Frick Coke Co. It is all due us." Later, on Carnegie's behalf, Moreland looked into their own records. He was unsuccessful, being frustrated by the secrecy that surrounded a very contentious issue: "You will understand we have no record anywhere that I can find that shows the bargain you refer to. Am sure allowance was never paid to us. Rates is a thing which don't want positive or strong records on."[91]

At the end of 1898, a decisive new stage was reached in the pricing of coke. On 9 December 1898, Schwab informed Carnegie: "The time has now arrived when we should fix the price of coke for next year. What are your wishes and views and how do you wish me to handle this matter?" He wrote again a week later, mentioning a permanent price of $1.35 per ton, with 25 cents for freight: "Am not sure that Mr. Frick will at once agree to this, but it is my belief that he should." A year later, Schwab tried to recollect the events that followed. His account, a full one, gives the impression that—in this aspect at least—they were running an extremely loosely conducted business. If this was not the case (and such an assessment would indeed be at odds with evidence from other aspects of their operations), he was trying to dissimulate. In any case, his memorandum points to the cumbersome and uncertain manner in which vital decisions were made. He recorded that, early in December 1898, there had been much discussion over the coke price. He talked it over with Carnegie and with Frick, but they arrived at no definite conclusion. Carnegie then asked him to agree on a fair price with Alexander Peacock, Phipps, and Lauder, and after that to take it up with Frick. Schwab and the three other partners agreed that $1.35 was a fair permanent rate, informed Carnegie of this, and asked him to cancel any back claims from H. C. Frick Coke for freight and interest on coke stored on their behalf at Braddock. Carnegie agreed; Frick did not but said he would take the matter up with Carnegie in New York that week. On his return from that visit, he told Schwab he had agreed to the arrangement, but before bringing the matter to the board, Schwab talked the matter over with him "very freely." Before it was submitted to their colleagues, they learned that Carnegie was coming to Pittsburgh the following week, and they decided to defer it until then. However, Carnegie changed his mind and did not come. As a result, Schwab gave Moreland instructions about the price to be paid, "making simply a pencil memorandum." Moreland showed this to Frick who confirmed his agreement.[92]

In mid January 1899, Lovejoy made a note of the approval of the $1.35 price for coke and the 25 cents addition for haulage to the furnaces. Sometime thereafter Frick changed his mind, deciding that neither he nor Carnegie had the right to make such a contract, such a power resting instead with Schwab and Lynch as presidents of the two companies. He said he would see Carnegie in New York and ask him to send Schwab the necessary instructions.

> I never heard anything from Mr. Carnegie, and he [Frick] went abroad. In the meantime, coke was billed to us for the first quarter of the year at $1.35 and vouchers for same were made out and receipted by the Frick Coke Co. as payment in full for coke at this rate (enclosed find voucher). Matters went on until Mr. Carnegie sailed for Europe in April, when the Frick Coke Co., without advising me, raised the price of coke. In view of the fact that re-organization was then being much discussed, it was thought advisable to not bring up the coke question at this time because the whole matter would be amplified after our firms were re-organized, consequently the Frick Coke Co.'s bills have not been recognized at the advanced price, all payments made to them being advances on account only and this continues to this day.[93]

Lynch, in mid December 1898, had made an immediate and careful response to the suggestion that a fair price would be $1.35. He defended the price H. C. Frick Coke had been charging, stressing that small stockholders in the coke company, individuals who had no interests in Carnegie Steel, should not be sacrificed to give that concern a low price for its fuel supplies. Normally, Carnegie Steel had obtained coke at a reasonable price as compared with the other steelmakers. For example, he pointed out, during the previous December when the combination price was $1.65 Carnegie Steel was paying only $1.50, and he could not recall any other purchaser getting a price under $1.60. He thought the solution might be for Carnegie Steel to buy out the other stockholders, after which it could legitimately fix prices to suit itself. In the meantime, he proposed that a contract should be entered into to supply all the coke Carnegie Steel needed for five or perhaps ten years at a fixed price of $1.50. He went on: "In view of the large and growing demand for Connellsville coke and the rapid exhaustion of the coal and the large decrease in the number of ovens in consequence thereof within the next five years, I regard $1.50 as a very low price." Rather than agree to one still lower, he favored submitting the issue to arbitration.[94] In fact, for more than three-quarters of 1899, the pricing of coke continued on a very unsatisfactory basis, neither the coke company nor the steel company regarding the payments received or made as anything other than interim settlements. Eventually this was to provide occasion for bitter disagreement, momentous in its results.

5

Aspects of Management

Process Plant

Modernization and Integration

As the scale of the Carnegie Steel Company operations increased, so it became clear that economic advantage could be gained by reducing any unnecessary duplication of plant, and by increasing the specialization of the mills. Their three main plants illustrate the process very well (see table 21). Edgar Thomson, built for the rail business, retained this as its main line of production throughout the independent life of Carnegie Steel. Homestead had been designed for the same trade, but when bought by them it was revamped for still heavier lines of business, especially beams, plate, and armor. The Allegheny Bessemer Steel Company installed a rail mill at their new Duquesne works, but after it was brought into the Carnegie group, it was turned over above all to production of billets and splice bars. At the same time, linkage between the plants—to permit "internal" movement of raw materials and of semi-products and to give them all improved connections to main line railroads—was secured by the building of the Union Railroad. In each of these works, a process of backward and forward integration was carried through: the first involved the provision of hot metal for steel-making operations either by the building of blast furnaces or by the purchase of existing ones; the second required more finishing mills to use the extending steel capacity. In all these activities, Frick played an important part. In some of them he had to battle against the resistance of other leading partners.

In the middle years of the nineteenth century, Pittsburgh had been a major market for pig iron brought in from outlying plants in Western Pennsylvania and eastern Ohio, notably from the Valleys district. In 1873 for in-

178

TABLE 21
Contrasts in Carnegie Steel Production, 1892, 1899

	April 1892	*March 1899*
Edgar Thomson		
Pig iron	47.2	90.6
Bessemer steel	36.1	66.4
Rails	28.6	a
Duquesne		
Pig iron	none	70.3
Bessemer steel	22.6	53.2
Billets and bars	20.3	48.0
Lucy furnaces	14.7	6.0
Homestead		
Bessemer steel	10.7	31.3
Open-hearth steel	11.6	90.1
Blooms and billets	—	95.6
Structural shapes	7.0	22.0
Plate	3.8	8.6[b]
Carrie furnaces	(not C.S. Co.)	18.9
Upper and Lower Union Mills		
Structurals, plate etc.	8.0	28.4
Beaver Falls		
Wire	7.7	(sold 1895)

Sources: Frick Papers 1899; Dickson 1938, p. 29.
Notes: Figures are in thousand tons.
[a] The estimated monthly capacity in 1899–1900 was about 55,000 tons rails.
[b] Excludes armor plate.

stance, as plans for the new Edgar Thomson steelworks began to take shape, 68 percent of the iron used in the Pittsburgh area still came from outside Allegheny County. After that, there was a rapid increase of local iron production, as new ironworks were built and old ones extended. By the 1880s, some of the biggest steel plants were linked with their own iron capacity, as at Edgar Thomson or Jones and Laughlin. Over seven years, the Carnegie associates purchased two major steelworks that had no iron capacity of their own—Homestead and Duquesne—and they tried different ways of making good this deficiency.

Immediately after they had taken over Duquesne, the idea of building blast furnaces there was mooted, but the labor troubles at Homestead, and after that the difficult trading conditions of 1893, delayed these plans. Next year there was a further postponement. In September 1894, the three principal owners of Carnegie Steel stock were all staying in southern England; there they made critical decisions about extensions in the Monongahela Valley. Frick spent the night of Friday, 2 September, with Henry Phipps at Knebworth House, Hertfordshire. Next day, from the Hotel Metropole in London, he wrote to Carnegie, who was then at Buckhurst in the Sussex Weald. Phipps, he reported, "heartily favors" building blast furnaces and a rod mill at Duquesne but "however is quite anxious for dividends." Phipps wanted a return from the business giving him a monthly income of $10,000. "We discussed various ways of meeting his wishes." Since leaving Phipps, Frick had been thinking further how to arrange "to give him the money he seems to think he needs." Three weeks later, he wrote that they had decided not to build furnaces at Duquesne that year, though plans for them were being drawn. Although the iron capacity was needed, their present financial situation did not warrant the expenditure. He also gave a more personal reason for not proceeding, one that throws an interesting sidelight on the wear and tear entailed in their business: "Have not yet forgotten the experience of the Baring and '93 panics, nor entirely recovered from the strain then endured."[1]

By the following summer, they were ready to go ahead at Duquesne, and Carnegie was eager to hear from Leishman what arrangements had been made. At this time, the company reckoned that iron could be made 43 cents a ton cheaper in the Valleys district, on either side of the Pennsylvania-Ohio line, than locally, but extensions made in steel capacity there were expected to take up more of its iron output. (In 1890 Valley pig iron capacity was almost 1.3 million tons and steel capacity negligible; by 1896 iron capacity had increased to 1.9 million tons, but steel capacity was already 0.58 million tons.) Carnegie wanted to give the press "an item" stating that the new Duquesne furnaces would be able to supply the general needs of the Pittsburgh district: "The idea is to keep it out of the heads of any of our friends that there will be a scarcity of pig in Pittsburgh. We want to do the Blast Furnace building ourselves." Two furnaces were built at Duquesne in 1895–1896, and two more in 1896–1897. By spring 1896, the first of these was ready for blowing in, an event of such interest as to cause Charles Kirchoff, editor of *Iron Age,* to correspond with Carnegie. The results were impressive in both furnace productivity and lowered costs. It was anticipated, Carnegie wrote Frick, that Duquesne No. 2 furnace would make iron for 50 cents a ton less than the Edgar Thomson furnaces.[2]

By this time, Homestead was rapidly replacing Edgar Thomson as their

Duquesne Steel Works and Furnaces, 1897. *Courtesy of USX.*

largest operation. In April 1898, Schwab wrote Carnegie that in March Edgar Thomson made 64,745 tons of ingots, Duquesne 49,900, and Homestead 77,420 tons, just under two-thirds of which came from its open-hearth plant. Though it was their biggest steelmaker, Homestead had no blast furnaces. It could obtain part of its iron requirements from other furnaces in the group, and by April 1898 it was expected that the Union Railroad would be in a position to bring in some hot metal from Duquesne.[3] Even so here was a point of weakness in their operating efficiency (see table 22).

Across the Monongahela and slightly upriver from Homestead was a large merchant iron-making plant, the Carrie furnaces. Late in 1897 and early in 1898, the desirability of acquiring this works became a matter for dispute between the principals of Carnegie Steel. On one or two occasions in the course of the previous years, steelmaking or steel-using concerns had been sounded out as possible purchasers by the Carrie owners. John W. Gate's Consolidated Steel and Wire Company, which had a mill at nearby Rankin, had been offered the plant, and Schwab considered they had miscalculated in failing to take it, rounding out their operations at the same time with a converting plant and a blooming mill between Carrie and their wire mills. At some time, probably in the mid 1890s, Carnegie Steel was also offered the furnace plant, but they turned it down. The asking price then had been $750,000. After this, the owners spent $150,000 to improve their operations.[4]

On Thursday, 18 November 1897, Frick was visited by Mr. Fownes of the

TABLE 22

Carnegie Steel Company,
Supply and Consumption of Pig Iron, 1897

	Pig Iron and Spiegel Production	Pig Iron Consumption
Edgar Thomson	1,012	650
Duquesne	700	515
Lucy	240	—
Homestead	—	740

Source: Gayley to Carnegie Steel board of managers, 1 Feb. 1898 (ACLC).

Notes: Figures are in thousand tons. For pig iron alone, production was 1,742 thousand tons and consumption was 1,905 thousand, the overall deficit for the three steel works was 163 thousand tons.

Carrie furnaces, who explained that his company was again in the market to sell its two blast furnaces. They produced about 575 tons a day, or some 170,000 tons a year—more or less equal to Carnegie's current deficit. In addition to the iron works, they operated 103 ovens that coked washed slack brought from mines along the Monongahela. The quality of their coke was not very good. The Carrie owners wanted to sell because outlets for their iron were becoming limited, and they recognized that to stay in business they would have to invest in more coke ovens and build a steel plant. They were now asking $800,000 for the plant—$100,000 in cash and the rest in seven annual payments bearing interest at 6 percent. However, Frick reckoned Carnegie Steel could get it for $700,000 and have the annual payments arranged to suit themselves. He suggested that Schwab write "generally" to Carnegie about this, and that with Thomas Morrison he should go to look at the plant they were being offered.[5]

On the same day, writing to Carnegie, Schwab mentioned he feared "a little" that the Carrie people would build an open-hearth plant and damage the Carnegie billet trade: "It is a question, of course, as to whether they fully appreciate the cheapness with which Open Hearth can be manufactured." Carnegie Steel could find a use for the Carrie iron at Homestead, and it "could be handled across the river with a wire rope haulage device without any great difficulty." On the other hand, Schwab reckoned they had more or less enough iron capacity in their group of works, and that for an equal cost they could build two more furnaces at Braddock, together making 800 tons a day, "so that, everything considered, it is indeed very doubtful if there would be any advantage in our owning this plant." But yet again, if angle

and universal plate mills were built at Homestead, more open-hearth furnaces would be needed and the iron situation would then be different.[6]

Frick made no mention of the matter to the board of managers until
their meeting on 11 January 1898. On the previous day, he had tried to persuade Carnegie: "Cannot but think that purchase of Carrie Furnace plant
would be a wise move on our part." To the board, he argued that, having
their own ore, coke, and transportation, and in view of the likelihood that
they would be making more steel extensions, it was better to make iron than
buy it. The matter was then open to debate. Curry reckoned that when they
brought in their new open hearths at Homestead, iron consumption would
increase by some 150,000 or 200,000 tons a year. On the other hand, Morrison pointed out that the Carrie furnaces were in a shape that required
much expenditure. If they decided to go ahead, rather than a wire rope
transfer (or a bridge, which would be expensive), he favored moving molten
iron by barge between floating docks on each side. There was dispute as to
whether purchase would really succeed in keeping another competitor out
of the steel trade for, as Lovejoy remarked, "there are other sites." Nine
members of the board spoke; at the end, Frick said they would take up the
matter again when they received Carnegie's views.[7]

Henry Phipps, renowned for his financial acumen, now took a hand,
being much more decisive than he had been almost four years before in
relation to the Duquesne furnaces. He strongly favored building new capacity rather than buying existing plant, and he summed up his views in a
striking postscript that drew on both personal and earlier company experience (the aftermath of the Kloman venture in the Upper Lakes): "An old
plant is dear at almost any price. I altered a house—I never want to again.
We moved a furnace from Escanaba [to Braddock]—got it for almost nothing, and lost largely, and we suffer by it today and perhaps always will." As
bearing on the matter, "let me work out some figures I had from Mr.
Schwab . . ." (see table 23). Though interesting, his calculations did not take
into account the economies of the full integration of operations, nor the
gain to be had as they extended their steel capacity at Homestead. Frick
replied that, in general, he too did not favor buying old plant, but Carrie
was in a good location, and if they did not buy it, then its present owners
would erect an open-hearth plant and a billet mill or something of the kind.
Despite his own original skepticism, Morrison had assured him that by
spending $300,000 he could make Carrie in every respect the equal of their
Lucy furnaces.[8]

On 27 January 1898, Carnegie agreed to the purchase, so long as they
could get it at a 4 percent rate of interest and over a long period. Although

TABLE 23

Costs and Returns of a Furnace at Edgar Thomson and
a New Furnace at Duquesne, 1897–1898

	Capital Cost	Iron Made	Cost per Ton	Profit or Margins on Transfer	Percentage Return on Capital
Braddock	600[a]	132[b]	9.25[c]	99[a]	16
Duquesne	1,100	192	8.90	211	19

Source: Phipps to HCF, 23 Jan. 1898, Frick Papers.
Notes: [a] Figures this column are in thousand dollars.
[b] Figures this column are in thousand tons.
[c] Figures this column are in dollars.

not "very enthusiastic about the matter," he had given his approval because he thought that in that year they would make sufficient money from Carrie to cover a large part of its purchase price. A few days later, seeing that pig iron prices had fallen, he went back on his decision and suggested instead that they would do better to put the money into a new furnace at Duquesne. Schwab reported to Frick that, "It seems difficult for him [Carnegie] to make up his mind." Schwab was reported as sharing his doubts, though he denied this.[9]

When the board of managers met on 1 February 1898, the general opinion was that they should continue to buy iron. Disagreeing with Carnegie, and probably with Schwab, Frick argued that if they were to build new furnace capacity, it should be at Braddock. Later that month, he cabled Carnegie urging purchase and stressing the value of the thirty-six-acre Carrie site and the need for more iron capacity west of the Appalachians in the near future. Carnegie and Lauder at once cabled their approval of the purchase. Two days later, Frick saw Fownes and offered to buy under more favorable circumstances than had been discussed earlier—a price of $750,000 of which $50,000 would be in cash and the rest in seven annual installments with interest at 5.6 percent. Fownes grumbled that outlay on a small steelworks might pay them better than selling, but after the Carnegie managers approved the purchase on 22 February, the transaction was completed within three days. Frick, having secured his long-term objective, now suggested they should use Carrie fully through the boom and only spend for repair work when business slackened.[10] Shortly afterward, a bridge was built across the Monongahela for the transfer of hot metal to Homestead.

By his persistence, Frick had achieved a further stage in full integration and thereby in cost reduction. Carnegie was quick to praise the decision

Henry Phipps in the mid 1890s. *Courtesy of Old Westbury Gardens Archives.*

they had come to: "I never felt so happy and contented in regard to our business as at the present time." In a second letter on the same day and another three weeks later, he included Carrie in the reasons for that contentment: "Yours of 19th received upon my return from yachting. You have been right upon Carrie from the start. I was thoroughly with you, but wavered when pig was down. . . . So glad you have secured the property," and "I have great satisfaction thinking over Carrie purchase."[11]

A further stage in the control of local iron production was contemplated but not carried through. Since the early 1870s, the Isabella furnaces of the iron tube firm of Spang, Chalfant, and Company had been making iron not far from their initially keen rivals, Carnegie Steel's Lucy furnaces. By now there were three Isabella furnaces. John W. Chalfant, their chairman, was dying in 1898, and it seems Frick proposed that they should negotiate to buy the furnaces, for in May Phipps wrote that he could say little about the matter until he saw figures of the "showing." Phipps wanted to know what their capacity was and how much metal came into the area from the Valleys: "In other words do you think there is a field for those furnaces? What are they able to do now in cost? What savings per ton can you confidently count upon? . . . No one wants those furnaces I imagine, Mr. Chalfant being in such bad health. We ought to get them very low."[12] Although Chalfant died, his firm survived, and the Isabella furnaces did not follow Carrie into the control of Carnegie Steel.

In addition to further integration of processes, there occurred extensions into new lines of finished products. Throughout the 1890s, Carnegie Steel mainly made heavy products or semi-finished steel—especially in the form of billets and largely for sale. Gradually their product range widened, especially at Homestead. Having been equipped with plate and beam mills and casting and forging plant, by the mid 1890s it produced blooms, billets, structural shapes, bridge steel, boiler, and ship and tank plate; it also had their armor plate department. By the late 1890s, there was some consideration of installing angle mills to complete its capacity to make ship-building steels, but instead, by spring 1899 the company was building a new mill to produce wider plate and two universal plate mills, increasing plate capacity by about 0.3 million tons, or more than one-quarter. By that time, the managers had given much thought to the need to diversify into lighter finished products. This involved the awe-inspiring question of reorganization within the whole of the nation's steel trade and is of such importance as to justify separate and fuller consideration.

Questions of Location

Speaking in Cleveland in 1895, Carnegie pointed out that the changes occurring in the raw material inputs for iron making and steelmaking had altered locational considerations to the detriment of some long-established leading centers of production. Pittsburgh was no longer the ideal place for manufacture. The situation was even more complex than he allowed, and in that complexity lay the possibilities of finding a way out of these difficulties. Five years after his Cleveland speech, a U.S. government review of the iron and steel trade quoted from *Iron Age:*

> It is not a mathematical problem pure and simple to determine the location of cheapest assemblage of materials or with reference to favorable position as to markets. No one can sit down and figure out where I must haul so many tons of coal or coke, and so many tons of iron ore, at a minimum cost freight, so that, adding freight on product to market, I reach the lowest figure.

Important considerations were such complicating factors as "normal" freight rates and concessionary rates, types of materials used, and degrees of integration. In an industry having a large commitment in fixed capital, although additions could be made in new locations, the wholesale abandonment of less well placed operations was not easy to justify. In such established areas, it was possible either to let changing circumstances gradually become overwhelming or to fight a rear-guard action. It is not surprising that Carnegie Steel both chose the latter course and conducted the struggle with the utmost success. Some years later (by which time locational considerations had taken a further turn), the Pittsburgh correspondent of the *American Metal Market* summed up the vital role of the area's human resources, the part played by initiative in responding to the drift of raw material and of technological and market changes:

> The strength of Pittsburgh as an iron and steel producing center does not lie so much in the fact that it is a good place at which to assemble raw materials and from which to dispatch finished products, although these advantages are extremely important. To the writer's mind the chief strength of Pittsburgh has been that it has the men—men with capital to embark in new enterprises; men with brains to manage and superintend new works; and men with skill to work in them.[13]

That there were limits to this process of response, and that an equal outlay of such outstanding qualities could reap even greater rewards if exercised in favorable locations were conclusions that were sometimes lost from sight in such fighting talk. Such considerations were to gain in significance later.

For many years Carnegie had been looking for ways to cut transport costs. In 1884–1885 he had been disappointed in his hopes of securing a route to the East to rival the Pennsylvania Railroad. Although he had subscribed to it, Vanderbilt's South Pennsylvania line was then sold to the Pennsylvania. From about 1889, there was much enthusiasm in the Pittsburgh area for a ship canal to link the Ohio River to Lake Erie. Carnegie wrote and spoke widely in its favor, but when the time came for commitment his own was decidedly modest. On 4 July 1896, he subscribed $1,000 to the $100,000 Guarantee Fund of the Lake Erie and Ohio River Ship Canal. Nor does he seem to have offered a warm welcome to an enthusiastic letter from W. C. Andrews of the New York Steam Company announcing his plan for "the most remarkable invention of modern times," a sixteen-inch-diameter pipeline with pumping stations from twenty to thirty miles apart. Its inventor intended it for movement of coal and reckoned it could deliver 8,000 tons in twenty-four hours.[14] Perhaps his own preoccupation with the movement of iron ore explained Carnegie's lack of response. Meanwhile he and his colleagues gathered data on freight charges and on assembly and distribution costs.

In the light of Carnegie's undoubted active concern for railroad freight rates, it is perhaps understandable that some have regarded Frick as luke-warm in this respect, as compared with his senior partner. Wall remarks that careful monitoring of freight costs was "a concern which Frick did not share," but this is less than fair. He had long been involved with negotiations over rates and with the quality of railroad service in respect of coke. Before he had either a managerial post or even a financial involvement in the Carnegie businesses, he took a lively interest in their rail freight situation. It is indicative of this that in May 1886, the general freight traffic agent of the Pennsylvania Railroad, John S. Wilson, sent him a copy of the memorandum of arrangement with Carnegie Brothers—and with the then associated Homestead concern of the Pittsburgh Bessemer Steel Company—for freight charges on materials (ore and limestone as well as coke) and on finished products dispatched from those works. An illustration of his keenness and willingness to bargain, and proof that he had done so on previous occasions, may be seen in the letter he wrote to George Roberts, the Pennsylvania's president in spring 1891, apparently immediately after an interview with him:

> You incidentally remarked today, after reading a letter from Mr. McCrea, that he took a rather gloomy view of the situation, and you also stated that we only gave you what ore we were compelled to do. You will pardon me for saying that I think Mr. McCrea may well feel as he does, in view of the fact that the policy of your Western people is rather to discourage business than encourage it. I know it to be a fact that the furnace men in the Valley had to stop operations because they were making pig iron at a loss. . . . We had a bargain with Mr. McCrea, by which we were to take dock space at Erie, on the line of your Road, on the same terms we had dock space at Fairport, on the Pittsburgh and Western, and at Ashtabula on the Lake Shore, but Mr. McCrea called the bargain off, for the reason, he said, that you would not approve of it. We are yet willing to make that bargain with you, and we are always willing to give you what you might say was your full proportion of what ore we ship; provided it does not cost us any more, delivered at our furnaces, than the ore received at

our furnaces over other railroads. I do not think that you can ask more than this, particularly as I have said before we are always willing to sell you rails as low as you can buy them from others, or, if we do not feel like taking the price named by others, we cannot blame you for not giving us a portion of your order. We are, at present, shipping from the lake ports to our Bessemer furnaces 150 cars of ore a day, so it is very plain why Mr. McCrea's business is dull. With the coke ovens idle, the Valley furnaces stopped, and our concerns being compelled to ship our ore by other roads, it certainly would have some effect on his traffic.[15]

One of Frick's early successes at the Carnegie companies was the planning and construction of the Union Railroad. This connected their various works in the Pittsburgh area, permitting an easy exchange of material and making such large savings in switching charges that these alone paid the interest on the capital tied up in the line. The railroad provided each works with direct connections with all the main railroads and, by ending the need for those companies to run their own trains into the yards of the steelworks, gave back the works full control of their own properties. Because of this line, Carnegies were allowed a rebate of 25 cents a ton on the freight charges on ore from Lake ports. In 1897 the railroad freight coming into the Carnegie works amounted to 7.49 million tons, and their dispatches by rail were 2.66 million tons.[16]

Frick's campaigns for lower rates were combined with an interest in the relative costs of iron production at various locations. This was brought out when, on 19 December 1894, he wrote to their general freight agent, George E. McCague, asking him to find out the transport costs at three competing rail-making locations—Edgar Thomson, and the expected new competition at Youngstown and at the Johnson steel plant, then being built at Lorain. Within eight days, McCague had made the requested return, which Frick immediately sent on to Carnegie. To McCague's data, he added for their own works the special rates they had negotiated with the railroads, which were often considerably lower than the official rates. It was clear that they were at a disadvantage, in some respects at least when compared with the Valleys, and very definitely when measured against the Erie shore (see table 24).

Their new rivals would have advantages too in marketing rails to the West and Northwest. McCague summarized with great clarity both the problem and the difficulty of meeting it:

It is self-evident from the above figures that Bessemer is at a disadvantage from a transportation standpoint, as compared with either Youngstown or Lorain, except in marketing rails to the south and east, and I feel a responsibility arising

TABLE 24

Transport Costs at Bessemer, Youngstown, and Lorain, 1894

	Pig Iron		Steel Rails
	Per Ton	Total	Total Costs for Transport
Bessemer			
1.6 tons ore at	1.15	1.84 (1.52)[a]	
0.85 tons coke at	.55	.468 (.30)	
0.4 tons limest at	.80	.32 (.29)	
Total		2.628 (2.11)	3.335 (2.71)
Youngstown			
1.6 tons ore at	.675	1.08	
0.85 tons coke at	1.25	1.062	
0.4 tons limest at	.30	.12	
Total		2.262	3.148
Lorain			
1.6 tons ore at		no land haul cost	
0.85 tons coke at	1.65	1.402	
0.4 tons limest at	.30	.12	
Total		1.522	2.425

Source: G. E. McCague to Frick, 27 Dec. 1894, Frick Papers.
Notes: Figures are dollars. Steel rail total transport costs include those for the pig iron needed per ton of salable rails and for fuel used in converting pig to steel and for rolling the rails.
[a] Entries in parentheses for Bessemer indicate concessionary freight charges for Carnegie Steel.

therefrom which it shall be my purpose to meet as far as possible, but as it is impossible to annihilate space, the result may not be satisfactory.

It is interesting to note that he believed they were being treated well by the railroads. Discussing the practical monopoly over much of their business by the Pennsylvania Railroad (neither the Baltimore and Ohio nor the Pittsburgh and Lake Erie had the equipment or facilities to handle their outgoing traffic), he went on:

[B]ut I must say they have pursued a liberal policy toward us during recent years, and, inasmuch as they cannot hope to secure very much of the business in or out of Lorain, and only a share of the business in and out of Youngstown, it is probable the Pennsylvania RR will see that it is to their interest to protect us against competition, whether it comes from favoritism from their competitors, or from geographical advantage in location.

On ore and coal movements he wrote:

> I have found with a few exceptions, our Railroad Companies are not only fair and in some cases liberal with us, but also active in protecting our interests at the various and very frequent meetings of their Associations. I need hardly add that a ship canal from Lake Erie, together with a continuous series of locks in the Ohio River would be of greater advantage to us than anything the railroads could do.[17]

There were further plans to associate with other railroads in order to break the grip the Pennsylvania held on the Carnegie business. In 1890 such a scheme envisaged a new East-West link through central Pennsylvania. It was to be built by the Pittsburgh, Beech Creek, and Eastern Railroad from Kittaning, where it could link with the Allegheny Valley Railroad, to Curwensville, Clearfield, and then down Beech Creek and on to Lock Haven, there to make junctions with eastern roads, including affiliates of the New York Central system. A branch line was contemplated from the Pittsburgh, Beech Creek, and Eastern south of Decker's Point to the town of Indiana, then to Saltsburg, and up the Kiskiminetas River and Loyalhanna Creek to Latrobe, with possible extension still further south to Connellsville.[18] The Pennsylvania Railroad was said to be surveying parts of the same route, but the Philadelphia civil engineer, John Wilson, stressed to the Carnegie interests that if they submitted their plans, they could frustrate the proposed alternative line. Neither this new route to the East nor the link from Decker's Point to Latrobe was ever built. Later that decade the president of the Pittsburgh, Beech Creek, and Eastern became associated with Carnegie Steel in a scheme that broke their dependence on independent railroads for transport to and from Lake Erie.

The idea for a company-owned rail link from Pittsburgh to a lake port seems to have come from an outsider. James H. Creery, general counsel of the Pittsburgh, Monongahela, and Wheeling Railroad wrote to Carnegie in the fall of 1895 suggesting that such a rail line was better than waiting for the "possible and yet problematical benefits of the canal." He pointed out that, since 1881, all freight rates in the Pittsburgh area had been based on a classification agreed by the Pennsylvania, Baltimore and Ohio, and Pittsburgh and Lake Erie railroads and had been arranged to their benefit. In his opinion, the appropriate response was "a line of railroad built between Pittsburgh and a Lake port, honestly built and honestly operated . . . entirely independent of any existing system, and put in such a shape as to remain independent," and handling business to and from the lakes "at as near cost as possible." Having taken engineering advice, Creery reckoned such a railroad could be built to Ashtabula or to Lorain for not more than $6 million and that it could operate profitably even if it charged no more than 50 cents a ton. After this, Carnegie quickly had surveys made of prospects for ore docks at Ashtabula and Fairport, and estimates of costs per ton mile for a completely new track were examined.[19]

However, soon afterward Carnegies made renewed contact with Colonel Saul B. Dick, who had been associated with the Pittsburgh, Beech Creek, and Eastern. He was now president of a rundown railroad (a concern that a later chairman recalled was on its "last legs"), the Pittsburgh, Shenango, and Lake Erie Railroad, which owned a line between Butler and the little lake village of Conneaut. In 1895 Conneaut Harbor handled only a quarter million tons of iron ore, but it was then being dredged at the expense of the U.S. government. Already the Pittsburgh, Shenango, and Lake Erie was looking into the prospects of building a connection from Butler to Turtle Creek and over to Bessemer. Attracted by the obvious relevance of these routes and plans to their own needs, Carnegie initially contemplated leaving the railroad to make the extensions itself. Carnegie Steel was to contract to provide at least one and a half million tons freight annually over a twenty-five-year period. Leishman reported to Carnegie, "I have spoken to Mr. Frick about the survey from Butler to Braddock which was made through Mellons and he thinks he will be able to find some of the papers."[20]

Early in 1896, Frick believed he had succeeded in using the threat that Carnegies might associate with or acquire and improve this line to obtain a Pennsylvania concession. The Pennsylvania Railroad would revise the rates charged, so long as Carnegie Steel abandoned the threatened new scheme. Carnegie, however, insisted on carrying it through. A few days later, Dick in turn tried to force their hands by pretending that other interests were in the market for his railroad. He telegraphed Carnegie: "new overtures on tempting terms made me which I have declined." By summer, the cost of the extension from Butler to Pittsburgh was put at $0.6 million.[21]

The operation on which they had now resolved soon ran into difficulties on the managerial side. By April 1896, Carnegie Steel had given Dick thirty days' notice of their intention to call off negotiations unless he proved he was vigorously pressing on with the work. From this time, most of the capital for the reconstruction and extension of the line came from Carnegie Steel, which ensured that it was effectively their private line. By July 1896, experience had convinced Carnegie that Dick "is a sloppy manager." He was soon emphasizing that the sooner they got control of the line the better, and then he had to rebuke Dick for an "insulting and abusive" letter.[22] That autumn, Dick transferred thirty thousand shares and much of the control in the Pittsburgh, Shenango, and Lake Erie to Carnegie Steel; in return he was paid $200,000 and made chairman for ten years with a salary of $20,000.

Carnegie thought Frick had been too generous in these payments, especially when reports showed that Dick had made false statements and that "the Railroad accounts were cooked," as Carnegie put it. Now, however, development went ahead rapidly. In the course of 1897, work that would normally have required two or three years was done on the old line. It was found that it had not been

> very well constructed, [and] had been suffered to run down, both the road bed and equipment being in bad shape. There was hardly a culvert over which we dared to run a heavy engine. All of the bridges and trestles on the main line were unsafe and the road is full of sags and inequalities which tend to break trains and which must be taken out before long trains can be safely run. The road was poorly equipped with passing sidings, rendering it difficult to pass the trains without delays.

The cost of the work to be done had been estimated at almost $2.5 million.[23]

Renamed the Pittsburgh, Bessemer, and Lake Erie, the extended line was in operation by October 1897, although that year it handled only 1 percent of the traffic in and out of the Carnegie works. Further improvement was still required. Carnegie responded with a touch of humor: "Her case is respectfully submitted to the attention of Dr. Henry Clay Frick, Surgeon and Physician (amputations may be necessary)." The roadbed north of Butler was reconstructed using blast furnace slag as ballast, and on it were laid new hundred-pound rails. Equipment was upgraded by the introduction of the first steel freight cars and the nation's heaviest locomotives. Given all this attention, the new line quickly established unexcelled standards for railroad freight handling. Costs per ton mile fell to as little as 1 mill, the lowest anywhere apart from Rockefeller's Duluth, Missabe, and Northern Railroad. (As late as 1886 the rate charged by the Pennsylvania had been 9.25 mills per ton [net] mile.)[24] Soon the vice-president of the Pittsburgh, Bessemer, and Lake Erie, J. T. Odell, could claim that the rebuilt line had

> the lowest rate per ton per mile, the highest average length of revenue haul in proportion to its track mileage, the greatest density of tonnage in proportion to its freight-train mileage, the greatest average paying load, and the lowest "ton-mile cost" of any road on the American continent reporting to the Interstate Commerce Commission.

Carnegie was jubilant about the consequences for their efficiency and was typically aggressive in the way he wanted to exploit them to the full. As he

anticipated in a December 1896 memorandum to his partners: "This Fall
Pittsburgh became a Lake Port, and I think next year the one thing we
should avoid is any combination that restricts our output." Two years later,
when the railroad had proved itself, he took the opportunity of a banquet
given in his honor by the Pittsburgh Chamber of Commerce to make clear
that he no longer favored a barge canal to Lake Erie. He was, he announced,
convinced that the capital invested in such a project would be wholly lost.
The only value a canal might have would be to ensure that the railroads kept
freight rates to and from the lakes at a reasonable level. But, if it was built
with this in mind, the federal government should finance it.[25] Meanwhile,
having obtained its own ore line, the company capitalized on the asset with
imagination and thrust.

By the mid 1890s, less than one ton of coke was used in making one ton
of iron. Even so, the freight charges on fuel were of concern to Carnegie
Steel for it used about 5,000 tons of coke each day. The Pennsylvania Railroad was charging them heavily; as Carnegie pointed out, although McCrea
had said he wanted coke traffic at 3 mills per ton per mile over short distances, he was in fact charging 5 mills. A railroad of their own could, Carnegie suggested to Frick, haul coke at 2 mills. At that time, Dick spoke of
building a line into the coke region and Carnegie promised him part of their
business. Setting the rate for this at one-third less than current charges
would, Carnegie suggested to Leishman, cause the other roads to make comparable reductions. Later that year, as they moved toward full control of the
ore line to Lake Erie, Carnegie Steel took up the idea of extending it to the
coke field. Three requests to the Pennsylvania for lower rates went unanswered. Writing yet again to Frank Thomson, vice-president of the Pennsylvania Railroad, Carnegie delivered an ultimatum: they had shelved their
original plan for a coke line, but "it will however be promptly done unless
the matter is closed between us by Saturday. It is all ready, and I have only
to say the word when I go to Pittsburgh on Monday." After that he added,
rather surprisingly, "Now please do not understand this in the light of any
threat. I simply tell you the truth that you may not reflect upon me for not
being entirely frank."[26] He was in fact bluffing. They were by no means
ready to proceed, being fully occupied over the next two years in recon-
structing the Pittsburgh, Bessemer, and Lake Erie. However, now and again
the idea of an extension to the coke region resurfaced.

In summer 1897, Carnegie suggested that the Union Railroad might make
a trackage arrangement to the coke region, and that Frick should see Frank
Thomson about it. Carnegie thought the Pennsylvania might see some advantage in it. He also thought that Carnegies in this way could avoid capital

outlay on making their own extension and could save as much as 15 of the 25 cents they were then paying on coke to Pittsburgh (or about $300,000 a year). But Phipps was still toying with the idea of their own coke railroad, a scheme going beyond Frick's thinking. Carnegie had written him about the Pittsburgh, Bessemer, and Lake Erie: "The Chairman is right, our new road will help coke, but extended to coke it would make our coke property a mine of wealth, let that be our next year's expenditure—I say." Phipps's own reaction was, "This matter will bear keeping in mind—important." Later that year Carnegie was again championing their own line, but as a less immediate project than the one he had presented to Thomson. He urged Frick to avoid doing anything "that will restrict us from taking the business of the country and running full" and made an unusually cryptic reference to the coke railroad:

I hope our friends are quietly attending to that remaining vital step, which taken, we can then rest. Do get everything necessary secured and be ready. We have probably undertaken quite enough for this and next year but for 1899 we should do the one thing lacking. I am more than ever satisfied that our great coke estate cannot be made to yield its harvest minus that indispensable appliance.

He had veered to advocating their own track for "no matter what the present railroads promise, they can never make you master of the situation."[27]

A key factor in this part of Carnegie Steel planning was the Monongahela Southern Railroad, a Mellon company. This included the Duquesne branch of the West Side Railroad Company but otherwise consisted less of physical plant than of potential and the opportunity to realize it—a charter, surveys, and a four-mile right-of-way. The plan was for Mellon to build an eighteen-mile railroad on this route and then sell or lease it to the Union Railroad. At Frick's request, Judge Reed made a valuation of this concern and put it at $100,000; Mellon had offered to sell it to Carnegie Steel for half that.[28] Understandably, Frick's assessment of their fuel resources was not less fulsome than Carnegie's: "Do not think we have anything that, in the long run, will prove more valuable than the Connellsville coal land," was how he put it early in 1898. Yet he was less bullish than his partner on the railroad. He wanted to use the threat of it to gain their ends. They should purchase Mellon's company in order "to be in a position to go ahead in future if it should prove to be necessary. It seems to me we are in the railroad business just as far as it is necessary for us to go—far enough to control the situation." His estimate of the cost of building the railroad was over $1 million.[29]

During that spring he came up with another idea for solving their problems. He pointed out that the Vanderbilt system regarded their railroad up the Monongahela Valley as their main access to the coal and coke district, and that therefore they might be willing to lease or sell their other line, which ran from McKeesport along the Youghiogheny to Connellsville. "If that could be brought about, it seems to me we would occupy a position that would be impregnable"—and without spending much capital.[30] In the end they neither acquired nor built a railroad to the coke region, but they had such projects, and their obvious ability to carry them through had beneficial effects on the way railroads could treat them.

All these efforts were expended in order to maintain and extend the competitive advantage of the Carnegie plants. In this sense they were the essential counterparts in the field of transportation of the company's unvarying readiness to scrap and rebuild process plant in order to increase efficiency and cut unit costs. Carnegie, in a memo, had once sent to the directors of the Pennsylvania Railroad a simple statement of faith: "It is all a question of transportation. Pittsburgh and the district around us can easily be made as cheap a place to manufacture iron and steel as the Lake front." But the situation was not so straightforward. As McCague had put it a few years before, space cannot be annihilated; by dint of undoubted enterprise and at substantial capital cost, Carnegie Steel retained their competitive edge, but they could not deny that an interior location was becoming less attractive. Indeed in his 1895 Cleveland address, Carnegie had already recognized the drift of locational considerations that increasingly favored lakefront works— which in his judgment meant, above all, those on the shore of Lake Erie. He had explained then why he thought the advantages of the Pittsburgh area to be fading:

> The reason is easily given and will be obvious to the dullest comprehension. It takes two tons of iron ore to make a ton of finished steel. It takes only one ton of coke to make one ton of steel or pig iron. Therefore a manufacturing plant situated upon Lake Erie, north of Pittsburgh, has not to transport by rail the two tons of ore at all; it comes to the manufacturer by water, and he only has to transport the ton of coke from Pittsburgh to the Lake. This gives the Lake Erie manufacturer so decided an advantage that if one were about to locate iron and steel works he would go there.[31]

There was a good deal of external evidence to support his contention. The Johnson Steel Company was already building, at Lorain, the Bessemer plant and mills that were to be the nucleus of a major integrated works. At the same time, encouraged by the success of merchant iron furnaces, a group of Lehigh Valley interests were planning four blast furnaces and a Bessemer plant for Buffalo. Over the next few years, there were more developments in the same area, culminating in the dramatic announcement, in 1899, that the Lackawanna Iron and Steel Company would run down its Scranton operation and remove to a virgin site near Buffalo.[32] When the Pittsburgh, Bessemer, and Lake Erie line was operating well, it seemed a good time for Carnegie Steel too to think about possible developments on the lakeshore. During the first half of 1898, the company's thoughts were still of Conneaut as a raw material handling point; in the latter part of that year, attention turned to prospects of processing there. It was soon recognized that this could bring with it considerable economies in overall movement costs.

By April 1898, the Carnegie managers were taking up Lauder's suggestion that, rather than store ore at their Pittsburgh furnaces, they should stock it for winter at the port, a change that would both economize in the increasingly scarce space in Monongahela valley works and also make better use of the capacity of their railroad during the period in which lake navigation was closed. Schwab, Lauder, and Phipps (presumably Lawrence Phipps, Henry's nephew) were to visit Conneaut in order to look into the best way to use the 212 acres of land they had bought for this purpose. Shortly afterward, the operating department discussed the possibilities of handling rails at Conneaut.[33] The first steps toward planning for processing there were taken by an outsider. Sometime during autumn 1898, Jay Morse—former president of Illinois Steel and now an associate of the Cleveland ore shipping firm of Pickands Mather—approached Frick concerning possible purchase of land at Conneaut for one or two blast furnaces. In presenting the matter to the Carnegie managers, Frick was aware that they had not yet thought out a development strategy of their own:

> The question is—Can we afford to sell land for the use of two furnaces without interfering with our own operations at Conneaut? I suppose no one here is prepared to give an opinion without better information as to what land we have and what we shall need; therefore if there is no objection, Mm. Gayley and Clemson are appointed as a Committee to investigate and report fully.[34]

A month later the committee reported that space suitable for iron-making plant was available east of the ore dock. Such operations would help give a better balance to railroad flow, for a 300 ton per day furnace would require 40,000 gross tons of limestone and 100,000 net tons of coke annually. They saw still further possibilities: "There is sufficient flat land adjoining the furnace location, of which the Dock company owns part, which if filled with slag would be suitable for steel works and other manufactories." As so often with Carnegie Steel, the scale of thinking mushroomed—a process helped along by the increasing disposition of rolling mills that, until now, had bought steel from them to acquire or establish their own sources of supply. Bridge seems to intimate that the idea of building a tube works at Conneaut originated with Frick. No evidence has come to light to support this opinion, but plans for works of this kind were soon being discussed by the Carnegie managers. Early in February, Daniel M. Clemson reported that, not long before, they had supplied almost all the plate needed by National Tube, but now the latter had built their own steelworks and furnaces to support their tube output of about 250,000 tons a year. He thought the pipe business was one Carnegie Steel could enter, although he did not specifically identify Conneaut as the favored location for such a plant.[35]

Carnegie's response was positive: "I have not heard of anything which strikes me so favorably—from ore to pipe." Phipps was much more doubtful—though perhaps, as so often, his caution was a necessary corrective to Carnegie's almost reckless enthusiasm. He wrote to Frick, "The objections to embarking in a large and new business are many and important"; material and machinery were "dear and hard to get"; costs of the existing producers were so low that "the margin to strike is not a large one"; and the business was already crowded "with plenty of capital and men of experience in it who will not be easily pushed aside." At the same time, it was "a line with which we have no acquaintance, and all will admit knowledge is a good equipment." He shrank from the unknown: "let us develop what we now have, and we can increase all we want, and in a business of which we are masters, and no groping in the dark, such as a new venture would involve." He recognized another limitation, which in their self-confidence others were in danger of overlooking, that of the physical capacity rather than competence of their managers. In the expansion of Carnegie concerns this had received little attention:

> The President and Staff have all they can do in justice to themselves and the firm—two of the Managers are now ill from overwork. The President, under the strain, has all he can do to keep well. If he had nothing else than to build the pipe works, with its adjuncts, and create a new business, it would be quite enough for a year, to tax his whole time and strength.

Phipps concluded: "For these and other good reasons, I beg you to postpone any action till at least next January, when a fuller consideration can be had." Whether his plea was respected or (as Bridge suggests) there was a wish to avoid alienating the Moore brothers (with whom the sale of Carnegie Steel was being negotiated during that spring and summer), large-scale developments at Conneaut were put off.[36] Before they were revived, Frick had ceased to be a Carnegie Steel executive.

In spite of his occasional loud protestations, Carnegie remained ambivalent about the locational advantages and disadvantages of Pittsburgh. He had once explicitly recognized that Pittsburgh's maximum attractiveness was reached when wrought iron was the dominant finished material and was reduced when the more fuel-efficient Bessemer process replaced the puddling furnace, but he retained a strong sentimental attachment to his home city and for their well-established plants. Carnegie rationalized these prejudices. He explained to Frick in 1894, he had an "instinctive aversion to making investments hundreds of miles away." He went on, "we should as near as possible get out of every investment we have except those in and around the City of Pittsburgh." Six years later—looking back on the century that had just closed, and as the early moves for the formation of the U.S. Steel Corporation were underway—he permitted himself a look into the future. He felt reassured: "So far as the writer sees there is nothing to change the center of steel manufacture in the new century; it is in the Central West already described, and there it is likely to stay." He had already written in the same article that the "Central West . . . has Pittsburgh as its metropolis."[37]

The Bessemer Railroad provided scope for realizing new economies from Pittsburgh. As early as 1896, Carnegie anticipated that "we shall market our product seven months in the year east and west via Conneaut and barges. The deepening of the Erie Canal is going to change the situation." At the same time, he was trying to induce the Pennsylvania Railroad to make concessions by stressing the advantages that the Lake Erie shore had over interior locations: "We . . . cannot shut our eyes to the fact that future development is to be in that region, under present conditions." He reckoned that on Lake Erie it was possible to save $1.70 on the ore to make a ton of steel, that a plant there would also save the $1.15 a ton on steel sent back to the Great Lakes from Pittsburgh and could deliver that steel in Chicago for $1 less than from Pittsburgh. A year later, considering further development of ore and product transport on the Great Lakes, he wrote Lauder, "You should look into the policy of building a few of the largest sized ore carriers; then I think that we shall find it advisable to have a few smaller craft running to lake cities with our finished product, coal and coke, returning with scrap etc." The company should also charter or own some boats that would cross the lake and go on through the Erie Canal to New York or even to Boston: "The greatest saving that can be effected now is in the cost of transport. . . . We shall never get full benefit from our railroad until it is part of a rail and lake route. This seems to me the most important question now before us."[38]

He eventually recognized that the logistic situation made Conneaut an excellent place for manufacture of iron and steel.

Although they shared Carnegie's confidence in the exceptional competitiveness of Carnegie Steel, not all his colleagues were persuaded by his interpretation of the geography of long-term locational advantage. In the early 1890s, Frick seemed convinced that Pittsburgh was the ideal location. At that time, they considered buying the Lassig Bridge works in Chicago. After this fell through, Frick reflected that events had shown there "is no doubt but we should concentrate our business and not have too many concerns to look after. One large concern with its plants all located in Allegheny, Fayette and Westmoreland counties will succeed the best."[39] As time went on, he modified these views, and in the course of that decade, he seriously contemplated plant purchase in the East and plant construction in the West.

Both these ideas were anathema to his senior colleague. The East was regarded by Carnegie as no longer suited for bulk steel production. This belief resulted from their long experiences of the rail trade. In spring 1898, he wrote to Frick about two of their eastern competitors: "Pennsylvania and Scranton reports shed a flood of light upon the situation—it is very clear that we can take the Eastern trade when we have to and still make a profit." Three years later, in his *New York Evening Post* article, he pointed to the concentration of Bethlehem Steel on specialties, the current mortal troubles of the pioneer Bessemer steelworks at Troy, and the removal of the Lackawanna works to Buffalo as various evidences that "for the making of ordinary steel," the East was not a favorable location. A partial exception was the Steelton works of Pennsylvania Steel and that company's associated operations at Sparrows Point, the latter of which he recognized possessed "advantages for export."[40] Yet it was all too easy to attribute contemporary difficulties of eastern works to inherent deficiencies of location when some of them were due to failures in management or to persistence in wrong lines of business. In some respects at least the area had great potentials. Frick had some grasp of these, but eventually it was to be Schwab who fully seized them. On a number of occasions, Frick considered Sparrows Point works as a possibly promising purchase, but each time his ideas received a cool reception from Carnegie.

By the 1890s, there were a considerable number of open-hearth steelworks in the coastal region of Eastern Pennsylvania and in northern New Jersey. Fully integrated tidewater operations there were confined to Sparrows Point. The iron ore deposits of Cuba had been proved in 1882, and in 1887 Pennsylvania Steel surveyed a site for a new works near Baltimore. It was originally conceived as an iron-making plant that would send its product on to Steelton for further processing, but instead it was soon extended into rail and steelmaking. Sparrows Point was a hundred miles nearer Cuba and sixty-five miles closer to the bituminous coalfields of Western Pennsylvania than was the district around Philadelphia. However, long hauls were involved with both materials, and as far as foreign ore was concerned, the delivered cost varied as tariffs on imported minerals went up or down in response to the respective pressures from home- or import-based interests. In marketing, Sparrows Point was well placed to supply the southeastern coastal states or outlets on the Gulf Coast or overseas. Projected in the expanding demand of the late 1880s, this plant came into production under the more difficult trading conditions of the early 1890s and suffered accordingly. It seems to have been at this time that Frick first suggested they might follow up their success in acquiring Duquesne by buying Sparrows Point, thereby removing what might eventually be another troublesome competitor. Carnegie was unshakably against this:

> Really I would not favor our taking Sparrows Point works for nothing, contingent upon our having to manage and run them. You know I have said from the first that Sparrows Point works were folly. New rail mills are not needed in the East—or in the West either for that matter. Our best policy is to divide with Chicago equally and have nothing to do with the East.[41]

However, other interests persisted in pressing the attractions of the East. In March 1893, Carnegie received a letter from D. C. Wedding of Baltimore with details of a plot of land on the Patapsco Estuary, a solid earth site having eighteen feet of water directly offshore and lying opposite Sparrows Point: "we all think it is best for us, and this community, to induce you if possible, to transplant some part at least of your own industries here, as has the Pennsylvania Steel Company of Harrisburg, Pennsylvania." That spring, it was reported in Pittsburgh that Carnegie had been to Sparrows Point and might buy it. Francis Lovejoy, as company secretary, issued a press statement to scotch this rumor. It was firm in tone and ended on the sort of jaunty note that might have been inspired by their head: "The policy of the Carnegie Steel Company is to concentrate all its works in and near Pittsburgh. . . . We have no idea of acquiring any plants in other sections of the country. Pittsburgh is good enough for this company."[42]

Throughout the years, Frick's name was time and again linked with Sparrows Point. However in January 1906, months before Frick became a director of the Pennsylvania Railroad, the president, Alexander Cassatt, received a report on the steel plant from William H. Donner, a young steelman for whom Frick had a high regard. Donner showed that the average cost of hot metal there was $3.25, one-third higher than in Pittsburgh, although he did not explain to what extent this was due to location or to deficiencies in plant or operations. His conclusion was unequivocal: "As an independent enterprise, I do not think the works of the Maryland Steel company, owing to their location, could ever be made an attractive proposition."[43] Ten years later, Sparrows Point was taken over by a revived Bethlehem Steel group led by Schwab. Frick, Donner, and above all Carnegie would have been surprised could they have known that, for a time, Sparrows Point would eventually be the largest steel plant in the United States.

The unchanging map of steel that Carnegie affected to see was still more patently wrong in the case of the Midwest. With the 1898 merger of Illinois Steel into the bigger group of Federal Steel, the Carnegie group feared keener competition. In June 1898, John A. Potter, their ill-starred former superintendent at Homestead, reported on a visit he had made to the Illinois works. Generally they were "losing considerable money by not looking more carefully after small economies, which amount to mountains in works of this kind," but South works—apart from an open-hearth plant that was in "a very bad shape"—was in fair condition, had a very good rail mill, and was busy.[44] Here clearly was not only a formidable competitor but a favored location.

Frick initiated a response involving at least the threat of Carnegie Steel operations in the Chicago area. At all stages, he had to fight doubts or opposition from his senior partner. In March 1898, Frick wrote, "Gates seems to have it in for us, but Illinois crowd may find, some of these times, a formidable competitor alongside of them, on Lake Michigan." On the other hand Carnegie was at that time captivated by the prospects opened up for their present location by the movement of steel products northward on the Pittsburgh, Bessemer, and Lake Erie Railroad, to be transferred near Lake Erie to the Erie, the Nickel Plate, or the Lake Shore and Michigan Southern railroads. In April, he moved on to the possibilities and advantages of water transport from Conneaut: "The most formidable competitor that Illinois Steel can ever find will not be one on Lake Michigan in my opinion provided we develop barge lines from Conneaut to Chicago, Milwaukee and lake ports, or even if the Pennsylvania Railroad will agree to carry other forms of steel at $1.40 to Chicago, the rate upon rails." He wanted Frick to help Schwab in getting lower rail rates. In May, he was even more specific: "I believe that when we get through with the present plans and have the railroad rates that we are bound to get, it will be better to continue filling the field from the great center."[45]

In spite of this barrage of ideas for building on the present situation,

Frick persevered with his own thinking about securing some presence on Lake Michigan. In June, he referred to the proposed consolidation of Illinois Steel with the Minnesota Iron Company, the second biggest ore producer in the Upper Lakes, and the still wider plans for both those companies. He thought that such a consolidation would be in a position to secure new money to improve their plants: "However money alone is not the only thing they will need. Have my doubts about conglomerate organization like that being able to secure right men or proper organization to spend the money." This led him on to the thought that they might do better than an extended Illinois group, and he then built on Carnegie's commitment to their existing location. He presented his ideas with careful moderation, even managing to work in an idea that Phipps had used a few months before in the discussion of the Carrie furnaces:

> Am with you as to Pittsburgh as manufacturing center, particularly as distribut-
> ing point for steel products generally, but still it may be that a compact little
> plant on Lake shore near Chicago may be of great value. Undoubtedly Chicago
> will continue to use more and more pig iron as time goes on and 468 miles is
> quite a distance to overcome. Even if these concerns do consolidate and secure
> money to modernize their plants it will be something like repairing an old
> house—cost will be great and even after it is done, it is never satisfactory. . . .
> With our new railroad as a lever, we could put fuel for blast furnaces down
> very cheaply in Chicago. During our time however there is nothing that can
> beat Carnegie Steel Company, in the management of which every man looks
> on himself as an owner. That would be very hard to get in any other organiza-
> tion. It is a matter of growth.

Carnegie did not concede, but he was reasonably conciliatory. He speculated what might happen if they shipped pig iron from Pittsburgh to Conneaut and from there by water at perhaps 50 cents a ton to Chicago. In those circumstances, they could put iron down in Chicago at what they reckoned was Illinois Steel's cost of making it there. He added, "All this does not militate against the purchase of the land there—it will do to hold, and its effect upon the owners of Illinois Steel Co., not upon the officers, cannot but be wholesome."[46]

Carnegie was now aware, as the last sentence suggests, that Frick had already acted in this district on his own account, having paid $105,000 for 300 acres of land, with a 4,000-foot frontage on the shores of Lake Michigan and lying about four miles east of the South Chicago works. It was a first step in provision for a future in which the balance of locational advantages might change. Frick believed the area chosen would provide "an ideal loca-tion for blast furnaces etc." It was estimated that a harbor having a depth of

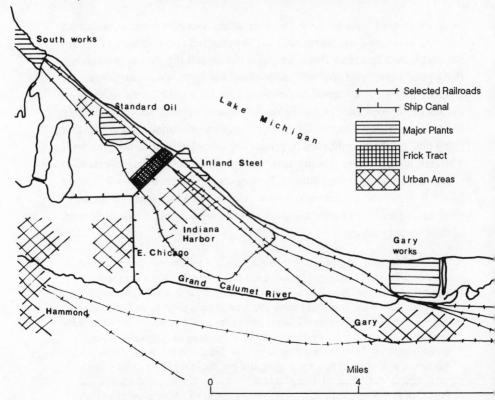

H. C. Frick Landholding, Indiana Harbor, 1912

twenty feet of water could be built in a year and for $100,000. The parties who sold him the land had agreed to contribute that sum of money if a works was built within five years. He had engaged Thomas Rodd, a Pittsburgh engineer, to survey a harbor and consider the site's suitability for a steelworks. Rodd pointed out that waste could be easily disposed of, railroads gave excellent access to major areas of consumption, and there was a large labor market not far away in Chicago but "without the disadvantage of being too near to it." Although he recognized that Frick was "no doubt better qualified to judge than [him]self" about the situation for bringing together necessary raw materials, he reckoned that "every natural and artificial circumstance affecting this site and harbor seem to be most favorable and to indicate an almost ideal point for a steel making plant." Frick had made his own more modest assessment: "I look on it as a good safe investment, whether it is ever used for a manufacturing plant or not."[47]

After seeing Carnegie and Phipps at Skibo, Frick wrote in August to the Carnegie Steel managers, enclosing his original letter to Carnegie and the correspondence from Rodd. Again he was restrained in his claims, stressing that, even if they decided to go no further, the land itself, or the land with a harbor added, "would be worth much more than the amount invested." He added the point he had made earlier to Carnegie: "In the proposed consolidation of Illinois and Minnesota companies (and likely Lorain), we may find it necessary to properly protect our large interests to have a small but complete establishment in Chicago."[48]

When the board of managers met on 16 August, Schwab stated that although at first he had not favored Frick's plan, he now believed they should start at once to develop the tract Frick had offered them. A month later, he even took the matter up with Carnegie. He pointed out that by handling direct from ore boat to furnace stockyard, as opposed to their present necessity of handling into ore trucks at the Erie shore and then from truck to yard in Pittsburgh, they could save a further 6 cents a ton. Even with the superb efficiency of their new Pittsburgh, Bessemer, and Lake Erie Railroad, the cost of haulage from lakeshore to furnace was 59 cents per ton. Each ton of pig iron required 1.6 tons of ore, and according to his calculations, this gave Pittsburgh as compared with Chicago a transport cost disadvantage on ore of $1.04 per ton of iron. On coke, on the other hand, Chicago had extra freight costs of $1.25 per ton, and Schwab allowed an additional cost to producers there of 15 cents for the wastage suffered by coke on such a long journey. Assuming nine-tenths of a ton of coke per ton of iron, the disadvantage on the Chicago coke account as compared with Pittsburgh was $1.26. Overall, he reckoned that they could perhaps produce pig iron 25 cents a ton cheaper than Chicago. Taking note of trends in fuel economy and that, as the *Chicago Tribune* had claimed three years before, plants there had no competitor in a natural market area of fully a million square miles (over one-third of the contiguous United States), Lake Michigan development began to look attractive. Schwab went further than Frick, envisaging a fully integrated plant devoted exclusively to rails: "If we ever do build such a plant in Chicago, we should think of nothing less than Basic furnaces and Rail mill with 4 blast furnaces—the total cost of which would not exceed $5 million to make from 50 to 60,000 tons per month, counting on using half mixture of scrap."[49]

The Carnegie Steel board of managers discussed investment in Chicago again in mid October. The idea was presented "with a view to whipping Illinois Steel into line, and better controlling the markets." However, not all the partners were in favor and it was stressed that unanimity would be needed for them to go ahead.[50] Three months later, Carnegie was present at a meeting whose proceedings indicated how compliant his partners were to his wishes. Frick asked whether the company wanted to take the land on Lake Michigan off his hands but remarked that he would really prefer to keep it as an investment. Reasserting his own faith in Pittsburgh (although his presentation of the case for it showed up as faulty), Carnegie now effectively killed the scheme. He argued that a division of the sphere of their operations would diffuse the power of the managers. This might well have been true, for their difficulties in watching over the management of their Hartman Steel Company at Beaver Falls had been part of the reason for its recurrent financial problems, from the time they acquired it in 1883 until they sold it to J. W. Gates in the mid 1890s. And Beaver Falls was only a thirty-five-mile rail journey from Pittsburgh, whereas Lake Michigan was 375 miles away.[51] On the other hand, when Carnegie maintained that the West was not so important an outlet as the East and overseas, his statement was flying in the face of the evidence. Schwab accepted his market assessment with the vitally important exception of rails, for which he recognized a Chicago location would be cheaper than their present one. Carnegie's response was essentially no more than a confession of faith that they could continue to cut costs if necessary: "I would rather manufacture rails in Pittsburgh at $15.00 and pay $1.00 freight to Chicago, than make in Chicago for $15.00. Our attitude should be that we do not need to go into any part of the country to compete in its local markets. This is our headquarters; let us grow here." To the doubtful logic of this clinching statement, Phipps added an extremely lame coda: "I agree with Mr. Carnegie and think also we should do in this matter whatever Mr. Frick wishes."[52] Not for the last time, the other members of the board meekly concurred with their senior partner. By general consent it was decided not to take and develop the tract Frick had bought. It was to be almost twenty years before this land became part of the site of a major steel plant. Even so it is clear that, in the late 1890s, Frick had foreseen the drift of national locational advantages more clearly and responded more definitely than most of his Carnegie Steel colleagues.

6

The Reshaping of Carnegie Steel

Change in the High Command

To the outsider, the Carnegie interests seemed to be almost always successful, both in their current business and in their extensions and new ventures. This was due to various causes, including their superb plant and efficiently conducted processes. Suppliers, rivals, and their own workers were kept firmly in place. For all these contributing factors there was a common cause: the excellence of the management at all levels from shop floor to boardroom. It could readily be thought that a single, unwavering commitment to commercial success united them all, dispelling all petty rivalries and personal ambitions. The quality and efficiency of the organization were real enough, but below the surface unanimity there was actually a great deal of dispute, accompanied by a willingness—especially on the part of Carnegie himself—to be rid of those who fell below the mark or who would not conform to type.

Carnegie always claimed that the most valuable asset his group of companies possessed was the quality of their men, especially of those at the top. He once remarked that he wanted his epitaph to read that he was one who knew how to pick men who were cleverer than he was himself. On another occasion he made the dramatic claim that, should their plants be destroyed but their organization remain intact, they would quickly recover their position at the head of the world's steel trade. He did not add that he was unfailingly a hard driver of those for whom he made such large claims, which came in part from his own insatiable ambitions. In 1868, at the age of thirty-three, he had written a warning to himself (a warning that over the years he would time and again fail to heed): "Whatever I engage in I must

207

push inordinately; therefore should I be careful to choose that life which will be the most elevating in its character." In later years he was able to drive others in order to fulfill his own ambitions. He once mentioned to Captain Jones the release he felt from business cares when he set out on his travels: "You cannot imagine the abounding sense of freedom and relief I experience as soon as I get on board a steamer and sail past Sandy Hook," to which Jones made the stout response, "My God! think of the relief to us!"[1]

Even when he was far away, Carnegie kept a close watch on what went on and, by mail or telegraph, could drive his colleagues with the same unremitting pressure. This was well brought out in an autumn 1889 letter to Abbott: "You seem to be alright now except at Beaver Falls. We have too much money and far too much lost prestige there to think of withdrawing. We must go ahead and put those works ahead of all kindred works—that's clear. I understand you have asked to be allowed to manage it—good—but *see you don't fail.*" He ended the letter by reapplying the pressure: "If I were you I would take care to be on the right side of estimates hereafter, especially at Beaver."[2]

Not everyone could survive under this pressure. Some did not make the mark; others proved incapable of following the approved route toward the goal. There was failure and dissension among the principals and on occasion this led to removal or expulsion, which was often represented as a wished-for resignation to pursue alternative careers or retirement to cultivate other interests. In these ways Carnegie secured the elimination of those he thought had failed him. At the same time, most of those who initially did not agree with him on some point of policy or management proved willing to compromise or to give up their views in order to keep their position or his regard. It is important to keep these general problems with senior colleagues in mind for otherwise the common myth will persist that Frick was exceptional in becoming an unacceptable colleague. It is true that he too was often willing to curb himself to retain harmony, but Frick was unusual not so much in disagreeing with his senior partner as in occasionally expressing his own opinions fearlessly. Eventually he was to challenge Carnegie's position, and in some sense at least, to manage to bring him to order. However, it must also be remembered that Frick had expressly chosen to place himself in a difficult position, the dangers of which both Tom and Andrew Carnegie had given explicit warning from the start.

Following the death of Tom Carnegie, the partners realized that when a major member of the association withdrew, for whatever reason, there would always be a danger that settling his interests or estate might mean an unacceptably large call on the partnership finances. In the case of Tom,

Andrew came to an agreement with his widow, Lucy, under which he bought his brother's interest over an extended period, but a similar happy way out of their difficulties might not be possible in other instances. In the extreme case, because of his preponderating interest, Andrew Carnegie's own death might necessitate the dissolution of the partnership. Some way out of this problem had to be found. On 10 January 1887, helped by legal counsel, Phipps drew up the first of the so-called Iron Clad agreements, which partners were required to sign. This included two important provisions. First, it allowed the company an extended period in which to purchase, at "book value" from his heirs, the interests of a deceased partner. Second, it provided a means for securing the withdrawal of any partner. This could be required if at least three-quarters of his colleagues agreed to request this, so long as they also owned three-quarters of the stock. Only three weeks after the Iron Clad Agreement was drawn up, Frick obtained his first financial interest in the Carnegie companies. On 31 January 1887, he acquired a $100,000 share in Carnegie Brothers for $186,000. For this he did not put up any cash, his share being held by Phipps until dividends from the company covered the full amount of his interest. Many years later, a penciled note was added to the article of agreement recording this arrangement, when, at a time of confrontation with Frick, A. M. Moreland was searching through their archives on Carnegie's behalf. He wrote:

> My Dear Mr. Carnegie, This will show that Mr. Frick entered the service in evening clothes (Iron-clad seems so cold an application) like the rest of us. Anything else find of interest in hunting ammunition for lawyers will send to you.[3]

For many years Moreland's note of acrimonious comment would have seemed inappropriate.

From 1889, as chairman first of Carnegie Brothers and then of the Carnegie Steel Company as well as head of the H. C. Frick Coke Company, Frick did not spare himself in the day-to-day pressures of business. His working day was long, and for years he took no holidays, but he seemed to revel in his enslavement. A few months after he became active in management, he let Carnegie know his reactions: "As I become familiar with the steel business it becomes more interesting; always something that can be done to reduce costs; but the business requires close attention." He wanted still more financial involvement. This was the subject of a letter he wrote to the senior partner in New York in March 1891, a letter interesting in tone as well as content:

> My Dear Mr. Carnegie: You have frequently kindly indicated your willingness to sell me a larger interest in these associations. When you come out would like

to take up the matter with you. Am now satisfied should like to continue my connection with them, but want to be more largely interested, if still agreeable in every respect to you, and satisfactory to all. I am, and always have been, afraid of debt or would certainly have owned today a larger interest in Frick Coke Company. In event of purchase, would like my liability limited, and beg to submit the following, viz: To purchase from you, on such time as mutually agreed upon, 11 percent and give you as additional security 1 percent of my present interest, leaving me 2 percent in each unencumbered. Making my interest in each 14 percent. My indebtedness to you to be evidenced by collateral note, or notes, and my liability limited to the 12 percent in each. Very Respectfully Yours, H. C. Frick.[4]

As this letter suggests, and other sources of evidence amply confirm, Frick's value to the Carnegie companies was fully acknowledged by his partners, including Andrew Carnegie. In spite of this, however, they were periodically at odds with each other. In this he was by no means unique. Before he arrived, William Shinn had left under a cloud, never to be reconciled to Carnegie. The departure of William Abbott did not lead to personal bitterness, but it was undoubtedly felt that he had not performed well enough as head of Carnegie, Phipps, and Company. In the cases of other high officials, Carnegie could be highly critical; in many instances he took Frick fully into his confidence about these views. This aspect of man management came out in a long letter he wrote from Milan in the immediate aftermath of Cleveland's landslide election victory and as the Homestead strike ended. With his thoughts very obviously developing as he wrote, his aim was to apply the brake of caution to Frick's wish to advance some of the top men in their works. At least some of his remarks may have contained reflections by implication on characteristics of Frick himself. In turn Carnegie considered Dillon, Schwab, and Gayley, and, more briefly, others:

> *Dillon.* Nothing too good for such a man, never had a Supt. a Manager, but he is apparently an exceptional man, and deserves the unique honor. . . . Election to the Board is a great honor for him. . . . Am glad you think him likely to develop so he could step in and handle whole business—a "big order" this however. A man must not only have decision, vigor and *fight,* but the much rarer quality of knowing how to win Victory without fight ninety nine times out of a hundred—Still I know of none of our men more likely to grow into a real wise general. *Schwab* of course deserves increase. Still it would have been appropriate time to give this *after* he had settled in Homestead and become a Homestead man exclusively—and made Homestead a success. . . . *Gayley*—I confess I can't see your reason for giving increased interest to him now—He may deserve it hereafter but has yet to prove capable of independent command—Two big plums given at once, Promotion and Increased Interest, only count for one, but the main objection is *He has not earned it*—He was given an interest for superb management Furnaces—He has done nothing else *yet.* You

and I blundered, as we agreed, about giving interests—What a line of failures we have—Potter (we were both so sure of him), Childs—Utley—All three admitted failures and Peacock, well; I have not heard your latest report of him, perhaps he is nothing more than "a nice young man" like Childs—worth $3,000 salary each if so much. When I see expenses at Homestead I feel Potter must be idiotic—How can you lose nearly $10,000 per day there?—Even if 2,000 nobodies were paid an average of $2.50 per day *doing nothing* it would not be so much. $2.50 is above average of former men at Homestead.—Much better have paid them to sit down—It's incomprehensible. . . . The fact is that nobody should be allowed to retain an interest in the Firm except he possesses and uses exceptional ability in an *independent command*—I have come to that conclusion—Assistants, etc., etc., should be required to wait—and at least five years' service be exacted before interest given. . . . Truly I rejoice to think you are to bring a man of Dillon's record closer to your side and to the General counsel Table—You have Brains in Leishman and Dillon anyhow—Scott at Union Mills not much grey matter there. . . . But Good night. Off for Venice tomorrow. Ever your AC.[5]

There were further episodes both of disagreement on the board of managers of Carnegie Steel, and of expulsion from it. As well as dissatisfaction from the top, there were also disputes between managers on the spot. Occasionally these came to light, specific disagreements being made stronger by longer-term tensions. For example, Schwab once wrote to Frick about the percentages they had secured in an agreement between the beam and channel makers: "Peacock as usual opposes. I think principally because he did not negotiate, as he can give no real reason for his objections." Frick himself was alternately loud in praise of Schwab and then critical of his tendency to what Frick regarded as lavish methods of doing business. Above all, this seems to have been due to a difference of temperament; Frick once summed it up very well: "There is too much of the fireworks order about every thing he does."[6] Despite his affection for his "boy," even Carnegie could now and then be severe on Schwab, although he was always ready to forgive him. In September 1897, a criticism of their president was shown to refer to Leishman, not to their present head, but Carnegie, in October, took the opportunity of this correction to take up another matter with Schwab: "*I cannot understand why you do not watch your figures. Believe me you will never obtain the confidence of your partners unless you are more careful as to your statements in figures.*"[7] Carnegie was soon full of praises for Schwab once more, however, and their harmony was restored.

With Frick, Carnegie's disputes were more serious. Partly this was because the chairman was apt to make a vigorous response to any censure or correction when the issue involved H. C. Frick Coke Company. There were various disagreements concerning coke in the 1880s. Though he might be overruled, in this field Frick was the expert; by contrast, he was a latecomer in steel, although very soon he was making clear his desire for freedom of action even there. At the end of his first year at Carnegie Brothers, he wrote to Morse in Chicago, "I cannot understand why Mr. C. should have written Mr. Potter [of the North Chicago Rolling Mill Company]. He never intimated to me that he thought of doing anything of the kind. He has been keeping hands off everything very well for some time." On the same day he informed Carnegie he had heard from Morse, "He tells me that you wrote to Mr. Potter on the subject [of ore]. I cannot quite understand why you should have done so." Late in 1890, Carnegie was pressing Frick about railroad rates; he received an impatient response. Frick explained that he had no intention of "letting up" on Vanderbilt or Roberts, but

> [t]here are other ways, and I do not desire to fool too much time away with those parties, for the reason that it may be fooling after all, and try to do something else in the present situation. There are plenty of other things that can be done and should be done by all of us. One man however can only do so much. . . . Regret that I do not have time to write you longer letters. We have a good many things to do here of much importance.

Later that month, tensions were building. Frick added a postscript to a letter: "What have you got against the Frick Coke Company bonds that you try to trade them off every opportunity?" Next day, he was writing about difficulties with the blast furnace men at Edgar Thomson: "I am glad to see that we are all in accord on this important matter." Gayley had matters well in hand, and "his policy is and has been to deal firmly and boldly with the men, the chief difficulty being only the most ignorant. . . . Mr. Schwab does not appear quite as sanguine of the situation . . . and does not seem to grasp the situation to my mind quite so well."[8]

There were further irritations, some of them little enough in themselves, but highlighting the different value systems of Frick and Carnegie. In mid August 1892, a time of pressing preoccupations (and while he was recovering his strength from the attempt on his life and the death of his baby son), Frick sent on their plans for the World's Columbian Exposition in Chicago due to open the following spring. He must have stiffened as he read the reply that came from the peaceful retirement setting of Rannoch Lodge:

> I must say that the proposed plans for the Chicago exposition received with your favor of the 19th ultimo, are altogether too Frenchy to suit my taste. It is most pretentious. The hanging chains upon it would do for a lot in a cemetery, and rather than have such a spread-eagled thing, I should vote to have no exhibit at all. The twisted columns are false from every point of view; material is not twisted that we have for use.

Carnegie deplored the scheme for a great arch spangled with "little bits of our various forms." What they wanted was "a pile that will impress people with its solidity—an armor plate for foundation, great 24 inch girders, etc." He ended, "I am glad you sent me this, as I would not have wished to visit the Exposition if we appeared in anything like the form suggested."[9]

After this they passed through the depression of 1893, but by the end of that year things seemed to be well. That Christmas, Frick sent a cheerful cable of goodwill on the company's behalf to the Carnegies' Manhattan home: "All things considered, we have every reason to be very happy today and to exchange the greeting—'Merry Christmas and Happy New Year.' Mrs. Carnegie and you have now, as always, our heartfelt good wishes; above all that you may both enjoy the best of health during the coming year—your Partners."[10] However, the coming year, which began so auspiciously, ended with hitherto unprecedented disagreement between Carnegie and Frick that brought on a change in Frick's status within the company.

DISAGREEMENTS IN 1894

In summer 1894, Frick visited Europe. During his travels he met up with Carnegie, who for the last eight years had leased the castle at Cluny on the River Spey near Kingussie, Scotland. There they shared the enjoyment of Highland scenery and recreations and also discussed the business situation. After that, Frick called on Henry Phipps at Knebworth House in Hertfordshire before going on at the beginning of September to London. Less than three weeks later he wrote from Pittsburgh. To this letter Carnegie gave the penciled title, "Frick and Schwab Animosities." Carnegie was also a participant in the dispute, which exposed the existence of factions in the company's top management. Apparently in their conversations at Cluny, Carnegie had made "very frequent" remarks about the extravagance of James Gayley. On his return Frick had taken up the matter with Gayley. As a result, he wrote:

> I have not been blind to the fact that criticisms of Gayley, and some other
> trifling matters, originate with Mr. Schwab, are brought to your attention by
> Mr. Lauder, and when they do not do rank injustice to an employee unable to
> defend himself I do not care, as very little harm is done, and some good may
> come out of any reports made you from that or any other source—no harm,
> because you rarely take other than broad views of such matters.

But he ended by giving Gayley his endorsement: "Gayley is by no means a perfect manager, but he is honest and attentive." A few days later, however, he himself with a strange change of views was ready to concede that not all was right:

> Spent most of the day at Edgar Thomson; went thoroughly over the property. While it is in prime condition, think we could get better results if we had a more active Manager. Gayley is honest and attentive, but does not have quite snap enough about him. Am glad to say he is willing to have as an assistant a more active and energetic man. In fact think he feels need of it. He is a great deal of a student himself, as you know.

Gayley had spoken of the possibility of making use of Alva Dinkey, "brother in law of Schwab," as a possible assistant, and Frick planned to "look him up," though as a general rule he deplored the dangers of nepotism.[11]

Although the Gayley affair only indirectly involved Carnegie, and in the end Frick had been conciliatory, other causes of disagreement were already emerging. In August, the House of Representatives report had been published on the armor plate scandal of the previous year. It confirmed the original findings against the company. Both report and press articles at the time fiercely denounced senior men in the mills, particularly Schwab and Corey, and members of the board, especially Carnegie and Frick. This alone must have increased the level of tension within the company.

Things were made worse by disagreements about their search for foreign orders for armor, especially in Russia. Millard Hunsiker was sent abroad to represent them. In September 1894, about a month after he had spoken with Carnegie at Cluny, Frick added to a general letter on the business of their various plants: "Did not break silence on armor matters on my return, as you advised, as I am absolutely opposed to newspaper interviews of any kind." But Frick's self-discipline was rendered ineffective by his senior partner's inability to resist the temptations of publicity. At the end of October, Frick expressed his anger about this to Lieutenant C. A. Stone in Washington:

> I was astounded this morning to find that the newspapers had obtained knowledge of Mr. Hunsiker's visit abroad. To my mind, this could only have reached the public through one source (through our leading stockholder) who, it seems, is not able to contain himself at any time or under any conditions. I will have this traced and ascertain. If it was an employee of this company, we would have no further use for his services.

To Hunsiker, he explained: "It is unfortunate of course that our leading stockholder is a little injudicious at times, but we cannot have everything as we should like it." In December it became known that Bethlehem Iron had beaten Carnegies in the competition to supply twelve hundred tons of armor plate to the Russian navy. The Bethlehem price was considerably lower than their own.[12]

Another disagreement stemmed from the negotiations to bring the

Rainey coke properties into the Carnegie fold. Carnegie had committed the indiscretion of seeing W. J. Rainey without including Frick. He was apologetic, but though he expressed the hope that Frick might join a second meeting with Rainey, he realized that, as the former had used such words about his fellow coke manufacturer as "thief" and "rascal," there was not much hope of a successful outcome.[13]

Both the armor and coke issues unlocked Frick's anger, and he reacted with increasing bitterness. He was prepared to be quite open with Carnegie about his feelings. A week before Christmas, replying to Carnegie's suggestion that they take up a particular issue with Robert Linderman of Bethlehem, Frick remarked that someone else would have to take up the matter:

> As I told you (and you seem to have forgotten it), I happened to be with Mr. Linderman when he received news of their success in Russia, and, of course, congratulated him most heartily. Bethlehem, as you say, is certainly a lively competitor, made more so from the fact that they were told by you, *before they put in their bid,* if they took the contract they would have to take it at a very low price. They entered the race with some other advantages over us, most unfortunately, which it would be well for you not to forget. These are some of these "little things" which it would be just as well to bear in mind when comparison is being made between one management and another.

Concerning Rainey, Frick told John Walker he felt that Carnegie had not kept an agreement with him, but "leaving my feelings out of the question, he has already done the Frick Coke Co. great harm." Finally he decided he must break off his association. On 17 December 1894, he informed Carnegie that he intended to retire from the chairmanship of Carnegie Steel. Next day, he reported that their affairs were in "splendid shape" and that, as the future looked bright, they should at once arrange for his successor and for the purchase of his interest in the company. He then touched on another matter, one whose impact may help explain some of the harsh words he used at this time. He would not have thought of retiring if their affairs had not been so healthy. But the "past six years have been trying ones to me, and my mind from necessity has been so absorbed in looking after the interests of this great concern I have not had time for anything else and feel now that I need such a rest as is only obtained by almost complete freedom from business cares."[14]

Carnegie responded on the same day with two letters. The second was, as his biographer put it, "ingratiating." He addressed Frick as "My friend and partner" and suggested gently that resignation then "might not fulfil the sacred obligations you recognize as due your partners." He was surprised by the strains that Frick had borne, because "I knew (though you didn't apparently) that no brain, not even yours, and your temperament (the latter as rare as the former) could stand it." He had recommended trips to Europe and the taking of recreation. Now he suggested a long holiday in Egypt and promised that he would remain in the United States and give Leishman all the advice he needed until Frick returned. Again he referred to the claims of his partners and then reverted to the state of Frick's health:

> As I write your face appears to me as it was the other night when you came to us to dinner. It was worn—you were tired, overstrained—long meetings, vital questions, discussions had worn you out. . . . If you can only be restored to pristine health you will soon return and smile at matters which now in your tired state seem gigantic and amazing, and your partners will be unable to contain their joy. All your partners ask (at least I ask) is that you will be patient and try the cure; not one of them would endanger your health. I'll see you soon. Yours ever, AC.

By this time Frick seems to have been so worked up that he was neither easily calmed nor willing to let pass other sources of irritation. On Wednesday, 19 December, he wrote that he had come across a broker who was selling thirty-two thousand H. C. Frick Coke Company bonds—bonds that Carnegie had taken as part of his interest in that firm. This revived his feelings about the negotiations in coke: "What will Rainey think of bonds selling below par? It strikes me increasing capital stock might have less effect on that remarkable gentlemen, if it was worth considering him at all in any of our affairs." When he received this letter, Carnegie penciled on it: "HCF you are mistaken and will be sorry—When have you found me selling or borrowing or doing anything underhand—I know nothing about these bonds—I should surely have spoken to you before offering—be just my friend."[15]

Meanwhile, Carnegie's letter of the previous day inflamed rather than helped the situation (which in view of the letter's tone is perhaps not surprising). Frick responded, "I think I understand what is due between partners and friends and that to a large extent has influenced my action." He then became calmer, although later reversion to a more intemperate style indicates that his anger continued to boil just below the surface. On Christmas Eve, he agreed to defer action on his retirement until early in January. Four days later he ended a letter, "I have no desire to do anything that would cause embarrassment to anyone, particularly to those with whom I have been so long and pleasantly associated." But on Sunday, 30 December, he reacted fiercely to an old theme: "And so Mr. Rainey is delighted to have anyone 'you desire' present at next meeting. How kind of him, how considerate of you, and what a Solomon he has proved himself to be in not mentioning my name." On New Year's Day, again writing from home, he launched into an unprecedented personal attack on Carnegie, an attack provoked by remarks Carnegie had made about him to Henry Phipps:

> Mr. Carnegie, it is high time you should stop this nonsensical talk about me being unwell, overstrained, etc., and treat this matter between us in a rational business-like way. . . . If ever a man penned a sillier lot of nonsense than you did when you wrote that letter to Mr. Phipps. . . . I should as a curiosity like to see it. It is from start to finish untrue and you know it. . . . I desire to quietly withdraw, doing as little harm as possible to the interests of others, because I have become tired of your business methods, your absurd newspaper interviews and personal remarks and unwarranted interference in matters you know nothing about.

When Carnegie replied to this tirade two days later, he was, understandably, much less conciliatory than he had been two weeks before, although he still managed to be courteous. All in all, he wrote a gracious letter. He was, as he put it, "one who likes and values you" and had spoken as Frick's "best friend," but circumstances had changed and so had his tone: "This is not the first time you have resigned." After the resignation over the 1887 coke strike,

> I had difficulty getting your shareholders to take you back. I put you back and *you knew* it. Well you resign again and I have tried my best to be your friend again. It is simply ridiculous, my dear Mr. Frick, that any full-grown man is not to make the acquaintance of Mr. Rainey, or anybody else, without your august permission—really laughable—but I did not do it until you had given approval. . . . No use corresponding any more. You are determined to resign. All right. I am forced to agree that the work of the Carnegie Steel Company and the Frick Coke Company is too much for any man. No one values you more highly as *a partner,* but as for being Czar and expecting a man shall not differ from you and criticize you, No. Find a slave elsewhere, I can only be a man and a friend. Your friend still, Andrew Carnegie.[16]

Henry Phipps, the other senior partner and major shareholder, was only fifty-five, but like Carnegie he had retired from active day-to-day involvement in Carnegie Steel. One of his major concerns was to guarantee himself a large regular income to support his comfortable lifestyle and frequent world travels. Experience over the years had convinced him that Frick's management of their affairs was the best security for this. At the time of this interchange between Carnegie and Frick, Phipps was at Knebworth House in southern England. He was deeply disturbed by events but kept in touch and did his best to calm the situation. On 22 December, he sent an important, frankly expressed message to Carnegie. Much later, John Walker was to tell Burton J. Hendrick that he doubted if Phipps had ever read an entire book purely for pleasure or for intellectual interest, but on this occasion he proved his ability to find a quotation that was apposite and that, from its provenance, would endear itself to Carnegie:

> Thanks for the cables, the last made me happy and I hope the Pittsburgh incident is now closed. For a year or two past, such an incident or occurrence has been in my mind, the hastiness of one and the touchiness of another rendering quite possible a misunderstanding of greater or less severity and probably ill consequence. In my opinion there is not in our country the equal of our Chairman, he fills more fields and does the duties better than any man I know in active business. . . . Macaulay well said a statesman must be judged by his whole policy and not by his isolated acts, and I think the same must be said of a businessman.

Writing to his son Jay, Phipps was less equivocal about where the blame for this violent dispute lay. He fully recognized the temperamental failings of Frick but concluded that, on the whole, on this occasion he was the wronged party:

> This Christmas to me has been marked by a series of serious cables from A.C. in regard to the Chm. leaving us; of course it is the egotism and bad temper of the one who is not unknown for his exhibitions. It looked on the 21st as tho' I must at once go home, and the strain has more or less continued until this morning when a cable from Mr. Frick said "Everything arranged satisfactorily." It seems A.C. must have climbed down a very long and steep way; in fact I went so far as to cable that unless something was done, I intimated I wished to retire. A.C. was awful hot at HCF who was the wronged one and had my sympathies and best support.[17]

The solution they found for this crisis was to leave Frick as chairman but to transfer the duties of the chief executive to a newly created post of president.

At 1 P.M. on Tuesday, 8 January 1895, a special meeting of the board of managers of the Carnegie Steel Company was held at their general offices. Frick was in the chair, and the other regular members present were Leishman, Curry, W. H. Singer, Phipps, and Lovejoy. Carnegie and Lauder also attended. Frick stated that for almost a year, he had wished for a change in their organization to relieve him of some of the "confining and exhaustive details which . . . constantly require the attention of the Chairman." The consulting partners—that is, those who were not involved in day-to-day administration—had not hitherto given their approval but now had done so. Carnegie then remarked that, although he had opposed change "more because he thought the time for it had not arrived, than because it might not be advantageous," he now "heartily" favored it. Unanimous approval was given for alterations in responsibilities. John Leishman was proposed for the new post of president. Final action on the matter was deferred to the meeting on 11 January 1895. It was then recorded that Carnegie had written to the managers on the day of their last meeting to confirm his agreement with the new structure. He recognized that Frick had been right when they talked about the organization in Scotland the previous summer: "It is better for him and therefore better for the firm that he be kept from numerous people which, as Chairman, he is compelled to see. Much better that he be not called away from home to Meetings, which the Chairman is bound to attend. He should be the *reserve.*" Until now Frick's share of the Carnegie Steel stock had been 11 percent, and 5 percent was now transferred from him to Leishman.[18]

The critical events of late 1894 and early 1895 have been presented by biographers in various ways. Strangely, Wall makes only passing reference to this crisis in the relations of Carnegie and Frick. Harvey describes them as a "difference of opinion" about coke, which "so nearly caused a break between the two partners that each offered to sell his interest to the other, but a final satisfactory adjustment of all points in dispute was finally effected at an unrecorded personal interview." He suggested that it was Frick's wish to cut his debt that caused his share of the Carnegie Steel stock to be reduced from 11 to 6 percent. His account is an altogether too gentle presentation of what was clearly a serious crisis within the company. By contrast, Hendrick points to this time as being the end of Frick's administration; after this he was merely chairman of the meetings of the board of managers. He quotes a memorandum from Carnegie, which intimated that Frick retained even this post only by Carnegie's own considerate action:

> Mr. Leishman was elected his successor. After this action was taken by the Board, Mr. Frick came to me, dejected, haggard, penitent and in sore distress. He asked me if I could not get my partners to create for him a nominal office, Chairman of the Board of Directors, to save him from humiliation. I was very strongly averse to creating an office which I feared would undermine the authority which the President, an executive officer, should possess in so extensive a firm. Against my business judgment and actuated solely by pity, and anxious to do everything I could to spare him humiliation, I did promise to consider the subject. I sent for the organization of the New York Central Railroad, as I knew it had a Chairman of the Board, and finding that his duties consisted solely of presiding over the Board of Directors when present, I suggested to my partners in the Board that we might go so far for our late Chairman.

There is indeed some evidence that Carnegie expected Frick to play a reduced part. A month after the meeting of the board that appointed Leishman as president, Carnegie wrote to their secretary, Francis Lovejoy, about the amendments to their rules. He pointed out that, now they had a president, they could not have a chairman and that, having chosen to resign, Frick was now only "Chairman of the Board of Managers." Hessen has suggested that Carnegie's willingness to approve Frick's retention of the title of chairman was in order to placate Phipps who, when he heard Frick was to resign, had written a letter anticipating that disaster would speedily follow: "Mr. Frick is first and there's no second, nor fit successor. With him gone a perfect Pandora's box of cares and troubles would be on our shoulders." Phipps foresaw "The Herculean labors that would confront us, troubles unnumbered—unending, life too short, the game not worth the candle."[19]

Whatever the thinking behind the reorganization, in practice the chairmanship of the board was to prove much more than a merely decorative position. Leishman remained president for two years, but as a business leader he was a pygmy compared with the man he had replaced. There was indeed some suggestion that Frick was happy to accept Leishman's nominal preeminence because he knew the real power would remain in his own hands. Charles M. Schwab, who replaced Leishman in February 1897, was unquestionably an outstanding industrial leader. Yet through his presidency too, both Frick's own correspondence and the records of the company prove that he continued to play a most important part in the control and development of the company.

He retained or regained a great deal of his power, although the routines of the office did not so completely dominate his days as they had since the beginning of 1889. He was able to widen his interests; for example, he now gave full rein to his art collecting impulses, "which had so far been sporadic." He had not acquired many pictures in recent years, but in a trip abroad in 1895 he bought fifteen.[20] In many respects even his relationship with Carnegie was restored. By 18 January 1895, the latter already felt confident enough to mention that he had seen two of the Raineys that morning to talk about possible forms of association. Even Frick's reactions became calmer. Within five weeks of the board meeting that displaced him from the top post, he could report, "met W. J. Rainey at Duquesne Club; had quite a pleasant chat with him."[21]

By that time, he had clearly recovered his usual equilibrium. Perhaps the most remarkable feature of the dramatic events of 1894–1895 was Carnegie's willingness for Frick to retain so much of his power and standing. He had been outspoken to an unprecedented degree; however, not only Henry Phipps but also Andrew Carnegie had realized how much they all would lose if his connection with them was severed. To avoid that, Carnegie was willing to accept from Frick an outspokenness that he would not tolerate from any other.

Under the presidency of John Leishman, Carnegie Steel continued to do well and indeed to advance its standing among the nation's steel firms. In both 1895 and 1896, there was an increase of $1 million in net profits; in 1896, net earnings were 50 percent above those of 1894. The company's share of U.S. crude steel production in 1896 was 26 percent (their highest to date and only to be exceeded once in their history). Contemplation of these indicators occasionally led to euphoria; in a happy moment at the beginning of 1896, Carnegie ended a letter to Lovejoy, "I think we never had the organization for managing our business so perfect as it is today."[22] More generally, however, there are indications that he realized they now had a less capable man at their head.

Carnegie's letters constituted a barrage under which their only recently appointed president must often have flinched. In July 1895, Carnegie congratulated him on the sale of the Beaver Falls mills and expressed a wish that "some good party" would buy their Lucy furnaces and the Union mills, so leaving them free to concentrate attention on the three major steel plants. Earlier in the same month, he had pressed him on the acquisition of new land for Edgar Thomson and about railroad rates, which at that time he reckoned meant that Valley furnaces could assemble materials for one ton of pig iron at 43 cents per ton cheaper than works in Pittsburgh. A few months later, he pointed out that their average coke consumption per ton of Bessemer pig iron had been 1,955 pounds: "This is at least 5 percent more than it should be and perhaps more. It should be investigated." Two weeks after that, he complained that they had too much money tied up in materials stocks: "Frankly, I must say, that if you do not look out, you will bring even our firm into serious trouble."[23]

There were a number of references to lack of communication of information so that those not on the spot were less well served than they had been under the previous administration. Writing from Cluny in 1895, Carnegie pointed out that many of the questions he had asked remained unanswered: "Mr. Frick used to send me monthly costs and also monthly reports of Blast Furnace products and these were very interesting. I wish you would kindly continue this." He ended, "The Squire [Phipps] was here for a day or two, and asking so many questions, which I was sorry to say I was not able to answer. Please remember how much you can oblige us by keeping us in touch with important events." Leishman then sent some of the operating statements that had been requested, and Carnegie thanked him on his own and on Phipps's behalf: "You can scarcely realize how anxious in these times your absent partners necessarily are, and how much they have missed Mr. Frick's admirable correspondence and statements." Later Carnegie was incensed by some of Leishman's business methods. Early in 1896, he found it deplorable that he had tried to hide that he was in debt; he also pointed out Leishman's wider responsibilities as their public figurehead:

> Every dinner you attend, every lunch at the Club at which you linger, every act, affects the Company; every word you speak; . . . every *financial* step in your private affairs has serious consequences. . . . We all appreciate your ability in some directions, but you have much to do before you regain the confidence of your partners as a *safe* man to be the Executive head of the Company.

At the end of 1896, Carnegie condemned the purchase of two "bankrupt" furnaces in the Valleys and took the opportunity to spell out his distrust of those who dabbled in risky investments. He stressed that he could not have Carnegie Steel "degraded to the level of speculators and Jim Cracks, men who pass as manufacturers, but who look to the market and not to manufacturing, and who buy up bankrupt concerns only to show their incapacity."[24] This aversion was to surface again some years later as a factor in his condemnation of a major scheme for reorganizing Carnegie Steel.

By 1897, Leishman was ready to quit his post. He wrote to Carnegie and then talked the matter over with Frick, who reported back, "Mr. Leishman came out to see me Sunday afternoon: told me he had decided to leave the Company. After long conversation, I suggested it would be far better for him to continue to hold his present position and interest, but go to England and represent us. This struck him very favorably." Frick mentioned that he and Carnegie had talked over some such arrangement some time ago and went on: "There is a great field abroad for a man of Mr. Leishman's ability. . . . Think it to interest of firm and certainly to Mr. Leishman's interest, that he should continue with us." Two weeks later, the board accepted Leishman's resignation. Carnegie wrote the typical notice for the press, which—while stressing that the initiative for the change had come from their president—contained all the indicators that he had been encouraged in his voluntary withdrawal: "Mr. Leishman has been urging his partners for some time to relieve him of the harassing duties of the presidency of the company, owing to the state of his health. . . . Mr. Leishman . . . intends to sail with his family for a long rest and period of travel in the early spring."[25]

Leishman was replaced by Schwab, who was to retain the presidency for over four years until Carnegie Steel was incorporated in a much wider organization. Very soon after his term of office began, the first moves were made toward amalgamation within the industry. Given its size and efficiency, Carnegie Steel was always a key consideration in such plans. The resulting uncertainties helped bring out further differences among the partners in their thinking about policy.

The Urge to Reorganize

Throughout the 1890s, as the business and the profits of Carnegie Steel grew massively, its nominal capital and distributions of profits to partners both remained small. Carnegie generally favored expansion involving unceasing expenditure on new plant and an aggressive stance to competitors. Among his senior partners, Phipps always argued for caution concerning extensions and was occasionally impatient for dividends. Although their interests and inclinations might differ from Carnegie's, when the junior partners had to make decisions, they recognized Carnegie's predominating interest and usually fell in with his wishes. Frick had already proved that he was willing to take an independent line.

Throughout the decade, the company held to the partnership organization that had served it so well in the past; but this was gradually recognized as being more of a restraint, as the business environment changed, as other companies were reconstructed and new ones were established. Carnegie urged the need for them to turn out a wider range of finished steel products in order to meet the challenge of new competitors; his partners began to press for a new company structure. Andrew Carnegie was away from the United States from May 1897 to October 1898. He spent Christmas 1897 on the Riviera, sending the managers a greetings cable whose enthusiastic tone gave no indication he was thinking a time for withdrawal or wholesale reconstruction was approaching: "Cordial good wishes and regards. Now for 98 and a record."[26]

Through much of the following year, relations between Frick and Carnegie were good. They were helped along by their affection and infectious enthusiasm for their young children. In March 1897, aged sixty-one, Carnegie had become a father. A year later, as Margaret Carnegie grew from a baby into child, she became an occasion for pleasantries, in letters that generally focused on business. Frick's daughter, Helen, was eight and a half years old when Margaret was born and was always the object of Frick's doting affections. In mid April 1898, he added a postscript to a letter to Carnegie that had dealt with the Bessemer Railroad and the threat of war over Cuba: "My experience is that little girls show their mamas preference until they are about three years old, and then the papas seem to be really

Charles M. Schwab in 1901. Schwab replaced John Leishman as president of
Carnegie Steel in February 1897. Leishman, Frick's successor, had served as
president for only two years.

appreciated." Meanwhile, Carnegie had written to express his hope that
Frick would be able to visit Skibo that year: "the best summer location in
the world," and after remarking that Margaret was "very cute," he added,
"I think when Helen and she are seen together the people will vote them a
prize pair." Shortly afterward, Frick wrote that he had been thinking of
holidaying in Strathpeffer "on account of its proximity to Skibo," but he
went on to make various excuses—that part of Scotland was too damp, and
although Adelaide Frick wanted a holiday abroad, he and Helen did not.
Eventually, recognizing that Adelaide needed a complete rest, he decided to
take her to the health resort of Aix-les-Bains. Andrew Mellon either traveled
with them or joined them there. The two men did not stay long in the south
of France but soon left Adelaide and the children in Aix to go on to Paris,
where Frick negotiated for Corot's *Ville d'Avray,* which at this time he re-

garded as "the gem of my collection." He felt sure that Carnegie would like it.[27]

Already, thought about reorganization of Carnegie Steel was developing. It was helped along by pressures from outsiders keen to contain the company's aggressive business practices. In the first week of January 1898, a party from Illinois Steel and American Steel and Wire made a visit to the works at Homestead, Braddock, and Duquesne. The group was led by Elbert H. Gary, who was then engaged in organizing American Steel and Wire for John Pierpont Morgan. Others in the party were Eugene J. Buffington, who became secretary and treasurer of American Steel and Wire, and a Mr. Shearson. Schwab took them round and was critical: "Mr. Buffington does not impress me as a man of ability or experience; knows nothing of the practical details of the business." The visitors took the initiative in broaching the question of some sort of association, and Schwab reported at once to Frick, who was at their New York office:

> The weather was the worst we have had here for some time and it made our trip around the works most disagreeable. They were exceedingly interested, however, and I am sure very much impressed. The Judge constantly talked of the possibility of inducing Mr. Carnegie to consolidate with them. Made no reply, but simply listened to what he had to say. Tells me he has some ideas about valuation to take up with you when he sees you. Told him I expected you to be in New York tomorrow and home Sunday morning. This made him more than ever anxious to go to New York tonight, and he leaves on the 10 o'clock train and will likely see you tomorrow.[28]

There were rumors of various forms of consolidation in the steel industry during the year. In April 1898, Frick mentioned talk of a possible link between Illinois Steel, American Steel and Wire, Minnesota Iron, Cambria Steel, and Lackawanna Steel. A few days later, in May 1898, he was surprised when, in conversation in New York, Gates suggested that Carnegie Steel should own his former company, Illinois Steel. It could be purchased on very reasonable terms, and he would be glad to undertake to bring it about. Frick reported his own response: "Told him was afraid it was almost too big an undertaking for us, but we were always willing to receive propositions." (Less than two years before in December 1896, he had written to Carnegie: "Do not think it would be difficult to use Illinois Steel Co. with an organization we could put there.") Now his own thoughts were moving in the direction of a consolidation, but one with a much narrower compass. Two days after speaking with Gates, he remarked, "It seems to me time may have arrived when Carnegie Steel should own all stake in H. C. Frick Coke Co."

He put a high valuation on the coke company and added that he thought they could perhaps incorporate the word *Coke* into the title of this new firm. Certainly, "One big perfect organization would have many advantages." Lauder and Carnegie were then about to sail from Scotland on the yacht *Argo* to attend the Stockholm meetings of the Iron and Steel Institute. Lauder suggested caution in responding to this proposal, although his own immediate reaction was heated:

> How comes it that the coke business has got so very valuable, has increased in a much larger ratio than the steel works? . . . really the Coke Co. are as much in a position to absorb the Steel Co. as vice versa—$30 million—whew—Let us take a breath anyway, there are a number of different points of view to look at this from, which we will talk over at sea.

The idea of a merger of steel and coke was to recur, though not always in a form that Frick found acceptable.[29]

Meanwhile, Carnegie was by no means consistent in his attitude to reorganization. In the course of one letter during his long absence overseas, he mentioned that he would be willing to dispose of his predominating share in Carnegie Steel. Even when he held to this, there were two very different approaches—to sell or to reorganize. He favored the latter; Frick and Phipps preferred the former. Their thinking was further complicated by continuing schemes for expansion. In a letter from Skibo that was read to the board of managers on 23 August 1898, Carnegie estimated the combined value of Carnegie Steel and the H. C. Frick Coke Company to be at least $300 million. Yet his attention was diverted from disposal to the alluring prospects of moving downstream to production of more finished products such as steel cars, boilers, or wire: "Why not steel pit-wagons and a thousand different articles of steel? . . . The trend of events is all in this direction and we are not to see subdivision of processes, but more and more processes united in one concern."[30]

Forward thinkers in other companies were also looking to reconstruction; now and again, their actions forced the pace of change at Carnegie Steel. On 9 September 1898, a $200 million corporation was formed through the agency of J. P. Morgan. The new Federal Steel Company included the plants, coal mines, and coke ovens of the Illinois Steel Company, the ore mines in the Upper Lakes region belonging to the Minnesota Iron Company, and the Lorain Steel Company on Lake Erie. Elbert H. Gary became president. Shortly after returning from Europe, Carnegie invited Gary, and another Federal Steel director, H. H. Porter, to dine with him and with Frick in his New York home. Although initially shocked when Gary demanded that his company should have half the rail tonnages of the contracts that jointly they had secured, Carnegie and Frick—convinced of the strength of their competitor—had to concede. This must have given a jolt to their own thinking about reconstruction. By November 1898, the movement to sell was gathering momentum. Almost all Carnegie's colleagues now wished to buy him out, but he still found it difficult to face up to parting with interests he had dominated for so long. Consequently, time and again, his opinions were to oscillate. On Wednesday, 23 November, Henry Phipps in some excitement wrote to Frick from the Arlington Hotel in Washington:

> Yesterday Mr. AC dined and stayed the evening with us, and walking to this Hotel he again mentioned the great question of selling out, and I mentioned my views to him mildly and on starting down this PM I received the enclosed, which seems at least a step in the right direction. It is a chance of a life time—comes to but few and is rarely repeated. If you were ten and myself twenty years younger I would prefer selling but a half of my interest. Please return the note and I will send it to GL [Lauder].

(Unfortunately Carnegie's memorandum is no longer with Phipps's letter.) On Monday, 28 November, both Phipps and Schwab wrote to Frick concerning Carnegie's undecidedness about reconstruction; the former reported his own conversations with Carnegie, the latter conveyed what Lauder had passed on to him. Phipps described what seems to have been a not uncommon setting for his discussions with Carnegie: "My friend and I had a long walk and talk on many subjects—especially the Phillipines [*sic*] and an occasional touch on the subject of selling." Phipps had asked what "Dod" [Lauder] thought of the idea and the answer had been that he was delighted. Carnegie had already thought out what he would do with "his great sum," including "a fine plum" for Pittsburgh:

> I think our Partner is shy of making an offer but would entertain one of the amount mentioned and he speaks very kindly and nicely of his old Partners and I am hopeful that he will consent to do what would be the greatest possible gratification to all his Associates. Whether he would take to the plan you ingeniously outlined and which seemed to me a good thing—I cannot say [he later inserted "am inclined to doubt it"]—but when you see him which I hope will be soon he may have something clear and positive, he asked whether you had seen Mr. Porter [presumably H. H. Porter of Federal Steel] and I said no—he was apparently anxious for some word from him. It seems AC is acting in a business-like way in the matter.

Phipps gave only incidental evidence of the plan that Frick was said to have devised: "While thinking favorably of the cash and stock plan—I should like to consider it further before deciding and have a further talk with you. Big things necessarily move slowly—so it will probably be with our project."[31]

Lauder had several talks with Carnegie before returning to Pittsburgh. He reported them to Phipps: "His mind is nothing like made up, sometimes one way and sometimes another, but I suppose he was talking his thoughts to me." Lauder reckoned it was true that, not knowing how they would be placed if Carnegie should die, the younger partners wished the sale to go through:

> If the Federal got in they could all have as much salted down as make them independent. I shall write AC to this effect but shall take care not to say too much. A little circumstance took place during one of our talks which it would be well you should know—Louise came in and sat down, he turned to her and told her what we were talking about, his thoughts were running favorably to the sale at the time—she remarked that when it was done she "would be the happiest woman in America"—He immediately turned on her quite savagely and went into quite a tirade on men who retired from business dying etc. etc.—that he would be laying down a crown etc. etc., so I judge the matter will make the most progress by being let alone as much as possible—He is in a considerably excited state about the Phillipines [sic] anyway and this coming on the back of it may have had physical effects I fear. Frick is in N. Y. today. I am going to talk to him in a minute or so and will tell him that my judgment is to say little or nothing about selling. If any thing important transpires perhaps we had better talk over the phone.[32]

Schwab wrote to Frick on the same day after speaking to Lauder. His account provided little more than a gloss on what he described as "selling to Federal," except that it also emphasized the commitment to the sale among their junior partners:

> Mr. Carnegie talks most freely about the matter but seems unable to make up his mind. From what Lauder says I believe if Mr. Carnegie was entirely satisfied that the Junior Partners would be satisfied he would not hesitate. Of course definite information on this point could only be obtained by speaking to each one individually. I feel satisfied however that the majority would strongly favor it. Mr. Lauder says that less than $200,000,000 would not be considered.

Schwab then related the incident of Carnegie's outburst to Louise Carnegie. He went on:

> Mr. Lauder says the strongest argument with Mr. C. is that there comes a time when the works could be disposed of to the best advantage, and he is inclined to believe that this is the best time. A little pressure from all his partners will make the thing go through in my opinion. Lauder has advised him to do it and is strongly in favor of it. . . . Nothing new here today. Everything moving along smoothly and quietly.[33]

Through December 1898 and on into 1899, Frick explored the possibilities of sale to either Federal Steel or to Rockefeller—at a price for Carnegie Steel of $250 million and for the Frick Coke Company of $70 million. The results were disappointing. Federal proved unable to contemplate such an immense outlay, and Rockefeller decided he did not want to go into steel on a large scale. The alternative approach was through a reorganization of their own operations with a more realistic valuation. On 10 December, Frick had submitted such a scheme to Carnegie. It provided for the formation of a new holding company for all their operations, under the title The Carnegie Company Limited. The capital would be $250 million.[34] Soon the whole issue was complicated not only by Carnegie's natural reluctance to withdraw from business but also by his anticipation that expansion would bring further increase to profits that were already snowballing (see table 25).

Such prospects whetted Carnegie's insatiable appetite. As a result—as shown in the schedule of their 1898 performance and projections for the next year, which he sent on to Lauder—he was now borne aloft in a state of high optimism, though he had not quite closed his mind to change. Profits in 1898 had been $11.5 million:

> I am certain that in 2 years hence we shall be on a basis of $25 million net yearly even at low prices—we have to supply the world. . . . Since we reach Atlantic ports at $1 per ton we have all the trade of the world. I favor holding on for 2 or 3 years. No question but we can sell our property at $400 million. . . . Why not then wait. . . . If you (want) to sell now then here is the plan.

This plan, which he apparently regarded as the second-best option for the future, involved formation of a $300 million corporation that would cover all their operations, mines, coke ovens, works, and so on. He, Frick, Phipps, and Lauder would retire from active business but for five years would act as "consultative partners." His letter ended, "This proposition is true, nothing held back."[35]

Yet for all his strange mixture of greed, aggressiveness, and romanticism concerning their situation, Carnegie's doubts about change still surfaced occasionally. Things were going so well with their present organization. His own 1898 income from earnings, dividends, and interest had been $10.52 million. At the end of December he wrote critically about combinations in the industry, and his words were quoted at the meeting of managers on 3 January 1899: "We should look with favor upon every combination of every kind upon the part of our competitors; the bigger they grow, the more vulnerable they become. It is with firms as with Nations, 'Scattered possessions' are not in it with a solid, compact, concentrated force." On the first Thurs-

TABLE 25

Earning Power of the Carnegie Steel Company, 1892–1898

	Capital and Surplus on 1 January	Earnings in Year	Percentage Earning Power
1892	25,750	2,000	7.77
1893	28,828	3,000	10.41
1894	31,021	4,000	12.89
1895	35,625	5,000	14.04
1896	40,768	6,000	14.72
1897	43,536	7,000	16.08
1898	49,144	11,500	23.40

Source: Carnegie Steel Company, 28 Jan. 1899 (ACLC).
Note: Figures in first two columns are in thousands of dollars (there was clearly rounding of the annual earnings figures).

day of the new year, a critical meeting was held at his home in New York. Those present were Carnegie, Frick, Phipps, Lauder, Schwab, Lovejoy, Peacock, and Phipps's nephew Lawrence Phipps, their treasurer. Carnegie opened their discussions by favoring a new organization that would consolidate the business in their own hands, but he "finally consented, though with great reluctance, and yielding to the wishes of his oldest Partner, to a sale at a price." They agreed they would be willing to sell the company stock for $250 million, half in cash and half in gold bonds. Negotiations with interested parties were left to Frick. On 11 January, Schwab sent Frick projections of output and profits for 1899; their bullish tone made selling yet again look less attractive. He reckoned that, in their Pittsburgh operations alone, increased output and reduced production costs would push up profits from the $11.5 million of 1898 to at least $19.37 million, a projection that he described as "conservative" (see table 26).[36]

On Friday, 13 January 1899, Frick's negotiations with the Morgan syndicate that had created Federal Steel came to an end. The syndicate was unwilling to accept Carnegie Steel terms and had wanted to pay in stock. Next day, he passed the information on to Carnegie who expressed himself delighted by the failure. He now favored going ahead with a reorganization to create a new Carnegie Steel Company—though with a capital of only $60 million—that would purchase all the properties of the H. C. Frick Coke Company. When the managers met on 16 January, Frick summarized these developments, and he, Peacock, Lovejoy, and Lawrence Phipps were appointed to pursue the new course.[37]

This was quickly followed by the beginnings of a fresh division on the

TABLE 26

Carnegie Steel, Projected Profit Increases, 1898–1899

Works	Increase
Edgar Thomson steelworks	1,200
Duquesne steelworks	1,100
Homestead steelworks	2,950
Upper and Lower Union mills	1,125
Carrie furnaces and ovens	150
Car shops and axle works (new 1899)	350
Savings in operating costs	1,000
Total	7,875
Add to profits for 1898	11,500
Projected 1899 profits	19,375

Source: CMS to HCF, 11 Jan. 1899, Frick Papers.
Note: Figures are in thousands of dollars.

board. Until now, Lauder had generally supported the line Frick had followed, but from this point he became a critic. On 16 January 1899, he wrote to Carnegie about the valuation of the H. C. Frick Coke Company. In earlier discussions, this had been put at $30 million, and he regarded that as excessive. The current figure was $35 million. The increase angered him: "there seems to me no earthly reason for the coke works to be jumped up 5 million ... if we keep fooling much longer it will go to 50 or 75 million without any trouble." His opinion was that steel and coke were separate businesses. He ended, "However, you are the boss." On the day he received this letter, Carnegie was visited by Schwab, who reported back to Frick: "I called to see Mr. Carnegie this morning. He talked a great deal about reorganization. Had a letter from Lauder on this subject this morning, reciting what we had done on the board, and advancing some views as opposed to it. Mr. Carnegie now talks as though he favors postponement of anything of this sort until next year." Meanwhile, Lauder did not give up easily. He met with some of the partners who had smaller shares—Peacock, L. C. Phipps, Clemson, Morrison, Moreland, Henry P. Bope, and Lovejoy—to discuss the purchase of the coke business. Although he spoke out against it, they generally favored the consolidation of coke with the iron and steel business. He passed on their opinions to Carnegie: "Naig,—Have just had the juniors together. They all seem to be in favor of taking the Coke Company at 35 million, or rather leaving it to you and Frick to fix the price." He ended, "I have nothing more to say on the merits of the question." However, he took it up again next day, this time passing on some thoughts on the subject from Clemson.

Generally, the partners were saying that whatever Carnegie found satisfactory was acceptable to them: "Moreland is perhaps an exception, he seems to reason more than others and from sounder ideas—It might not be amiss to let him go through the Coke Co. figures before taking it over, if you decide so to do. . . . Of course you can count out my views now, I am so hopelessly in the minority." At the end of the month, Carnegie informed the managers that he was not opposed to consolidation of coke and steel but did not favor going ahead yet. If coke operations remained separate, they would be better managed by Frick.[38] With that, agitation for a radical restructuring subsided for a time. When it broke out again, Frick was soon more deeply and more obviously at odds with his senior partner.

An Option to Buy

At the end of March 1899, when discussion of reorganization was again underway among the partners, an approach was made by William H. Moore for the purchase and combining of the Carnegie and Frick companies. This bid failed, but it was accompanied by circumstances that soon afterward helped bring about the dramatic final stages of the association between Frick and Carnegie. Judge Moore had already shaped two major combinations of steel and finishing operations, the American Tin Plate Company in December 1898, and the National Steel Company in February 1899. At the time of the discussions about Carnegie Steel, he was completing his third trust, the American Steel Hoop Company. Carnegie strongly disapproved of stock manipulators like the Moore brothers, who had previously been involved with other industrial amalgamations such as the Diamond Match Company and the National Biscuit Company. He could be scathing in his expression of these opinions. On one occasion, his feelings were made very public with the remark, "The Carnegie Steel Company are [sic] out of fashion in these days, a back number. They only know how to make and sell steel, and nothing about making securities, preferred and common stocks and bonds."[39] Thinking this way, he refused to deal directly with outside parties but required that negotiations for sale of Carnegie Steel be conducted through his principal partners, Phipps and Frick. It was these two therefore that became associated with the Moore syndicate in this particular scheme for amalgamation.

For the purposes of the negotiations, Carnegie Steel was valued at $250 million, of which Carnegie's share was $158 million. His interest in the $70 million now assessed as the value of the H. C. Frick Coke Company was $17.5 million. A ninety-day option on these investments was secured for a million dollars. Subsequently, he raised the option money to $1,170,000; Frick and Phipps together put up the extra $170,000. This addition to the option money was agreed on April 24. Bridge suggests that Carnegie undertook that if necessary he would later return this portion of the deposit because it came from his two partners. There seem to be at least some reasons for this assumption, but in fact the initial draft agreement read:

> Should this option not be completed and its terms complied with within the 90 days named within, second parties [presumably including Phipps and Frick] shall forfeit the deposit made with the Carnegie Steel Company Ltd. to the credit of the first party [Carnegie], and any and all rights, duties and obligations created under this instrument shall cease and determine, and the parties respectively shall stand in relation to the subject matter thereof as if this agreement had never been executed.

The agreement was read to the Carnegie Steel board of managers on 26 April 1899 and was discussed by them very briefly. The revised option was outlined in a note of 19 May. This too seemed to envisage forfeiture of the option money, which it referred to as given "with the understanding that, in the event of failure to reorganize and consolidate the companies, each party was to lose but the amount contributed, and no further obligation was created between them."[40]

A prospectus was prepared giving details of the various works and properties and outlining financial performances. It indicated that improvements already underway would increase pig iron output from the current 2.2 million to 2.37 million tons, and steel production from 2.8 million to 3.15 million tons. There was to be provision for "a limited amount of stock" to be made available to the general public. At the same time the principal officers, who were to retain much of the rest of the capital, committed themselves to maintain the company's exceptional levels of efficiency. The statement ended by becoming a paean of praise, although one that might seem to the discerning reader to be attempting to combine some incompatible qualities; it reported (presumably in anticipation) that the Carnegie Steel staff, down to workers and clerks, had subscribed for stock, thus

> demonstrating their faith in its future and ensuring the same bold yet conservative management which has rendered possible such an aggregation of capital as this; making large profits, yet earning them; largely controlling the market, yet never abusing its power; encouraging the wider use of steel by the reduction in its cost, yet paying the highest wages in the World. Such has been the past, such is the present and such is expected to be the future of the Carnegie Steel Company.

At the same time as the prospectus was prepared to commend them to
the general public, Schwab outlined to Frick his own anticipations of their
prospects:

> While we have been highly successful in the past, as every one knows, I believe
> we are only now getting in shape to be truly successful and truly profitable. . . .
> With prices anywhere near today's selling prices we would easily make over
> $3,000,000 per month, and then our new works to be started in two months
> will, I estimate on present prices, bring us an additional profit of $600,000 per
> month or total of $3,600,000 per month.

But he was sure that they could run well at lower prices and that, as he put
it, the business of the world was within their grasp:

> I know positively that England cannot produce pig iron at actual cost for less
> than $11.50 per ton, even allowing no profit on raw materials, and cannot put
> pig iron into a rail with their most efficient works for less than $7.50 per ton.
> This would make rails at net cost to them of $19.00. . . . You know we can make
> rails for less than $12.00 a ton. . . . As to the works, any competitor will tell you
> that we are far ahead of any one, and, if plans which we have for the future are
> carried out, we will be farther ahead than ever. I have no fears for the earnings
> in the future. I believe they will much exceed any estimate we have made,
> provided, however, that the same methods of organization and operation as
> now exist, are fully carried out in the future. It must not be run as other con-
> cerns are run, but as it is now conducted. This is most important. I believe the
> earnings will fully justify the capitalization and as a proof of my belief in this, I
> am quite willing to take every dollar I own in the stock of the new concern on
> the basis proposed.[41]

For a time, discussions with Moore seemed to go well. The outside world
looked ahead to the completion of the sale. On 6 May, John W. Gates even
went so far as to send his congratulations to Frick:

> [U]pon the consummation of what I know must have been the great desire of
> your life—to put the affairs of the Company that you have so ably managed for
> many years through adversity and prosperity, in such shape that you are, I feel
> positive, in absolute control. No man in the iron and steel business in the world
> could hope to accomplish what you have done since your connection with the
> Carnegie Steel Company; and I cannot congratulate you too earnestly for your
> great achievements, which I think will result in the closer alliance of the iron
> and steel manufacturers of the entire world. If I can assist you in any manner,
> either personally or in a business way, I am at your command: and in the
> meantime remain, Yours very truly, J. W. Gates.

A few days later, *Iron Age* published a leader under the heading "Andrew
Carnegie's Retirement." The editor was clearly convinced that now was the
time for the evaluation of an era that was ending. Its author recognized that

although Carnegie had relied on the day-to-day labors of a group of able and active partners, "his master mind guided the great concern which bears his name in all hours of crisis." But the same issue contained a fuller outline of "The Carnegie Interests," and in the course of this, particular attention was paid to Frick, who—whatever the importance of Carnegie to whom the leader had paid tribute—was regarded as the key man. He was "the principal factor in its phenomenal development," and also "one of the principal factors in the industrial development of the United States, to which the country owes much for its place as the foremost commercial nation of the world." His exceptional qualities had earned him this place and were detailed:

> In business Mr. Frick is wonderfully quick of comprehension and accurate in his judgment of men and affairs. It appears easy for him to select the best man for a particular duty. He never lacks courage to vigorously carry out his decisions. He is equally firm and courageous in opposing any measure of which his judgment or strong sense of right disapproves.[42]

On 13 May, writing to Carnegie, Schwab remarked that matters seemed to be progressing favorably toward the goal of reorganization. He presumed Frick had kept him informed—although Wall seems to imply that Frick and Phipps, knowing Carnegie's aversion to stock gamblers of the Moore stamp, had not revealed the names of the parties negotiating, until they sent a cable that Carnegie received on 10 May. (On the face of it this seems most unlikely; Carnegie was not the sort of man to even initiate discussions for the disposal of his steel empire without full inquiry into the credentials of hopeful bidders.) Meanwhile, the uncertainty brought with it other problems: as Schwab had found, it was "very difficult to keep things up to a standard with the minds of so many of our young people occupied with prospective riches. . . . hope something may be settled soon."[43]

Before Schwab wrote this letter events had already occurred that quickly frustrated the reorganization plans. Moore's expectations that he would have no difficulty in raising capital were dashed by the disturbances in the financial world brought on by the death of the financier Roswell P. Flower, on Friday, 12 May 1899. The following Tuesday, Schwab saw Moore briefly at their New York offices. He reported to Frick:

> Had a few moments' conversation with him and it struck me that he feels decidedly blue over the outlook. He don't speak nearly so confidently as he did. Seems anxious for you to come to New York. Says however that the condition of the market is most unfavorable and that very little can be done at this time. He showed me list of Chicago subscribers, principally National Steel Corporation crowd headed by Reis for $350,000. I think he felt discouraged over the showing but did not say so.

The initial plan fell through. So Moore, Phipps, and Frick promptly came up with another scheme to buy the properties and charter a new company in Pennsylvania, capitalized at $250 million—to be divided into two and a half million $100 shares. On Monday, 22 May, Frick informed the Carnegie Steel board of managers that he and Phipps had met Moore in New York on the previous Friday. The minutes of the board meeting record a letter from Philander Knox, explaining that the charter they would have received a week later under their first scheme now needed to be amended. Frick remarked that he had not been satisfied with the high capitalization that Moore had wanted and that, under the changed circumstances, he and Phipps had "insisted on our plan being adopted. . . . There is no water in this. We are not putting the price as high as Mr. Carnegie sold out for. I really think the property is worth that money and will take stock for all my investment in the present companies, provided the same management remains in charge." Even Lauder was reconciled: "I felt very much relieved, indeed, when you told me in New York that this plan had been decided upon. It is no stock jobbing arrangement now, but is on a proper basis." Indeed, contentment with the proposed scheme seemed universal: "Each member present expressed his satisfaction with the reorganization as now proposed, believing it very much better for all concerned than at first outlined." Following this endorsement from the board, Frick wrote to Carnegie: "Beg to enclose copy of agreement reached last Friday [19 May], after hard struggle, and after an offer to Mr. Moore to return his money, which he refused to accept. . . . Mr. Moore is an honest man, but very sanguine." Frick mentioned that Moore had wanted a high capitalization, but he had opposed it. He also noted the disturbance caused by Flower's death.[44]

There is no reason to doubt that Carnegie anticipated this would mark his withdrawal from the steel scene. He went so far as to prepare what his biographer has called a "sentimental" letter to be released to the press when the sale was agreed. His old friend and business competitor, Benjamin F. Jones, in a newspaper interview lauded a career that was regarded as ending or even ended:

> Mr. Carnegie has just closed a remarkable career in the world of steel. . . . he had a wonderful faculty for surrounding himself with the strongest and brightest men in the business as soon as they gave promise of development. . . . Mr. Carnegie's name will go down as that of the greatest ironmaster in the history of the world.

It is clear that as late as the end of May, Carnegie was intending to go ahead. He received a note about the close of his career in the industry from Leo

Bullion, a long-term servant of the company—who five years before had been involved in controversy at the Homestead plate mill. In reply, Carnegie wrote, "I am very much touched by your letter. There is a painful side to it. Retiring from business is not with me a question of money one way or other, the wrench comes from leaving the younger men I have been associated with, yourself among the number."[45] But just at the point when the buying out of Carnegie, the achievement of company reconstruction, and supreme power all seemed within Frick's grasp, things went wrong.

In his letter of 23 May 1899, Frick had said that if there were any problems, he might sail with his family to sort it out with Carnegie "in which event would have Mr. Phipps accompany me." A week later, on 30 May, Phipps was obviously troubled when he wrote to Frick, although his letter failed to spell out the details: "I think well of your letter to Mr. Moore—he should meet us surely and relieve us of a great moral responsibility. . . . I presume you will think out some good plans for various circumstances with Mr. Andrew Carnegie."[46] It had become obvious that, in the difficult financial circumstances, the selling of bonds and the raising of cash to pay for the purchase could not be completed by the closing date of 4 August. Frick sailed for Europe on 6 June. Arriving in Britain, he and Phipps traveled up to Skibo. Carnegie had somehow been informed at the end of May that his two partners were to receive $5 million for their work in arranging the option. Disapproving of this sort of commission, he was not disposed to sympathize with their request for an extension of the time for raising the capital to complete the purchase. Their conversations in the house or during their walks and drives in the extensive grounds of Skibo Castle must often have been strained.

On 23 June, writing to Lauder, Carnegie reported on his meetings with Frick and Phipps. His letter was in pencil and is not easily legible. Even so the main points are clear enough and show a strange, almost perverse interpretation of the outcome of the meetings on his part:

> HP and HCF came and told me Moore wished an extension. I said not one hour. They were delighted, both wished the matter ended, although they left me to decide not knowing their views. I said business was to be so fine next year would show 40 to 50 million . . . they concurred. . . . I said no trouble getting up to 320 million—That I thought partners would be glad to take it for themselves and on that basis. Frick said just his idea. Harry ditto.

He mentioned that the option ceased on 4 August and added that their partners "needn't be thinking over anything but attention to business." On 24 June, Phipps and Frick cabled back to the board: "Pleasant interview at

Skibo. Will not extend or modify present option. Have advised Chicago" (the center of the Moore group activities).[47]

The option lapsed on the agreed date. Although he had earlier written concerning the option money, "of course any part paid by my partners I shall refund," Carnegie now refused to do so, allegedly because he had found out about the $5 million bonus his visitors would have received if the reorganization had gone ahead.[48] Much later, Frick stoutly maintained that Carnegie had been wrong concerning this alleged bonus. Pointing out Carnegie's failure to keep his part of the bargain to return the additional option money they had subscribed, Frick recalled in a letter to Bridge that he had been told this was because Carnegie had learned of the bonus, but in this, Carnegie was "entirely mistaken. . . . I repeat, there was never any understanding, secret or other, with Judge Moore by which Mr. Phipps and I were to have any advantage over our associates."[49] On Carnegie's side, dissatisfaction over the planned association with a man like Moore may have given extra strength to the reluctance to give up his powers and his desire to stay on top, to reap the even richer harvests of profits being forecast. On the other side, even as he sat back to think through their Skibo discussions, in the train carrying him south from Bonar Bridge Station, "delight" and "pleasure" can scarcely have been the terms to describe Frick's emotions. The initial frustration of his plans for consolidation was soon to be further colored by resentment over the loss of the option money.

Before these positions solidified into confrontation, however, consideration of reconstruction continued, although apparently without any clear sense of direction. Phipps was again speculating about the matter in midsummer. That year, the Phipps family rented Beaufort Castle, to the south of the small Highland town of Beauly and a journey of some sixty miles from Skibo. In the first half of July, before his unwillingness to return the option money had been revealed, Carnegie stayed with the Phippses for two days. He was in good health and excellent spirits, but his conversation seems to have confirmed the impression that a good deal of the cause for the repeated failures of attempts at reconstruction was to be found in the volatility of his views. He and Phipps enjoyed their time together: "Andrew was made happy by catching two fine salmon—17″ to 18″ long—hooked and landed them unaided—his first salmon. The first caught he sent home—the other, mentioning the fact, to his Uncle Lauder. I landed three the other morning. Water now in fine condition and our place never seemed to us so nice." But Phipps realized that Frick's main interest would not be in his reports of the recreational delights of the Highlands: "You will naturally like to hear what his views are on the great question in which we are all so much

interested." There followed a rather muddled report. As they had been preparing to go into lunch on Friday, 14 July, two cables had arrived. One of
them brought the news that June profits had been $1.766 million:

> Our friend was quite frank about the business—its prospects etc. during the
> luncheon, and that the Creator did not make many such Coal and Ore proper-
> ties as we possessed! The day before Andrew had said that a 4 percent bond was
> all we ought to ask for, and driving to the station he was quite jubilant and said
> that from this on, our gains would [be] two [presumably $2 million] monthly
> and next year's around forty [million dollars] and that he could write a pro-
> spectus that would sell our concerns—even thought Judge Moore would yet
> arrange to take before Aug. 4th—to which I replied impossible—that even if he
> thought advisable to try it, the movement of so much ready money at one time
> would cause a disturbance approaching a panic, and he said he didn't want
> money he was willing to take more bonds and gave me the impression that the
> settlement could be made in almost any form. Four percent is all he aims at
> and is all we should expect. With your means and mine it is surely all we should
> dream of. Your opportunities and abilities are superior to Carnegie's and mine.
> Mrs. Phipps thinks that Carnegie is very anxious to sell. . . . You will have some
> good ideas on the subject when we meet. Let me hear from you when conve-
> nient. . . . We eagerly hope you will come to see us. I honestly believe a week
> here with such weather as we are having will be worth double the time in the
> Adirondacks and if gain is great don't limit your stay but delay your sailing.
> Surely wisdom. . . . Don't fail to come. Will try to arrange a special car like AC
> mentioned to you if you can give me early notice.[50]

By the time of Phipps's next letter (unfortunately undated), Carnegie had
declared his refusal to return the option money, and therefore not surprisingly the tone is noticeably different. It was another glorious morning and
the Phipps family were just about to start out for Glen Affric with their
visitors, the Choates (Joseph H. Choate was now beginning his six-year term
as U.S. ambassador to the United Kingdom). Notwithstanding the beauties
of the natural setting and the distinction of his guest, Phipps's thoughts were
preoccupied with company reorganization. Again he stressed his dependence on Frick's competence and opinions:

> A visitor says the Senior is desperately anxious to sell. An obvious fact. If it had
> not been for you and me AC would never have gotten his $1,170,000. Mighty
> little thanks we get for our part. Unless a right sum and terms are agreed
> upon—some sort of a reasonable compromise—I shall vote *No*—this is the way
> I feel. . . . Having been one of several who paid the large sum for an option at
> $320,000,000 I am not willing to pay that figure which we rejected. You are the
> Atlas in this matter and therefore double reason why you should see this matter
> most clearly. . . . Bon Voyage.

Frick arrived back in New York on Tuesday, 5 September. At the end of the
following week, Phipps, still at Beaufort Castle, replied to a cable from him.

Carnegie still could not make up his mind about a sale. In view of what was to happen in a few month's time, his references to the Iron Clad agreement are interesting:

> [O]ur friend claims that next year will be the harvest year, puts the figure as high as 40, and he may be averse to consolidate on the basis on which there is, otherwise, a perfect unanimity of opinion. Under these conditions it may be necessary, as a dernier resort, to make some modification of agreement with him, to let him down easy; and that would be, if we reach such a figure as he expects in 1900, we will give him his share of it as a supplement to the price at which we buy him out. One thing sure, we are not compelled to purchase, and as to the Iron Clad, in strength it is not even a rope of sand; merely a reminiscence, as Mr. Walton would say. I expect to sail on the 4th of November,—perhaps the 11th,—unless you or Mr. Walker would wire me that I had better come earlier; but there has been so much talk by Mr. Carnegie, and so much changing of his ground after we thought it was understood, that even a few weeks may not amount to much or delay the negotiations appreciably.[51]

Frick had by now formulated yet another scheme for an increase in the capitalization of the Carnegie Steel Company and the buying out of their senior partner. On 11 September, he was back in the chair for the board and asked the members to consider the matter carefully for later discussion and decision. But this new scheme for reorganization came to nothing. Soon after the whole matter was swept up and lost in a final crisis.

The Crisis of Fall 1899

It is difficult, probably impossible, to find objective history. Historians rewrite the past in every age, seeing forces, values, or principles that were ignored or undervalued by their predecessors. The interpretation of events is affected by partisanship, either conscious or unrealized—nationalism or religious bias provide obvious examples.

The same thing is true in the consideration of economic development. The extreme instance here is in radically different structures "imposed" on the flux of forces and their results by capitalist and by socialist writers. At a lower level, in the consideration of the history of an industry or firm, there may be a conventional wisdom and a conflicting perspective. There can be few clearer illustrations of different perspectives than the accounts of the final dispute between Frick and Carnegie in autumn 1899. The generally accepted view is that Frick was a disturbing element, who had to be evicted for the greater good of the company as a whole. This is the approach of Hendrick and, with refinements, of Wall's magisterial biography. The case for Frick is presented in Harvey's biography and in the remarkable "inside" history by Bridge. Inevitably perhaps, all parties present a one-sided view of the situation.

Bridge observed that what Carnegie called "ejectures" of partners had marked major steps in the consolidation, growth, and change of the Carnegie interests and pointed to Miller, Coleman, and Kloman in the early years and Shinn and Abbott later. In the mid 1890s, Leishman was displaced. Now it was the turn of Frick. Carnegie had never been willing to tolerate any possible rival. But this argument is incomplete. There is another common feature to a number of these instances, and that is Carnegie's need for a single person on whom he could depend completely. From the early 1890s, he had spoken and written of Frick as his successor, but by the late 1890s, he was grooming Schwab for power and showed no envy of his outstanding talents or rapidly growing success. On the other hand, Bridge certainly exaggerated when he wrote that Frick emerged from the Homestead contest "with the admiration of the country."[52]

It is not the case that there had been any sudden change in Frick's position or attitude that required his elimination from the company. Perhaps the most reasonable interpretation of the events of the fall of 1899 is that fundamental differences of character and views of the future of business organization now crystallized. In this sense, the analogy used by Bridge—of a sudden blow setting off a chemical change for which the other conditions were already in place—may be helpful. However, it may be argued that, rather than personal conflict initiating change, the changing circumstances for operations and organization brought about the final divide. In respect of these conditions, it must be concluded that Frick discerned the signs of the times more clearly than Carnegie, who in this respect as in others was often strongly influenced as much by sentiment as by logic.

Time and again, Frick had asserted his independence of view, usually with a frankness that contrasted sharply with the readiness of most partners to concur with Carnegie's opinions. An example from early 1899 shows this well. It also points to an interesting pricing policy. The managers were discussing iron, and Frick remarked:

> As criticism of the views of Partners on the purchase of Pig Iron seems to be in order, I submit that the Senior is somewhat off in his views. Lovejoy's suggestion is just right for normal times, but what we want now is to establish immediately a high price for Bessemer Pig, in order to get the benefit of our finished products sold on a sliding scale. It seems to me that this is clear. The Senior has the last guess and the power to decide the policy on these matters, which he does, frequently regardless of the Board, but for some time he has stumbled badly.[53]

Over the next few months there were negotiations for the reconstruction of the steel and coke companies, followed by discussions with Carnegie in Scotland. Then, in the weeks of summer that remained after the Skibo meetings, the "delight" with which Carnegie convinced himself Frick and Phipps had left him soon disappeared. It was replaced by anger when they learned he would not return the option money, despite what they at least believed had been his word. For his part, Carnegie remained disturbed that they had been willing to sell the company to men such as those of the Moore group. According to Bridge, he was at that time discomforted by the publicity and near ridicule to which he was subjected when it was believed that, in retirement, he might become the owner of an almost unprecedented fortune. The general increase in resentment from his two senior partners—and potentially from junior ones too, frustrated as they were in their hopes of fortunes—provided a distracting background for normal business. By autumn, it seemed both Carnegie and Frick were almost looking for points of disagreement.

There were a number of steps toward the explosion that made further reconciliation impossible. The uncertainties of summer 1899 made for a peculiar operating environment within the Carnegie works. On 1 September, while Frick was still traveling home across the Atlantic, Schwab spoke to the meeting of the operating departments in a way that indicated how unusual those circumstances were:

> The President opened the meeting by calling attention pleasantly to the tendency on the part of everybody in communicating with the different departments to color their communications to suit their desires to an extent which caused them to be discounted by the parties receiving them. This tendency, from which he was not exempt, he felt was due to the enthusiasm arising from great interest in the work but he believed it would be safer in all communications to state the exact condition of the case and suggested this be made the rule hereafter in all cases.[54]

Frick was back for the managers' meeting of 11 September. Before it began, he briefed his colleagues:

> During the luncheon preceding the more formal part of the proceedings, Mr. Frick gave in detail his discussions while abroad with Messrs. Carnegie and Phipps on the question of Re-Organization, and a letter on the subject from Mr. Henry Phipps to Mr. Frick, received by the latter at the time of sailing for home, was read. The members present were asked to consider the matter carefully and be prepared to give their respective opinions when the subject shall be taken up later.

In the course of the meeting that afternoon, Frick showed signs of irritability, in part with his colleagues but also in part because of a deeper disagreement with Carnegie's written opinions. A question of arrangements with Cambria Steel over ferromanganese provided an instance of the former. He suggested giving immediate notice that they wished to cancel this contract. Schwab responded, "It is worth something to have Cambria out of the market," which elicited from Frick, "But not as much as we have been paying them."[55]

Carnegie had sent a number of criticisms of board actions. They were addressed to his partners generally, not specifically to Frick. But the absent senior partner seemed especially critical of those who were bearing the heat of everyday business, and his words, although general, contained references to topics that must have revived memories of the summer's disappointments. He was dissatisfied with their sliding scale contracts in general, and with one in particular that had been concluded with the American Tin Plate Company. This had been "made without submission to the Board, or without time for absent partners to speak—I pronounced at the time one of the most unnecessary give aways I ever knew in business. . . . The Tin Co. would have given us a rich prize to keep out of their domain. . . . This Tin Co. miss may cost us several millions." In sales to the steel finishing companies, "It is heads they win, tails we lose, under present scales, as I see it." He was pleased that a Russian order had not gone ahead:

> The minutes of the last meeting—(Mr. Peacock's letter)—should be expunged. If ever it is dragged to light the Armor misfortune will be as nothing. Personally, I have always done honorable business, and believe that not only is fair, square open business the only right business, but that it is the most lucrative as well. We do not need to take up with speculators, or adopt unbusiness methods— besides there is only loss and disgrace probably from doing so. I am glad that such are also the views of Mm. Phipps and Frick who have had the most experience in business. The North-Western Railroad Company owes us a part of its Rail order, and *it could have been secured*. It is not good management to let the Federal Steel company exceed its proportion, and you will find that the fact that it does, will require you to exert much force to hold to equality.

The secretary recorded Frick's testy response to this trail of criticisms, a response that ended with a short but pointed attack on Carnegie:

> These contracts have been made, and we must live up to them. If Mr. Carnegie wishes to review past actions, we have as much right to review other things. Take the Rail Agreement, for instance; we had a splendid Agreement made, to which possibly the only objection was the appointing of a General Selling Agent, but this might have been otherwise arranged. Mr. Carnegie objected to it, and it was upset. This, under all the circumstances attending the making of

the Agreement, had a bad effect on our selling organization, and had a bad effect on the minds of every one. I think we have blundered about in proportion to our interests in the concern.[56]

As tension mounted, the junior partners had to decide where to place their allegiance, and it was by no means an easy choice. Frick had quarreled with Carnegie before and had returned to his top post on the board. That summer he had almost achieved supreme power with the buying out of Carnegie. Might he still succeed? These uncertainties were shared by Schwab. In him, as with Carnegie, sentiment and emotion were important both in character and in business relations, in a manner completely foreign to Frick. As president, Schwab had a major role in the success of the Carnegie Steel Company, but even he was uncertain about the future disposition of power. Over the next few weeks, Schwab would have to decide between his two senior partners: for the present he tried to ride both horses. This was vividly brought out in his attitude to Frick at the end of September. There was a board meeting on Monday, 25 September. That evening Schwab set out for New York for discussions between the main rail-making concerns. Next morning, he saw Moore who, he informed Frick, "Seems very pleasant, but did not mention reorganization matter. Of course I did not either. Sent his kindest regards to you and asked when you were coming East." Schwab then went on to mention that his man had let him know Frick had sent him the Thaulow painting of which they had spoken. (Its identity is not known. Frick had bought one Thaulow in 1898 and two, including *The Smoky City*, in 1899.) The news of this gift brought forth expressions of unqualified affection and loyalty, protestations similar to those he had made, and was soon to make again, to Carnegie. If genuine, they show his inherent affection for Frick and therefore the fickleness, treachery, or agony involved in his subsequent conduct; if false or merely a front, they indicate a certain lack of principle in protecting himself whatever the outcome of the struggle he could see looming between his two senior colleagues. It is not known which scenario is true, but there was no equivocation in the general drift of the words he used, although some of them may have important implications and others seem to bear the burden of impending crisis:

> Dear Mr. Frick permit me to write what I would find difficult to say to you, because you would not listen, and say that while I fully appreciate the value of such a picture it counts as naught compared with the consciousness of having won your fellowship and regard. I regard that with more satisfaction than anything else in life—even fortune—you have been so eminently fair and good to me that I can never forget it, and be assured if I have anything of value in me your method of treatment will bring it out to its full extent. Working with and

for you is a great pleasure, and I am yours to command always. I do not write this as a formal and set letter but as a spontaneous expression of my true feeling.[57]

A few days later, there were signs that the time of crisis had arrived, and that awkward choices concerning allegiances would soon have to follow.

There is evidence that, at the beginning of October, the record of Carnegie Steel business discussions was tampered with. The first page of the minutes of a meeting that probably occurred on 1 October is missing. When the managers met on 16 October, a letter from Carnegie was read. He was conciliatory in his reaction to their decisions taken on 11 September, seemingly not even taking offense at Frick's blunt remarks: "The Chairman says that we all have blundered. True, and always will blunder; no one is infallible, but suggestions of a change do not imply personal reflections. It is simply a business question as to what is best, and experience should teach us to change when thought best." Frick as usual chaired the meeting.[58]

On Wednesday, 25 October, the board of the H. C. Frick Coke Company met. This was the occasion for a dramatic deepening of the conflict. Carnegie's copy of the minutes was headed by him, in pencil, "The Carnegie-Frick Coke Contract"; in the corner of the front page of the record, he added another note: "*No Contract. Declaration of War.*" The proceedings bear the mark of contrivance, of steps that had been previously rehearsed. In this instance, the stage management was undertaken by Frick and Lynch. At one point of the meeting, Frick asked, "Mr. President, have you anything to report?" Lynch then listed their contracts for coke in 1900 (see table 27). After he finished his statement, Frick said, "Have you anything else Mr. President?" In response, reference was made to the fact that Carnegie Steel was paying for coke at a fixed price, which that company claimed had been agreed on 1 January 1899 although, Lynch observed, "We have no record of any such contract, and I have repeatedly so informed the proper officers of the Carnegie Steel company." They had billed Carnegie Steel at $1.45 per ton fob for the first quarter of 1899, $1.60 in the second quarter, and after that at $1.75, although "the claim of the Carnegie Steel Company is that the price should be only $1.35 under the terms of the contract alleged to have been made by Mr. Carnegie and Mr. Frick." At this point Lauder, the only Carnegie Steel appointed director present, remarked, "I think this is a question between Mr. Frick and Mr. Carnegie." Frick seemed reasonable, "Mr. Carnegie and I had considerable talk about what the price of coke should be for, as he called it, a 'permanency.' For the sake of harmony, I was personally willing to agree to almost anything. I am willing to talk over the matter with Mr. Carnegie any time. Mr. Lynch, what action do you wish the Board to

TABLE 27

H. C. Frick Coke Company, Examples of Contracts, 1900

Purchaser	Monthly Tonnage	Delivered Price	Price at Ovens
American Steel Hoop	15,000	na	2.50
Duluth Furnace	na	7.00	3.25
Corrigan McKinney (Scottdale)	na	na	3.00 first half 2.25 second half
Lackawanna	50,000	4.55	2.65
Federal Steel (Lorain and Chicago)	35,000	na	2.60
Ohio Valley Iron	na	na	3.00

Source: T. Lynch to H. C. Frick Coke Company, 25 Oct. 1899 (ACLC).
Note: Prices are given in dollars per ton.

take in this matter?" It was Lynch's turn to be inflexible. He proposed they should deny the existence of the contract and notify Carnegie Steel that no claim to settle according to it would be recognized. John Walker supported this motion. Lauder opposed and again suggested that Frick and Carnegie sort out the matter. Frick now responded, in a manner at odds with his earlier remarks, "I have no authority to make contracts for the H. C. Frick Coke Co." To this, Lauder made the commonsense reply, "You and Mr. Carnegie represent a vast majority of stock in the two companies, and if you cannot fix the matter it is a strange thing." His suspicions were now aroused: "Let me look at the Resolution. It seems too much like a declaration of war." Lynch's motion was supported by himself, Walker, and G. B. Bosworth of the coke company; Lauder dissented. Toward the end, he made a remark that again inflamed the mood of the meeting. Referring to the price of coke, he said, "it is a question that can be fixed without any trouble. But I think that if it had not been for the Carnegie Steel Company the Coke Company would not be as big a company as it is today." Frick, as always stung by any remark that seemed to demean the concern he had created, reacted sharply: "I don't know about that." Lauder then moderated his tone but defended his position:

Well, that is a matter of opinion. That is my opinion and you can give yours. That is all right. Through good times and bad, the Coke Company has been supported by the Carnegie Steel Company. The question is surrounded by a great many circumstances that should be taken into consideration. If you and Mr. Carnegie will take it up I am sure I would be delighted to submit it to arbitration.

From the other side, John Walker welcomed this suggestion: "It strikes me that that would protect my interests nearly as well as they could be protected." With that the meeting closed.[59] When the managers of Carnegie Steel met on the next two Mondays, there is no record that either Frick or Lauder mentioned this controversy. Even so it continued to smolder. When it burst out again, it was associated with another matter of dispute.

While negotiations were underway with the Moores in spring 1899, Frick in private purchased the Wylie properties located on the left bank of the Monongahela River, well to the south of the existing Carnegie plants. The 260 acres were reported to have cost him $165,000, or about $635 an acre. Clearly this farm was bought as a prospective industrial site. The steel company was already contemplating building finishing mills to meet the challenge of the great horizontal combinations, whose purchases of semi-finished steel from other companies were set to fall away as they developed their own capacity still further. In June 1899, National Tube was formed; within a few months, Carnegie Steel was beginning to plan its own tube mills. It considered locating them on the site that Frick had acquired at the mouth of Peters Creek. Lawrence Phipps now valued this at $4,000 an acre; Frick offered it to Carnegie Steel for $3,500, more than five times the price he had paid only a few months before.[60]

At this time there was some further progress concerning the merging of the coke and steel interests. The valuations adopted were modest as compared with the open market assessments of the properties. Carnegie was still cautious in his figures, but Frick was much less so and pressed for more realistic costings. Forms of address and the general tenor of the letters between them had now become noticeably less friendly. On 18 November, Frick wrote:

> I understand your proposition to be as follows: The Carnegie Steel Company to be taken at its book value as of November 1 1899 which is $68,399,816.41. The Frick Coke Company and Allied Companies to be taken at their book values as at 1 November 1899, which is $17,906,146.51. Merge them and give me for my interest in Frick Coke company and Allied Companies on the basis of their book values such additional percentage in the Carnegie Steel Company at its book value as the value of the former will purchase. To this I will assent, on condition that, after the merger, the book value of the Steel Company including Coke and Allied Companies, is made not less than $150,000,000.

He added a handwritten note: "This does not include Union Supply Company Ltd. Under the Law, Steel Co. could not hold, its stock can be properly divided and paid for by all parties at proper values." Carnegie replied two days later, effectively rejecting the idea of inflating the stock: "You are slightly off in regard to the suggestion I made, which was that when the books of the Carnegie Steel Co. were balanced for the year and adjusted in the usual manner, I would favor issuing additional stocks for the Frick Coke Co., actual cost value, no water." Even so, he reckoned all would be reasonable: "Whatever there is will be done in fair square manner, most liberal to the Frick Coke party."[61]

Room for maneuvering and will for adjustment were now disappearing, as was shown that same day at a decisive meeting of the Carnegie Steel managers. Frick chaired the meeting, and all proceeded normally until he asked Moreland to submit a statement concerning their financial situation. Commenting on this, Frick drew attention to the low rate at which they had contracted for rails for 1900 delivery, a price almost $8 a ton below current prices. He then went on from one ground of dispute to another, managing to inflame each in turn:

Mr. Carnegie continually referred while here, to the low prices obtained under sliding scale contracts, entirely ignoring that he alone was to blame for creating the atmosphere in which these sliding scale contracts, and other contracts, were made, by insisting last Fall, against the almost unanimous protest of his partners, on selling rails far into the future at $16.00 and $17.00 per ton. . . . although, it must be said for Mr. Carnegie, that he gave as his reason for wanting such low prices . . . that it was for the purpose of breaking up eastern Rail companies. I learn that Mr. Carnegie, while here, stated that I showed cowardice in not bringing up question of price of coke as between Steel and Coke companies. It was not my business to bring that question up. He is in possession of the Minutes of the Board of Directors of the Frick Coke Company, giving their views of the attempt, on his part, to force them to take practically cost for their coke. I will admit that, for the sake of harmony, I did personally agree to accept a low price for coke, but on my return from that interview in New York (within the next day or two) President Schwab came to me and said that Mr. Lauder said the agreement should provide that, in case we sold coke below the price that Mr. Carnegie and I had discussed, the Steel Company was to have the benefit of such lower price. I then said to Mr. Schwab to let the matter rest until Mr. Carnegie came out. . . . He changed his plans, and did not come out. . . . Mr. Schwab, I believe, never heard from him on the subject, and Mr. Lynch . . . very properly, has been billing the coke, as there was no arrangement closed, at a price that is certainly quite fair and reasonable as between the two Companies, and at least 20 cents per ton below the average price received from their other customers. We have By-Laws and they should govern. If not, why do we have them? It is the business of the Presidents of the two Companies to make contracts of all kinds. Mr. Carnegie has no authority to make a contract that would bind this Company. Neither have I any authority to make any contract that would bind the Frick Coke Company, and, at any rate, why should he, whose interest is larger in Steel than it is in Coke, insist on fixing the price which the Steel Company should pay for their coke? The Frick Coke Company has always been used as a convenience. The records will show that its credit has always been largely used for the Steel Company, and is today, to the extent of at least $6,000,000. The value of our coke properties, for over a year, has been, at every opportunity, depreciated by Mr. Carnegie and Mr. Lauder, and I submit that it is not unreasonable that I have considerable feeling on this subject. He also threatened, I am told, while here, that, if low price did not prevail, or something was not done, that he would buy 20,000 acres of Washington Run coal [in the area south from Perryopolis on the Youghiogheny River toward Tippecanoe] and build coke ovens. That is to say, he threatened, if the minority stockholders would not give their share of the coke to the Steel Company at about cost, he would, if possible, attempt to ruin them. He also stated, I am told, while here, that he had purchased that land from me above Peters Creek; that he had agreed to pay market price, although he had his doubts as to whether I had any right, while Chairman of the Board of Managers of the Carnegie Steel Company, to make such a purchase. He knows how I became interested in that land, because I told him so in your presence, the other day. Why was he not manly enough to say to my face what he said behind my back? He knew he had no right to say what he did. Now, before the Steel Company becomes the owner of that land, he must apologize for that statement. I first became interested in that land, as I told you, through trading a lot in Shadyside that I had owned for years. The land is six miles away from any land owned by the Carnegie Steel Company. Steel Company does not need it now, and will not need it for a long time in the future, if at all, but, of course, if they owned it, it might keep another large works from being built, or enable Steel Company to go into competition with some other large industry. Harmony is so essential for the success of any organization that I have stood a great many insults from Mr. Carnegie in the past, but I will submit to no further insults in the future. There are many other matters I might refer to, but I have no desire to quarrel with him, or raise trouble in the organization, but, in justice to myself, I could not at this time, say less than I have.

The secretary closed his minutes of the meeting soberly: "There being no further business, the Meeting, on motion, adjourned at 1.45 pm. Lovejoy." As the members dispersed, some of them at least must have felt burdened with premonitions of doom. Next day, writing to Frick, Carnegie seemed conciliatory:

> If I have insulted you I have known it not. . . . All my sins about last year's rail policy I freely confess. . . . I shall receive your unmerited invective in silence. . . . When you get your usual calm and if you come to me, I shall tell you all the circumstances just as they occurred and you will be sorry for your hasty outburst to your partners. I am not guilty and can satisfy you of this, also of the folly of believing tale bearers, a mean lot."[62]

However, during the next two or three days, he and some of his leading partners began to make definite preparations for the expulsion of Frick from his position of power in Carnegie Steel.

Opposition to Frick was gathering; in this Lauder was active in strengthening Carnegie's resolve. Carnegie later filed a letter from Lauder under the penciled heading, "Letter from Dod—fight it through." It referred to the "crisis," and then to illustrate his proposition that "no one in our firm has given so much trouble as Mr. Frick has done," Lauder mentioned past dissensions—first the coke strike of 1887, then "his sudden turn on you and determination to sell out regardless of his partners' wishes or interests: third this present angry craziness, which seems to be prompted altogether by personal feeling." On this he built a case for eliminating Frick, an argument well calculated to keep his cousin up to the mark. "Now the question keeps intruding itself into my mind all the time—would any possible sacrifice that could be entailed be too much in order to cut loose altogether from such a disturbing element?" He referred to the possibility that, if he left them, Frick might be involved with "an opposition steel works," but "to my mind the Chairman seems to have deliberately burned his boats and the issue is now Carnegie or Frick pure and simple." If Frick retained his power, "every one here will look on the settlement as your virtual abdication." He added that some thought this would indeed be the outcome. Finally he shifted the blame on to some irrationality within Frick. He too had cause to feel aggrieved with Frick, but "I have considered ever since this controversy about coke began that he is scarcely responsible for many of his sayings and doings and, now that the sting of failure last summer is added, the less said about his condition of mind the better, it is probably more a misfortune than a fault to be thus constituted."[63]

It seems to be about this time that Carnegie became determined to break with Frick. He wrote three decisive letters, to Lauder, to Schwab, and to Phipps. His reply to Lauder's letter was immediate, written on his own sixty-fourth birthday. His spirits had been raised and his resolve strengthened by his cousin's advice, and he was now ready to focus his hopes for the future on Schwab. Even so, he was not thinking of immediate action, and he tried to rationalize the decision in order to convince himself. There were inconsistencies, inaccuracies, and uncertainties in what he wrote:

> You voice my views exactly—Frick goes out of chairmanship of board next election or before—that's settled days ago—Have no fear of opposition— none—He could not manage a big concern—beside we will have opposition anyhow—He's too old—too infirm in health *and mind*. Now I have long felt that Chairmanship was a mistake—It overshadows President and you know how Frick got Phipps to urge me to make Chairman the Executive officer and I told him NO NEVER. I was with Schwab always—Schwab has behaved far too kindly to Frick, but this was best after all—You may tell CMS he will be the

man and the only man and that next election Chairmanship will be abolished—Now CMS must see that his men stand firm for this policy . . . must express opinion No Chairmanship and be loyal to CMS. CMS can manage all this nicely—Everyone likes him at heart, not like Frick. I have nothing but pity for Frick, not one iota of temper—this recent exhibition is childish—He sent HP to arrange meeting with me at Union League Club or HP's rooms, Manhattan [hotel]. I said if he wished to see me he knew my office, No 5 West 51st—no further word. My resolve is taken and cannot be shaken—I have given CMS and his brother and a few others control in my will and in life. Shall stand by him—"Who wouldna fecht for Charley" Yours Naig.

He added a postscript:

You may show this to CMS and let him lay his plans accordingly—once again we are to be a happy and united family. . . . My birthday—never better nor happier especially since I decided to tell Mr. Frick in kindest manner that I mean divorce under "Incompatibility of Temper." I shall tell him never had anything but happy family until he came into it—and I am not going to have anything else—it is divorce between us as far as management of our business is concerned—no feeling—only I believe our best business interests demand an end of quarreling. . . . Mr. Frick has no right to ask what passes between partners, all being confidential and sacred, and if any of our boys asked they should at once decline to be made tale bearers.

At about the same time, he wrote to Schwab, revealing in his manner that as always he was looking for compliant rather than independently minded partners: "I give up the long-continued attempt to cooperate satisfactorily with Mr. Frick. Three times now he has broken out . . . call it my fault or his fault, or the fault of neither which is best, but simply 'incompatibility of temper.' " He had concluded that Frick was "an able man, possessed of many virtues, who cannot however harmonize with me, somehow or other, much." Then Carnegie approached Phipps to try to secure his cooperation in persuading Frick to quit without making the occasion one for bitter and perhaps public dispute. His letter is undated, but the mode of expression indicates it was written at about the same time as those to Lauder and Schwab:

My Dear Harry, You know I have decided not to try co-operation with Mr. Frick again. It is a clear case of "Incompatibility of Temper," always sufficient cause for divorce. . . . I shall ask the stockholders to abolish the chairmanship. . . . I shall not vote for Mr. Frick as manager believing that his presence on the Board would not be beneficial. I shall soon be in Pittsburgh and present to various partners my reasons for these conclusions. That they will be adopted by almost everyone I have no reason to doubt. I wish Mr. Frick to know this because I would shield him from being, as it were, ousted from a position he covets. He can resign, stating that he wishes to relieve himself of routine duties and join the veteran brigade. . . . A short note in the newspapers makes it all right and leaves unshaken his position before the public. . . . If he concurs it will never be necessary for me to open my mind to the partners and I will not. . . . Agreement to part company is best for both of us. I must beg you in laying this before Mr. Frick to say that the question of adjusting this in any other manner than that I indicate be not raised. It would be useless.[64]

It is not known when, or indeed, if Phipps showed this letter or conveyed its meaning to Frick, but given his thorough and painstaking nature it is probable that he did. If so, Frick was well prepared for what was to come.

Frick chaired the managers' meeting on Monday, 27 November. Later that day Schwab reported to Carnegie how things had gone. There had been no signs of imminent collapse. Frick "seemed cheerful and happy and apparently took much interest in the usual business before the Board. Don't think he has any idea of resigning." If Carnegie had made up his mind to abolish the chairmanship, he should inform the board to that effect; Schwab believed Frick would then resign. An alternative was to abolish the office at the next annual election. Carnegie could count on them all, although they had some fears that might qualify their reliability: "the Board would not hesitate to do as you wish. . . . The boys are, I am sure most loyal to you, but knowing Mr. Frick's power in the past, will hesitate to do anything against him, fearing the matter might ultimately be fixed up and if it was would injure or end their career." Therefore it was imperative that Carnegie take the initiative. If he wanted Frick's resignation he should say it was because the two of them could not work in harmony, but "the best way is for you to come to the offices and arrange matters with Mr. Frick direct." He went on to vow his own unswerving support, as usual with excessive ardor:

> Regarding myself, permit me to say first, *I am always with you.* Aside from deep personal regard and feeling for you, you have heaped honors and riches upon me and I would indeed be an ingrate to do otherwise. My interests and best efforts will always be for you and the old firm, and when they don't want me any more, I shall even then never give a thought to any other. Believe me, Dear Mr. Carnegie, I am always with you and yours to command. I want to be straightforward toward all. I believe the great majority of important partners feel as I do.

At the end of his letter, Schwab mentioned he would be in New York for a meeting of rail makers in the first days of December. He would call to see Carnegie then. After they had met, he returned to Pittsburgh on the morning of Sunday, 3 December. In the course of that day he wrote a confidential letter to Frick, in which he attempted to cover himself against all eventualities. In doing so, he presented himself in a light that is perhaps rather more favorable than scrupulous:

> Mr. Carnegie is en-route to Pittsburgh today, and will be at the offices in the morning. Nothing could be done with him looking toward a reconciliation. He seems most determined. I did my best. So did Mr. Phipps. I feel certain he will give positive instructions to the Board and Stockholders as to his wishes in the matter. I have gone into the matter carefully and am advised by disinterested and good authority that, by reason of his interest, he can regulate this matter to suit himself—with much trouble no doubt, but he can ultimately do so. I believe all the Junior members of the Board and all the Junior Partners will do as he directs. Any concerted action would be ultimately useless, and result in their downfall. Am satisfied that no action on my part would have any effect in the end. We must declare ourselves. Under these circumstances, there is nothing for us to do but obey, although the situation the board is thus placed in is most embarrassing. Mr. Carnegie will no doubt see you in the morning, and I appeal to you to sacrifice considerable if necessary to avert this crisis. I could say much on this subject but you understand and it is unnecessary. Personally, my position is most embarrassing, as you well know. My long association with you and your kindly and generous treatment of me makes it very hard to act as I shall be obliged to do. But I cannot possibly see any good to you or any one else by doing otherwise. It would probably ruin me and not help you. Of this, as above stated, I am well advised by one most friendly to you. I beg of you for myself and for all the Junior Partners, to avoid putting us in this awkward position, if possible and consistent. I write you this instead of telling you, because I cannot, under the circumstances, well discuss this subject with you at this time, and I wanted you to know before tomorrow. Please consider confidential, for the present, and Believe me, As Ever.

In spite of what he had written, in the course of that Sunday Schwab decided to deliver his letter personally to Frick, a resolution that shows his strength of character. Accordingly, he went over during the evening to Clayton and was there shown into the sitting room. When Frick came in, Schwab handed him the letter and waited while he read it. The effect was dramatic. Long afterward, he recalled that he had seldom seen a person more enraged. He left with the expressions of Frick's anger ringing in his ears.[65]

Next morning, Carnegie arrived, called a meeting of the board, and asked its members to sign a request that Frick resign. He told them he wanted this document in case Frick required such evidence of the general will. He then called on Frick, who responded with an unexpected willingness to give up the chairmanship in the interests of harmony. On Tuesday, 5 December, Frick sent a formal letter to the board of managers: "Gentlemen, I beg to present my resignation as a member of your Board." A special meeting was called at 12.30 that day at which seven ordinary members were present, in addition to Carnegie, Lauder, Phipps, and Singer. On a motion from Clemson and Peacock, the resignation was accepted, with the sincere thanks of the board "for efficient, zealous and faithful service as a member of this Board from January 14 1889, to the present day."[66] The eviction had proved unexpectedly easy.

Far more contentious episodes were to follow. Sometime during November, Carnegie had contacted Lauder concerning the bylaws of the Frick Coke Company, which indicates that he may have already been edging toward the idea of gaining control. Next month, perhaps immediately before Frick's resignation, he wrote twice to Frick about coke—in neither instance was the date indicated. Reference to Christmas may point to dates sometime after the resignation, although Harvey suggests the letters antedated it. Some features of the correspondence support Harvey's view. Whatever the date, the principle remained the same: Carnegie's necessity was to get favorable coke prices for the steel company. If required, Carnegie Steel would take control of the coke company. Justifiably, Harvey refers to Carnegie's first letter as written "with all his former sprightly and ingratiating pungency." He wrote, "This for yourself—don't let the others know we consult together on this." He referred to the new charter they might need if and when they issued stock to the public, and to the "new ground" that Carnegie Steel was getting (this may have been Frick's land at Peters Creek). Then he turned to the main business: "There's one question I wish you would fix—coke prices. Schwab wrote me about them." Carnegie thought the $1.35 price was right; he did not think a change was justified but that the best thing was "to get a fixed price for all time and relieve us of friction which has arisen. . . . Do get at this and fix it and always please remember none of your partners will or can regard you as only the representative of a Seller Co. to them—they will not argue or object freely, but they *think* all the same." He also complained that Frick Coke had not handed over a 15 cent concession on coke freights or interest on coke stored at Braddock. It was, he conceded, as much the steel company's responsibility to take action about this as the coke company's duty:

> [B]ut you see how it is—None of them want to stir up things with F. C. Co.— very foolish when it's only business with nothing personal in it, isn't it. Yet so it is. Do get a permanent arrangement and greatly oblige—you want to make your pard a Christmas gift any how—I'll not look for a $40,000 thing. Give me a settlement on Coke and I'll bless you. Yours ever AC. We never had friction before. It annoys me more than dollars even than Phillipines [*sic*].

Frick seems to have replied, and Carnegie wrote again a few days later. His second letter retained a generally friendly approach, though it was mixed with some blunt speaking. Subject matter and tone together suggest that it came after Frick had resigned the chairmanship:

> Excuse me, I have no time to waste upon the Prest. of the F. C. Co. who begins saying he didn't know the bargain—that's all I read—It's gone to waste basket. It is all settled any how. Schwab writes me they are all willing to pay *$1.35 permanently*—of course F. Co. has no business with C. S. Co. . . . 2nd rate that's clear. This is more than I should have given if I had to decide as a *permanent thing*—I think it's high. It is your own terms and ends it. Don't fool yourself about Lauder and I being alone. Lauder never told me about interest on coke at ET being promised by you and he never knew till told himself that 10c per ton of C. S. Co.'s freight rate was not paid over—he didn't believe it nor did I. My friend you are so touchy over F. Co. Co. (fortunately the only point). . . . Your partners will not speak to you freely about coke, that's decided, but it's a pity. But now all's over you have a mighty good bargain . . . . and a big profit even if fight comes and any other coke field is opened—Washington Run for instance. . . . I believe all back things are also settled—so now all's well. [And he added in a postscript] This is all the Christmas Gift I ask.[67]

For a time, things seemed to be going as smoothly as could be expected in the light of the decisive step just taken. A week after his meeting with Frick that secured the resignation, Carnegie wrote to Schwab:

> My Dear CM, Am glad Mr. Frick is so philosophic but I don't believe he can content himself out of active business, few business men can, they try it and are miserable, fish out of water scarcely more so—no, it rarely seems possible. Mr. Frick should get control of his Frick Co., this would not trouble him, but give him a proper business position among his fellows. He would really be the Coke King he is reputed. If it transpires at next election that he is only a shareholder of less than a quarter, it cannot be pleasant for him. At any rate he will only have himself to blame. I have given him his chance on fairest of terms.

Carnegie had offered Frick most of his own interest in the coke company, and although the two of them had agreed they would no longer cooperate in business, "I shall be sorry for Frick's future happiness if he does not take the position of King in Coke." He expected Frick's response when he had considered this matter. Two days afterward, Carnegie described a very different outcome to Lauder. He had seen Schwab who was "very happy—so are we all," but now Carnegie was contemplating taking over the Frick Coke Company. As a result, "He will be in a ridiculous position not being Coke King."[68]

Interpretation of events at this juncture becomes complicated because there was clearly further tampering with the company records. The evidence now available is not complete. The meeting of managers on 18 December read and approved the minutes of a meeting a week earlier, but no such minutes survive. There is also a gap in the correspondence between 4 and 10 December. Even so, on Frick's fiftieth birthday, 19 December 1899, he received a cable at his home in Pittsburgh: "Mr. and Mrs. Carnegie cordially wish you many happy returns. Yours is a great record to date which they hope and believe the future is still to enhance."[69]

By the latter part of December, there were fears that Frick might cancel the coke contracts that had given Carnegie Steel such cheap fuel for that year. Carnegie denied he could do this: "He can't repudiate contracts for any company in which myself and friends control—we are not that kind of cats." They decided on a very firm response, Carnegie wrote Lauder: unless the old contract was renewed, when elections were made to the board of the H. C. Frick Coke Company on 9 January 1900, Frick would lose his place there too. Lauder seems to have advised caution: "see what Frick does, I have not lost hope that he will come to terms with you and take control of his own company." Carnegie was by now too euphoric to be cautious. As he put it to Lauder next day, "So well and all so happy, business an unalloyed pleasure as I think of every partner now—no rift in the lute."[70]

Meanwhile, Schwab had let Carnegie know that Frick had gone to the South for a holiday of about ten days. Before his departure, he and Schwab had arranged matters for the coke board—Frick was to name two members, Carnegie Steel five. Frick wrote to Lynch, "You are to be President and there will be no Chairman of the Board." He seemed conciliatory but added a note that showed his lowly state: "I have dictated this in the presence of Mr. Schwab." In spite of his apparently compliant mood, next day Schwab reported that Frick would not sell his coke interests for less than $50 million.[71]

While Frick was on vacation, preparations were made for the next round of the conflict. As in the dispute five years before, Phipps supported Frick. He began in his systematic fashion to prepare the defense of their interests. Three days after Christmas, he wrote to their ex-chairman from Laurel in the Pines: "Away from New York I have ample time on my hands and so I have concluded to go over the papers I lent you in Pittsburgh and put them in shape and write out what I want to ask my Attorney."[72] There was not long to wait for the time his "going over the papers" would be of relevance. Early in the new year, further decisive steps were taken.

A meeting of the Carnegie Steel Company was held on Tuesday, 2 January 1900. After some normal business, notice was given of a special meeting of the H. C. Frick Coke Company called for the following Tuesday in Scottdale. Lauder was to act on behalf of the steel company, and Schwab, Peacock, Lawrence Phipps, Clemson, Morrison, Gayley, Moreland, and Lovejoy were each given five shares, "the purpose being to qualify each member of the Board of Managers to act as a member of the Board of Directors of the H. C. Frick Coke Co. should occasion arise."[73] On the day before the coke meeting, there was a special meeting of the Carnegie managers, at which Carnegie won approval for the use of the Iron Clad agreement against Frick if necessary. The H. C. Frick Coke meeting worked out as Carnegie had planned. The chairmanship was abolished, the number of directors was increased from five to seven, and although Frick and Lynch were reelected, five Carnegie men were also appointed. Frick left the meeting in protest.

On the morning of Wednesday, 10 January, Frick was in his office in the Carnegie Building reading a letter from A. R. Whitney, a friend and a stockholder in the steel company, when Carnegie arrived. He sent in a messenger to ask if it was convenient to see Frick. He went in and shook hands with him, and then, when they sat down, took up the matter of his threat to enjoin Frick Coke not to continue deliveries of coke to Carnegie Steel under contract at $1.35 a ton. Frick sat in stony silence while his voluble partner argued for his acceptance of the situation. At the end, he asked what would be done if he did not cooperate. Carnegie replied that in that case they would use the Iron Clad agreement to compel him to give up his financial interest in Carnegie Steel. In his office next door, Schwab heard heated words, raised voices, and the air becoming "thick." Frick jumped from his chair, shouting to his partner words he had not heard for many years, if at all: "For years I have been convinced that there is not an honest bone in your body. Now I know that you are a god damned thief. We will have a judge and jury of Allegheny County decide what you are to pay me." With fists clenched he advanced on Carnegie, who speedily withdrew. Accounts vary as to what happened next. The more dramatic suggest that Carnegie fled, closely pursued along the corridor. Another indicates that Frick slammed his door so loudly the workers in the outer offices were all startled. In his own memorandum of the event, Carnegie was content to represent himself as a calming, sobering influence against Frick's passion: "He became wilder and I was forced to leave."[74]

Later that day, Frick went to the office of John Walker, now a leading figure in the coke concern, whom Carnegie had attempted to win over with an offer of a place on the board of the steel company. Frick told Walker what had happened and explained that he had lost his temper. They decided that, if Carnegie carried through his plans for coke as proposed, they would both present suits against the Carnegie partners, one to prevent the sale of coke at a low price and the other to force a fair evaluation of Frick's interest in the steel company. Walker would take charge of the publicity for their cause. At Walker's suggestion, Frick at once reserved the services of the distinguished trial lawyer John A. Johnson. In so doing he managed to forestall Carnegie.[75]

As he fled the frank speech and menacing postures he had inspired in Frick's office, Carnegie sought immediate sanctuary in Schwab's room. "Charlie, let's go for a little drive," he said, and in the carriage, he revealed what Frick had said to him.[76] On their return to the offices, he called the managers to a special meeting, at which he briefly reported all (or some) of what had happened and asked them to begin proceedings for depriving Frick of his financial interest. On that day and the next, a resolution to this effect was signed by thirty-two partners, the signatures of Schwab and Carnegie heading the two columns of names. The transfer was to be made by the close of business on 31 January, Frick's interest being paid for under the terms of the Iron Clad agreement. It was stressed that, in accordance with the requirements of that document, those who signed represented more than three-quarters of both members of the association and of the value of all holdings required to compel the surrender of a partnership interest.

Frick replied to Carnegie Steel and to Schwab as its president under the date of 10 January. It was a short, but inflexible note:

> You are hereby notified that there is no contract or offer to sell in existence by which either of you can purchase or take from me my stock or interests in the Carnegie Steel Company Limited, and that neither you, as President, nor any other officer of the Carnegie Steel Company Limited, is authorized to transfer any of my stock or interests in the said Company. If there ever was an offer to sell or authority to transfer on my part I have heretofore, and do now, wholly revoke and withdraw the same.

Three days later he took the process further, essentially holding his colleagues collectively responsible. He complained that the board of managers had been called five days earlier without his knowledge and had taken action that he regarded as illegal:

> At the instigation of Andrew Carnegie you now speciously seek without my knowledge or consent and after a serious personal disagreement between Mr. Carnegie and myself, and by proceedings purposely kept secret from me, to make a contract for me under which Mr. Carnegie thinks he can unfairly take from me my interest in The Carnegie Steel Company Limited. Such proceedings are illegal and fraudulent as against me, and I now give you formal notice that I will hold all persons pretending to act thereunder liable for the same.[77]

The battle lines were drawn.

More interesting in some ways than Frick's response, which must have been expected, was how the others reacted. The crisis acted to winnow the

Under the provisions of a certain Agreement between The Carnegie Steel Company, Limited, and the partners composing it, known as and generally referred to as the "Iron Clad" Agreement, we, the undersigned, being three-fourths in number of the persons holding interests in said Association, and three-fourths in value of said interests, do now hereby request Henry C. Frick to sell, assign and transfer to The Carnegie Steel Company, Limited, all of his interest in the capital of The Carnegie Steel Company, Limited, said transfer to be made as at the close of business January 31, 1900, and to be paid for as provided in said Agreement.

Done at Pittsburg, Pa. this 10th and 11th days of January, 1900.

Resolution passed by the managing partners.

```
To

  THE CARNEGIE STEEL COMPANY, LIMITED,

              AND

  C. M. SCHWAB, PRESIDENT OF THE CARNEGIE STEEL COMPANY, LIMITED:

          YOU ARE HEREBY NOTIFIED that there is no contract or of-
  fer to sell in existence by which either of you can purchase or
  take from me my stock or interests in the Carnegie Steel Company,
  Limited, and that neither you, as President, nor any other offi-
  cer of the Carnegie Steel Company, Limited, is authorized to
  transfer any of my stock or interests in said Company.

          If there ever was an offer to sell or authority to trans-
  fer on my part I have heretofore, and do now, wholly revoke and
  withdraw the same.

  Pittsburgh, January 10, 1900.

                              H. C. Frick        (SEAL).
```

Frick's reply.

moral fiber of the leaders of both the coke company and the steel company. Millard Hunsiker, who had once been Frick's personal assistant, chose (as others had already done) to protect himself. He wrote from London, where he represented Carnegie Steel, to revoke Frick's power of attorney for him:

> I know nothing about your plans and am too poor to stand out alone. . . . Of course I don't know much about what's going on but imagine it will be made as uncomfortable for you as possible. Truly I am *very, very* sorry. I beg of you however not to consider any action I may be forced to take as in any way lessening my faith and confidence in you.[78]

Through Schwab, he had already put his name to the request that Frick turn his interest over to Carnegie Steel.

For various reasons others were more supportive. A. R. Whitney was away in California and could not be contacted in time; later he was to prove less than enthusiastic for the majority cause, although Moreland, through Peacock, was anxious (as he put it) to avoid Whitney's trying to "parley" with them and therefore tried to pressurize him. Henry Phipps, rejecting the invitation to support the eviction of Frick, wrote formally to Carnegie Steel: "As I have heretofore stated, I am opposed and object to any attempt not only to force from any partner his interest in our Company, but, also to the right of our Company to use its capital in the purchase of any such interest." Henry Curry had been with Carnegies for much longer than Frick. He was now desperately ill, but even so the resolution that they should invoke the Iron Clad agreement if Frick did not sell his stock was taken to him on his sickbed. He refused to sign, telling Moreland that he wanted to "go to my grave with the marks of an honest man, just as I lived." Another account implies that Carnegie also visited him but Curry remained adamant, saying, "Mr. Frick is my friend." Carnegie asked, "And am I not also your friend?" to which the sick man is said to have replied, "Yes, but Mr. Frick has never humiliated me."[79]

At 2.46 P.M. on Monday, 15 January 1900, Lovejoy visited Frick in his office at 920 Carnegie Building. He handed over the petition from thirty-two of his partners requesting that Frick sell his interest in Carnegie Steel. Frick's only response was "I accept service." Next day, letters from him and from Phipps opposing this action were read to the Carnegie Steel managers. On Wednesday Lovejoy, who had refused to sign the petition he had delivered to Frick two days before, resigned as secretary and member of the Carnegie Steel board. His resignation was accepted, he was thanked for his services, and Moreland was appointed in his place. That day, Lovejoy wrote to Carnegie, "I have no desire to discuss the question, nor, I am sure have you; so I will only add that I can now have no regret whatever for my decision, since, while I have not affronted one of my best friends, I have retained the esteem of the other."[80]

The campaign against Frick was taken a step further on 24 January, when an agreement was concluded by the newly constituted board of H. C. Frick Coke Company to supply all requirements of Carnegie Steel for five years— from 1 January 1899—at the price that had been so contentious during the previous autumn, $1.35 free on trucks at the ovens. At that time, the open market price for coke was at least $3.50 a ton; the difference would mean an annual loss to the coke company of about $4 million. The so-called over-pricing of the past year was to be repaid, representing a further $596,000 call on the finances of H. C. Frick Coke. Both J. Walker and S. L. Schoonmaker wrote to protest. Schoonmaker resigned. Walker had been first associated in business with Carnegie in 1873, through the Lucy furnaces. From 1886 to 1888, he had served as chairman of Carnegie, Phipps, and Company. Since 1882 he had owned a minority interest in the H. C. Frick Coke Company and from 1887 was a director. These were the material interests that may have inclined him to support Frick. Long after the deaths of Frick and Carnegie, he pointed out to Hendrick that, although he never admired Frick as he did Carnegie and thought Frick too narrow in interests and lacking in humor, he supported him in this dispute because he believed wrong was being done in trying to force his interest from him at book value. His own suit against Carnegie denounced the directors who had been appointed by Carnegie Steel to the H. C. Frick Coke board as designed to act in "utter and fraudulent disregard" of the interests of the minority stockholders.[81]

On 29 January, Frick and Phipps together complained that the correct value of Carnegie Steel was not shown on its books. At this time the capitalization was only $25 million, but they put the true value at "considerably" more than $250 million. Three days after this, Schwab informed Frick that, in the absence of his agreement, he, acting as Frick's Attorney in Fact, had that day transferred the latter's financial interests to the Carnegie Steel Company.

Attempts were made to detach Phipps from Frick, but these proved ineffective. By mid January he was already finding deficiencies in the Iron Clad agreement, the chief weapon for Frick's dislodgement (and one for which he himself had produced the first draft thirteen years before). As he pointed out in a memorandum sent to Frick on 17 January, in each of the forms of that agreement—1887, 1892, and 1897—the provision for compelling partners to withdraw and to sell their interests to the company specifically excluded senior partners who fully owned the interests credited to them, that is, who were not in debt to the company for their share. Frick came in this category. A considerable further embarrassment to the company was that the 1892 agreement was found to have not been signed by any of the partners.[82]

Frick filed a suit against Carnegie Steel in the Court of Common Pleas of Allegheny County in the second week of February 1900. He prepared a draft of his case, which spoke bluntly of the ill treatment he had received from Carnegie:

> For various reasons, all of which will appear in the evidence, Andrew Carnegie has conceived a personal animosity to me. Chiefly I believe this grew out of the fact that myself and others held during part of 1899 an option from him to purchase his interest in The Carnegie Steel Company Limited for the sum of $ which we were unable to carry out. . . . Since then his animosity against me grew until on the   day of   AD 1899 he, without good cause, demanded my resignation of the office of   in the said Company.

Carnegie had "secretly" held a meeting of the board of managers, which had passed a resolution to take over his interest:

The resolutions recited as fact much which was not true and which Mr. Carnegie must have known to be untrue. . . . On   he came to my office and endeavored to frighten me into selling my interests in the Steel company at much below their value. . . . Your orator has hoped and has made all reasonable effort to accomplish an amicable solution of his present difficulties with Andrew Carnegie and The Carnegie Steel Company Limited.

The brief of Frick's counsel brought out more details. For the first time, the public learned of the true size of the profits that had been made. The nature of the Iron Clad agreement was exposed to public scrutiny. The "considerable animosities" between Frick and Carnegie in 1898 and 1899 over the conduct of the company were revealed, as was the fact that, although he had been willing to sell in January 1899 for $270 million, when the sale fell through that summer Carnegie had refused to renew the option except at a price of $500 million, saying that business had greatly improved. After obtaining Frick's resignation from the chairmanship, Carnegie had had his way:

Since then he has completely domineered his partners and dictated the policy of the Company toward me, even resorting to threats and menaces of loss of the official positions, salaries and interests of his junior partners, to persuade and coerce them into cooperation with him in his declared intention of driving me out of the firm and appropriating my interest at less than one quarter of the value he demanded of his own and at less than one sixth of what he declares is the value of it at this time.[83]

Frick indicated how inadequate the valuation had been and that the true value had been hidden:

The books of the Company do not now and have not recently contained a reasonable valuation of its assets. A very large quantity of its assets on January 1 1900 stood upon its books at very inadequate valuations. Some of the assets did not there appear at any valuation. This was known to Carnegie and the other partners. The fair valuation of your orator's interest therein could not be determined from what now appears on the books of said company.

On 1 November 1899, the book value of the three steelworks, the Lucy and Carrie furnaces, and the Upper and Lower Union mills was $33,097,000; their net profits in 1899 had amounted to $17,121,000.[84]

The response to Frick's suit was the "Joint and Several Answer of The Carnegie Steel Company Limited and Andrew Carnegie," filed in the first week of March. It made complaint that, although Frick was "a man of ability and we should have been glad to have him continue in the business of said Association," he was also of imperious temper, impatient of opposition and disposed to make a personal matter of any difference of opinion, even on questions of mere business policy. At times, moreover, he gives way to violent outbursts of passion, which he is either unable or unwilling to control. He demands absolute power and without it is not satisfied. After January 11th 1895, when he ceased to be chairman of said Association, and became merely chairman of its board of managers, the plaintiff was and continued to be restless and dissatisfied. He sought an enlargement of his powers, which could not properly be granted for the reason that such action, it was thought, would create a lack of confidence in the president of the Association and would tend to destroy the influence and authority of his position as the chief executive.

Indeed it was represented that, over the past five years, apart from chairing meetings, his services had been merely advisory and he had spent most of his time on his own interests. Even within Carnegie Steel, his work was not presented as constructive. "His time has been largely employed in various speculative schemes for placing the property of the Association in the hands of promoters to be floated in marketable securities on the public." In some respects, this reply was unsatisfactory. Much later, as Carnegie admitted to a congressional committee, their valuation of their properties had been wrong. When asked whether it had not been a sworn statement, he replied, "Yes. My partners sent this on as an answer prepared by our lawyers. I no doubt glanced over it and signed it, but I did not read it all."[85]

Although by no means without some foundation, the situation outlined by the defense was a misrepresentation. First, Frick was quite clearly willing to recognize that powers had been transferred from him to others. His remarks to Gates about Schwab's full responsibility to negotiate rail agreements on behalf of Carnegie Steel is one indication, as was his insistence—after an initial weakness on the point—that the power to sign contracts for coke resided not in him as chairman of both coke and steel companies, but in Lynch and Schwab, as their respective presidents. Second, and on the other hand, it is quite clear from letters from Carnegie or from Schwab as well as from outsiders that Frick's role in the company, although officially diminished after January 1895, was still quite central. He was consulted on policy; he was one of those whom Carnegie had written of in 1899 as senior partners who after reconstruction would act for five years as "consultants" to their junior partners; and it was Frick who, in the schemes for sale, was marked out to take the supreme command when Carnegie withdrew. In short, there is prima facie evidence that the company defense was to some degree building on and helping to confirm a picture of Frick's position in the firm that exaggerated his insistence on imperial powers and underrated his work and value on their behalf. His role in the company had emphatically not been a minor one.

An interesting light is thrown on the association's reply to his complaint by an earlier draft, with annotations by Moreland. Moreland had been their accountant long before he became their secretary. He was recognized by Lauder as a partner who thought things through more than most and was exceptional in taking an independent line if he felt this was justified by the facts. Obviously he was not an easy person, as was to be seen in the course of 1900; equally clearly he was also a man of broader perception and greater education than most of his partners. Moreland's suggested emendations of the draft reply indicate that he agreed that Frick had followed a different path than his colleagues, that he was essentially a lone wolf, but that he was not of the "imperious temper," nor in the normal way given to the violent outbursts of passion of which he was accused. It is unlikely that at this time of tension Moreland would indulge in irony; if not, his marginal annotations must have been made with serious intent. Most of his suggestions were not adopted in the company submission.

It is difficult to strike the right balance here. There can be no doubt that Frick had been violent with Carnegie and would remain ever afterward unforgiving toward him. On the other hand, the case against him exaggerated the circumstances and conditions. This may have been normal in the courts, but in this instance it was to contribute to the creation and confirmation—over many decades in the future—of the myth that Carnegie was a benevolent gentleman, the head of a generally happy brotherhood of industrial leaders from whom a persistently uncooperative member had been expelled for the general good. There was just sufficient truth in the accusation for the whole, damning statement to seem plausible. Building on the legacy of Homestead, Frick's reputation as perhaps the hardest and least human of American business leaders was thus firmly established.

Henry Phipps continued to oppose the action of the managers, stressing to Carnegie that he did so as a matter of principle. But although firm in this opinion, he was reasonable in tone, assuming the role of a bridge builder. To Carnegie he pointed out that usually he

> would do pretty much as you would wish, as it always gives me pleasure to concur with you—when I can properly do so. A right decision in this matter is less important to me in its effects upon my pocket than its influence upon my mind. To feel that I have been rightly treated is a greater pleasure to me than any probable or possible gain in money; that is subordinate, the first is everything; and next to it is the feeling that the business in which my heart has ever been, has been dealt with on time honored, safe and just business principles.

He set to work to bring the parties together. Schwab reported to Carnegie that, accompanied by Walker, Phipps had called on him at the beginning of

February to ask whether Carnegie would come to a financial settlement with Frick for his interest in the steel company on a valuation for those properties of $250 million. Schwab told them Carnegie would not consider it for a moment, and they had therefore decided to go ahead with the suits against Carnegie Steel.[86]

Eventually Phipps proved two things: both the weaknesses that underlay a case based on the enforcement of the Iron Clad agreement and also that others who had withdrawn earlier (notably Abbott) had been paid more generously than the Iron Clad agreement could have provided for. Pressures were building. In addition to conducting these cases at law, the managers were also striving to carry on business at a high level of intensity. As Moreland remarked early in March in response to an inquiry Carnegie had sent to him nine days before: "Should have answered this earlier, and while inclinations strong to do so, was kept so busy on papers and statements for lawyers that it seemed to be impossible for me to grasp this matter."[87]

Meanwhile, uncertainties increased in both camps about the strength of their cases, as well as about the desirability of much that had been secret becoming public knowledge. Mutual friends of Carnegie and Frick were pressing for settlement, in part no doubt by reason of their regard for them, but also because they feared revelations about the workings of major business corporations. These outsiders included George Westinghouse and Mark Hanna, the latter especially casting an eye to possible adverse effects on the Republican cause in a presidential election year. One of their old customers—A. B. Farquhar of York, Pennsylvania—let Frick know that he was "deeply grieved" at their divisions. From Niagara Falls, F. W. Haskell—who until the late 1890s had been secretary and treasurer of the South West Connellsville Coke Company but who was now vice-president of the Carborundum Company—wrote to Frick in a different and memorable vein. He had, as he put it, frequently received the Pittsburgh papers, "containing various allusions to the relations between yourself and the great Egotist."[88]

Together, internal and external circumstances and pressures eventually made Carnegie willing to come to some understanding with Frick. Again Phipps seems to have acted as intermediary. Frick is reported to have responded positively to the idea: "It is useless now to talk about anybody buying or selling. The fair thing to do is to make the consolidation of the two companies upon the terms agreed to by everybody a year ago before the Moore offer was received. That will solve the whole problem justly and honestly. I am willing."[89] There is no evidence at all that Carnegie ever entertained the idea of a reconciliation like those that had occurred after earlier disputes. In contrast to the reconstruction they had considered in 1899, it soon became clear in this case that Frick would have no further part in management.

On the evening of Saturday, 17 March 1900, a meeting of the two parties was held in Carnegie's New York home. Carnegie, Schwab, and Phipps were there; Lovejoy represented Frick's interests. Phipps submitted the Frick suggestion that they carry through the amalgamation of the steel and coke companies as planned during the previous year. This was favorably received. The discussions were then taken further at meetings held in Atlantic City, which in turn led on to an agreement that was signed there on Monday, 19 March. It was resolved to merge Carnegie Steel and H. C. Frick Coke, "substantially" along the lines planned in the previous June, increasing the capital of the first to $250 million and of the latter to $70 million. Frick was to receive stocks and securities representing 6 percent of the capital of the new company; in return he was to withdraw his suit. The dispute over the price for coke—an all-important flashpoint in the controversy—was solved so quietly as to prove that, had there been a will to do so, a solution could have been found long before: "neither party shall be held to be right or wrong, both shall be considered equally so, therefore the difference will be split in two, each party yielding one half of its claim."[90]

There was, even now, some hesitation before the arrangements were finalized. Frick pointed out that some of the language used in the drafts made in Atlantic City was too vague. On 21 March, Schwab wrote to him in Pittsburgh to clarify the matter, the letter being delivered by hand. At 2 P.M. on Saturday, 31 March 1900, a special meeting of the Carnegie Steel Company was held in the Carnegie Building. Twenty-seven members, including Phipps, were present. Carnegie, Lauder, and Frick were among the six who were represented by Attorneys in Fact. The agreements as worked out in New York and in Atlantic City, with minor subsequent modifications, were confirmed. A new holding company, The Carnegie Company, controlling both the steel and the coke companies was approved, to come into being on 1 April 1900. Frick retained his financial interest but was excluded from management.[91]

Although in some respects he seemed to have been vindicated, Frick's relations and personal contacts with Carnegie would never be restored. The new tone was set in a telegram sent by Frick to A. R. Whitney, who had refused to be stampeded into the camp of those opposing him: "Settlement made. I get what is due me. All well. I, of course, have not met this man Carnegie and never expect nor want to. It is not my intention to be officially connected with the reorganized concern."[92] Apart from the deep alienation from Carnegie this message discloses, it also indicates that Frick realized his active involvement with these particular steel and coke operations—which together had covered thirty years—had now come to an end.

Some thought Frick had vindicated himself. Long afterward, the nestor of the Valleys iron trade, Joseph G. Butler, reckoned he had "done inestimable service in blazing the way for a better understanding of business honor and rectitude," showing that "in the steel business, as in other walks of life, ability usually wins." Others, nearer to the issues, were not so sure. Almost thirty years after these events, Burton J. Hendrick interviewed some of the former Carnegie Steel partners. He was impressed by their intense loyalty and affection for Andrew Carnegie:

> An absence of enthusiasm for Frick is just as apparent. The chairman is regarded with a positive but detached respect. His old co-workers admire his ability, his force, and, in certain phases, his character, but they do not regard him as a friend. . . . "The young partners were all afraid of Frick" is the most frequent comment heard.

The truth of the remark, quoted by Bridge, of one of the junior partners about their relations with Carnegie—"We were simply a band of circus horses and we all jumped as the ring-master cracked the whip"—cannot cancel out the evidence unearthed by Hendrick. As Hendrick recognized, Frick paid a high price after the so-called resolution of the dispute. "The wrongs he had suffered from Carnegie became an almost pathological obsession, on which he would dilate at all times and to all persons, even comparative strangers."[93] In this sense, the wounds inflicted in the winter of 1899–1900 were never to heal.

7

Years of Transition

The Carnegie Company Without Frick

During the first few months of 1900, public attention was attracted away from the operational successes of Carnegie Steel to the controversy between its managing partners and Frick and his supporters. However, these conflicts did not affect the company's profits, which reached higher levels than ever before. Although he was in litigation with the company, Frick was still interested in their successes. In April, he wrote to Andrew Mellon, "The profits for March 1900 were as follows—Steel company $4,394,588.48, Coke company $666,142.41. Pretty satisfactory figures are they not?"[1] Maintained at that rate, they would have equaled the total for 1899 in less than five months.

On 1 April, The Carnegie Company came into existence, controlling both the Carnegie Steel Company and the H. C. Frick Coke Company. The capitalization was $320 million, of which Carnegie held stock of $174.5 million and Phipps $34.8 million. In the old Carnegie Steel Company, Frick's 6 percent share represented $1.5 million of the nominal capital of $25 million; in the recapitalized concern his interest was $31.3 million. Despite an increase in his share, Schwab—although chief executive and the major resident driving force of the new organization—owned only $19.2 million of the capital. On the other hand, although Frick held such an important interest, he (unlike Phipps) was debarred from a place on the board.

In the middle months of 1900, trade fell away at the time when the company was in the middle of its dispositions, including plans for new plant, to meet the challenge of backward integration from firms that had previously bought their semi-finished steel in the open market. At the year's end, there occurred the first moves toward a great consolidation, which was to come forth onto the public stage fully formed in spring 1901. Frick remained a keen observer and critic of all these aspects. Although no longer a prime mover, he played a minor part from the sidelines. No one could then have realized how short this period of transition was to be.

After Frick's removal, Carnegie had expected that they would all be a happy family again. That this was not so clearly indicates that Frick was indeed not the only source of irritation. Given the internal stresses of their fast-driven business, this is hardly surprising. The next source of dissension proved to be A. M. Moreland, who had succeeded Lovejoy as secretary in January 1900. In the campaign against Frick, Moreland had been in charge of the securing of support from the partners. When The Carnegie Company was formed, he received $1.6 million of its stock. He remained active in the new company throughout the summer; but at the end of August at a meeting of the board, he made a critical statement about their Pittsburgh Steamship Company, which, eighteen months after its formation, already operated thirteen ore boats. James Gayley responded with outraged vigor at the next meeting: "I wish to say, after hearing the tirade against the Steamship Company by Mr. Moreland, I did not suppose that there was a man of influence connected with this institution who could give so many false statements as in the statement read, which is absolutely false in its entirety." Later in the meeting, a letter from Moreland was read; in both content and tone, like Gayley's outburst, it speaks of the pressures of the time:

> Please accept my resignation as a Director and as Secretary of the Carnegie Steel Company, to take effect at once. I am quite unwilling to continue working as I do for the salary that is paid me at the present time, when I know that I can command positions of more power and more money elsewhere and where worth and honest work count for something.

Schwab had cabled asking, unsuccessfully, that Moreland should remain until his own return home: "Can not have any foolishness and dissatisfaction in our ranks; everything working too smoothly for that."[2]

Controversy with Moreland dragged on over the next few months. For some time he neglected to send in his formal resignation. He also asked for $500,000 as the price of surrendering his position as a Carnegie Company trustee. The issue was not resolved until after the formation of U.S. Steel, at which time he was paid one-tenth of the compensation he claimed. Schwab had talked the matter over with Judge Reed, who advised him to obtain a court order compelling Moreland to hand over his stock, claiming "there is no doubt that we can do so, fearing only that Moreland's answer will be of a vindictive nature." Schwab thought they must take their chance on that but wanted all members of the board to approve before such action was taken.[3] His caution seemed to point (as with the earlier arrangement with Frick) to fears that, if the matter were taken to court, Moreland might reveal more than his former colleagues would wish.

During 1900, Carnegie Steel was actively planning to meet new challenges. Some of the most serious of these concerned railway access and rates of freight to Pittsburgh. Carnegie still entertained ambitious ideas of teaching the Pennsylvania and Vanderbilt systems a lesson, by the Steel Company obtaining its own access to independent main lines both east and west. At the same time, he was brimming over with ideas for meeting the competition of both old and new rivals in steel. One by one, the great finishing groups formed in the course of the previous year had begun producing more of their own steel, thus reducing their purchases from longer established concerns making both iron and steel, and above all from Carnegie Steel. For example, American Steel and Wire had at one time bought up to 14,000 tons of Carnegie billets each month, but by early 1900, it had already cut this to 6,000 tons. Carnegie Steel considered reacting by building a continuous billet mill and two merchant bar mills at Duquesne, costing respectively $150,000 and $650,000. Within a week, because of the financial situation, they had decided to hold back on the bar mills but to go ahead with the billet mill, from which (rather puzzlingly) Schwab reckoned they could make $3 a ton profit on billet sales.[4]

During the second quarter of 1900, there were difficult negotiations with Rockefeller over new ore contracts. The issue was settled by midsummer. At this time, Carnegie Steel also agreed to sell the Keystone Bridge works to the new American Bridge Company for $3 million of its stock and an undertaking to buy 51 percent of its steel purchases from Carnegie. Should American Bridge not take 75 percent of U.S. bridge work, Carnegie Steel was to have the right to build its own bridge works. Soon after this, it was reported that American Steel Hoop was only taking 3,000 tons of their steel a month, as compared with their previous order of between 15,000 and 20,000 tons. Undaunted, Carnegie recommended in a letter to Schwab dated 20 June 1900 that they should promptly prepare to make the products turned out by the steel hoop company. Two days later he returned to the same theme, arguing that this sort of forward integration "will not only give them but others a lesson, which I am sure we will have to give sooner or later."[5]

At the midsummer meeting of managers at which Schwab announced that American Steel and Wire had given notice of the cancellation of their contract, there was read out a cable that Carnegie had sent two days before from Scotland. Approaching his sixty-fifth birthday, he was in fighting mood. It was almost as if he was possessed by the excitement of a man entering business for the first time, rather than reacting as one who had already dominated it for many years:

> My recent letters predict present state of affairs; urge prompt action essential; crisis has arrived, only one policy open; start at once hoop, rod, wire, nail mills, no halfway about last two. Extend coal and coke roads, announce these; also tubes. Prevent others building; not until you finish most staple articles can you get business among them sufficient to keep mines and furnaces in full operation; should also run boats Conneaut to Chicago, even if costs are high. Never been time when more prompt action essential, indeed absolutely necessary to maintain prosperity. It will be made poor affair if failure now when challenged; have no fear as to the result, victory certain. Spend freely for finishing mills, railroads, boat lines. Continue to advise regularly by cable.[6]

Meanwhile, other progressive but less spectacular improvements or extensions were going ahead. These included the demolition of the Bessemer shop and complete dependence on the open-hearth process at Homestead. Later, there were plans for further upgrading of the Pittsburgh, Bessemer, and Lake Erie Railroad and for better materials handling at Conneaut.[7] Not surprisingly, given the wide financial interests of the house he headed, J. P. Morgan began grumbling that Carnegie seemed likely to destabilize both steel and rail transportation. Yet, in spite of its immense resources and exceptional achievements, there also seemed a danger that Carnegie Steel would find itself overextended as it tried to deal with challenges from all directions.

Some of the partners were more cautious than Carnegie. Even Schwab, generally expansive, deferred the tube mill following Carnegie's July cable. A week later, Lauder also opposed further appropriations for extensions, saying he preferred to wait until mid September by which time he would have discussed the matter with Carnegie. Responding to his caution, Schwab explained that, taking account of the trends in the major finishing groups, he thought it likely they would eventually lose all the outlet for between 35,000 and 40,000 tons of billets that they had been shipping monthly (a tonnage equal to about one-sixth of their crude steel capacity). Already Duquesne had been forced to stockpile 32,000 tons of pig iron; delay in installing their own finishing mills might cause its closure. Schwab pointed out that, if they had held back in previous periods of bad trade, they would not have entered the open-hearth steel or the structural businesses under such favorable conditions. He ended with what for the sixty-two-year-old Lauder must have seemed a cutting remark: "If we want to drop back into an old-fashioned way of doing business, I want to be counted out of it." Before the meeting ended, they had approved expenditure of $1.4 million for rod, wire, and nail mills for Duquesne. Of the seven partners present, Lauder was the only one to vote against.[8] By September they were planning to build sheet mills.

At the same time as they faced the loss of outlets for semi-finished steel, they were affected by recession. Early in July, a lack of orders was already closing some departments at Homestead, and by the end of the month the company's business generally was 40 percent lower than in June (when the recession could already be sensed) and promised even worse. Slackening trade had been one reason for Lauder's caution about going into new lines of production. Like Schwab, Carnegie saw it differently. For him a time of "reaction" was, as always, an opportunity for aggressive development: "Better prices can only come when several of our competitors cease operations just as before when Penna Steel Co. and others closed times began to improve."[9]

The biggest challenge they planned to mount to the various finishing trades was in tubes. National Tube, the main producer, possessed no lake ore reserves and relatively small holdings of coking coal. In 1900 it made only 250,000 tons of crude steel, or just over one-twelfth as much as Carnegie Steel. However, it was already integrating backward, having authorized expenditure of $2,500,000 for a blast furnace plant and open-hearth furnaces at Wheeling at the end of 1899. Its 1900 earnings were not only larger than those of any other finishing group but also in excess of those of Federal Steel, although only one-third those of The Carnegie Company. In 1898 the Carnegie Steel board of managers had discussed the building of tube works at Conneaut.[10] This project was now taken up again.

In the course of their July discussions about development, Lauder remarked, "It is also well to consider carefully where is the best place to locate our new plant." His question was particular relevant to tube manufacture, for which two possibilities were under consideration—a revised Conneaut scheme or a riverside site near Pittsburgh. There was much to be said for the latter. Their established capacity and infrastructure were there, opening up for a new works the possibility of at least partial integration through the Union Railroad. Close management (the secret of their past successes) would be easier in the vicinity of Pittsburgh. This was the locational aspect of Carnegie's old advice to put all the eggs in one basket and then watch that basket with great care. However, a serious obstacle was that the district's expansion in the last few decades meant there were no longer many suitable sites left. Moreover, the very existence of their massed capacity in Pittsburgh meant that there were operational economies to be won from having counterbalancing capacity on the shores of Lake Erie.[11]

There is evidence that, until mid 1900, they were thinking only of a tube works, presumably bringing in supplies of semi-finished steel from existing works that were losing their present outlets. In early June, Carnegie wrote to Lauder, "We ought to go into tubes because we have a combine at our mercy and lost trade we used to have before National Tube left us. We can spend a few millions (no blast furnaces at present) and divide with the Trust. It is clear sailing." He expected recession would bring down the prices for properties. Over the next few weeks, the partners on the spot looked for sites along the Monongahela River. They found none large enough for the works they had in mind nearer than forty miles upriver, a distance beyond what they referred to as "the Mellon plant" (Donora) and nearer to Monessen. It was recognized that they could build on sites away from the river but this was not favored by Schwab. One place considered was the tract along Peters Creek, which Frick owned and whose attractions were set to increase with the plan that the Wabash Railroad extension, giving independent access to Pittsburgh from the west, would have a branch down this creek to McKeesport. Carnegie hoped they would not have to buy this site, and Schwab informed him that Frick would only sell at above the previously agreed price.[12]

After this, search around Pittsburgh switched to the Allegheny Valley. Options were secured on land at Tarentum, and Lawrence Phipps and Daniel Clemson examined the prospects there. Serious site limitations soon became obvious. Schwab complained that there was no room for expansion due to the closeness of the valley's hillsides and explained that he regarded their interest there as useful mainly as a bargaining counter with the railroad companies. For their part, the latter seemed willing to cooperate, Cassatt contacting Carnegie to assure him that the Pennsylvania Railroad would contemplate giving them trackage rights to the junction with the Pittsburgh, Bessemer, and Lake Erie Railroad.[13] Even so attention moved to Lake Erie.

On Sunday, 11 November, some weeks before all discussion about Tarentum ended, Schwab discussed plans for their tube works with Carnegie and they agreed that Conneaut was the place for the plant. At Tarentum, a 540-acre site would have cost $190,000 and they had reckoned their own rail connection to the Pittsburgh, Bessemer, and Lake Erie Railroad might take another $750,000; at Conneaut they could buy a 2,500-acre site and connect it to their railroad for not more than $1 million. Half a million dollars were said to have been paid to two hundred farmers to quit their land. However, they could sell one thousand acres of this site for housing for perhaps $2,500 an acre, thus recouping their initial outlay two and a half times over.[14]

Logistically, Conneaut was even more attractive. Compared with existing works, Schwab reckoned they would have lower assembly costs for all raw materials of $1.07 per net ton; for distribution it would be no worse than Pittsburgh, "and would probably be better." At one point, he is said to have assured Carnegie that they would be able to produce tubes at least $10 a ton below the National Tube cost. (Prices for tubes were volatile. Before National Tube was formed in 1899, they had been $30 a ton. During 1899, they rose to $67 and early in 1900 reached a maximum of $89.)[15]

Conneaut would have further advantages. Between April and December, they would be able to ship tubes both east and west by water. On 8 January 1901, Schwab made a public statement of their intention to spend $12 million on the new tube works. It would have two and possibly four blast furnaces and twenty fifty-ton open-hearth furnaces.[16] Active planning for Conneaut went on into the last week of January 1901; at that time it was submerged by discussions that, within two months, were to issue in the formation of an amalgamation to include both The Carnegie Company and National Tube.

During 1900, Frick—having a 6 percent interest in Carnegie Steel but debarred from participating in its direction—was critical of both the operations and what he could glean of the development planning of those now in charge. It is important to put his dissatisfaction within the context of the increasingly difficult trading situation. Amalgamation, new construction, and recession all meant that in some respects business was less easy to secure than it had been in 1899. Federal Steel had decided to go into the structural trade; Lackawanna was putting up new works near Buffalo; National Tube was building blast furnaces and steel plant at Wheeling; and in the Valleys district, National Steel was entering the rail business. When the trade recession began, Carnegie Steel executives were busy planning new works or railway extensions. The pace must have been exhausting—a sidelight on its effects is seen in yet another fighting letter to Schwab from Carnegie who was then in Scotland: "All very well here and Skibo finer than expected. Tell any of the managers that in case of a collapse they can be cured here upon most reasonable terms." His remark was probably not quite so lighthearted as it seemed. The final factor affecting Frick's criticism of his former colleagues came from within himself. Writing at this time, J. Burnley suggested that Frick felt no bitterness toward them for what had happened; but any summarily displaced top executive would have felt some animosity to those who dealt with him in that way, and given Frick's character and past experience, it is understandable that he kept a keenly critical eye on them.[17]

There is every reason to believe that Carnegie Steel continued to monitor its costs in detail. A careful breakdown of categories was kept for each major unit of plant (see table 28). Frick pressed his former colleagues for as much information as possible. Early in August, he asked Schwab for statements about their business. Sending them on, Schwab pointed out that he could not let him have the daily product reports. Later he sent on four more statements. A month afterward, he thanked Frick for returning three of them but asked for the fourth, promising when he received it to send a copy. Frick was embarrassed to have to admit that Miss Williams, his secretary, had lost the original and had been unable to find it.[18] In August, Frick attacked the way they were conducting business in a cable that was probably his last direct communication with Carnegie. He criticized their purchases of coal and scrap at high prices and pressed Carnegie to look into these matters himself. All in all, he seems to have overstated his case:

> Do not let them hide things from you. You cannot trust many by whom you are surrounded to give you facts. You need commercial rather than professional ability to cope with the concerns managed by brainy and honest men trained to the business. You are being out-generalled all along the line, and your management of the Company has already become the subject of jest.

Carnegie's reaction to this gratuitous advice is not recorded. However, it appears that Frick did not contact Carnegie merely to irritate him, for at the same time he wrote to Phipps, identifying unnecessary losses amounting to millions and calling him to account for not attending more closely to his duties as a director. Phipps, who was again staying at Beaufort Castle, was not convinced that Frick's outspoken approach to Carnegie had been the right one: "If any good is to be accomplished at this stage it is by patient and gentle methods, and in view of policy I was very sorry that you sent the cable you did to Mr. Carnegie." A few months later, Frick also communicated his doubts about their commercial standing to Schwab: "You are dealing with some very able men and I hope they are not getting the best of you in your pool arrangements."[19]

Frick's other point of disagreement with his successors' policies concerned Conneaut. At the end of December 1900, he mentioned to Jay Morse that Carnegie Steel had complete plans for a new works fully integrated from blast furnaces to tube mills:

> It will be a model plant, I am sure, and it is their present intention to start work early in the year. I have every reason to believe that they will build a complete plant, but I doubt the advisability of it. Far better, in my opinion, to make some arrangement with the National Tube Co., to furnish them with a certain quantity of steel month by month.

TABLE 28

Carnegie Steel Company, Cost Analyses for Plants, October 1900

Type of Plant	Number of Operating Units for which Figures Produced	Number of Cost Categories for Each Type of Plant
Bessemer works	3	13
Open-hearth works	3	13
Blooming mills	5	12
Sheared plate mills	3	13
Universal plate mills	4	13

Source: Carnegie Steel board of managers, minutes, 16 Oct. 1900 (ACLC).

Whatever the reasons behind his doubts, he seemed in this remark to be unaware of National Tube's choice to phase out its purchases from Carnegie Steel. Moreover, as Schwab had proved, the logistics of the business were now strongly in favor of providing balancing capacity at the lake end of the Pittsburgh, Bessemer, and Lake Erie Railroad. A more persuasive argument might have been that they should complete the rounding out of their existing plants with more finishing capacity, before embarking on a new plant on a wholly new site, a type of expansion of which they had no experience at all since Edgar Thomson was completed in 1875. A few days later, Frick took up this theme in a talk with Schwab in New York and followed their conversation with a letter, in which he questioned whether they were wise to spend large sums on a new plant. Before they did so, he wrote, "put yourself in position to finish the pig iron you make at the various plants you now have. You are at a great disadvantage it seems to me in depending on many of these strong steel companies for a market for your product."[20]

Whatever the force of his arguments concerning their development strategy, Frick was in error in believing the business was not being operated with care. Early in 1901, Schwab sent Carnegie figures comparing the situation of The Carnegie Company with a group of their main rivals. In 1900 Federal Steel, National Steel, National Tube, American Steel and Wire, and American Sheet Steel had together produced only 84.5 percent as much crude steel as they had done. Yet their capital was $411 million as compared with Carnegie's $320 million ($160 million of this in bonds, $160 million in preferred stock). Carnegie earnings in 1900 had been $40 million; those of their combined rivals $42 million. The Carnegie resource base was far stronger, with 65 percent more ore—almost nine and a half times the Connellsville coal acreage and over five times as many ovens (see table 29). Notwithstand-

TABLE 29

The Carnegie Company and Some Major Rivals, 1900

	Steel Output	Lake Ore Reserves	Coking Coal Holdings	Ovens	Capital	Earnings
Carnegie	2,970[a]	162,250[b]	38,000[c]	11,637	320[d]	40[d]
Federal	1,225	66,000	7,500	2,400	126	10
National	1,400	13,500	2,850	1,300	63	8
Nat. Tube	250	—	938	—	80	13
Am. S&W	490	18,750	9,350	1,760	90	6
Am. Tin Plate	—	—	—	—	46	4
Am. Sheet	150	—	—	—	51	5
Am. Steel Hoop	—	750	130	—	33	2

Source: CMS to AC, 24 Jan. 1901 (ACLC).
Notes: [a] Figures this column are in thousand tons.
[b] Figures this column are in million tons.
[c] Figures this column are in acres.
[d] Figures this column are in million dollars.

ing Frick's doubts, operating statistics and financial results alike suggest that Carnegie Steel was at the peak of its excellence. Throughout the 1890s, one of the most impressive demonstrations of their efficiency had been the way the company increased its share of national production in times of depressed trade. In 1900, national steel production fell by 4.2 percent below the 1899 tonnage; the Carnegie Steel share of the total went up from 25.03 to 29.15 percent. Net profit per ingot ton was still mounting, indeed more sharply than ever ($4.15 in 1897, $5.30 in 1898, $7.88 in 1899, and $13.47 in 1900). Above all, there seemed to be even brighter prospects ahead. In 1899, production averaged 222,000 tons of crude steel a month, and in 1900, this was 247,000 tons. Schwab reported production running at 300,000 tons a month in January 1901. He looked ahead five years to monthly outputs of 500,000 tons (a target 50 percent higher than the turnout of all the steel plants in Britain in 1900).[21]

However, there were some less satisfying aspects of the situation, providing at least some support for Frick's doubts. In May 1899, Schwab had reckoned that within two months at current prices they should be earning at an annual rate of $43.2 million. Three months later, Carnegie projected their 1900 profits as $40 million; Frick reckoned that they could reach $42.5 million. In March 1900, before the recession, Carnegie Steel profits were at an annual rate of $57 million. That month (the last for which the H. C. Frick figures were separately available) the coke company earnings were 15 percent as large as those of the steel company. For many (though not all) products,

1900 prices were higher than those of 1899, but profits in that year at Carnegies amounted to only $40 million, and that figure included the earnings from coke. More important still, the large increase in profits per ingot ton in 1900 was in part due to inclusion of the coke company profits. In negotiations with Morgan, early in 1901, Carnegie still assumed $40 million as the profit for 1901. Most important of all, the attitudes and actions of their rivals indicated that in future the struggle would be harder.

On the evening of Wednesday, 9 January 1901, the first dinner of The Carnegie Company was held at the Schenley Hotel, Pittsburgh. It was a magnificent occasion. The grand white banqueting hall was thickly decorated with bushes and arches of greenery. The tables were arranged in the form of the cross section of a single steel rail, and on them were laid covers for ninety-one guests. Resplendent in evening dress, each with a colorful buttonhole, the guests posed for a photograph to record the achievement and glory of Carnegie Steel. Letters of regret for their absence from Phipps and from Hunsiker (among others) were read. Carnegie sent a letter of happy, familial greetings, which the toastmaster, Judge Reed, read out:

> Much of the success of the Carnegie firm has come from the fact that we were always partners and friends. My recent visit to Pittsburgh satisfied me that you were more closely knit together than for many years past. . . . To one and all I feel like an elder brother, liking you all and recognized as one of you in return.

Among the toasts that evening, Schwab gave one under the intriguing title "Expectations."[22]

If The Carnegie Company had gone ahead with the ambitious plans maturing in these first weeks of 1901, they might reasonably have expected, sooner or later, to far exceed their past achievements. If that had been the case, Frick would have played no active part in the result, although he would have enjoyed the financial benefits produced. A month before that Pittsburgh dinner, however, another celebration in New York initiated a series of events that through the winter and into spring 1901 created a new situation, in which Frick not only returned to a key role in decision making in a greatly widened steel concern but eventually displaced both Carnegie and Schwab from their central roles. In the meantime, he was involved with other big industrial projects.

New Interests in Steel and Shipbuilding

Throughout the 1890s, steel production was dominated by rails. Although there had long been a certain amount of re-rolling of old rails, almost all the tonnage came from fully integrated works. However, during this period there was a growing output of other products, some of them made by plants lacking iron capacity or even steelworks, that is, they were purely re-rolling operations. Structurals and plate—although produced in the main by big companies and in large works—were also still made by smaller, less integrated firms such as Phoenix Iron, Pencoyd, and Lukens, each of them in the old iron district of Eastern Pennsylvania. In the course of the 1890s, there was rapid growth of an American tinplate industry. Another impressive growth line was wire products, and it was with this business that Frick was to become briefly involved following his rift with Carnegie Steel. His contact with it had begun long before.

Much of the increased wire production was absorbed by the wire nail makers, whose product had rapidly replaced the cut nail. In 1899, cut nail production was only 23.3 percent that of 1886; for wire nails, on the other hand, the proportion was 1,269.66 percent. The expansion in the use of wire itself, including barbed wire, was also most impressive. The Great Plains had become one of the main areas for railroad expansion in the 1880s and 1890s. By 1880, for instance, Kansas had 3,104 miles of track; in 1899, the mileage was 8,777. At the 1900 census, 77.5 percent of that state's population still lived outside settlements of 2,500 or more, and this rural population represented a large market for wire in many of its forms (especially nails and fencing wire), for in this state there was a dearth of material for stone walling and wooden rails, and hedges would not grow well (if at all). The need for labor economy made such elaborate boundaries unattractive anyway. The very large expansion in cattle numbers and then in grain growing made easy wire fencing attractive. Similar situations applied throughout the rest of the Plains. Additionally, by the mid 1890s, some entrepreneurs were beginning to realize that the United States, with its advantages for large-scale, low-cost steel production could perhaps displace European producers of wire products in other pioneer areas of the world where farmers found they had similar needs. Overall, although small compared with the market in rails, the market for wire products was growing dramatically. Between 1888 and 1898, rail output increased by 569,000 tons; in wire rods, the increase was 790,000 tons (increases of 42.6 percent and 282.1 percent respectively). Additionally, with the single exception of 1896, wire avoided the wild yearly oscillations of the rail business (see table 30).

The growth of their business encouraged wire makers to extend their operations, from drawing mills to the production of rods, and then to steel, pig iron, and even into mineral working. In this process of backward integration, these operations impinged on the positions of the bigger, more es-

TABLE 30
U.S. Output of Steel Rails and Consumption of Wire Rods,
1888, 1893–1898

	Rail Production	Wire Rod Consumption
1888	1,386	280
1893	1,129	536
1894	1,016	668
1895	1,300	788
1896	1,167	621
1897	1,644	969
1898	1,976	1,070

Source: AISA; W. H. Donner to HCF, 13 Sept. 1899, Frick Papers.
Note: Figures are in thousand tons.

tablished steel firms from which they had earlier bought their supplies. In 1888, for example, there were forty-nine wire nail works, of which only two were integrated back into rolling mills. Six years later, one-quarter of all wire nail works had rolling operations. As expansion, competition, and backward linkage occurred, the wire products industries began to make an impact in the Pittsburgh area. For instance, in the mid 1870s, J. Wallace Page had begun to make wire fencing for his own farm. He then mortgaged the farm and began to produce fencing on a small scale at Adrian, in southern Michigan. Eventually the Page Woven Wire Fence Company became a big concern, and decision was taken to build a wire mill at Monessen, thirty-five miles up the Monongahela River from Pittsburgh. Page seems to have planned to use local steel (though at that time much rod was imported), but when he was ready for business, he found that rods were in scarce supply and the price was higher than he had anticipated. The company therefore built its own rod mill and open-hearth steel works.[23] Carnegie's friend Henry Oliver followed a not altogether dissimilar course. In 1881 the Oliver Wire Company was formed and built a wire-drawing plant in Pittsburgh. The company also acquired a barbed wire plant at Joliet, Illinois, which was later removed to Pittsburgh. Later, the company integrated forward to nails and backward to rods and the control of steel supplies.

By far the biggest and most disturbing factor in the wire trade was the midwesterner John Warne Gates, a man who, although important in the growth of the steel industry, was in many aspects a striking contrast to the more stable, conventional, and publicity-avoiding Frick. Gates had worked his way up from wire salesman to manufacturer and, in the 1890s, played a prime role in the consolidation of the industry. He had interests in the Pittsburgh area through the Braddock Wire Company, but the main sphere of his operations was for long in the western parts of the manufacturing belt. In 1892, he promoted the Consolidated Steel and Wire Company, which in the course of subsequent acquisitions and rationalization had, by 1895, purchased the wire nail capacity of the Carnegie Steel Company at Beaver Falls (a plant that Gates was to make successful although the Carnegie associates had never done so). Between 1894 and 1896, Gates was also president of the Illinois Steel Company. By 1897, he was beginning to shape up an association of firms under the title of the American Steel and Wire Company, which was to have a capital of $80 million (although Morgan later valued it at half that figure). Gates had been in contact with Frick on many occasions when at Illinois Steel, and he now consulted him about wire in a letter he characterized as "strictly personal and absolutely confidential." The letter dealt with a specific issue but also illustrated the wider implications of the consolidation he was working on:

> The wire business of the United States is about 800,000 to 900,000 tons per annum. The wire business of Europe is about 2,000,000 tons per annum. The exportation of wire, in the shape of plain wire, barbed wire, wire rods and wire nails, is probably at the present time 125,000, possibly 150,000 tons per annum. With the wire concerns all consolidated into one company there can in my judgment within the next five years be an export business of at least 1,000,000 tons of wire per annum. Australia is a very large buyer of wire: next comes Africa and South America. On account of the superior shipping facilities, a great portion of this wire is now exported from Hamburg, Antwerp and Bremen—very little now being exported from the United Kingdom. . . . Within five years the wire business of the United States can easily be made two million tons per annum . . . we can have agents in all foreign ports. . . . It will help the shipbuilding and shipping of this country very materially, consequently help the iron and steel business generally. . . . It means volumes to the coke business, to the iron ore business . . . and also means a large additional sum of money, in my judgment, to such concerns as the Carnegie Steel Company and the Illinois Steel Company. If the concerns are all in one company, there will not be the temptation to hammer the price of soft steel down to such a point that there will be practically no profit left to the maker.

Apart from his obvious desire to placate suppliers of steel and to encourage a man with special interests in coke, Gates wanted Frick's help to persuade Henry Oliver to drop his opposition to the consolidation and to bring in his firm. Gates said he had looked on Oliver as "a very broad-gauge, level-headed man when a proposition was put before him properly." He ended his letter with a plea: "I earnestly urge you to take this matter up with

Harry Oliver in your own way and advise me at Chicago the result of your conversation with him so soon as you have seen him, and by so doing greatly oblige."[24] The sinking of the *Maine* in February 1898 caused Morgan to withdraw his support for the merger, but in the following month Gates and his collaborators managed to form a consolidation under the title of the American Steel and Wire Company of Illinois. Within a year, with the backing of other financial interests, this was transformed into the even bigger American Steel and Wire Company of New Jersey, and the Oliver works were included.

The implications for the major integrated steel concerns were soon seen to be threatening. American Steel and Wire of New Jersey had a rod mill capacity of 1.1 million tons and a wire nail capacity of 10.5 million kegs (1.5 million kegs in excess of the record national output of 1897). The company planned further backward integration. Soon it was making a good deal of its own steel and pig iron and had acquired considerable iron ore and coking coal properties.[25]

Notwithstanding Gates's earlier vision of benefits all round, the creation and expansion of American Steel and Wire (AS&W)—as with the other combinations of the period in finished product lines—threatened to reduce the wire market for semi-finished steel products of the major heavy steel firms, and particularly of the Illinois and Carnegie companies. On a number of occasions in Frick's last year as chairman, Gates had tried to reassure him on these matters and to adopt a generally cooperative approach. Thus, in mid February 1899, he wrote to suggest that Carnegie Steel could buy Schoenberger and Company at "a fairly reasonable figure, everything considered." That firm was of some importance in plate, and "we might be willing to render some little financial aid in this matter conditional upon your not going into the manufacture of wire rods." A week later, he was assuring Frick that his company was and would remain a large customer for Carnegie Steel, and a few days afterward he wrote, "I . . . certainly think we can work in harmony so there will be some money in both our branches of the business."[26]

His persuasiveness did not bring the hoped for results. By autumn 1899, he was protesting that at $42 a ton quoted by Carnegie Steel for steel supplied to AS&W (the average Pittsburgh figure that year was only $31.2), "we are absolutely out of the export market." At that time, both Carnegie Steel and AS&W were considering buying the small reconstructed steelworks at Troy. Gates explained he wanted it only to look after their export business, and that "It will not cause us to buy one ton less of steel off your company." AS&W had for a time an almost monopolistic position in wire, controlling

in 1899 some thirty-six plants. In 1899, after paying depreciation and preference dividends, its earnings were equal to 18.7 percent of the common stock.
Next year they fell to 8.4 percent. Gates had already shown himself to be (as
always) a manipulator. In the spring of 1900, his firm closed down much of
its capacity, laying off what were variously said to be four thousand or ten
thousand of its employees. Not surprisingly, shares in AS&W slumped.
Gates took the opportunity to increase his interest, and when the works
reopened he was one or two million dollars richer as a result.[27]

Meanwhile, the existence of the consolidation provided encouragement
for other concerns to enter the wire trade. In 1901, facing the challenge of
the backward integration of steel finishing concerns, Carnegie Steel planned
large incursions of its own into steel products. The greatest of these was to
be the new tube works at a fully integrated Conneaut operation, but one of
the others was a rod mill and wire plant at Duquesne. Displaced from the
industry, Frick became linked with yet another Pittsburgh area wire project.

One feature of consolidations was that they often displaced formerly independent managements. At the same time, by holding up prices, they provided an umbrella that sheltered newcomers to the trade. Encouraged like
so many others by the raised duties of the McKinley tariff of 1890, in 1894
the thirty-year-old William H. Donner had organized the National Tin Plate
Company and built a works at Anderson, Indiana. Three years later, he
added another at Monessen. The American Tin Plate Company acquired
both works in 1898, so that Donner had to look for new outlets for his
entrepreneurial talents. In September 1899, he wrote to inform Andrew Mellon that he proposed to build rod and wire mills and a nail plant to meet
the competition of AS&W. He quoted the impressive figures of the growth
of national consumption of wire rods over the last decade. Two months
later, he organized the Union Steel Company and began to build a works at
the place that became Donora, well up the Monongahela River. Leaving
Carnegie Steel, Frick joined Mellon as a partner in this project. Even before
he did so, Carnegie Steel considered selling billets to Union Steel at competitive prices.[28] Later that year, there was some consideration of Union being
taken over by Carnegie Steel.

Frick and Carnegie were no longer in contact with each other, and the
responsibility for negotiations concerning Donora fell to Mellon. Carnegie
wrote to him at Hertford Castle in southern England. The letter was a peculiar mixture of sound business sense, journey details, and sentiment. He
clearly saw Donora as a threat. He pointed out that Carnegie Steel was being
driven to enter more finishing lines. They were going into tube manufacture
at once and were considering putting in a rod mill for foreign business, and

although not yet decided they might find it necessary to enter the wire trade. Schwab was on his way to Skibo, "and the whole matter will be taken up." Carnegie could not see how a Donora rod mill could run against AS&W unless they were willing to build blast furnaces, have their own coke,

> and get down to lowest costs. This I believe you will have to do ultimately. . . .
> I think it would not be a bad thing for you to run up here and see Messrs.
> Schwab, Lauder and myself. We shall give you a Highland welcome, and rest
> assured that the feeling I have for your father and yourself is genuine and
> everything I can do to preserve amiable relations will be done.

Carnegie added a postscript, and after that, a note in his own hand: "The 8 o'clock from Euston brings you direct to Bonar Bridge by next noon and we meet our guests at Bonar Bridge station. Are you married yet?"[29]

Mellon reported his visit in Scotland to Frick. He arrived at Skibo on Sunday, 30 August. Schwab came the following day. On Monday evening, Carnegie, Lauder, Schwab, and Mellon had a general discussion about the situation. It seems Mellon made some offer of the plant to Carnegie Steel. He explained they were thinking of a monthly output of 12,000 tons of billets, but Schwab thought they needed to go for 20,000 tons. Schwab also objected to buying the Donora plant because construction costs had been high, its location was not good, and he would want to run a mill direct. Mellon stoutly replied that it was not competition they feared but the unpleasantness of competing with friends. On the Tuesday morning, Carnegie, Lauder, and Schwab went into session after breakfast and did not appear until Mellon was ready to leave that evening. During the whole day he "had no drift of what was on hand." The Carnegie Steel party talked about going on at once with a railroad to the coke region, Schwab brought out maps, and they consulted Mellon about location and other matters.[30] The impression is that Carnegie's interest was above all in the opportunity to construct this strategic railroad, which would have completed the full integration of the Carnegie Steel properties and for which Mellon owned valuable rights of way. The purchase of Donora would probably have been only (or mainly) a step toward that end. The arrangement with Carnegie Steel was never carried through, however, and the Donora project of Donner, Frick, and Mellon went ahead independently.

The capital of Union Steel was increased far beyond the $1 million originally envisaged. At one stage, one-quarter of its stock was held by Frick. The scope of the plant was widened, and in September 1901, when all attention was focused on the recently formed U.S. Steel Corporation, the Donora mill came into operation. It then was reckoned to have an annual capacity of

200,000 tons of rods, 200,000 tons of wire, and a million kegs of nails. By this time, it had also been decided to equip it with blast furnaces, open-hearth steelworks, and pipe mills. There were even plans for a rail mill. Holdings of Connellsville coking coal and Lake ore were bought, the latter eventually amounting to 40 million tons. The route of the Connellsville Central Railroad—the line that Schwab had hoped to acquire—was graded through to the coal district, and a new and independent railroad was projected to new ore docks, to be built at Elk Harbor near Girard on Lake Erie. Thus, in miniature, here was the model of the organization of Carnegie Steel, including a prominent part in development thinking from the man who had filled such a central role in that company's success.

Soon there was further evidence of the growing significance of the new concern. In November 1902, Union Steel merged with a similarly new and expanding company, Sharon Steel, that had been organized in October 1899 and had since erected a blast furnace, steel and semi-finished products plant, and then rod and wire mills, nail works, and tinplate production. The merger created a company with a capacity of 0.75 million tons of pig iron and 0.85 million tons of steel, which controlled six thousand acres of coal land (over three-quarters of it containing coking grades), all in the Lower Connellsville district and therefore near the navigable Monongahela River. In addition to its own Upper Lakes ores, there were contracts for long-term supply with the Minnesota Iron Company. Plans were formulated for new works and for the acquisition of other firms in the fields of wire, sheet, and pipe.

In December 1902, the announcement came that the U.S. Steel Corporation had paid $45 million to absorb this small but rapidly expanding concern. The considerable price paid for Union Steel reflected the potential earning power of its further extended operations and the benefits of securing still more reserves of ore, which raw material was increasingly seen as determining future success in the industry. A final factor may have been the wish of J. P. Morgan to have Frick more fully involved in the counsels of the U.S. Steel Corporation. Certainly the *Financial Weekly* concluded that: "For the purpose of inducing Mr. Frick to become active in the Steel Corporation, Mr. Morgan purchased the Union Steel Works." He did so at a price that, as Andrew Mellon laconically remarked, "yielded a fair profit to all around."[31] It is by no means sure that the matter was as simple as the *Financial Weekly* represented it, but the purchase indicated the value put on Frick and his associates as competitors, however David-like they seemed by the side of Morgan's corporate Goliath.

With yet another project in the area, Frick was involved not as a participant in the works but as a developer of the site. His offer in 1899 of land along Peters Creek at a price far above what he paid for it had been among the causes of his last, violent clash with Carnegie. After he left Carnegie Steel, he bought the little community of Blair Station just south of Peters Creek, a place containing about two hundred people. As a result, it was said that he controlled three miles of riverfront and a similar distance back from the river. His plans were initially reported in the *New York Times* as involving removal of the houses in order to build "magnificent plants."[32] A few weeks later, it was decided that the Crucible Steel Company of America would build two large blast furnaces and a twelve-furnace open-hearth melting shop there. Frick and associates were reported to have formed the St. Clair Improvement Company in order to lay out a new town on land around the new works.[33] In this way at least, he was involved with the establishment of Clairton works and town. In May 1904, the Clairton Steel Company was brought into U.S. Steel.

Frick's later steel ventures were much less substantial. In April 1901, almost at the same time as U.S. Steel was formed (and not unrelated to that event), a new holding company, the Pennsylvania Steel Company of New Jersey, was formed to take over the former Pennsylvania Steel and Maryland Steel companies. The Pennsylvania Railroad, the Philadelphia and Reading Railroad, and W. H. Donner each held a controlling interest. Frick was eventually involved in Pennsylvania Steel, either as a director of the two railroads or as a former business colleague and friend of Donner's. In turn, Pennsylvania Steel acquired interests in Cambria Steel.

In late 1905 and early 1906, before he became a director of the Pennsylvania Railroad, Frick was involved in a general assessment of the efficiency of the Cambria works, which then employed fifteen thousand men. The report on its operations was made by Donner for A. J. Cassatt of the Pennsylvania Railroad. Average monthly costs of metal there were found to be $12.30 per ton, as compared with under $10 at Pittsburgh—although the difference was largely due to lower cost materials. Donner found that the Johnstown rail mill had never been operated with a view to the lowest costs; whereas in Pittsburgh the spread between the costs of pig iron and rails was $5 or less, at Cambria the lowest spread had been $7.39, and the average was $8.21. For the year, the cost of production of rails was over $5 greater than in Pittsburgh, at a time when the product was selling at $28 a ton. It appears that some months later Cassatt expressed to Frick his doubts of Donner's competence to criticize a long-established regime, for in reply Frick stressed that he too did not think Cambria got the output it should from furnaces or mills and that the profit and loss account showed this. In his condemnation of the old management, he showed his commitment to the old Carnegie Steel doctrine of volume of output as a vital consideration: "Do not think Cambria is securing the output it should, which is one reason why it is not securing low costs." He also indicated that he was open-minded about newer methods and the leadership of younger men: "probably Mr. Donner might be the man needed on the directory; and it may be that as he was born after Mr. Stackhouse became a steel man, is something to his advantage" (Powell Stackhouse [1840–1927] had been associated with Cambria since 1876).[34]

Ten years later, the Clayton anti-trust act required the Pennsylvania Railroad to dispose of its interests in both Pennsylvania Steel and Cambria Steel. Frick and Donner were reported as wishing to secure control of these interests, but at the same time Schwab, now at Bethlehem Steel, wanted Pennsylvania Steel in order to extend capacity for war material. Early in 1916, Bethlehem acquired the Steelton and Sparrows Point works. Cambria Steel was brought into an extended Midvale Steel and Ordnance group, in which the central place was now occupied by another man prominent since Carnegie Steel days, William Corey.

SHIPBUILDING

The revival of the eastern steel industry at the turn of the century was partly associated with a new emphasis on shipbuilding, both merchant and naval. This in turn reflected a transformation in America's place in the world economy and a new conception of its role in international politics. When it appeared in 1902, *Census Bulletin 166*, dealing with shipbuilding in 1900, celebrated the recent growth of the industry but ended with a comment that would have sounded strange in any of the major industrial countries of the Old World, which had more or less continuous growth in shipbuilding:

> The growth of the shipbuilding industry in the United States during the last ten years, as shown by the census reports, exceeds that of any preceding decade, and the tonnage constructed during the census year ending May 31, 1900, was greater than during any preceding year in the history of the United States, with the possible exceptions of 1854 and 1855.[35]

In the 1850s, in an age when shipping was still largely built of wood, American yards constructed an annual average of 366,000 tons, as compared with only 234,000 tons in the United Kingdom. Conversion to iron construction and then to steel came later in the United States than in Europe; and as its national economic development took a continental rather than oceanic course, U.S. shipbuilding fell behind that of the Old World. During the

1880s, the annual average of new tonnage built had fallen to 211,000 tons; in the United Kingdom it had increased to 647,000 tons. At this time, the combined tonnage of Germany and the Scandinavian countries was also in excess of the American output. By 1900, over 90 percent of U.S. foreign commerce was being carried in foreign bottoms. In the course of the 1890s, however, the value of the product of American yards had almost doubled, and the capital invested in the industry increased by 183 percent.[36]

Even so, the slower development of shipbuilding and the continuing vitality of railroad construction meant that—whereas in Britain the steel industry moved from rails to plate and angles (and also from Bessemer to open-hearth steel)—adjustments, both of product mix and process, could be more leisurely in the United States. However, as shipbuilding advanced in the 1890s, the steel industry responded. Expansion in this field was helped along by the new determination that the United States should have a major navy, a resolution that, before the end of Frick's life, had become a commitment to naval power second to none.

In the 1890s, manifest destiny brought the United States to the annexation of Hawaii and, after the war with Spain had given vivid evidence of the value of naval power, to the control of Cuba and the Philippines. By 1900, America was championing the Open Door policy in China, and soon after that, the creation of the state of Panama and construction of the Isthmian canal marked her arrival as the prime influence of affairs in Latin America. As writers of the time—especially Alfred T. Mahan—recognized, such an outward turning required a navy comparable with that of other powers.

But in this respect, the Republic was starting from a low base. On 1 July 1890, the U.S. Navy consisted of sixty-five war vessels, of which seven were sailing ships. The total complement of men and officers was nine thousand. This was scarcely a force for greatness in the power broking of the world. The Spanish American war (which officials of Carnegie Steel seem generally to have considered an inconvenient interruption of normal business) was recognized by others as requiring a new scale of thinking about naval power.

Strangely, given his pacific inclinations and his denunciation of annexation of parts of the old Spanish empire, Carnegie gave this movement some encouragement. In the first half of 1898, he suggested that a first-class shipyard and dry dock should be built on New York harbor. E. C. Potter, son of the former president of their keen Chicago rival the North Chicago Rolling Mill Company, wrote to convey his enthusiastic support for such an idea:

> This country *must* become a great sea power. . . . The present war is fraught with the most tremendous consequences for this country. It will accomplish

the rehabilitation of our merchant marine, the material increase of our navy, the construction of the Nicaraguan Canal and an enormous extension of our commerce. In my estimation the country is about to enter upon the most glorious period of her history.[37]

A few months later, another correspondent informed Carnegie that he and friends had both the sort of site and the sort of shipbuilding plans Carnegie was advocating. Already, Carnegie Steel was benefiting from the associated increase in shipbuilding. They had closed with the Union Iron Works Company of San Francisco to provide steel for one of the battleships in the current naval program and had provisional orders for the material for the other two, one to be built by Cramp and the other by the Newport News yard.[38]

By 1902, the U.S. Navy already had ten first-class battleships and eight more were building. At the same time, Russia had ten in each category, France had nineteen built and three building, Great Britain had thirty-seven built and fifteen either building or in preparation for building. Over the following few years there was further dramatic change, and by spring 1910, the United States with thirty battleships ranked behind only Germany with thirty-three and Britain with fifty-six.[39]

The growth of a world-ranking navy required the establishment of a whole complex of support industries. At the start of the twentieth century, Britain possessed a number of Admiralty naval yards and a much larger number of private yards capable of building capital ships. She had five armor plate mills and a number of firms capable of building heavy naval guns. By this standard, the United States was relatively ill-equipped. Since the late 1880s, Bethlehem and Carnegie had made armor plate, and the former also produced heavy guns. Midvale Steel of Philadelphia had made moves to produce both armor and ordnance but had not yet become an important factor in either.

There was a widespread feeling that more needed to be done. For a few years around 1900, there were ideas of creating a major East Coast arsenal and naval yard on the model of some of the bigger British examples, and two English firms—Armstrong Whitworth and Vickers—were separately involved in negotiations with American parties about this scheme. Eventually it failed to materialize. In merchant ship building, although the United States had had an illustrious past, its current position remained an undistinguished one. In 1900, it launched 191,000 gross registered tons, 8.85 percent of the world total. It was outbuilt by Germany (205,000 tons). United Kingdom yards launched 7.5 times the U.S. tonnage.

These circumstance provided the context within which Henry Clay Frick was involved with schemes for shipbuilding. At least as early as 1898, he was in touch with those planning a new East Coast shipbuilding center. Initially, the hope had been that Carnegie Steel would become involved. The contact in shipbuilding was Henry G. Morse, in age almost an exact contemporary of Frick's. Morse had been in railway work and other engineering. From 1896 to 1899, he was president of the Harlan and Hollingsworth shipyard in Wilmington, Delaware. At the end of the 1890s, he was ready to strike out in another direction. After looking into such questions as depth of water, he wrote to Frick in September 1898: "I have partly estimated costs etc. and will I trust finish and be ready to see you during the latter part of next week." By the end of that month, he had spent four days in and about New York harbor, "in search of a proper location. They are very scarce and expensive." He looked up the Hudson at Weehawken but reported back that there was only a shoreline there and the costs would be prohibitive. At the beginning of December, he had an interview with Carnegie, Lawrence Phipps, and Homer Lindsay, the former Homestead overseer who now had a nominal $0.3 million interest in Carnegie Steel and Frick Coke. Morse reported to Frick his impressions of what had proved a friendly but ultimately unsatisfactory discussion. Carnegie had been in a frustrating mood,

> very cordial, talked a little about my location, argued that the Delaware was better. Asked no question about size of plant proposed and declined to look at plans "because he knew nothing of such things, had no doubt they were excellent." *Repeatedly* stated Carnegie Steel Company would not become interested, to which subject I had not referred. Declined to give me a letter (which I stated would help me get subscriptions) by saying he had already written a letter covering every point. I was very guarded in my conversation. He did almost all the talking. I am puzzled and cannot understand his attitude, unless he did not wish to talk before his audience.[40]

Morse proved to be a man not easily diverted from the course he had chosen. Shipbuilding was on an upward course—the merchant tonnage built increased from an average of 220,000 tons in the ten years from 1888 (and 230,000 in both 1896 and 1897) to 303,000 in 1900, although some of this increase was connected with activity on the Great Lakes rather than in oceanic shipping. Morse wrote enthusiastically about his experience at Harlan and Hollingsworth: "more work than they have ever had under contract at one time." He was gathering together a technical staff for his new venture. Theodore Lucas, who was with Cramp, had offered his talents in the organization of shipbuilding, and now "I can outline to you or others with you interested quite complete plans for the technical and commercial side of such an enterprise and should be pleased to have an interview with you for further particulars." He was still searching for a suitable location: "A great many locations have been rejected because of lack of depth of water for launching, bad bottom for foundations, distance from homes for workmen, etc., etc."[41]

Eventually things began to work out. Andrew Mellon became associated with the scheme as "organizer." In spring 1900, Mellon reported from London that Morse was in Belfast—presumably seeing there the great operations of Harland and Wolff. By that summer, the New York Shipbuilding Company was in existence with Morse as president. Notwithstanding the company's name, the location chosen for its yard was Camden, New Jersey. By September 1900, there were already 1,350 men employed. Building began at the start of 1901 and, within nine months, they had done $1.05 million of work. Employment reached 2,400 early that autumn and was increasing by about 200 men a month. Unlike so many yards that had grown piecemeal, Camden was designed to operate on a logical plan. Morse wrote, "The various departments (some 15 in this business) depend on each other and cannot be started separately, but follow one after the other. We anticipate that we will be running full by next spring."[42] Morse was to win recognition for his achievements in developing an excellent shipyard layout, material coming in by rail at one end of the site and progressing under cover through successive stages from keel laying to completion.[43] It seems to have been from this shipyard project that the idea of a major East Coast steel and forgings plant was derived.

Almost as soon as the rupture with Carnegie Steel became public knowledge, Frick's name became associated with shipbuilding. The matter came up time and again. When he was said to be associated with the New York Shipbuilding Company, he told a Pittsburgh newspaper: "I have nothing to say on the matter. I am not a shipbuilder." A week later, another of the city's papers ran a story that, with Andrew Mellon, Frick wanted the Sparrows Point works of Maryland Steel to make plate for the New York Shipbuilding Company. Shortly after this, the *New York Times* reported that he had long anticipated a movement of British armament firms into the market as suppliers to the U.S. Navy and had suggested moves to meet this challenge. Carnegie had not approved (the story went), and now, following the break between the two men, Frick was to take this up on his own account. He was to make armor plate on a scale comparable with Bethlehem or Carnegie Steel and to invest at Camden, New Jersey, in association with Henry Phipps, along with the financier and magnate of western railroads Collis P. Huntington (who had been involved in the earlier discussions with the British armament firms) and the New York Shipbuilding Company.[44] These reports proved to be intriguing amalgams of hearsay, falsehood, and some truth.

In August, Collis Huntington died, but this did not kill off the project. Shortly afterward, the secretary of the board of harbor commissioners for Philadelphia wrote to Frick, "It may be within the bounds of possibility that I might be of service in connection with the increase here in the works in which you are interested, more particularly the addition of a steel plant as part of the New York Shipbuilding Company's plant." After this, the idea of an East Coast arsenal brought Frick once more into contact with John Potter, who had been sacrificed as superintendent at the end of the Homestead strike and, despite Schwab's suggestion, had not then been offered control of their armor department, and who had left Carnegie Steel in 1893. Sometime in 1900, Potter was in contact with Frick about the East Coast project and, on Christmas Eve, wrote in great enthusiasm with estimates of costs and profits for "one complete steel casting, forging and machinery plant, in place on the Delaware River, Camden, New Jersey." His ambitions for it were unbounded:

[It would make] the largest and heaviest parts required for large ships, engines, ordnance and any other heavy work demanded by modern undertakings, not only for our own country and Government, but for the world, as it is my idea, should I succeed in bringing this proposed plant to a reality, to make it the best plant in the world for the purpose for the next 20 years to come, and, as I have already informed you, I am ready to back my belief in its success from the start with my savings and patents which by their use will assist in producing a better steel than is now made by any other process.[45]

Soon after this, the relationship became clearer between Morse's shipyard and the new steel and forge plant. They were to be separate but associated enterprises, the yard already being developed at Camden, the proposed forge some miles further south at Paulsboro on Mantua Creek. At the same time, notwithstanding Potter's bold claims for the excellence of the plant he was planning, in this field at least technical dependence on the Old World was not yet completely ended. In March 1901, Morse spoke with Mellon and then wrote to Frick suggesting that Potter communicate with Albert Vickers about "you[r] undertaking the manufacture of their guns at your forge plant. They are apparently anxious to have them manufactured in this country (or may possibly only wish to sell the rights etc.)." That summer, Potter asked if he could arrange for Mellon and Frick to visit the Openshaw steel plant of Armstrong Whitworth (from which he had made inquiries concerning casting and fluid compression mechanisms, presses, and other machine tools) and the Crossley Gas Engine Plant, also in the Manchester area, "as there you would see what I am figuring on for Paulsboro," where they had just acquired the site. The public was informed that Frick was to build an "immense" steel plant on Mantua Creek, which—although fully equipped with labor-saving equipment—would nevertheless employ as many as two thousand.[46]

Negotiations and rumor concerning transatlantic cooperation on an East Coast arsenal and on naval yards dragged on for a few more years. In autumn 1901, Millard Hunsiker—still in London but now representing U.S. Steel there—wrote to Frick to introduce John Strain of Cassillis, Ayrshire, Scotland. Strain was visiting Pittsburgh with Dr. Francis Elgar of the Clydeside yard of the Fairfield Shipbuilding Company, who (Hunsiker had heard) was a consultant for Morse's yard. Strain himself was an interesting man, a civil engineer but also managing director of one of the leading Scottish steel firms, the Lanarkshire Steel Company. Hunsiker mischievously added another reason he thought Frick might like to meet Strain, for "he has one of the best fishing and shooting estates in Scotland."[47] In the end, this proved to be more or less the measure of the resulting collaboration.

The arsenal project was eventually to founder. Vickers had other contacts in the U.S. steel and engineering industries and, in any case, adopted a superior attitude to the Americans, which cannot have endeared them to potential partners.[48] However, the Camden Yard of the New York Shipbuilding Company survived and expanded, although in the course of 1903 it suffered the shock of the death of Henry Morse. Three battleships for the U.S. Navy were put out to tender that summer. Frick asked Morse if they would tender for them but later concluded the company could not bid for them at prices that would secure the order. As a result, he thought the only thing to do was to quote a price that would, as he put it, "protect other shipbuilding concerns." Some time later, Frick was contacted by T. Jefferson Coolidge of the Old Colony Trust Company, which had recently "reorganized" the Fore River Shipbuilding Company of Quincy, Massachusetts, a yard contemporary in date with Camden. Fore River was eager to get the contract for one of the new government warships. Coolidge deplored the reckless bidding between shipbuilders and suggested that the owners of yards should look into the matter of costs and direct "their subordinates, the manufacturers, to make only fair bids and not cut-throat bids for these vessels." To this end he hoped to see Frick before he left for Europe, remarking that his own involvement had already saved one series of negotiations from failing.[49] It is not known how long Frick was associated with the New York Shipbuilding Company. Even before the death of Henry Morse in 1903, he was becoming more involved with a vastly bigger venture, one that brought him back into the mainstream of the steel industry.

8

The Shaping of the
U.S. Steel Corporation

Formation and Early Operations

During the late 1890s, major amalgamations produced a number of great steel trusts—horizontal integrations of most of the firms in a particular line of business. The breadth of their scope may be appreciated by the example of American Tin Plate, which linked more than forty previously rival firms. Initially, these were mainly or wholly finishing concerns, buying semi-finished steel from the large integrated companies. However, at the end of that decade, the firms began to integrate backward to supply more of their own needs. At the same time, a new primary steelmaking firm—the National Steel Company—was formed, largely to supply their finishing operations. Such developments caused previous suppliers, and especially Carnegie Steel, to react by preparing to make a wider range of finished products. Already, the industry was marked by very large overcapacity and therefore increased overheads (see table 31); the new situation threatened still more expansion and sharper competition. From a vague ferment of threats, schemes, and thoughts about remedial action the U.S. Steel Corporation took shape.

Plans for a major amalgamation of competing steel firms can be traced back into the 1890s, although if carried through they would have resulted in something less comprehensive than U.S. Steel. In spring 1899, Frick and Gary discussed merging their two concerns and put tentative values on the various properties. Both this and the slightly later negotiations with Moore (which Gates thought might produce a billion-dollar corporation and which caused such bitter feeling between Frick and Carnegie) came to nothing, and for the next eighteen months the companies continued to fight for mar-

TABLE 31

Production, Capacity, and Utilization Rates in the Steel Industry, 1900–1901

	Production		Capacity	Excess Capacity over Average Production
	1900	1901	end 1901	1900–1901
Pig iron	13,789[a]	15,878[a]	24,812[a]	67.3[b]
Bessemer steel	6,685	8,713	12,938	68.0
Open-hearth steel	3,398	4,656	8,290	105.8
Rolled iron and steel	9,487	12,349	23,220	112.7
Tinplate	303	399	605[c]	72.4[c]
Rails, all kinds	2,385	2,875	4,630[d]	76.0[d]
Structurals	815	1,013	e	na

Source: Based in part on Jeans 1902, p. 312.
Notes: [a] Figures this column are in thousand tons.
[b] Figures this column are percentages.
[c] Capacity of twenty-five out of sixty-three works only.
[d] Capacity of eleven Bessemer rail mills only; forty-eight mills in all could roll rails.
[e] Sixty-nine mills had capacity for structural shapes.

kets and to prepare for yet fiercer battles ahead. A still wider amalgamation might remove these animosities. More particularly it could contain and harness the competitive power of the Carnegie Steel Company.

There was no possibility of overlooking the awesome quality of that power. In 1900 Carnegie Steel made 29 percent of the nation's steel. It had long dominated the rail business. On November 1900, it was reckoned to have plate orders for home consumption that were five times greater than those of all other producers combined. What demoralization might such a concern create in the tube trade? Or in sheet or wire? Herein lay a perennial nightmare for the capital-inflated steel trusts. The New York Times soon afterward wrote of the attractions of wider associations: "Those who know the facts understand that it has been formed primarily to eliminate Mr. Carnegie from the trade. His competitors could make no plans for their own protection until his vast capital and masterful intelligence were devoted to philanthropy rather than to business."[1] Such were the causes; the more immediate antecedents and occasions for amalgamation came in autumn 1900.

At the meeting of Carnegie Steel managers on 6 November 1900, Schwab reported that, during his visit to New York the previous week, he had received a message that J. Pierpont Morgan would like to see him. Thinking this concerned their plans for railroad construction, he did not go. Afterward, Morgan's assistant Charles Steele told him that the aim had been to talk about the tube business, whose good order Morgan feared would be disturbed by Carnegie plans.[2]

A more immediate opportunity to set in motion massive changes in the steel industry came at the famous dinner given for Schwab at the University Club in New York on 12 December 1900. In his speech as guest of honor, he outlined the benefits of a merged, rationalized, and extended steel industry: there would be a higher degree of product specialization in individual rolling mills; the less efficient operations would be brought up to the standard of the better (or closed, though this implication seems not to have been spelled out until later); and the huge extra costs involved in cross hauling from a wide spread of competing mills could be eliminated. Outlined with the authority of a professional but presented with all the magic of his infectious enthusiasm, self-confidence, and particular style of eloquence, Schwab's vision was followed with close attention by his audience from the world of finance and industry.

Most important, the vision bewitched J. P. Morgan, who was beginning his conversion to the idea of a uniquely wide-ranging new grouping—one that would make it possible to avoid the demoralization of both steel and railroads that he so much feared. Carnegie made only a brief appearance that evening, before going on to another engagement. There is no evidence that Frick was present, and every reason to assume he was not, as he was then engaged in a generally acrimonious correspondence with Schwab. However, Frick was consulted in the course of the discussions and arrangements that proceeded from that evening. At the end of December or in early January, at Morgan's request, Elbert H. Gary produced a draft scheme for the amalgamation of Federal Steel and Carnegie Steel, and the inclusion of some of the firms created in the previous round of horizontal mergers, including National Tube and American Steel and Wire. Morgan commissioned the world-renowned steel consultant Julian Kennedy to survey and value the various properties that were to be included in the amalgamation. Carnegie heard rumors of these plans and inquiries before mid January, but not until the end of that month did Schwab present him with details or ask his price for selling. Early the following month, in order to satisfy a public which was aware that something dramatic was underway, Gary made a public announcement that steps were being taken toward the formation of a big new grouping. On 2 March 1901, J. P. Morgan and Company issued an official statement that made specific reference to a new "United States Steel Corporation." The new company began trading a month later.

In size, and still more in competitive power, the plants of Carnegie Steel dominated the new grouping. The overall capacity of Carnegie Steel was from 40 to 50 percent bigger than that of Federal Steel and about half as big again as that of National Steel; but, allowing fully for the indebtedness of these companies, U.S. Steel paid four times as much for Carnegies as for Federal and seven times as much as for National, paying, as the Commissioner of Corporations later put it, "not only for tangible assets, but also— and very liberally—for earning power, and perhaps more important still for the elimination of Mr. Carnegie." Although the price was high, as Corey remarked some years later, "No value too high or too great could be put on the organization of the company." Perhaps the most striking evidence of the excellence of both its plant and its organization was Corey's contention that costs in that section of U.S. Steel had not been lowered further in the twelve years since its formation.[3]

An essential step in providing for the support of the new corporate giant was to ensure that it possessed abundant reserves of raw materials. As far as fuel was concerned, the inclusion of the properties of the H. C. Frick Coke Company—as well as the smaller coal and coke subsidiaries of Federal Steel and American Steel and Wire—was to guarantee these reserves for many years. However, in iron ore, there were some weaknesses. Federal Steel had its own Minnesota Iron Company; but much of the Carnegie ore had come from its long-term supply contract with Rockefeller's Lake Superior Consolidated Iron Mines Company. Concerned to secure these ore reserves for U.S. Steel, Gary approached Morgan, who met Rockefeller's son but obtained no satisfaction.

Frick was then commissioned by Morgan to approach J. D. Rockefeller direct in order to find out the price he wanted for his ore fields. Rockefeller asked him if he agreed that the figure Gary had offered was too low, and then, to Frick's surprise, asked his own assessment of its value. Frick came up with a figure $5 million in excess of the figure Gary had suggested. This was acceptable to both Rockefeller and Morgan. At the adjourned U.S. Steel board meeting of 1 April 1901, it was decided to pay $270 a share for the Rockefeller ore.[4] By this negotiation alone, Frick made a vital contribution to the future success of U.S. Steel.

For Carnegie, the creation of the new group marked his retirement from business. He wrote to Lauder, "Pray sleep soundly—all is fixed—your Bonds and mine go as our partners' go—into vaults." For most of the other ex–Carnegie Steel directors and top executives, the new corporation marked a major stage in their business careers. In exchange for his interest in The Carnegie Company, Frick received bonds, preferred and common stock amounting to $61.4 million in the U.S. Steel Corporation. He had, from the first, one of the largest interests. His place in the new corporation's hierarchy of control was less obvious. It had been decided that he would be a director. However, many of the top officials had previously been his colleagues at Carnegie Steel and were among those who had ousted him less than eighteen months before. Burnley claimed that his feelings for his former associates were "absolutely free from resentment, vindictiveness or jealousy," but it is difficult to believe that Frick can have been wholly without antipathy to those he was convinced had wronged him.[5]

Frick was convinced of the great power the new corporation would exercise, but he did not know how large a part he would be called on to play in it. A letter he wrote to Jay Morse is interesting in this respect:

> It seems to me that the United States Steel Corporation will be so large that it is bound to command the best talent in managing it. With the large amount of ore they control, the fuel, and the splendid manufacturing plants, it should be a great money maker. I don't know that they would want me to take hold of the matter, but I have had a great number of prominent individuals speak to me regarding it; but you, of course, know that at my age it would be a very great mistake to assume such a responsibility. I have enough of my own to look after and to occupy my time very fully.[6]

Such words seem to indicate that some at least of those involved were pressing for him to be made the chief executive officer; Carnegie on the other hand endeavored to ensure that he had no powerful position.

The U.S. Steel Corporation began business on 1 April 1901. Judge Elbert H. Gary was appointed chairman of the executive committee. At the 16 April meeting of the board, Charles Michael Schwab was elected a director and, there being no other nomination, was also appointed president. The same meeting elected Frick to the board. A few weeks later, Schwab wrote to explain to Carnegie why, notwithstanding his earlier promises, he had again agreed to serve on a board containing Frick. He pointed out that the board's final composition had not been decided until ten days or two weeks after his election (in light of the above, this seems not to have been the case). It was only then, he said, that he learned of Frick's membership. He was surprised by this, "especially after what [Morgan] had said to me and knowing your feelings as well as my own in the matter." Schwab went to Morgan, pointing out that "this was not according to our understanding," and that he could not serve with Frick. Morgan replied that Frick had agreed never to attend a board meeting, and he pleaded with Schwab to continue. "After much reluctance, I agreed to do so, but I do wish to say this, that if at the end of this year Frick does not resign from the Board, I shall. . . . I trust this explanation will be entirely satisfactory."[7] The episode shows how much

Morgan valued both Schwab and Frick. After the year had passed, neither Frick nor Schwab had resigned.

Other divisions soon appeared among the leaders of U.S. Steel. There were early hints of disagreement along the lines of old company loyalties. Within two weeks of the corporation's inauguration, there were differences about coke properties. Schwab wanted to leave Lynch with much independence of action; Gary thought the executive committee should know more about his plans. Gary also remarked that "in his opinion the properties and plants controlled by the Illinois Steel Company in the coke region had men there who were the best constructors of plants and that their showing is the finest of any one." It was not the sort of statement likely to commend him to those who had for many years been associated with the H. C. Frick Coke Company.[8]

There were arguments too about attitudes toward competitors. Schwab and other old Carnegie Steel men, including Frick, could not easily accept Gary's more open and cooperative approach. Their reservations were shared by directors from some of the other formerly independent companies. Discussions were held during the first meetings of the executive committee concerning the amount of freedom of action that should remain with constituent concerns rather than with the central decision makers. Schwab and the former independent company presidents Daniel Reid (American Tin Plate), Edmund Converse (National Tube), and William Edenborn (American Steel and Wire) spoke out in favor of more devolution of powers; Gary and Henry H. Rogers, who had come from Standard Oil, favored centralized control. Here in embryo was the division between control from 71 Broadway and control from the industrial centers, whose resolution in favor of the former was, over the decades, to help bring about the gradual erosion of the position of the corporation now beginning its career with such apparent promise. However, in the meantime, plant executives often seized the initiative—as Garraty put it, they "sometimes found it difficult or inconvenient to comply with orders from New York; when this was the case they often kept silent and did as they pleased." At the center, Schwab—schooled in the hard, ceaselessly combative regimen of Carnegie Steel—was an opportunist. At the beginning, he thought the U.S. Steel Corporation should raise the price of rails, for then, "in his judgment, it would attract but little attention." Converse suggested they should welcome a level of railroad freight rates "just as high as it can be, if they will give us some definite and distinct rebate or preference in some other way." Gary responded that this was to expect an unfair preference for them (which Converse had clearly intended).[9]

From an early stage there was dispute over precedence between the chairman and the president. At the meeting of the executive committee on 1 July 1901 while Morgan was away in Europe, Schwab tried to establish his primacy but was outvoted. After that defeat, he revealed the depth of his disappointment to a fellow director, Morgan's partner, the banker George W. Perkins:

> I have suffered every torture on Mr. Morgan's account to make matters move smoothly until his return. I have been hampered, criticized and goaded by incompetent critics, who do not understand the whole steel situation. . . . I feel most deeply for that great man, Mr. Morgan, who must find this condition upon his return. I'll do anything he may ask me, no matter what, except that I will not continue as President of this Company under any condition.

In spite of this, he stayed on. A year later, coke caused another disagreement. The question of the development of properties in the Pocahontas region was in the hands of Gary; but (as Charles Steele, a Morgan representative on the executive committee, remarked) insofar as it was a manufacturing question it should be in Schwab's control. Schwab was conciliatory. He reacted to Gary's remark, "I think it does not refer at all to operation," by stating his own opinion, that coal development was so closely associated with operations that "I do not think you can very well separate them," but he added, "It does not make the slightest difference to me, however."[10] Such differences were signs of a struggle for the effective leadership of U.S. Steel. Schwab's denial that it was important to him may indicate that he was already reconciling himself to withdrawal from the corporation that his vision of the industrial future had inspired.

The opinion of Hessen, a usually sympathetic biographer, was that Schwab "accomplished very little as president of U.S. Steel."[11] This is an unduly harsh assessment. Schwab set in train a search for yet more ore reserves, attempted to rationalize freight shipments, pursued further the interworks comparisons that had been so successful at Carnegie Steel, and integrated the foreign sales organizations that the amalgamation inherited. However, for all but a few months between the end of December 1901 and spring 1903, he was in Europe or ill at home. Given Frick's own ideas of business propriety, it was understandable that he was one of those who criticized Schwab most strongly.

There were troubles associated with Schwab's illness and with his reported gambling exploits when holidaying in Europe. He was away from the United States for some seven months from July 1902, and his absence gave Frick an opportunity to attend the directors' meetings. He was first at the meeting of 22 September 1902 and then at five of the next six meetings, from all of which the president was absent. In this period, he gave some indication of his thinking about the situation. In October, when earlier confusion about Schwab's gambling at Monte Carlo had been superseded by concern about his health, Frick wrote to John Strain in Scotland. He expressed pleasure with their business organization but not with its top direction. U.S. Steel directors "have certainly whipped the organization into very good shape and are getting good results. It is unfortunate that its President does not stand as well as the President of such an organization should, but the organization contains some very good men." It was rumored that Frick might replace Schwab. He gave his reaction to these suggestions to a reporter on Christmas Day 1902, at the same time stressing that, "I am most averse to newspaper interviews." He denied that the presidency of U.S. Steel was vacant and that he might take it even if it was, for he was too occupied with his own affairs. By March 1903, Perkins was suggesting that Schwab should step down. It is not clear what Frick's recommendation was at this time, but undoubtedly he was consulted both by Schwab and by others. On 20 March, he wrote to Gary, "I saw Judge Reed today and find that he has not yet seen Schwab. When he does I think he will advise him as I did regarding the Presidency."[12]

After his return from his extended visit to Europe, Schwab assured the board on 7 April 1903 that "I have come back with renewed health and vigor and in condition to go on with the work that is so interesting to us all." Frick was absent from the meeting at which that statement was made. Schwab was away again in May, and Frick again attended. The meeting of Tuesday, 2 June, was the first at which both men were present. Frick also attended the meeting of 7 July, at which Gary gave notice that he wished to bring forward some amendments to their bylaws. At this meeting, another event took place that retrospectively may be seen as important, the election of Corey to a directorship. On Tuesday, 4 August, Frick again sat at the same directors' table as Schwab. The events of that day must have reminded both men of the meetings and communications in January 1900 when Schwab had acted as the chief agent in the removal of Frick's powers at Carnegie Steel. Gary moved his motion to amend the bylaws in order to abolish the executive committee and create the office of chairman of the board with supreme powers. The motion was accepted and he was thereupon elected to the new post. The minute recording this was followed by the sentence, "Mr. Charles M. Schwab tendered his resignation as President of the Corporation." In explaining his decision to resign to representatives of the press, Schwab sought refuge in his health problems and put a favorable gloss on the role played in the affair by his old colleague:

> On my return from Europe six months ago I tried to get Mr. Morgan and the directors to accept my resignation, but was unable to do so. That does not look as if I had been forced out. Later I appealed to Mr. Frick and through him have finally succeeded in inducing the directors to accept my resignation. . . . I want to say that I think I have been treated very unfairly by the newspapers in regard to the reasons for my retirement. . . . My retirement is on account of ill health—nervousness. I have been in bad health for six months or more.

Many years later, testifying in the Mellon tax evasion case, he was more open as to his motivation: "There were too many people to consult with and advise with. I craved the old authority I had in the Carnegie Company. In other words, I wanted to be 'It.' "[13] He was succeeded as president by William Corey. For the next few months Schwab remained a U.S. Steel director and member of its finance committee. He last attended the finance committee on 5 April 1904; twelve weeks later, his resignation from the board was accepted.

Over the first three years of full operations, the steel output, employment, and sales of U.S. Steel declined. In all these respects it performed less well than the rest of the industry. Harvey believed that the $45 million purchase of Union Steel in December 1902 was sanctioned not only to remove a small competitor but also to secure the fuller involvement of Frick as a key man. If so, the results were delayed; the standing of the common stock declined, its high and low points being 46.75 and 29.75 in 1902, 39.87 and 10.00 in 1903, and 33.62 and 8.75 in 1904. In response to this worsening performance, Frick sold all his common stock and most of his preferred stock.[14]

Interviewed some years later, Frick was critical of the way the business had been run. He thought U.S. Steel had started with too little in the way of ready cash and had made a "great mistake" from the first in paying dividends on its common stock.[15] Now as Schwab's power faded, Frick became more involved. He had been appointed a member of the finance committee at the board meeting of 6 January 1903, at the time that the acquisition of the Union Steel properties was completed. Within a few weeks, he was involved in negotiations for the purchase of the ore properties of the Chemung Iron Company; with Gary, he was asked to look into a proposed acquisition of the Clairton steelworks; he acted as a member of the subcommittee considering a contract between the Union and the Wabash railroads and considering plans for river coal shipments by the H. C. Frick Coke Company.[16] Time and again over the next fifteen years, he was to serve similarly as one of the principal assessors of policy options for U.S. Steel. He thereby became closely associated with Gary.

Except for the first two years, in which he was establishing his precedence over Schwab, Elbert H. Gary was for over twenty-six years the undoubted leader of U.S. Steel. He was the only chairman of the executive committee, serving until it was abolished on 4 August 1903. That day, he was elected chairman of the board, and on 26 February 1907 chairman of the finance committee. He held both offices until his death in 1927. Gary was a man who, in the judgment of a later generation, was "overly serious, pompous and restricted in imagination"; his was a very different sort of business leadership from those of the previous decade. He liked to present himself as a new-style, progressive industrialist in his attitudes to other firms and to his own workers. He summed up this unusual approach in a 1914 address to his steel industry peers: "I ask you to consider not only the propriety, but the necessity and more than that, the pleasure of being fair, reasonable and generous in our treatment of our employees, and in our treatment of one another."[17] Yet his attitude to workers or their representatives was always paternalistic and sometimes patronizing. Coming from outside the industry, he had no conception of the hard labor of the men who toiled through the long shifts, and he was always a bitter opponent of unions. The steel strike of 1919 was to throw a revealing light on his eulogies about relations with labor.

Gary generally followed the policy of cooperation with other firms that he advocated, a remarkable contrast with the preceding period in steel. This for a time confounded his colleagues. *Fortune* later summarized their confusion: "Directors, worthy members of a cruder age, were honestly puzzled. It was bewildering to hear their Chairman preach the community of interests of all steelmakers, to see him consistently refusing to use the Corporation's size as a club over the rest of the industry." The central feature of his drive for cooperative action was his concern to maintain reasonable and steady prices. To outsiders, the most suspect of all the devices he adopted to secure this end were the so-called Gary dinners—social occasions for top steel executives, at which (as he later put it to the Stanley Commission) "what has been said has been serious."[18]

The first was held at the Waldorf-Astoria, New York, on the evening of Thursday, 10 December 1908, at a time when steel prices were falling alarmingly. Gary spoke then of conciliation, cooperation, stability as resulting in "the best interests of ourselves and all others." His audience was a group of 150 leading steelmen, including the presidents and vice-presidents of Lackawanna, Cambria, Maryland, Pennsylvania, Bethlehem, Youngstown Sheet and Tube, and Inland Steel. Schwab was there; and so too were other leading ex–Carnegie Steel partners, now occupying high positions in the corporate structure of U.S. Steel—William Corey, Alva Dinkey, William Dickson. In fact, Gary had set this course for his corporation even before he achieved unchallenged preeminence there. In November 1902, with Schwab recuperating in Europe, Gary had replied to questions concerning their prices:

> The policy of our corporation is to maintain reasonable and steady prices. We use our influence against an increase in prices and also against a decrease in prices if those which obtain are fair and reasonable. . . . We desire and seek the friendship of our competitors, but look first to the protection of our customers.[19]

Ex-Carnegie men understandably found it difficult to accept this new attitude, although some of them eventually recognized its benefits. James Gayley told the Stanley Committee, "I was brought up in a different school, and I must confess that I did not receive his ideas very favorably. . . . But I began to see that Judge Gary's perspective was a good one." Hunsiker decided to sever his connection with U.S. Steel in 1906. Frick too had to adjust. In the mid twenties Tarbell talked over these early days with Gary, and as a result she linked Frick with those who had wanted to take full advantage of their vastly superior power, who advocated more aggressive attitudes to labor, and who resented that they were not allowed to benefit from insider knowledge of the corporation's business for personal gain on the stock market.[20] Yet Frick too was won over.

In 1905, the *New York World* published an article about Frick, quoting his views on business methods. The account seems a paraphrase rather than a direct quotation, but the tone is interesting as it suggests a half-grudging recognition of the need for and benefits of the new order:

> The tendency of our modern industry is sound and helpful to the whole human race. Such evils as may exist are incidental and temporary. . . . The tendency of our modern methods of commerce and finance is to give courage and stability to enterprise. No important business has to stand alone, exposed to the shocks of fortuitous conditions. It can command credit, support and sympathy from the world around it. Gradually the whole fabric of American industry, commerce and finance has grown into intersupporting relationships, the result of a sensible understanding of the present and the future. . . . It is true that the development of modern methods of business has disturbed old conditions and that there has been some consequent suffering. That however is an incident of progress. It is a temporary phase of a great, necessary and wholesome growth.

Many years later, the board of U.S. Steel, and above all Gary, recognized Frick's initial doubts quite openly:

The Corporation at the beginning decided upon policies which, in several respects, were somewhat different from those which had been previously pursued in the management of large business affairs. Therefore, during the early period of Mr. Frick's connection with the Corporation he was somewhat doubtful in regard to some of the policies adopted, but was quick to appreciate the reasons presented and readily became a strong supporter of all including the idea that large corporations should openly recognize their obligations to others.[21]

Not surprisingly, their competitors welcomed the change. George Verity of the American Rolling Mill Company expressed appreciation on behalf of new firms and, in doing so, unconsciously contrasted Gary's policies with the predilections of so many of the Carnegie partners, including Frick: "If a man of another type, harder, colder, less human, less committed to right dealing, less anxious that a high ethical code should prevail in business, had come in to the Corporation, it would have brought endless disaster."[22] One result of Gary's live-and-let-live policy was to make it easier for a new generation of competitors to emerge, firms that were to grow more rapidly than the old leaders. Examples of such newcomers were Inland Steel, Youngstown Sheet and Tube, and the American Rolling Mill Company. At the same time, older firms that had suffered badly in past struggles now reconstructed and recovered, as with the transplanted Lackawanna operation and Cambria. Colorado Fuel and Iron, on the original shopping list of those putting U.S. Steel together, was bought by a new group and extended. Frick made a $30 million offer on behalf of U.S. Steel for Jones and Laughlin, but the offer was unsuccessful and the long-established firm was reconstructed as a more efficient but still independent operation. Perhaps most noteworthy of all was the case of Bethlehem Steel, to which Schwab now turned his energy and talents. From his new situation he could at last recognize some of the benefits of Gary's approach: "The policy of the Steel Corporation has not been to stifle or destroy, but by naming a fixed open price, to help stabilize conditions."[23]

Such policies enabled other companies to increase their share of production at the expense of U.S. Steel, which—although it could offer the advantages of plant specialization that Schwab had anticipated in his after-dinner speech in December 1900—was too big and too unwieldy in its organizational structure to cope with so many smaller, leaner, and more aggressive firms. When formed, U.S. Steel produced almost two-thirds of the nation's crude steel; by 1914, it produced only half. If more forceful policies had been followed, it might not have survived government attempts to break it up as being in restraint of trade; in that sense, Gary's policy was perhaps the wisest or at least the only practicable course.

It is clear that whereas Carnegie Steel had been a radical force, indeed a pacemaker, in the industry, its much bigger successor became a conservative influence, and in some respects a laggard. This is shown most strikingly when the production record of Carnegie Steel in the 1890s is compared with that of its successor during the next decade. In every year in which national output fell, Carnegie increased its share of the national total; U.S. Steel's performance always worsened in years of reduced production (see table 32).

Gary was to achieve much in the development of the U.S. Steel Corporation, and there is a good deal of evidence of the high regard he held for Frick; for many years, he depended heavily on his advice, and Frick's standing in U.S. Steel deliberations undoubtedly grew. Morgan had a high opinion of Frick from the start, and this regard was fully reciprocated. A few weeks after the new company began trading, writing to the British shipbuilder Arthur Hill, Frick had been unstinting in his praise of the financier: "It is conceded by all that he is the only man who could have carried the consolidation through." Over the years, his relations with their chairman also became closer. On 17 July 1906, Gary left on a visit to Europe. Next day the *New York Herald* carried what it represented to be the record of an interview given by him before he sailed. In it he spoke of their earnings and other developments. When he got to Paris he wrote personally to Frick to explain that he had had no conversation with a reporter. He went on, "I trust you are enjoying your new mansion as you deserve. Hope you will be within early reach of our office during the summer. With kind regards, I am, cordially yours, E. H. Gary." Early next year, Frick was in Palm Beach. He had recently recommended that the Steel Corporation take some Pennsylvania notes. Gary did not wish to do so, but after conveying his disagreement he added, with a strange mode of expression he was to use again later: "As you know, your opinion to me is potential." Two years after this, while staying at the Hotel de France in Paris, Frick received a cable from Gary:

> Privately yourself. Careful inquiry demonstrates that all competitors materially cutting prices much to our detriment. Our presidents all here agree the only way of protecting our customers favor thoroughly meeting competitive price. After long deliberation our Finance Committee unanimously concur. Have you any suggestions to make? Immediate action seems necessary.[24]

Such a message indicates that Frick was not regarded as a merely decorative member of the U.S. Steel central counsels.

This was emphasized still further in his relations with their new president. William Ellis Corey had followed Schwab up the ladder of promotion in the Carnegie concerns: he became superintendent at the Homestead plate

TABLE 32
Shares of U.S. Crude Steel Production

Year	Carnegie Steel	Year	U.S. Steel
1890	15.4	1901	65.7
1891	20.4[a]	1902	65.2
1892	17.8	1903	63.1[a]
1893	21.5[a]	1904	60.6[a]
1894	25.3	1905	59.9
1895	23.9	1906	57.7
1896	26.0[a]	1907	56.1[a]
1897	23.6	1908	55.9[a]
1898	24.3	1909	55.7
1899	25.0	1910	54.3
1900	29.1[a]	1911	53.9[a]
		1912	54.1
		1913	53.2
		1914	50.3[a]

Source: Carnegie Steel and U.S. Steel records (USX).
Note: Figures are percentages.
[a] Years in which national steel output fell below the level of the previous year.

mill in 1889 and, four years later, was superintendent of armor, in whose production he made important technical improvements. He took over from Schwab as general superintendent at Homestead in 1897, and as president of Carnegie Steel in April 1901. He was appointed president of U.S. Steel in August 1903 when he was thirty-seven, two years younger than Schwab had been when appointed to the same office in 1901. Like Schwab, he was voted an annual salary of $100,000, but in contrast to his predecessor, he knew from the start that his position ranked below that of the chairman. Corey seems to have been rough and blunt and less able to cover his defects with the genuine charm of his predecessor, and within a few years of his promotion, he had created a scandal far worse than Schwab's reported gambling exploits in Monte Carlo. In 1907, he divorced the wife he had married in his Monongahela Valley youth to marry the "actress" Mabelle Gilman (essentially a chorus girl). His second wedding was accompanied and followed by spectacular (and well-reported) examples of lavish bad taste. The whole episode fell lamentably short of the high moral tone Gary looked for in the figurehead of what was then the world's biggest industrial concern. It would have been equally outrageous to Carnegie.

In correspondence with Frick, Corey was sometimes very outspoken in

William Ellis Corey succeeded Charles Schwab as president of United States Steel Corporation in 1903.

criticism of Gary. In March 1909, he reported that at a recent meeting of the American Iron and Steel Institute, Gary had suggested that a number of overseas visitors be invited to their New York annual meeting. They would then be taken by special train to various works and ore fields, "all to advertise the Chairman." Corey put himself on record as "opposing this horde visiting our works." A few weeks later, he criticized the reluctance of Gary and the finance committee chairman, Perkins, to agree to a reduction in wages. It brought out his Carnegie Steel aggressive instincts:

> [T]hey seem to want to keep wages up so that steel prices can be advanced at the first opportunity. This is a great mistake for the policy of the past four years has doubled the capacity of our competition. We should operate our mills to full capacity and sell at reasonably low prices. We have expended $300 million on new plants and remodelling old. What is the object in spending money if we are going to have our plants stand idle? There is too damn much harmony, too much politics and too many axes to grind for personal advantage financially, socially and politically. Our company should be conducted on plain business principles and not used to exploit theories.

That same year, he wrote, "I notice that J. P. Morgan sailed yesterday so that he will be home for the meeting. What would you think of an increase of 3 percent while the two devils are away? This would be considered conservative and would be well received." That October, the American steel industry gave Gary a testimonial dinner. Corey refused to attend, saying he disagreed with his chairman's views and so would not "inconvenience" himself to honor him.[25]

Despite the frankness of Corey's letters to him, it is by no means clear that Frick thought highly of their president. Indeed, he was to play a part in Corey's fall from power—although, as with Schwab's removal, this was perhaps not so much the exercise of powers of an ambitious kingmaker but more the work of a wise and much respected senior colleague. However, in the early stages of the dispute that set this process in train, Frick's sympathies were with Corey. The question of the relative standing of the office of president and that of chairman was again the central issue. In autumn 1909, Gary had a consultation with the superintendent of the U.S. Steel ore subsidiary, the Oliver Iron Mining Company, without informing that division's president. The superintendent observed the confidentiality, but his secrecy was eventually found out and he was dismissed by the Oliver president. At this point, the superintendent appealed to Gary who, with Morgan and others, decided that he should be reinstated.

This brought out the still latent production-company sympathies of former industrial executives within the board, in opposition to financial and other colleagues. Both Corey and Frick supported the Oliver president. At the turn of the year, some extraordinary letters crossed between Gary and Corey, and there was a series of critical finance committee meetings. On 31 December 1909, Gary asked Corey to "please recommend" the reinstatement of the superintendent. On the same day, Corey replied that "after most careful consideration, I regret I cannot comply with your request." Having failed in several attempts to make contact by telephone over the New Year weekend, Gary again wrote to him, "I certainly think you are wrong in your conclusion and in your position. . . . I hope that you will withdraw your letter of refusal and promptly comply with my request." At this point, Corey took the extraordinary step of summoning the presidents of many of the subsidiary companies to New York to back him in his struggle against the centralizing (and largely the finance) sector of the board. There seemed every prospect of an open and very damaging breach.

On Tuesday, 4 January 1910, a special meeting of the finance committee was held. Both sides presented their case. Corey argued that Gary's way of operating would "result in great demoralization to the organization." Some members—notably the bankers, including the Morgan representatives, George Perkins and J. P. Morgan Jr., and George Baker of the First National Bank—wanted Corey's resignation at once. Frick was among those who urged moderation, but he now realized that Corey could not be saved unless he recognized Gary's superior authority. Frick therefore took Corey aside and argued the case with him, and as a result Corey gave way and agreed to reinstate the ore superintendent. The committee resolved that "the action of the Chairman in directing the President . . . was within the authority of the Chairman under the by-laws, and is, therefore, ratified and approved."[26]

It was appropriate that a further episode in the humbling of Corey should take place in the heart of U.S. Steel's manufacturing activities. It was in some ways a counterpart to the New York City dinner at which the financial and industrial establishment had honored Gary three months before. On 8 January 1910, the officials of U.S. Steel's Carnegie Steel subsidiary gave a hundred-dollar-a-plate dinner for Corey in the Fort Pitt Hotel, Pittsburgh. As was usual on these occasions, the room was lavishly decorated; and the guests each received solid gold necktie pins. (That year, the average weekly wage of a manufacturing employee in the United States was $10.73).[27] Morgan was outraged by what he judged a prodigal display, although his displeasure seems to have been activated more by business prudence than from concern for the impression left on the common man. As George Perkins put it to Corey in a letter written on Morgan's behalf, "people in charge of such matters" should remember "that it is not their money but the stockholder's money that is being spent for such things."[28]

Even after this episode, Corey survived another year until, on 2 January 1911, Frick sent on to Morgan the Corey resignation, which presumably he had been delegated to obtain. He wrote in his covering note, "The resignation of Mr. Corey desired by you is herewith enclosed." Next day at the meeting of the finance committee, Corey took a normal part in the business, but at the end of the meeting Gary presented his written resignation, "to take effect at the pleasure of the Board." It was left to Gary to decide whether a public statement should be made. Corey was last present at the meeting of 31 January 1911. A week later, it was resolved to pay him an additional $25,000 allowance for his presidency, and that he should be issued with his stock in U.S. Steel as represented by his participation certificates.[29] Like Schwab, he was later to try to build up a major new steel group in the East, but with less success.

Corey's withdrawal had further consequences. Two former Carnegie men followed him in resigning their posts—Thomas Morrison as a director, at the last meeting Corey attended, and William B. Dickson as a vice-president, three months later. Meanwhile, Gary was consolidating his hold at the top. The previous year, following the dispute about the ore superintendent, he had asked for a clearer definition of his status. He obtained the following addition to the bylaws, an addition that increased the powers he had secured when Schwab had left seven years before: "The chairman of the Board of Directors shall be the chief executive officer of the Corporation and, subject to the Board of Directors and the Finance Committee, shall be in general charge of the affairs of the corporation."[30] The powers of Corey's successor were thus further reduced even before he was chosen.

There was some question about the need for a president, and apparent divergence of opinion about who should be appointed if the post was retained. Schwab later reckoned that Gary had wanted E. J. Buffington, the man who thirteen years before had not impressed him as "a man of ability or experience" when he had visited Carnegie Steel with Gary. Buffington had long been president of Illinois Steel. In his letter to Morgan on 2 January 1911, Frick had given his opinion: "It seems to me there is no necessity of having a President, [but] if so I would favor Mr. Farrell." James A. Farrell had come into U.S. Steel with American Steel and Wire and had been put in charge of their export division, initially known as the U.S. Steel Products Company, later U.S. Steel Export Company. Frick added to his recommendation of Farrell that such a choice would "avoid any friction" within the various branches of the corporation. Much later, Tarbell reported that Farrell's promotion had been "at the insistence of Judge Gary."[31] In January 1911, Farrell was elected both to a directorship and to the presidency of U.S. Steel. At the same time, both he and others were given irrefutable evidence of the relative decline in the status of the office of president. Schwab and Corey had each received salaries of $100,000 a year. When Corey's replacement was being considered, Morgan is said to have remarked, "The trouble with U.S. Steel is to find a President of ability who does not need all his time to spend his salary properly." To ease this burden on his time, Farrell was voted only $50,000.[32]

Like most top executives, Farrell worked hard, according to Schwab trying to do too much without deputizing. Having reached this position his nature changed and he became domineering and aloof. Whether this is true or merely the soured perspective of a predecessor who was later a competitor, Frick was soon on happier terms with him than he had been with Schwab or probably with Corey. Farrell regularly sent him details of their monthly performance. Soon Frick was encouraging him to ease off (which perhaps indicates Schwab was right in his opinions). On Tuesday, 23 July 1912, the president added a note to his regular report: "I am going to Pittsburgh tonight; Greenville and Conneaut Thursday, thence as far as the Soo on one of our ore boats, returning by rail, so as to be at my office [in New York] on Monday morning." Frick wrote back immediately from Prides Crossing, his Massachusetts coast home: "Am delighted that the outlook seems so bright. Am also pleased to see that you are taking the trip on the boat. This will give you a rest and you should do it frequently."[33] In spite of the stresses of his post, Farrell remained president for over twenty-one years, and his relationship of respect and friendly relations with Frick continued to the end of the latter's association with the U.S. Steel Corporation.

New Districts, New Plant, New Problems

Its vast size meant that U.S. Steel spent much time rationalizing its initially overextended operations. At incorporation, it owned 213 manufacturing plants; by the end of 1909, it was still operating 143.[34] Its appetite for absorbing others was relatively slight, both for this reason and because it was fearful of attracting the anti-trust attentions of government. For particular purposes it would risk this, as in the case of its 1901 purchase of Shelby Steel Tube, a firm that already monopolized seamless steel tubes, or in the accumulation of ore properties, which was partly the motive for the Union, Sharon, and Clairton steel purchases. However, within little more than six

years of incorporation there had been two major developments, each of
which indicated how locational considerations in the industry were changing. These developments involved the entry of U.S. Steel into the South and
a major increase in its Chicago area capacity, and Frick played an important
part in both.

Southern steel production was insignificant at the beginning of the twentieth century. Prospects seemed poor. The industry was largely unconnected
with the operations of the great northern companies. Republic Iron and
Steel was exceptional. It had important southern ore and coal properties but
had nonetheless chosen to expand mostly in the North. Although it was the
biggest regional company, the Tennessee Coal, Iron, and Railroad Company
(TCI)—whose mines and plants were concentrated in the Birmingham, Alabama, area—was an extremely small operation as compared with U.S. Steel.
In 1907 TCI made only 1.05 percent of the nation's steel and 2.4 percent of
its iron (as compared with U.S. Steel's 56.4 and 41.8 percent respectively),
and in terms of quality TCI's ore and coking coal were much poorer. On
the other hand, these minerals were very close to each other and were abundant at a time when the coming exhaustion of both Upper Lake direct shipping ore and the coking coals of Connellsville and neighboring fields could
already be dimly discerned. TCI could produce pig iron cheaply, but it was a
poor quality iron, ill-suited for steelmaking except in the basic open-hearth
furnace. However, the company was now making and finding buyers for
basic open-hearth rails, although apparently not yet at a profit. In 1906 and
1907, large-scale spending was under way to improve and extend its operations. The *Manufacturers Record* of Baltimore sensed that great things might
lie ahead for both company and region:

> [I]t is a matter of the deepest interest to the South that this corporation, so
> long the football of unscrupulous speculating and gambling in Wall Street, is
> now being legitimately developed on very broad lines and for the fullest utiliza-
> tion of the remarkable advantages possessed by this and other companies in the
> Birmingham district. If the men who now control this property carry out its
> development . . . as has been stated they will do, for the enlargement of its
> operations . . . they will not only add vastly to their own wealth, but they will
> be great benefactors to the South.[35]

The major factor that now increased northern interest in southern concerns
was the latter's large ore holdings. Carnegie Steel had been paying royalties
that ranged from 15 to 35 cents a ton. In the five years from 1902 to 1906, the
average royalty at those Upper Lake mines that furnished information to the
Bureau of Corporations (mines involving a total annual production of over
64 million tons) was 26 cents a ton. A sharp break occurred in October 1906,

when U.S. Steel leased from 400 to 500 million tons of ore from the Great Northern Railroad (James J. Hill) at a royalty of 85 cents a ton. This lease was variously interpreted. Some thought the reason was that the rate of new ore discoveries was falling; others emphasized a wish to deny its use to rivals. Discerning commentators recognized that iron companies might need to look to southern ore fields. At first consideration the U.S. Steel Corporation did not seem the most likely firm to take this next step. But *Iron Age* saw further implications: "The Hill deal suggested to men of large capital that the psychological moment had arrived for investment in Alabama ore and coal, and in the plants already existing to turn them into steel." The economist Abraham Berglund drew what seemed a logical conclusion: "It is in the interests of this region that the Steel Corporation is likely to meet its most formidable competitors in the future," and he reported rumors that appraisals had already been made of southeastern and western companies, with a view to their ultimate absorption. Although Colorado Fuel and Iron (CFI) had been on the shopping list of those shaping U.S. Steel, southern properties were apparently not considered at that time.[36]

Since then, on their own initiative, individual TCI directors had now and then suggested that U.S. Steel might take over their company, but they received no sympathetic response.[37] Two estimates were made in 1904–1905 of the investment needed to bring TCI up to the efficiency levels of better northern plants. The figures were between $20 and $25 million. Expenditure on this scale was beyond the capacity of local financing. In 1906 at last, it began to look as if funds might become available to realize the area's potential. At that time, control was gained by a group that included John W. Gates and some of the leading men from Republic Iron and Steel. They made big plans and spent about $8 million on improvements over the next eighteen months. There was now at least the distant prospect of a powerful southern competitor.

The large TCI ore reserves and a technological change in steel were other important considerations. Basic open-hearth steel rails commanded a slight premium over Bessemer rails. U.S. Steel was now committed to their manufacture on a large scale in Chicago. Potential threats in this market took early shape when in spring 1907 the Harriman railroads ordered 157,000 tons of open-hearth rails from TCI's Ensley mill. At about the same time, TCI announced more ambitious developments, involving outlay of from $25 to $30 million for a modern steel plant and new rail mill, doubling the output of each and cutting costs. New evaluations that had been made the previous year credited TCI with huge mineral reserves—700 million tons of iron ore and 2,000 million tons of coal, much of it of good coking grade.[38]

Even so, by 1907 U.S. Steel was reputed to have turned down the idea of acquiring TCI because the price would be too high—although this seems inconsistent with its willingness to spend to deny others the Great Northern ore. (Opposition within U.S. Steel to the Hill lease led to its cancellation after five years.) The financial crisis at the end of 1907 gave the company a second chance to consider investment in the South. The first moves in this direction came at the beginning of the crisis, and well before firms associated with TCI were directly involved in it (see table 33).

The financial panic of 1907 broke on Monday, 21 October. When J. P. Morgan reached his office two days later, he found Henry Clay Frick, the financier Thomas Ryan, and the magnate of western railroads Edward Harriman waiting to see him. At this stage, their main concern was with the security of leading financial institutions. However, later that day U.S. Steel made a first move toward the acquisition of a small interest in TCI. Finance committee meetings were usually held on Tuesdays at 2 P.M., but on that Wednesday, Gary chaired a meeting that opened at 11.30 A.M. Four other members of the committee were present, Frick and the bankers Perkins, Baker, and Norman B. Ream. They considered a submitted agreement and, after "some discussion," voted unanimously to exchange $1.2 million par value of U.S. Steel Gold Bonds for $2 million par value of TCI stock.[39]

After this for a time there seemed some improvement in the general financial situation, but ten days later on Saturday, 2 November, the crisis deepened and this time pressed directly on TCI. The house of Moore and Schley, prominent New York brokers, was threatened with collapse. It had sold TCI stock and, through making loans as collateral, effectively still held $6 million of it. Grant B. Schley was a member of the TCI executive committee. The attorney Lewis C. Ledyard, through Morgan, suggested that U.S. Steel should rescue them by buying TCI. Morgan consulted Gary and Frick who were agreed that TCI stock was not worth more than $50 or perhaps $60 a share. Frick proposed an alternative approach, that they should help by offering Moore and Schley a loan of $5 million, but this was rejected as inadequate. The evidence suggests it was not easy to shift U.S. Steel from its opposition to purchase. However, that weekend details were worked out for U.S. Steel to acquire TCI as a means not only of saving Moore and Schley, but also thereby of helping stop the slide into a national financial collapse. At 11 A.M. on Saturday morning, the finance committee met. The same members were there as on 23 October, with the addition of J. P. Morgan, "by request." The minutes recorded, "The subject matter of the purchase of the properties of the Tennessee Coal Iron and Railroad Company on terms suggested was fully discussed and thereupon the meeting adjourned without

TABLE 33
Production by TCI and U.S. Steel, 1904, 1906

	TCI		U.S. Steel	
	1904	*1906*	*1904*	*1906*
Coal	2,756	3,208	13,718	18,533
Iron ore	1,208	1,483	11,763	23,123
Pig iron	475	642	8,254	12,619
Steel	155	402	9,422	15,153

Sources: TCI; BAISA, 15 May 1907; U.S. Steel Annual Reports.
Note: Figures are in thousand tons.

action." They met again at 9 P.M. with the same result, and this was repeated on Sunday morning at 11 A.M. There was yet another meeting on Sunday evening at 9 P.M. This time the outcome was different—"Upon motion, duly seconded, it was: *Resolved:* To recommend to the Board the purchase of the properties of the Tennessee Coal Iron and Railroad Company on terms suggested, and that the whole subject-matter be referred to the Chairman, with power."[40]

In their talks with Morgan, Gary had argued that the situation would not be helped if attempts to purchase TCI caused President Roosevelt to initiate proceedings against U.S. Steel for attempting a monopoly. In order to avoid the danger that purchase would bring down upon them the full force of government anti-trust powers, Gary and Frick were deputed on Sunday evening to seek Roosevelt's approval. They caught the night train to Washington and arrived at the White House as the president was breakfasting. Their importunate pressure ensured that he left his table to talk with them. With the advice of Elihu Root, Roosevelt wrote a note about the situation to his Attorney General concluding with the words, "I felt it no duty of mine to interpose any objection." With this rather less than whole-hearted endorsement (what Frick was once to refer to as Roosevelt's "attitude of tacit acquiescence"), they felt in a position to go ahead.[41]

On their return to New York, another meeting of the finance committee was held on Monday night, which again decided to advise the board to purchase, but the terms approved were slightly different from those of twenty-four hours earlier. Further meetings followed, at 9 P.M. on Tuesday and at 3 P.M. and 3.30 P.M. on Wednesday. The intention now was to exchange $30 million of U.S. Steel bonds for TCI. On Wednesday, 6 November, the board gave its approval. In this way U.S. Steel acquired at very reasonable cost a property requiring considerable further capital outlay, but having great potential. Overall, its value was much higher than the price paid (though it is impossible to be sure by how much). Although he may not have been in close touch with Alabama conditions and was speaking well after the event, Julian Kennedy, the steel consultant, reckoned that when acquired the TCI properties were worth from $90 to $100 million. When U.S. Steel took over, there were $3 million of TCI debts to be paid. By 1913 a sum of $23.5 million had been spent on improvements and diversification. In the assessments and decision making involved in this development process, Frick played a not unimportant part. He was appointed along with Perkins and Ream and with ex-officio members to a special committee to consider expenditure on large-scale developments there. As a result of these experiences, over the years he became a champion of the virtues of southern steelmaking. In 1919 in a moment wilder than most, he is said to have predicted that in twenty years Birmingham would be a greater steel center than Pittsburgh.[42]

The major focus for U.S. Steel development turned out to be in another direction, however. In retirement, Carnegie reckoned that the corporation had made a mistake in not choosing to build a plant on his company's Conneaut site. Land haulage of ore would be avoided there, and operations could benefit from cheap back-haul freight on coke or coal. For much longer, Frick had considered possible advantages in some shift of emphasis to the Chicago area. Growth in consumption was most rapid in the West, but although well located to do so the existing Chicago plants had been unable to satisfy that demand. For a long time a major check on the westward drift in production had been Carnegie Steel's efficiency and aggression. Now that company was incorporated in U.S. Steel, the logical processes of locational change could be resumed. Evidence from shares in national production shows that the competitiveness of Pittsburgh reached its peak in the late 1890s and fell away after that (see table 34).

In 1898 Schwab had calculated that, taking movement costs into account, Carnegie Steel was disadvantaged in ore by $1.04 as compared with Chicago works; for coke their costs were lower by $1.26. These were small differences but, if anything, Pittsburgh was then at a marginal overall advantage. Ten years later when Gary gave evidence to the Tariff Commission, the distortions Carnegie Steel had introduced had largely been removed. In part for this reason but in part also because of changes in production processes, the trend of costs had moved against Pittsburgh. Within U.S. Steel, transportation costs on the coke required to make a ton of pig iron were now said to be $1.95 less to Pittsburgh than to Chicago, but on the ore required, Chicago

TABLE 34
Allegheny County Share of U.S. Steel Production

	Crude Steel	Rolled Iron and Steel	Rails	Structurals
1897	39.5	31	32	62.9
1901	38.1	32.3	24.7	60.0
1905	32.9	30.1	22.0	n.a
1907	29.5	28.4	21.2	45.8
1908	32.0	24.2	14.0	42.7
1909	27.9	26.2	16.0	39.9
1910	27.4	26.2	14.7	41.9
1911	27.2	23.6	15.1	37.5
1912	24.9	24.4	11.4	37.3
1913	24.5	24.3	11.4	38.1
1914	24.9	22.8	12.5	34.7
1919	22.0	23.3	13.8	35.1

Sources: AISA and AISI.
Note: Figures are percentage of U.S. total.

was reckoned to have a $2.16 advantage.[43] There was a long-term tendency for the grade of Lake ores to decline and for greater coke economy in smelting. These considerations and hopes of using coke made from nearer coals, or made in by-product ovens at the works, meant that Chicago's small overall advantage on the ore and coke account of 21 cents a ton of iron could be expected to increase. As a center of production, Chicago as always benefited from major local outlets and good access to the great markets and even greater potential demand in the West.

During U.S. Steel's first years, the geographical pattern of plant extension showed no clear signs of the westward trend. Indeed, by the acquisition of Donora and Clairton works, 0.7 million tons of capacity was added in new plants in the Pittsburgh area. Between 1901 and 1904, the rated ingot capacity of the four longer-established main works there—National Tube at McKeesport, Edgar Thomson, Homestead, and Duquesne—went up by a mere 4.4 percent, from 4.20 to 4.38 million tons. However, early in 1903, the decision was made to spend $0.94 million for a new 140-inch-plate mill at Homestead. Two years later, after considerable discussion, it was agreed to allocate $11.5 million for the rebuilding of the McKeesport works. In the Chicago area over the same years the already idle Union works was dismantled and two plants—Joliet and South works—were expanded, but only by 8.6 percent or 145,000 tons. In 1904, a further 250,000 tons was being added to South Chicago.[44]

There soon followed the first steps to much bigger developments in that district. In June 1905, the finance committee considered what was recorded as "Additional Land for Extension of the Business in the Neighborhood of Chicago." At that time, they could obtain two tracts—one at Rockdale, southwest of Joliet, and the other near Whiting on Lake Michigan. The latter seems to have included the land lying just west of the Indiana Harbor Canal that Frick had owned since 1898. When he bought it, it had seemed adequate for a major plant (as late as 1904, Homestead covered only 156 acres), and now there were negotiations with Frick over this land, apparently as a site for fabricating operations. He responded by outlining what he held, but he went on, "I would not care to dispose of this, unless of course at full value. If you should desire to locate the bridge works in that locality it might be possible that you could secure land from other parties there at a lower price than I would be willing to take." He was absent from the finance committee meeting when the two sites were first discussed, but he was appointed with Gary, Rogers, and Ream to a special committee to look into the question. It was decided to produce a comprehensive report on further development of their properties. Within ten weeks, piecemeal extensions around Chicago had been superseded by decision on a major greenfield development.[45]

On the day of the meeting of the finance committee to decide on this project, Frick was in the Black Forest spa town of Baden Baden. He cabled Gary with his acquiescence and with his usual shrewd advice: "Strongly favor purchase. Firm offer, however, might secure much lower price. You have no competition for tract so large, far from center and no harbor." This was the beginning of what was soon to be known as the "Gary project," which created what was for many years the world's biggest steel plant. Frick was appointed one of five members of a special committee that was to take final decisions on the size and equipment of the new works. The public announcement in U.S. Steel's fourth annual report on 16 March 1906 referred to the failure of capacity in the Chicago area "to keep pace with the increased and rapidly increasing consumption tributary to this location: and therefore a large percentage of this tonnage is now supplied from Eastern mills."[46] Now, a central command could do something to remove the inefficiency in the locational pattern of production and haulage which this represented.

By summer 1906 the Chicago project had gone far beyond the possibilities of the Frick site. About five thousand acres had been acquired but even so, although large, the new plant was initially no bigger than some of the existing Pittsburgh area plants. Its planned ultimate steel capacity was then 1.75 million tons. In summer 1906, Corey forecast that with "reasonably good luck," they might be finishing steel there by spring 1908. When Gary reported that forecast, all seemed well commercially; as he put it, "our . . . prospects are very bright indeed. There is no speck on our horizon from what we have seen and what we can see."[47] In 1906 and 1907 they established new levels of prosperity, but in 1908 depression cut the operating rate to only a shade over 50 percent and earnings fell by almost $60 million. The schedule for the new works was disrupted. The first of the main finishing mills (for rails) was brought into production in February 1909. Over the next few years, more rolling mills and other plants were erected nearby for some of the corporation's specialized subsidiaries.

The inauguration of the Gary works marked an important stage in the relative decline of the Pittsburgh region. In the mid and late 1890s, competition from Pittsburgh had been effective right into Chicago; now, by contrast, the new plant shut Carnegie Steel out of huge territories it had long supplied. In 1911, speaking to the Pittsburgh Realty Club, the vice-president of U.S. Steel's Carnegie Steel division explained the situation:

> [T]he plant in Chicago, in the neutral freight zone of course, can do as well as ourselves; but our neutral freight zone only goes to the western Ohio lines.
> Everything west of that is in the domain of Chicago and Birmingham. Therefore it becomes necessary for us to look in other directions; first, to find new fields; second, to find new uses for steel.[48]

There was a good deal of slippage in Allegheny County's share of national production even in Frick's lifetime. Pittsburgh could still claim that it was the world's center for steel, but U.S. Steel was already following the commercial logic that would reduce that leadership.

Initiative in this process was not wholly within the control of their own corporate planners. Growth by other companies was also important: U.S. Steel's share of the nation's output was falling. In some lines the decline was greater than in others. Old products were still important, but there were new growth sectors. Rail production was increasing slowly now; after 1907 it began to fall away. Plate, sheet, and structural output was rising. In many lines U.S. Steel was clearly failing to hold its own. Old companies were being restructured to become more effective competitors, and there were new concerns, often specializing in the growth lines and driven forward by young managements. These companies were to continue to grow much more rapidly than their bigger, established rivals (see tables 35, 36).

TABLE 35

Main Finished Steel Products, 1901, 1913, 1919

	Rails	Plate and Sheet	Wire Rods	Structural Shapes
1901	23.3	18.2	11.1	8.2
1913	14.1	23.2	9.9	12.1
1919	8.8	29.4	10.1	10.4

Source: AISI.
Note: Figures are percentages of all rolled products.

TABLE 36

U.S. Steel Production of Finished Steel

	Rails	Plate and Sheet	Wire Rods	Structural Shapes	All Finished
1901	59.8	64.6	77.6	62.2	50.1
1913	55.5	49.1	58.4	54.0	47.8
1919	62.0	44.3	55.4	43.8	44.6

Source: AISI, quoted in Cotter 1921, p. 308.
Note: Figures are percentages of U.S. total.

An interesting example of product change that seriously affected U.S. Steel was in heavy structural shapes, of which Homestead had long been the nation's leading producer. The trade was now deeply affected by a change in technology. During the 1890s Henry Grey first turned out a wide-flanged beam that could be rolled as a single section instead of in separate sections that had to be rivetted together. He achieved this in the rather out of the way setting of a small plant in Duluth, Minnesota, and other producers showed little interest in his invention. Eventually the first mill built specially for the Grey beam was put up in 1902 in Luxembourg. At about this time Grey approached Schwab, who brought his proposal before the U.S. Steel finance committee, which rejected it. At the end of 1905 Schwab—now president of Bethlehem Steel—decided to build a Grey mill there, and he was honorable enough to inform Gary of his plan. Gary had the scheme examined by experts, who again decided not to recommend adopting the new-style mill. Schwab proceeded and completed the new Bethlehem mill in January 1908. (Ironically, he was helped in nursing it into full production by a loan from Carnegie—of U.S. Steel bonds to be used as collateral.) After a short, difficult trading period, Bethlehem established a high reputation for the new product. Schwab proudly told the Tariff Commission, "The new mills which I have built at Bethlehem have made a radical change in the character of structural steel, so that most of the structural steel plants of the United States will have to be changed within the next five years."[49] The U.S. Steel Corporation felt the impact of their competition much sooner than that.

In the latter part of 1908, Corey wrote to Frick that Gary was "considerably worried over something, don't know what." Then he went on to discuss the situation created by Schwab's initiative: "I believe it would be advisable to make an arrangement with Schwab on a fair basis, say for not over three years. This would give us time to build a mill, strengthen the structural situation which is rather mixed up, and Schwab will not make a great deal of money." Corey wrote again in the uncertain period before that year's election, in which Bryan was again challenging for the presidency. This time he referred to the Grey mill and to the wider effects of their policy of holding prices steady:

> Gary may bring up the question of an arrangement with Schwab during my absence. Am very decided in my opinion that nothing should be definitely decided until after election for we shall want our hands free in case the unexpected happens. At times I almost wish for a change, for our present policy is building up competition all over the country some of which is cutting our throat. We should make a good fair bargain with Schwab and am certain we can if we are only careful and patient.

In fact they suffered a sharp loss of structural business to Bethlehem Steel. In 1899 about 69 percent of Pennsylvania's tonnage of heavy and light structurals had come from Allegheny County. In 1909, the second year of operation of the Grey mill at Bethlehem, this share was down to 55.2 percent. By 1912 it was only 51.8 percent.[50] Eventually this was to lead the Carnegie Steel subsidiary of U.S. Steel to infringe Schwab's monopoly of the Grey patent, but Corey and Frick had both ceased to be directors long before that happened.

Through to the outbreak of war between the major European powers, Frick was deeply involved with the U.S. Steel Corporation. It was still by far the world's biggest steel operation, in 1913 producing well over a fifth of the world's total output. Yet there were already signs that all was not well. Between 1901 and 1914 the U.S. Steel share of national production had fallen in every year except one, and in times of difficulty (when Carnegie Steel had shown its virtuosity by increasing its proportion of a reduced output), U.S. Steel now did noticeably less well than others. In 1908 national production of crude steel was 60 percent the level of the previous year; for U.S. Steel the proportion was only 58.7 percent. The year 1913 was a banner year nationally with output 0.12 percent above the record level of the previous year, but U.S. Steel production was 1.45 percent lower than the 1912 figure. The corporation's income per ton of steel products shipped was $10.13 in 1902, $7.42 in 1910, and $6.06 in 1913. This record did not compare well with that of the old Carnegie Steel Company.

Culmination and Decline in the Coke Region

At the turn of the century, 46.5 percent of all the coal carbonized in U.S. beehive coke ovens was charged in plants located in the small Connellsville district; only 5.2 percent of all the oven coke produced in the nation came from by-product ovens. It was already recognized, however, that the life expectancy of the old coke field was limited and many experts acknowledged the superiority of the by-product method of coking. In the course of testimony to the Industrial Commission in spring 1901, as the newly appointed president of U.S. Steel, Schwab estimated that if steel consumption continued to increase at the rate of the previous few years, reserves of Connellsville coking coal would be exhausted within thirty years—about half the expected productive life of the known iron ore resources of the Northwest.[51] Through his directorship of U.S. Steel, Frick was to remain identified with the coke industry until the tonnage of beehive coke was exceeded by that of by-product coke and the decline of the Connellsville region was undeniable. By then he had played his own part also in the reshaping of the industry that he had dominated for so long.

There were a number of possible alternatives or complementary strategies for meeting the prospect of a long-term decline in Connellsville's ability to supply coke. One was to secure the largest possible share of the declining resources of that field. A second was to open neighboring fields where the coals, though of poorer quality, could still produce an acceptable furnace coke. A third was to widen the range of usable coals substantially by using a retort rather than a beehive oven. The retort ovens usually had arrangements for recovering by-products, the hitherto wasted constituents of the coals that had been coked—tar, gas, ammonia, and so on. Both the iron and steel industry in general and the U.S. Steel Corporation in particular adopted all three approaches.

Time and again during the more than sixteen years that Frick was an active member of U.S. Steel's finance committee, consideration was given to further acquisitions of coal lands or of rival coke companies in the Connellsville district. During summer 1901, the executive committee considered and rejected the idea of purchasing the properties belonging to the Hostetter-Connellsville and Rainey companies, the latter at an offered price of $40 million. During 1902, and again two years later, they considered buying coal lands from J. V. Thompson at $1,000 an acre.[52] In summer 1904 Lynch applied for permission to build two thousand more ovens; he was given authority to build one thousand in the Connellsville district. The Hecla Coke Company was bought in 1905 for almost $2 million. Two years later Frick was a member of subcommittees that considered further purchases of companies or tracts of land—the Hostetter-Connellsville Coke Company, the coking coal owned by the Thaw family between the Mammoth and Standard coke works, and the McLaughlin tract of fifty-five acres of coal lands near Leisenring. For the latter they paid $1,400 an acre. A few years later, during World War I, there was a good deal of selling of what were judged to be useless tracts of property held by H. C. Frick Coke in the coke region; at the same time the search went on for new coal or better arrangements. Only four weeks before his death, Frick was empowered by the finance committee to act with Gary in deciding on an exchange of undeveloped land between the H. C. Frick Coke Company and Thomas Thompson and S. E. Taylor. However, by then, despite this continuing interest in Connellsville, the emphasis in coke development had shifted elsewhere.[53]

To the west of the old Connellsville region there were higher volatile coals. This area became known variously as the Lower Connellsville, Masontown, or Klondike region. Development of it began in the mid 1890s, but as late as 1900 it contained only twelve coke works, whose ovens consumed only 3.9 percent as much coal as did those of Connellsville proper. Until that time, much of the investment made there had been by two Chicago-based groups, the American Steel and Wire and the Federal Steel companies. Soon after the formation of U.S. Steel there was more development, and later that decade, U.S. Steel was making railroad extensions in that area. By this time increasing interest was bringing with it rising development costs. Corey reported in spring 1909 that land offered by the Isabella Connellsville Coke Company, priced a year or so before at between $1,200 and $1,300 an acre, was now in the market for $500 more.[54] During the rest of Frick's life, Lower Connellsville continued as a major area of growth. By 1919 it contained seventy-one coke oven plants as compared with ninety-two in the traditional coke district; its ovens dealt with 82.9 percent as much coal.

Another area of interest lay far to the south in the Pocahontas coalfield of West Virginia, centered on the town of Bluefield. This district was as well placed as Connellsville to supply Chicago furnaces. At the end of 1901, Lynch wrote to Schwab explaining that although they needed more ovens he did

not think these should be in Connellsville. He suggested looking to the Pocahontas field. Gary believed they should buy at least fifty thousand acres
there. In the summer of 1902 the executive committee agreed to the building
of twelve hundred ovens in that district. In 1903 Frick, Corey, and Gary were
asked to look into the "Pocahontas Coke Question." Next year they had to
buy Pocahontas coke to make up a shortfall in supplies, and by 1905 it had
been resolved to spend $1 million to build more ovens, miners' housing, and
other facilities there.[55] At various times coal lands were offered to U.S. Steel
in other parts of West Virginia, including the counties lying southwest of the
coking coal districts of Pennsylvania—Preston, Barbour, Taylor, and Marian
Counties—and, later, in the panhandle district in Brook County.[56]

In spite of numerous piecemeal additions, the reliability of long-term
supplies of coke continued to worry the directors of U.S. Steel. In 1908, for
example, a Special Committee on Securing a Safe and Permanent Supply of
Coal in Pittsburgh and Chicago Districts was appointed, with Frick as a
member. Attention focused increasingly on the opening of higher volatile
coals and the related investment in by-product coking. The coals concerned
were largely in Greene County, west of the Monongahela. They could be
bought at much lower prices than those of Connellsville proper and were
even cheaper than those of Lower Connellsville. Because of their location,
their coke or coal could be carried by water to Pittsburgh. Early in 1902
before Frick became a member, the finance committee approved the purchase—for $348 an acre—of 247 acres of coal lands lying on the edge of the
Monongahela and near some coal land already owned by American Steel
and Wire. By the following year, Frick had looked into possibilities for river
coal shipments. Naturally even here, as demand increased, so too did the
price of mineral land. By 1911, the price asked for the Ross Farm coal on the
river in Greene County was $553 an acre.[57]

Yet Frick was sufficiently convinced of the prospects of the new area that
when he sold land for urban development in Pittsburgh he invested much
of the proceeds in more Greene County coal. Toward the end of World War
I, he was warmly advocating to Gary that they should buy sixty thousand
acres there offered to them by the Thompson interests—a compact body of
coal averaging 8 feet in thickness and said to be all the coking coal left
unsold in that county. He warned him not to be put off by suggestions that
it might be high in sulphur (which could be easily washed out) or that it all
should be drilled before purchase was decided: "It is all right I assure you
and I hope that you will promptly contract for it." The price asked was $500
an acre, or only 50 cents a ton, and they would save 40 cents by being
able to ship the produce of this area by barge to riverside works. This was

"something that cannot be duplicated in the world. . . . We are in such splendid position to make a purchase of this kind, and even if we had to go into debt I should favor it. . . . There is no body in the world equal to it both as to quality and location."[58] Naturally he was delighted when they decided to go ahead. The value of this coal was particularly related to the switch to by-product coking, a process that Frick had for so long and so firmly resisted.

By-product coking plants were more costly in capital terms than bee-hives, but they offered a number of operational advantages over the older method. They could use poorer coals, thus cutting transport costs on fuel to some iron-making districts. The yield of coke per ton of coal was higher, and the by-products provided additional income to counterbalance the higher outlay of capital. Before the war, sulphate of ammonia was not a particularly attractive product for the price was low. On the other hand, gas from the ovens was seen as a good fuel for open-hearth furnaces. From the start the committee recognized that the ideal location for by-product ovens was near the iron and steel plant, not in the coalfield. Location at the point of consumption of the coke also meant that its watering and abrasion in the course of long-distance transport could be avoided. For U.S. Steel with its wide scatter of plants, by-product coking was particularly attractive in loca-tions distant from the Connellsville coalfield. For a time it seemed possible that they might be able to coke coals from other northern fields, away from the Appalachian plateau, and in 1904 Frick was a member of a subcommittee looking into the question of purchasing Illinois coal lands. Eventually the committee recognized that these coals, though satisfactory as a general works fuel, were not suitable for coking, even in the new-style ovens. Their limited use was reflected in their low value: in 1909 when U.S. Steel bought almost four thousand acres of coal lands at Clinton, Illinois, the purchase price ranged between $50 and $55 an acre. Gradually by-product coking was seen as generally more advantageous. In 1907 the finance committee decided to spend $2.05 million to build 275 Koppers ovens at Joliet. Two years later, on the basis of experience gained there, they resolved to install by-product ovens at Gary.[59] At this time U.S. Steel lagged slightly behind the industry as a whole in turning to the new technology. In 1909, of U.S. Steel output of coke, 87.5 percent was still made in beehive ovens as compared with 82.3 percent for the rest of the industry. Six years later, the proportions were 66.9 percent for U.S. Steel and 65.8 percent for the others. Increasing shortages of good coking coals and the pressures of demand for more coke (and also for the chemicals required above all for explosives) ensured that during World War I by-product capacity was largely extended.

In 1914 Andrew Mellon acquired control of the patents of the Koppers by-product oven for $300,000 from Heinrich Koppers. Some accoutns suggest that he was advised in the matter by Frick, although no material evidence for this has come to light. If true, this would indicate that Frick had changed his opinion of the new process completely. Within a few years, the Koppers Company was to move its headquarters from Illinois to Pittsburgh and to greatly expand its capital and its business. A major new coking development in the Pittsburgh area at this time improved the value of the Greene County coal lands (in which Frick had invested on his own account and to which he had pointed U.S. Steel) and marked a decisive stage in the declining present and future status of Connellsville.

By autumn 1915, the depression in steel that had begun the year had already changed into a frenzy of activity. On 15 October, the finance committee recommended the installation of the first important by-product plant in the Pittsburgh area. This plant was to be of two hundred ovens, located on the banks of the Monongahela at Clairton. Five months later this plan was replaced by a much more ambitious one—a $12.4 million investment in 640 ovens and coal-carrying craft to supply them. A further $850,000 was to be spent on a pipeline system to carry coke oven gas to Duquesne, Homestead, and Edgar Thomson. By summer 1917, with inflation of prices and further elaboration of plans, the 640-oven installation was expected to cost as much as $25 million.[60] The average haul from H. C. Frick mines on the 4.1 million tons of coal needed annually would be 47 miles. The ovens were expected to produce 2.74 million tons of coke a year for the 24 blast furnaces at Duquesne, Homestead, Braddock, and Clairton works, a coke tonnage equal to 28 percent of all the beehive coke produced by U.S. Steel in 1915, the year in which the first decision to build the plant was taken. *Iron Age* anticipated that later the 640 ovens would be duplicated.[61] The first Clairton ovens were at work in 1918. For a time, the needs of a war-inflated industrial economy required the output of both old- and new-style ovens, but after the Armistice the beehive industry (and especially Connellsville) suffered severely from the contraction in trade. The 1919 output of coke in the United States was 21.8 percent down on the 1918 figure. For by-product coke the decline was only 3.3 percent, but Connellsville shipments were 28 percent less. That year for the first time the tonnage of by-product coke was greater than that from beehive ovens (see table 37).

Frick had been one of the champions, as he was over so many years the leader, of the beehive coke industry of Connellsville. His career spanned its growth, its peak, and the beginning of its decline into the role of reserve capacity. In 1870 there had been 7 coke oven plants in Connellsville district,

TABLE 37

Coal Coked in the Area of the Pittsburgh Bed,
1910–1929

Year	In Beehive Ovens	In By-Product Ovens
1910	33,762[a]	2,230
1915	32,597	2,049
1918	33,462	10,100
1919	21,559	11,808
1929	7,777	27,924

Source: Eavenson 1939.
Notes: Figures are in thousand tons. The districts involved
were in Western Pennsylvania, northern West Virginia, and
Ohio.
[a] Estimated

in 1910 the industry reached its high point with 118 plants, and by 1919 only
92 remained.[62] A man who would never allow sentiment to interfere with
good business principles, he had played his part in the change of emphasis,
recognizing the inevitability of mineral exhaustion and the advance of a
more appropriate technology. The result of that high-level decision was to
desolate the coke industry, and the society dependent upon it, in the area
whose earlier expanding activity had laid the foundations of his wealth.

9

From Industrial Manager

to Finance Capitalist

New Business Interests

At the turn of the century, Frick was at the height of his powers and still driven by the endless aspirations of the great businessman. He had no doubts of his ability to succeed in new fields and had many qualities that meant he was well equipped to do so. Conscious of the value of time, he wasted none of it in the course of business. In conversation he would go straight to the point, he gave orders clearly and briefly, and he evaluated propositions with striking facility. He was a keen analyst of men. An associate once said of him that he could bore his way through to the innermost soul of a man with one penetrating glance of his clear grey eyes, which looked straight into the visitor's face.[1] At the same time, according to the *Pittsburgh Times,* he was full of energy and of a civilized demeanor, an interesting combination of seemingly incompatible qualities:

> [A] short, chubby, fastidious and methodical man, but quick, determined and possessing a powerful constitution. He was polished and agreeable and had none of the roughness which the public associates with the men who suddenly made so many millions out of steel. He was quiet and silent, but aggressive and active in the extreme.

Noting his love of paintings, one visitor early in the new century recorded that on the wall of his inner business office there was a magnificent oil painting of tigers hunting their prey. In his last few months as chairman of Carnegie Steel he was described as cordial to most individuals,

> but rather constrained, confining his conversation to the business in hand. When necessary he can express himself with vigor and decision, but even then his voice does not rise above a modest monotone, his most vigorous condemna-

330

tion of men and measures taking the form of cutting sarcasm instead of expletive.

Yet he adjusted his manner according to circumstances. A. Lardy in the *Pittsburgh Post*—a rather unkind, but clearly informed, commentator— recalled:

> A martinet in dealings with men less powerful than himself, he was blandness itself when his business was to be aided thereby. He never used his voice, even in anger, but when he told some caller: "Well, is there anything else?" there was an undernote of finality in the smooth low voice which invariably terminated the interview.[2]

In 1900 there remained ample time for the exercise of these talents and qualities. When he left Carnegie Steel and soon afterward lost control of the company that bore his name, two-fifths of Frick's working life still lay ahead of him. He was fifty, the very age at which, a few years earlier, he had told Carnegie he would retire and enjoy himself. Now, although already a multimillionaire, he chose not to withdraw to enjoy the fruits of his labors or to distribute his wealth to causes he thought worthy, but rather to use his profits in coke and steel for further investment. An important part of this wealth went back into steel, but his interests now became far wider than before. He had been an outstanding industrial executive; now that stage was past and, in Harvey's words, he became a "capitalist of the first rank." This phase of life was to give him not only a new role, but a new operational space. Again Harvey summed it up well, his "interests were no longer confined to a manufacturing town but now lay in the financial center of the country."[3] In short, he became an important agent of the transition from industrial to finance capitalism, moving from the great manufacturing city to the centers of national and even international economic power.

Inevitably he had to move from Pittsburgh. For many years Carnegie had lived in New York and only visited Pittsburgh occasionally. By contrast, Frick not only remained deeply involved in the business life of the Pittsburgh area but for a time after leaving Carnegie Steel continued to reside there. He was then eulogized as "purely a Pittsburgher; his heart and soul are wrapped up in the welfare of his home city. He is the leading spirit of all progressive movements."[4] He was to retain his Pittsburgh suburban mansion of Clayton for the rest of his life, but after 1902 he used it only occasionally. Yet although his residential connection with Pittsburgh fell away, his investment interests there remained important and he continued to have a high regard for the city's prospects.

Pittsburgh was then at the dizzy peak of its eminence in American manufacturing and was, for many, the very epitome of the virtues (and for others of the defects) of industrial capitalism. In 1900 the value of manufactured products in Pittsburgh and Allegheny City alone (not to mention all the outlying mill towns) was greater than the combined total for Cleveland and Detroit. It was at this time in its history that the area was visited by the British social and economic writer Arthur Shadwell, who had much first-hand knowledge of industrial districts both in his home country and in continental Europe. Shadwell recognized that the area had some good houses, some suburbs free from smoke, fine shops and fairly good public buildings, and streets not lacking in dignity though much too narrow to carry the swarming traffic. He was repelled, however, not only by the general extreme smokiness and the rough and unfinished appearance of the city's outskirts but by what he sensed of the ethos of the place:

> It gathers up and concentrates the restless energy, the reckless hurry to make money and the contempt for everything else, of the newer industrial world. I suppose some of the English manufacturing towns passed through this stage once. Grime and squalor unspeakable, unlimited hours of work, ferocious contests between labor and capital, the fiercest commercial scrambling for the money literally sweated out of the people, the utter absorption by high and low of every faculty in getting and grabbing, total indifference to all other ideals and aspirations—these marked the rise of the great English industrial edifice, and they mark the center point of the much vaster American one today.

Presumably, if given the opportunity to respond to that indictment, some of the leading businessmen of Pittsburgh would have echoed the puzzled reaction of the representative "middle-class gentleman" with whom Engels had discussed the environment and social conditions as they walked into Manchester just sixty years earlier: "And yet there is a great deal of money made here. Good morning, Sir!"[5]

This was the environment in which Frick continued to operate and occupy a prominent place. Much of his new investment in Pittsburgh was in real estate, and the scale was such that by 1904 he was the largest owner of property in the city. Two projects illustrate different facets of the man. The first involved the construction of major office accommodation. In 1900 Saint Peter's Episcopal Church at the intersection of Grant and Diamond Streets was bought for redevelopment. A local newspaper noted, "For the sake of old times, it would be a nice thing to keep, but the spirit of progress and enterprise has dictated that it must go." Frick acquired the building and the ground for $180,000. Within two years, the Frick Building stood on the site, a dominant feature of the central business district, resplendent in its twenty stories of white granite. It was widely praised as a magnificent project. Many referred to its fine lobby and to La Farge's stained glass window of Fortune and her wheel—a strange image to be chosen or approved by a man who once said of achievement, "There is no secret about success; it simply calls for hard work, devotion to your business at all times, day and night." Few of those who praised the new block recognized how the city landscape now bore evidence of competition and assertion; the Frick Building rose well above the once magnificent fifteen-story Carnegie Building, built some eight years earlier and regarded as the city's first skyscraper. Looking back later, one writer took a sour view of the rivalry perpetuated by these two neighboring office blocks:

> The personal relations between Carnegie and Frick took on a somewhat puerile phase, but not without the expenditure of millions. To build a 14 [*sic*] storey building and then to have your former chum build a 22 [*sic*] storey building to shut out its light is not much different from the temper displayed when one boy, building a sand mound, finds that his former chum is undermining it to build another beside it.[6]

This is a simplistic comment, but it does contain some truth. In January 1902, two months before the first tenants moved into the Frick Building, the announcement came that Frick would also build a hotel to surpass any in the nation. It was to be at Sixth Avenue and Grant Street and was expected to cost $5 million. The thirteen-story building was to have exterior walls of either marble or granite, and decorations and furnishings of high quality. As the architects D. Burnham and Company of Chicago were reported to have said, this new William Penn Hotel would be exceptional: "they have seen every hotel of note in the world, and the Frick venture will excel all." Construction was delayed for many years, however, and by the time the hotel was opened in spring 1916, it had cost $6 million. Frick had sold the site in March 1914 and used the proceeds to invest heavily in Greene County coal lands.[7]

He was also involved in financial ventures in the region. In 1899 he joined Andrew Mellon in founding the Union Trust Company. Three years later the banking business of T. Mellon and Sons, which thirty years before had helped him with loans in the vital early stages of his investment in coke, was incorporated as the Mellon National Bank, and Frick became a director. For many years after this, he retained his belief in the economic potentials of his home region, and according to his daughter, his advice to young men just starting on a business career and eager to make their fortunes was often "Go to Pittsburgh." Already some individuals were thinking about the improvement of this great but polluted industrial district. In 1906 the president of the Pittsburgh Chamber of Commerce wrote to seek Frick's support in getting through the councils of the city an ordinance providing for the prevention of as much smoke as possible.[8] It is not known how Frick responded. The city's first Bureau of Smoke Control was instituted that year, but effective local legislation was delayed another thirty-five years.

In spite of his continuing and important Pittsburgh investments, Frick's main interests now lay elsewhere, and they were various in nature. In summer 1901 he accepted an invitation to join a large number of other prominent businessmen on the board of the huge Equitable Life Assurance Society. Before spring 1905 he was also a director of the National City Bank of New York, the Equitable Trust Company of New York, the Mercantile Trust Company, the Franklin National Bank of Philadelphia, and the Commercial Trust Company of Philadelphia. He added directorships of the Union Insurance Company and the National Union Fire Insurance Company and became secretary and treasurer of the Diamond Light and Power Company. By this time serious problems were developing in the first of these concerns. The life insurance business in general was going through a difficult period, sometimes involving growth without regard for the security of either policyholders or the companies themselves. Large amounts of money were accumulated and not properly accounted for. By spring 1905 it was clear that the top direction of Equitable Life (a company established for over forty-five years) was now unsound. A committee of "outside" directors was formed to investigate the situation. Frick chaired this committee, among whose other members was Edward H. Harriman. They found that, from the president downward, "extravagant, loose and irregular methods" had become general. The president and vice-president had by now secured the support of other directors, however, and they rejected the committee report. Frick resigned his seat on the board.[9]

More important, and longer lasting, was his involvement in railroads. By April 1905 he was on the board of the major anthracite region system, the Reading Railroad. He also became a director of a number of the major western lines, the Chicago and Northwestern, the Union Pacific, and the Atchison, Topeka, and Santa Fe. He played some part in the efforts made by Harriman around 1905 to secure cooperative agreements between the Union Pacific and the Santa Fe, which involved Union Pacific investment and directors in the other system. Soon afterward, he added directorships of two more eastern companies, the Baltimore and Ohio and the Norfolk and Western. In December 1906 he replaced the recently deceased Amos R. Little as a director of the Pennsylvania, of which he already owned 168,000 shares.[10]

In each of these railroads he at one time invested at least $6 million, and when the Interstate Commerce Commission published the names of the largest investors in railway stock in 1906 his name headed the list of individual owners. After 1911 he reduced his commitments, retaining directorships only in the Reading, the Santa Fe, the Chicago and Northwestern, and the Pennsylvania. Circumstances were changed by the Clayton Act of 1914, which aimed to strengthen anti-trust provisions by preventing collusion between railroads and manufacturing concerns and which outlawed interlocking directorates. Railway companies were prohibited from having dealings in excess of $50,000 with concerns with which they shared directors, officers, or agents. Frick was unhappy with the new legislation and was anxious to defend the status quo. He wrote with some heat to the board of the Pennsylvania Railroad:

> Important considerations arise in connection with the policy of yielding without a struggle to the Attorney General's demand that the Pennsylvania Railroad should divest itself of its Norfolk and Western stock which should have careful thought. It is a complete, radical and dangerous power that the Attorney General is now exercising in relation to the business of the country.[11]

In spite of his opposition to the new law, in October 1915 he resigned his directorships of the Reading Railroad and of the Philadelphia and Reading Coal and Iron Company.

During his business career he acquired interests in non-ferrous metals. As early as the mid 1880s, on his behalf surveys were made of copper, silver, and iron in Colorado and other parts of the West, but he declined at that time to become deeply involved. In the twentieth century his interests extended even more widely, and he became financially interested in copper mining in Peru through the exploration and then the long-drawn-out development work of the Cerro de Pasco Mining Company. To some extent he linked this with his other interests. For instance, in 1910 he put this mining company in contact with James Farrell at U.S. Steel in the hope that they could do business with each other. Two years later he again referred to this business connection when he asked Farrell to ensure that a special effort be made to get plates delivered to W. B. Pollock of Youngstown, a firm engaged in supplying Cerro de Pasco: "I would greatly appreciate anything you will do in the matter."[12] He retained his Peruvian connection at least into World War I.

Apart from business, he now had more time for other interests, and one of these was politics. Throughout his adult life he was connected with the Republican party. Even his business letters to Carnegie now and then contained news or speculation about elections or electoral prospects. And there was more direct involvement as well. According to Harvey, in 1880 he might have been diverted from a business career when he was invited to accept a Republican nomination for Congress. After brief consideration he decided it was not the right course for him. His closest political associate was Philander C. Knox, for long the Carnegie Steel lawyer. In 1896 Frick approached the newly elected president, William McKinley, with the suggestion that he should appoint Knox as Attorney General. Four years later Knox was offered and accepted this post. In 1904 Knox unsuccessfully asked Frick to replace Matthew S. Quay as senator for Pennsylvania. More than once, Frick was invited to take high federal office. In 1899 Congress set up an Isthmian Canal commission to examine the best prospects for a Central American canal. Four years later Roosevelt offered Frick the chairmanship of this commission. Twice between 1899 and 1907, Frick is also said to have declined offers of the secretaryship of the U.S. Treasury, the post that Andrew Mellon was to occupy with distinction between 1921 and 1932.[13]

Frick's relationship with Theodore Roosevelt followed an uneven course. Initially their dealings were cordial enough. On Independence Day in 1902, the president visited Pittsburgh and addressed a crowd of around a hundred thousand on Flagstaff Hill. He lunched that day at Clayton. It was a grand occasion that had taken weeks of preparation. The house was decorated with bunting, roses, and orchids. Twenty-one guests (all male) sat down to a magnificent eight-course meal. On occasion also, the Fricks were guests at the White House. Frick paid $20,000 for Chartran's painting of the signing of the peace protocol between the United States and Spain, which he presented to the president. In his early years, Roosevelt did not interfere much with big business, and Frick gave $50,000 for his 1904 campaign fund and followed up the election result with an enthusiastic telegram: "The endorsement of yourself and your policies by your fellow citizens is magnificent and truly well deserved. Cordial congratulations. H. C. Frick."[14]

The later activities of Roosevelt sometimes exasperated Frick. Tarbell reported that, at one U.S. Steel meeting, he who "as usual" was speaking out against the president cried out "what man has he ever helped?" Even so, there were still occasional friendly contacts, including the mutual use of their relationship to help others. In 1905, for instance, when Elihu Root followed John Hay as secretary of state, Roosevelt contacted Frick in his search for new employment for ex–Assistant Secretary of State Loomis. (Frick could suggest no immediate prospects, however.) A few months later Frick in turn was trying to secure a post on the Interstate Commerce Commission for Woods of Pennsylvania, only to be told by Roosevelt that it would be very hard to justify another member from the Northeast. He had earlier mentioned that "If the Bill passes I shall gladly take Mr. Woods' name into careful consideration—as I need hardly say would be the case with any recommendation of yours." Late in 1907, and only a few weeks after the Tennessee Coal, Iron, and Railroad Company takeover by U.S. Steel, the president wrote, "I should always be glad to see you and Judge Gary on any matter."[15]

Later Roosevelt became more radical. His message to Congress in April 1908 denounced those who preached hatred of honestly acquired wealth, but he was also outspoken against some aspects of big business:

> [A]mong the many kinds of evil, social, industrial and political, which it is our duty as a nation sternly to combat, there is none at the same time more base and more dangerous than the greed which treats the plain and simple rules of honesty with cynical contempt if they interfere with making a profit; and, as a nation we cannot be held guiltless if we condone such action.

A few weeks later he held a three-day conference of governors to consider the waste of resources and the destruction of the national environment. In the address with which he opened the meeting, he deplored the rapid destruction of the nation's natural resources. The first presentation that afternoon concerned "The Conservation of Ores and Related Minerals." Its author was Andrew Carnegie. He took the opportunity to deplore waste in the mining and the using of coal, pointing out that much coke making was still "extravagant."[16] To a man such as Frick who had until this time conscientiously turned his back on by-product coking, the theme and some at least of the participants in this conference must have seemed objectionable.

Roosevelt's "Progressive" phase for a time broke the power of the long-established Republican party boss of Pennsylvania, Boies Penrose. Penrose was on the Republican National Committee from 1904 until his death seventeen years later, except for the years 1914 to 1916. As Bridge put it, although Penrose controlled the state's Republican machine, he "was himself controlled by Henry Clay Frick." Early in 1914 Penrose's loss of power brought about a rare exchange of letters between Frick and Schwab. Schwab had helped Penrose's cause financially in exchange for support for duty-free entry of foreign iron ore. Frick wrote in reply to him, "My Dear Schwab, Replying to your note. Always glad to see you, but I am afraid I can do nothing for Penrose. I had the matter up, but owing to the suit [the U.S. Government's Dissolution Suit against U.S. Steel] and other things, I know nothing can be done at this time."[17]

Apart from the calls of new business interests and the distractions of politics, there was much else to preoccupy Frick. One of his joys was in fine houses. In this field, although his scale of operation reflected his great wealth, his taste was decidedly conservative as compared with that of some of his business colleagues. For many of them rank ostentation was the outstanding quality informing their designs. Schwab, Peacock, Clemson, Morrison, Lawrence Phipps, and other Carnegie Steel partners had built great mansions in the more salubrious districts of Pittsburgh. Some of them (notably the homes of Schwab and Clemson) owed a good deal to Clayton as a model, as can be appreciated from Schwab's Braddock home, which still survives, a century after it was erected.[18] Those who went on from Pittsburgh to wider spheres of business took their passion for building with them. Schwab, moving to U.S. Steel's New York office, put up a massive, hybrid French château in Manhattan.

Frick too was moving into national rather than regional spheres of business and, although he retained Clayton, he recognized the need for a home in New York. In 1902 he rented a family apartment at Sherry's Hotel. Initially, the *Pittsburgh Dispatch* reported, he did this to make it easier for Helen to complete her education. Then, for nine years from 1905, he leased the Vanderbilt mansion on Fifth Avenue, a house he had coveted since his first visit to New York in the company of Andrew Mellon, a quarter century before. Eventually he purchased the beautiful Lennox Library at Fifth Avenue and Seventieth Street. He offered to pay for its removal and re-erection at any place in New York City but then had it demolished. In its place a large neoclassical mansion in white limestone was designed for him by the architects of the New York Public Library, Carrere and Hastings. He moved into his new home in 1914. In spite of a grandeur that sometimes earned it the name of a "palace," it was in a more solid, conventional idiom than the homes of many other princes of industry and commerce. Yet even so, as with the Frick Building, it was alleged that his determination was to outdo his former partner. Carnegie's house on Ninety-first Street had cost over a million dollars; Frick spent $5.4 million, partly in order (he is alleged to have told friends) to "make Carnegie's place look like a miner's shack."[19] In 1906 the Fricks built another home, at Prides Crossing in the fashionable resort area of the "North Shore," some eighteen miles northeast of Boston. This "summer" house, named Eagle Rock, was itself palatial, having 104 rooms.

Into his various homes Frick poured still more of his wealth, in fine furniture and furnishings, sculpture, paintings, and music. When Eagle Rock was built, he paid $20,000 to the Aeolian Company for a pipe organ, and a little later another $1,000 for an extra console. This was dwarfed by the organ that was installed in his Fifth Avenue home, which was said to have cost $100,000. The noted organist Archer Gibson was hired by the hour. For years he played before, during, and after lunch and dinner, the great sounds reverberating up and down the fine stairway and out through the main picture gallery. Often there might be two hundred guests or more in the house, and as they gathered, chattered, and dined (one of the visitors thought) Gibson's playing "served to emphasize the owner's happiness in his own hospitality." Yet as Frick built up his grand houses, the popular press remained always ready to mock his taste or manners. Anna Robeson Burr thought it both anomalous and an opportunity for amusement to report that he had once been seen "in his palace, seated on a Renaissance throne, under a baldacchino, and holding in his little hand a copy of the *Saturday Evening Post.*"[20]

In plays and in music Frick's taste seems to have been conservative rather than adventurous. He had a box at one of the New York theaters and would often attend—apparently more often with Helen than with Adelaide, and taking care to keep out of the limelight. He was generous in providing his friends with similar facilities. In December 1913 James Farrell's wife, Catherine, wrote to him from their home in Brooklyn, "I wish to thank you for the delightful evening we spent at the opera. It was indeed most kind and thoughtful of you to give us the use of your box."[21]

Of Frick's reading habits there is little enough to go on. Carnegie once made a scathing general indictment of his fellow businessmen, claiming that most of them were incapable of coping with anything other than an account book. Certainly use, misuse, or failure to employ led here as elsewhere to the shaping of the faculties still available in later life. An instance of this was that, in his maturity, Frick had little interest in current fiction. On the other hand, he enjoyed biography and books on self-improvement. In the latter category he was apparently especially interested in the views of William George Jordan, a contemporary author who covered an impressively wide field. He read religious literature of a rather special type, apparently circulating copies of Jefferson's writings to friends. Thus in spring 1905 he wrote a note to the banker Alvin W. Krech: "I neglected to bring with me, from your house, the production 'Immortality' by Jefferson, that I handed Mrs. Krech to read. Will you kindly have it mailed to me?" A few months later he thanked Philander Knox for copies of Jefferson's *The Life and Morals of Jesus of Nazareth.*[22]

His leisure pursuits extended also into sport. In Pittsburgh he had walked part of the way to and from work, but when he moved to New York he lost this exercise, so instead, recognizing the possibilities of his new place of residence, he planned to take up yachting. He even went so far as to have a boat designed, only to decide eventually that such a recreation would be too confining. He found moving at high speed a terrific excitement, a thrill that in later years he found in motoring. Even so his chief outdoor pleasure came from an activity with a very different pace. Although he originally frowned on the sport as being too slow, he became a keen golfer, managing to carry over into his play something of his business impatience. When he played at Myopia, not far from Prides Crossing, it was customary for everyone to step aside when a caddy shouted, "Look out, Mr. Frick is coming through!" In 1910, staying in Butt Cottage in Augusta, Georgia, he played about thirty holes a day. But in spite of this pace and dedication, when writing to a friend in August 1915, he could manage a lighthearted response to what, in his judgment, was his lack of ability in the game: "I am having quite a pleasant summer—feeling first class; a game of golf daily, hoping that I am going to do better the next. It is remarkable that I never become discouraged, although I think my game this year is worse than it has ever been."[23] Golf remained one of his chief sources of enjoyment to the last few weeks of his life.

An indoor relaxation to which he was almost as much addicted was cards. He played with a few friends, including George Westinghouse, Andrew Mellon, and Philander C. Knox, who made up an interesting group. Westinghouse was two years Frick's senior, an industrialist more concerned with technical innovation than business practice and who lacked the essential patience for steady success. In 1907 his firm went into receivership and (although he later regained control) remained unprofitable. Knox was three years Frick's junior and came from the Upper Monongahela Valley. As secretary of state under Taft he pursued an interesting mix of conservative and progressive policies. The youngest member and the closest to Frick was Mellon. Each had been the means of securing the introduction of the other to his future wife (a step that in Mellon's case had not led to long-term happiness). They had shared interests in art since at least the early 1880s. Above all they had in common many traits of character and manner, although measured by the standards of the other man, Frick was relatively mellow, warm, and relaxed. Mellon had chill gray-blue eyes. His lips were usually kept tightly closed, he rarely smiled, and when he spoke he was so hesitant as to seem almost inarticulate. Shaking hands, he presented only the tips of his fingers. One reporter summed up the impression he made as being "like a tired double-entry bookkeeper who is afraid of losing his job."[24] They must have been a fascinating group as they relaxed in each other's company: the solidly built, walrus mustached Westinghouse; the full-faced, clean-shaven, cigar-smoking Knox; the pale, frail-looking Mellon, nervously smoking small black-paper cigarettes to the very limit of their length; and the fastidiously dressed Frick with his finely trimmed, greying beard. They were all prominent Western Pennsylvanians, and the record of their conversations would have provided invaluable insights into the industrial history of the nation.

Another recreation was travel. There is no full record of the journeys made by Frick and his family, but they were clearly frequent and widespread. At home there were holidays or periods of extended residence in the warmer regions. Before they came to live in the Vanderbilt mansion in New York, they had a long stay in The Breakers, Palm Beach, a town that was then still a reasonably fashionable resort for the wealthy, with a population of only a few hundred. Frick visited Europe often before 1914. Early in 1912, he made a rather more interesting holiday trip, to Egypt. This was the occasion for a letter from James Gayley, who wrote to tell him that Theodore N. Davis—once a part owner of the Norrie mine on the Gogebic iron range, bought by Carnegie Steel in 1897—now spent his winters in Egypt "excavating among the Kings' tombs." Gayley thought he was at Luxor, and as he was a man of "very charming personality, . . . this might be the means of adding considerably to your pleasure and interest in your trip to the Nile, as Mr. Davis is always glad to meet interesting Americans." No further record of this Nile holiday has come to light. When Frick traveled he did so in some style, as befitted his rank in society. For instance, in 1899 he inquired of the Paris office of Nordeutsche Lloyd the rate for the captain's room and suite for his party of four adults, two children, and one servant. (The cost for an Atlantic crossing was $2,600.)[25]

In this period Frick was able to enjoy his growing collection of fine paintings and had more time and wealth to augment it. Between his first purchase in 1881 and the time he left Carnegie Steel, there had been many years when he made no purchases at all. This was especially so in the late 1880s, when he was preoccupied with management in coke, and in the early 1890s, during the most active part of his chairmanship of Carnegie Brothers and of Carnegie Steel. According to Harvey, he bought sixty-seven paintings altogether during those years, but there were in fact many more. Over the next twenty years he made purchases each year. It has been suggested by Holbrook that he never "really cared for art except as an expensive hobby." This is an unfair criticism: in the process of collecting, Frick became ever more expert in what he bought, and as Schwab once admiringly put it, when Frick had finished, "he knew art."[26]

He made some mistakes but on the whole bought through reputable dealers. Roland Knoedler of New York was prominent, although Joseph Duveen also was involved after 1910. The range of his interests was wide, although he did not favor nudes of either sex. (But see the comments by Hellerstedt on *Une Révélation,* the second painting he bought.) Nor did he buy paintings of life in the lower orders of society—with the notable exception of Goya's *The Forge,* acquired in 1916, whose subject matter was sufficiently remote in time to lack close linkage with contemporary industrial conditions.[27] For some of the art he paid high prices, notably the Fragonard panels, the *Romance of Love and Youth,* that he bought from the J. P. Morgan collection for $1.25 million in 1915. He was also subjected to a good deal of sales propaganda from the dealers. An interesting example, which highlighted the connection between the state of business and the art market, came in a letter from Frau Hermann Linde in February 1906. Linde tried to build on both his goodwill and his feelings of affluence:

> Your sweet smile the other morning when I met you on 5th Ave., denoted to me that you were very happy, and a few days later, I did read in the papers that you had great cause to feel satisfied. I congratulate you upon your great achievements, having made 7 million dollars in one year on Reading etc. This would be the right time, indeed, to start in now on some great old masters. I mean really great. I will put myself entirely at your disposal and will honestly and satisfactorily work in your best interests. I could never understand why you would not buy from me any of the great Rubens paintings. *If any scoundrel at any time ever* intimated to you, *or wrote* to you, *or expressed to you verbally, that these great works are not, as what they are described in the Rubens* literature and by the greatest authorities on Rubens,—then you should kindly tell me, that I can defend myself. They are absolutely guaranteed. I will exhibit them at the Rubens headquarters in *Antwerp* at the Royal Museum, if you so desire. I should like very much to have an interview with you, and I should like to see what you have acquired since I saw your collection in Pittsburgh.

There is no record of Frick's reply to this torrent of enthusiasm, but according to Harvey's list he did not acquire his first Rubens until 1910, and only ever bought two. For many years before the benefactions in the cause of art provided in his will, he had been generous in his more general support. In 1905 for instance he gave $100,000 to the American Academy of Arts in Rome. He helped talented young artists of slender means, in some instances financing the completion of their studies in Europe.[28]

Thus, like his peers, Frick filled his life with interesting pursuits and beautiful things. It is a good idea to set their acquisitions, buildings, and journeyings within the context of the conditions of life of that great underclass from whose labors their wealth was largely derived. The industrial areas in which Frick's wealth had been accumulated were still dark and, for most of their inhabitants, provided poor rewards for long and often harsh exertions. In Pittsburgh the water supply was of low quality, and the strains of life were so great that Allegheny City, in which Frick had lived when he first moved from the coke region, was often referred to as Suicide City. The mill towns out along the Monongahela River were still—and were long to remain—horrors of company domination, of exploitation and unrest. U.S. Steel's new company town of Gary had been announced as a "magic city" with a residential district "providing for all the necessities, comforts, educational and spiritual advancement and amusement of its inhabitants." There was claimed to be "a marked absence of the hovels, dirt and squalor, so pronounced a feature of most manufacturing cities." Instead, municipal cleanliness was to be a leading virtue in what was to be "a city of homes, each on its own lot and surrounded by its own lawn." Yet even there, in a new setting, the reality speedily turned out different. As a Croatian physician in Chicago put it to the visiting academic A. E. Zimmern in 1912, "Go to Gary by all means, if you would see the Sodom and Gomorrah of my race." Compared with the huge sums expended by the successful, often for luxuries, the mass of Americans even now lived in near penury. As late as 1910, a prosperous year in which pay had risen a good deal from the levels of the 1890s, the average annual wage in the American steel industry was only $697.[29]

In this period of his life Frick showed that he was not unaware of the needs of the poor and disadvantaged. He practiced an unostentatious giving to good causes. For instance, in autumn 1906 the prominent medical pioneer Lawrence Litchfield wrote to him about the International Congress on Tuberculosis to be held in Washington in 1908. He painted a vivid picture of the scourge caused by this disease of poverty and deprivation:

> Tuberculosis costs the United States about 200,000 lives a year and helps to fill orphan asylums, houses of correction, insane asylums and prisons by the wrecks which it leaves in its path. It costs the world over 3 million lives a year, and is a drag on civilization and prosperity beyond the grasp of the human mind.

Three months later Litchfield wrote to thank Frick for a donation of $5,000. Given Frick's personality, it is perhaps not surprising that even in his charitable giving he was very precise or even over-organized. An example was the letter he wrote in February 1908 to his old colleague, Thomas Lynch, at the H. C. Frick Coke Company, in the Carnegie Building in Pittsburgh: "Gentlemen, Will you please ship a carload of coke to Sisters of Mercy, Lowellville, Mahoning County, Ohio, via Pittsburgh and Lake Erie Railroad, sending bill to me? Send about same quantity as in similar shipments here-tofore."[30]

Although he retained his sharp response to criticism, he now showed signs of mellowing. He even showed some interest in his public image. In 1906 he let J. H. Bridge know that he would take twenty copies of his *Inside History of the Carnegie Steel Company,* a book that presented him in a favorable light. He was annoyed by the way he was represented in the *Pittsburgh Leader,* whose cartoons at one time always portrayed him with a large dollar sign on his back. His reaction was to send his secretary to try and buy the paper, but soon after he recognized that he had acted impulsively. Some years later, however, he sent a sharp telegram to A. P. Moore, the editor of the same newspaper: "In view of the slanderous editorial in your paper about 2 weeks ago based on an untrue report of a gift to my son [Childs] on his marriage, it seems to me you rather presume to ask a favor of me. What do you think?" Now and again there was now even a glimmer of humor, although (as Harvey acknowledged) it was usually of the sort to be appreciated with a "slow, understanding smile" rather than a laugh. When he learned that Millard Hunsiker had been given a military rank, he immediately began to address him as "Colonel." He graciously showed his appreciation of gifts. In summer 1907 he wrote to Hunsiker in London, "The Scotch has arrived. I have not sampled it yet, but expect to do so in the near future. It is very kind of you to remember me so handsomely. I had it shipped direct to Prides Crossing where we are now located."[31]

As he aged and moved into wider spheres of business and as he extended his leisure activities, Frick was changing both in appearance and in personality. In his fifties he had become a robust broad-shouldered man whose fine features, grey and gradually whitening beard, and tasteful suiting gave him an air of impressive distinction. He spoke quietly, but his eyes could turn quickly from a pleasant twinkle to a steely gaze. He smiled easily and his smile, according to Bridge, "invested his handsome features with a charm that invited the confidences he was so reluctant to return." According to an admiring Harvey, even as he lay back thinking in his office chair, "he personified power—under restraint," and when he moved he was extraordinarily nimble. He expected from his colleagues a like commitment to his own. Of his Carnegie Steel partners he once remarked, "When they saw what their Chairman was doing they all followed suit gladly and enthusiastically. So we all got on very well."[32]

In spite of the maturing of his character, he was still liable to strong personal animosities, however. He believed that Theodore Roosevelt was guilty of some breach of faith after the purchase of the Tennessee Coal, Iron, and Railroad Company and, as a result, cherished an ill will toward him throughout the rest of his life. With his former Carnegie Steel colleagues his relations were varied. He was still in regular contact with those who, like him, moved over to U.S. Steel. Now and then he corresponded with and exchanged hospitality with Schwab (although the latter for some reason tried to give the impression they were not in contact). Henry Phipps had been his close ally, but although from 1901 he too lived along Fifth Avenue where it fringed Central Park, there is no record in Frick's correspondence of any further contact with him. In 1915 the seventy-five-year-old Phipps fell ill and made no more appearances in public, although he survived for another fifteen years. Throughout the years Frick implacably opposed any attempt to bring about a reconciliation with Andrew Carnegie. On at least one occasion it seems that Carnegie specifically sought a friendly meeting only to have his overtures refused intemperately.[33]

There is other evidence of this inflexibility. In 1911 and 1912 the U.S. government attempted to prove that U.S. Steel was a restrictive trust and therefore should be broken up. Carnegie took the stand in January 1912. (Frick never gave evidence.) It was during this time that Bridge once again met the man for whom he had acted as secretary a quarter century before. After this, Bridge called on Carnegie many times in his New York home, and in their conversations found that Carnegie still regretted his estrangement from his senior partner. As a former associate of both men, Bridge determined to attempt a reconciliation. In February 1912, he sent a letter to the banker J. Horace Harding who was then in Egypt with Frick. He expressed his wish to bring together two men who, although "the most prominent in American industry[,] . . . are now linked only in antagonistic memory." On their return, Harding arranged for Bridge to meet him and Frick in Frick's office. It was to no avail. Bridge was "surprised at Frick's outburst of angry denunciation of the man with whom he shared so much of success and fortune. I had never suspected such indignation in this usually quiet and undemonstrative man."[34]

Frick was more than merely passive in his bitterness toward Carnegie. In summer 1912 he drafted a challenge to him to retract statements made in evidence to the Stanley Committee, which implied that in 1899 Frick had played a dishonorable part in the negotiations for the reconstruction of their company. Frick's draft (which may never have been sent) pulled no punches:

Although made by you under oath, these statements are false both in fact and in all their implied charges of untruth, dishonesty and double-dealing; and the purpose of this communication is to demand a full and complete withdrawal of the charges in such manner as will assure a wide publicity to such withdrawal.

The letter went on in a provocative manner to refer to the "great many inaccuracies" in the Carnegie evidence:

[M]isstatements of facts, dates, places, persons; which suggests that some of the injurious charges made against Messrs. Frick and Phipps may be due to failing memory. For this reason no insistence is laid on the legal aspects of your action, which Mr. Frick is willing, for the present, to regard as an involuntary lapse of memory rather than as a wilful act of perjury.

The letter then turned to the evidence given concerning the disagreements that led to the forfeiture of Frick's and Phipps's $170,000 of the option money:

These statements, which are false in every particular, were disseminated broadcast throughout the country, and further were incorporated into the proceedings of the Stanley Committee. The result is there is now in the public archives a permanent record of charges against Messrs. Frick and Phipps of untruthfulness, chicanery, dishonesty, infidelity to associates, avarice and double-dealing; and these perjured records are backed by the name of a man whose public gifts may hereafter erroneously be supposed to represent his private virtues. This is an intolerable condition and must be relieved.

After he had made the first draft of this letter, it seems Frick consulted Lovejoy, who replied that he had reworded it to introduce a "little milder tone . . . as showing righteous anger but no irritation." As so often, the opposing camps were setting the record as they would like posterity to see it. Thus in spring 1913, Peacock wrote to Carnegie about Lovejoy: "He seems to have gone all to pieces, physically and mentally."[35]

Frick paid a high price in psychological health for his continuing animosity to Carnegie. E. R. Graham—who had been assistant director of works at the Chicago Exposition and later a partner of the architects D. H. Burnham and Company, designers of the Frick Building—knew both Carnegie and Frick well. He told the editor of the *Wall Street Journal* Clarence W. Barron, "Frick poisoned himself with hatred for Carnegie. He hated Schwab because he was with Carnegie."[36] That there is truth in the first of these statements seems incontrovertible; independent evidence in relation to the second suggests that the case was being made too simplistically. Here was myth in the making.

World War I

Most of the partners of the old Carnegie Steel Company had severed their links with the U.S. Steel Corporation by 1914. Schwab had long ago committed himself to the reconstruction and revival of Bethlehem Steel. Corey was also looking to the brighter prospects of hitherto ailing eastern operations. James Gayley and Thomas Morrison had resigned some years before. In February 1914, Henry Phipps retired from the board in his seventy-fifth year. By contrast Frick remained fully involved, showing remarkable regularity in his attendance at the meetings of the board of directors and the finance committee, and frequently serving on special committees. His opinions were highly respected. Though now sixty-four, he was still a businessman of formidable powers.

The steel industry was entering a challenging phase in its development. Nationally the industry had attained record outputs in 1913. In that year, U.S. Steel alone produced over 38 percent more steel than all the works in the country had done in 1901. The following year brought a sharp contraction to levels (for both pig iron and steel) that were lower than at any time since the depression year of 1908. Not a single new blast furnace was blown in, and by the end of the year, 287 of the 451 existing furnaces were idle. During that summer, however, external events already heralded a complete transformation of trade prospects. The assassination of Archduke Franz Ferdinand in a little Bosnian provincial town on Sunday, 28 June 1914, marked the start of a five-week period during which the European nations drifted into war. As these tragic moves were made, Andrew Carnegie was staying in his summer cottage on the Highland moors at Aultnagar, finishing his autobiography. The events unfolding as he wrote brought an abrupt end to his memoirs. He could no longer find comfort, let alone meaning, in the adage that for him summed up the worldview of Herbert Spencer and that for so long he had made his own motto: "All is well since all grows better." Although he tried many times to resume writing, according to Louise Carnegie his life had been blighted by "the failure of his hopes . . . his heart was broken." He had expounded his vision and had worked to achieve an end of militarism. Now he managed just one more paragraph in which he recognized the failure of those hopes: "As I read this today [1914], what a change! The world convulsed by war as never before! Men slaying each other like wild beasts!" The only hope he had now lay in the idealism of Woodrow Wilson.[37]

Others saw the same events but traced different implications in the confusion and bloodshed of the time. For them, war between the great powers of Europe could have benefits, causing a business revival. In the longer term it promised unquestioned American leadership in the world economy. Under a leader headed "War Madness," the *Evening Post* pointed out that a general war would have a disastrous effect on Europe's commercial, financial, and industrial supremacy in the world. The *New York Sun,* repeating that diagnosis, drew the obvious conclusions, hoping that the United States would be equal to the opportunity. Not only would America be freed from its debtor status, but its horizons would be immeasurably widened:

> Anything resembling a general European war would seem likely to guarantee that the economic future will belong to the American continents, especially North America. The paralysis of European finance and commerce during any such upheaval and their subsequent prostration will leave the way clear for nations whose energies have not been debilitated.[38]

Henry Clay Frick had been in Europe in spring 1914, apparently on his last transatlantic vacation. The exact dates of this visit are not known, but the period of his absence may be marked roughly, because after attending the finance committee on 14 April he was not present again until 3 June. On Tuesday, 28 July, the day of the Austrian declaration of war on Serbia, he attended the finance committee in the corporation's New York offices. By the beginning of the following week, he was at Prides Crossing, laid low by an old complaint. On Monday, 3 August, as the chancelleries of Europe sent out their last desperate peacetime messages, and as droves of young men left factory towns and farms all over the continent to join their regiments, some of them torn reluctantly from their families, others fired by a wild enthusiasm, Frick was lying at home (as he wrote to J. P. Grier), "helpless as a baby, having to be carried to and from the bathroom—muscular rheumatism of the very worst kind. It has been coming on for some time." His bodily infirmity did not affect the clarity of his mind, but the course his thoughts followed was quite different from that of Carnegie's. He wanted to make sure that he was informed of the march of events: "The situation certainly looks serious. I would be greatly obliged if from time to time you get anything new or important you would call me." On Thursday, he wrote to the banker Henry C. McEldowney of the Union Trust Company, of which he was a director, expressing his regrets that McEldowney's vacation had been interfered with by the crisis, but "nothing greater could have happened than a general war in Europe." He made the same point that day to James Farrell and went on to consider the matter-of-fact consequences: "Are your foreign shipments interfered with? It looks to me as if you had commenced to put prices up at about the right time in view of what has happened. . . . I would like to have your views on the situation generally." With McEldowney he had allowed himself to look ahead as well as at the immediate situation: "Of course in the end we will be the gainers, meantime it is difficult to say just how things will shape themselves. If we only had a good merchant marine, what a difference it would make to us." By Saturday, he reported that he had learned from the Cerro de Pasco Mining Company that the war had brought on a financial panic in Peru, where all banks had been closed for a week. He wrote with unusual familiarity next week to "My Dear Lote" (Sylvanus L. Schoonmaker, the former Carnegie Steel agent): "Well it is too bad we are to have a war, but it seems it had to come sometime, and it is just as well it should be over."[39] In hindsight the words "too bad" may seem a modest enough assessment of what was beginning in Europe; but to a nation still at peace, enjoying the usual distractions of the dog days of summer, the baseball series and family holidays, his reaction was unexceptional. No-one could have realized that a major epoch of world civilization was coming to an end.

By late August Frick had been on his back, "perfectly helpless," for almost a month. Over the next four weeks or so he improved, although into October he was still moving with difficulty. Long before, his interest in the impact of war had inevitably become mingled with more immediate, routine, mundane concerns. On 10 August he wrote to explain that uncertainty about his rheumatism meant he could not play in a return golf match at the nearby Essex Club on the following Saturday. A week later he contacted Alexander Morton in Broad Street, New York: "You might send me a list of the wines you have set aside for me, giving prices, and I will decide at once." Early in September he was negotiating membership of the Montserrat Golf Club at Prides Crossing for his organist Easthope Martin, "a very quiet, interesting little man whom I have known for about six months," and for Mrs. Martin. However, the disciplines of a lifetime also ensured that he kept an eye on world events and their commercial implications. Apparently Farrell offered to come up to visit him. Perhaps this suggestion revived memories of Atlantic crossings and long train journeys to Skibo to report and discuss with Carnegie; at any rate on 21 August he wrote back:

> I would of course be glad to see you, but it is too much to ask for you to spare the time to come up here. A little note will give me the information I want—the daily bookings; the daily shipments; cash collections and cash on hand. . . . Is there any increase in the orders from abroad, or are you having cancellations?[40]

Gary had a more direct experience of the conflict to report to him in mid September: "I have just returned to the office after an interesting and somewhat exciting sojourn in Paris." By that time the German armies had re-coiled from the Marne, and before the situation stabilized into the entrenched positions of a stalemated conflict, it looked for a time as if French and British forces would continue their counteroffensive and go on to a speedy victory. So Frick, replying the following day, took an optimistic view: "You must have had an interesting time. I presume it is just as well to have this trouble in Europe. It was bound to come some time and it now looks as if it is going to end as it should." However, others were already anticipating a much longer struggle. On the day Frick responded to Gary, he also wrote to J. H. Dunn in London, touched on the same themes, but then introduced a new note: "This war, of course, is a terrible thing, but I presume it had to come sooner or later, and has got to end only one way. I am sorry however if you think that it will be as long as two or three years."[41] By autumn, the wide-ranging seesaw battles on the western front were over, warfare had settled into the trenches, and there began the long haul that was to double Dunn's first figure. It was this phase of steady attrition and occa-sional massive but futile offensives that was to ruin the economies of Europe and to hand over both the commercial markets of the world and the oppor-tunity of supplying much of the insatiable demand for munitions for the Allies to the factories of the United States.

During summer 1914 the American economy had been sliding into reces-sion: a sign of its impact on the basic industries was the decision of the Oliver Iron Mining subsidiary of U.S. Steel to cut wages by 7 percent in late June. By the time Gary arrived back from Europe in mid September, trade was thoroughly depressed and things were getting worse. All over the coun-try, men were walking the streets looking for work. U.S. Steel profits fell to levels far below those of the depressions of 1903–1904 and 1908. The worst three months of earnings in those earlier years had averaged $3.35 million and $5.26 million respectively; the average for November and December 1914 and January 1915 was only $2.35 million. The dividend on common stock was passed and almost fifty thousand men were laid off. By the close of December 1914, the tonnage of unfilled orders on the U.S. Steel books was less than half that of two years earlier. Just before Christmas the finance committee gave the matter "careful consideration" before deciding that "at present" it would not recommend a general reduction in wages and sala-ries.[42]

However, after adding an initial further blow to confidence in the general downward trend, the war in Europe contributed to a revival and then went on to sweep business up to unprecedented levels. As he recovered from his illness, Frick was involved in the frenzy of activity caused by these new opportunities and needs. In January 1915, pig iron output was at an annual rate of about 19 million tons; by December that year, it was double that level, tonnages being far in excess of any ever reached before. In some centers of manufacture, prices for pig iron went up by well over 50 percent during the same period. There were similar dramatic increases in steel. In 1914 seventeen new open-hearth furnaces were completed; next year twenty-nine. Even this was completely overshadowed by the following two years, in which the annual average completion of new open hearths was 102 furnaces, together representing 9.4 million tons of new steel capacity. During 1915 electrical steel capacity was doubled, and in 1916 there was a further increase of 86 percent in the number of electrical furnaces installed. Altogether in 1916 and 1917, capacity for steel of all types went up by one-quarter; output in 1917 was not far short of half as great again as in 1913, itself the best ever peacetime year.

Naturally the specialized armament makers were particular and early beneficiaries of war-related demand, and none more than Bethlehem Steel, with its armor plate mill, gun foundry, and shipyards. So thrilled was Charlie Schwab with their flood of business and the earnings it brought that he sent Frick a copy of their annual report for the year ending 31 December 1914. Thanking him, the latter promised, "I shall enjoy looking it over carefully."[43] The Midvale Steel Company, now under the control of William E. Corey, was another specialized munitions maker that was well equipped for war business. Although the Carnegie Steel Company division of U.S. Steel also made armor and guns, it was above all concerned with commercial products. However, modern all-out warfare was soon calling for large increases of all categories of steel production, and profits at U.S. Steel benefited accordingly. By the end of 1915, their order book was twice as large as at the start of the year; and it reached a peak at the end of the first quarter of 1917 that was three times the level of the end of 1914. Earnings grew even more, those of March 1917 (the best month) being $43.6 million, over twenty-five times as great as at the low point of the depression just over two years before. For shareholders prospects were transformed (see table 38).

The immediate preoccupations of the European belligerents excluded them from traditional overseas markets, and so an unprecedented share of international trade fell to American industry. In the case of the Russian Empire, which came to Frick's notice, efforts to keep up the struggle at the front led to terrible strains and shortage. To make room for military transport and the most urgent movement of food supplies, train services between Moscow and Petrograd were officially suspended for weeks. Dire necessity made it desirable to make important extensions to the rail network, and in

TABLE 38

U.S. Steel During World War I

	Steel Products Shipped	Employees	Earnings per Share of Common Stock
1913	13,387[a]	228,906	$11.02[b]
1914	9,935	179,353	nil
1915	12,826	191,126	$ 9.96
1916	17,105	252,668	$48.46
1917	16,919	268,058	$39.15
1918	15,570	252,106	$22.09

Sources: U.S. Steel Annual Reports; Allen 1935, p. 207.
Notes: [a] Figures this column are in thousand tons.
[b] Figures this column are in dollars.

the first two years of the war the length of line was increased by a thousand versts (about 650 miles). American mills were an obvious source of supply for the rails. In summer 1915, Frick received a cable about the situation from Hunsiker who was then in Petrograd. Some of the points he touched on revived memories of the old rail association: "Cambria's agents account lack experience made bad mess their rail negotiations here. Believe additional large quantities may be required. Suggest endeavoring arrange my negotiations for all firms thereby saving time, trouble and middleman's large profits. Won't you discuss with Farrell?" Widening the contact, Frick cabled back: "Will confer at once with Farrell and Donner." He sent Hunsiker's telegram to Donner, who since U.S. Steel had taken over Donora had widened his involvement in the steel business. Frick himself took another step at this time. By November 1915 he could write to Farrell, "I am out of everything in the steel line (having sold my Cambria stock) except my investment in United States Steel and I think I had better keep in that position."[44]

He was still devoted to the interests of the Steel Corporation but also showed a wider vision of the needs and responsibilities of basic industry under war conditions. This was brought out by developments in the market for plate, a product in which Carnegie Steel had long been a leader. Early in 1915, plate prices were about $1 a ton below those for many other categories of ordinary finished steel; by the year's end prices were already about $14 a ton higher than the price of most other rolled products. A further boost was given during the following year when Congress authorized a three-year naval building program involving sixty-three warships. In 1917, after the United States had entered the war, the Emergency Fleet Corporation embarked on its dramatic merchant ship building program, and the steel industry responded to this sudden if temporary emergence of the United States as the world's biggest shipbuilding nation. An impressive instance was the erection in six months of a new mill for ship plate at West Homestead. Another plate mill was built by the Illinois Steel division of U.S. Steel at South Chicago. Shortly after this, U.S. Steel Corporation decided to begin shipbuilding on its own account. To this end it formed the Federal Shipbuilding Company and built a yard with ten building ways on the Hackensack River and another on Chickasaw Creek near Mobile. The latter required extensions to their TCI works at Fairfield.[45] Plate production reached unprecedented levels in 1916, and two years later output of plate and sheet together was only just less than 50 percent greater than in any pre-war year. In 1913 these products amounted to 23.2 percent of the national output of rolled products; in 1918 they amounted to 28.2 percent.

After the United States entered the war, Bernard Baruch—soon to be a member of the materials purchasing commission for the Allies and chairman of the War Industries Board—was asked to investigate complaints that excessive prices were being charged for ship plate. At a conference with steelmakers at the U.S. Steel offices he obtained no satisfaction. Gary, who represented the views of the industry, insisted that 4.25 cents per pound was a fair price, and he was inflexible when Baruch pressed him on this. Baruch called next on Frick and, stressing that he was acting on a commission from the president, asked him "as a patriotic citizen" what was the production cost for ship plate. Frick revealed that at U.S. Steel it was 2.50 cents a pound. This led to the Allied purchasing commission standing firm against the steel companies. A compromise price of 3.41 cents a pound was eventually agreed.[46]

As a director and a member of the key finance committee, Frick was involved with both the U.S. Steel expansion program and the general oversight of its increasing production. He was now entering his late sixties but was as conscientious as ever in the exercise of his responsibilities. He remained regular in his attendance at the finance committee and the full board of directors. During summer 1915, in the absence of others who were sometimes on holiday, he occasionally chaired the finance committee. He acted as a member of special subcommittees of the finance committee. In spring 1916, for instance, he was involved with the examination of plans for building a steelworks at Ojibway, Ontario. Nor was he merely interested in deliberations around the boardroom table in New York. When the finance committee visited Alabama in connection with extensions in June 1917, he was a member of the party. It is not known whether he took the same part in U.S. Steel's "social" events, but he received invitations to the 1915 annual

Members of the Finance Committee of United States Steel at Bayview, Alabama, June 7, 1917 (from left to right): George Baker, Frick, George W. Perkins, Percival Roberts, Jr., E. H. Gary. Courtesy of Frick Art and Historical Center, Frick Archives.

Steel Corporation dinner at the Waldorf and the 1916 dinner at Judge Gary's home at 856 Fifth Avenue.[47]

In this time of massive expansion, as in the 1880s or 1890s, Frick had an eye to the securing of additional mineral supplies, especially coal. He now showed himself free from commitment to old allegiances. In midsummer 1914, before the threat of war appeared on the horizon and when trade was declining, he commended the prospects of Greene County coal to Gary. He suggested that they should buy fifty thousand acres of it as a long-term investment, pointing out that once it had been possible to get Klondike coal lands for between $50 and $100 an acre, "but some of our people reported against it and we did nothing and you know how values have gone up in that district." He owned ten thousand acres of Greene County coal, "which

I would not sell at anything near what similar coal can be purchased for—in fact I would not sell it at all as I bought it for a long pull." In December 1916, he sent Gary another memorandum about mineral resources: "I spoke to you on Tuesday, as you will remember, about a very valuable tract of coal situated on the Norfolk and Western Railway and within two miles of the Chesapeake and Ohio Railway—in West Virginia in what is known as the Tucker field. . . . It will be an excellent purchase for the Steel Corporation."[48]

His continuing keen business sense was shown in other ways too. In 1898, he had acquired land at Indiana Harbor and, in 1906 and 1908, had added further small plots to this holding, which gradually assumed greater industrial potential. Even in 1915, he had valued the 129-acre site at $5,000 an acre. The Indiana Harbor Canal, which edged it on the east, was suitable for use by large ore vessels and beyond the canal was the expanding works of Inland Steel Company. During the war there was great business expansion in the Chicago area. Between 1914 and 1917, whereas the rolled steel production of Pennsylvania went up by 65 percent, the increase was 90 percent in Illinois and 100 percent in Indiana. In the first nine months of government regulation of the steel industry—that is, to July 1918—Chicago was made a basing point for steel products. A large growth of steel-using industries occurred under the new conditions of activity and pricing. Between 1917 and 1919, 150 new industrial plants were built in the Calumet district alone, an increase of 57 percent.[49] In 1916 the new plant of the Steel and Tube Company of America was built on the west side of Frick's land. During 1917 interest was expressed in the area he owned, but in 1918 it was decided that its development potential was more long-term than immediate.[50]

There were other instances of Frick's business acumen. On Sunday, 3 June 1917, he played golf with John S. Phipps, Henry Phipps's son. Next day, he reported to Gary that he had found him

> willing to sell quite a block of bonds. I think that he offered you some of them at the price he has given me on the slip which I enclose, but you thought you should have them at a fraction less. It seems to me now that he offers you such a substantial block, it would be a most excellent purchase, and I hope you will buy them from him at his price.

Yet, while thinking expansively, in accordance with his old established practice, he also concerned himself with details of costs. In February 1916 he asked Gary, "Will you please have a statement prepared for the Finance Committee at its next meeting, showing the costs of our various products for the following months: January 1915, October 1915, January 1916. I think a comparison would be interesting to see."[51]

During wartime expansion and disturbance in the industry, he saw familiar features swept away, or well on the way to disappearance. Nowhere was
this more marked than in coking technology. As late as 1914, the tonnage of
by-product coke made was less than half that of beehive coke; in 1919 the
by-product ovens established a primacy in production that they were never
to lose. In 1915 U.S. Steel decided on a major investment in by-product
ovens at Clairton. Yet even in the midst of such changes, Frick remembered
and honored obligations from a very different era. Early in 1916 he contacted
Farrell in order to introduce W. S. Paddock, "the son of Mr. J. H. Paddock,
who was formerly in the employ of the Frick Coke Company and lost his
life during the strike in the coke region many years ago in defending the
property of the Company. I should like very much if you could place him
somewhere. He will tell you what he is fitted for and what he would like."[52]

He had wider concerns as well, some reflecting his other directorships,
others appropriate to the standing of a man who was now one of the elder
statesmen of the nation's business. He had been a director of the Norfolk
and Western Railroad since about 1905; in 1916 he acted on their behalf with
Farrell. He noted that the railroad was hauling a great deal of coal for U.S.
Steel, "and on the whole I think giving you good service." They now needed
a thousand new cars, which they could build at their Roanoke shops. Frick
had told them that he thought U.S. Steel would make a great effort to deliver
the steel required and at a competitive price. An industry-wide perspective
was shown in another letter to Farrell, written in June 1917 shortly after the
United States entered the war. Frick pointed out that there was steel in semi-
finished form waiting at various ports for shipment overseas, and he suggested that it would be good to have a statement made of this and, if it could
not be forwarded promptly, "to get the consent of all parties, through the
assistance of our Government, in having it shipped to mills in this country
where it could be used and put in shape to build cars, locomotives etc." He
was still on the outlook for good men and was prepared to use his influence
on their behalf. In April 1918, he drew Farrell's attention to a potentially
valuable addition to their team of experts on war material:

> I learned yesterday of a man, Archibald B. Hubert, now a Major in the Ord-
> nance Department in Washington, who was with Midvale in the Gun Depart-
> ment; left them for the reason that he did not think they were pushing that
> department as they should. He is well connected; Midvale sent him abroad for
> a short time looking into gun plants. He is about 36 years of age and a Virgin-
> ian. He is well known in the Ordnance Department and he knows the Depart-
> ment in Washington is in bad shape for big guns. He might be of use to you in
> the future in some capacity, and it is for that reason I call your attention to
> him.

At this time the Secretary of War, Newton D. Baker, had asked Gary to obtain his board's approval for U.S. Steel to build a complete plant for large guns and projectiles. This was agreed in spring 1918, and work began on a site on Neville Island, in the Ohio River just below Pittsburgh. By October the failure of Congress to provide additional funds had led to a decision not to order more materials or machinery.[53]

Another aspect of Frick's wider involvement was his contact with the leaders of delegations sent from the Allied powers. In spring 1917, a few months after his removal from supreme command of the armies of France, Marshal Joffre was sent to the United States with a French mission. When Joffre visited New York, Frick gave over the whole of his Fifth Avenue home to him and his suite, moving his own family to a hotel. However, his faith in the hero of the Marne, who he had thus so generously acknowledged, was shattered when he saw him kiss the American Federation of Labor leader Samuel Gompers on both cheeks.[54]

Japan, too, was eager to secure a hearing in the United States. Its industry was in need of supplies from outside, but its high-handed actions in China had aroused the latent suspicions of Americans. In October 1917, the chief of the special mission from the House of Representatives of Japan, T. Masao, called on Frick with a letter of introduction from Charles W. Eliot of Harvard. Masao wanted to talk with him about the possibility of purchasing structural steel and especially ship plate. Frick referred him to Farrell. A year later, he was visited by the elderly Masayoshi Matsukata, a man whose efforts many years earlier had put Japan on a firm financial basis, and who had other interests that made him a congenial visitor. Frick reported, "Mr. Matsukata called yesterday and saw my collection. I found him a very interesting, modest gentleman."[55]

The expansion in steel continued to the end of the war. The output in 1917 and 1918 averaged 45.48 million tons (90.4 percent higher than in 1914). U.S. Steel Corporation expansion was a good deal less, however. Its 1914 shipments of products had been 9.93 million net tons; the average of 1917 and 1918 was 16.24 million (an advance of 63.5 percent). High levels of activity and extension of capacity not only required large additional outlays but also took their toll of men and managers. It was in reaction to one aspect of this situation that Frick showed perhaps most conclusively how much he had matured. In autumn 1917, he wrote in a fatherly tone to James Farrell: "I was sorry to hear of your illness. I hope you will take good care of yourself, and take a little rest now that you are not feeling well and not bother too much about business until you are in first class shape again."[56]

In his varied life—attending meetings of the finance committee and the full U.S. Steel board; acting the various parts of intermediary, liaison officer, assessor, and industrial elder statesman; writing extensively from Prides Crossing and from Fifth Avenue; mixing in the purchase of works of art; playing golf—Frick passed through the war years. His role in the war was not the flamboyant one of Charlie Schwab—negotiating for and building guns, submarines, and other supplies for the Allies; basking in the newfound wealth of his company; or stumping the country to rouse worker enthusiasm and produce the astounding results of the Emergency Fleet Corporation. Nor, on the other hand, was Frick prostrated by the barbarities of the time as was Andrew Carnegie. At last it was all over. A letter he wrote in New York on the day of the Armistice made no reference to the fact, but four days later, contacting a British art friend, Sir Charles Allom, he took a sanguine view of the outcome. Allom's family had played their part: "You certainly have done your share towards winning the war. How gratified we all are it is ended and that the victory has been so complete."[57] For Frick the Armistice was a short break in an active life; it also marked the beginning of its final phase.

Back to Normalcy

Peak wartime activity at U.S. Steel was reached in 1917, but production continued at a high level through the following year. After the Armistice a contraction in industrial activity generally was marked by a sharp decline in steel demand, output, and shipments. By the end of March 1919, unfilled orders on hand at U.S. Steel were valued at only 65.4 percent of the level six months earlier. It is noteworthy that, although things were soon to change, the declines in Allegheny County and in U.S. Steel were less than in the nation as a whole. National output in 1919 was only 77.98 percent of the 1918 level, whereas U.S. Steel shipments were 86.51 percent as high and Allegheny County production was 89.5 percent. It was during this year that the Western Association of Rolled Steel Consumers began an onslaught on the "Pittsburgh Plus" system of steel pricing, but generally it was a good year for the conclusion of the career of one who had for so long proclaimed the virtues of a Pittsburgh location, and who had been one of the more influential, if not most public, figures in U.S. Steel's direction during its eighteen-year life.

Henry Clay Frick was now in his seventieth year; he still retained and actively cultivated wide interests and was very much in possession of all his faculties. As he had remarked to Bridge sometime during 1917, he thought that he was as strong as ever and he expected to live for another ten years. From his Fifth Avenue home or from Prides Crossing he still journeyed to

board meetings, committee meetings, and the golf course. In both homes he
could enjoy the pleasures of gracious living and the quieter, more personal
satisfactions of his pictures and of his family. The following year was to be
full and varied almost to its end. In this respect he was more fortunate than
Carnegie, of whom his wife Louise wrote in midsummer that he was "so
frail and feeble and so very weak."[58] However, Carnegie was fourteen years
older than Frick.

Apart from U.S. Steel, art, sport, and personal considerations, there were
great national themes with which Frick was actively concerned. Two of these
were the return to a peacetime economy and the place of America in the
international politics of the post-war world. About each of them, he had
definite opinions that were characteristically conservative. The stance from
which he viewed industrial affairs, his belief in the almost sacred status of
the great institutions he had helped shape, and his unwillingness to countenance any radical departures in considering how capitalist structures might
be modified even for their own long-term benefit—at a time when scares
about Bolshevism were common—may be sensed by the words with which
he commended to Elbert Gary a work of art commemorative of J. P.
Morgan:

> It is with feelings akin to reverence for the founder of the Steel Corporation
> that we have commissioned J. Massey Rhind to make a portrait bust of the late
> J. Pierpont Morgan and in presenting this bust to the corporation which he
> created, we feel that we are honoring ourselves rather than adding to the unique
> distinction which is his. For Mr. Morgan's monument is the Steel Corporation
> itself—the greatest and most beneficent industrial organization conceived by
> the brain of man. At the same time those of us who knew him best like to think
> of Mr. Morgan as a man—as a human personality, strong, self-contained, dig-
> nified; and that is the aspect which the sculptor has so skillfully presented in
> the enduring bronze of his art. That coming generations may know him as we
> knew him, his bust may fittingly stand in some conspicuous place in the Steel
> Corporation's building; and to this end we have pleasure in presenting it to you
> as head of the great corporation he founded and which you administer so wisely
> and with such distinction.[59]

Even now, in relation to business opportunities Frick was often as farseeing
and as eager as younger men. One of his interests was the further development of the coal resources of the Appalachian plateau. The focus by this
time was in its middle districts, in southwest Virginia and the neighboring
parts of West Virginia, the area whose coking coal prospects he had deprecated to his Chicago associates thirty years earlier. By this time, however,
Connellsville was obviously teetering on the edge of a period of rapid decline. By 1919 C. M. Schwab's Bethlehem Steel "flier" of spring 1901 had

become a giant corporation and was endeavoring to extend its mineral resources. Schwab consulted Frick about coking coal, who replied to a telegram from his former partner in July. His letter indicated no animosity toward the man who, twenty years before, he thought had betrayed him:

> My Dear Schwab, . . . I came down from Prides Crossing Sunday night and am returning there tonight. I am having all the reports, maps, analyses and information about the Faraday property gathered together and will send them to you in a few days with a man who is thoroughly familiar with the property— Earl F. Overholt, who is a nephew of mine. He will be prepared to take any man or men you might wish to send, should you make up your mind to look into it, to the property and show them over it. It is really the only Pocahontas coal that is unsold and I think is just what you ought to have.[60]

Later that year his interest in the same Appalachian region showed itself in a scheme with international dimensions. Italy had depended on outsiders for the fuel for its industrialization, modest enough though that process had yet been. Some of Italy's coal had been railed in from Germany; much of it had come from Britain. The war disrupted the trade, which proved difficult to reestablish in its aftermath. By 1919 Italian customers were paying four times as much for British coal as users in the United Kingdom; naturally they considered other sources of supply. Between 1909 and 1913, Italian coal imports from the United States had been less than 1 percent as large as purchases from British mines, but in 1919 they were only a shade under 25 percent. One problem in expanding this flow was that, during the war, the Italians had lost over half their merchant shipping tonnage. In turning to America for fuel they were also interested in acquiring ships to carry it. Having been approached for help, Frick wrote to James Farrell about the matter late in October 1919:

> This will introduce Mr. Leopoldo Belloni who is figuring to purchase a large tract of coal in Virginia and to establish a steamship line from Norfolk to supply Italy with coal. I am familiar with the coal tract he is negotiating for and I told him I thought you would be willing to build him a fleet on fair terms and to be paid for in instalments. He will explain fully what he desires, and I trust we will be able to make a deal with him to furnish him such vessels as he may need. He is also interested in securing some steel for Italy, but will explain all this to you fully.[61]

Amid the everyday round of business commitments, there were other distractions. The Treaty of Versailles, formally ending the war with Germany, was signed on 28 June 1919. From the beginning of the previous December, American troops had started to return from Europe. By July 1919, more than 2.9 million men had been demobilized by the War Department. In towns and cities across the nation, innumerable parades were organized to welcome local men home. In midsummer Frick was invited to be present at the return of troops to the coke region. He was unable to accept, but he sent a response that revealed not only his sentiments for the sons of men he had fought so bitterly in the labor battles of the 1880s and 1890s, but also the background to his attitudes to such contemporary issues as the return of business to a peacetime footing, labor questions, and the international order for which some of the Connellsville men had died on the battlefields of France:

> [If the letter had arrived earlier,] I should have made an effort to rearrange my plans so that I could join in welcoming home the Connellsville boys on their return from the war. I have read over their names and rejoice to see how thoroughly American in spirit they have become, despite the foreign origin of many of them and I beg you to convey to them individually and as a whole my hearty thanks, as well as my most cordial congratulations that they have returned safe and sound. Besides the memories of great experiences, they will always have the inspiring recollection of having fought for humanity and the rights of the individuals, as truly as did the fathers of the Republic with whom the boys of Connellsville have now identified themselves.[62]

Another issue that meant much to someone with his industrial background and more recent financial involvement was the state of the nation's railroads. Increased wartime business had put them under unprecedented strain; congestion and delay had resulted. In spring 1917, the American Railway Association produced a form of agreement to be signed by all railroads, committing them to so reorganize their business as to lead to the greatest expedition in the movement of freight.[63] Pressure mounted further (the movements of freight by rail in 1917 being 38.4 percent above the level of 1914), and on 1 January 1918, the railroads were taken over by the government in order to secure improved coordination. After the Armistice, there were further problems. Employees pressed for concessions, strikes resulted, and inefficiencies in the system became still more obvious. Frick had been conscious of the importance of rail transport from his earliest days in business, and his directorships of a number of major railroads in the early twentieth century made him familiar with their possibilities and problems. In October 1919, he was sufficiently concerned about the situation to write to the director general of railways, Walter D. Hines, a man he had known for many years on the board of the Santa Fe. It was a plea for a return to stability and the avoidance of economic collapse:

> In common with many others, I am deeply distressed by the appalling conditions which now confront us as part of the aftermath of the war. . . . something

must be done to avert overwhelming disaster. . . . What the whole country needs now above all is restoration of confidence. . . . Anybody realizes that adequate railway service is the keystone of the entire arch of industrial progress and prosperity. Even more vital than the circulation of money is the circulation of goods. . . . Manufacturers are now overwhelmed with orders which they cannot fill and they naturally refrain from making necessary enlargements of their plants while in doubt as to their ability to make deliveries.

Hines argued that an important cause of the current difficulties was stubbornness on the part of the railroad companies, and he succeeded in converting Frick to his views.[64]

Labor problems plagued the early post-war steel industry. Although wages had risen over the last few years of intense activity, there was a strong, though not undisputed, opinion among commentators that a large number of workers in the lower grades of the industry even now did not have a wage that guaranteed them a fair standard of living. As before there was much concern about hours of labor. A large proportion of the men in U.S. Steel plants were still working twelve-hour shifts. In the mill towns, the hand of the companies as always pressed heavily. John Fitch had studied them ten years before. Even now he wrote, "One who has not seen with his own eyes the evidences of steel company control in the towns where their plants are located will have difficulty in comprehending its scope and power."[65]

A related but even more central issue was the industry's continuing opposition to unionization. Since the Homestead strike, the Amalgamated Association of Iron, Steel, and Tin Workers had shrunk almost to the point of disappearance. When U.S. Steel was formed, the Amalgamated had only 13,800 members—one in every thirty-one workers in the industry nationally. The strike of 1909, which lasted in some places as long as fourteen months, almost ruined the association; after that, it retained very few members, mainly in sheet and tinplate mills. As the war ended, a new, more widely backed move for unionization and better conditions was underway. The American Federation of Labor meeting in St. Paul in summer 1918 resolved on "one mighty drive to organize the steel plants of America."[66] A year later, Samuel Gompers and the president of the Amalgamated, Michael Tighe, wrote to Gary asking for a conference. He refused to communicate with representatives of associations that he did not approve of and that he maintained did not represent his workers.

The outcome was a strike, which began on 22 September 1918 with 365,000 men out nationally. Support varied dramatically from plant to plant. Gary in Indiana—loudly proclaimed by U.S. Steel as a model town ("a beautiful city . . . with a splendid school system" was how James Farrell eulogized it)—had an almost total withdrawal of labor. Around Pittsburgh the strike was nearly complete at Monessen, but it was very slight in the city works of Jones and Laughlin. Among Steel Corporation mills, there was full support at Donora, but much less at other plants. At Homestead, Duquesne, Clairton, and McKeesport in the third week of the strike it was reported that 23,514 out of a "normal" workforce of 28,200 were working.[67] It seems that the industry carefully "managed" the news media, however; it is not at all certain that these published figures of men at work are accurate. The union side was weakened by disagreements between "radicals" and "conservatives." As the dispute dragged on, up to and then beyond Christmas, support from the men weakened, and when the strike ended on 20 January 1920, only about a hundred thousand were still out. Some five months afterward, a commission of inquiry from the Interchurch World Movement published a report on the strike that was highly critical of the steel firms. As part of its response, U.S. Steel circulated 1.2 million copies of a sermon by a New England clergyman who derided the report as "industrial heresy" and tried to find biblical backing for that conclusion. The clergyman observed that the report

> advocates gradually and reasonably reducing "the hours of labor to the lowest practicable point." This is the hobo's doctrine. It glorifies leisure and denounces toil. . . . How can we advocate reducing work to its lowest practicable point if we have left in us any of the spirit of him who said, "I must work the works of him that sent me while it is day; for the night cometh when no man can work."[68]

It was a defense worthy of William Graham Sumner. Whether drudgery in the rolling mills of industrial America came within the scope of that New Testament definition of the urgency of work seems not to have been considered.

Although the steel conflict was national, rather than confined to one company or one mill town, and although he was no longer in the public eye as a principal protagonist, there was much in the early phases of these events to remind Frick of the Homestead strike. Mills were again fortified and had to be provisioned against siege. There was frequent brutality—in Pennsylvania from the state constabulary, and in Gary from federal troops that were called in on 7 October and stayed until the end of the strike. Inevitably, the men were not free of guilt, either. During the Homestead strike, Frick had been remarkably reticent in public. Now Gary—speaking before the Senate Committee on Labor and Education—tried to justify corporation employment policy. He did so with an astounding lack of fluency. He admitted that sixty-nine thousand of their employees were on a twelve-hour day but argued that their tasks did not involve hard manual labor such as he claimed to have known as a boy on an Illinois farm. Much of the time their workers were merely overseeing mechanized processes: "That is not to say there is no work in that, because of course there is, and I would not belittle it, of course. It is hard work to work hard whatever one does, and to the extent one does hard work, he, of course, is doing hard work." Frick supported his chairman in resisting the men's pressure. Early in October, he wrote to congratulate Gary on his continuing refusal to negotiate with Gompers: "I was glad to see . . . that there would be no compromise . . . that's the kind of stuff."[69]

During that summer and autumn, Frick was involved in a movement with even more momentous consequences than this great industrial dispute. It resulted in defeat for the attempt to make the United States a founder member of the League of Nations. America had entered the war in a spirit of idealism and with a zeal for reform of the relations between states that had led to the international anarchy. On 8 January 1918 in an address to a joint session of Congress, Woodrow Wilson outlined, under fourteen headings, his conception of a post-war settlement. The last of his "Fourteen Points" was that "A general association of nations must be formed under specific covenants for the purpose of affording mutual guarantees of political independence and territorial integrity to great and small states alike." In a vague form this idea for preserving peace had been in the minds of visionaries and men of goodwill from various nations for many years. Before 1914, one of the most enthusiastic supporters of the idea—if not of the comprehensive form now envisaged to carry it over into practice—had been Carnegie. Speaking at the Peace Palace at the Hague less than a year before the war began, he had advocated an "International Court" for the abolition of war: "I submit that the only measure required today for the maintenance of world peace is an agreement between three or four of the leading Civilized Powers (and as many more as desire to join—the more the better) pledged to cooperate against disturbers of world peace, should such arise."[70] It was this idea that Wilson took up, developed further, and continued to advocate after the initial announcement of the Fourteen Points. In the first half of 1919, he secured the inclusion of a commitment to the establishment of a League in the peace treaty with Germany that was signed in Versailles on 28 June 1919. Yet when he returned home, he had to face a Congress in which his party had lost its Senate majority and whose Foreign Relations Committee was controlled by political and personal opponents. At the head of this committee was Henry Cabot Lodge who was committed to fight the League proposals. Many were angered by Wilson's insistence that approval of the peace treaty with Germany should be inextricably linked to acceptance of the League of Nations. As he fought to secure popular support so as to win the two-thirds Senate vote for ratification, Wilson's health broke in late September.

Long before this, Frick had been brought into the campaign against American membership of the League of Nations. In spring 1919, things seemed to be going well for League supporters. Not only Democrats but also some Republicans, led by former President Taft, favored U.S. participation. Many bankers and industrialists were with them. Sometime in May the opposition group—the "Irreconcilables" as they liked to be called—took the opportunity of Frick's apparently genuine uncertainty and open-mindedness to win him to their cause. It all happened in the conversation following a dinner that he gave in New York in honor of General Leonard Wood, then considered a political heir to Theodore Roosevelt and a possible 1920 Republican presidential candidate. Wood was an ultra-nationalist obsessed with the "Red Scare," who, a few months after Frick's complimentary dinner, headed the military intervention in Gary during the steel strike. Harvey, himself strongly opposed to the League, gave an account of the brief exchange at this dinner, which he suggested converted Frick to that cause. After asking many questions, Frick summed up what he had learned:

> As I understand it, then, the proposition is to pledge the United States, now the richest and most powerful nation in the world, to pool its resources with other countries, which are largely its debtors, and to agree in advance to abide by the policies and practices adopted by a majority or two thirds of its associates; that is, to surrender its right of independence of action upon any specific question whenever such a question may arise.

His informant replied, "That is substantially it." Frick then came to his conclusion: "Well, I am opposed to that. Of course I am. I don't see how any experienced business man could fail to be. Why, it seems to me a crazy thing to do."[71] With that he committed himself to the fight, and his adherence seems to have helped to secure that of Andrew Mellon. Together they brought in essential fighting funds to back the public front of the campaign conducted by such congressional leaders as James A. Reed of Missouri, Philander C. Knox of Pennsylvania, the bitter opposition from Hiram Johnson of California and of the hectoring William Borah from Idaho. Eventually the Senate defeated the Wilson proposals. This decision helped the United States make its way back to "normalcy" and into the wild expansion of the Golden Twenties. As an American historian was to put it many years later, the nation had been put off further international political involvement by "above all, the discovery that 'to make the world safe for democracy' would demand continued effort and sacrifice on the part of the United States."[72] Perhaps the decision that Frick took at the end of that happy dinner in his home on a spring evening in 1919 was to have wider and more unfortunate implications than anything he had done in a long and in many respects distinguished life.

In early autumn 1919, his life entered its last phase. It was one in which happiness was still intertwined with sadness. In mid October Frances, the wife of his son Childs, having already a family of three girls, gave birth to a son. In honor of his renowned grandfather, he was named Henry Clay. Two days later, Frick went over to their Long Island home to see the new baby. During the same month he was present at one of the receptions for the visiting King Albert and Queen Elizabeth of Belgium. On Friday, 24 October 1919, sixteen hundred members of the American Iron and Steel Institute meeting in New York gave their enthusiastic support to Gary's strike leadership. It is not known whether Frick was at the daytime sessions, but it was a matter of remark that he attended the annual dinner in the Hotel Commodore that evening, an almost unprecedented sign of his involvement in the industry's collective power—displayed beneath the Institute's motto "Right Makes Might." In this grand display of the size and wealth of American steel—at a time when, in terms of capital invested, it could still claim to be the nation's leading industrial sector—Frick was given a place of honor. He sat in the central part of the top table, only two places from Gary and nearer than James Farrell, the president of U.S. Steel. At this time he looked well, holding himself erect among his colleagues when they stood for a photograph of the vast assembly. His white beard and hair gave him great distinction, the air of an outstanding elder statesman of the industry. It was to be his last great public occasion.

Although he was still involved in some of the major movements or events within the nation, there were signs that he mellowed as he aged. He was often generous, and there is evidence that he valued personal relationships. He continued to give to charity. On 6 November 1919, in response to an All Saints Day letter, he sent $10,000 to Reverend Leighton Parks toward the "expenses and benevolences" of Saint Bartholomew's Church on Manhattan's east side. Yet even in charitable giving he could still react strongly against unwanted publicity. In the past he had donated to the New York American Christmas Fund, but his secretary now wrote to the fund's manager, J. Smith, "Mr. Frick declines to renew his annual subscription to the Christmas Fund, only for the reason that you violated your agreement with him regarding publicity." He showed a desire to maintain old friendships and to repair some of those that had grown rusty. There is no mention in his correspondence of his reaction to Carnegie's death on 11 August 1919, but Schwab later recorded that he chanced to meet Frick outside the latter's Manhattan home and was invited in for a chat. Frick wrote to his old coke region friend, Father Lambing, in November letting him know that he had recommended that the Frick Coke Company should assist "liberally" in the work Lambing was doing there. He added, "If you come to New York do not fail to come to see me: I should be very glad to see you again."[73]

At the end of October he made a business trip to Pittsburgh. The steel dispute was still dragging on, and a coal strike was beginning that was to involve 435,000 miners nationwide. On Saturday, 1 November, after his return from Pittsburgh, he had his secretary write to George Wyness at Prides Crossing: "Mr. Frick is quite anxious that you and all the men employed by him should vote for Governor Coolidge on Tuesday and hope that you will quietly arrange to have this done."[74] Next day, Childs brought his family over to visit his parents. On Tuesday, 4 November, the day of the elections, Frick gave a lunch for James A. Reed, one of the leaders of the "Irreconcilables." After this he fell ill with what was diagnosed as ptomaine poisoning. Together with a cold, which he had caught in a day's golfing at Roslyn, Long Island, this brought on an attack of inflammatory rheumatism, which in turn threatened his heart. The board meeting of the U.S. Steel Corporation on Friday, 7 November, had to be held at his home. He was confined to bed for another twelve days, but on Wednesday, 19 November, he was allowed downstairs—"to sit with my pictures" as he put it. It was on that day that a test vote in the Senate produced 55 votes in favor of ratifying the Versailles Peace Treaty and 39 against, thus failing to deliver the necessary two-thirds majority.

Two days later, against the wishes of both Adelaide and his daughter Helen and the specific advice of his doctor, he ordered his car and traveled to Long Island to visit Childs and Frances's family. When he returned, he was exhausted and soon was ill again. Next day, as his secretary reported to Senator Reed, he was once more confined to bed. On Tuesday, 25 November, while he was still bedridden, a memorial service was held in the Carnegie Music Hall in Pittsburgh for Andrew Carnegie who, had he lived, would have been eighty-four on that day. Frick must have read the accounts of Charlie Schwab's eulogy of his former head in the next day's papers. His reactions are not recorded. For five days after this, there seemed to be a slow improvement in his condition. At 11 A.M. on Monday, 1 December, his old colleague James Bridge called on him. He found him sitting up in bed with newspapers spread around him. He asked his visitor to pull up a chair and launched into discussion of the affairs of the outside world with the question "Who will be the next President?"[75]

Early on Tuesday morning, Frick woke and asked his butler for a glass of water. After drinking it, he lay back on his pillow and said, "I think I will go to sleep."[76] A few minutes later, in his splendid bedroom overlooking the wintry landscape of Central Park, he peacefully passed away. In less than three weeks he would have been seventy years old. The cause of death was initially attributed to the ptomaine poisoning he had contracted a month earlier, but his physician, John S. Conner, later issued a statement: "Mr. Frick for the past month has shown signs of an organic affection of the heart which presumably was the late result of the severe attacks of inflammatory rheumatism to which he was subject in earlier life."

The next day a brief funeral service was held at the Fifth Avenue home. By his own wishes, Frick was to be buried in Pittsburgh, and that evening a private train carrying his casket, members of the family, and a few New York friends left Pennsylvania Station, arriving at East Liberty Station in Pittsburgh the next morning. At noon on Friday, 5 December 1919, a fifteen-minute service was conducted in the music room at Clayton by the Reverend Dr. Edwin J. Van Etten, rector of Calvary Protestant Episcopal Church. The service was attended only by close relatives and a few intimate friends. Christine Clemson, the wife of one of his partners at Carnegie Steel, sang three hymns, one of which was "Lead Kindly Light." The honorary pallbearers included longtime friends and associates such as U.S. Senator Philander C. Knox, Andrew W. Mellon, Richard Beatty Mellon, and Henry Clay McEldowney.

Following the service, a funeral procession bore the casket to the family plot on the highest elevation of Homewood Cemetery, just behind Clayton. There, under an overcast sky with scattered snowflakes carried on a chill wind, Henry Clay Frick was laid to rest beside his beloved daughter Martha, who had died at the age of six in 1891. Two graves away, to his right, lay Henry Clay Jr., the infant who had survived his birth in the dreadful summer of 1892 by only one month.

10

Images and Perceptions

Assessing Frick's Life

—————

F rick had always been an intensely private man, who always tried to avoid attention and seemed to care little for it when it proved unavoid-able. Now his death and his will became matters of major national interest. Over the next two years more than forty-five hundred obituaries, news and feature stories, or editorials appeared in newspapers across the United States. Fortunately for the historian, the family decided to collect these re-cords of public perception. On 4 December, a letter was sent to Burrelles Press Clippings Bureau in New York, asking for a bound collection of the obituary notices from New York and Pittsburgh papers, and an unbound version of reports in the more prominent of the other papers from all over the country. Next day a further letter changed this request to one for two bound books of clippings from newspapers throughout the nation.[1]

With the exception of the Homestead strike, the attempted assassination by Berkman, and the bitter quarrel with Carnegie, the population at large had little prior knowledge of Frick. The national press had widely reported the Homestead conflict, at which time his notoriety was at its most intense. But these events had occurred a generation or more before, and now, gener-ally speaking, the newspapers were more awed by the passing of a pioneer of national economic greatness than concerned to rake over the reputation of a strike breaker. A *New York Tribune* editorial recognized that "the name of Frick was abhorrent to great numbers of his fellow citizens" but contin-ued, "time softened this acerbity, and he has long been recognized as a strong man who on the material side was one of the makers of America of his generation." Other editorials too were nostalgic, viewing him as an ex-emplar of the archetypal self-made man of another era. The *Wall Street Journal* compared his career to that of Rockefeller, in the sense that each

369

had built his wealth from the development of previously almost unexploited natural resources. Both introduced order to the chaotic methods and trading practices they had found when they entered their respective mineral trades, and both had used the capital they accumulated for further investment in mining, manufacturing, and railroads.[2]

Frick had gone further by involving himself in the tertiary sector of the national economy, in banking, insurance, and trust funds. Showing itself rather out of touch with real circumstances, the *New York Times* marveled at the transformation hard work could bring about: "Born to salutary poverty, a Pennsylvania farm barefoot boy, at seventeen or eighteen he was earning seven or eight dollars a week. Before he was thirty he was a millionaire." The *Times* went on to point out that Frick and his contemporaries "belonged to a race of creators of industry" who played "the game fairly as they understood it and as it was played in their time." In contrast, the *Lexington (Kentucky) Herald* sought a moral for today: "If there is any lesson for the present generation in the career of this admittedly remarkable man, it lies in the proof that America still offers to the boy who has the will and determination, the realization of unlimited aspirations."

Some newspapers introduced a sourer note. The *New York Evening Sun* remarked that "the death of Mr. Henry C. Frick, following that of Mr. Carnegie within the year, accents the close of another of those remarkable careers of the last century in which the personal ability of the man turned the wheel of fortunate chance to his own spectacular advantage." The *St. Joseph (Missouri) Herald* let bad taste take over with the headline "Frick, Last of Old Guard on Millionaire's Row to Face Great Adventure." The editorial verdict of the *New York World* was harsh, claiming that his attitude to labor had never softened, though it recognized he was hard on others too:

> He was uncompromising. Business with him was a battle to be fought to a finish, and he was as full of zest in enforcing this view on protesting workmen as upon the financial gladiators with whom he occasionally came into conflict. . . . if at any time he took notice of the broadening tendencies of humanity, as displayed in the careers of some of his associates, he gave no proof of it by word or deed.

Most criticism was accompanied by a grudging admiration for his business genius and his determination. Although allowing that Frick "lacked the more human qualities that made Carnegie so beloved," the writer of the editorial in the *Lexington (Kentucky) Herald* admitted, "Frick was a fighter. The anarchist's bullet that laid him low for a brief period . . . had no more effect on him than the pleas of the distressed families of the [Homestead] strikers. . . . He was that kind."

The regional newspapers were proud of the achievements of a man born and reared in their midst, and of his unrivaled contributions to the growth of their coal, coke, and steel industries. They were aware of his lifetime personal loyalty to Western Pennsylvania, an area then perceived by much of the nation as a grim land of industrial filth. More was known of his philanthropy here than in the nation as a whole. Understandably, therefore, their praise was virtually unstinted. The Pittsburgh papers quoted the city's mayor on the day of Frick's death: "The towering monuments which he created in Pittsburgh express faith in its future. He was an inspiration and example for us all."[3] For the *Pittsburgh Post-Gazette,* he indeed

> typified the Pittsburgh spirit of enterprise and energy . . . [and] no matter how much of his time he spent in New York . . . it was in Pittsburgh that he maintained his voting residence, and in many ways he showed his affection for this community. [He was] a many-sided man who . . . had tenderness where tenderness was called for, just as he had unflinching courage and sternness where those qualities were demanded.

The *Pittsburgh Press* labeled the enemies he had won at Homestead "radicals," thereby neatly sidestepping any question of his inhumanity to ordinary workingmen. It described his management of "the famous strike" as "vigorous." When it was learned he was to be buried in Pittsburgh, the news was given front-page banner headlines.

In the coke region, the debt to Frick was great. An editorial in the *Connellsville Courier* noted that, whereas he might be remembered by the world at large as one of the nation's great industrial leaders, "as the founder of the greatest coke company in the world he will never be forgotten in the Connellsville coke region, the commanding importance of which was so largely due to his farsighted vision . . . energy, and vigorous leadership." A few days later, after it became known that he had left $500,000 to the Cottage State Hospital in Connellsville, another *Courier* editorial suggested that "[t]hose who have not known him and have harshly and incorrectly judged him cannot but have a different opinion on the views he held as to the responsibility he recognized as a possessor of large wealth." A balanced summing up came from another small newspaper from the scene of his early business triumphs, the *Uniontown Herald.* It may fairly stand as a concluding contemporary statement of his stature:

> The name of Henry Clay Frick stands very near the top of the list of builders of America. . . . He worked long hours. His conception of life he expressed in terms of work. The difference between him and many thousands of other men . . . was that as he labored he dreamed. The humdrum years of his modest toil were illumined by the light that has led every great doer of the world's work.

His dreams took form and substance in vast structures of steel, in long lines of rails, in roaring furnaces fed by an improved fuel, in one of the most notable art collections the world ever saw. There are some things that Frick did that other men would have done otherwise or left undone. But, as a great constructive personality his name is destined to be perpetuated in the amazing annals of America's material development.[4]

Judging by the press coverage, the nation was impressed and probably surprised by Frick's generosity in disposing of his estate. Carnegie benefactions had been widely publicized for many years; Frick's philanthropy so far had been private. Now, in death, this taciturn man received a degree of public approval he had seldom if ever enjoyed in life. His estate was valued at $145 million: $117 million of this was left in the form of gifts from which the general public could benefit. The art collection, which was alleged to have cost $50 million, was bequeathed to New York City with an endowment of $15 million for its maintenance and extension. His house on Fifth Avenue was to be reconstructed to become the home of the Frick Collection after the death of Adelaide Frick, which occurred in 1931. He was generous in his educational endowments, which, as Thomas Lamont put it, reflected that he had more and more realized the value of trained minds in business. He left $15 million to Princeton (where Childs, his only surviving son, had graduated) and $5 million each to MIT, Harvard, and the Educational Commission of Pittsburgh. To Pittsburgh, he gave a 151-acre park with $2 million for its upkeep; and $500,000 went to each of fourteen philanthropic institutions in Pennsylvania, including the hospitals in the leading coke region centers of Uniontown, Connellsville, Mount Pleasant, and Greensburg, and the steel towns of Braddock and Homestead. There were gifts also for the Mercy Hospital, Pittsburgh, at which he had been treated after the attempt on his life, and for the Lying-In Hospital in New York. A further $6.5 million passed to the thirty-one-year-old Helen Clay Frick to be spent for whatever charitable and educational purpose she chose. A residue of $25 million was left to his wife, son, and daughter, four grandchildren, other relatives, friends, and employees.

The recent death of Carnegie was frequently mentioned in the obituaries. Loss of these two giants of nineteenth-century American business within four months seems to have encouraged the sentimental tone of some of the verdicts on Frick. Alexander Berkman who had unwittingly won public sympathy for Frick by the violence of his attack during the Homestead strike now made an unexpected reappearance. Ironically, it was on 2 December 1919 that an order was issued for Berkman's deportation. "Well," he is reported to have said when he heard that Frick had died that morning, "he left the country before I did." Three days later, on the day that Frick was buried in Pittsburgh, Berkman was moved to Ellis Island to await a ship to carry him to the Soviet Union.

The press reactions to Frick's passing were based on public perceptions and values. His business associates were also called upon for comment. They had known him as well as anyone outside his family or a small group of close friends. Relationships with him would not encourage cant, and therefore their opinions provide useful insights into his character and achievements. They brought out his attention to detail, sound judgment, implacable determination, and organizational abilities—a formidable combination of qualities. References to his charms or personal warmth were less prominent, though not completely absent. Elbert H. Gary, speaking for U.S. Steel, observed that Frick "talked little but . . . said much"; he emphasized his sound judgment, "natural ability . . . unfailing courage and fixed determination." James Farrell, the U.S. Steel president, was rather more expansive. He mentioned that Frick "had the soundest judgment and one of the keenest minds I have ever known." The J. P. Morgan partner, Thomas Lamont, made a particularly interesting comment: "Mr. Frick had a mind that was brilliant and at the same time sound." He added that almost every enterprise he touched "showed the results of his acumen and thorough-going, painstaking efforts."[5]

Business associates made clear that Frick was slow to make friends but could be relied upon when he had done so. As an anonymous statement from U.S. Steel put it, a month after his death, "Intimate acquaintance was necessary in order to fully estimate his fine qualities of heart and mind." Robert Walker, who had known him in Pittsburgh for thirty years, reckoned he was

> less understood than any other who has occupied so prominent a part in the business world. [He] did not seem to possess to large degree the happy facility of cultivating friendships in business, and yet those who knew him best swore by him. . . . He was at times brusque in manner, but he had a kindly heart, and to those who were fortunate enough to be counted as his business and personal friends he was loyal to the last degree.

Philander C. Knox, who had grown up in Brownsville and served as lawyer to Carnegie Steel before entering government, strongly affirmed Frick's allegiance to those he knew well: "An intimate friendship since boyhood has given me firm impressions of the character, abilities, and temperament of Henry Clay Frick. . . . Charity, generosity, justness, and patriotism were Mr. Frick's outstanding virtues. His generosity did not demand obsequious acknowledgment."[6]

At the time of Frick's death, Charles M. Schwab praised his business rather than personal qualities, not sharing in the expressions of personal regard expressed by some other colleagues. In the mid 1930s, he cast caution aside and in a series of long interviews with Sidney B. Whipple of the *New York World-Telegraph* revealed his true opinion of Frick. By this time Schwab was aging rapidly and the accounts he gave of his former partner presented a one-sided though intriguing perspective. It was a forthright and damning assessment, one well calculated to make or to reinforce a myth, but it also contains valuable insights overlooked by others:

> He was to me a curious and puzzling man. No man on earth could get close to him or fathom him. He seemed more like a machine, without emotion or impulses. Absolutely cold-blooded. He had good foresight and was an excellent bargainer. He knew nothing about the technical part of steel, but he knew that with his coke supply tied up to Carnegie he was indispensable—or thought he was. . . . His assets were that *he was a thinking machine, methodical as a comptometer, accurate, cutting straight to the point* . . . the most methodical thinking machine I have ever known. . . . He seemed to lavish on art all the passion that he might have bestowed on human beings. . . . He had *no friends* and was *a very unhappy man.* . . . He . . . was not cultured, had no instinct for books or learning; was cold-blooded, ignorant of everything except the steel and coke business; had no love for his fellow man, nor indeed for anybody around him; was cold and austere and unlovable even in his family; ruthless, domineering, icy. [He lacked patience and his] temper was violent. Even in his family life he was cold, austere and occasionally had flareups. He rowed with his son, and the only fondness for any human being he seemed to have was for his daughter—who was exactly like him in temperament. . . . He had no friends because he was totally incapable of demonstrating friendship. I believe he softened towards me at the last, for he met me outside his New York home, by chance, and shook hands with me. "Charlie," he said, "I don't believe I have ever said to any man that I was sorry. Won't you come in the house for a while?" I went in and we had a chat, and that was the most human thing I ever knew him do.

Whatever the truths of his assessment, Schwab must have forgotten the letter he had written thirty-six years before, thanking Frick for a painting and for his "fellowship and regard." Presumably he could not forget that early December evening in 1899 when he had faced Frick's towering wrath in the drawing room at Clayton.[7]

Perhaps one of the most remarkable features of the success of Carnegie Steel had been that the temperaments of its three central partners were so different. A most valuable insight into two of them, Carnegie and Frick, was provided by a man who had known them closely for thirty-five years. The Englishman James H. Bridge had been Herbert Spencer's private secretary before he moved to the United States in 1884 to become a "literary assistant" to Carnegie, helping him write *Triumphant Democracy,* published in 1886. Bridge first met Frick in 1885. When Bridge was writing his excellent book *The Inside History of the Carnegie Steel Company: A Romance of Millions* (1903), Frick gave him access to some of the company's papers. In the first years of the century Bridge saw Frick almost daily, and from 1914 he was the curator of Frick's art collection. As Bridge wrote in *Millionaires and Grub Street* (1931), Frick and Carnegie were—"although each man tried to conceal the fact from each other—as unsympathetic as oil and water." Carnegie was "the most consistently happy man I ever knew. He enjoyed the perpetual miracle of life. . . . [He was] the Star-Spangled optimist." On the other hand, in spite of his innumerable meetings with Frick, Bridge felt that he never got as close to him as to Carnegie. He was well aware of Carnegie's faults but yet, almost mysteriously, was engaged by some unexpected qualities. In Frick there was

> an imperious demand for recognition of his rights and an unforgiving remembrance of what he deemed his wrongs. The courtly manner of his earlier years grew a protective armor as time went on. [But] the materialistic aspect of his life . . . was qualified by his love of children and of art. It is in these gentler phases of his character that he is remembered by those who knew him best. . . . despite his disconcerting taciturnity, his inflexibility so defiantly demonstrated in the Homestead tragedy, his unrelenting enmity toward Carnegie which he carried to his grave, and which Colonel Harvey in his book carried beyond it, despite all this and more, there was a singularly charming, humane and charitable side to the character of Henry Clay Frick.[8]

This has about it the ring of truth.

For those who built up the great American fortunes of the late nineteenth and early twentieth centuries, there were two main ways in which their wealth could be spent—conspicuous consumption and philanthropy. These were not mutually exclusive, but one or other tended to dominate, according to the character of the individual concerned. Given their particular arrays of talents and aims, it is not surprising that most business leaders gave no evidence that they ever sat down to ponder the purpose of it all. For most of them the thrill of building, of competing, and of winning was probably the all-important thing. The *New York City Globe* wrote discerningly about this at the time of Frick's death: "It's the conflict, the battle for power that holds the interest of forceful men in business enterprises, and the money profits, once they have realized enough to keep them comfortably, must seem a casual matter, a by-product that accumulates with irritating rapidity and has to be taken care of." Carnegie, too, recognized that the race was more important than the prize, though he put a slightly different gloss on the matter. At the end of a letter to Schwab, written at the time of the break with Frick, he observed: "We are not in for dollars; fortunately you and I and all our partners have plenty or are getting plenty. We have pleasure in business, performing useful parts—this is our great reward. Money comes far behind, indeed the more we get after competence the less happiness."[9]

Most of these men regarded the disposal of their fortunes as a matter for them alone. Though he was by no means an ungenerous man, Charles M. Schwab was to remark that he did not feel an obligation to give away his wealth. (In the end this was just as well, for before he died little of it remained.) Henry Phipps devoted much of his money to humanitarian purposes, including the building of sanitary tenements in New York and liberal endowments of research into tuberculosis and mental illnesses. In his philanthropies as well as in his various writings about business and its relations to society at large, Carnegie was quite exceptional. Yet even in his case puzzles remain. Winkler was economical in the words he used to sum him up: "Andrew Carnegie, I suspect, was the greediest little gentleman ever created." Yet, on the other hand (and almost certainly in good faith), Carnegie wrote of the wider responsibilities of the great capitalist and of the rights of workers. From an early stage of his industrial career he was eloquent concerning the shame of dying rich. A few years before the end of his life, he spelled out what business meant to him and what faculties it called on:

> Service to the community must always be the root of business. . . . I confidently recommend a business career as one in which there is abundant room for the exercise of man's highest power and of every good quality in human nature. . . . Business is not all dollars. These are but the shell—the kernel lies within and is to be enjoyed later, as the higher faculties of the business man, so constantly called into play, develop and mature.

To his unquestionable honor, Carnegie spent most of his retirement ensuring that his wealth would benefit future generations. Yet even here there remained an annoying, persisting anomaly stemming from the unremitting campaigns he had conducted in cutting costs. It was summed up in the pithy words of one economic historian: "Carnegie built libraries from the wage savings."[10]

Frick's position was less clear. He made no public protestations about the rights of man or of the calls society could justifiably make on successful capitalists. He refuted the claims of outsiders to interfere or to judge. There is no evidence that he ever sat down, as Carnegie did, to puzzle out what all the effort—the exploitation of earth resources, the driving of workers and

managers, and of himself—was for, and thereby in the widest sense to rationalize or defend the position of the capitalist. Yet he was quietly generous in
disposals from his wealth, with others as well as with his family. In his later
years he determined that after his death much of it should be made available
to the general public. One gets the impression that his apparent frigidity and
ruthlessness owed much to his awkwardness when in the public eye and to
his unwillingness to pretend that, at the end of the day, all his exertions
were for the wider good. He was loyal to his deputies and to working men
who had served his companies well (though he retained to the end an implacable opposition to organized labor). Others, including both Carnegie and
Schwab, happily paraded as champions of the American worker. Nothing
would have been more out of character for Frick.

Through art Frick felt a transcendence that had no other parallel in his
life. A central mystery of this hard-headed, very rich businessman lies in his
lifelong aesthetic instinct and his passion for collecting. Unlike many of the
outstanding entrepreneurs of his generation, he did not view purchase of
works of art as merely another competitive activity, a cultural extension of
a business career. Near the end of his life, confined to his room in his New
York mansion, when his illness permitted he would say, "I think I would
like to go down and sit with my pictures." His longtime friend, Andrew
Mellon, also built up one of the world's great collections, as well as the
National Gallery of Art in Washington. When Mellon's son was asked how
his father had learned how to judge art, he answered without hesitation,
"Clay Frick taught him"—referring to the trip to Europe the two young
men made in summer 1880. Frick delighted in the art that the wealth he
made in coke and steel enabled him to accumulate. Carnegie distributed
much of his immense profit from steelmaking to philanthropy but often
referred to Skibo as his "heaven on earth." (At the same time Shadwell was
characterizing Homestead as "hell with the lid off.")

Over the generations since that time, much of the material base from
which fortunes and squalor alike had been made has been swept away. The
Connellsville region, which after mushroom growth became the world's
greatest center for the manufacture of metallurgical coke, now has an economy that has been stagnant for years. The median taxable income in the
region is less than two-thirds the figure for Pennsylvania. Population has
declined. On the positive side, the landscape has made a remarkable recovery from the savagery with which mining and coke making had treated it
and is once again an area of rolling, pleasant, reasonably prosperous rural
scenery. The beehive coke industry reached its peak in Frick's last years and
then began a long decline, its downward course being checked temporarily

at times of exceptional activity at the nation's blast furnaces. The last considerable battery of ovens—Shoaf, built by H. C. Frick Coke in 1904–1905—were last in production in 1972. After that the only coke made in the region has been to demonstrate an outmoded technology or on festival occasions. The branch railroads that ran widely through the district in its heyday have gone, their tracks either torn up or overgrown by rapidly growing secondary woodland. Amid these wasted areas are to be found the remnants of the coke works, broken or decaying as their brickwork collapses onto the old railroads, their abandoned equipment—larries, drawing machines, long iron rakes, old coke trucks—rusting undisturbed as weeds, bushes, and small trees take root everywhere, speeding but also softening and hiding the decay. Some of the "patches"—the old miners' and coke workers' settlements—remain, often as rather uninspiring low-quality residential areas, though many of the wood-framed former company houses have been remodeled and are now in good condition. Generally, the industrial relics of the region are quietly crumbling away, with no adequate recognition of the unique quality they add to the nation's heritage.

The industrial plants and the towns that grew up around them in the Monongahela Valley have also decayed, but here the process occurred later and is less advanced. Here too there can be no parallel to the coke region's return to something like rural gentility, and accordingly the results are much less mellow. For years after they closed, the skeletons of once great iron and steel works still stood, strung out alongside the river on the small meander-core flats that, in this highly dissected country, were the only suitable sites even for late nineteenth-century scales of production. Homestead works—famed worldwide for its industrial achievements, and equally notorious for its labor relations—now lies dead; Duquesne is partly dismantled; Donora went out of production thirty years ago. At Clairton the iron and steel plant was closed in the 1960s; only the blackened hulk of the massive coke oven plant remains active. The single important iron and steel mill still operating is the so-called Mon Valley works, a hybrid as its name suggests, involving much of the old Edgar Thomson mill. By the early 1980s the towns of Braddock, Homestead, and Duquesne already contained only one-third as many people as at the time of the deaths of Carnegie and Frick.

Yet Pittsburgh, the economic center of the district, has diversified and prospered. The decline of its basic industry, following pollution control ordinances, has transformed it from the archetypal Smokey City into a prosperous postindustrial metropolis. The dramatic sweep of its new skyscraper office cityscapes can best be seen and appreciated—both by day and perhaps even more impressively at night—from the heights of Mount Washington, which once looked out on a drab central city and on foul rivers across whose surfaces an endless commerce of workaday barges shuffled to and fro.

It would, however, be quite erroneous to conclude from this that the efforts of the industrial pioneers, the urgent toil of thousands of working-men, and the patience and often the poverty of their families were in vain. Foundations were being laid for the very different economic and social structures of the present day. This, with all qualifications and doubts, may legitimately be claimed as an achievement of the age of coal and steel. Whether Carnegie, Frick, Schwab, and all the other leaders of late nine-teenth- and early twentieth-century industry are to be celebrated as heroes of American economic growth or castigated as robber barons (two catego-ries that are not mutually exclusive), it is indisputable that they contributed much to the modern situation. They provided the leadership and organiza-tion that molded together the capital—originally of others, then increasingly that accumulated as profits from their own early operations—with the labor of the masses. On that basis has been built the more widely diffused afflu-ence of the late twentieth century.

Apart from the modern economy, there are other legacies from the lead-ers of the heroic age of big business. The wealth of Carnegie remains pro-ductive in the foundations he set up, and still more in the large number of libraries that he financed in the United States and in Great Britain. The great art of the Frick Collection in New York and, more modestly, of the two Frick galleries in Pittsburgh represent resources for today's society—resources that, like the great houses and estates of England, would not have been produced in, but can now be enjoyed by the members of a more egali-tarian society.

There was a heritage of fine buildings. Some it is true have made way for utilitarian structures. Carnegie's beloved "castle" of Skibo degenerated in semi-dereliction and has recently been harrowed by fire. "Riverside," the grand Manhattan château that Charlie Schwab built at Riverside Drive and Seventy-second Street was sold even before he died. Offered to and spurned by New York City, it was later demolished. In this respect the Frick legacy has fared better. His summer retreat of Eagle Rock has been demolished, but its gargantuan stable block still towers behind its high fence and, though designed for a humble role, possesses all the grandeur of a mansion. Num-ber One East Seventieth Street has been the splendid home for over fifty years of the Frick Collection. Clayton—by the standard of such houses a very modest home—has been lovingly restored at high expense and opened to the public as an exceptionally fine example of a wealthy businessman's late Victorian home.

Perhaps what above all remains at this distance in time is reputation or myth—of virtuous but exploited workers, of self-made men, of the iron heel of capitalism, of robber barons. In each of these, fact is inextricably interwoven with fiction. Carnegie, understandably, continues to appeal, as the Croesus who was at the same time a silver-tongued apologist for big business. There is continuing interest in his presentation of the rapacity of the capitalist as at the same time in accordance with the laws of evolution and a means to benefit society as a whole, the very pith and marrow of triumphant democracy. He is regarded as the most farseeing and generous of the capitalist-philanthropists, and the strange anomalies of his character make him one of the most interesting of all the great leaders of this unrivaled age of industrial giants. Schwab's reputation is much more narrowly based, but he retains it for industrial genius combined with an easy and widely extended bonhomie. Both men were more complex characters than is often supposed.

Frick's business abilities have been generally recognized, but it is understandable that his inflexibility, insensitivity, and ruthlessness—never so openly displayed as during the Homestead strike—have dominated the often vague public consciousness ever since. For the man or woman in the street, especially in Western Pennsylvania, these qualities still color the image of Frick. Since Clayton was reopened after restoration in September 1990, it has become a popular destination for tourist visits in the region. Yet, in some instances, when members of coach parties have learned for the first time on their arrival whose home they were about to enter, some of them have refused to go in. Here indeed, the evil that men do lives after them.

The great industrial magnates of the turn of the century were outstanding men. Such a description does not automatically justify the use of the additional adjective *admirable*. Henry Clay Frick was a worthy member of their front ranks. He was typical of his peer group in his attitudes and values, nineteenth-century standards that may not now be esteemed so highly. Yet he was much more complicated than his stereotype. Here indeed was one who, like the rest of humankind, was partly the maker of his fate, but who was also largely shaped by heredity and upbringing and by the external circumstances of place and time. He was not after all "the Man" of Carnegie's dreams, or of Harvey's adulation, but he was an outstanding man for all that.

Appendix A

Statistical Tables

━━◄〰〰►━━

TABLE 1
The Connellsville Coke Industry, 1880–1919

Date	Ovens	Shipments	Average Price	Bessemer Pig Price
1880	7,211	2,206[a]	1.79[b]	na[c]
1881	8,208	2,639	1.63	na
1882	9,283	3,043	1.47	na
1883	10,176	3,552	1.14	na
1884	10,543	3,192	1.13	na
1885	10,471	3,096	1.22	na
1886	10,952	4,180	1.36	18.96
1887	11,923	4,147	1.79	21.37
1888	13,975	4,955	1.19	17.38
1889	14,458	5,930	1.34	18.00
1890	16,020	6,464	1.94	18.87
1891	17,204	4,761	1.87	15.95
1892	17,256	6,329	1.83	14.37
1893	17,513	4,806	1.49	12.87
1894	17,834	5,454	1.00	11.38
1895	17,947	8,244	1.23	12.72
1896	18,351	5,412	1.90	12.14
1897	18,628	6,915	1.65	10.13
1898	18,643	8,460	1.55	10.33
1899	19,689	10,130	2.00	19.03
1900	20,954	10,166	2.70	19.49
1901	21,575	12,610	1.95	15.93
1902	26,329	14,139	2.37	20.67
1903	28,092	13,345	3.00	18.98
1904	29,119	12,427	1.75	13.76
1905	30,842	17,896	2.26	16.36
1906	34,059	19,999	2.75	19.54
1907	35,697	19,029	2.90	19.43
1908	37,842	10,700	1.80	17.23
1909	39,158	17,786	2.00	16.40
1910	39,137	18,690	2.10	na
1911	38,904	16,334	1.72	na

(*continued*)

TABLE 1 (*continued*)

Date	Ovens	Shipments	Average Price	Bessemer Pig Price
1912	38,884	20,001	1.92	na
1913	39,067	20,098	2.95	na
1914	37,965	14,076	2.00	na
1915	38,986	17,921	1.80	na
1916	38,362	21,654	2.58	na
1917	38,110	17,806	6.25	na
1918	37,061	16,138[d]	7.25	na
1919	35,758	10,255[d]	4.70	na

Sources: Coke data are from annual statistics quoted in the *Connellsville Courier* (note that these figures do not coincide with those quoted by Eavenson). For later dates, the figures clearly include outlying districts as well as Connellsville "proper." Bessemer pig prices are from AISA.

Notes: [a] Figures are in thousand net tons.

[b] Figures are dollars per ton.

[c] Figures are dollars per gross ton.

[d] Figures are for production, not shipments.

TABLE 2

H. C. Frick Coke, South West Coal and Coke, and All Connellsville

	H. C. Frick Coke		South West		All Connellsville	
	Works	Ovens	Works	Ovens	Works	Ovens
1870	—	—	—	—	7	300
1876	2	201	—	—	45	3,455
1882	9	1,022	3	674	67	8,430
1886	13	2,639	4	672	72	12,918
1894	27	7,202	4	1,202	85	17,613
1899	na	na	na	na	na	18,643
1901 +	41	10,473	4	1,232	96	21,919

Sources: The *Connellsville Courier, Coal and Coke,* etc.

Note: Figures for 1901 refer to 1 January 1901.

TABLE 3

H. C. Frick Coke and Rival Companies, 1882–1901

	Frick	Cochran	Schoonmaker	McClure	Rainey
1882	1,022	280	662	294	313
1886	2,639	160	1,016	1,264	436
1894	7,202	108	—	2,153	1,422
1901	10,473	108	—	—	2,905

Sources: The Connellsville Courier, Coal and Coke, etc.
Note: Figures are numbers of ovens.

TABLE 4

Bessemer Rail Production, 1867–1907

Year	Total U.S. Production	Price	Percentage of Total U.S. Production			
			Edgar Thomson	Other Pennsylvania Mills	Illinois Mills	Other States
1867	2,277[a]	166.00[b]	—	na	na	na
1868	6,451	158.50	—	na	na	na
1869	8,616	132.25	—	na	na	na
1870	30,357	106.79	—	na	na	na
1871	34,152	102.52	—	na	na	na
1872	83,991	111.94	—	na	na	na
1873	115,192	120.58	—	na	na	na
1874	129,414	94.28	bldg	46.16	33.31	20.53
1875	259,699	68.75	2.25	36.54	38.23	22.98
1876	368,269	59.25	8.75	40.65	32.42	18.18
1877	385,865	45.58	12.65	45.32	20.71	21.31
1878	491,427	42.21	13.13	42.85	26.12	17.90
1879	610,682	48.21	12.45	41.38	28.93	17.24
1880	852,196	67.52	11.75	40.19	26.99	21.07
1881	1,187,770	61.08	12.76	38.98	26.03	22.23
1882	1,284,067	48.50	11.18	41.63	23.37	23.82
1883	1,148,709[c]	37.75	13.48	50.22	17.98	18.32
1884	996,983[c]	30.75	14.45	53.90	25.99	5.66
1885	959,471[c]	28.52	13.20	55.34	28.68	2.78
1886	1,574,703	34.52	10.99	52.02	24.44	12.56
1887	2,101,904	37.08	9.18	45.06	30.95	14.81
1888	1,386,277[c]	29.83	10.70	49.21	32.89	8.62
1889	1,510,057	29.25	18.37	49.11	30.87	1.65
1890	1,867,837	31.78	17.82	52.47	28.08	1.62

(continued)

TABLE 4 (*continued*)

Year	Total U.S. Production	Price	Percentage of Total U.S. Production			
			Edgar Thomson	Other Pennsylvania Mills	Illinois Mills	Other States
1891	1,293,053ᶜ	29.92	20.45	49.24	28.21	2.10
1892	1,537,588	30.00	21.49	41.07	29.30	8.13
1893	1,129,400ᶜ	28.13	20.39	44.08	20.69	14.83
1894	1,016,013ᶜ	24.00	21.69	48.68	22.27	7.36
1895	1,299,628	24.33	24.99	41.53	25.21	8.27
1896	1,116,958ᶜ	28.00	26.93	33.42	27.87	11.77
1897	1,644,520	18.75	29.03	33.48	26.55	10.94
1898	1,976,702	17.63	28.42	24.87	27.78	18.93
1899	2,270,585	28.13	26.62	27.33	25.92	20.14
1900	2,383,654	32.29	26.30	23.85	25.38	24.47
1901	2,870,816	27.33	24.66	24.31	24.52	26.50
1902	2,935,392	28.00	24.18	14.94	25.09	35.79
1903	2,946,756	28.00	24.94	15.32	22.02	37.72
1904	2,137,957ᶜ	28.00	25.77	11.87	23.77	38.73
1905	3,192,347	28.00	22.57	na	na	na
1906	3,791,459	28.00	21.80	na	na	na
1907	3,380,025ᶜ	28.00	22.39	na	na	na

Sources: Iron Age, 14 April 1904, p. 18; AISA annual statistics, U.S. Department of Commerce, *Historical Statistics of the United States,* 1960, p. 123.
Notes: ᵃ Figures this column are in thousand gross tons.
ᵇ Figures this column are in dollars.
ᶜ Indicates years that U.S. production fell from previous year.

TABLE 5
Capacities in the Bessemer Rail Trade, 1890–1904

Leading Rail Mills	Date Established	1890	1896	1901	1904
Pittsburgh and Valleys					
Carnegie Steel					
Edgar Thomson	1875	380	450	c.650	c.650
Duquesne	1889	200	c.400	—	—
National Steel					
Youngstown	1899	—	—	c.600	c.600
Subtotal		580	850	1,250	1,250
East					
Pennsylvania/ Maryland Steel					
Steelton	1867	180	180	180	300
Sparrows Point	1891	—	c.300	c.300	c.400
Troy Steel, Troy	1866	110	110	—	—
Bethlehem Iron	1873	205	205	205	—
Lackawanna, Scranton	1875–1883	400	c.450	c.630	—
Subtotal		895	1,245	1,315	700
Erie Shore					
Cleveland Rolling Mill	1868	90	c.100	c.150	—
Lorain Steel	1895	—	180	c.500	c.550
Lackawanna Steel, Buffalo	1903	—	—	—	600
Subtotal		90	280	650	1,150
Chicago					
Illinois Steel					
Union works	1871	270	270	—	—
North Chicago	1872	170	120	—	—
Joliet	1873	190	300	540	—
South Chicago	1882	270	360	c.675	720
Springfield Company	na	135	135	—	—
Subtotal		1,030	1,185	1,215	720
West					
Colorado Fuel and Iron, Pueblo	1882	55	120	200	300
Total capacity		2,650	3,680	4,630	4,120
Annual average output previous five years		1,506	1,255	1,878	2,681

Source: AISA works directories and annual statistics.
Note: Annual average output from 1903 to 1907 was 3,090.

TABLE 6

Net Profits of the Carnegie Associates, 1875–1900

Year	Profit	Year	Profit
1875	18.6	1888	1,941
1876	171.8	1889	3,540
1877	190.4	1890	5,350
1878	300.3	1891	4,300
1879	512.1	1892	4,000
1880	1,557.8	1893	3,000
1881	2,000.4	1894	4,000
1882	2,128.4	1895	5,000
1883	1,019.2	1896	6,000
1884	1,301.2	1897	7,000
1885	1,192.0	1898	11,500
1886	2,925.3	1899	21,000
1887	3,441.9	1900	40,000

Source: Carnegie Steel Company records in Frick Papers.
Note: Figures are in thousands of dollars. The figures cover the
Edgar Thomson Steel Company, 1876–1881; Carnegie Brothers and
Company, 1881–1892; Carnegie, Phipps, and Company, 1886–1892;
and the Carnegie Steel Company, 1892–1900. Profits for 1900 in-
clude those of the H. C. Frick Coke Company.

TABLE 7

Production of Steel by Carnegie Steel Company, 1888–1900

	USA	Carnegie Steel	Carnegie Steel as Percentage of USA
1888	2,899	332	11.5
1889	3,386	537	15.8
1890	4,277	660	15.4
1891	3,904	797	20.4
1892	4,928	878	17.8
1893	4,020	863	21.5
1894	4,412	1,115	25.3
1895	6,115	1,464	23.9
1896	5,282	1,375	26.0
1897	7,157	1,686	23.6
1898	8,933	2,171	24.3
1899	10,640	2,663	25.0
1900	10,188	2,970	29.1

Source: AISA and Carnegie Steel Company (USX).
Note: Figures are in thousands of gross tons.

TABLE 8

Indicators of the Efficiency of Carnegie Steel, 1890s

	Net Profit Per Ingot Ton	Value of Products Shipped	Net Profits as Percentage of Value Shipped	Wages Paid	Wages as Percentage of Value Shipped
1892	4.56[a]	46,225[b]	8.65[c]	7,271[b]	15.73[c]
1895	3.41	52,494	9.52	7,294	13.89
1897	4.15	62,897	11.13	7,546	12.00
1899	7.88	104,999	20.00	10,992	10.47

Source: Carnegie Steel Company (ACLC).
Notes: [a] Figures this column are in dollars.
[b] Figures this column are in thousand dollars.
[c] Figures this column are percentages.

TABLE 9

Capacity of U.S. Steel Corporation and Companies, 1901

	Pig Iron	Bessemer Ingots	Open-Hearth Ingots	Finished Products
Carnegie Steel	2,740	2,000	1,900	3,866
Federal Steel	1,855	1,760	240	2,360
National Steel	2,325	2,100	110	2,000
National Tube	605	480	—	996
American Steel and Wire	1,030	935	365	2,645
American Steel Hoop	500	—	10	730
Lorain Steel	400	550	—	506
American Sheet Steel	—	—	247	920
American Bridge	—	—	230	na
American Tin Plate	—	—	—	534
Shelby Steel Tube	—	—	—	44
Troy works	—	—	—	275
Total	9,455	7,825	3,102	14,876

Source: Jeans 1902, p. 185.
Note: Figures are in thousand tons.

TABLE 10

U.S. Steel Corporation and Total U.S. Production, 1902, 1909, 1919

	Percentage of Total Output		
	1902	1909	1919
Iron ore (all)	45.1	45.7	42.1
Lake Superior ore	60.4	51.4	45.9
Coke	37.4	34.6	na
Pig iron, etc.	44.7	45.0	44.0
Bessemer steel	73.9	62.7	65.8
Open-hearth steel	52.4	51.8	46.0
Steel rails	65.4	57.3	62.0
Plates and sheets	59.4	49.8	44.3
Total finished rolled	50.8	48.9	44.6

Sources: U.S. Commissioner of Corporations 1911, pp. 360–63; Cotter 1921, p. 308.

TABLE 11

U.S. Steel Corporation Coke Production, 1901–1919

	Beehive	By-Product	Total	Percentage U.S. Total
1901	8,968	—	8,968	41.1[a]
1902	9,521	—	9,521	37.4
1903	8,639	19	8,658	34.2
1904	8,539	113	8,652	36.6
1905	11,930	313	12,243	37.9
1906	12,900	395	13,295	36.5
1907	12,716	829	13,545	33.2
1908	7,591	579	8,170	31.3
1909	11,896	1,694	13,590	34.6
1910	11,641	2,008	13,649	32.7
1911	9,491	2,629	12,120	34.1
1912	11,545	5,164	16,709	38.0
1913	11,062	5,601	16,663	36.0
1914	7,093	4,081	11,174	32.3
1915	9,702	4,799	14,501	34.9
1916	12,479	6,423	18,902	34.7
1917	11,177	6,284	17,461	31.4
1918	9,962	7,795	17,757	31.4
1919	5,933	9,530	15,463	35.0

Source: U.S. Commissioner of Corporations 1910; Cotter 1921, pp. 310, 311; Bureau of Mines annual.

Note: Figures in first three columns are in thousand tons.

[a] Figures this column are percentages.

TABLE 12
Steel Capacity of U.S. Steel Corporation, Pittsburgh and Chicago, 1901, 1920

	1901	1920
Pittsburgh area		
Edgar Thomson	1,000	1,380
Homestead	1,900	2,130
Duquesne	1,000	1,356
McKeesport	300	689
Donora	built 1902–1903	750
Clairton	built 1901–1902	650
Total	4,200	6,955
Chicago area		
Union	325	dismantled
Joliet	600	732
South Works	1,075	2,345
Gary	—	3,045
Total	2,000	6,122

Source: AISI, *Directory of the Iron and Steel Works in the United States and Canada.*
Note: Figures are in thousand gross tons.

TABLE 13
Allegheny County Share of Total U.S. Output, 1891–1919

Year	Pig Iron	Ingot Steel	Year	Pig Iron	Ingot Steel
1891	17.6	35.3	1906	22.5	29.9
1892	19.4	32.6	1907	21.1	29.5
1893	23.8	39.6	1908	24.6	32.0
1894	26.8	42.9	1909	21.3	27.9
1895	21.7	39.4	1910	19.5	27.4
1896	23.9	41.9	1911	21.6	27.2
1897	27.6	39.5	1912	20.5	24.9
1898	25.7	38.4	1913	19.4	24.5
1899	23.9	38.9	1914	20.0	24.9
1900	22.6	39.8	1915	19.9	24.1
1901	23.2	38.1	1916	18.3	21.7
1902	23.9	37.9	1917	16.1	19.9
1903	23.4	37.2	1918	16.3	19.1
1904	26.6	38.0	1919	18.4	22.0
1905	23.5	32.9			

Source: AISA, AISI annual statistics, and U.S. Department of Commerce 1960.
Note: Figures are percentages.

Appendix B

Biographical Notes

━━◅ⅉ⟡ⅉ▻━━

ABBOTT, WILLIAM L. 1852–1930. b. New Haven, Conn. Joined Carnegies as clerk, 1871. Worked at Edgar Thomson, then as superintendant of Union mills. Vice-chairman of Carnegie, Phipps, and Co., 1886. Chairman, 1889. Director of Carnegie Brothers, 1889. Retired, July 1892.

BRIDGE, JAMES H. 1856–1939. Private secretary to Herbert Spencer, 1879–1884. Emigrated to USA, 1884. "Literary assistant" to A. Carnegie, 1884–1889. Curator Frick Art Collection, 1914–1928.

CARNEGIE, A. 1835–1919. b. Dunfermline, Scotland. Came to USA, 1848. Worked in cotton factory, as telegraph boy, then on Pennsylvania Railroad. Went into iron trade with Keystone Bridge Company and Union Iron Mills after Civil War. Entered steel trade of Pittsburgh area, 1872, through Carnegie, McCandless, and Co. with the building of Edgar Thomson works (in production, 1875). Acquired Homestead, 1883, and Duquesne steelworks, 1890. Carnegie Bros. and Carnegie, Phipps, and Co. merged as Carnegie Steel Co., 1892. This reconstructed and amalgamated with H. C. Frick Coke Co. as a division of the Carnegie Co., 1900. Agreed sale of Carnegie interests to become part of U.S. Steel Corp., 1901. Retired to practice philanthropy, advocacy of world peace, etc., 1901.

CARNEGIE, TOM M. 1843–1886. b. Dunfermline, Scotland. Worked on Pennsylvania Railroad, in oil transportation, and in telegraphs. Partner with brother, Andrew, in iron enterprises, from 1865. Associated with building of Lucy furnaces (the first Carnegie iron-making plant), 1870–1872, and of Edgar Thomson works, 1873–1875. Chairman of Carnegie Bros., 1881–1886. Shared in forming Carnegie, Phipps, and Co., 1886.

CONVERSE, EDMUND C. 1849–1921. Educated as an apprentice in the tube trade while father was president of original National Tube Co. Associated with early stages of U.S. Steel Corp.

COREY, WILLIAM, E. 1866–1934. b. Braddock. Entered chemical laboratory at Edgar Thomson, 1882. Transferred to Homestead, 1887. Superintendent plate mill, 1889. Superintendent armor plate mill, 1893. General superintendent Homestead, 1897. President Carnegie Steel Co., 1901–1903. President U.S. Steel Corp., 1903–1911. Later interested in Midvale Steel and Ordnance Co.

DINKEY, ALVA C. 1866–1931. b. Weatherly, Pa. Brother to Rana (Mrs. C. M. Schwab). Water boy at Edgar Thomson works, 1879. Assistant to general superintendent Homestead, 1899–1901. General superintendent Homestead, 1901–1903. President Carnegie Steel Co., 1903–1915. President Midvale Co., 1915–1923.

DONNER, WILLIAM H. 1864–1953. Organized National Tin Plate Co. at Anderson, Indiana, 1894. Built tinplate mill at Monessen, 1897. Sold both Anderson and Mones-

sen mills to American Tin Plate Co., 1898. With A. Mellon and Frick set up
Union Steel Co. at Donora, 1900. Undertook assessment of Cerro de Pasco copper
mining project for Frick. Interested in Cambria Steel Co., 1905. President Pennsylvania Steel Co., 1914. Purchased New York State Steel Co. and organized Donner Steel Co., 1915.

EDENBORN, WILLIAM. 1848–1926. b. Westphalia, Prussia. Emigrated to USA, 1867.
Worked as mechanic in St. Louis and became practical wire drawer. President St.
Louis Wire Mill Co., 1877–1882. President Consolidated Steel and Wire Co., 1890s.
Vice-president American Steel and Wire Co., 1898–1901. Member executive com-
mittee and then advisory committees of U.S. Steel Corp., 1901–1904.

FARRELL, JAMES A. 1863–1943. b. New Haven, Conn. Began work as wire drawer locally
in 1879. Joined Oliver Iron and Steel Co., 1888. Worked for Pittsburgh Wire Co.,
by 1889. General manager, sold over half their output in hitherto neglected foreign markets during depression of 1893. When Pittsburgh Wire Co. absorbed by
American Steel and Wire, became general manager export division, 1899. Head
U.S. Steel Products Export Co., 1903. Established sixty agencies and warehouses
in South America, South Africa, Europe, China, and Australia, and a steamship
fleet to carry export products. President U.S. Steel, 1911. Succeeded Gary as chief
executive, 1927. Retired, 1932.

FELTON, EDGAR C. 1858–1937. Joined Pennsylvania Steel Co., 1880. President, 1896.

GARY, ELBERT H. 1846–1927. b. Wheaton, Ill. Practised law in Illinois, 1867–1892.
Helped form amalgamation that produced the Consolidated Steel and Wire Co.,
1892, became counsel, then director. Helped form American Steel and Wire Co.,
1898, then Federal Steel Co., 1898, became president of latter. Chairman U.S. Steel,
1901–1927.

GATES, JOHN W. 1855–1911. b. Turner Junction, Chicago. Worked in hardware store, to
1878. Salesman, partner, and manufacturer in wire firms, to 1892. Leading partner
Consolidated Steel and Wire Co., 1892–1897, and American Steel and Wire Co.,
1898–1901. Succeeded Jay Morse as president Illinois Steel Co., 1894. Active with
Moore brothers in unsuccessful negotiations for a major trust in steel including
Carnegie Steel, 1899. Played marginal part in forming U.S. Steel, then was excluded from it. Involved in forming Republic Iron and Steel Co., 1899. In a northern group that took over Tennessee Coal, Iron, and Railroad Co., 1906.

GAYLEY, JAMES. 1855–1920. b. Lockhaven, Pa. After college, chemist in iron works at
Catasauqua, on Lehigh River, 1877–1880. Superintendent Edgar Thomson blast
furnace plant, 1885. Later superintendent Edgar Thomson works and partner of
Carnegie Steel Co. First vice-president U.S. Steel Corp. in charge of ore, 1901–
1909.

HARVEY, GEORGE B. M. 1864–1928. b. Vermont. Journalist, 1880s. Built and managed
electric railroads, 1890s. Formed syndicate to acquire lines in Cuba, 1898. Returned to publishing, 1900–1914. Supported Wilson for president, 1912. Estranged,
gave support to Charles E. Hughes (Republican), 1916. Established *North American Review*'s *War Weekly*, later known as *Harvey's Weekly*, which bitterly denounced the Wilson administration, 1918. Harding's ambassador in United
Kingdom, from April 1921 to Dec. 1923. Produced various books before *Henry
Clay Frick: The Man*, 1928.

KENNEDY, JULIAN. 1852–1932. b. Poland, Ohio. Worked in iron industry of Valleys district, then to Edgar Thomson and Lucy furnaces. General superintendent Carnegie, Phipps, and Co., 1885–1888. Installed first American basic open-hearth furnaces at Homestead, 1886. Designed Homestead armor plate mill. Chief engineer Latrobe Steel Co., 1888. Consulting engineer in Pittsburgh, 1890. Sir Lowthian Bell (d. 1904) once remarked that in Britain Kennedy was considered the greatest engineer in the world. Appraised plants for J. P. Morgan when shaping U.S. Steel Corp., 1901.

KNOX, PHILANDER, C. 1853–1921. b. Brownsville, Pa. Admitted to bar, 1875. Member law firm of Knox and Reed, 1877 onward. Legal counsel Carnegie Steel Co. Attorney General of USA, 1901–1904, and U.S. Secretary of State, 1909–1913.

LEISHMAN, JOHN G. A. 1857–1924. b. Pittsburgh. Worked for Schoenberger. Then senior member Leishman and Snyder, steelbrokers, Pittsburgh, 1881–1886. Joined Carnegies, 1886. President Carnegie Steel Co., 1895–1897. Entered diplomacy, U.S. representative in Switzerland (1897–1900), Turkey (1900–1906), Italy (1909–1911), and Germany (1911–1913) in turn.

LINDSAY, HOMER J. 1860–? Private secretary to Tom Carnegie, and later assistant to president Carnegie Steel Co.

LOVEJOY, FRANCIS T. 1854–1932. b. Baltimore, Md. Worked in Pennsylvania oil region as telegrapher, stenographer, bookkeeper, newspaperman, oil producer, refiner, 1870–1880. Moved to Pittsburgh, 1880. Joined Carnegie group as clerk, 1881. Auditor to Carnegie companies, secretary Carnegie Bros., 1889. Member board of managers Carnegie Bros. and Carnegie, Phipps, and Co., 1891. Secretary Carnegie Steel Co., from 1892 to Jan. 1900. Conducted negotiations on behalf of H. C. Frick with Carnegie Steel, March 1900. Took up gold mining, 1902–1903. President of one and vice-president of three mining companies, by 1904–1905.

LYNCH, THOMAS. 1854–1915. b. Uniontown, Pa. Began work as country store clerk, 1872. In company store in Connellsville district, 1875–1876. Superintendent of a mine and plant of H. C. Frick Coke Co., 1877. General superintendent, 1882. General manager, 1890. President H. C. Frick Coke Co., 1897.

MELLON, ANDREW W. 1855–1937. b. Pittsburgh, Pa. Banker and industrialist, and later Secretary of the Treasury. Took over from his father, Thomas Mellon (1813–1908), the control of the Pittsburgh banking concern that became Mellon National Bank. Widely associated with coal, coke, and steel enterprises, etc., including Union Steel, Alcoa, the Koppers Co. From late youth a close friend and later business associate of H. C. Frick.

MOORE, WILLIAM H. 1848–1923. b. Utica, N.Y. Practised law, especially corporation law, in Chicago, from 1872. With his brother, James H. Moore, engaged in trust promotion. Produced the "Moore Group" of steel concerns (with capitalization $187 million), National Steel Co., American Tin Plate Co., American Sheet Steel Co., and American Steel Hoop Co. Negotiated unsuccessfully to acquire Carnegie Steel Co., 1899.

MORGAN, JOHN PIERPONT. 1837–1913. b. Hartford, Conn. U.S. agent for London banker Peabody and Co., 1860. Member of Drexel, Morgan, and Co. and of J. S. Morgan, 1971. Financed reorganization of railroads, industrial companies, and ocean transport, 1890s. Organized U.S. Steel Corp., from Dec. 1900 to March 1901.

MORRISON, THOMAS. 1861–? b. Scotland. To USA, 1886. Entered Homestead machine shops. Superintendent Duquesne works, 1891. Superintendent Edgar Thomson, 1895–1903.

OLIVER, HENRY W. 1840–1904. b. Ireland. Moved to Pittsburgh, 1842. With brother formed Oliver Wire Co., 1881. Bought barbed wire plant from Joliet and moved it to Pittsburgh, c. 1881, built wire rod mill, 1882, also wire nail works. Interest in Hainsworth Steel Co., Pittsburgh, 1889. Early interest in Upper Lake iron ore led to form Oliver Iron Mining Co. and close association with Carnegie Steel.

RAINEY, WILLIAM J. 1834–1900. Sold coal in Ohio, starting as an agent for coke, before 1877. Entered coke production with Fort Hill ovens, 1879. Eventually major producer.

REED, JAMES H. 1853–1927. b. Allegheny City, Pa. Admitted to bar, 1875. Member Knox and Reed Co., 1877–1902. President Pittsburgh, Bessemer, and Lake Erie Railroad.

REID, DAVID G. 1858–1925. b. Indiana. Banker. Became interested in tinplate industry, 1890s. Involved in organizing American Tin Plate Co. and later National Steel Co., American Steel Hoop Co., and American Sheet Steel Co., late 1890s. Director and member executive committee U.S. Steel, 1901.

ROBERTS, PERCIVAL. Civil and mining engineer who became president American Bridge Co.

SCHWAB, CHARLES M. 1862–1939. b. Williamsburg, Pa. Worked as engineering corps stake driver at Edgar Thomson works, 1879. Later draughtsman. Chief engineer and assistant manager there, 1881–1887. Superintendent Homestead, 1887–1889. General superintendent Edgar Thomson, 1889–1892. General superintendent Homestead, 1892–1897. President Carnegie Steel Co., 1897–1901. President U.S. Steel Corp., 1901–1903. Bought controlling interest Bethlehem Steel Co., summer 1901. President, then chairman Bethlehem Steel Corp., 1904–1939. Director general U.S. Shipping Board Emergency Fleet Corp., from April to Dec. 1918.

STACKHOUSE, POWELL. 1840–1927. Joined Cambria Iron Co., 1856. President Cambria Iron and its successor, Cambria Steel Co., 1892–1910.

Notes

━━◈◈◈━━

Unless otherwise noted, all correspondence to and from Henry Clay Frick is to be found in the Henry Clay Frick Papers, Helen Clay Frick Foundation, Pittsburgh (referred to throughout as Frick Papers).

ABBREVIATIONS USED IN THE NOTES

AC	Andrew Carnegie
ACLC	Carnegie Papers, Library of Congress
AISA	American Iron and Steel Association. (Later this became the American Iron and Steel Institute [AISI].)
BAISA	Bulletin of the American Iron and Steel Association
CMS	Charles M. Schwab
HCF	Henry Clay Frick
TMC	Tom M. Carnegie
USX	Carnegie Papers and U.S. Steel Corporation Papers, Pittsburgh.

PREFACE

1. H. N. Casson 1907, p. 175, see also pp. 175–81.

1. PROLOGUE: FOUNDATIONS FOR A BUSINESS LIFE

1. Rostow 1971, pp. 6–10.
2. E. L. Godkin quoted in Kirkland 1952, pp. 27, 31; W. G. Sumner quoted in Blum et al. 1973, p. 432.
3. Temin 1964, p. 5.
4. Henry Clay Frick (hereafter HCF) quoted in Bridge 1903, p. viii.
5. Hendrick 1932, pp. 415–16.
6. Wall 1970, p. 479; Bridge 1903, p. 170.
7. Jenkins 1904.
8. Overman 1850, p. 174; Lesley 1859; Fulton 1905, p. 153.
9. Harvey 1928 makes no mention of this, but it is referred to in a short biographical note that appeared in HCF's lifetime, Jordan 1915.
10. Overholt, Frick, and Company, Day Book, Frick Papers; Harvey 1928, pp. 29–31.
11. Harvey 1928, pp. 38–41; quotation is from Lorant 1988, p. 233;
12. Harvey 1928, p. 62.

13. Hendrick 1932, pp. 172, 173.

14. For the Connellsville Locomotive works, see BAISA, 10 and 17 June 1878, p. 165.

15. Harvey 1928, p. 51.

16. Ibid., chap. 4, is good on this period. See also J. Moore quoted in Weingartner, 1988, pp. 9, 10.

17. HCF to M. Twombly, 12 Dec. 1882.

18. HCF to T. Lynch, 25 Nov. 1882.

19. HCF to Lynch, undated (1880s).

20. HCF to J. G. A. Leishman, 6 July 1885.

21. HCF to J. Maclean, HCF to J. H. Norton, 22 Sept. 1882.

22. HCF to W. N. Page, 22 June 1881.

23. HCF to C. C. Beggs, 3 Oct. 1881; HCF to W. J. Hitchorn, 1 May 1883.

24. HCF to G. D. Nickel, 13 June 1881; Nickel to HCF, 1 Aug. 1881; HCF to Nickel, 28 April 1883.

25. Shinn 1879–1880, p. 24; Harvey 1928, p. 66.

26. HCF to Thomas Carnegie (hereafter TMC), 6 April 1883.

27. Harvey 1928, pp. 55–57, has an interesting if rather bland account of this practice.

28. *Annual Report of Secretary of Internal Affairs of Pennsylvania* 1878–1879; HCF to TMC, 6 April 1883.

29. Harvey 1928, pp. 68–74; quotation is from J. Moore, in Weingartner 1988, p. 11.

2. COMPLEXITIES IN COKE AND STEEL

1. AC to F. B. Hubbell, 5 Oct. 1872; G. Lauder to AC, 19 Feb. 1872 (both in USX).

2. AC to E. C. Biddle, 19, 22 May 1873 (USX); see also Lauder to AC, 16 April 1873.

3. AC to TMC, 2 Feb. 1872 (USX).

4. Lauder memorandum to Carnegie brothers, Dec. 1879 (USX).

5. Wilson, Boyle, and Playford to Lauder, 1 Dec. 1879; Lauder to AC, 2 Dec. 1879 (both in USX).

6. AC to S. M. Felton, 6 Feb. 1880; D. A. Stewart to AC, 28 Feb. 1880 (both in USX).

7. Phipps to AC, 28 Feb. 1880; Stewart to AC, 6 March 1880 (both in USX).

8. Phipps to AC, 1 Jan. 1880; Lauder to AC, 25 Feb. 1880 (both in USX).

9. AC to W. J. Rainey, 4 March 1881 (USX).

10. Lauder to AC, 2 March 1880; TMC to AC, 8 March 1880 (both in USX).

11. Lauder to AC, 2 March 1880 (USX).

12. Lynch quoted in Keighley 1900.

13. AC to A. Cassatt, 18 March 1881 (USX).

14. Hendrick 1932, p. 249; Carnegie 1920, pp. 221–222.

15. Phipps to AC, 16 Jan. 1880 (USX).

16. HCF to AC, 18 Nov. 1882 (USX).

17. HCF to TMC, 30 Nov. 1881; see also AC to Carnegie Brothers, 15 Dec. 1881 (both in USX).

18. TMC to AC, 13 Dec. 1881 (USX).

19. This account is taken from Harvey 1928, pp. 74, 75, and Wall 1970, pp. 483, 484.

20. AC cable to TMC, 23 or 24 Dec. 1881; AC to R. Garrett, 28 Dec. 1881 (both in USX).

21. Phipps to AC, 4 Jan. 1882 (USX).

22. Phipps to AC, 29 March 1882 (USX).

23. AC to HCF, 6 Jan. 1882 (USX).

24. AC to Cassatt, 11 Jan. 1882 (USX).

25. AC to O. W. Potter, 25 April 1882 (USX).

26. AC to HCF, 22 Dec. 1882; HCF to TMC, 6 April 1883.

27. HCF to AC, 13 Aug. 1883.

28. H. C. Frick Coke Co. records (USX).

29. HCF to A. Tinstman, 5 June 1882; HCF to J. Overholt, 6 Nov. 1882; HCF to Dillinger and Tarr, 12 Aug. 1882.

30. HCF to Chicago and Connellsville Coke Co., 4 Dec. 1882; HCF to Lynch, 25 Nov. 1882.

31. HCF to AC, 18, 19 Nov. 1883, in Frick Papers; letter and report from Lauder to AC, 14 Nov. 1883 (USX).

32. HCF to AC, 1 April 1885, and Carnegie Steel Co. records, in Frick Papers.

33. The only source found for this story is Frick's obituary notice in the *New York City Mail*, 2 Dec. 1919. See also *Engineering and Mining Journal*, 12 Jan. 1884, p. 19, and 16 Aug. 1884, p. 108.

34. Phipps to AC, undated (before fall 1886) (USX).

35. AC to W. P. Shinn, 10 April, 28 Aug., 1876, and Oct. 1878 (all in USX).

36. HCF memorandum, 9 Dec. 1884; J. S. Wilson to HCF, 18 May 1886.

37. Bridge 1931, pp. 67, 68.

38. TMC to HCF, undated penciled note in Frick Papers.

39. AC to HCF, 25 Feb. 1886.

40. Carnegie 1920, p. 142.

41. Recording Tom's death in his own *Autobiography* almost thirty years later, Andrew Carnegie provided another example of his faulty recollections: "My Mother and my brother passed away in November within a few days of each other" (p. 212). Margaret Carnegie died on 10 November, Tom on 19 October.

42. H. Curry to HCF, 8 Nov., 1 Dec. 1886.

43. AC to HCF, undated (early 1886).

44. *American Manufacturer*, 19 Feb. 1886, p. 10, and 26 Feb. 1886, p. 10.

45. M. A. Lambing to HCF, 23 Feb. 1887.

46. *Pittsburgh Times*, 27 June 1887.

47. *Keystone Courier*, 17 June 1887.

48. J. M. Schoonmaker to HCF, 4 May 1887.

49. HCF to Phipps and Walker, 13 May, 7 June 1887, quoted in Harvey 1928, p. 85.

50. Lynch to HCF, 2 June 1887.

51. AC to HCF, 1 June 1887; HCF to Phipps, Walker, and others, 7 June 1887; Cambria Iron Co. to HCF, 4 June 1887; J. H. Bailey to HCF, 14 June 1887.

52. Lynch to HCF, 7 Nov. 1887.

53. HCF to AC, 3 May 1882; AC to O. W. Potter, 25 April 1882 (USX); HCF to AC, 20 Dec. 1883.

54. Press report, 4 Feb. 1884; HCF to J. Morse, 19 Sept. 1885.

55. HCF to Cambria Iron Co., 8 July 1884; Minutes of H. C. Frick Coke Co., 25

Nov. 1885, 27 Jan. 1886, in Stanley Committee 1912, pp. 4127, 4128; W. R. Stirling to HCF, 4, 11 Nov. 1885.

56. J. Morse to HCF, 26 Nov. 1886; Stirling to HCF, 5 April 1888.

57. J. Morse to HCF, 23 Nov., 17, 23 Dec. 1886, 5, 13 May 1887.

58. M. Ramsay to HCF, 11 June 1887; R. Spencer to HCF, 14 June 1887; Stirling to HCF, 25 June, 2 July 1887; R. Spencer to HCF, 27 June 1887.

59. H. A. Gray to HCF, 5, 12, 13 July 1887.

60. Stirling and Gray to E. M. Ferguson, 26 Aug. 1887, in Frick Papers.

61. J. Morse to HCF, 1 June 1887; Stirling and Gray to Ferguson, 25 July 1887; Gray to HCF, 24 Aug., 20 Sept. 1887, all in Frick Papers.

62. Gray to HCF, 20 Sept. 1887; J. Morse to HCF, 29 Nov. 1887.

63. HCF to J. S. Wilson, 19 July 1888; HCF to Stewart, 10 Aug. 1888.

64. Phipps to Carnegie Brothers board of managers, 16 Oct. 1888 (USX).

65. HCF to AC, 4 Feb., 13 March, 13 June 1889.

66. HCF to AC, 9 Aug. 1889; AC to HCF, 3 Sept. 1889; Phipps to AC, 1 Nov. 1889.

67. Harvey 1928, p. 99.

3. CARNEGIE COMPANY GROWTH AND THE HOMESTEAD CRISIS

1. AC in *Forum* (April 1886), pp. 114–25; *New Jersey Mail*, 25 March 1886; Burgoyne 1893, pp. 7–9; U.S. Congress, House of Representatives 1892, p. ix.

2. AC to HCF, 3 Sept. 1889; Phipps to HCF, 6 April 1890.

3. *Pittsburgh Commercial Gazette* quoted in BAISA, 2 Oct. 1889.

4. W. R. Jones to HCF, 11 March 1889.

5. HCF to O. W. Potter, 27 Sept. 1889; HCF to J. Morse, 27 Sept. 1889; BAISA, 2 Oct. 1889.

6. Wall 1970, p. 533; Frick in memorial to W. R. Jones, noted in Carnegie Papers, 27 Nov. 1889 (ACLC).

7. HCF to C. M. Schwab (hereafter CMS), 17 Oct., 9 Nov. 1889.

8. HCF to Phipps, 6 Jan. 1890.

9. *American Manufacturer* quoted in BAISA, 20 Feb. 1889; HCF to AC, 13 June 1889.

10. HCF to AC, 25 July 1889; Lauder to HCF, 6 Aug. 1889.

11. J. Morse to HCF, 25 July 1889; HCF to AC, 2 Jan. 1890; J. Morse to HCF, 19 Feb. 1890.

12. HCF to AC, 3 April 1890; HCF to J. Morse, 24 April 1890; HCF to AC, 3 July 1890.

13. Hogan 1971; HCF to AC, 9 Jan., 3 July 1890.

14. HCF to AC, 14 Nov. 1890; *Pittsburgh Commercial Gazette*, 18 Nov. 1890; BAISA, 19 Nov. 1890. Note that BAISA incorrectly reported the price paid as "somewhat above $1,800,000."

15. Schwab's estimate referred to in HCF to AC, 14 July 1891; Leishman to HCF, Aug. 1891.

16. D. A. Ashworth to HCF, 14 Dec. 1893.

17. Wall 1970, p. 498; HCF to AC, 9 Sept. 1891.

18. Peto 1866; Sienkiewicz 1876; AC to HCF, undated (1885–1886).

19. For a general discussion, see Habakkuk 1967 and Temin 1964.

20. Wallis 1854. Statistics collected by the newly formed national association in the iron trade in the late 1850s indicated that the cost of labor then made up 60 percent of the total for pig iron, 66 percent in the case of rails, and as much as 75 percent in smaller and finer lines of finished product (E. Smith quoted in Lesley 1859, p. 765).

21. Hewitt 1870.

22. *Transactions of the American Institute of Mining Engineers* 1 (1871–1873), p. 281.

23. Quoted in Brody 1960, p. 17.

24. CMS quoted in Hessen 1975, p. 32; see also Barron 1930, p. 82; *Journal of the Iron and Steel Institute* 1 (1881), pp. 129–45.

25. Brody 1960.

26. Brody 1960, p. 51.

27. W. R. Jones quoted in Casson 1907, p. 132.

28. Wall 1970, pp. 527, 528; Bridge 1903, pp. 189, 190; BAISA, 24 Aug. 1892; Carnegie Steel Co. Papers (USX).

29. HCF to CMS, 25 Feb. 1890; CMS to HCF, 2 Oct. 1890.

30. The quotations and information in the preceding two paragraphs are from CMS to HCF, 2 Oct. 1890.

31. HCF to AC, 30 Aug. 1889; HCF to CMS, 30 Oct. 1889; CMS to HCF, 20 Oct. 1890.

32. HCF to AC, 10 Dec. 1890; HCF cable to AC, 1 Jan. 1891.

33. HCF to AC, 1, 2, 3 Jan. 1891.

34. CMS to HCF, 1 Jan. 1891 (two letters); HCF to CMS, 1 Jan. 1991; HCF to AC, 1 Jan. 1891.

35. CMS to HCF, 1 Jan. 1891 (third letter).

36. HCF to J. Gayley, HCF to CMS, 2 Jan. 1891.

37. HCF to CMS, 13 Jan. 1891.

38. HCF to CMS, 17 Jan., 27 April 1891.

39. HCF to CMS, 28 Sept. 1891; CMS to HCF, 22 Oct. 1891.

40. HCF to CMS, 28 Oct. 1891, 8 Jan. 1892, 14 Oct. 1891.

41. Carnegie associates telegram to AC, 25 Dec. 1891; AC to HCF, 3 Feb. 1892, both in Frick Papers.

42. C. C. Foster quoted in Annual Report for 1887 of Secretary for Internal Affairs of Pennsylvania 1888, p. 246.

43. AC to W. L. Abbott, 4, 25 July, 13 Aug. 1888 (ACLC).

44. AC to Abbott, 29 Dec. 1888 (ACLC).

45. HCF to AC, 13 June 1889.

46. AC to Abbott, 7 Aug. 1889 (ACLC); HCF to AC, 21 Oct. 1889, in Frick Papers.

47. AC to HCF, 17 March 1891; CMS to U.S. Industrial Commission 1899–1901, vol. 13, p. 460.

48. Letter of Cramp representative, 8 Jan. 1892, quoted in B. F. Cooley Papers, Hagley Library.

49. Bridge 1903, pp. 204, 205.

50. Meeting and memo referred to in HCF to AC, 12 Oct. 1892; HCF to AC, 21 April 1892.

51. HCF to AC, 31 May 1892; HCF to J. A. Potter, 30 May 1892.

52. AC to HCF, 7, 17 June 1892 (ACLC); *Forum*, April 1886, quoted in BAISA, 31 March 1886, p. 82.

53. HCF to AC, 2 June 1892.

54. HCF to W. C. Whitney, 9 June 1892; HCF to S. L. Schoonmaker, 11 June 1892; J. C. Fleming to HCF, 19 Aug. 1892.

55. HCF to J. O. Hoffman, 11 June 1892. In 1912, when he was giving evidence to the Stanley Committee, Carnegie was asked whether they had ever employed Pinkertons before the 1892 strike. He replied, "To my best knowledge and belief, I never heard of such a thing. And, of course, I did not know that they were employed at Homestead at that time" (AC to Stanley Commission, 12 Jan. 1912, p. 2529). In fact, the more-than-five-month struggle that resulted in the elimination of the eight-hour day at Braddock in the winter and spring of 1889 had been policed, with Carnegie's knowledge, by Pinkertons (Bridge 1903, pp. 188, 189).

56. HCF to AC, 24 June 1892.

57. HCF to Hoffman, 1 July 1892.

58. The fullest and most authoritative account is probably Krause 1992.

59. HCF to AC, 4 July 1892; Foner 1955, p. 209.

60. Harvey 1928, p. 123; Burgoyne 1893, p. 92; Wall 1970, p. 559; Lorant 1988, p. 655.

61. HCF to *Philadelphia Press*, quoted in BAISA, 13 July 1892, pp. 202–03.

62. AC to W. E. Gladstone, 24 Sept. 1892, quoted in Hendrick 1932, p. 356; HCF to AC, 11 July 1892 (two letters).

63. AC cable to Frick, 14 July 1892; HCF to AC, cable and letter, 14 July 1892.

64. HCF to Congressional Committee, quoted Harvey 1928, p. 128; HCF to O. H. Childs, 15 July 1892.

65. HCF to P. R. Dillon, 11, 19 July 1892; HCF to Wrigley, 15 July 1892; HCF to T. Morrison, 19 July 1892.

66. HCF to J. Wannamaker, 15 July 1892; HCF to Major Bent, 15 July 1892; HCF to AC, 18 July 1892; HCF to vice-president Pittsburgh and Lake Erie Railroad, 21 July 1892; HCF to Sheriff of Allegheny County, 22 July 1892.

67. HCF cable to AC, 23 July 1892; AC to Leishman, undated (July 1892) (ACLC).

68. J. E. Milholland, memo of visit to HCF, 30 July 1892, in Harrison MSS., vol. 145, Library of Congress.

69. HCF to AC, 19 Aug. 1892; HCF to J. Morse, 25 Aug. 1892.

70. HCF to H. Oliver, 12 Sept. 1892; HCF to Bent, 24 Sept. 1892; HCF memo of 27 Sept. 1892.

71. HCF to AC, 17 Aug., 12 Sept., 31 Oct. 1892.

72. AC to HCF, 28 Sept. 1892; Pennsylvania Department of Internal Affairs 1893, pp. D1–11; HCF to AC, 31 Oct. 1892.

73. BAISA, 30 Nov. 1892; Pennsylvania Department of Internal Affairs 1893, D11; HCF to AC, 21, 28 Nov. 1892.

74. U.S. Congress, House of Representatives 1892, p. x.

75. AC to Lauder, 17 July 1892 (ACLC); HCF to AC, 23, 27 Aug. 1892, in Frick Papers.

76. AC to Gladstone, 24 Sept. 1892, quoted in Hendrick 1932, p. 357; Lord Rosebery to AC, 10 Oct. 1892, and J. Morley to AC, 31 Dec. 1893 (both in ACLC).

77. CMS cited in Whipple 1935, pp. 70–73; HCF to AC, 12 Oct., 8 Sept. 1892.

78. Bridge 1931, p. 67; personal note from AC to HCF, quoted in HCF's reply, HCF to AC, 12 Oct. 1892.

79. AC to HCF, 17 Nov. 1892; AC to Reid, 20 March 1893 (ACLC).

80. *Commercial Gazette*, 27 Jan. 1893; AC quoted in *New York City Herald*, 7 Dec. 1919, and in part by Bridge 1903, pp. 251–53; T. Mellon to AC, 30 Jan. 1893 (ACLC).

81. Garland 1894, p. 3; Spahr 1900, p. 148; Fitch 1910, p. 233.

82. HCF to AC, 31 Oct. (two quotations), 1 Nov. 1892.

83. AC to Lauder, 17 July 1892 (ACLC); CMS to HCF, 16 Oct. 1892, in Frick Papers.

84. *Pittsburgh Times*, 6 Nov. 1892; CMS to HCF, 21 Nov. 1892.

85. HCF to CMS, 22 Oct. 1892.

86. Bridge 1903, pp. 295, 296; CMS cited in Hessen 1975, p. 40.

87. HCF to CMS, CMS to HCF, HCF to CMS, 19 Oct. 1892.

88. CMS to HCF, 21, 26 Oct. 1892; CMS cited in Hessen 1975, pp. 39, 43.

89. HCF to CMS, 14 Nov. 1892; HCF to Dillon, CMS, and Fleming, 17 Nov. 1892; HCF cable to Miller et al., 18 Nov. 1892; HCF to J. Vandervort, 19 Nov. 1892; HCF to C. O. Johnson, 1 Dec. 1892.

90. HCF to CMS, 21 Nov. 1892.

91. *Pittsburgh Chronicle Telegraph*, 1 Feb. 1893.

92. CMS to HCF, 26 Oct. 1892; HCF to P. C. Knox, 27 Oct. 1892; note on Jones in Krause 1992, p. 87; CMS to HCF, 23 Nov. 1892.

93. HCF to CMS, 6 Dec. 1892, 9 Jan. 1893; CMS to HCF, 7 Jan. 1894; HCF to CMS, 9 May 1894; HCF to J. R. Skewis, 11 Oct. 1894; HCF to CMS, 11 Oct. 1894 (last two) (ACLC).

94. HCF to CMS, 6 Jan. 1893; H. J. Lindsay to HCF, 10 Jan. 1893.

95. CMS to HCF, 17 May 1893.

96. Reverend J. J. McIlyar quoted in Burgoyne 1893, p. 93; HCF to J. Barton, 13 Dec. 1892.

97. T. S. Newton to CMS, 27 June 1893; HCF to CMS, 5 June 1894, both in Frick Papers.

98. HCF to AC, 7 Sept. 1895.

99. H. M. Howe and R. Roberts quoted in Brody 1960, pp. 27, 34.

100. CMS to HCF, 11 Dec. 1894; for party from Bethlehem, see Johnston 1896; AC to Leishman, 21 Aug. 1896 (ACLC).

101. W. E. Corey to CMS, 27 Jan. 1898 (ACLC); CMS to HCF, 3 Dec. 1897; CMS to AC, 9 Dec. 1897 (ACLC); Meade 1901.

102. CMS to HCF, 20 Sept. 1893; HCF to CMS, 2 Oct. 1895 (ACLC); AC cable to HCF, 27 Nov. 1892.

103. CMS to AC, 21 May 1896 (ACLC); *Iron Age*, 6 April 1899, p. 31.

104. For a restrained but depressing description of the works and its setting in the late 1890s, see Dreiser 1899 and the later, fuller analysis by Margaret Byington of the *Pittsburgh Survey*, in Byington 1910, and in Byington 1912, pp. 3034–37. B. Webb quoted in Wolff 1965, p. 236; Shadwell 1906, vol. 2, pp. 327, 328; Krause 1992, p. 6.

4. ASPECTS OF MANAGEMENT:
PRODUCTION AND SUPPLY

1. AISA statistics; U.S. Department of Commerce 1960. For a valuable discussion of the economies of pools in steel products as well as much detailed evidence, see Lamoreaux 1985.

2. E. C. Potter in *Iron Age*, 17 Feb. 1898. The Tariff Act of 1870 set a duty of $28 a

ton on Bessemer rails. The duty was $17 in 1883 and $13.44 in 1890. The average price of steel rails per gross ton in the same three years was $106.79, $37.75, and $31.78 respectively. Production of steel rails was 30,000 tons in 1870 and 260,000 tons in 1875 when Edgar Thomson works began production. It continued to rise steeply, reaching 1,210,000 tons in 1883 and 2,119,000 tons in 1887. After that demand was more variable and production did not again exceed 2 million tons until 1899. The average output of the eleven years between 1887 and 1899 was 1,436,000 tons, or less than 68 percent of the 1887 figure.

3. Wall 1970, p. 350.

4. *Iron Age*, 8 March 1888; AC quoted in *Iron Age*, 4 April 1889, p. 510; AC to J. S. Wilson, 18 April 1887, in Frick Papers.

5. AISA statistics; Clarke 1929, vol. 2, p. 444.

6. Lamoreaux 1985, fig 3.6, p. 79.

7. HCF to AC, 22 Feb. 1889, 15 July 1890; CMS to HCF, 27 Sept. 1890.

8. J. Morse to HCF, 18 Dec. 1889.

9. J. W. Gates to Stanley Commission, 27 May, 8 June 1911. I am grateful to John Ingham for pointing out the contrasting attitudes of Carnegie and Frick.

10. HCF to AC, 15 July 1890; HCF to J. Morse, 16 Dec. 1890; Lamoreaux 1985, p. 79; HCF to J. Morse, 10, 16 Jan. 1891.

11. HCF to J. Morse, 1 April 1891, 28 April, 3 May 1892 (see also HCF to AC, 10 Jan. 1891); HCF to J. Morse, 25 Aug. 1892; HCF to CMS, 22 Sept. 1892.

12. HCF to J. Morse, 16 Nov., 10 Dec. 1891; statistics are from *Iron Age*, 16 Nov. 1892.

13. Both quotations are from HCF to Leishman, 8 April 1892; Gray to HCF, 3 Nov. 1893.

14. AC to HCF, received 6 Sept. 1893; HCF to Lauder, 8 April 1892.

15. HCF to J. Morse, 9 Nov. 1891.

16. HCF to G. B. Roberts, 24 Feb. 1891; HCF to Lake Shore and Michigan Southern Railroad, 27 Oct. 1893.

17. *Iron Age*, 22 Feb. 1894, p. 364.

18. *Pittsburgh Post*, 11 Nov. 1893; quotation is from *Pittsburgh Dispatch*, 10 Nov. 1893; HCF to S. L. Schoonmaker, 7 Nov. 1893; Memorandum of Agreement Between the Illinois Steel Company and Carnegie Steel Company, 18 Oct. 1893, in Frick Papers.

19. *Pittsburgh Dispatch*, 2 Dec. 1893.

20. HCF to AC, 2 Nov. 1894; November 1894 meetings referred to in *Iron Age*, 11 Feb. 1897.

21. E. H. Gary to Stanley Commission, cited in *Iron Age*, 5 June 1913, pp. 1394, 1395.

22. J. M. Swank in BAISA, 20 Feb. 1897, p. 44; *Iron Age*, 11 Feb. 1897, p. 18; *Iron Trade Review*, 11 Feb. 1897; *Philadelphia Public Ledger*, 11 Feb. 1897; Ripley 1905 pp. 80, 81; Lamoreaux 1985, pp. 80, 81.

23. HCF to J. Morse, 16, 18, 20 April 1894; HCF to Chisholm quoted in HCF to Morse, 20 April 1894.

24. T. C. Carson to HCF, 18 Oct. 1893; HCF note, 29 Aug. 1894; Fleming to HCF, 6 Dec. 1894.

25. Gates to HCF, 29 Jan., 6 April, 28 Sept., 23 Dec. 1896.

26. AC to HCF, 15 Jan., 7 Feb. 1897; Lamoreaux 1985, p. 82.

27. HCF to CMS, 10 Sept. 1897; CMS to HCF, 17 Sept. 1897.

28. CMS to HCF, 29 Sept. 1897.

29. All quotations in this paragraph are from A. M. Moreland to CMS, 15 Nov. 1897 (ACLC).

30. HCF to W. Scranton, 16 Dec. 1897; AC to HCF, 20 Sept., 9 Oct., 7 Dec. 1897.

31. Gates to HCF, 28, 29 Dec. 1897; AISA annual statistics.

32. HCF to Scranton, 16 Dec. 1897; HCF to CMS, 25 Nov. 1897; AC to HCF, 31 Nov. 1897, 5 Feb. 1898.

33. CMS to HCF, 5 Jan. 1898; Agreement of 5 Jan. 1898, in Frick Papers.

34. AC to Carnegie Steel board of managers, 19, 21 March 1898 (ACLC); HCF to AC, 4 April 1898; HCF to Carnegie Steel board of managers, 5 April 1898 (ACLC).

35. Carnegie Steel board of managers, 27 Sept. 1898 (ACLC).

36. CMS to HCF, 26 Sept. 1898.

37. Carnegie Steel board of managers, 6, 20 Dec. 1898 (ACLC).

38. Carnegie Steel board of managers, 14 March 1898 (ACLC).

39. *American Manufacturer* quoted in BAISA, 7, 14 Dec. 1887.

40. For Carnegie on Thanksgiving Day, see *Commercial Gazette*, 26 Nov. 1885; *Triumphant Democracy* quoted in Wall 1970, p. 646.

41. Wall 1970, p. 646; for Carnegie to the Republican Club, see *New York Herald*, 8 Jan. 1911, quoted in Wilson 1915, p. 2.

42. Hessen 1975, p. 29; see also AISA 1899.

43. AC to Abbott and AC to HCF, summer 1890, both quoted in Wall 1970, p. 649.

44. AC to Abbott, 4, 25 July, 13 Aug. 1888 (ACLC).

45. AC to HCF, first letter received 22 Jan. 1890, second letter undated (middle 1890).

46. AC to B. F. Tracy, 27 June 1890 (ACLC). Krause 1992, ch. 19 and Appendix 1, examines the doubtful means whereby Carnegie, Phipps, and Co. acquired the Poor Farm from the City of Pittsburgh. AC to Tracy, July 1890 (ACLC); HCF to AC, 3 July 1890.

47. AC to HCF, 3 Aug. 1890.

48. Lauder to HCF, 6 Aug. 1890; AC to Abbott, 27 Aug. 1890 (ACLC); AC to HCF, 28 Aug. 1890, 7 Oct. 1891.

49. CMS to Leishman, 7 July 1896 (USX); AC to HCF, 4 Sept. 1894.

50. M. Hunsiker to HCF, 16 Dec. 1892.

51. AC to HCF, 3 Dec. 1891; HCF to AC, 5 Feb. 1892.

52. AC to Tracy, 5 July 1890 (quote); HCF to AC, 22 June (quote), 26 Dec. 1891, 12 Jan. 1892 (quote).

53. HCF to AC, 29 Dec. 1891; HCF to I. M. Scott, 9 July 1892; AC to HCF, 28 Sept. 1892.

54. HCF to CMS, 6 Dec. 1892; HCF cables to AC, 17, 23 Feb. 1891.

55. AC to HCF, 14 Aug. 1891, 12 Oct. 1894; Lauder cited in CMS to HCF, 30 Oct., 11 Dec. 1894.

56. W. M. Folger to HCF, 15 and 17 Feb. 1893; quotations are from HCF to AC, 16 Nov. 1892.

57. AC to HCF, 9 Nov. 1892; Hessen 1975, pp. 42–58.

58. BAISA, 14 Sept. 1892.

59. AC to G. Cleveland, quoted in Hessen 1975, pp. 46, 47; Wall 1970, pp. 650, 651.

60. Hessen 1975, pp. 46–58.

61. HCF telegram to H. A. Herbert, 15 Sept. 1893; quotations are from HCF to CMS, 16 Sept. 1893; HCF to Herbert, 20 Sept. 1893.

62. HCF to Herbert, 13 Dec. 1893, 11 April 1894.

63. CMS to HCF, 12 Dec. 1893; *Pittsburgh Dispatch*, 12 March 1894; CMS to HCF, 12 April 1894.

64. CMS to HCF, 27 March 1894.

65. L. Bullion to HCF, 2 April 1894.

66. Bullion to HCF, 2 April 1894; CMS to HCF, 2 April 1894.

67. HCF to CMS, 4 April 1894; CMS to HCF, 4 April 1894.

68. AC to HCF, 7 Sept. 1894; HCF to AC, 19 Sept. 1894; Hunsiker quoted in HCF to CMS, 7 Dec. 1894.

69. Carnegie Steel Co. figures (USX); Dickson 1938, p. 29.

70. HCF to AC, 17 July 1890.

71. Baron 1897, pp. 341, 342; Birkibine 1897, p. 519.

72. Wall 1970, p. 589; HCF to AC, 26 June, 15 July 1890 (quote); HCF to J. Morse, 16, 18 April 1891.

73. CMS, June 1939, quoted in Nevins 1953, pp. 248–50.

74. CMS quoted in Nevins 1953, p. 253; Winchell 1892–1893, p. 685. See also Jeans 1902, p. 33.

75. Lon Merritt quoted in Wall 1970, p. 594; AC to HCF, 29 Aug. 1892.

76. For Carnegie's skepticism, see Wall 1970, p. 596; AC to HCF, 4 Sept. 1894; HCF to C. A. Turner, 13 Jan. 1893; HCF to AC, 13 July 1895.

77. Wall 1970, p. 597; AC to HCF, undated (1896), in Frick Papers; quotation is from AC to Leishman, 21 Aug. 1896 (ACLC).

78. BAISA, 1 Oct. 1896; AC to J. D. Rockefeller, 30 Oct. 1896 (ACLC); Frick quoted in Hendrick 1932, p. 395; Carnegie Steel board of managers, minutes, 12 Dec. 1896 (ACLC).

79. *Engineering and Mining Journal*, Jan. 1897; *Iron Age*, 18 Feb. 1897, quoted in BAISA, 1 March 1897; HCF to AC, 30 Nov. 1896.

80. Oliver to HCF, 27 July 1897; AC to HCF, 9 Oct. 1897, quoted in Harvey 1928, p. 195; Wall 1970, pp. 601–11.

81. AC memorandum on ore, undated (ACLC); Harvey 1928, pp. 191, 195.

82. Minutes of H. C. Frick Coke Co., 28 Jan. 1899, 24 Jan. 1900, in Stanley Committee 1912, vol. 6; CMS quoted in Whipple 1935, p. 6.

83. AC to HCF, 21 March 1899; report by C. McKibbin to H. B. Tate, 2 April 1891; HCF to J. Morse, 2 April 1891; AC to HCF, 22 April 1891, all in Frick Papers.

84. *Connellsville Courier*, 6 April 1894; HCF to W. Ramsay, 24 May 1894.

85. Lynch memorandum 1899 (ACLC).

86. Both quotations are from HCF to AC, 13 Aug. 1883.

87. CMS report to Carnegie Steel board of managers and comments of HCF, concerning visit of 13 July 1898 (ACLC).

88. Carnegie Steel statement of purchases, 24 Jan. 1900 (ACLC); Lynch to HCF, 8 Feb. 1899.

89. Carnegie Steel board of managers, minutes, 28 Jan. 1896; HCF, note to board of managers, 5 Jan 1897; board of managers, minutes, 27 June 1897 (all in ACLC).

90. AC to F. Lovejoy, 19 Aug. 1898; Lovejoy to AC, 8 Sept. 1898; AC to Lauder, 21 Sept. 1898 (all in ACLC).

91. Carnegie Steel Company board of managers, minutes; Lovejoy to AC, 8 Sept. 1898; Moreland to AC, 8 March 1900 (all in ACLC).

92. CMS to AC, 9, 16 Dec. 1898; CMS memorandum, 8 Dec. 1899 (all in ACLC).

93. Lovejoy note, 17 Jan. 1899; quotation is from CMS memorandum, 8 Dec. 1899 (both in ACLC).

94. Lynch memorandum, 17 Dec. 1898 (ACLC).

5. ASPECTS OF MANAGEMENT: PROCESS PLANT

1. HCF to AC, 3, 25 Sept. 1894.

2. AC to Leishman, 2 July, 5 Aug. 1895; C. Kirchoff to AC, 27 April 1896 (all in ACLC); AC to HCF, 18 Sept. 1896.

3. CMS to AC, 14 April 1898; operating department minutes, 22 Jan. 1898 (both in ACLC).

4. CMS to AC, 7 March 1898 (ACLC); HCF to CMS, 19 Nov. 1897.

5. Carnegie Steel board of managers, 3 May 1898 (ACLC); HCF to CMS, 19 Nov. 1897.

6. CMS to AC, 19 Nov. 1897 (ACLC).

7. HCF to AC, 10 Jan. 1898, in Frick Papers; Carnegie Steel board of managers, 11 Jan. 1898 (ACLC).

8. Phipps to HCF, 23 Jan. 1898; HCF to Phipps, 25 Jan. 1898.

9. Carnegie Steel board of managers, minutes, 27 Jan. 1898 (ACLC); AC to HCF, 2 Feb. 1898; CMS to HCF, from Cannes, 29 Jan. 1898.

10. HCF to AC, 8, 19 Feb. 1898; AC and Lauder to HCF, 19 Feb. 1898; HCF to AC, 25 Feb. 1898.

11. AC to HCF, 7 (two letters), 29 March 1898.

12. Phipps to HCF, 21 May 1898.

13. AC speech quoted in *Iron and Coal Trades Review* (U.K.), 27 Dec. 1895, p. 812; *Iron Age* quoted in U.S. Bureau of Statistics 1900, p. 203; *American Metal Market* quoted in BAISA, 1 Sept. 1908, p. 93.

14. Wall 1970, pp. 509–17; Carnegie Papers, 4 July 1896, and 1896–1897 in general (ACLC).

15. Wall 1970, p. 518; J. S. Wilson to HCF, 18 May 1886; quotation from HCF to G. Roberts, 4 March 1891.

16. Bridge 1903, pp. 256, 257; Carnegie Steel records 1897 (ACLC).

17. G. E. McCague to HCF, 27 Dec. 1894.

18. J. A. Wilson to HCF, 27 Jan. 1890; J. A. Wilson to S. B. Dick, 27 Jan., 1 Feb. 1890, all in Frick Papers.

19. J. H. Creery to AC, 25 Oct. 1895; AC to Champlin, 29 Oct. 1895 (both in ACLC).

20. AC to Dick, 3 Feb. 1896; AC to J. A. Stewart, 18 April 1896; AC to A. D. Smith, 14 Nov. 1895; Dick to AC, 9 Dec. 1895; Leishman to AC, 9 Dec. 1895 (all in ACLC).

21. Hendrick 1932, pp. 402, 403; Dick to AC, 20 March 1896; R. A. Franks to AC, 14 July 1896 (both in ACLC).

22. AC to Dick, 6 April 1896 (ACLC); AC to HCF, 28 July 1896, in Frick Papers; AC to J. H. Reed, 14 Sept. 1896; AC to Dick, 15 Sept. 1896 (both in ACLC).

23. AC to HCF, 28 July 1896, 9 Oct. 1897, in Frick Papers; Report of J. H. Reed to

NOTES TO PAGES 193–06

Carnegie Steel board of managers, 14 Dec. 1897 (ACLC); Report of R. A. Franks, 4 June 1897, in Frick Papers.

24. J. T. Odell to Reed, 15 Dec. 1897 (ACLC); quotation from AC to HCF, 30 March 1898; J. S. Wilson to HCF, 18 May 1886.

25. Odell quoted in Bridge 1903, p. 271; Meade 1901, pp. 532–41; AC memorandum to "The Chairman, President, and Managers of Carnegie Steel Company," 31 Dec. 1896 (ACLC); AC at the Pittsburgh Chamber of Commerce quoted in *Iron Trade Review*, 17 Nov. 1898, pp. 16, 17.

26. AC to HCF, 7 Feb. 1896; AC to Leishman, 4 Feb. 1896 (ACLC); AC to F. Thomson (of the Pennsylvania Railroad), 5 May 1896, in Frick Papers.

27. AC to HCF, 2 June 1897; Phipps to HCF, 25 June 1897; AC to HCF, 9 Oct., 4 Dec. 1897.

28. AC to HCF, 4 Dec. 1897; A. W. Mellon to HCF, 20 Jan. 1898; HCF to AC, 20 Jan. 1898.

29. Quotations are from HCF to AC, 25 Feb., 20 Jan. 1898; estimate from HCF to Carnegie Steel board of managers, 26 April 1898 (ACLC).

30. HCF to AC, 12 May 1898.

31. AC to Directors of Pennsylvania Railroad, 1896 (ACLC); AC speech quoted in *Iron and Coal Trades Review* (U.K.), 27 Dec. 1895, p. 812.

32. *Iron Age*, 31 Jan. 1895; Warren 1988, p. 102.

33. Carnegie Steel meeting of managers, 5 April 1898; operating department minutes, 16 April 1898 (both in ACLC).

34. J. Morse to HCF, 13 Dec. 1898; Carnegie Steel board of managers, 13 Dec. 1898 (quote) (ACLC).

35. Carnegie Steel board of managers, 16 Jan. (quote), 7 Feb. 1899 (both in ACLC); Bridge 1903, p. 358.

36. AC to Carnegie Steel board of managers, 21 Feb. 1899 (ACLC); Phipps to HCF, 17 April 1899; Bridge 1903, pp. 358, 359.

37. AC to HCF, 4 Sept. 1894; AC article in *New York Evening Post*, 12 Jan. 1901, quoted in BAISA, 9 Feb. 1901.

38. AC to "The Chairman, President, and Managers of Carnegie Steel," 31 Dec. 1896 (ACLC); AC to Lauder, 1 Jan. 1898 (ACLC).

39. HCF to AC, 30 Jan. 1891.

40. AC to HCF, 29 March 1898; *New York Evening Post*, 12 Jan. 1901.

41. AC to HCF, 19 Sept. 1891.

42. D. C. Wedding to AC, 8 March 1893 (ACLC); *Pittsburgh Chronicle*, 8 May 1893.

43. W. H. Donner to Cassatt, 15 Jan. 1906 (copy in Frick Papers).

44. J. A. Potter to CMS, 23 June 1898 (ACLC).

45. HCF to AC, 22 March 1898; AC to HCF, 30 March, 5 April, 23 May 1898 (22 March and 5 April (ACLC); others in Frick Papers).

46. HCF to AC, 10 June 1898, in Frick Papers; AC to HCF, 20 June 1898 (ACLC).

47. HCF to Carnegie Steel board of managers, 15 Aug. 1898; T. Rodd to HCF, 13, 15 Aug. 1898; HCF to AC, 2 June 1898.

48. HCF to Carnegie Steel board of managers, 15 Aug. 1898 (ACLC).

49. Carnegie Steel board of managers, 16 Aug. 1898; quotation is from CMS to AC, 20 Sept. 1898 (both in ACLC).

50. Carnegie Steel board of managers, 18 Oct. 1898 (ACLC).

51. Wall 1970, pp. 489, 490.
52. Carnegie Steel board of managers, 14 Jan. 1899 (ACLC).

6. THE RESHAPING OF CARNEGIE STEEL

1. AC, Dec. 1868, quoted in Heilbroner 1970, pp. 86, 94.
2. AC to Abbott, 28 Oct. 1889 (ACLC).
3. Moreland to AC, undated (probably early 1900) (ACLC).
4. HCF to AC, 25 July 1889, 26 March 1891.
5. AC to HCF, 9 Nov. 1892.
6. CMS to HCF, 6 Nov. 1897; HCF to AC, 7 Aug. 1893.
7. Carnegie Steel board of managers, 18 Sept. 1897; CMS to AC, 5 Oct. 1897; AC to CMS, 16, 18 Oct. 1897 (all in ACLC).
8. HCF to J. Morse, 4 Dec. 1889; HCF to AC, 4 Dec. 1889, 8, 29, 30 Dec. 1890.
9. AC to HCF, 3 Sept. 1892.
10. HCF cable to AC, 25 Dec. 1893.
11. HCF to AC, 20 Sept., 3 Oct. 1894.
12. HCF to AC, 25 Sept. 1894; HCF to C. A. Stone, 30 Oct. 1894; HCF to Hunsiker, 8 Nov. 1894; HCF to Stone, 19 Dec. 1894.
13. AC to HCF, 26 Dec. 1894, and AC note to Phipps (both in ACLC).
14. HCF to AC, 18 Dec. 1894 (ACLC); HCF to Walker, circa 26 Dec. 1894; HCF to AC, 18 Dec. 1894.
15. Hendrick 1932, pp. 429–31 covers these events. AC to HCF, 18 Dec. 1894; HCF to AC, 19 Dec. 1894.
16. HCF to AC, 20, 24, 28, 30 Dec. 1894, 1 Jan 1895; AC to HCF, 3 Jan. 1895.
17. John Walker interviewed by Hendrick in 1928, quoted in Wall 1970, p. 425; Phipps to AC, 22 Dec. 1894 (ACLC); H. Phipps to J. Phipps, quoted in Boegner and Gachot 1986, p. 17.
18. Carnegie Steel board of managers, minutes, 8, 11 Jan. 1895 (ACLC).
19. Wall 1970, pp. 660, 661; Harvey 1928, pp. 183–86; AC quoted in Hendrick 1932, pp. 432, 433; AC to Lovejoy, 11 Feb. 1895; Phipps to AC, 22 Dec. 1894 (both in ACLC); Hessen 1975, p. 66. Harvey (p. 184) suggests that the idea of creating the new post of president came from Frick.
20. K. Hellerstedt quoted in Weingartner 1988, p. 65.
21. HCF to AC, 14 Feb. 1895.
22. AC to Lovejoy, 20 Jan. 1896 (ACLC).
23. AC to Leishman, 24, 2 July 1895, 15, 26 Jan. 1896 (all in ACLC).
24. AC to Leishman, 22 July, 26 Aug. 1895, 4 Jan., 4 Dec. 1896 (all in ACLC).
25. HCF to AC, 27 Jan. 1897; Carnegie Steel Co., notice of 12 Feb. 1897, quoted in BAISA, 20 Feb. 1897.
26. AC to Carnegie Steel board of managers, 25 Dec. 1897 (ACLC).
27. HCF to AC, 19 April 1898; AC to HCF, 23 April 1898; HCF to AC, 24 May, 18 June, (quotation is from) 2 Aug. 1898 (all in ACLC).
28. CMS to HCF, 6 Jan. 1898.
29. HCF to AC, 28 April, 10 May 1898, 10 Dec. 1896 (in Frick Papers), 12 May 1898; Lauder to AC, 24 June 1898 (all except one in ACLC).
30. AC to Carnegie Steel board of managers, 23 Aug. 1898 (ACLC).

31. Phipps to HCF, 23, 28 Nov. 1898.

32. Lauder to Phipps, 28 Nov. 1898, in Frick Papers.

33. CMS to HCF, 28 Nov. 1898.

34. HCF to AC, 10 Dec. 1898 (ACLC).

35. AC to Lauder, Dec. 1898 (ACLC).

36. AC letter of 30 Dec. 1898, and Carnegie Steel board of managers, minutes, 3 Jan., 16 Jan. 1899 (ACLC); CMS to HCF, 11 Jan. 1899.

37. Carnegie Steel board of managers, 16 Jan. 1899 (ACLC).

38. Lauder to AC, 16 Jan. 1899 (ACLC); CMS to HCF, 17 Jan. 1899, in Frick Papers; Carnegie Steel Co. meeting, 19 Jan. 1899; Lauder to AC, 19, 20 Jan. 1899; AC to Carnegie Steel board of managers, 31 Jan. 1899 (all in ACLC).

39. AC quoted in Iron Age, 9 Feb. 1899,

40. Bridge 1903, pp. 304, 305; Carneige Steel Co., draft agreement, April 1899; Carnegie Steel board of managers, 26 April, 19 May 1899 (all in ACLC).

41. Prospectus is in Carnegie Papers (ACLC). Bridge 1903, p. 312, quotes a slightly different form of the draft prospectus. CMS to HCF, 15 May 1899, quoted in Bridge 1903, pp. 312–14.

42. Gates to HCF, 6 May 1899; Iron Age, 11 May 1899, pp. 16, 27, 28.

43. Wall 1970, p. 728; CMS to AC, 13 May 1899 (ACLC).

44. CMS to HCF, 16 May 1899, in Frick Papers; Carnegie Steel board of managers, minutes, 22 May 1899; HCF to AC, 23 May 1899 (both in ACLC).

45. For Carnegie's prepared letter, see Wall 1970, pp. 725–27; B. F. Jones quoted in BAISA, 1 June 1899; AC to Bullion, 31 May 1899 (ACLC).

46. HCF to AC, 23 May 1899 (ACLC); Phipps to HCF, 30 May 1899.

47. AC to Lauder, 23 June 1899; Carnegie Steel board of managers, 27 June 1899 (both in ACLC).

48. AC quoted in Bridge 1903, p. 320; Wall 1975, pp. 732, 725 (but note reservation expressed p. 1094, n. 17).

49. HCF to J. H. Bridge, 20 May 1913.

50. Phipps to HCF, 15 July 1899.

51. Phipps to HCF, undated (circa 20 or 25 Aug.), 15 Sept. 1899.

52. Bridge 1903, pp. 316, 317.

53. HCF to Carnegie Steel board of managers, 20 Feb. 1899 (ACLC).

54. Minutes of operating departments meeting, 1 Sept. 1899 (ACLC).

55. Carnegie Steel board of managers, minutes, 11 Sept. 1899 (ACLC).

56. Ibid.

57. CMS to HCF, 26 Sept. 1899.

58. Carnegie Steel board of managers, Sept. and Oct. 1899; AC letter dated 28 Sept. 1899, read to Carnegie Steel board of managers, 16 Oct. 1899 (ACLC).

59. H. C. Frick Coke Co., minutes, 25 Oct. 1899, in U.S. Congress, House of Representatives 1912, vol. 6, pp. 4135–4137.

60. Bridge 1903, p. 322.

61. HCF to AC, 18 Nov. 1899, in Frick Papers; AC to HCF, 20 Nov. 1899 (ACLC).

62. HCF to Carnegie Steel board of managers, 20 Nov. 1899 (ACLC); AC to HCF, 21 Nov. 1899.

63. Lauder to AC, 24 Nov. 1899 (ACLC).

64. AC to Lauder, 25 Nov. 1899; AC to CMS, undated (late Nov. 1899); AC to Phipps, undated (late Nov. 1899) (all in ACLC).

65. CMS to AC, 27 Nov. 1899 (ACLC); CMS to HCF, 3 Dec. 1899; Whipple 1935, p. 117.

66. Bridge 1903, pp. 325, 326.

67. AC to Lauder, undated (Nov. 1899) (ACLC); Harvey 1928, p. 225; AC to HCF, undated (marked Dec. 1899), in Frick Papers; AC to HCF, undated (Dec. 1899) (ACLC).

68. AC to CMS, 11 Dec. 1899; AC to Lauder, 13 Dec. 1899 (both in ACLC).

69. AC to HCF, 19 Dec. 1899 (ACLC).

70. AC to Lauder, undated (Dec. 1899); Lauder to AC, 26 Dec. 1899; AC to Lauder, 27 Dec. 1899 (all in ACLC).

71. HCF to Lynch, 26 Dec. 1899; CMS to AC, 27 Dec. 1899 (ACLC).

72. Phipps to HCF, 28 Dec. 1899.

73. Carnegie Steel board of managers, 2 Jan. 1900 (ACLC).

74. Wall 1970, pp. 752, 753; Hendrick 1932, p. 467; CMS quoted in Whipple 1935, p. 4. There is considerable confusion about the H. C. Frick Coke meeting. Printed minutes suggest it was held on 10 January 1900 and in Pittsburgh (Stanley Committee 1912, pp. 4138, 4139).

75. Bridge 1903, p. 328; Wall 1970, pp. 755, 756.

76. Whipple 1935, p. 64.

77. HCF to Carnegie Steel Co., HCF to CMS, 10 Jan. 1900; HCF to Carnegie Steel Co., 13 Jan. 1900 (all in ACLC).

78. Hunsiker to HCF, 24 Jan. 1900.

79. A. R. Whitney to Moreland, 20 Feb. 1900; Moreland to A. Peacock, 23 Feb. 1900; Phipps to Carnegie Steel Co., 15 Jan. 1900 (all in ACLC). For the Curry incident, see Wall 1970, p. 754; Bridge 1903, p. 344, Winkler 1931, p. 253. There is some corroborative evidence for the situation that Curry is reported to have indicated. Many years later Bridge recognized that Andrew and Tom Carnegie were equal as geniuses in the selection of men: "But his brother left to every man his own individuality. Andrew Carnegie assimilates the best of everyone he touches. He absorbs other people as certain of the amebae [sic] absorb each other" (Bridge 1931, p. 61).

80. All the information in this paragraph is taken from Lovejoy to AC, 17 Jan. 1900 (ACLC).

81. For the pricing of coke, Iron Age, 1 March 1900; Bridge 1903, p. 329. For letters of protest, see Carnegie Papers (ACLC); J. Walker, Bill of Complaint, quoted in Harvey 1928, p. 246.

82. Phipps to HCF, 17 Jan. 1900, quoted in Harvey 1928, pp. 251–53; Wall 1970, p. 757.

83. Frick brief against Carnegie and the Carnegie Steel Co., spring 1900 (draft brief and extracts in Appendix, Bridge 1903, pp. 365–69).

84. Bridge 1903, p. 332.

85. "The Joint and Several Answer of The Carnegie Steel Company, Ltd., and Andrew Carnegie" (ACLC); Iron Age, 15 March 1900, p. 15.

86. The A. M. Moreland amendments are in the draft of "The Joint and Several Answer . . ." (ACLC); Phipps to AC, quoted in Boegner and Gachot 1986, p. 18; CMS to AC, 3 Feb. 1900 (ACLC).

87. Moreland to AC, 8 March 1900 (ACLC).

88. Wall 1970, pp. 761, 762; A. B. Farquhar to HCF, 9 March 1900; F. W. Haskell to HCF, 12 Feb. 1900.

89. Frick quoted in Harvey 1928, p. 254.

90. Copy of Atlantic City Agreement in meeting of shareholders of Carnegie Steel Co., 31 March 1900 (ACLC).

91. Harvey 1928, pp. 255, 256.

92. HCF to Whitney, quoted in Harvey 1928, p. 256.

93. Butler 1917, p. 91; Hendrick 1932, p. 463; Bridge 1903, p. 346; Hendrick 1932, p. 474.

7. YEARS OF TRANSITION

1. HCF to A. Mellon, 19 April 1900.

2. The Carnegie Company, minutes of board meeting, 4 Sept. 1900 (ACLC).

3. CMS to directors of Carnegie Steel, 17 May 1901, and minutes of board meeting, 29 Aug. 1901 (ACLC).

4. Carnegie Steel board meeting, 5, 12 Feb. 1900 (ACLC).

5. Carnegie Steel board meeting, 10 March, 23 April, 3 July 1900; AC to CMS, 20 June 1900; AC to Carnegie Steel board meeting, 22 June 1900 (all in ACLC).

6. AC cable to Carnegie Steel board meeting, 9 July 1900 (ACLC).

7. Johnston 1900; Carnegie Steel board meeting, 12 Nov. 1900 (ACLC).

8. Carnegie Steel board meeting, 9, 16 July 1900 (ACLC).

9. AC to Lauder, 3 June 1900 (ACLC).

10. Carnegie Steel board meeting, 27 Nov. 1899; CMS to AC, 24 Jan. 1901 (both in ACLC); Bridge 1903, p. 358.

11. Carnegie Steel board meeting, 16 July 1900 (ACLC).

12. AC to Lauder, 3 June 1900; CMS to AC, 19 June 1900 (both in ACLC).

13. Carnegie Steel board meeting, 27 Nov. 1900; Cassatt to AC, 10 Dec. 1900 (both in ACLC).

14. Carneige Steel board meeting, 12, 27 Nov. 1900 (ACLC); BAISA, 15 April 1901.

15. Carnegie Steel board meeting, 12 Nov. 1900 (ACLC); Jones 1922, pp. 196, 197.

16. J. Kennedy to Stanley Committee, in Iron Age, 4 April 1912, p. 892.

17. AC to CMS, 4 June 1900 (ACLC).

18. CMS to HCF, 14 Aug., 18 Sept. 1900.

19. HCF quoted in Harvey 1928, p. 257; Phipps to HCF, 11 Sept. 1900; HCF to CMS, 7 Jan. 1901.

20. HCF to J. Morse, 31 Dec. 1900; HCF to CMS, 7 Jan. 1901.

21. CMS to AC, 24 Jan. 1901 (ACLC).

22. Iron Trade Review, 10 Jan. 1901.

23. Lamoreaux 1985, p. 63; BAISA, 1 Jan. 1890.

24. Gates to HCF, 24 Sept. 1897.

25. U.S. Commissioner of Corporations 1911, pp. 91, 92, 207.

26. Gates to HCF, 13, 21, 27 Feb. 1899.

27. Gates to HCF, 11, 20 Oct. 1899; Burnley 1901, p. 441; Hogan 1971, pp. 261, 262 (these two accounts of the slump in AS&W shares differ in important respects).

28. Donner to A. Mellon, 13 Sept. 1899, in Frick Papers. Carnegie Steel board meeting, 2 Jan. 1900 (ACLC)

29. AC to A. Mellon, 28 Aug. 1900, in Frick Papers.

30. A. Mellon to HCF, 7 Sept. 1900.

31. *Financial Weekly* and Mellon both cited in Harvey 1928, p. 273. For more detail and a slightly different paraphrase, see also Ingham 1989.

32. *New York Times,* 6 Feb. 1901.

33. BAISA, 25 April 1901.

34. Donner to Cassatt, 27 Nov. 1905; HCF to Cassatt, 8 May 1906, both in Frick Papers.

35. Quoted in BAISA, 10 July 1902.

36. Ibid.

37. E. C. Potter to AC, 1 June 1898 (ACLC).

38. A. C. Machen to AC, 22 Dec. 1898; Carnegie Steel board of managers, 6 Sept. 1898 (both in ACLC).

39. *Encyclopaedia Britannica* 1902 and 1911 editions, articles "Navy and Navies." See also *Whitakers Almanack* annual.

40. H. Morse to HCF, 23, 28 Sept., 8 Dec. 1898.

41. H. Morse to HCF, 20, 22 Dec. 1898, and undated (late 1898).

42. A. Mellon to HCF, 4 May 1900; H. Morse to HCF, 1 Oct. 1901.

43. Biographical note on H. Morse in *National Cyclopaedia of American Biography.*

44. *Pittsburgh Post,* 28 Jan. 1900; *Pittsburgh News,* 2 Feb. 1900; *New York Times,* 17 Feb. 1900, p. 4.

45. F. Knauff to HCF, 28 Aug. 1900; for Potter's leaving Carnegie Steel, see CMS to HCF, 21 Nov. 1892, in Frick Papers, and J. A. Potter to AC, 19 Oct. 1893 (ACLC); J. A. Potter to HCF, 24 Dec. 1900.

46. H. Morse to HCF, 27 March 1901; J. A. Potter to A. Mellon, 22 July 1901, both in Frick Papers; Burnley 1901, p. 405.

47. Hunsiker to HCF, 17 Oct. 1901.

48. The matter is outlined from the standpoint of Vickers in Trebilcock 1977, pp. 135–39.

49. HCF to H. Morse, 21 May 1903; T. J. Coolidge to HCF, 27 Oct. 1904.

8. THE SHAPING OF THE U.S. STEEL CORPORATION

1. Quoted in Wilgus 1901, p. 25.

2. Carnegie Steel board meeting, 6 Nov. 1900 (ACLC).

3. U.S. Commissioner of Corporations 1911, pp. 163, 164; Corey cited in *Iron Age,* 30 Jan. 1913.

4. Harvey 1928, pp. 261–67; Tarbell 1925, pp. 118–20; U.S. Steel directors meeting, 1 April 1901 (USX).

5. AC to Lauder, 12 March 1901 (ACLC); Burnley 1901, p. 406.

6. HCF to J. Morse, 4 March 1901.

7. CMS to AC, 20 May 1901 (ACLC).

8. U.S. Steel executive committee, 11 April 1901 (USX).

9. Garraty 1957, p. 117; U.S. Steel executive committee, 9, 10, 11 April 1901 (USX).

10. CMS to G. W. Perkins, 3 July 1901, quoted in Garraty 1957, pp. 96–97; U.S. Steel executive committee, 1 April 1902 (USX).

11. Hessen 1975, p. 128.

12. HCF to J. Strain, 8 Oct. 1902; *New York Times,* 26 Dec. 1902; HCF to Gary, 20 March 1903.

13. U.S. Steel directors meeting, 7 April, 4 Aug. 1903 (USX); CMS press statement, 4 Aug. 1903 (USX); CMS in Mellon tax case quoted in O'Connor 1935, p. 71.

14. Harvey 1928, pp. 272, 273 (but note his chronology is uncertain and in some respects seems inaccurate).

15. Quoted in BAISA, 1 Dec. 1906.

16. U.S. Steel finance committee, 6 Jan., 3, 17 March, 28 April, 12 May 1903 (USX).

17. Cochran 1974, p. 411; Gary quoted in Cotter 1928, p. 32.

18. *Fortune* (May 1936), p. 157; Gary to Stanley Commission, 8 June 1911.

19. *Iron Age*, 17 Dec. 1908, pp. 1794, 1795; quotation is from BAISA, 25 Nov. 1902.

20. J. Gayley testimony to Stanley Committee 1912, p. 372; HCF to Hunsiker, 11 July 1906; Tarbell 1925, pp. 134, 143, 345.

21. "Mr. Frick on Business Methods," *New York World*, quoted in BAISA, 1 June 1905; U.S. Steel directors meeting, 30 Dec. 1919 (USX).

22. Verity quoted in Tarbell 1925, p. 351.

23. Casson 1907, p. 211; CMS to Stanley Commission, quoted in *Iron Age*, 22 May 1913, p. 1263.

24. HCF to A. Hill, 23 April 1901; Gary to HCF, 30 July 1906, 21 Feb. 1907; U.S. Steel Corporation to HCF, 18 Feb. 1909 (USX).

25. W. E. Corey to HCF, 1 March 1909, undated (April–May 1909), undated (1909); for Gary's testimonial dinner, see Garraty 1957, p. 120.

26. Information in these two paragraphs is from Garraty 1957, pp. 112–24; quotations are from U.S. Steel finance committee, 4 Jan. 1910 (USX).

27. Calculations of Paul Douglas quoted in J. R. Commons article "Wages," in *Encyclopaedia Britannica* 1926.

28. Perkins to Corey, quoted in Garraty 1957, p. 125.

29. Frick quoted in Garraty 1957, p. 125; U.S. Steel finance committee, 3, 31 Jan., 7 Feb. 1911 (USX).

30. U.S. Steel finance committee, 31 Jan., 25 April 1911 (USX). The resolution is quoted from Tarbell 1925, p. 219, who dates it as 1 March 1910, whereas Garraty 1957 dates it as 1 May 1910.

31. CMS quoted in Whipple 1935, p. 244; Garraty 1957, p. 125; Tarbell 1925, p. 252.

32. U.S. Steel finance committee, 10, 17, 31 Jan. 1911 (USX); the quotation is from O'Connor 1935, pp. 57–58.

33. CMS quoted in Whipple 1935, p. 244; J. A. Farrell to HCF, 23 July 1912; HCF to Farrell, 24 July 1912.

34. Berglund 1907, p. 78; Goodale 1931, p. 247.

35. *Manufacturers Record*, 2 May 1907.

36. This issue is discussed in U.S. Commissioner of Corporations 1911, pp. 259, 260, 322; *Iron Age*, 22 Nov. 1906, pp. 1388, 1389; Berglund 1907, pp. 158–62.

37. Cotter 1921, p. 78.

38. *Manufacturers Record*, 2 May 1907; mineral resources cited in Seager and Gulick 1929, p. 231.

39. U.S. Steel finance committee, 23 Oct. 1907 (USX).

40. U.S. Steel finance committee, 2, 3 Nov. 1907 (USX).

41. Barron 1930, pp. 78, 80; Harvey 1928, p. 306.

42. J. Kennedy to Stanley Committee, quoted in *Iron Age*, 4 April 1912; Frick quoted in Barron 1930, p. 87.

43. CMS to AC, 20 Sept. 1898 (ACLC); Gary to U.S. Tariff Commission 1908, p. 1694.

44. U.S. Steel finance committee, 10 Feb. 1903, 14, 21 Feb. 1905 (USX); for Chicago, see AISA Directory.

45. U.S. Steel finance committee, 13 June 1905 (USX); HCF to Gary, 17 May 1905; U.S. Steel finance committee, 24 Aug. 1905 (USX).

46. HCF to Gary, 24 Aug. 1905; *U.S. Steel Corporation Fourth Annual Report*, 16 March 1906 (USX).

47. Corey quoted by Gary to directors of U.S. Steel Corporation, 26 June 1906 (USX).

48. *Iron Age*, 2 Feb. 1911, p. 304.

49. CMS to U.S. Tariff Commission, 1908–1909, p. 1669.

50. Corey to HCF, undated (early autumn 1908), 2 Oct. 1908; AISA annual statistics.

51. Bureau of Mines; Eavenson 1942, pp. 579–82; CMS, 11 May 1901 to U.S. Industrial Commission 1901, vol. 13, p. 464.

52. U.S. Steel executive committee, 8 July, 25 June 1901; U.S. Steel finance committee, 14 Oct. 1902, 13 Dec. 1904 (all in USX).

53. U.S. Steel finance committee, 28 June, 30 Aug. 1904, 29 March, 5, 25 April 1905, 22 Jan., 23 July, 13 Aug, 17 Sept. 1907, 3 Nov. 1919 (USX).

54. U.S. Steel finance committee, 6 April, 9 Feb., 7 Dec. 1909 (USX).

55. U.S. Steel executive committee, 15 Nov. 1901, 3 July 1902; finance committee, 27 Oct., 4 Nov. 1903, 22 Nov. 1904, 25 April 1905 (USX).

56. U.S. Steel finance committee, 11, 25 Sept. 1906, 11 April 1911 (USX).

57. U.S. Steel finance committee, 17 Nov. 1908, 18 March 1902, 12 May 1903, 7 March 1911 (USX).

58. HCF to Gary, 12, 23, 29 Aug. 1918.

59. U.S. Steel finance committee, 13 July 1904, 17 Jan. 1905, 23 Feb., 16 March 1909, 28 May 1907, 4 May 1909 (USX).

60. U.S. Steel finance committee, 15 Oct. 1915, 14 March 1916, 24 July 1917 (USX).

61. *Iron Age*, 3 Jan. 1918, p. 83.

62. Eavenson 1942.

9. FROM INDUSTRIAL MANAGER TO FINANCE CAPITALIST

1. *Philadelphia Press* quoted in BAISA, 15 July 1899; quotation from *Wall Street Journal*, 6 Dec. 1919.

2. *Pittsburgh Times*, 3 Dec. 1919; description of Frick's last few months as chairman is in Casson 1907, p. 179; A. Lardy in *Pittsburgh Post*, 3 Dec. 1919.

3. Both quotations from Harvey 1928, p. 269.

4. *Successful Americans*, undated (1904–1905), p. 6.

5. Shadwell 1906, vol. 1, p. 322; Engels 1845, p. 301.

6. *Pittsburgh Dispatch*, 7 April 1900; Frick quoted in *Wall Street Journal*, 3 Dec. 1919; observer's remarks from *New York City Commercial*, 3 Dec. 1919.

7. Quotation is from *New York Times*, 22 Jan. 1902; *Pittsburgh Leader*, 2 Dec. 1919.

8. Helen Clay Frick, recorded recollections from the 1950s, in Weingartner 1988; H. D. W. English to HCF, 5 Nov. 1906.

9. *Greater Pittsburgh Directory* 1906; Harvey 1928, p. 280.

10. *Pittsburgh Leader,* 2 Dec. 1919; BAISA, 15 Jan. 1907.

11. Harvey 1928, pp. 277, 281; HCF to Pennsylvania Railroad, 13 Jan. 1914.

12. F. Ballou to HCF, 11 Sept. 1885; HCF to J. A. Farrell, 8 June 1910, 11 Nov. 1912.

13. Harvey 1928, pp. 289–91; T. Roosevelt to HCF, 9 June 1903; HCF to Roosevelt, 12 June 1903; BAISA, 10 May 1907.

14. Lorant 1988, p. 657; J. Moore in Weingartner 1988, p. 15; BAISA, 10 Dec. 1903; telegram is cited from Allen 1935, p. 74.

15. Tarbell 1925, p. 195; Roosevelt to HCF, 16 Oct. 1905; HCF to Roosevelt, 27 Oct. 1905; Roosevelt to HCF, 22 Feb., 29 June 1906, 30 Nov. 1907.

16. Roosevelt quoted in BAISA, 1 June 1908; AC quoted in Proceedings of a Conference of Governors 1908, vol. 1, p. 22.

17. Bridge 1931, p. 68; HCF to CMS, 29 Jan. 1914.

18. See also Lorant 1988, pp. 268, 269.

19. *Pittsburgh Dispatch,* 25 March 1905; Frick quoted in *New Yorker,* 15 July 1939, p. 24.

20. HCF contracts, 8 Sept., 29 Oct. 1906, in Frick Papers; *New Yorker,* 15 July 1939; visitor quoted from Bridge 1931, p. 72; Anna Robeson Burr quoted in Allen 1935, p. 108.

21. Catherine Farrell to HCF, 13 Dec. 1913.

22. Harvey 1928, pp. 364, 369; HCF to A. Krech, 30 May 1904; HCF to Knox, 8 Dec. 1904.

23. *New Yorker,* 15 July 1939, p. 24; HCF to Gary, 10 March 1910; HCF to anonymous friend, Aug. 1915.

24. Nevins 1958; quotation is from Murray in Garraty 1974, p. 750.

25. Gayley to HCF, 4 Jan. 1912; Nordeutsche Lloyd to HCF, 8 July 1899.

26. Harvey 1928, list of Frick's paintings on pp. 337–43; K. Hellerstedt quoted in Weingartner 1988, pp. 62–66; Holbrook 1954, p. 363; CMS quoted in Whipple 1935, p. 238.

27. Hellerstedt quoted in Weingartner 1988, p. 63; *New Yorker,* 2 Dec. 1985, p. 125.

28. H. Linde to HCF, 7 Feb. 1906; Harvey 1928, pp. 337–43; BAISA, 1 Aug. 1905.

29. Quotations are from *Iron Trade Review,* 21 Nov. 1907, and article on E. H. Gary in *National Cyclopaedia,* 1917; Zimmern 1912, p. 207; Brody 1960, p. 48.

30. L. Litchfield to HCF, 25 Oct. 1906, 31 Jan. 1907; HCF to Lynch, 6 Feb. 1908.

31. HCF to A. P. Moore, 3 Nov. 1913; Harvey 1928, p. 357; HCF to Hunsiker, 11 June 1907.

32. Bridge 1931, p. 70; Harvey 1928, p. 357 (Frick quoted, p. 358).

33. For Roosevelt, see Bridge 1931, p. 125; for Schwab, see Whipple 1935; for Carnegie, see Wall 1970, p. 764.

34. J. H. Bridge to J. H. Harding, 3 Feb. 1912, quoted in Bridge 1931, pp. 84–85; for Frick's reaction see Bridge 1931, p. 85.

35. HCF, draft letter to AC, 17 July 1912; Lovejoy to HCF, 2 Oct. 1912; Peacock to AC, 29 May 1913, quoted in Wall 1970, p. 764.

36. Quoted in Barron 1930.

37. Louise W. Carnegie, 16 April 1920, quoted in Carnegie 1920, p. vi; Carnegie 1920, p. 371.

38. *Evening Post* and *New York Sun* quoted by the New York correspondent of the *Times*, in *Times* (London), 28 July 1914, p. 7.

39. HCF to J. P. Grier, 3 Aug. 1914; to H. C. McEldowney, 6 Aug. 1914; to Farrell, 6 Aug. 1914; to McEldowney, 8 Aug. 1914; to S. L. Schoonmaker, 13 Aug. 1914.

40. HCF to C. Bohlen, 10 Aug. 1914; to A. Morton, 18 Aug. 1914; to secretary of Montserrat Golf Club, 3 Sept. 1914; to Farrell, 21 Aug. 1914.

41. Gary to HCF, 14 Sept. 1914; HCF to Gary, 15 Sept. 1914; HCF to J. H. Dunn, 15 Sept. 1914.

42. For Oliver Iron Mining, see U.S. Steel finance committee, 23 June 1914 (USX); Tarbell 1925, pp. 250, 251; U.S. Steel Corporation records, 1914–1915 (USX); U.S. Steel finance committee, 22 Dec. 1914 (USX).

43. HCF to CMS, 27 March 1915.

44. Hunsiker to HCF and HCF's reply are enclosures with HCF to Donner, 2 Aug. 1915; HCF to Farrell, 11 Nov. 1915.

45. Goodale 1931, passim; U.S. Steel finance committee, 17 April, 8 May, 10 July, 20 Nov. 1917 (USX).

46. Harvey 1928, pp. 319–22.

47. U.S. Steel finance committee, 11 April 1916 (USX); Tarbell 1925, p. 266; invitations to social events in Frick Papers.

48. HCF to Gary, 12 June 1914, 9 Dec. 1916.

49. *Iron Age*, 6 March 1919, p. 611; 3 April 1919, p. 898; 15 May 1919, p. 1287.

50. Frick 1909; HCF to G. J. Bader, 16 Sept. 1915; Smith, Bader, and Davidson to HCF, 28 Nov. 1917; Pickands Brown and Co. to HCF, 23 July 1918.

51. HCF to Gary, 4 June 1917, 21 Feb. 1916.

52. HCF to Farrell, 31 Jan. 1916.

53. HCF to Farrell, 29 Nov. 1916, 27 June 1917, 24 April 1918; U.S. Steel finance committee, 23, 30 April, 29 Oct., 6, 12 Nov., 24 Dec. 1918 (USX).

54. Bridge 1931, p. 87.

55. HCF to Farrell, 31 Oct. 1917, 26 Oct. 1918.

56. HCF to Farrell, 9 Oct. 1917.

57. HCF to A. Allom, 15 Nov. 1918.

58. Bridge 1931, p. 69; Louise Carnegie quoted in Wall 1970, p. 1039.

59. HCF to Gary, 7 May 1919.

60. HCF to CMS, 8 July 1919.

61. HCF to Farrell, 20 Oct. 1919.

62. HCF to J. Angle and H. B. Brown, 7 July 1919.

63. U.S. Steel finance committee, 17 April 1919 (USX).

64. HCF to W. D. Hines, 17 Oct. 1919; Harvey 1928, pp. 281–88.

65. J. Fitch in Foster 1920, p. vi.

66. St. Paul convention of American Federation of Labor quoted in Yellen 1936, p. 261.

67. J. A. Farrell in *Encyclopaedia Britannica* 1929 article on E. H. Gary; Tarbell 1925, p. 284.

68. New England clergyman quoted in Yellen 1936, pp. 290, 291.

69. Gary quoted in Yellen 1936, p. 253; HCF to Gary, 2 Oct. 1919.

70. AC at The Hague, 29 Aug. 1913, quoted in Carnegie 1920, p. 284 n.

71. Harvey 1928, pp. 327, 328 (Harvey uses the word *issues* but this seems inappropriate in the context and is assumed to be a misprint for *resources*).

72. Craig 1966, p. 556.

73. HCF to L. Parks, 6 Nov. 1919; HCF's secretary A. Braddel to J. Smith, 10 Nov. 1919; HCF to Lambing, undated (Nov. 1919).

74. Braddel to G. Wyness, 1 Nov. 1919, in Frick Papers.

75. Harvey 1928; quotation is from Bridge 1931, p. 68.

76. C. F. Chubb to J. E. Frick, 2 Dec. 1919, in Frick Papers.

10. IMAGES AND PERCEPTIONS: ASSESSING FRICK'S LIFE

1. Unless otherwise noted, quotations in this and the following paragraphs are taken from the volumes of press clippings of newspaper obituaries for HCF in Frick Papers.

2. *Wall Street Journal,* 16 Dec. 1919.

3. *Pittsburgh Leader,* 2 Dec. 1919.

4. *Uniontown Herald,* 5 Dec. 1919.

5. Gary quoted in *Wall Street Journal,* 3 Dec. 1919; *Iron Age,* 4 Dec. 1919, pp. 144, 145; J. A. Farrell in *New York City Tribune,* 3 Dec. 1919.

6. R. A. Walker in *Iron Age,* 11 Dec. 1919; Knox quoted in *Encyclopedia of Pennsylvania Biography* 1967.

7. CMS quoted in Whipple 1935; CMS to HCF, 26 Sept. 1899.

8. Bridge 1931, pp. 35, 56, 61, 67, 70, 95-97.

9. *New York City Globe,* 8 Dec. 1919; AC to CMS, 31 Jan. 1900 (ACLC).

10. Winkler 1931, p. 3; AC quoted in *Iron Trade Review,* 14 Aug. 1919; Shannon 1940, p. 521.

Bibliography

GOVERNMENT MATERIALS

Bureau of Mines. Annual. *Mineral Resources of the United States.* Washington, D.C.: Government Printing Office.

Pennsylvania Department of Internal Affairs. 1878–1879, 1888. *Annual Report of the Secretary of Internal Affairs.* Harrisburg.

———. Industrial Statistics Bureau. 1893. *The Strikes During 1892.* Harrisburg.

Proceedings of a Conference of Governors in the White House. May 1908. Washington, D.C.: Government Printing Office, 1909.

Stanley Committee. 1912. *See* U.S. Congress, House of Representatives. 1912. Hearings Before the Committee on Investigation of U.S. Steel Corporation. Vol. 6.

U.S. Bureau of Statistics. 1900. *Monthly Summary of Commmerce and Finance.* Washington, D.C.: Government Printing Office. August.

U.S. Bureau of the Census. Periodic publication of census material.

U.S. Commissioner of Corporations. 1911 and 1913. *Report on the Steel Industry.* 2 vols. *Organization, Investment, Profits, and Position of the United States Steel Corporation* and *Cost of Production.* Washington, D.C.: Government Printing Office.

U.S. Congress, House of Representatives. 1892. *Employment of Pinkerton Detectives: Labor Troubles at Homestead, 1892.* Washington, D.C.: Government Printing Office.

———. 1909. Tariff Hearings Before the Committee on Ways and Means. 1908–1909. 60th Cong. 2nd sess. Washington, D.C.: Government Printing Office.

———. 1912. Hearings Before the Committee on Investigation of U.S. Steel Corporation. (Stanley Committee). Washington, D.C.: Government Printing Office.

U.S. Department of Commerce. 1960. *Historical Statistics of the United States.* Washington, D.C.: Government Printing Office.

U.S. Industrial Commission. 1899–1901. Reports. Vol. 13. Washington, D.C.: Government Printing Office.

U.S. Tariff Commission. 1908–1909. *See* U.S. Congress, House of Representatives. 1909. Tariff Hearings Before the Committee on Ways and Means. 1908–1909.

ARCHIVAL COLLECTIONS

Bethlehem Papers. Hagley Library, Wilmington, Delaware.

Carnegie Papers. Library of Congress, Washington, D.C. (ACLC).

Carnegie Steel Company Papers. U.S. Steel Corporation, Pittsburgh, Pennsylvania (USX).

Cooley Papers. Hagley Library, Wilmington, Delaware.

Frick Papers. Helen Clay Frick Foundation, Pittsburgh, Pennsylvania.

H. C. Frick Coke Company Papers. U.S. Steel Corporation. Pittsburgh, Pennsylvania (USX).

Harrison MSS. Library of Congress, Washington, D.C.

U.S. Steel Corporation Papers. U.S. Steel Corporation, Pittsburgh, Pennsylvania (USX).

S. Whipple. 1935. Notes of conversations with C. M. Schwab in 1935 and 1936. Hagley Library, Wilmington, Delaware, and Bethlehem Steel Corporation Library, Bethlehem, Pennsylvania.

BOOKS AND ARTICLES

Allen, F. L. 1935. *Lords of Creation*. London: Hamish Hamilton.

American Iron and Steel Association (AISA). Later, American Iron and Steel Institute (AISI). 1866–1912. *Bulletin* (BAISA).

———. 1899. *History of the Manufacture of Armor Plate for the United States Navy*. Philadelphia: AISA.

——— (AISI). Occasional. *Directory of the Iron and Steel Works in the United States and Canada*. Philadelphia: AISA/AISI.

———. Annual Statistics.

Barber, W. J. 1967. *A History of Economic Thought*. Harmondsworth, England: Pelican.

Baron, D. H. 1897. The development of Lake Superior iron ore. *Transactions of the American Institute of Mining Engineers*, vol. 27.

Barron, C. W. 1930. *They Told Barron*. New York: Harper.

Bell, T. 1976. *Out of This Furnace*. Little, Brown, and Co., 1941. Reprint, Pittsburgh: University of Pittsburgh Press.

Berglund, A. 1907. *The United States Steel Corporation*. New York: Columbia University Press.

Birkibine, J. 1897. The ore supply. *Transactions of the American Institute of Mining Engineers*, vol. 27.

Blum, J. M., et al. 1973. *The National Experience: A History of the United States*. New York: Harcourt Brace.

Boegner, P. P., and Gachot, R. 1986. *Halcyon Days: An American Family Through Three Generations*. New York: Old Westbury Gardens.

Bridge, J. H. 1903. *The Inside Story of the Carnegie Steel Company*. New York: Aldine.

———. 1931. *Millionaires and Grub Street*. New York: Brentano.

Brock, M., and E. Brock. 1982. *Herbert H. Asquith's Letters to Venetia Stanley*. Oxford: Oxford University Press.

Brody, D. 1960. *Steelworkers in America: The Non Union Era*. Cambridge: Harvard.

Burgoyne, A. G. 1893. *The Homestead Strike of 1892*. Pittsburgh, Pa.: Rawsthorne.

Burnley, J. 1901. *Millionaires and Kings of Enterprise*. Philadelphia: Lippincott.

Butler, J. 1917. *Fifty Years of Iron and Steel*. Cleveland: Penton Press.

Byington, M. 1910. *Homestead: The Households of a Milltown*. Vol. 4, *The Pittsburgh Survey*. New York: Russell Sage Foundation.

———. 1912. Evidence to the Stanley Committee. U.S. Congress, House of Representatives, 1912.

Carnegie, A. 1886a. An employer's view of the labor question. *Forum* 1 (April): 114–25.

————. 1886b. *Triumphant Democracy.* New York: Scribners.

————. 1920. *Autobiography.* Boston: Houghton Mifflin.

Casson, H. N. 1907. *The Romance of Steel.* New York: A. S. Barnes.

————. n.d. (circa 1930). *The Meaning of Life.* London: The Efficiency Magazine.

Clarke, V. S. 1929. *History of Manufactures in the United States.* 3 vols. New York: McGraw-Hill.

Cochran, T. 1974. Entry on E. H. Gary in Garraty 1974.

Cotter, A. 1921. *United States Steel: A Corporation with a Soul.* New York: Doubleday, Page.

————. 1928. *The Gary I Knew.* Boston: Stratford.

Craig, G. A. 1966. *Europe Since 1815.* New York: Holt, Rinehart, and Winston.

Crowe, H. 1902. "A visit to the United States of America." Paper and discussion. Middlesbrough, England.

Daddow, S. H., and B. Bannan. 1864. *Coal, Iron, and Oil.* Pottsville, Pennsylvania.

Dickson, W. B. 1938. *History of the Carnegie Veterans Association.* Montclair, N.J.: Mountain Press.

Dictionary of American Biography. 1927–1958. 22 vols. New York: Charles Scribner's.

Dreiser, T. 1899. *The Carnegie Works at Pittsburgh.* Privately printed.

Eavenson, H. N. 1942. *The First Century and a Quarter of American Coal Industry.* Pittsburgh: privately printed.

Engels, F. 1845. *Condition of the Working Class in England in 1844.* Reprinted, London: Panther, 1969.

Fitch, J. 1910. *The Steel Workers.* Vol. 3 of *The Pittsburgh Survey.* New York: Russell Sage Foundation.

Foner, P. S. 1955. *History of the Labor Movement in the United States.* New York: International Publishers.

Foster, W. Z. 1920. *The Great Steel Strike and Its Lessons.* New York: B. W. Huebsch.

Frick, C. 1909. Report relating to Mr. H. C. Frick's property at Indiana Harbor. August. Privately printed.

Fulton, J. 1884–1885. Coal mining in the Connellsville coke region of Pennsylvania. *Transactions of the American Institute of Mining Engineers* 13, p. 334.

————. 1905. *Coke.* Scranton: International Textbook Company.

Garland, H. 1894. Homestead and its perilous trades. *McClure's Magazine,* 3 June.

Garraty, J. 1957. *Right Hand Man: The Life of George W. Perkins.* New York: Harper.

Garraty, J., ed. 1974. *Encyclopedia of American Biography.* New York: Harper and Row.

Goodale, S. L. 1931. *Chronology of Iron and Steel.* Cleveland: Penton Publishing Company.

Greater Pittsburgh Directory of Directors. 1906. (Source in Carnegie Library, Pittsburgh.)

Habakkuk, H. J. 1967. *American and British Technology in the Nineteenth Century.* London: Cambridge University Press.

Harvey, G. 1928. *Henry Clay Frick: The Man.* New York: Charles Scribner's.

Heilbroner, R. L. 1970. Andrew Carnegie: Captain of industry. In *Historical Viewpoints,* ed. J. Garraty, vol. 2. New York: Harper and Row.

Hendrick, B. J. 1932. *The Life of Andrew Carnegie.* New York: Doubleday.

Hessen, R. 1975. *Steel Titan: The Life of Charles M. Schwab.* New York: Oxford University Press. Reprinted, Pittsburgh: University of Pittsburgh Press, 1991.

Hewitt, A. S. 1870. *The Production of Iron and Steel in Its Economic and Social Relations.* Reports of U.S. Commissioners to the Paris Exposition, 1867. Vol. 2. Washington, D.C.: Government Printing Office.

Hogan, W. T. 1971. *Economic History of the Iron and Steel Industry in the United States.* 5 vols. Lexington, Mass.: D. C. Heath.

Holbrook, S. 1954. *The Age of the Moguls.* London: Victor Gollancz.

Hughes, J. 1973. *The Vital Few: American Economic Progress and Its Protagonists.* New York: Oxford University Press.

Ingham, J. N. 1989. Henry Clay Frick. In *Iron and Steel in the Nineteenth Century,* by P. F. Paskoff, in *The Encyclopedia of American Business History and Biography.* New York: Bruccoli Clark Layman, 1989.

Jeans, J. S. 1902. *American Industrial Conditions and Competition.* London: British Iron Trade Association.

Jenkins, H. M. 1904. *Pennsylvania: Colonial and Federal.* Philadelphia: Pennsylvania Historical Publishing Association.

Johnston, A. 1896. *Report on Visit to Homestead Works.* In Bethlehem Papers.

———. 1900. *Report on Visit to Homestead Works.* In Bethlehem Papers.

Jones, E. 1922. *The Trust Problem in the United States.* New York: Macmillan.

Jordan, J. W. 1915. *Encyclopedia of Pennsylvania Biography.* Vol. 4. New York: Lewis Historical Publishing Company.

Keighley, F. C. 1900. *History of the Connellsville Region.* Uniontown: Privately printed.

Kirkland, E. C. 1952. *Business in the Gilded Age.* Madison: University of Wisconsin Press.

Krause, P. 1992. *The Battle for Homestead.* Pittsburgh: University of Pittsburgh Press.

Lamoreaux, N. R. 1985. *The Great Merger Movement in American Business, 1895–1904.* Cambridge: Cambridge University Press.

Lesley, J. P. 1859. *The Iron Manufacturer's Guide to the Furnaces, Forges, and Rolling Mills of the United States.* New York: American Iron Association.

———. 1885–1886. The geology of the Pittsburgh coal region. *Transactions of the American Institute of Mining Engineers* 14, p. 619.

Lorant, S. 1988. *Pittsburgh: The Story of an American City.* Lenox: S. Lorant.

Meade, E. S. 1901. The genesis of the United States Steel Corporation. *Quarterly Journal of Economics* 15 (August): 532–41.

Mulhall, M. G. 1899. *The Dictionary of Statistics.* London: George Routledge.

National Cyclopaedia of American Biography. 1892–1964. 58 vols. New York: J. T. White.

Nevins, A. 1953. *Study in Power: John D. Rockefeller, Industrialist or Philanthropist?* New York: Charles Scribner's.

Oates, S. B. 1973. *Portrait of America.* Vol. 2. Boston: Houghton Mifflin.

O'Connor, H. 1935. *Steel, Dictator.* New York: John Day Company.

Overman, F. 1850. *The Manufacture of Iron.* Philadelphia.

Paskoff, P. F. 1989. *Iron and Steel in the Nineteenth Century.* In *The Encyclopedia of American Business History and Biography.* New York: Bruccoli Clark Layman.

Peto, Sir M. 1866. *The Resources and Prospects of America.* London: Strahan.

Platt, F. 1876. *Special Report on the Coke Manufacture of the Youghiogheny Valley.* Harrisburg: Commonwealth of Pennsylvania.

Ripley, W. Z. 1905. *Trusts, Pools, and Corporations.* New York: Ginn and Company.

Rogers, H. D. 1858. *The Geology of Pennsylvania.* 2 vols. Harrisburg: Commonwealth of Pennsylvania.

Rostow, W. W. 1971. *The Stages of Economic Growth: A Non-Communist Manifesto.* Cambridge: Cambridge University Press.

Seager, H. R., and C. A. Gulick. 1929. *Trusts and Corporation Problems.* New York: Harper and Brothers.

Shadwell, A. 1906. *Industrial Efficiency.* 2 vols. London: Longmans.

Shannon, F. A. 1940. *America's Economic Growth.* New York: Macmillan.

Shinn, W. P. 1879–1880. Pittsburgh: Its resources and surroundings. *Transactions of the American Society of Mining Engineers* 24.

Sienkiewicz, H. 1876. Notes made during travels in the United States.

Smith, A. 1776. *The Wealth of Nations.* Vol. 1. London: Dent, 1910. Reprint, London: Everyman's Library Edition.

Spahr, C. B. 1900. *America's Working People.* New York: Longman.

Successful Americans. N.d. (circa 1904–1905).

Tarbell, I. 1925. *The Life of Elbert H. Gary.* New York: Appleton.

Temin, P. 1964. *Iron and Steel in Nineteenth-Century America.* Cambridge, Mass.: MIT.

Trebilcock, C. 1977. *The Vickers Brothers.* London: Europa.

Wall, J. F. 1970. *Andrew Carnegie.* New York: Oxford University Press.

Wallis, G. 1854. *Report on the New York Exhibition.* British Parliamentary Papers.

Warren, K. 1988. *The American Steel Industry, 1850–1970.* Oxford: Oxford University Press, 1973. Reprint, Pittsburgh: University of Pittsburgh Press.

Weingartner, F., ed. 1988. *Clayton, the Pittsburgh Home of Henry Clay Frick: Art and Furnishings.* Pittsburgh: The Helen Clay Frick Foundation.

Wilgus, H. L. 1901. *The United States Steel Corporation in Its Industrial and Legal Aspects.* Chicago: Callaghan.

Wilson, M. B. 1915. *A Carnegie Anthology.* New York: Privately published.

Winchell, H. V. 1892–1893. The Mesabi iron ranges. *Transactions of the American Institute of Mining Engineers* 21.

———. 1896–1897. The Lake Superior iron ore range, USA. *Transactions Federated Institute of Mining Engineers (UK)* 13.

Winkler, J. 1931. *Incredible Carnegie.* New York: Vanguard.

Wolff, L. 1965. *Lockout: The Story of the Homestead Strike of 1892.* New York: Harper and Row.

Yellen, S. 1936. *American Labor Troubles.* New York: Harcourt Brace.

Zimmern, A. E. 1912. Seven months in America. *Sociology Review* 5, no. 3. July.

Index